MONGOLIA'S CULTURE AND SOCIETY

Sechin Jagchid
and
Paul Hyer

With a Foreword by Joseph Fletcher

Westview Press • *Boulder, Colorado*
Dawson • *Folkestone, England*

Copyright © 1979 by Westview Press, Inc.

Published in 1979 in the United States of America by
  Westview Press, Inc.
  5500 Central Avenue
  Boulder, Colorado 80301
  Frederick A. Praeger, Publisher

Published in 1979 in Great Britain by
  Wm. Dawson and Sons, Ltd.
  Cannon House
  Folkestone
  Kent CT19 5EE

Library of Congress Catalog Card Number: 79-1438
ISBN (U.S.): 0-89158-390-4
ISBN (U.K.): 0-7129-0892-7

Printed and bound in the United States of America

CONTENTS

ILLUSTRATIONS

FOREWORD

There is no field of history in which further understanding of the economic, social, and cultural setting has been more badly needed than in the history of the Mongols, creators of the greatest of the Eurasian steppe empires. Despite the Mongols' obvious historical importance and despite centuries of writing on the subject, the conditions of life in nomadic Mongolia remain unreal for readers of English. It is difficult or impossible for twentieth-century people who live in industrialized agricultural societies to imagine the needs and constraints that shaped the Mongols' unique historical career or to imagine the perspective from which the Mongols viewed the settled civilizations that they overran.

The very topic of nomadism itself confounds the modern reader. In considering the history of continental Asia, are we faced with a single nomadism or several? Was there a Turco-Mongolian nomadism, or were there basic functional differences distinguishing socioeconomic structures of the Turkic-speaking peoples in the western steppes from those of the Mongolian-speaking peoples of the east—differences that the Mongols' expansion may have obscured by putting the entire Eurasian steppe under a single rule? To what extent, even in Mongolia, was the Mongols' way of life identical with that of the Turkic-speaking peoples who preceded them, or with that of the earlier Hsiung-nu or the still earlier Iranian-speaking Scythians? And how much did the lives of any of these earlier pastoral peoples resemble the nomadic life of the Mongols in the late nineteenth and twentieth centuries that Chinese, Japanese, European, and American travelers have witnessed and described?

Readers seeking answers to these questions would do well to begin with the present work, which paints a picture of nomadic life and culture in Mongolia depicting the patterns of the Ch'ing period (1644-1912), in which all the Mongols—apart from a small fraction under Russian rule and a tiny group in Afghanistan—lived under the administration and control of the Chinese empire, and the patterns of the subsequent revolutionary period, in which new technology, new ideologies, and new political divisions and configurations sharply altered the conditions of life and thought.

Sechin Jagchid and Paul Hyer have framed this picture against a broad historical background, highlighting continuities within the nomadic environment and outlining the recurrent forms of interaction between the nomads of the Mongolian pastures and the peoples of agrarian China. The influence of Tibet is also clearly to be seen in these pages. In describing nomadic life of a more recent period, the authors are keenly aware of historical antecedents dating from the time of Chinggis Khan and even earlier periods. They see kinship, social stratification, political structure, the organization of the Mongols within the framework of the Ch'ing empire, and the fate of these structures after the Ch'ing collapse against the continuities and discontinuities of eight centuries of Mongolian history.

The book represents more than a decade of work by two scholars who have devoted most of their professional lives to Mongolian studies. Sechin Jagchid, himself a Mongol of Kharachin in Inner Mongolia, brings to bear his personal recollections of Mongolian life, his experiences as an Inner Mongolian administrator in the turbulent 1940s, and over three decades of reading and thinking about Mongolian history in contemporary and earlier times. Not least, the fundamental insights of his valuable *Peace, War and Trade Relationships Between the North Asian Nomadic Peoples and the Agricultural Chinese,* published in 1972 in Chinese, and therefore inaccessible to readers of English, are represented in the present volume. Paul Hyer contributes the perspectives of an American-trained historian and social scientist and a detailed knowledge of twentieth-century East Asian power politics, with special emphasis on Inner Mongolia.

Together, they have produced a clear and readable account of Mongolian society and culture. Their work contains much that cannot easily be found elsewhere in any language and will therefore be of value to the specialist. But more important, Sechin Jagchid and Paul Hyer have written this book for a wider public, at last making available to the general reader a glimpse of the color and motion of Mongolian life and history.

Joseph Fletcher
Professor of Chinese and Central Asian History
Harvard University

PREFACE

The society and culture of the nomads of Mongolia have fascinated many people for centuries. Before the Manchu conquest in the early 1600s, Mongolia was an area that had a great impact on China and Russia and also periodically influenced the entire Eurasian continent far into the West during the time of the great nomadic expansions. The pivotal position of Mongolia, in particular, and Inner Asia, in general, in the entire premodern Eurasian continent was not unlike that of the Mediterranean Sea in the classical world of Greece and Rome and throughout most of the medieval era. Today, Mongolia is the focus of a crucial confrontation between China and Russia. Once a pivotal area in world geopolitics for close to two thousand years, Mongolia is now a pawn in a great power competition. The great steppe region no longer serves either as a base of operations for nomadic incursions into the agricultural areas of Asia or Europe or as a refuge from expeditions such as those launched by Han Wu-ti and the Ming emperor, Yung-lo, or from the constant pressures exerted in modern times by warlords, the People's Liberation Army, China's Red Guards, or Maoist-type Production-Construction Corps.

Modern Mongols reject the proposition that Mongolia is Chinese territory and are also distressed to think that their people are a client-state of Russia. Mongolian national consciousness was late emerging, but since the turn of this century, the Mongols have made a valiant attempt to survive and to maintain their identity. Recently, there has been some effort to present the Mongolian story. The leading Mongolist of Europe, Walther Heissig, entitled his book *Ein Volk Seicht Sein Geschicht* [*A People Seek Their History*]. While seeking to retrieve a lost heritage, the Mongols, nevertheless, have very deliberately avoided an attempt to revive a dying culture. They stress that Mongolia, the nation, will live, but nomadic culture cannot. The fact that social, economic, and political institutions must inevitably pass through a metamorphosis in the process of modernization has been accepted by leaders, though resisted by some common nomads.

Presently, the Mongolian People's Republic, population one and a half million, is the sole political entity, in the contemporary world, representing the heritage of historical Mongolia. It is seated in the United Nations and recognized by the major powers of the world and scores of minor ones. However, Mongols do not feel that they have arrived, and they continue to make a self-conscious attempt to consolidate the gains they have made and to move forward.

The society and culture or life-style of the nomadic people of Mongolia are keys to understanding the mobility, power, and amazingly important role in history of a comparatively small group of nomads.

Nomadic society and cultural institutions are complex, and it is useful to observe their evolution rather than merely note their structure and function in a flat perspective of modern times. Thus, some care has been taken to show nomadic life in a time dimension. The time focus of this book is the first half of the twentieth century or pre-Communist Mongolia. During this period of great change, as Mongols became more sedentary in their life-style, there was a gradual attrition in many traditional nomadic institutions. The traditional culture is emphasized here, but limited attention has been given to culture change and to the transition of Mongolian society in the modern period. Changes stemming from the Communist period in Mongolia require a separate study.

This work is intended primarily as an introductory study of traditional nomadic institutions with no attempt to go into great depth in any particular area. It is not intended for Mongolists or specialists on nomadic societies but rather for a wider public; therefore, the style is less formal and while much behavioral-science jargon has been avoided, an attempt has been made to project life in Mongolia with some insights of the social scientist. This book, we hope, will be useful to students and teachers of Asia, in general, and China, in particular, as a detailed treatment of the nomadic peoples of Inner Asia who were a constant threat to China—against whom the Great Wall was built and who actually ruled much of China for half of the long period of empire (221 B.C.-A.D. 1911) as dynasties of infiltration or conquest—the same nomads, moreover, who made their mark on Russia and western Asia.

From one point of view, this work may be considered a case study of the culture and society of China's most important frontier, a nomadic society that came very close to being set by geographical determinism—whether one considers diet, transportation, dwellings, or other aspects of a broad socio-cultural index. Among the many Inner Asian nomadic peoples, the focus here is on the Mongols—so-called barbarians of ages past. But, actually, the pattern is broader, for the Mongols are a sociological "ideal type" of nomad from which one may generalize in many ways regarding such other peoples as the Hsiung-nu (Huns?), Juan-juan, Turkic-Uighur, the Kitan, and other peoples vaguely referred to as Tatars, and also, to a lesser degree, to Tungusic Manchu and Tibetans.

We have made an effort to record a nomadic life-style that is rapidly disappearing. Indeed, it is now virtually impossible for the anthropologist to carefully observe traditional life in modern Mongolia because of the changes that have taken place under a socialist economy in the Mongolian People's Republic and because of the socio-economic changes in the areas of Mongolia under the People's Republic of China.

The just criticism may arise that some sections of the work are premature, for basic monograph work is nonexistent in some areas. Consequently, at times, the treatment is fragmentary and impressionistic. Much important information presented here comes from direct experience in Mongolia or from long contact with Mongols now living in China, Japan, and elsewhere.

Some material is available in Western literature on the various nomadic peoples who have inhabited Mongolia; there are writings of foreign visitors to Mongolia from the time of Marco Polo to that of Sven Hedin. Accounts by foreign observers present advantages and disadvantages. Persons from a vastly different culture give perceptive insights by way of contrasts and comparisons; although at times the view is distorted, foreign observations contribute much to the understanding of nomadic life. At the same time, a bias characteristic of, for example, Chinese reports is the condescending discussion of nomadic culture as inferior and barbaric. These Western accounts are readily available, but the Chinese sources freely drawn upon here are generally unknown to the average Western reader. Comparatively little has been written by the Mongols themselves about nomadic institutions—aspects of a mundane existence they take for granted.

The authors have tried to exercise objectivity in writing but also to approach nomadic culture and society sympathetically, hoping to avoid perpetuating the distorted views of those who come from a sedentary background and who project a nomadic, "barbarian," syndrome in discussing nomadic civilization. Occasionally, cross-cultural comparisons are drawn; these most often use the sedentary society of China as a point of reference since it is such a marked contrast with Mongolia and, moreover, is the society with which the nomads of Mongolia have had the most prolonged and intensive interaction.

A note on the Romanization of Asian words is in order. There is no clear consensus on the matter, and inconsistencies constantly crop up. The authors have generally adopted what may be termed a modified Mostaert-Cleaves form of Romanization for Mongolian terms. The kh/gh/sh/ch forms are used in place of the q/j/s/c forms, respectively. Finally in some cases a spoken form is used, arbitrarily, while in most instances a written form is used. Diacritical marks are omitted in some cases. For Chinese terms, the Wade-Giles system of Romanization is used, and, for Japanese, a modified Hepburn system has been adopted.

This work would not have been possible without the support and cooperation of the Joint Committee for Contemporary China (Social Science Research Council and the American Council of Learned Societies) and the staff of Brigham Young University—the Research Division, department chairmen De Lamar Jensen and Ted Warner, and the dean of the College of Social Sciences, Martin Hickman. Appreciation is extended to the staff of the Graduate Institute of China Border Area Studies, Chengchi University.

S. J.
P. H.

1
LAND AND PEOPLE OF THE MONGOLIAN STEPPES

A line drawn through East Asia from the middle of Manchuria to the southwest, following the Great Wall toward Tibet and on to Arabia, naturally divides the Asian world into two parts: the arid world of the nomads to the north and the intensively farmed monsoon lands to the south. Within these two spheres there developed radically different societies and cultures. The historical succession of nomadic societies and cultures to the north was based on the domestication of animals and a migratory style of life; to the south, the economic base of society was primarily wet rice agriculture and a concentrated settlement pattern. The nomadic peoples and the sedentary Chinese struggled continually for power, for control over resources, trade routes, and strategic areas. Under strong dynasties, there were campaigns from China into the steppe, but the dominant trend was invasions of the nomadic peoples into North China. Major events or developments in the heartland of Inner Asia, either natural disasters or political changes, almost inevitably impinged on the fate of the surrounding territories governed by sedentary peoples in China, Russia, and West Asia.

In East Asia, the Chinese model of civilization dominated, and its institutions were naturally dispersed widely, northward into Korea and Japan and southward into Indochina. North of the wall, Chinese culture has had very little influence upon the society and cultural development of the nomadic peoples until recently. Conversely, while the nomadic peoples gained political dominance, they exerted very little cultural influence southward into China. While the geographical distance was short, the cultural distance between these two spheres remained very great. Just as Confucian patterns of society in China established a model

1

or common denominator for other East Asian societies, various nomadic peoples out in the steppe to the north (Turkic, Mongolian, or other) perpetuated certain common aspects of their life-style for centuries.

The unstable relationship between the nomadic Altaic people and the sedentary Chinese, and the lack of an institutionalized and continuous trade or co-prosperity between them, was due to the economic dependence of the nomadic people of the steppe on the agricultural people south of the wall and, concurrently, the antipathy of the Chinese toward their northern nomadic, "barbarian" neighbors. The steppe inhabitants had abundant meat for food and wool and hides for clothing, but they lacked such necessities as grain, cloth, and agricultural products. When they could not obtain these items through trade, they resorted to invasion and conquest.[1]

The scope of power and activity north of the wall was broad and expansive from the beginning of history until modern times. From the Mongolian plateau, as a heartland, dominion was thrust eastward into Manchuria and Korea or westward to control the trade routes, Central Asia and the lands of western Asia, the Near East, or even eastern Europe. From Manchuria to western Asia, there are virtually no major geographical barriers, so various nomadic rulers were able to control, for periods of time, the great Eurasian steppe area, far into southern Russia. From their excellent strategic position on the high steppe plateau of Mongolia, nomadic peoples looked down upon and constantly thrust themselves into the rich areas of China for exploitation and trade. Thus, through the centuries, the plateau served as a strategic military and geopolitical position. Because of an imbalance in supply and demand between these two spheres, the tension and conflict were never resolved.[2] Peace and trade between them did not exist for extended periods of time except during the Ch'ing, the last imperial period, which was actually one of Manchu rule rather than Chinese.

The nature of the relationship between the two spheres may be seen in the writings of Pan Ku (A.D. 32-92), second great historian of the Han dynasty.

> As for customs, food, clothing, and language, the barbarians are entirely different from the Middle Kingdom. They live in the cold wilderness of the far north. They follow the grazing fields, herding their flocks and hunting game to maintain their lives. Mountains, valleys and the great desert separate them from us. This barrier which lies between the center and the alien outside was made by Heaven and Earth. Therefore,

the sage rulers considered them beasts, neither establishing contacts nor subjugating them. If any agreements were established it would involve our troops in vain and cause the enemy to fight back if an invasion were carried out. Their land is impossible to cultivate and it is impossible to rule them as subjects. Therefore, they are always to be considered as outsiders and never as intimates. Our administration and teaching have never reached their people. Our imperial calendar has never been bestowed upon them.[3] Punish them when they come and guard against them when they retreat. Receive them when they offer tribute as a sign of admiration for our righteousness. Restrain them continually and make it appear that all the blame is on their side. This is the proper policy of sage rulers towards the barbarians.[4]

In the late Han period, many similar sentiments were current, demonstrating a deep breach and incompatible differences in life-style between the steppe and China.

The date of the earliest inhabitation by man in the steppe areas is still a moot question. However, archaeologists have discovered paleolithic sites inhabited by man in northern Mongolia in the Selengge, Tula, and Orkhon river-valleys and in eastern Mongolia in the Khalkha River valley. Other paleolithic sites have been found in the northwest region of the Altai Mountains and around Khobdo. All of these sites are recent finds. Sites inhabited by man from the late paleolithic age into the neolithic age are found in the great loop of the Yellow River (the Ordos) in southwestern Mongolia and also at Jalainor in the Nonni River valley in eastern Mongolia. Bronze Age and Iron Age implements as well as neolithic artifacts are found continually in various parts of northern and southern Mongolia, which are habitable by man. Mongolia thus served both as a cradle for many nomadic peoples and as a base for their expansion and the establishment of their empires. The major groups of Altaic people who dominated the area were the Hsiung-nu, the Hsien-pei, the Juan-juan, the T'u-chüeh, the Uighur, the Kitan, the Mongols, and the Manchu.

The geographical expanse of the Inner Asian steppe belt was well suited to the people who lived there since their activities continually required broad movements in search of water or pastures, or escape or refuge from natural disasters. Survival and security in the steppe, which offered so few of the necessities of life, depended upon the movement of families and clans or powerful khans over many clan federations. An increasing number of peoples, whose lives were based on a pastoral economy, settled in the area.

There were some common denominators among the people inhabiting these areas, but there were also important differences in life-style. The pastoral nomadic life was dominant, with important ancillary groups such as hunters; there were groups with a mixed hunting and pastoral economy and others with a mixed hunting and agricultural or a mixed agricultural and nomadic economy.

About one century B.C. in the classic history of the *Shih chi*, Ssu-ma Ch'ien wrote:

> The Hsiung-nu live in the Northern Barbarian lands and wander, follow-ing their herds, moving from place to place . . . searching for water and pastures. They have no cities, no permanent dwellings and no cultivated fields. . . . Their children ride on the backs of sheep and shoot [arrows] at birds and rats. As they grow older, they shoot fox and rabbits for food. The men are able to pull heavy bows and they are all armored horsemen. According to their custom, during times of peace they follow their herds and hunt animals and birds to sustain life; in crisis everyone uses their unique tactics for an attack and invasion. Their long distance weapons are bows and arrows and their hand-to-hand weapons are swords and daggers. When it is profitable they advance; when it is unprofitable they withdraw, never being ashamed of retreat. . . . From their rulers down everyone eats meat, wears animal hides and puts on felt and furs.[5]

This brief description confirms that hunting and pastoral pursuits were the bases of the livelihood of the ancient inhabitants of the Mongol steppes.

It seems to be the consensus of most students of Inner Asia that rather than being an ancient, primitive form of society out of which men evolved an agricultural society, nomadism was a comparatively late development made possible only after men had mastered the domestication of animals and developed techniques for survival in the steppe. By watching natural phenomena, men may learn how to plant seeds and deal with the comparatively simple world of agriculture, but it is much more difficult to develop processes to domesticate and handle herds of wild animals. Pastoral life depends on a critical ecological balance. It is necessary to know the lowest consumptive limitations of man, comparative birthrates in developing herds, and methods of avoiding or compensating for natural disasters. It is impossible to live by heedlessly drawing from the herds. For example, when taking milk, one must leave enough for the young nursing animals, and when shearing wool, one must make allowances for the protection of the animal in cold weather. This form of livelihood is more complex than agricultural life.

Food, clothing, transportation, and all other factors in the lives of nomadic peoples are directly dependent upon their animals; therefore, man and animal are inseparable. The milk and meat of the sheep, cattle, horse, and even the camel are the food of the nomad; the wool and hide of the animals are used for clothing; and even dwellings are made from animal products. The horse, the most important means of communication and mobility was also crucial to warfare. Cattle and camels also provided means of transportation; in extreme desert areas, only camels can be depended on. Naturally, the wealth of a nomadic family or ruler is determined by the size of the herds. In order to maintain or increase this wealth, it is necessary to constantly seek better or larger grazing areas. Disease, catastrophes due to weather, or other types of disasters force the nomadic group to move to a new area. Migrations inevitably lead to conflicts over good pasture areas.

Sedentary agricultural people consider their main source of wealth to be the land on which they raise their crops, but for nomads, land is only indirectly a necessity for increasing or maintaining viability.[6] The key element for nomadic people is the animal subsisting between man and the land. This is the basic difference between the two types of society.

Federated clans of nomads gradually coalesced into an empire—a "state on horseback."[7] Due to the precarious nature of the pastoral economic base, it was necessary to maintain a wide distribution of the herds. At the same time, it was necessary to maintain unity and coordination of the clan federation through a hierarchical structure of vassalage. It was not possible for the nomads to maintain large, tightly knit units like the Chinese family lineage (*ta-chia-t'ing*), nor was it possible in their geographical environment to integrate the nomadic population into a monolithic unity like the traditional Chinese state. Thus, inherent in the nomadic state (*ulus*) was a strong tendency to fragmentation and the dissipation of power.

The basic factors of nomadic life influenced unique developments in every phase of culture. Nomadic institutions or customs, then, are generally in marked contrast to those of sedentary agriculturists. Because of the great cultural distance between the thought and the customs of these two worlds, strong prejudices militated against any close relationship.

The term "Mongol," so awesome and famous in the Middle Ages, was earlier the name of an obscure and neglected group of people, a seemingly insignificant tribal people in the remote areas of northern Mongolia. The name soon became important as it was imposed upon smaller tribal neighbors and as these people became unified by the Mongols. As the empire expanded under the military and administrative genius of Chinggis Khan, the Mongol name was applied to the great empire that unified many ethnically related tribes. The name is still applied to the people and land of this same region. Mongolia remains today the homeland of its age-old inhabitants, still known to our contemporary world as the Mongols.

According to one theory, the term "Mongol" comes from the T'ang dynasty, when a nomadic group, known as the Meng-wu or Meng-wa, emerged. Some Chinese scholars confuse or mistakenly relate the word Mongol to the Mongolian word *mönggü(n)* ("silver") and explain that while the Jurchen people refer to themselves as the "golden" people, the Mongols called themselves the *mönggü(n)* or "silver" people.[8] Another theory, subscribed to by some Mongolian scholars and intellectuals, is that the term Mongol historically involves a linguistic combination of two Mongol words, *möngke* and *ghol,* which are interpreted to mean "the eternal center." This idea seems to come from Sagang Sechen, author of *Erdeni-yin tobchi,* who explained the origin of the word *Mongghol* as follows: "After Chinggis became the Great Khan he proclaimed: 'we suffered and struggled (*mong*) and have now become the center (*ghol*) of the universe, . . . therefore we should be called the *Köke Mongghol* [Blue Mongols]. One must remember that blue, the color of the heavens, symbolized everlasting power to the Mongols.' "[9] This is a pleasing notion from the viewpoint of the Mongols, which, while it cannot be disproven, seems to be a rather romantic interpretation.

Mongols commonly identify themselves and others by various triballike names. One important group is the Buriyad Mongols, who live in the vicinity of Lake Baikal in Siberia. In eastern Mongolia, in the Nonni River valley, are the famous Dakhur Mongols who speak a dialect of mixed Mongolian and Tungusic-Manchu. The most prominent Mongol group in western Mongolia, centered during certain periods in the T'ienshan mountain region and in the lower Volga River valley, are the Oirad Mongols, known more popularly in the West as the

Kalmuck. In the heartland of central Mongolia, to the north and south of the Gobi, are Mongols identified as the Khalkha-speaking group, but divided into various subdialects. It is this group that is frequently referred to in both Asian and Western texts as the Inner and Outer Mongols.

The terms "Inner" and "Outer" Mongolia, as the different spheres came to be known, are political terms not derived from the Mongols themselves, but rather from the Manchu rulers during their two and one-half century reign. These terms, which are distasteful to nationalistic Mongols, are useful in historical analysis. The Mongols do make a somewhat related distinction in that they refer to Mongols living north of the Gobi as the *aru* Mongols, literally the "back," and to people living south of the Gobi as the *obör* Mongols, literally the "bosom." Implicit in these terms is the idea that the back and the bosom are inseparable, that all Mongols are one.

Calculating the total population of Mongolia presents many knotty problems because of the widely dispersed population and the complex political situation, which places Mongolian peoples under various governments. Reliable estimates of the Mongolian population indicate, however, that it does not exceed a total of four million persons. The population of the Mongolian People's Republic approached one and one-half million in 1975. The population in southern Mongolia, in the Chinese sphere, is estimated at approximately two million persons, and the remaining numbers are scattered in various areas under Soviet and Chinese rule. Mongolians abroad—often elite leaders who have been forced to flee from Chinese or Russian rule for various reasons—number perhaps one thousand in the United States, four to five hundred in Europe, five to six hundred in Taiwan, and perhaps several hundred dispersed in India, Nepal, and Japan.

It is equally difficult to define Mongolia as a land because of the conflict between political boundaries and cultural institutions. However one may view it, cultural Mongolia today is far larger than the political boundaries represented by the Mongolian People's Republic. The common Mongolian view is that people who speak the Mongolian language are Mongols and that the land that they inhabit is Mongolia, irrespective of the present, temporary, political circumstances. Projecting this rather ideal scope of cultural Mongolia, it extends in the east from the Nonni River valley in Manchuria, latitude 125 degrees east, westward to the T'ienshan (Turk. Tenggeri Tagh) mountain range in eastern Turkistan (Sinkiang), latitude 80 degrees east. A north-south geographical projection extends on the south from the Great Wall in the Ordos Desert, longitude 37 degrees north, northward to Lake Baikal in Siberia, longitude 53 degrees north. The Mongols would also claim, as separate Mongolian fragments, the land located between the lower reaches of the Volga and the Don rivers and a rather large area in the heart of Kökönor (Chinghai).

Political Mongolia, as currently determined, has the Siberian Buriyad and Volga Kalmuck areas fully integrated into the Union of Soviet Socialist Republics (USSR) as subordinate republics of Russia; their people are Soviet citizens. To the south, within the Chinese sphere, eastern, southern, and western Mongolia and the Mongols of the Kökönor and Sinkiang (Turkistan) areas are integrated into autonomous regions or districts of the People's Republic of China, which leaves only the Mongolian People's Republic (MPR), the old heartland of the Mongols, as an independent state recognized by over sixty nations and admitted with a permanent mission to the United Nations. The area is about equal to that of Germany, France, and England combined.

It is not possible to treat the culture and society of all the subregions of Mongolia if one is to accept the broad definition. At the same time, the intent here is not to be limited to the current, politically recognized Mongolia. This work tends to draw upon the more often neglected areas of Inner Mongolia for material in discussing nomadic society and culture, except for certain historical considerations.

The broad plateau, which dominates a great basin, is surrounded by mountains: on the Chinese border to the east and south are the Hsingan, Yin, Ch'ilien, and T'ienshan ranges; on the border of Russian Turkistan to the west are the Altai and Tengnu ranges; and to the north in Siberia are the Sayan Mountains. Thus, the major territories surrounding geographical Mongolia—Manchuria, China, Siberia, and Turkistan— are lower in altitude.

Mongolia is a desiccated, arid area because it is cut off from the prevailing monsoon winds which would otherwise bring moisture into the area and make greater vegetation possible. In the center of this predominantly steppe area is the famous Gobi, a semidesert with a powerful wind, a hard surface, and a strong grassy stubble for growth. Through the ages the Chinese called it the *han-hai,* the "dry sea," and Chinese historical materials also frequently refer to the area as "the land of no hair" (*pu-mao chih ti*). Actually, the Gobi is not a desert in the classical sense of a great expanse of shifting sands (a type of desert found in Alashan, west of the great loop of the Yellow River and north of the old Silk Route). It tended to separate various Mongol groups in pasturing their animals, the north from the south, the east from the west, thus making it difficult for nomadic powers to maintain unity.

A misconception exists about the broad Gobi and its historic role; many feel it was an impossible barrier dividing nomadic peoples and blocking travel or contact, particularly with the West. The truth is that while the Gobi is an inhospitable place, its difficulties have been exaggerated and it actually has served as an important highway, continually traversed by various nomadic peoples in broad movements from the east to the west and from the north to the south. It also has served as an important bulwark for the Mongols against the Chinese military forces.

The popular view of Mongolia as a broad expanse of monotonous geography with little differentiation is incorrect. The topographical diversity of Mongolia includes lofty mountains with snowtopped peaks and rich, wooded areas with rivers, streams, and lakes. The Mongolian plateau, for example, is the origin of many important Asian rivers including the Amur, Nonni, Liao, Yenisei, Ili, and Irtish. Even the famous Yellow River passes through part of Mongolia and, in southern Mongolia, the Chinese have been saying since ancient times, "the Yellow River has its hundred disasters, but only enriches one section," meaning the *ho-t'ao*, the top of the loop of the Yellow River, where it curves northward deep into the Ordos Desert. The valleys of these rivers generally form rich pasture areas, which have been the key economic areas of Mongolia throughout history and, thus, the objects of endless struggles.

The northwestern area of Mongolia is notable for its hundreds of lakes, large and small. Most famous among them is the Baikal in the north of Siberia, the largest and deepest freshwater lake on the face of the earth. Another important lake in the northwest is the Köbsügül, the most important waterway for transportation between the Mongolian People's Republic and the Soviet Union. Other notable lakes are the Hulun in northeastern and the Kökönor in southwestern Mongolia. The rivers and lakes are generally on the outer fringe of Mongolia; the geographical center of the area is arid, with some usually dry riverbeds or smaller streams, which disappear into the earth.

However, it is true that the dominant topography of the Mongolian heartland is a broad expanse where one sees only the heavens as a bowl covering an enormous sea of grass. The only variation is rolling hillocks. A fitting description of this aspect of Mongolian terrain is found in an appealing poem, "Song of Ch'ih-le," written by an author of the ancient nomadic Hsien-pei people; today only a Chinese version from the Northern Ch'i period (550-77) remains.

> As a great yurt are the heavens
> Covering the steppe in all directions
> On the plain of Ch'ih-le
> Under the mountains of Yin
>
> Blue, blue is the sky
> Vast, vast is the steppe
> Here the grass bends with the breeze
> Here are the cattle and sheep.[10]

The Chinese viewed the same geography differently. As Ch'iü Ch'u-chi, the famous Taoist poet, left China to travel to Afghanistan to meet with Chinggis Khan, he wrote: "Passing northward over the peak of Mount Yeh-hu, gazing downward over the mountains of the T'ai-hang Range, I beheld scenery beautiful and lovely; but looking toward the north, the only thing I could see was the cold desert with its arid grass. The atmosphere of the Middle Land absolutely ceased from here!"[11]

Certain key subregions of Mongolia deserve special mention. Most important is the old heartland of the Mongols, the cradle or political center of gravity where the ancient khans located their headquarters (*ordo*). This significant locality lies in the upper reaches of the Orkhon and Tula rivers, headwaters of the Yenisei River; also important is the region between the Kerülen and Onon rivers, which form the upper waters of the famous Amur River. The great center of Karakorum, the capital of the Mongol Empire, was located in the valley of the Orkhon River. A short distance east of this old capital, on the northern bank of the Tula River, is the site of Ulan Bator, present capital of the Mongolian People's Republic. Lines drawn from the various outlying areas of Greater Mongolia (or cultural Mongolia) will intersect very near Ulan Bator. Not too far south of Ulan Bator, the landscape merges into the Gobi. In the opposite direction, just north of the present political boundary between the MPR and the USSR, in the vicinity of Lake Baikal, is the former homeland of the historical Barghujin (Bargha) people, now inhabited by the Buriyad Mongols.

The site in which Chinggis Khan laid the foundation of his great empire lies in a corridor to the north of the present capital of Ulan Bator, between the Kerülen and Onon rivers, and extending eastward to Hulun Lake. Adjacent to this area, on the east, in the vicinity of the Nonni River, is the center of Dakhur Mongol development—a semihunting, semiagricultural people. Southeast of the Gobi, along the range of the Hsingan Mountains and centered in the valley of the Shira-müren River (headwaters of the Liao River)—a land referred to by the Chinese as the "land of pine trees and desert"[12]—was the center or heartland of the Kitan peoples who established the important Liao dynasty (907-1125).

Further west, in the present location of Chakhar, was the old center of Shangtu, the capital and important base of Khubilai Khan from which he extended his power southward over much of China. This Chinese realm of Khubilai formed the richest and most populous khanate of the great Mongol Empire when it extended over into Russia, Persia, and other areas of the West.

The region of the Yin Mountains and the Ordos was, for many centuries, the realm of the Hsiung-nu; their origins are lost in prehistory, but they were a great threat to the Chin-Han dynasties (256 B.C.-A.D. 220), contemporary with the ancient Roman Empire. Situated on the west in the present Alashan region was a center of the ancient Tangut people, famous for their rule over the so-called Hsi-Hsia dynasty (990-1227).

In the westernmost region of historical Mongolia, on the northern boundaries of the T'ienshan Mountains and in the Jungarian basin, was located the key base of Chinggis Khan for his conquest of Khorezm. Another important historical subregion of Mongolia is present-day Tannu Tuva, a land of forest and lakes in the northwest region of the Altai Mountains. This area was the origin of a number of ancient hunting peoples famous in Mongolian lore as *Oi-yin-irgen,* the "people of the wood,"[13] ancestors of the famous Oirad Mongols, among others.

The broad expanse of Siberia, forming the entire northern border of Mongolia, was of little significance to the Mongols historically; it was inhabited mainly by minor tribes, who were usually subject to whichever nomadic people dominated Mongolia. The area has always been thinly populated because of its wet, cold climate.

The large subregion of Kökönor served as a refuge, into which flowed many peoples from steppe areas further north and east as they were conquered by successive waves of nomadic peoples. Thus, Kökönor has served as a melting pot in which the Mongolian culture merged with that of the Tangut or Tibetan peoples.

The oasis area of the southwest never became the locus of a dominant power, but nevertheless was a key region because of its rather stable economic base, which was a mixture of pastoral, agricultural, and commercial elements, and because it lay across and controlled the famous Silk Route of East and West trade. The main activity of the oasis people was serving as intermediaries in trade and caravan activity. Consequently, the oasis belt was usually the pivot or the pawn of the large powers who controlled the area. Characterized by fragmented oasis city-states, it never emerged as a dominant power in Asia but was continually overshadowed by more powerful neighbors, both nomadic and sedentary.

The single most important and famous artery of East-West contact was the famous Silk Route, the beginning of which is lost in prehistory. Over it, goods flowed from the great capital of Ch'angan and other places in China, west through the Kansu corridor to Tunhuang, across Chinese Turkistan (Sinkiang) to such central Asian oasis-states as Bukhara and Samarkand, and on to the Persian and Mediterranean worlds. There have been momentous struggles throughout history by various nomadic peoples of Inner Asia against outsiders for control of the route. Only occasionally, for short periods in history, has it been controlled by the Chinese. A faster, cheaper, and safer alternative to the Silk Route was developed in early medieval times: a water route from the Arab world around India through the Straits of Malacca to South China. It was long dominated by the Arabs, but passed into European control in the 1500s with the expansion of Portugal, Holland, and Britain. This sea route is still the most important link between Asia and Europe. In early modern times, another alternative to the ancient Silk Route was developed from Peking via Urga (Ulan Bator) and Kiakhta through Siberia to Moscow and on to Europe. Finally, after the Opium War (1839–42) between China and England, and with the opening of treaty ports in China, the northern trade routes fell into disuse. The struggles for control of the trade routes ended only in recent history with the rise of the Manchu-Ch'ing and the expansion of tsarist Russia.

The climate of Mongolia is typically continental except for the land lying southeast of the Hsingan mountain range, and there are severe changes in temperature from night to day and winter to summer. The weather year-round is clear and dry, and there is little precipitation; there is less rain in the summer than snow in the winter. Throughout the year, the prevailing winds are from the northwest to the southeast and are a little stronger in the spring. The spring season begins in May, and fall or winter, with the fall of snow, begins at the end of September or the beginning of October. In the winter, it is not uncommon for the temperature to fall to forty degrees below zero centigrade. No measurement of the average temperature for summer is available, but travelers consistently complain of the hot, dry climate. The mean temperature of the various regions of Mongolia is also unavailable.

In spite of dryness, coldness, and bareness, Mongolia is a land greatly loved by its nomadic peoples; their sentiment regarding their homeland is expressed in verses chosen from "My Native Land" by the contemporary writer, D. Natsaghdorj:[14]

The fertile virgin-lands between Altai and Khanghai;
Land of our eternal destiny where ancestors lie;
Land grown mellow under the golden rays of the sun;
Land grown eternal under the silver moon.
    This is my native land,
        Mongolia the beautiful!

Homeland of our ancestors since the days of the Hsiung-nu;
Land of great might in the days of the Blue Mongols;
Land we become more accustomed to with every passing year;
Land where now the crimson flags flutter.
    This is my native land,
        Mongolia the beautiful!

Beloved country of us all who were born and die here;
The enemy who dares invade our soil shall perish;
Let us build our revolutionary state on the land ordained;
Then let us march head high toward the brave future new world.
    This is my native land,
        Mongolia the beautiful![15]

The last verse of this beautiful masterpiece indicates that a natural love for Mongolia is made more profound, in modern times, by an awareness of history and a strong national consciousness.

Due to the extremely dry and cold climate, Mongolia is not a paradise of botanical growth. Nevertheless, because of its broad geographical expanse, there are unique varieties of flora and fauna in each region. In addition to the grass that covers much of the steppe area, there are many varieties of wild onions and smelly *kömöl* plants, which are very nourishing for grazing animals. Even the famous Gobi is not totally barren; it has a stubblelike growth, four to six inches high, and clumps of sagelike plants or bushes. The stubble is of little use for most animals, but is grazed by camels. Vegetation is found mainly on the northern surface of hillocks where there is more moisture. The characteristic trees of southern Mongolia are the pine, the birch, the elm, and the aspen. Trees characteristic of northern Mongolia are the birch and the larch, a species of pine that drops its needles in the winter. Over the steppe, there are virtually no trees or wood for fuel or lumber—only scant growth in places where there is a stream or where the water table is close to the surface of the earth. Thus much of Mongolia is a semidesert region, although along the rivers there is frequently a willowlike growth. The *jagh,* a crooked cedarlike tree useful only for fuel, is characteristic of the Alashan region.

A variety of edible food plants are found in Mongolia, unlikely as it may seem. In the rainy season of July and August, one frequently finds an edible, fragrant mushroom on the chilly plateaus. In southeastern Mongolia, which has been under cultivation for over a century by Mongols as well as Chinese migrants or colonists, there are many fruit trees and crops such as wheat, barley, oats, buckwheat, millet, corn, and *kaoliang* (a maizelike crop). Irrigation is common, and even rice is grown in certain places. In northern Mongolia, which has a short growing season like Siberia's, grains such as wheat, oats, buckwheat, and corn as well as some vegetables can be grown. But it should be remembered that any sustained agricultural development in Mongolia by the Mongols themselves is a comparatively recent development.

There is also a complex variety of both domestic and wild animals in Mongolia, depending on the area. In most places, where there is sufficient pasturage, one will find the traditional "five types of animals," always listed hierarchically by the Mongols in a sort of stereotyped categorization: namely, the horse, cattle, camels, sheep, and goats. In some areas, large herds of wild antelope, herds of wild horses (*khulan*), and various species of fox, wolves, rabbits, wild rats, and marmots are found. In mountainous areas, there are wolves, bears, deer, foxes, wild goats, and valuable game animals (particularly ermine and sable), which are plentiful and have been important in the fur trade for centuries. Earlier, in the famous Hsingan mountain range, there were many tigers, but these are now almost extinct, partly as a result of the famous tiger hunts of the Kitan emperors and later khans, particularly the Mongol princes and the Manchu emperors. In the western Mongolian area of Kökönor, a large animal of the cat family, the *shülüsün,* and many musk deer are found.

Two types of large birds common in Mongolia are hawks and vultures. In addition, there is a widespread variety of larks and other songbirds. Around bodies of water, there are various geese and ducks, including the colorful mandarin duck. In semidesert areas, pheasants are plentiful and are easily caught. In the deserts and around temples and monasteries, magpies, pigeons, and sparrows (continually criticized by the Mongols for their dirty habits) abound. The famous *todogh,* a large game bird, is common on the steppe; there is a popular saying that the meat of one *todogh* will fill a large pot. The *todogh,* gray cranes, and wild ducks, are seasonal migratory birds. Snakes inhabit the steppe, but they are not plentiful nor do they seem to be poisonous. A yellowish gray lizard, some five or six inches in length, is found mostly in desert or semidesert areas. A large variety of fish is to be found in the freshwater lakes and larger rivers.

Ancient Mongolia was the pivotal area of nomadic peoples who conquered surrounding territories, but modern Mongolia became a pawn set upon by the larger powers because of the widely dispersed, fragmented, triballike groupings of the nomads and the stress placed upon them by their more powerful neighbors. In the process of modernization, Mongolian nomads have been very flexible and progressive, but have had severe limitations placed upon their development. They have been disadvantaged by a very weak economic base from which to develop cities, industries, transportation systems, and modern institutions. In the past century or more, Mongolia has seen considerable trauma and turmoil as the Mongols have tried to maintain their self-determination and viability while confronted by overpowering outside forces with which it has been always difficult and sometimes impossible to cope—given modern means of transportation, weapons, and other technology, all controlled by much more powerful nation-states. In modern times, Mongolia has become rather a vacuum in terms

A comparison of Mongolian and Chinese historical periods

	Nomadic Peoples		Agrarian Chinese World		Chinese periods
	South/West Mongolia	North/East Mongolia	North	South	
B.C. 1500	Tu-fang (Kuei-fang)		Shang (or Yin) Dynasty 1766? 1122 B.C.?		
1000	Yen-yün , Jung, Ti		Western Chou 1122-770 B.C.		
900	Hu				
800					
700			Eastern Chou 771-256		
600					
500					
400					
300	Hsiung-nu 200s B.C. 220s A.D.	Tung-hu			722-481 Spring and autumn Period
200			Ch'in 221-207		403-221 Warring States Period
100	Yueh-chih		Former Han 206-B.C. -A.D.8		
A.D. 0					
100		Hsien-pei	Hsin, A.D. 9-23		
		Wu-huan	Later Han 25-220		
200					
300	T'o-pa	Hsien-pei	Three Kingdoms, Wei, Shu, Wu 222-280		Six Dynasties Period or
			Western Chin 265-316		
			Sixteen Kingdoms 304-439	Eastern Chin 317-420	
400					

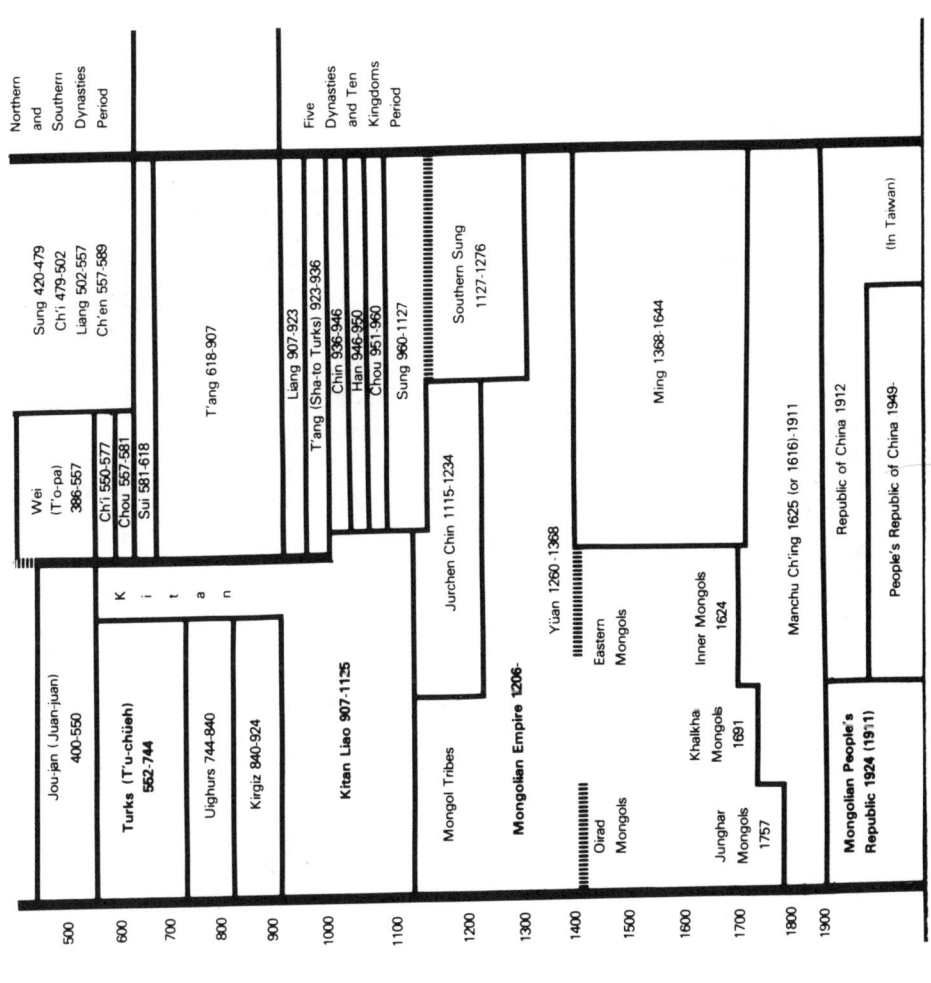

of population density or power, and its leaders have been greatly concerned because of the wide disparity between Mongolia and its neighbors with their vastly greater populations. The problem has become more acute with the growth of national consciousness among the common people and their reawakening to the historic role of the Mongols and their ancient glories of empire.

The power of the nomadic peoples has disappeared, but the strategic position of neither Mongolia nor Inner Asia has been lost in the geopolitical scheme of world power. Sino-Soviet confrontation is clear evidence of that fact. Some observers feel that with the end of the American involvement in Vietnam, the political center of gravity in East Asia has moved once again to Northeast Asia and the multipolar relationships between China, Russia, Japan, and the United States. In this context, Mongolia has been described impressively, if rather romantically, as not merely a great empty range for horses and sheep and cattle, not only the historical locus of Chinggis Khan and his hordes, not simply an interesting example of a nomadic people attempting to find a transitional path to sedentary agriculture and industrialization, but rather, as Chinggis Khan once put it, "the hinge of the earth."[16]

2

ELEMENTS OF NOMADIC CULTURE

HERDING

Herding and hunting are the most common traditional ways of life and production among the Altaic nomads. A Chinese account of the Hsiung-nu style of life, in the *Shih chi,* written in the first century B.C., indicates that at that date herding and hunting were extremely important in the daily life of the people and had conditioned certain attitudes and patterns of behavior. The dress of the people, their daily diet, and virtually every part of their life was influenced by their herding and hunting.[1]

In describing the livelihood of the Juan-juan nomads, an ancient Chinese chronicle, the *Wei shu* (ca. 560), notes that in the summer the tribes moved north beyond the "dry sea" (the Gobi) to a cooler climate and better pastures and in the winter they moved south, closer to the Great Wall where it was warmer.[2] While this may be an oversimplification, at least it is determined that the nomadic tribes wandered great distances in a circuit according to the season, not for their own convenience but mainly because of their animals. Later historians writing the *Sui shu* (ca. 600) noted the Turkic T'u-chüeh's custom of herding "their animals following the water and pasturing places; having no set place to live they dwell in tent-like yurts, eat meat, drink milk, and wear wool and hides. They are experts in shooting bows and arrows and in riding."[3] From such quotations it may be deduced that the lives of both Turkic and Mongol ethnic groups were basically the same in herding and hunting.

Old Mongols say that Chinggis Khan predicted that, if his descendants ever lived in houses of mud, it surely would be the beginning of the end for his people,[4] which is an expression of the importance of the pasturing or herding way of life to the nomadic people. Even when Chinggis Khan captured Chungtu (present-day Peking), capital of the Chin dynasty, he apparently did not stay within the city but sojourned on the outskirts,[5] indicating his avoidance of the sedentary way of life.

The famous Mongolian chronicle, *Altan tobchi,* contains the following story:

> One day as the Mongol princes were sitting about discussing what they considered to be the supreme moment or the happiest way of life, Jochi [eldest son of Chinggis Khan] said, "To me the greatest pleasure is found in herding our animals and finding the best area for pasture, in determining the best place for the royal camp to settle and in having all our people there together with a great feast, this is the best." . . . [The fourth son of Chinggis Khan] Tolui felt "To mount a well trained stallion, carry an excellent falcon and hunt in the wild lake for the coo-coo bird, then to ride on a fine spotted horse, carry a red falcon and go to the valleys of the mountains and hunt the spotted birds, this is the happiest time of life."[6]

To the degree that they can be taken at face value, these comments by the sons of Chinggis Khan give some idea of the pleasure the nomads felt for herding and hunting.

Nature compels nomadic life in steppe areas to follow a cycle according to the season. The spring season, officially February but actually late March, is considered the worst in the Mongolian steppe. The pastures are depleted, the grass is dry, and there are patches of snow. Often a severe wind arises, blowing dust and pebbles which is uncomfortable for both man and beast. (The blown dust builds up the topsoil in other areas, replenishing or developing good pastures.) The animals are skinny and weak in the spring after a severe winter season, and the herds are often depleted. A cold rain during this season can mean tragedy for the nomadic community because water freezing on the animals may kill them. In contrast, rain during this season is important for peasant farmers. A late snow is likewise a catastrophe; the animals lack the strength they had during the fall and winter to dig under the snow cover for what by now might be green grass. In 1204 Chinggis Khan made his famous surprise attack on the Naiman tribes in the spring because of the usual weakness of the herds during this season and because an attack at this time was never expected.[7]

Among the Mongols, the summer season, generally from May to September, is considered to be the best of all seasons. At this time, the pastures are green, the skies are blue, the animals are fat and healthy, and the small ones are being born.

Mongols speak of the autumn as a rich season when the sky is high, the air clear, and the horses full of spirit and stamina. In the agricultural areas, this season is a time of harvest and thanksgiving, and the peasants work in the fields gathering in their crops. This, consequently, is an additional reason why autumn was a good time for the nomads—they were able to exploit the situation by sweeping inside the Great Wall and plundering for grain, wives, and treasure.

Winter is usually from November on, and while the animals are still in good condition they are slaughtered and the meat is dried to supply provisions for the difficult season ahead. Even a severe winter does not confine the nomad to his yurt for he must go out to care for the animals. This is also an important season to hunt for game in order to stretch the family supplies.

Until recently the pastures of Mongolia remained uncultivated, just as they were in ancient times. Because of the arid nature of much of the region, there were salt and soda deposits and even the grass at times had a comparatively large salt or soda content which is good for the animals. In the *gobi*-like desert areas, there is only low, bushtype foliage, and while this is not good for most animals it is useful as fodder for camels. To one unaccustomed to the steppes, the pastures may all appear to be the same, but in reality there are great differences. Some types of pasture are not good for sheep (because of the burrs or grassheads, which penetrate the wool of the animal) but are useful for grazing horses. Other areas, not good for horses, are suitable for camels. A wise nomad knows as second nature which kind of pasture will be good for which type of animal according to the season.

All animals do not graze a pasture in the same manner. Horses generally eat the top of the grass; using their tongues, cows are able to graze the grass shorter. Of all animals, sheep nibble the grass the closest to the ground and deplete the pasture to such a degree that Mongols generally feel it is impossible to pasture in the same area twice a year. When a heavy snowfall completely covers the ground, it is possible for horses to use their hoofs to uncover the grass and graze. Cows and sheep, however, do not do this instinctively, and unless they are fed by man they die. For this reason the Mongols speak of a "white disaster" (*chaghan juda*), a winter with a great deal of snow. A winter with very little snow is called a "black disaster" (*khara juda*).

There is a sort of "class structure" or hierarchy of animals among the Mongols for they invariably speak of the five *mal* or animals in a set order: the horse, cattle, the camel, sheep, and goats. Each of the five *mal* serves a function in the nomad's life. The horse is used for war, hunting, and individual travel and pleasure. In semidesert areas, the camel and to a lesser extent cattle play a very basic role. Yurts are packed on camelback or ox-cart—not horseback. In alpine areas, yaks are used for this purpose. Sheep or goats provide meat and wool, but almost as important is their milk. Cattle, horses, yaks, and camels are prized because they provide milk in addition to their other attributes. Mare's milk is especially valued for the mild liquor that is made from it through fermentation. In regions of Mongolia where wood or other types of fuel are rare, *argal*—dried, pressed animal dung—is the most common fuel. A useful animal product, *argal* is neither messy nor smelly, and the collection of *argal* is one of the most important chores for the women and children.

The horse is the most prized of all animals, the leader or aristocrat. Some scholars have analyzed the various systems of nomadic life according to the type of animal that is the basis of the economy, and they have found that the life-style of nomads using the yak, as in Tibet, is different in certain respects from the Mongol nomadic community based on the horse, cattle, camels or sheep. Horse nomads are an "aristocratic" type with greater mobility but also greater dependence upon others who specialize in sheepherding or upon the plunder of agricultural communities. Nomads living deep in the steppe with few or no horses are greatly handicapped in their activities—traveling, hunting, herding, attacking their enemies, or escaping. A Mongol proverb notes, "the greatest misfortune is for one to lose his father while he is young or his horse during a journey."[8] For many centuries, the horse was the basis for the great mobility and striking power of nomadic armies in attacking south of the Great Wall and into the heart of Europe as well as in establishing great empires. Conversely, the horse made it possible for the Mongols to escape from the domination of intruders. The great value placed upon the horse can be seen in the specialized terminology or Mongolian vocabulary, which has many terms for color,

A horse herd at a princely residence

size, age, generation, and other factors. In contrast, the Chinese or Japanese have but a single common term for the animal. In a Mongolian camp, flags are strung along a rope; a special flag, the *kei-mori* or wind-horse flag, is stamped with the design of a horse. Mongols feel that as the flags wave in the wind, joy is brought to the family. The flags also symbolize that the family and their "horse of destiny" will always be galloping forward. The Mongols felt that in death one rode to heaven on a horse.[9]

Physically, the Mongolian horse is distinct from most breeds found in other parts of the world. It is generally rather small but has a relatively large head. While it is not considered to be as intelligent as the Arabian horse, it is noted particularly for its toughness and endurance. It can be used at great length and is tireless during the campaign or the hunt.

Horses require much greater territory for grazing and accordingly are not pastured near the base camp but out on the steppe. While women and children may herd sheep, horses require special handling, and this job is reserved for the best men of the camp. Constant attention and great skill are necessary for control and protection. One must guard particularly against the danger of stampedes during thunderstorms or blizzards, for this is when the wild wolf packs of the steppe attack the ponies. In normal conditions the stallions, as leaders of the herd, make a natural division of the animals among themselves and control and protect their own group. The conditioning of steppe life developed the famous warlike characteristics of the Mongols: fearlessness and adeptness with horses and bows and arrows.

In addition to the "aristocracy of animals," which places the horse as the number one animal, there is a priority according to color. There are regional differences, but white seems universally to be more prestigious, and leaders of some banners invariably ride a *saaral* (whitish horse). This custom is particularly prominent in the Üjümüchin Banner, which remained for the longest period the most traditional of all Inner Mongolian banners. (The color choice is not unique; there are similar customs in other parts of Asia—the white elephant in South Asia and the white horse of the Japanese emperor.) The tribute to the Manchu emperor from the Khalkha khans and the Jebtsundamba Khutughtu was the "nine whites" (yesun-chaghan)—one white camel and eight white horses.[10] The *Secret History* indicates that this custom had already become traditionalized when Chinggis Khan decreed that the famous shaman (*begi/beki*), Usun Ebügen, was allowed to "wear a white robe and ride on a white horse."[11]

There is a common lore among Mongols that the environment affects the color of the horses. For example, greater amounts of snow in Üjümüchin, it is felt, account for the greater number of white horses there than in other neighboring regions. In the Sünid Banner, where there is less snow and where the earth is generally a reddish brown, the most common horse coloring is bay or a reddish brown color (*ke'er* or *je'ered*—terms used only to describe horse coloration).

Men are commonly reluctant to ride mares, except in some areas of eastern Inner Mongolia where there are few horses. Stallions or studs also are not usually ridden; the preference is to ride geldings (castrated horses). In nomadic areas, Mongol leaders or people of distinction ordinarily would not ride a spotted horse or a horse of mixed color;[12] they rather prefer a horse of solid color. An exception to this rule is the dapple-gray horse referred to as *köke* or blue, a color prized for horses.

In contrast to the horse, cows live much closer to the nomadic settlement and graze near the yurts. They leave by themselves early in the morning to pasture and return in the evening, requiring very little attention during the day from herders. Cattle are important to the nomad, not only as a source of meat and milk, but also as a means for transporting tents, pulling carts, and especially journeying long distances by caravan. If no one is caring for the herd, the bulls take charge. The bull (*bukha*) is the symbol of strength and boldness to the Mongols. In the steppe and plateau areas of western Mongolia, there are large herds of yak, which is also a useful animal.

The camel native to Mongolia is of the two-hump (Bactrian) variety, useful particularly for long-distance travel in the desert or *gobi*. They are usually herded some distance from the main camp and require little close care. Male camels are especially difficult to handle, particularly during the mating season when they seem insane, are quick to anger, quick to fight, and dangerous to be around. Camels are used during the winter, but Mongols prefer not to use them during the summer when they shed their hair, look poorly, and are weak.

Sheep in Mongolia are differentiated into two types; the most common has a large, fat, round tail and a black head, the other has a long, large tail. The sheep with the large, fat tail is more common in eastern Mongolia while the sheep with the longer tail is more common in western Mongolia. The fat in the tail is important for nourishment of the animal during the winter season. The wool of the Mongolian sheep is quite coarse, but very white. A fine sheep herd in a summer pasture is beautifully described by the Mongols as "pearls on green velvet." Sheep live near the camps, usually to the rear of the yurt, and require a great deal of attention in being moved to and from pasture areas and in being watered. They are mainly tended by the women and children with the help of dogs. The sheep is probably the most important single animal to the nomad because it supplies not only meat and milk, the basic Mongolian diet, but also wool and hides for clothing and for felt, the main covering for the yurt dwelling and carpeting for the inside. Lambs are often kept inside the family yurt if the mother is lost or if the animal is weak, born in cold weather, or otherwise in need of special attention. In winter especially, or when the sheep are pastured at a distance, they need the care of adults, and several families may pool their resources for the task. Goats mix freely with sheep and are usually black and gray.

Moving herds was a complex and critical operation in old Mongolia. Grazing was only allowed within the circuit of the common lands held by the banner group (*khushighun*), and migration outside this region could mean war or, in Ch'ing times (1644-1911), would bring some kind of punishment for the herder and possibly for his prince.[13] Traditionally the control or enlargement of grazing fields was the main reason for a coalition of tribes into a confederation. Normally nomadic groups tended to restrain their grazing along a prescribed circuit in order to avoid clashes with neighboring groups, but on occasion natural disasters forced groups to move into new areas, leading inevitably to negotiation or trouble.

Recently, in all areas of Mongolia, the pattern of care and movement of the herds are rapidly changing, but, traditionally, when the snow melts in the spring, herders seek new pastures for their animals. Then, in the summer, herders try to find a raised area where there is a breeze for better air circulation among the animals and where they possibly may graze for a longer period. This movement also seems to be intended to protect the animals from disease. In the autumn, the more conscientious herders drive their animals out in ever-enlarging circles seeking better pastures to fatten their animals. In the winter, the object is to seek a basin or the southern slopes of a hill or mountain for protection against severe winds. Thus, although migrating frequently, the Mongols tend to remain longer at the summer and the winter camps; but in spring and autumn, they are constantly moving, and there really are no designated spring or autumn camps except for the very rich or aristocratic people who have a more settled camp or dwelling.

The ancient Kitan had an institution spoken of as the *nai-po* or "four-season court."[14] The cycle of seasonal migrations brought them to four official residences, each having a particular environment. A grazing area must have both grass and water. Many potential grazing areas lack a spring, well, or lake, which makes them unusable. The ideal is a pasturing area near a stream or freshwater lake. In the winter, it is possible for the animals to gain water by eating snow. If there is no natural water source, the only alternative is to dig a well, which means a great deal of labor for the herder in drawing water for the animals.

The dogs of Mongolia are notorious, and every traveler has dramatic stories about the ferocious Mongolian dogs kept around the camps for protection and assistance in handling the animals. In general, the Mongols maintain four types of dogs (*nokhai*). One is a large mastiff or Persian-type hunting dog called *taigh,* with a large snout, large shoulders, and a small rear end. This type of dog, found only in rich families, is used mainly for hunting. A second type of dog, a Tibetan breed, is also a large animal with long hair. It is usually all black, very ferocious, and especially helpful in animal herding. A third type of dog is a nondescript mongrel-type of many different colors and sizes. A fourth type of dog, according to the system of classification used here, is the Pekinese, the small house pet also known in the West. It is referred to as a *khab* and was introduced into Mongolia by princes returning from their annual visit to Peking. This dog is common only among more elite families and around Lamaist temples.

The Mongol fondness for dogs is second only to that for horses. For one to beat even a ferocious dog while making a visit would be tantamount to striking the host. Before the Communist takeover, the Prince of Üjümüchin Banner, Sodnamrabtan, maintained a collection of over one hundred dogs. An earlier aristocrat in the Kharachin Middle Banner had such an extraordinarily large number of dogs that he was nicknamed the "dog duke" (*Nokhai-yin Kung*). In the Ch'ing period, he presented dogs at the Manchu court as tribute.

Because of the great dependence of the nomad upon his animals, there is a deep feeling of appreciation, love, and respect for animal life which can be seen in the poetry, proverbs, and other arts of the Mongols. The misuse or maltreatment of animals is considered by Mongols to be depraved and sinful. Biblical metaphors, such as "I will recognize my sheep and my sheep will recognize me," and other such sentiments of Hebrew herders are not readily understandable to agricultural people, but they are very natural and appealing expressions to Mongols who have had contact with Christian churches. A good Mongol herder recognizes not only his own sheep but even knows which lamb belongs to which ewe.

In modern times, particularly in the Mongolian People's Republic, the old romantic pasturing life of the Mongols is passing away as new techniques of animal handling and care are developed (such as feed production, collectives, permanent corrals, barns, and new and numerous wells). Some of what is described here is already history, but many elements and influences persist.

HUNTING

Hunting serves economic, military, political, and diversionary functions in a nomadic life-style. Economically, it is an important means of sustenance—an alternative to pastoral production by which natural game is killed in order to save the domesticated herds from depletion. In addition, it is a source of goods, mainly pelts, which are important for trade with agricultural people. Hunting trains men in military techniques, and it serves as amusement and sport. The Mongols divide hunting into two general categories: first, regular hunting by individuals, which is called *ang;* second, a more specialized type involving many men in special tactics similar to encirclement or siege, referred to as *aba.* This large-scale battue type hunt is now very uncommon.

Ssu-ma Ch'ien (145?-90? B.C.) recorded in his *Shih chi* the importance of the hunt for the livelihood of the Hsiung-nu ("Huns"?). He noted that hunting supplements products from the herds in the areas of food, clothing, and items, such as pelts, for trade.[1] P'eng Ta-ya, in the thirteenth century, also noted: "The encirclement or siege tactics in hunting are used from the ninth month to the second month and they feed on the particular game killed according to the season. In this way, they kill fewer of their own animals."[2]

Good hunting preserves are as important to hunting peoples as good pasture and grazing areas are to herding peoples. When mutual agreement cannot be arrived at regarding their use, clashes occur and the groups separate. The *Secret History of the Mongols* notes that, among the Khori-Tümed tribe of the northwest forest area who engaged in more hunting than peoples further south in the steppe, a decision was made not to hunt particular animals such as sable and ermine. According to the record, Khorilartai-mergen, one leader, very unhappy with this decision, took a group who followed him, separated from the main body, and formed a new clan-lineage known as the Khorilar. Aware of an excellent game area in the region of the Burkhan Mountain, he and his group migrated to that place.[3]

The *Hou Han shu* (fifth century A.D.), in speaking of hides gained from trade among the Hsien-pei tribes, notes that they were sable and *na* and "the best under heaven."[4] Throughout the various dynasties extending over many hundreds of years and involving different nomadic peoples, furs or hides were an important medium of exchange in the border trade.

The military aspects of hunting were noted by General Chao Hung of the Southern Sung dynasty (1127-1276) in his *Meng-ta pei-lu:* "Among the Tatar [a general term for Northern nomadic people], children grow up on horseback and everybody learns the techniques of warfare. From springtime to winter, they hunt daily as a livelihood. Accordingly, they have no infantry, but only cavalry."[5] This description of Chao's may actually, with little qualification, fit all the nomadic warring peoples from the ancient Hsiung-nu down to the Mongols of modern times. The *Liao shih,* a record of the Kitan people, mentions the *nai-po* ("royal camp"), which moved according to the seasons: during the winter *nai-po,* the main activities were discussions on affairs of state and occasional hunts led by the emperor for the purpose of training men in military maneuvers.[6]

The military importance of the hunt is further illustrated in the life of Emperor Shih-tsung of the Chin (Jurchen) dynasty, one of the most Sinicized of nomadic emperors. This ruler, a scholar deeply steeped in classical Chinese Confucianism, maintained the hunt, and his biography, found in the *Chin shih,* records an incident in which one of his Chinese ministers petitioned him to give up the hunt, stressing that he was advanced in age and that the affairs of state were very pressing. However, Shih-tsung declined the petition, saying that the hunt was very necessary for him in order to give due attention to the military (*wu*) aspects of Chinese culture as well as its literary (*wen*) aspects.[7] Juvaini, a Persian historian of the thirteenth century, wrote in the *History of the World Conqueror* that to become proficient in military techniques and tactics, a Mongol must first be familiar with the use of weapons and with great, coordinated hunting activities. Through the hunt, men learn to track animals, to coordinate the movement of a large number of men, and to besiege the prey according to the number of hunters in a party. Before the hunt, scouts were sent out to make observations as a spy would during wartime. Juvaini stressed that if the Mongols were not warring, they were hunting; these activities were continuous and uninterrupted. The object of the hunt, he noted, was not merely sport or practice in the use of weapons, but also to condition the men to endure hardships.[8] The medieval missionary Carpini, in his famous visit to the Mongol Empire, also observed that there was little difference between the hunt and warring campaigns.[9]

Another aspect of hunting activity is politics. In the large-scale *aba*-type hunt, which was impossible to carry out with the men of only one kinship group, great skill was required in negotiating and coordinating with other clans to organize a confederation for the best possible success of all concerned. Highly skilled leadership was necessary, not only in negotiations and in the coordination of operations, but also in the disposition of the "take" or the booty, as in wartime. Either a consolidation of the confederation or a dispersion may result from wise or unwise disposition of the results of the hunt. The writer of the famous Mongol chronicle *Altan tobchi* indicated a number of important aspects of the *aba* in a poem.

Küdei Sechen said:

You, the ten sons of Ambaghai Khan, listen to me!
Hunting in the jagged mountains
You killed male and female mountain goats.
Following the division of the meat of the male and female
    mountain goats,
You killed each other, split and broke off from each other.

Hunting in the misty mountains,
You killed stag and hind.
Following the division of the meat of stag and hind,
You deserted each other, split and broke off from each other.

. . . .

The friendliness of the seven sons of Khabul Khan is as follows:

Hunting at the Turbikhan Khachar
They killed the fawn-colored baby antelope.
Dividing up and taking the meat of the fawn-colored baby
    antelope,
They said: "Let us feast once more,
May there be blessing and good fortune,"
And so they departed.

Hunting in the misty mountains,
They killed the wild musk deer.
Dividing up and taking the meat of the wild musk deer,
They said: "Let us honour each other once more"
They spoke fine words as of good-will
And so departed.

. . . .

You, the ten sons of Ambaghai Khan
Are of bad character and behavior.
You will become subjects and commoners.
Those seven sons of Khabul Khan

Through the strength of their amity
Will become the kings of all, the lords of the people.

Do not be angry because I, a poor old man, have said this.
You older and younger brother should live nicely, in mutual
    friendship.[10]

In the great hunts of the Mongol rulers, there was a contractual duty on
the part of their vassals to accompany the court in the hunt. The *Secret
History* mentions that Temüjin was supported by Khuchar, Altan, and
Sacha Beki as the leader of all the Mongol tribes and bearer of the title
Chinggis Khan. In their oath, they proclaimed:

> We will support you as khan [emperor] and we will be your
> vanguard to precede you in the attack when the enemy is before us.
> And to capture the beautiful and intelligent *khatun* [ladies], and
> the fine rumped horses from foreign peoples. Counting and dis-
> playing the booty we will offer it to you. At the time of the hunt,
> as we encounter the wily animals, we will press forward to encircle
> them for you and in the wilderness we will press them together
> until their bellies are side by side and in the valleys we will encircle
> them about and press them together so that their front legs and
> back legs are as one [and we will let you shoot them]."[11]

The quotation clearly states that the duty of a vassal was to follow the
khan in war and the hunt alike.

After establishing their capital in Peking, the Manchu descendants of
the former Jurchen (Chin), set aside a special preserve beyond the Great
Wall of China in present-day Inner Mongolia. The western part of the
region was called *muran* ("hunting ground"), and they established a
summer palace at Jehol. Those sections of the palace that were designed
on the model of the Tibetan Potala in Lhasa are the most famous. At the
height of the Manchu dynasty, the imperial court sojourned in this area
each year to take part in the royal hunt. The Manchu court required
their Mongol allies, as vassals, to attend the great battue hunt or *aba* at
the *muran*, as a form of tribute duty symbolic of a vassal-like relationship
in the Manchu-Mongol alliance.[12] The great *aba* hunt was used in a political context for the last time during the middle Ch'ing period (1700s).

Amusement or sport is a fourth important aspect of the hunt in
Mongolian culture. Tolui, a son of Chinggis Khan and father of the two
famous Mongol emperors, Möngke and Khubilai felt that the greatest

enjoyment of life was to be found in hunting with a beautiful horse and a fine gyrfalcon.[13] During the Yüan period, hunting continued to be the most important form of sport or recreation among the elite.[14] In this connection, Marco Polo made a number of perceptive observations regarding the Mongol hunt:

> You must know that . . . the Great Khan . . . has ordered that up to a distance of some sixty days' journey all round, everyone should hunt and fowl . . . every lord in the province takes with him all the hunters in the country . . . to the places where the animals are to be found; there they surround them, and kill them by means of dogs, or, more often, with arrows. . . . And when the Great Khan goes on this expedition . . . there is no lack of fine sights in the way of birds and beasts. There is no amusement in the world to equal it. And the Great Khan always goes on four elephants, in a beautiful wooden chamber, all lined inside with cloths of beaten gold, and covered outside with lions' skins. . . . There are also many barons and ladies to amuse him and keep him company. The Great Lord watches the sight, remaining in his bed, and finds great pleasure and amusement in it. And truly there never was, nor do I believe there is now, any man on earth able to have so much pleasure and delight as the Khan, and procure it with such ease.[15]

Another vivid account was written in 1233 by Yeh-lü Ch'u-ts'ai, famous Sinicized Kitan adviser to the Mongol khans, while he accompanied the great winter royal hunt of the camp of Ögödei Khan. He was a prime minister in the Mongol Empire at the time, a cultured Confucian gentleman from the great city centers, who found himself "roughing it," as it were, on a great hunt out in the Mongolian steppe. As a profound scholar of Chinese philosophy, Yeh-lü Ch'u-ts'ai was also deeply influenced by Buddhism, which may explain his lack of enthusiasm at the mass killing of animals on the great hunt.

> The winter hunt of the Emperor of Heaven is as a great
>   expedition of a military campaign.
> The white royal banner is unfurled as a signal for all
>   the warriors to establish the long, extended flanks and begin
>   the hunt.
> No one knows how many thousands of miles the flanks
>   extend.
> The liberating dragon trembles with fear and the mountain
>   gods are distressed.

The great flanks extend in a vast encircling pincer.
Tens of thousands of horsemen gather as the clouds, file
    into the center one after another.
Wild horses by the thousands intermingle with the wild
    mountain rams.
Red bears and white deer run with the gray antelope.
The warriors frame their bows and kill the exotic wild
    beasts.
The tigers and leopards are released to seize the greedy
    wolf. [In the royal camp, trained leopards are used.]
Only this weary traveler, the prime minister, reclines in
    the tent during the excitement.
Dropping the door flap of the yurt, I turn to a reading
    of the *I ching*.[16]

On another occasion, Yeh-lü Ch'u-ts'ai followed the emperor on a royal
hunt at Langshan (Wolf Mountain) and, as the imperial order was given
to release the animals caught in the great encirclement of the hunt, thus
saving them from death, he composed the following poem:

Do you not recall Han Wu-ti hunting in the Great Birch
    Forest, as noted in Ssu-ma Ch'ien's long poem exaggerating
    the extravagance of the imperial hunt?
Did you not observe T'ang Ming-huang practicing his military
    powers and tactics on the foothills of Lishan as noted
    by O-yang Hsiu in his history condemning the absence of
    mourning for the flight of the birds?
The deeds of these two emperors are poor examples.
For ages to come, the actions of these leaders will be condemned.
The royal hunts of my emperor are all carried out according
    to the moral precepts of the *Chou li*.
The circumference of the encircled flanks of the hunt is
    over a thousand miles.
The white gyrfalcon circles above while the golden whistling
    arrow signals below.
The elusive wild rabbit and the fox die with a snap of
    the bowstring.
The Imperial Decree is handed down as His Majesty arrives;
    in four directions, the great hunting encirclement is released
    and the animals are not all killed.
The animals and birds all bathe in the compassionate tide

of the Son of Heaven.
The flora and fauna of the Langshan mountain rejoice in
   happiness.[17]

The imperial decree stopped the slaughter before all the animals
gathered were killed. Juvaini observed a sort of customary ritual closing
the hunt, according to which one of the elders would come forward to
ritualistically beseech the khan to cease the slaughter of the animals.[18]
The action had the economic function of allowing some animals to live
in order to continue multiplying, but was made to appear as an act of
compassionate mercy by the khan.

According to the *Hei-ta shih-lüeh,* the main hunting season in the
Mongol Empire period was from the ninth to the second month of the
lunar calendar.[19] In contrast, the main season of the Manchu court hunt
was in the autumn.[20] Actually, nomadic rulers were hunting continually
in all seasons for different types of game. In more recent times, hunting
has been restricted to the period from early winter to the turn of the
winter equinox in December because after the equinox, pelts and hides
tend to lose their fine quality and the meat has become very lean. A fur
trader will not hunt after this period until the next hunting season, but
nomads, needing food, will continue to hunt.

An interesting note, useful in understanding the historical development of the Mongol hunt in the Ming period (1368-1644), is found in the
writings of Hsiao Ta-heng, who had close contact with the Mongols in
his role as a commander of Chinese troops on the frontier. He explained
in his *Pei-lu feng-su* [Customs of the Northern Barbarians]: "archery and
hunting, although a customary way of life of the barbarians, is still
handled judiciously. They may be expected to be wasteful in hunting
wild game, but on the contrary they are not so inclined." Hsiao
explained that, in the springtime, the Mongols did not hold large
encircling hunts which would kill female animals, who are about to give
birth, or young animals. Also, in the summer, no mass hunting was
carried on; small groups of from five to ten men hunted to gain food, but
did not kill for sport. Hsiao described a fascinating picture:

When the wind of autumn blows and the grass is withered, the bow
is strong and horses are powerful, the game is fast and the falcons
are swift.

Then he continued:

> The chieftain of the barbarians orders a great gathering to be held
> in the pine forests. Thousands of horsemen move like thunder and
> ten thousands of horses gallop as a cloud. They hunt in the Yin-
> shan mountain for days on end. The game is piled up like hills and
> mountains and by an unchangeable tradition it is divided evenly.[21]

Hsiao explained that there is reward and incentive, in that he who
brings down the game is given the pelt, hoofs, and horns of the animal,
but the meat is divided to all evenly. If arrows were lost, no one hid them
for fear of severe punishment.

In a record of the Southern Sung dynasty (1127-1276), the *Hei-ta
shih-lüeh,* the famous general and observer, P'eng Ta-ya, wrote about the
riding and shooting customs of the Mongols.

> When their children are very young they are bound with a cloth
> on a board which is then tied to the horses and they ride with their
> mothers on horseback. By the age of three, they are bound in the saddle in
> such a way that they may follow the others. At four or five years of age
> they are given their own little bows and arrows. As they grow older they
> follow the hunt in all four seasons. . . . It is their custom when they gallop
> to stand semi-erect in the stirrup rather than to sit down. Thus, the main
> weight of the body is upon the calves or lower part of the leg with some
> weight upon the feet and ankles. They gallop like the wind and their force
> is as a mountain avalanche. They can turn freely from left to right as a
> bird on the wing. As they gallop along they can shoot to the left even
> though they are facing to the right and this they do without holding on to
> the reins or saddle. [In shooting while] Standing on the ground they take a
> stance in the form of the [Chinese] character eight (*pa-tzu*) with legs
> spread far apart and the back and buttocks lowered. They are powerful
> shooters and are able to penetrate distant objects.[22]

The art of the hunt requires long, arduous practice to perfect tracking,
marksmanship, training of dogs and falcons, knowledge of animal habits
and psychology, and many such details. Shooting birds, for example, is
very difficult when one considers the necessity of judging the speed of
the bird, the trajectory of the arrow, the wind, and other factors. In
Mongol society, a man adept at shooting birds on the wing is especially
admired, and the term *mergen,* which in modern times commonly means

"wise" or "expert," in ancient times meant "good archer." Mongol hunters familiar with the unique behavior of the antelope found on the Mongol plain know that they have a tendency to race with a horseman and to cross in front of the path of his horse. It is important to shoot the antelope just as he passes in front of the horse and to select a single animal rather than to shoot wildly at the entire group. Mongol hunting techniques vary with the animal hunted. If the objective is taking the pelts, it is naturally important not to damage the hide in killing the animal. Before the introduction of the gun in Mongolia, hunting was done not only with bows, arrows, and spears, but also with the mace, which was used to beat the animal on the head. Among the Kharachin Mongols, a long spear was used particularly to hunt tigers. The many large wolves and packs of wolves in Mongolia are a great scourge to the herds. Ordinarily, the hunting of wolves would be of economic importance, both to protect the herds and also to gain hides for trade. However, there is surprisingly little mention of wolf hunts in early Mongolian records. Some feel that an early reluctance to hunt wolves, if in fact it existed, probably stemmed from the influence of early totemism, according to which the wolf was something of a sacred animal. The carved head of a wolf was mounted on the staff of the battle standard of the ancient T'u-chüeh (Turks).[23]

An alternative interpretation may be seen in the language of avoidance in that the term *chino* for wolf is avoided, even in modern times, by older people due to a feeling that the animal may be attracted; instead, they use the term *nokhai*, "dog," or alternatively, *khamut*, an adjective that has come to be used as a noun describing a springtime disease of dogs, which causes them to lose their hair. Thus, the use of the word "wolf" makes him more dangerous—it sharpens his teeth. The Panchan Lama enjoined the Mongols during his stay in the 1930s not to kill wolves. Young Mongols criticized the prohibition as superstitious nonsense. In informal conversation, Prince Demchügdüngrüb (De Wang), prominent nationalist leader, encouraged young men not to kill the wolf, but rather to emulate its firm will and determination. Still, many common hunters were not influenced by such romantic sentiments and killed wolves as they had always done.

The main season for wolf hunting is November, during the mating season. In tracking wolves in the pack, the Mongolian approach is to shoot the last wolf in the pack rather than to kill the lead wolf, ordinarily a female, so as to avoid having the entire pack attack the hunter. A wounded wolf is a formidable animal to be avoided.

Next to tigers and wolves, the most fearsome animals hunted in Mongolia are bear and wild boar. For furs, the most prized animals are the fox and marmot, which are most common, and the sable and ermine, which are the most expensive. Animal habits and hunting techniques are common knowledge among Mongolians.[24]

Bird hunting, usually with a falcon but sometimes with dogs, was almost totally for amusement. The best falcon, frequently noted in the Chinese records, was the *hai-tung-ch'ing,* or bluish gray falcon obtained from the Amur region of the Siberian Maritime Province. Another well-known type was the white gyrfalcon, the source of which is not known, but it seems to have been from west Central Asia and was obtained through the tribute system.[25] After the occupation of Persia, the Mongols used trained leopards in the hunt. A specialist who looked after the falcons was referred to as *shiba'uchi,* and the man who cared for the hunting leopards was termed *barschi.* The Yüan records note that many Mongol aristocrats had *ta-pu ying-fang,* which were hunting and eagle houses.[26] In addition to being an important form of amusement, the hunt was useful in obtaining special types of feathers, bones, and other materials necessary in the manufacture of weapons and for decorative luxury items.

FOOD

The diet common among nomads is unique and quite distinct from that of agricultural people. In the *Shih chi,* Ssu-ma Ch'ien explained that the main diet of the Hsiung-nu, largely meat, was the same for both nobility and commoner. However, it may be established from ancient records that while nomadic peoples had sufficient animal products for their diet they lacked certain other elements, such as grain and wine, which they greatly desired[1] and were forced to acquire either by trade or plunder. Ssu-ma Ch'ien (145?-90? B.C.) noted that with Emperor Han Kao-tsu's dispatch of an envoy in treaty relations, each year the Chinese sent to the northern nomads wine, rice, and other foods, in addition to silk. The same source discusses an account of the surrender of a Chinese official, Chung-hang Yüeh, who claimed that the nomads were very fond of Chinese food.[2]

Nevertheless, the nomads were often forced to be self-reliant, and, accordingly, developed the ability to subsist entirely upon their herds and hunting if necessary. The Chinese writer Chao Hung, in a thirteenth century work, noted: "in the territories of the Ta-tan [Mongols], there is abundant pasture grass and water for the herding of sheep and horses. For their livelihood, they drink only mare's milk to satisfy hunger and thirst. The milk of one mare is sufficient to satisfy three people."[3] P'eng Ta-ya, a contemporary, observed: "The foods they obtain from hunting are rabbit, deer, wild pig, ram, antelope, and wild horses, also fish from the rivers. The domesticated animal which they slaughter for cooking is mainly the sheep and secondly the cow. Horses are killed only for large banquets. Nine-tenths of the nomads' meat is roasted; a lesser amount is boiled. Their drink is limited to mare's milk and the fermented milk of cows and sheep. Their only spice is salt."[4]

Throughout the *Secret History of the Mongols,* the main items of diet before and during the early period of the Mongol Empire are mentioned in context. A hunter feasted on barbecued deer and its innards.[5] During the spring season, boiled mutton, which had been previously dried, and wild duck are eaten.[6] A passage refers to fermented mare's milk (*airagh*) and fermented cow's milk (*esüg*).[7] When Temüjin (Chinggis Khan) was a boy and his widowed mother and family were in difficulty, the record notes that they ate berries, crab apples, a type of artemisia, wild onion, wild garlic, and leeks.[8] Young Temüjin fished with his brother for food on the Onon River;[9] a man prepared a fat lamb for Temüjin during an escape;[10] Temüjin's family survived on marmots in particularly bad conditions.[11] The drinking of fermented mare's milk at banquets is noted often,[12] and a type of yogurt, *taragh,* is mentioned.[13] Wild ram is eaten by people in the mountains.[14] Mutton soup, a staple, is served each morning, and sheep are prepared as soup in the court kitchen.[15] Finally, the *Secret History* notes that Ögödei Khan (1229–41) reproached himself for drinking too much grape wine.

From Mongol and Chinese records of the thirteenth century, one may reconstruct the diet of the Mongols during this period and note some changes. Fermented mare's milk, referred to as *airagh* or *chige,* continued to be widely used. This, the famous *kumis* mentioned in travel accounts by Westerners in the Mongol Empire, is consistently stressed as the favorite beverage of the Mongol people and was the most common drink at banquets, particularly royal banquets. Because of the fermenting process involved in its preparation, there is some alcoholic content, which presented a problem for the European ambassadors Carpini and Rubruck. As emissaries from a Christian nation or as Christian missionaries, they did not wish to drink; but refusing to drink would be refusing the hospitality of the Mongols.[16]

An interesting and fairly detailed account of the Mongolian process of making *kumis* is given by the medieval traveler Rubruck; the technique has not changed for seven hundred years.

Cosmos [*kumis*], that is mare's milk, is made in this way: they stretch along the ground a long rope attached to two stakes stuck into the earth; and at about nine o'clock they tie to this rope the foals of the mares they want to milk. Then the mothers stand near their foals and let themselves be peacefully milked; if any one of them is too restless, then a man takes the foal and, placing it under her, lets it suck a little, and he takes it away again and the milker takes its place.

And so, when they have collected a great quantity of milk, which is as sweet as cow's milk when it is fresh, they pour it into a large skin or bag and they begin churning it with a specially made stick which is as big as a man's head at its lower end and hollowed out; and when they beat it quickly it begins to bubble like new wine and to turn sour and ferment, and they churn it until they can extract the butter. Then they taste it and when it is fairly pungent they drink it. As long as one is drinking, it bites the tongue like vinegar; when one stops, it leaves on the tongue the taste of milk of almonds and greatly delights the inner man; it even intoxicates those who have not a very good head. It also greatly provokes urine.[17]

Medieval Western travelers invariably mention *kumis,* but none go into detail as to its special characteristics. While Yeh-lü Ch'u-ts'ai, accompanied Chinggis Khan on an expedition against Khorezm, he wrote the following and included it in a letter requesting a friend to send him some *kumis:*

The heavenly horse migrated west
     the juice of the jade was brewed.
The mild fragrance of the wine
     arises from the place where the skin sack is poured.
In beholding the "light-white" [*kumis*], one feels cool
     as though gazing upon pale green jade juice.
The sensitive sweetness of the kumis
     prompts a longing for cool sugarcane nectar.
Ssu-ma Hsiang-ju[18] would love this [*kumis*]
     to quench the inner fiery thirst of his spirit.
I long to receive this from you,
     that I may be refreshed daily.

When Yeh-lü Ch'u-ts'ai received the *kumis* from his friend, he thanked him with a second poem:

> While eating meat I joyfully sip the kumis.
> It is most fragrant and smooth and the taste is slightly
>   tart.
> Your *kumis* is as Tsunhsun wine brewed in the skin sack of Han
>   Hsiang of the Eight Immortals of T'ang.
> I repeatedly pour the *kumis* into the birch-bowl until it is overflowing.
> Gnawing hunger pangs are immediately soothed and satisfied.
> My anxiety and thirst are thoroughly dissipated, I am refreshed and cool.
> Do you recall the poet Chia I[19] who forbid all to partake of his wine
>   except another poet?[20]

In these poems by a Sinicized Kitan, one sees an intimate hedonistic acquaintance with the famous Mongol drink. Noted are the mode of its preparation, the type of containers used, its smell, appearance, taste, and the satisfying sensation of drinking it.

Unfermented mare's milk has never been a common drink because it acts as a strong laxative or purgative. Fermented milk in general, such as buttermilk, is spoken of by the Mongols as *esüg*. Customarily, they dislike drinking fresh cow's milk, so it is common to make a sort of yogurt (*taragh*) of it; the same is true of sheep's milk. A common drink is hot salted tea with milk.

Marmots were traditionally eaten only by poor people and hunters, and the same is true today. The most common method of cooking marmot was a primitive process of heating stones and placing them in the stomach of the animal; the food is called *ghorhogh*. In early times, rabbits also were freely hunted and eaten, but now Mongols poke fun at and shame a rabbit eater. The common game animals eaten during the imperial Yüan period were the same as those eaten during the period of Chinggis Khan.

Among domestic animals, mutton and beef were the most common stock eaten by the khan as well as the common folk. Dried meat, spoken of as early as the *Secret History,* was prepared in the early winter, when the animals were in good condition, and stored for use as necessary. From ancient times to the present, Mongols have used the vitals or innards of animals they slaughter, but never in banquets. Cows are not commonly slaughtered during the hot months because of the problem of storing a large quantity of meat. The killing of animals is discontinued during the early summer season, in the fourth lunar month (May), because the flocks and herds increase as animals give birth and the birth of the Buddha is commemorated. During this month, milk is almost the only food eaten by many nomads except for meat dried the previous fall. Contrary to the custom of ancient times, it is more common now for Mongols to boil meat rather than roast it.

The famous Mongol record, *Altan tobchi,* speaks of Chinggis Khan's eating horse meat.[21] In the latter part of the sixteenth century, with the conversion of the Mongols to Tibetan Buddhism, the practice of slaughtering and eating horses was forbidden by the Third Dalai Lama and ceased to be a general practice. Particular mention is made of this fact in the *Erdeni-yin tobchi.*[22] However, among the Oirad Mongols in the west, the custom of eating horseflesh has continued to the present.

Early records dealing with the Mongols mention fish as part of their diet. Ancient Mongol dictionaries list many names of fish (the meanings of which are no longer understood), which indicates, contrary to common belief, that the Mongols did eat fish at one time. However, the practice of fishing also ceased with the introduction of Tibetan Buddhism, which inculcates the doctrine of many grades of incarnation, the lowest of which is water animals and fish. Formerly, one of the most sinful acts was to eat fish, but in contemporary Mongolia, with the weakening of Buddhism, eating of fish has been resumed.

Wild berries, onions, garlic, and other such foods have continued to be part of the Mongol diet to the present. The *Secret History* makes no mention of the use of grain for food during the rise of the Mongols; nor does the *Hei-ta shih-lüeh,* the important Sung period (960-1276) record. The Mongols may have been handicapped in obtaining grain, since they were a considerable distance from the Chinese frontier, or they may not have developed the custom of using grain in their diet. If such was the case, the situation did not last long, for the records of the Yüan period indicate that the use of grains and other agricultural products rapidly became common among the Mongols, even to the extent that limited plowing and marginal agriculture were practiced by the Mongols themselves or by Chinese living among them. From the fifteenth century on, there is considerable recorded evidence that animals were exchanged by the Mongols for agricultural products as foodstuffs.

Strange as it may seem, the oldest Chinese cookbook extant is apparently a non-Chinese compilation; the *Yin-shan cheng-yao* ("the proper management of food and drink") by Hu-ssu-hui was published during the Mongol-Yüan dynasty in 1503 (third year of the T'ien-li reign period) by the order of Öljeitü Khan (Wen-tsung). Hu-ssu-hui, a royal chef in the imperial kitchen, noted in his book that the diet of Khubilai Khan was prepared strictly according to proper nutritious principles. The preface of the book states that Khubilai Khan's favorite dishes are among the recipes. These are mainly lamb or mutton dishes drawn from old Mongolian or Uighur-Turkic cuisine rather than the Chinese. Even many of the ingredients are referred to by their Mongolian or Turkic pronunciation. The text indicates that during Mongolian rule of China, the food of the royal household was prepared not only delicately, but also nutritiously. It is also evident that while the Mongols were in China, they still prized Mongol-Turkic food and continued to eat their traditional diet, gradually accepting some elements of Chinese cuisine.

Hsiao Ta-heng (1590s), a Chinese border expert, noted many Mongol eating habits, among them a tendency to eat their meat rather rare, on the theory that it is better for the body and would satisfy hunger longer. Mongols continue to believe that meat that is too well done is not good for the body. They served sheep instead of beef to a guest. While they ate grain, on balance Hsiao felt that they ate more meat. Hsiao noted that a favorite food of the nomads was a thick soup prepared from boiled meat to which was added rice or millet; a type of mortar was used to husk rice and a round stone grinder to prepare flour. One common preparation of the nomads, according to Hsiao, was flour noodles mixed with milk or cream. He was greatly impressed with the ability of the nomads to bear hunger; often, they survived for several days on a lump of cheese with some water. In his opinion, the Mongols liked sweets somewhat more than the Chinese did. Hsiao confirmed that the Mongols of his day had a large variety of fermented or distilled drinks, mostly made from milk and some so strong that only several cups made a person drunk. These beverages were kept in sacks prepared from animal skins.[23]

In ancient times, the alcoholic beverages of the Mongols were restricted to airagh or kumis. Whether cow's milk was also used to provide a fermented beverage in earlier times is not known since no mention is made of it in the Secret History or other early records. Yüan dynasty records make particular note of the fact that wine was used by the Öngghüd tribe, then migrating near the Great Wall, as a tribute to Chinggis Khan. Chinggis declared that it was all right to drink a little wine, but that it was unwise to drink a large quantity because a person would lose control of himself.[24] The evidence seems to indicate that before contact with the Chinese, there was no real wine, as such, among the Mongols. The use of wine became common only with the expansion of the Mongol Empire, contact with the Chinese, and particularly contact with the "western regions" (Hsi-yü) or western Asia. Eventually, a *boro darasu*-type wine, made of grapes, came to be the most common wine among the Mongol elite. While Chinggis Khan did not usually drink wine, he did not strictly prohibit it in the famous Mongol law code, the *jasagh* (*yasa*). D'Ohsson, in his well-known *History of the Mongols,* included the following:

> Chinggis Khan objected to the habitual drinking of wine and said, "A drunkard is like one who is blind, deaf, and insane, he cannot even stand erect but is like a man that is struck upon the head. Regardless of what talent or training a person may have, to the drunkard these things are useless, all he will receive from others is insults. The ruler who becomes addicted to wine can never undertake a great enterprise. A general who likes wine can never control his troops. Whoever it may be who has this evil habit it will certainly lead to disaster. The person who cannot desist from this habit it would be better for him if he would get drunk but three times a month. If only one time this would be even better. However, best of all is total abstinence. But where may I find such a man?"[25]

While the empire was being established, wine became popular among the troops, and some have said that wine saved Europe from the Mongol conquest because the Great Khan Ögödei died of a stroke (1241) after drinking wine. Upon his death, the Mongol armies ceased moving into Europe as the generals withdrew to hold a great assembly and elect a new khan. The *Yüan shih* records that the Emperor Ögödei went hunting, retired at night to drink wine, and died the following day.[26] Apparently, the most famous prime minister of the Mongol dynasty, Yeh-lü Ch'u-ts'ai, attempted to stop the Emperor Ögödei from overdrinking. It is recorded that, on one occasion, the minister took the iron mouth of a liquor jug to the emperor, showed him how it had rotted the metal, and pointed out that if the metal could corrode, his stomach would not be able to withstand the corruption.[27] Mongols deplore the fact that distilled drink brought great damage to the empire and the people, but liquor continues to hold a great attraction for them to this day.

The *Secret History* does not mention tea, which later became very important to the Mongols. The only morning beverage noted is a meat soup prepared for the court. At the present time, tea is an integral part of the diet. The first mention of tea in a Mongol record is in the *Altan tobchi:* in the fifteenth century, the *khatun* or empress, Sain Mandukhai, in anger, poured tea on a minister who made a proposal with which she did not agree.[28] From this anecdote one may deduce that tea was used then, at least among the aristocrats. When Tibetan Buddhism was reintroduced in the late sixteenth century, the habit of tea drinking was adopted concurrently with the new religion because it was a universal custom among the Buddhist monks and an aid to their meditation. Long before the sixteenth century, tea was traded to the Tibetans by the Chinese in exchange for horses; however, this type of trade did not develop very early with the Mongols. When Altan Khan (d. 1583) desired to entertain high Buddhist monks, he negotiated with the Ming court to inaugurate tea trade. The Ming refused, saying that there was no precedent for such trade, though they did allow a little to be given to Altan himself.[29] The evidence suggests that, before the 1570s, tea trade and drinking was not common among the lower levels of Mongol society.

Customarily, the Mongols have three meals per day, and tea is drunk in the morning and at noon. The most popular type of tea during the late Ch'ing period and in this century was transported from Hankow. For easy transportation, the tea was first steamed and pressed into hardened bricks. A lower grade of tea, commonly called *shira chai* ("yellow tea"), was one of the common products exported in the late Ch'ing dynasty into Outer Mongolia. A common method of tea preparation among the Mongols is to break up the brick tea in a large pot, in which it is boiled, and add a little salt; then, while the tea is still boiling, milk or cream is added. For breakfast and lunch, toasted or roasted millet may be added to the tea and milk. The millet is ordinarily very hard, having been toasted, but becomes soft when put into the hot tea. Sometimes tea is drunk with *öröm* or *khuruud,* a sort of milk curd, or with cheese. The mixture will often be eaten with cold boiled mutton, left over from the previous day.

There are many types of milk curd in the Mongol diet. One of the most common means of preparation is to let milk set until the cream rises and then skim it off. The milk is then boiled until a curd begins to form, so the water or whey can be removed. Butter and sugar are added to the remaining curd, which may be eaten or dried and prepared for storage for later use. Another method of preparation, commonly found in the

West, allows the milk to curdle; the whey is poured off, and after the curd sours, it is eaten as a form of sour cheese. Sometimes, the whey removed from the buttermilk is distilled to prepare an alcoholic drink.[30]

The evening meal is the most important in Mongolia, and a common dinner dish is a piece of boiled, sliced meat mixed with noodles made of flour, or millet mixed into a meat soup. In the past, rice has been considered a luxury. When tea replaced meat soup in the morning meal, meat soup gradually became part of the evening meal. A type of dessert is prepared by boiling flour cookies called *borsogh* in oil or butter. With various foods prepared from milk, sugar is commonly added as sweetening.

In more recent times, vegetables and fruits have been produced in the agricultural areas of Mongolia, but these still are not commonly available in the pastoral or nomadic areas, though some dried fruit is imported. A type of pickling process is used to preserve wild leeks, mushrooms, garlic, and other such items. The older generation, ridiculing the younger people about their diversified diet that includes vegetables, commonly says, "Grass is for the animals and meat is the food for man, and if you eat grass, you will not have a strong body." This sentiment is indicative of the traditional predominance of meat products in the Mongol diet.

Probably the most important evolutionary change in the diet of the Mongolian nomads was the introduction of grain and tea. However, far more meat and milk products have continued to be used than in the neighboring agricultural regions of North China.

Ceremonial offerings indicate foods that were selected for special consideration. The Monograph on Worship and Offerings (*Chi-ssu chih*) of the *Yüan shih,* dynastic history of the Mongols, notes that they built magnificent ancestral temples in Peking on the Chinese style, but the offerings were largely a perpetuation of nomadic custom. A horse of pure color, either white or some other, was offered along with sheep, oxen, and pigs. Before certain ceremonies, a high official was dispatched with a group of hunters to bring in game, particularly deer and rabbits, for offerings. Swan, wild horses, a type of marmot (*tarbagha*), pheasant, antelope, a wild dove (*khujar*), mare's milk, grape wine, wild pigs, fish, and foods from the western regions of China were offered in customary state rituals of the Mongol nation.[31]

Horses, most prized of Mongol animals, were used symbolically as offerings in the worship of heaven (*Tenggeri*) and for special feasts.

During the Yüan period, the court urged people to kill only one horse rather than many for a banquet. A white horse was especially prized, and it is significant that this type alone constitutes the great offering at the sacrificial ceremony at Ejen-khoroo in the Ordos, where the cult of Chinggis Khan is centered.

The use of tobacco began fairly early in Mongolia, but the earliest source of its adoption is unclear. It seems certain that the Manchu first acquired tobacco from Korea, and there is the possibility that it first came to Mongolia via the Manchu rather than China. However, Chinese merchants during the Ch'ing period soon came to monopolize the tobacco trade.

DRESS

Clothing, like food, is largely determined by environment for the nomads of the Mongolian steppe. The climate is dry and cold, and nomads, from the ancient Hsiung-nu to the contemporary Mongols, require garments that furnish protection from the cold, freedom when riding horses, and a suitable covering when camping out in the wilderness.

In addition to their usual purpose, fabric and clothing were exchanged in tribute, taken as booty, and obtained as items of trade. From the time of Han Kao-ti (206-195 B.C.), the Chinese sent as tribute each year a considerable amount of cloth, silk, and other items to the threatening Hsiung-nu *shan-yü* or emperor, Mao-tun (209-174 B.C.).[1] The nature of the tribute indicates the need of nomads to obtain cloth from settled agricultural peoples. During excavations in 1924-25, Russian archaeologist P. K. Kozlov discovered the tomb of a Hsiung-nu aristocrat in the Noyan mountain range,[2] in which were found both the woolen textiles of the Hsiung-nu, with animal motif or designs, and Chinese silks, indicating that from very early times, even before the Christian era, Chinese silk was valued by the nomads.

The *Secret History* indicates that the undergarments of women were made of fine wool or from silk and cloth imported from China. The red-colored dress of the women and the interlocking ring-design of silk found in the dress of babies were obtained from China even prior to the height of the Mongol Empire.

Some Mongol leaders had ambivalent feelings about wearing the finery acquired from people they conquered, and when Chungtu

A Mongolian lady in formal dress and customary polite posture

(Peking), capital of the Chin was captured, the leader, Shigi-khutughu, refused a Jurchen gift of a bolt of silk decorated with a golden design. His puritanical sensitivities constrained him to reject it.[3] Similarly, fine clothing or material was offered to Chinggis Khan by a surrendering Uighur ruler who came to court petitioning to become an adopted son and presenting pearls, silks, and *nachid* (Chs. *na-shih-shih*), a particular type of silk of all golden Persian design.[4]

Prior to the capture of the Chin capital, Chungtu, the Mongols had difficulty in acquiring silk and woven goods, but after the conquest these goods were readily available until Ming times, after the fall of the empire. *Nachid* became most highly prized and was later in great demand and common use among the Mongol nobility. However, the most ancient reference to nomadic dress, found in the *Shih chi*, notes that all— from the ruler of the Hsiung-nu down to the common people—wore the pelts of animals.[5]

There are passing references to Mongol clothing and headdress of the steppe period in the *Secret History,* among which are: (1) the undergarments of the mother of Chinggis Khan;[6] (2) the male hairstyle *kegül;*[7] (3) a special female hairstyle called *shibülger;*[8] (4) the *boghta* (Chs. *ku-ku*) hat, distinctive of a married lady;[9] (5) a special black sable garment, which was a present from Börte, the wife of Chinggis, to her parents-in-law;[10] and (6) a baby shawl, also made of sable.[11] When Bo'orchu, a chief among the companions of Chinggis Khan, came to join him, he was wearing a brown woolen garment.[12] Since Bo'orchu was wealthier than Chinggis,[13] it appears that at this stage, Chinese silk was still not commonly used. The record also notes a belt worn on an all-purpose gownlike coat;[14] a *de'el*, a robe made of a fur-lined sheepskin worn by an old lady;[15] the costume of a boy, including a sable hat or cap, boots of doeskin, and a long coat of unlined bleached hide with an otter-skin border;[16] a baby's garment, a sable jacket lined with silk and bearing a design of interlocking rings;[17] and a woman's red coat.[18]

In the thirteenth-century Chinese record *Hei-ta shih-lüeh,* Mongol dress is described:

> As to headdress, the hair is allowed to hang down freely over the forehead and the sides of the face with a plait on each side in front of the ears. In the winter, a fur hat is worn, and in the summer a straw hat. On top of the head, women wear a *ku-ku*. Their robe buttons to the right with the neckline or collar cut so as to form a square just below the neck.

Anciently, hides, wool and felt were all used in place of textiles. More recently, they use linen, silk, and golden silk. There is no difference between the higher classes and the lower classes in design or style. The colors generally worn are red, purple, green, and yellow. The most common designs are the sun, moon, dragon, and phoenix.[19]

An analysis of the *Hei-ta shih-lüeh* establishes that textiles in use before the rise of the empire differ markedly from those used later. Decorative symbols also changed; the sun, moon, dragon, and phoenix designs are not typical Mongol designs, but were derived from the Chinese. The Chinese, among whom color and style of textiles were carefully restricted and prescribed according to rank, were very surprised to find that, for the nomads, color and style had no particular class distinction. Mongol dress in the steppe, compared to the rather conservative colors of the Chinese, is customarily quite bright, emphasizing blues, purples, and reds. A study of nomadic influence on the dress of the Chinese, *Hufuk'ao* ("examination of barbarian dress") by Wang Kuo-wei indicates that the nomads had a much greater influence on the dress of the agricultural people than has been commonly thought.[20]

Carpini, the first Roman Catholic envoy to the Mongols, observed in the account of his visit at the time of the enthronement of Güyüg Khan (1246-48) that all Mongol leaders wore a different color of dress (*jisün*, a formal, ceremonial coat worn at imperial parties or special occasions)[21] each day and that all men would wear the same color on the same day.[22] No explanation for this practice is given. In the *Yüan shih*, the Mongol dynastic history, there is a very excellent, detailed description of the dress of the khan and ranking members of the Mongol court. The Yüan court costume mixed Mongolian and Chinese style.[23] Among the Mongol khans the first to wear Chinese dress was Möngke (1251-59). An account in his biography[24] notes that on one occasion he wore the robes of the Son of Heaven, typical dress of the Chinese emperors in the very important ceremony of worshiping heaven; however, it is felt that particular mention is made of this case because it was an exception rather than the general rule.

William of Rubruck, who was sent to Karakorum (1253-54), the Mongol capital, by Emperor Louis of France, observed that the dress of the Emperor Möngke was "a speckled and shiny furlike sealskin."[25] The portraits of the Mongol emperors and empresses, presently held by the Palace Museum in Taiwan, give an excellent and authentic model of Mongolian courtly or aristocratic dress. Judging from these portraits there has been a strong persistance in the style of male dress from the Yüan period to the present century; however, the costume typical for women during the Yüan period has long since disappeared. Descriptions of Mongol male dress in ancient Tibetan chronicles note a "winged-swallow" hat and a "pig-snout" boot with a turned-up toe. These Tibetan records confirm a long-standing tradition from early times to the present in these items of dress.[26]

According to Hsiao Ta-heng, who wrote in the 1590s, the traditional gown or robe of both high and low classes had sleeves that were very tight and had very distinct pleats. In cold weather, it was common to pull the sleeves down over the hands. The gowns reached to about one foot below the knee and were decorated along the bottom and on the overlapping fringe across the chest with the fur of tigers, leopards muskrats, sable, and seal. The gown itself, it appears, was made of leather, but, Hsiao stressed, "recently the Mongols have been offering tribute to us [Chinese] with great care and we usually give them golden, embroidered and designed silk; therefore, the tribal barbarians have begun to wear robes of silk. Their chieftains especially delight in adopting such clothing."[27]

Sable pelts or fur, which are symbolic of honor and good fortune, have been used to cement alliances. The sections on religion and worship in the *Yüan shih* note that emperors were dressed in sable gowns and placed in "golden coffins" for their funerals.[28] Later, a custom institutionalized during the Ch'ing period (1644-1911) had the tribes situated north of the Altai mountain range bring sable pelts to court as tribute, a custom which persisted down through late Ch'ing times.[29] The *Secret History* notes that Börte, wife of Chinggis Khan, came to him at a low period of his career bringing a sable gown as part of her dowry. The sable was very shrewdly used by Chinggis to gain status and power in political dealings with his neighbors. He brought the sable gown as a present to Ong Khan (To'oril), leader of the Kereyid tribe, who was the most powerful of the tribal leaders of the steppes, and said: "You are the sworn brother of my father and thus are as a father to me. Now I am married and my wife has brought a present to her father and mother-in-law, and I now bring this to you as my father." Ong Khan was greatly pleased and replied: "As a reward for this black sable gown, I will do as follows: Your people are scattered, and I will gather them for you; your followers are dispersed and I will bring them together for you."[30] This speech was recited in a sort of chant to Chinggis. The two immediately formulated an alliance, which was an important stage in the beginnings of the Mongol Empire. Of various types of sable pelts, black was particularly prized. Among aristocratic families, the treasured garment was a sable fur cloak for babies; these were uncommon among the masses of the people.

Headgear and hairdos have changed over the centuries. A broad, peaked straw hat that became popular after the conquest of China is spoken of in the *Yüan shih* as part of the court dress; but it seems to have had no functional value in Mongolia, although in China it may have served as protection from the sun. The *ku-ku*, a typical female headdress, was popular from the twelfth to the fifteenth century and was restricted to married women of the aristocratic class. According to portraits found in the Palace Museum, the *ku-ku* style was about one foot tall, narrow in the center after rising from the head, and wider and flat on top. Large jewels were usually worn on the front of this unique headgear, which disappeared several centuries ago. The *shibülger,* another early headdress typical of married women, was a style in which the hair was parted from the forehead and brought to both sides of the face in plaited braids. It persisted until very recent times.

In the typical male hairdo, or *kegül* of the empire period, the hair came down over the forehead and was parted to the sides of the face; long tufts of hair hung from the temples down to the shoulders. Early Franciscan and Dominican missionaries in the Mongol Empire mentioned a style in which the hair was worn long around the edges and the center of the head was shaved in a monklike tonsure. Other medieval sources mention a pigtail worn down the back, but it is difficult to say just when this custom began. As early as the fourth century, the Chinese spoke of the braided headdress of the nomads as *so-lo,* and implied that it indicated the status of a chained slave.

Long after the empire, Hsiao Ta-heng gave a description of traditional Mongol headdress. He noted that Mongol males, both young and old, shaved the forepart of the head except in winter, leaving the back hair to grow long and be braided. Young women wore several braided plaits on both sides and in the back of the head until marriage. Upon meeting the parents of her husband, a young bride then parted her hair in the middle and wore only a simple braid on each side over the ear. Young women often pierced their ears and attached gold and silver ornaments to them. Hsiao observed that Mongol women used a type of powder, both red and white, on their faces; compared to Chinese custom, he felt it was used excessively.

Hsiao described the hats worn by Mongols as being similar in shape to those of the Chinese, though smaller, so as to cover only the forepart of the head. He mentioned a special small hat that covered only a small area in the middle of the head and was tied down. It is not yet possible to trace the origin of this hat, but its description resembles the traditional hat worn by Korean men, and some Korean scholars report that this headgear was adopted under Mongol influence. The brim on all Mongol hats, according to Hsiao, was narrow with a red tassle hanging down and a small silver image of the Buddha affixed to the front. Some of these hats were made of felt, others of leather. Straw hats similar to those of South China are also mentioned.

The hat style found on the most common portrait of Chinggis Khan is still typical of the hat worn, particularly in the winter, in the early decades of this century. It is a capelike covering with a band or border around the edge going down the sides of the face to the back of the neck. It ordinarily had lambskin on the inside and fox skin around the borders of the outside with a cloth center that was generally brown, blue, or maroon. On the top was attached a red button with red silk threads forming a tassle toward the back. One style of hat, with a broad brim or circular band, worn by all classes resembles a sailor's hat. During the summer season, the brim was black velvet and during the winter, it was otter, black lambskin, or sealskin. A similar style also had a sailorlike brim, but came to a point on either side of the head, and the further north one traveled, the taller became the peak or center of the hat. Mongol male and female hat styles are similar, except that women's brims are more decorative. The most common hat found among the Mongol nomads, often seen in pictures taken by Western travelers, has ermine-lined earflaps used in cold weather. During the hotter summer periods, a popular headdress among the common people is merely a piece of cloth tied around the head.

Women's decorations are worn mostly on the head. Unmarried women commonly wear a single braid down the back with bits of turquoise or coral attached to the braid. Unmarried girls may, on occasion, wear a necklace, but married women generally prefer profuse ornamentation. The traditional decorative headdress has beaded streams from the forehead to the shoulders or breast; rich ladies wear pearls, less wealthy ladies wear coral, and silver is used by the least well off. On the end of the ladies' plaits, coming down from the temple

Sechin Jagchid and his wife in front of a yurt

toward the breast, was worn a small box and above that a ring, both
carefully decorated with different types of coral, jewels, or stones. An
amulet or protective fetish, always highly decorative, was worn on a
necklace. Married ladies among the Khalkha Mongols traditionally
wore a hornlike wig extending upward and outward from both sides of
the head. The women of the Bargha (Barghu) tribe wore a similar
headdress, except that the wig extended up from the side of the cheeks
and back toward the rear of the head.

In ancient times, the nomads of Mongolia wore belts; however, in
modern times, Mongols wear sashes, not true belts. If we can judge by
the fasteners, a belt worn in early times on the steppe is still found in the
west among the Kazaks. The belt, or sash, of the traditional Mongol
costume is made of silk and worn by both men and unmarried women.
Belts, sashes, and hats came to be symbolic of power and dignity. When
worshipping, Chinggis Khan removed his hat and expressed gratitude to
Tenggeri, the highest god of Mongolian Shamanism.[31] Upon marriage, a
woman removes the sash as a symbol of obedience to her husband.
Formerly, a common appellation for men was "sashed ones" and for
women, "sashless ones." While this terminology, regarded as
feudalistic, was abolished after the revolution in the 1920s, the wearing

of sashes continued; even married women began to wear them.

Mongolian nomads are constantly outside during the winter, and a sheepskin coat is their single most important item of clothing. It is worn quite long and full in order to protect the legs, and a belt or sash is used to keep it in place while involved in such activity as horse riding. The belt is cinched tight around the midriff but the chest and shoulder sections of the coat are very full to allow movement. The sleeves are long, coming down past the fingertips. Formerly, the cuff of the sleeve, which, in winter, protected hands that handled horse reins or metal objects, such as weapons, was distinctive: wealthy people wore valuable furs whereas the common people wore velvet in the summer and lambskin during the winter. However, the cuff was seen as a needless luxury, and its use among the elite was considered "feudalistic"; therefore, it was abolished when the Communists came to power in Mongolia.

For protection against the strong winds on the Mongol steppe during the winter season, clothing is usually made of heavy sheepskin, young camel, or wild goatskin. In early spring and late autumn, lambskin or other lighter pelts are used. The common Mongol *de'el* or robe, worn in the winter, is generally sheepskin; the smooth side of the hides are turned outward and tanned to a fine texture by using milk while the fur side is worn toward the body. Along the hem of the garment is sewn a bias of velvet or silk. In early spring or late autumn, a quilted lining may be added to the dress for additional warmth. During the summer season, a garment of double-layered common cotton cloth is worn instead of skins. Only in the vicinity of the Great Wall, where the climate is warmer, do the Mongols wear a single-layered cloth garment. The pelts used for all clothing, of course, are native to Mongolia; cotton and silk are imported from China with the most popular silk coming from Shantung province.

The most common colors worn now are blue, red, purple, brown, green, pink, and white. Mongol cuffs are consistently light blue, except in winter when fur is used. Black is worn for mourning, except for black silk which is occasionally worn as a vest, originally a Manchu style. The vest is worn on ceremonial occasions and may be of different colors in contrast to the Chinese who universally wear black.

Traditionally, the dress of unmarried females differs little in style from that of males except that it is more colorful. When a girl marries, she begins to wear a long sleeveless garment over her gown. This garment is a conservative dark color, but is always bordered with bright designs, and totally covers the body except for the arms. Men's trousers are always very full for horseback riding, and horsemen or herders frequently wear a type of chaps or leather leggings, often beautifully designed, pulled over the legs and tied to the belt. Frequently, the chaps and vests are made of pelts obtained from the deer hunt.

Because of the prevalence of sand in the desert and steppe areas, both male and female wear long boots. The Mongol boot is commonly broader at the top than Western boots, and, in some regions, the toe turns up. The boot is made of black oxhide with a yellow or green oxhide design; the sole and heel are very thick. Felt boots are common in the winter because they are warmer than leather. But felt boots are not worn at other times of the year because felt is hot and wears out rapidly. Mongol socks, worn inside of the boots, are made of either felt or many layers of cloth.

For decoration, the Mongol male ordinarily fastens hanging ornaments on both sides of his sash. On the right side, he attaches a pouch or kit containing a knife and chopsticks. On the left side is attached a flint, formerly used for making fires but now merely an ornament. The decorations are always skillfully carved; the most expensive ones are made of steel embedded with gold designs, while less expensive ornaments are made of silver. On the left side, men also wear a *dailur,* or pouch, lapped onto the belt. For tobacco or snuff, the *dailur* may be as long as a foot and four or five inches wide, and it is usually carefully embroidered or designed by the women. The snuff is in a smaller agate container with a stopper on the top, which is placed in the pouch. A common traditional Mongol greeting was a quick exchange and sample of snuff containers; the container was then returned to its customary place.

The headdress, the gown cuff, the ornament hanging from the sash, and so forth were typical up until the 1930s and 1940s, after which dress became increasingly more simple with the passage of time. The earliest move was to abolish the headdress of the married women, the cuffs on the gowns of the men, and the ornaments on the sashes.

One should not underestimate the importance of details regarding clothing among all Mongol tribes; the coat is traditionally buttoned from left to right. In 1688, during the critical period of struggle between the Jungar Mongols and the Khalkha tribes, the nobility of the Khalkha debated whether protection should be sought from the Chaghan (white) Khan (Russian Tsar) or the Manchu court. The powerful Living

Buddha, the First Jebtsundamba, stressed that the religion of the Manchu and the Khalkha was the same and that both peoples buttoned their robes to the right, therefore, an alliance with the Manchu would be blessed. This view was supported by the Khalkha princes and an alliance with the Manchu followed.[32]

TRANSPORTATION

The very basis of Mongol society is mobility, and all aspects of nomadic livelihood—diet, dress, dwelling, and so on—are conditioned by or subordinated to this mobility. On the "sea of grass," the Mongolian steppe, the horse is the single most important means of transportation. Horses are also obviously important for herding, hunting, warfare, and sports. If a nomad can control and maintain horses, he has great potential for movement. On horseback, nomads have striking power to raid and plunder agricultural areas and then retreat to safety. However, each time nomadic peoples invaded China to exploit the agricultural areas and then lost control of their horse breeding areas and pastures, they lost control of the entire steppe area. They then fell prey to new waves of nomadic peoples moving in from the steppe.

The Mongol nomadic state (Chs. *ma-shang hsing-kuo*) first raided, then invaded, and finally conquered the Chinese empire (*t'ien-hsia*). However, after Khubilai Khan ascended the dragon throne as the first real "Chinese" emperor of Mongolian descent, he lost control of the old horse breeding grounds and strategic areas of the steppes; this was the beginning of the end of his dominance in the inner Asian homeland. Khubilai could no longer mobilize and unify the nomadic tribes against opponents as his grandfather, uncle, and brother had done before him.[1] This event emphasizes the importance of the horse to politics, economics, and military defense or offense.

A satisfactory means of communication is prerequisite to successful geopolitical control; therefore, after the establishment of the Mongol Empire, the first step in consolidation of its administration was the establishment of way stations for postriders on the imperial circuit of communications. This facilitated the rapid dispersal of commands to every point of the empire and the quick reception of any news or report of impending trouble. Mongol leaders either dispatched their own men to strategic points to establish poststations, called *jam*, or they directed local people in outlying localities to establish them.[2] *Jamchi*, men who served at these stages on the imperial road, were exempt from duties other than facilitating commands, news, and transportation, and assisting officials who were traveling the road. Their service was to supply horses, living quarters, and other assistance. Official travelers on the imperial roads of the Mongol Empire were given a chit or document, called a *paiza,* designating their rank and entitling them to accommodations or assistance according to rank. Thus, the khans established a very complex and efficient network of communications within the empire.[3] This type of system extended to non-Mongol areas and with modifications continued down to the 1930s or 1940s in those areas inhabited by the Mongols. In modern times, the system came to be known as the *örtöö.*

After occupying China, the Manchu reestablished a system of communication and transportation on the earlier model of the Mongol khans, at least into such areas as Chinese Turkistan and Tibet. In the middle of the eighteenth century, during the great struggle between the Manchu and the last Mongol resistance—Jungar—the Khalkha Mongols in Outer Mongolia maintained a *jam*-type system of communications as allies of the Manchu, but when a change of policy occurred, the Khalkha withdrew all the stages of the *jam* system, very nearly causing a collapse of the entire Manchu effort to crush the Jungar. There are many such indications of the significance of the *jam* or *örtöö* system.

Traditional Mongol administration during the imperial period was closely tied to the use of horses. Princes, royal relatives, important generals, and other representatives from the empire were customarily called to periodic *khuraltai* assemblies for the purpose of discussing high affairs of state and important decisions or even to elect a successor to a former khan. The *khuraltai* depended on rapid transportation throughout the empire and an efficient *jam* system.

When the princes or nobles were called to a *khuraltai* at the camp of the khan, there were always predetermined places for hitching horses. The arrangement, called *kirü'es* (during the Yüan period, the Chinese name for this institution was *ch'üeh-lieh-ssu*),[4] was a key aspect of the communication and transportation system. The superintendent of the operation had to be very trustworthy, and it is recorded that when Chinggis Khan had certain critical matters to take care of, his brother Belgütei was entrusted with responsibility for the *kirü'es.*[5] In delicate discussions concerning affairs of state or in cases of potential conflict in the assembly, the tight regulations of the horse hitching area were also applied to the individual *kirü'es* of officials who came to court with a large retinue of counselors and attendants. The strict regulations avoided quarrels and trouble that arose on occasion from conflicts over lost and stolen horses. Also, unless the horses were properly secured, it was impossible for people to pass freely through the horse hitching areas. After the consolidation of the empire, when China became the focal point—and the most populous and richest part of the empire—the Mongol capital was transferred from the steppe area to what is present-day Peking. The Mongol khans continued to give careful attention to the *kirü'es*. The Monograph on Law and Punishment (*Hsing-fa chih*) of the *Yüan shih* states:

> If a thief with a record of stealing transgresses the regulations of the *kirü'es* and steals a horse, camel, or cow, he and all who assist him or combine with him in this action . . . shall be punished with one hundred seven strokes, and shall be exiled to Nuerkhan [an area just north of the Amur River in the Maritime Province of Siberia]. In a case where the thief does not have a record and this is his first offense, he shall be punished with one hundred and seven strokes and shall be exiled to farm in Chao-chou [a place in the Fu-yu district of present-day Kirin province near the present Mongolian Banner of Ghorolos].[6]

As indicated, in addition to horses there were camels and oxen tended at the *kirü'es*. The earlier punishment for stealing—execution—had been lightened. These and many other laws related to nomadic peoples compiled in the *Hsing-fa chih* during the Ming period (1368-1644) are intended for Chinese-related situations and were edited out of the great compilation of the *Ta-Yüan t'ung-chih* (a survey of the laws of the Yüan dynasty), made during the reign of Emperor Ying-tsung (Mongolian: Gegen Khan, 1321-23). These records indicate some evolution or change in the attitude of Mongol leaders regarding the *kirü'es*.

The size of a prince's or noble's *kirü'es,* the number of horses hitched there, indicated the preeminence or power of the man. After Chinggis Khan ascended the throne (1206) as the great leader of all Mongol tribes, a very ambitious and capable shaman named Kököchü, whose *kirü'es* was even larger than that of Chinggis, was deemed a threat to the absolute power of Chinggis Khan and was killed.[7] This act was important in establishing the supreme power of Chinggis Khan.

Even today it is traditional for a visitor approaching a Mongol yurt to circle so as to approach from the left and dismount from the left side to tie up his horse. It is a great insult to approach a yurt from the front or from the right side of the camp. All Mongol dwellings have a hitching post a short distance away and on the left side of the yurt, and even the head of a house will not dismount at the door of his own yurt. Unless a person is going to use a horse almost immediately, it will not be hitched at the hitching post, but will be hobbled to graze in the vicinity of the yurt. It is released to graze with the herds if it is not needed for a longer period of time.

Although Mongol ponies are known for their endurance, stamina, and ability to take abuse, a person traveling any great distance would take with him a string of horses. Otherwise it would be necessary to use the horse relay system available to official travelers (until the Communist takeover), by which one would be furnished horses at stages on the route by presenting an official chit. The shoeing of horses is rare in the Mongolian steppe because there are so many horses that can be exchanged and such careful attention to the hoofs of one horse is unnecessary except in mountainous areas.

Mongols do not usually use a Western-style lariat. A rope loop at the end of a long pole is used to catch a horse; a trained horse in turn is used to control others.

Oxen also are important for transportation in Mongolia, particularly for drawing carts which are frequently used in plains regions. For distant journeys, most often undertaken in the autumn, oxen and wagons are hitched in single file alternately and arranged in such a way that one outfit follows directly after another. These wagons commonly have a deep or heavy-toned bell hitched under the axle. The silhouette of a wagon train against the evening sky, with the silence of the steppe being broken only by the ringing of the wagon bells is a very poetic scene.

Camels, too, are used for riding and for caravan transportation of goods, especially during the winter and in very sandy or desolate areas which would be impassable by horse or oxen. Camels must be cared for and given rest during the summer months and are then used beginning in the autumn for the winter months. The camel's nose is pierced and fitted with a ring for easier handling. Caravans of camels or oxen travel comparatively slowly, averaging only about thirty or forty kilometers

A camel cart on the Mongolian steppe

per day. A day's journey begins in early morning before dawn to take advantage of the cool of the day, stops before noon to rest until late afternoon when the journey is resumed, and continues until almost midnight. Generally, camel caravans are used to cover much greater distances than oxen caravans. However, in eastern Mongolia ox-cart caravans are traditionally much more common than camel caravans. When camels are used for riding instead of for caravan service, speed or the distance covered in a given time differs little from that of horses.

The early development of Mongol transportation and caravans can be seen through references from the *Secret History:* a beautiful girl seated on a "black cart";[8] high-wheeled carts with a covering pulled by camels for transporting the family of the khan or nobility;[9] the use of carts for storage of wool;[10] the mention of Börte, wife of Chinggis Khan, riding on an ox cart equipped with a covering over the top and a door on the front;[11] a cart transporting a large tent;[12] the appointment of a general overseer of all carts, commissioned by Chinggis Khan immediately upon his assuming leadership as the khan of the Mongol tribes.[13] The large carts with yurts mounted upon them, common in the literature of the period of the Mongol Empire, later fell into disuse and disappeared, while the so-called black cart seems to have been a painted cart with a covering and, according to the accounts of the *Secret History,* was used for transporting the court ladies. A cart referred to as a "black cart" was still in use until the 1940s and, although it actually was *not* painted black, it was still reserved for the transportation of ladies of the elite. A poem entitled "Holin" (Karakorum), composed by Liu Ping-chung,[14] a Chinese minister of Khubilaı Khan, describes the magnificent capital of the khan:

The sounds of the black carts constantly penetrate our ears
    and the white tents continue without end
Whether impressed by dignity and power or by the dragons and
    lions above the palace
At Holin you will be struck by the great capital of the
    Khan.[15]

The countless tents and the innumerable black carts were a common sight and symbolic of an empire on horseback. From the period of the empire to the present, carts pulled by horses, oxen, and camels have been an important part of Mongolian transportation. A distinctive feature of the khan's cart was that its wheels were larger than those of other carts. In ancient times, the Mongols called these high-wheeled carts *khasagh,* and even today the Mongols of the Ordos region, believed to be descendants of the elite guard of Chinggis, retain the ancient name *khasagh* for their carts, which are somewhat larger than those found in other areas of Mongolia.

Usually the Mongols stack wool and other items on their carts for storage as well as for transportation. In nomadic areas, carts are commonly made of wood; the wheels also are wooden and are very seldom rimmed with iron. Frequently, a cart is pulled by a single animal, a horse, ox, or camel, but occasionally two animals are tied in tandem as a team. A man will sometimes ride a horse alongside an animal drawing a cart to urge the animal along.

The use of donkeys or mules for transportation or as beasts of burden was not introduced into Mongolia until recently when Chinese began to migrate in large numbers and settle outside the Great Wall. Eventually, in parts of Inner Mongolia, Mongol carts have become more like Chinese carts, which was natural since most carts are produced in Chinese shops. Donkeys and mules are not too useful in the interior of

Mongolia because of the cold winter temperatures. Thus, these animals and Chinese-style carts are found only near the Great Wall and are not typical of traditional nomadic society.

DWELLINGS AND CONCEPT OF SPACE

Mongolian dwellings have evolved with nomadic life. The *Secret History of the Mongols* mentions (1) an *embüle*,[1] a domed hutlike structure made of grass; (2) a standard yurt;[2] (3) both tents and yurts pitched together in a large circle to form an enclosure (*küriyen*);[3] (4) a tentlike structure called *khoshiligh*;[4] (5) a cart pulled by oxen on which was placed a yurt or tent;[5] (6) the famous *ordo* or magnificent encampment of the Mongolian imperial court; and (7) the removal of the imperial tents of Chinggis Khan as he broke camp.[6] The writer of the *History* recorded that Ong Khan of the Kereyid tribe held a banquet in a great tent spoken of as *altan-terme* or "golden pavilion."[7]

Grass dwellings, *embüle,* are still found in Mongolia, but are now called *obookhai* and are used only as temporary shelters by hunters or herders. They are made of birch willows covered with felt; grass is no longer used. It can no longer be determined just what type dwelling the ancient *khoshiligh* was. It is mentioned in Yüan dynasty poetry as *huo-shih*[8] (a "*huo-shih* dwelling"), but this sheds no light on its form since *huo-shih* is merely a Chinese transliteration of the Mongol *khoshiligh.* Early in the modern period the Mongol prince of the Kharachin Banner[9] had a ceremonial tent with a roof shaped much like the eaves of a Western house, and, judging from citations in old dictionaries, it seems possible that there is some connection between this type of tent and the ancient *khoshiligh.* The old yurtlike dwellings transported by carts have not been seen in Mongolia for centuries. All yurts in contemporary use are collapsible so that they can be easily transported. The term yurt, it should be noted, is not Mongolian but is derived from Turkic. Apparently, it came into the English dictionary from the Russian language.

A dwelling of comparatively recent development is a solid structure of Chinese-style architecture, called *baishing.* According to one theory, the word was adopted from the Chinese in the sixteenth century and originally meant the common people (*pai-hsing*).[10] Another theory, which is gaining support, holds that the word appears much earlier in Sanskrit and comes into Mongolian through Persian and Turkic. As used by the Mongols, the term *baishing* has a connotation of condescension, which indicates the early Mongolian attitude toward the alien innovation. The generic Manchu term for all dwellings is *bao* and, accordingly, Mongol dwellings were early spoken of as *Mengu-bao*. This term came into the Chinese language as a loanword, *Meng-ku pao,* from Manchu and is today commonly mistaken for a native Chinese term.

A description of the traditional type of nomadic dwelling is noted in detail in Carpini's account of his travels in Mongolia.[11] And, in his discussion of Khanbalic (Chs. Taitu), the Franciscan Odoric de Prodenone gave a detailed description of the magnificent vehicle of the Mongol emperor, which was actually a portable yurt.[12]

The *Hei-ta shih-lüeh,* an important early Chinese record of observations on nomadic life, notes:

> The Mongols live in a felt yurt which has no heavy or permanent walls, ceilings or rooms. Since they are continually moving with their herds in seeking new grass they have no set place for their dwelling. The hunting camps of the Mongol rulers are called *ordo.* When they break camp to move they transport their tents by means of camels, horses and cows. They use a tented cart on which they may sit and sleep [as they travel] . . . and when they reach water they make camp. . . . There are two types of yurts—in the type common in the area of Yench'ing (Peking) willows are used to form a frame or lattice work for the yurt. . . . This framework forms a wall and may be expanded or collapsed. There is a door in the front and the ceiling is also formed of a framework like an umbrella; in the center is a hole spoken of as *t'ien-ch'uang* [sky-window]. The whole framework of the yurt is covered with felt. It is possible to transport the yurts on horseback. In the steppe grazing areas, yurts are formed of willow stakes which are not collapsible and the whole yurt is transported on a cart. When the grass is depleted, an entire camp may be freely moved to a new place.[13]

The need for a portable dwelling is obvious for a people following their herds and seeking new pastures. The yurt or Mongol *ger* was developed by the nomads in ancient times and has continued to be used to the present day, although in recent decades it is rapidly giving way to permanent housing.

The walls of the Mongolian *ger* are made from thin birch willows formed into a lattice and held together by leather strips. Sections of the lattice are put together in a large circle to form the walls. Each section is approximately five to six feet high and seven to eight feet long. Mongols call the collapsible lattice *khana.* The size of a yurt is determined by the number of *khana* used; the number is always even, and Mongols commonly refer to the size of yurts by the number of *khana* used in erecting them. A six- or eight-*khana* yurt is average; a twelve-*khana* yurt is considered large. Door sections are separable units, and the ceiling is formed from an umbrellalike framework also of slender poles referred to as *oni*. In the center of the ceiling is a hole, called *toono* or *öröke (erüke)*, which is approximately one yard in diameter; it allows smoke to escape and fresh air and light to enter, and it may be covered when necessary by a flap manipulated by ropes. The entire outside surface of the yurt is covered with felt tied in place by woolen ropes. One layer is sufficient in the summer season, three layers in winter. The bottom of the felt covering the *khana* framework on the sides, called *khayaa,* is arranged so it can be raised or folded up one foot away from the ground at the bottom, particularly in the summertime, to allow for better ventilation. During the winter, dirt or wood is placed against the *khayaa* to keep cold air and rain from entering the yurt. Also, during the winter, the *toono,* or opening in the ceiling, is closed most of the time. The door, formed of wood, is ordinarily a single door folding outward or two single doors folding inward. In addition, there is a flap to cover the door in bad weather.

A Mongol yurt always faces southeast, mainly because the winds come from the northwest, but also because, from ancient times, Shamanism in Mongolia has held that the east, origin of the rising sun, is a sacred direction for worship.[14] Customarily, upon entering a yurt, a Mongol will open the door flap with the left hand and will always leave from the right side. There is a superstitious taboo against entering or departing from the wrong side;[15] it is considered bad luck. The threshold of a Mongol's yurt is also traditionally a sensitive place that involves taboo. The belief among the common people is that to step on the threshold of a yurt is tantamount to stepping on the neck of the owner. This common custom, however, is not documented in recorded tradition. During the Mongol Empire, there were reports of foreign emissaries being killed for stepping on the threshold of the royal pavilion as they entered and of guards being placed on either side of the door to lift up and carry in foreign emissaries in order to avoid this fate.[16]

In areas where a nomadic family has a set place to make camp in their nomadic migratory circuit, there will often be a platformlike, raised area built up of packed earth upon which the yurt is placed in both winter and summer. This also guards against rain or water entering the yurt.

The floor of the dwellings in any culture is important, and Mongolia is no exception since the floor surface of a nomad's yurt receives more use than floors in most societies. Ordinarily, in laying out their accommodations, a family places as many hides as they have next to the ground. On top of these is then placed older felt. The final layer is newer felt, which may have designs on it; wealthy families may cover the yurt floor with rugs on top of the felt. Rich families cover the walls with drapes, the most prized type being woolen decorated textile imported from Tibet. Seating is on rug-covered felt cushions, or silk cushions in more aristocratic dwellings. Wooden boards form a small platform just inside the entrance where there is most wear. Also, a wooden frame, perhaps two inches high and four inches wide, encloses the hearth, which is situated in the center of the room in a raised area, to protect the hides and the felt of the floor covering. The hearth itself is about one and one-half feet in diameter and is placed within an earthen rectangle a yard square in the wooden frame.

The interior arrangement of the yurt varies from region to region, but in most places in Inner Mongolia a small bed, which is symbolic of the marriage bed of the man and wife, is placed opposite the entrance. It is not actually used as a bed by the couple because it is too narrow and uncomfortable; it is a place to stack quilts, pillows, clothing, and so forth, particularly in the winter and colder periods. Still, it is special furniture in that, regardless of rank, a visitor may never sit on this bed. A traveler in Mongolia who visits a family with only limited bedding customarily sleeps in his large *de'el* or robe. It is not uncommon, in the wintertime, for hearty nomads who travel on the steppe or work at some distance from their yurt to curl up in their heavy *de'el* and sleep in the snow, arising the next morning to brush off and take up their tasks.

Because of the life-style, the furnishings of Mongol homes are quite simple and consist of several standard chests with doors that open and shelves upon which objects are placed. Smaller tables are always present, but play a less important function. Mongols never sit on a table or put trousers, underwear, or other such objects upon it. The family altar, the bed of married couples, and other such objects are precisely defined as to function, which is maintained in a rather formal fashion. Furnishings are placed in a definite position, and members of the family or visitors coming in ordinarily never move the heavy cushions used for seating from one place to another. Moreover, a visitor in a Mongol yurt will never take liberties in shifting the furniture about or in opening chests and drawers.

Contrary to Chinese custom, Mongols regard the right side of the host as the honored side. Thus, just right of the bed is the traditional place for the Buddhist altar, sutras, or other religious objects. When Shamanism was strong, *ongghon* ("images") or small sacred figures used by the Shaman were also situated here. Next to the wall, small cabinets or closets are ordinarily placed, and by the door, fuel for the fire is stored. Between the yurt walls and the central fireplace is a felt- or rug-covered area in which are situated small tables. Between the draped walls and cabinets and central hearth area, people sit, sleep, eat, and carry on other family functions.

The carpeted area opposite the door, just in front of the marriage bed, is the honored spot in the yurt and is where the head of the family usually sits. When visitors come to the yurt, the host may seat himself to the right of the door and urge the guest to be seated in the honored place. A grandfather, favorite uncle, or some other such person ordinarily sits in the honored spot, but a common visitor without status sits just right of the door in front of the fuel-storage place, unless strongly urged by the host to be seated in another more favored place.

The central hearth area is regarded as sacred, for fire is sacred to the Mongols. The hearth is a metal container in which fires are built. It is made of iron bands in the form of a circle approximately one and one-half feet in diameter and is supported by four or six iron legs.[17]

The interior arrangement in Khalkha areas differs from that in Inner Mongolia: the hearth is still in the middle, but the arrangement of the cushions is often in the form of two converging lines of a triangle rather than in a rectangle.

Nomadic Mongol families usually have only two or three yurts; the largest, for the family head, is situated the farthest west (right) and the other yurts extend to the east (left). In the last one are the kitchen facilities, storage, and so forth.

The princely Mongol dwelling (the *ordo*) is much more elaborate than the yurt of the common nomad. The *khana* latticework, the *toono* ceiling opening, the *oni* ceiling framework, and also the cabinets or cupboards are painted red, which, in contrast to the white felt, is considered very beautiful by Mongols. Yurts of only six *khana* do not require supporting center poles, but yurts of eight or more *khana* need additional support. The Mongol *ordo* and aristocratic dwellings have red center poles decorated with gold dragons. The princely tent of Demchügdüngrüb (De Wang) of the Sünid Banner, outstanding nationalist leader in the

1930s and 1940s, was large enough to accommodate two hundred people, and the princely *ordo* of the Üjümüchin Banner of Inner Mongolia, until recently at least, accommodated as many as five hundred people. The supporting poles of these yurts were very large and attractively painted. When the Lamaist tent temples of Urga, in Outer Mongolia, were still moveable, they must have been very large and magnificent.

Japanese Professor Yanai has made a careful comparative study of the *ordo* or tent compounds of the Mongol khans.[18] The residence of the Prince of East Abagha of the Shilin-ghol League of Inner Mongolia seems most typical of the traditional type. Judging from the model, there were a few permanent storehouses at the summer camping site, but none at the winter camping site. Usually there would be many large and small yurts in the *ordo* compound, and the tent or yurt farthest west was a temple, on top of which was placed a gilded metal piece with concentric circles, a typical Buddhist symbol. Next to the temple was the tent of the elderly prince, and from this tent extending to the east were ranked the yurts of the sons and daughters according to age from the eldest son down. On the end, farthest east, was situated the prince's office, kitchen and servant facilities, and a storage area. On the outside surface of the top of the prince's tents were placed decorative cross symbols in red with an ornate black border. The entrances to the yurts of the prince and his sons each had a red, wooden porch structure with eaves. Surrounding the tent complex of the prince was a fencelike structure, forming a yard or compound. The prince's yurt, situated farthest to the west, designated the most important section of the yard, and thus Chinggis Khan forbade anyone to approach his camp from the west or right side.[19] The influence of this traditional arrangement can be seen in modern times.

In 1933, when the rise of Mongolian nationalism led to an autonomous movement, many princes from different banners suddenly gathered at Batu-kha'alagha (Pailingmiao) in the Ulanchab League, Inner Mongolia, forming, overnight as it were, a tent city. From pictures of this modern gathering, one can imagine earlier scenes when the great khans and their governments traveled from place to place, when the great Jebtsundamba Living Buddha of Outer Mongolia moved his tent temples in nomadic fashion, and when Urga, though not yet settled, still formed the focal point of government among the tribes of Outer Mongolia.

Urga, capital of Outer Mongolia before the Communist revolution, was a name used by foreigners, a corrupted term derived from the Mongolian word *örgö,* for "princely yurt." The Mongol term for Urga, Küriyen, is found in the *Secret History of the Mongols* with the meaning "great circle."[20] Originally, the prince's yurt was the center point in the formation of a camp, and others set up their yurts in a broad circle around it, somewhat like the circle of wagons made during the great westward movement of American history. The circle formation originally signified protection or honor. Later, when the migratory temple camp of the Jebtsundamba Living Buddha became settled in the area of modern Urga, his tent temple was placed in the center with those of his followers around it, forming a great encirclement; hence, the term *küriyen* was given to this encampment. The center point came to be called *örgö* and by extension of meaning and corrupted pronunciation we derived Urga, former name of the present capital, Ulan Bator.

Ong Khan, famous ancient chieftain of the Kereyid tribe, was noted for his "golden pavilion" (*altan-terme*). But it is not certain just what was meant by this term or just what his tent was like.

In modern times, on ceremonial occasions or for a great banquet at a prince's residence, a large, special blue and white tent (*chachir*) is erected. It is a rectangle, with four high posts in a line in the center and canvas coming down from the peak to form eaves. Many small pillars support the edge, and there are coverings on the outer side. The *chachir* is tightly pitched with ropes and stakes; sticking up on the outside poles or on top of the tent are gilded decorations. The tops of the blue tents have many white decorations, and several *chachir* with gilded trimmings, arranged on a green pasture in the summer against the blue sky and clouds, present a magnificent sight. This pavilionlike tent ordinarily accommodates from two hundred to three hundred persons.[21] The common people also have smaller rectangular tents, blue outside and white inside, large enough to accommodate from five to ten people; but these are used mainly for traveling.

Permanent dwellings in Mongolia date back very early—probably to the pre-Christian period when the Hsiung-nu settled Chinese who had surrendered to them. During the tenth and eleventh centuries, the Kitan people built small cities in the southern part of the present Mongolian People's Republic.[22] The first mention of permanent dwellings among the Mongols is in the period of Ögödei Khan; he built the great city of Karakorum (1235) in the vicinity of the Orkhon River. The second instance of permanent dwellings was Khubilai Khan's building of the city of Shangtu near Dolonor in the present area of the Chakhar League, Inner Mongolia. Unfortunately, war and time have eradicated all but the bare foundations of these once great cities and other smaller cities built during the Yüan period. In the latter part of the sixteenth century, Altan Khan built a famous city and many great temples at Köke-khota (Hohehot), present capital of the Inner Mongolian Autonomous Region.

Since that time, with the rapid growth and eventual domination of Lamaist Buddhism, large permanent temples of brick, wood, and stone have been built in various places throughout the steppe. There are two styles of architecture of the temples: one with a Chinese tiled roof and painted red wooden beams, and the other a square, Tibetan architecture with white walls, windows, and a flat roof with red borders. In some instances the two styles are mixed, so there are Tibetan walls and a Chinese roof. Surrounding the main temple halls are other fixed dwellings of the monastic complex for the accommodation of the monks or lamas. Most of these dwellings are whitewashed on the outside. These temple settlements have come to be an important part of the scenery on the steppe.

Modern cities have begun to grow in various parts of Mongolia over the past few decades, but around them are still clustered the traditional yurt dwellings. It is difficult to say just how long these old dwellings will continue to be used.

Mongolian herdsmen raised in the steppe notice, on coming into the city, a distinct difference in the way people relate to space or respond to their environment. It seems to them, for example, that city dwellers are much more inclined to survey their surroundings with quick eye movements and without turning their heads. In contrast, Mongols who live in the expansive steppe, turn their heads much more and use less eye movement to maintain a surveillance of the surrounding territory. A Mongol who was transported rapidly from a nomadic area to a large hotel in Shanghai in the 1930s felt comfortable inside the hotel, but said it would have been much better if the buildings had been erected in the steppe. He felt claustrophobic in the city. The dense environment and the lack of space greatly detracted from the buildings; a large, beautiful temple out on the lonesome steppe was all the more magnificent when enhanced by the space around it.

During the 1930s and 1940s, many Japanese had extended periods of residence in Mongolia, and their almost unanimous experience was one of exhilaration. They were greatly impressed with the expansive nature of Mongolian life in contrast to the tightly confined environment of their homeland. Japanese raised in the confines in Tokyo had the sensation in Mongolia that the sky was distinctly different: rather than being a square patch of blue-gray above them, it was a great kettle placed over the earth—expansive blue above, shading off to gray on the horizon. Among the Chinese there also is a general feeling that northern Chinese are more "expansive" in their feelings or mind in contrast to southern Chinese and, moreover, that those who go beyond the Great Wall find the nomadic people to be even more expansive than people south of the wall.

An abundance of space naturally has an influence on how the Mongols relate to those around them; for example, when walking or riding horses, Mongols are never concerned with avoiding collisions with others. In this respect, they vary greatly from city dwellers or people in more densely inhabited places. In talking to each other, Mongols ordinarily maintain more personal distance between speakers than do people in most other societies, and they begin to feel uncomfortable if, in conversation, a person comes too close to them. Observers of Mongolian life-style see a unique situation in the confines and restrictions within the yurt. Young people are conditioned to living in close quarters with a minimum of stress or competition for space. The situation within the yurt is naturally compensated for by the expansive environment without; however, it seems that Mongols, in their attitudes and conditioning, are less inclined to strife and social conflict than people in urbanized areas where more priority is placed on space and where there is greater competition for it.

Mongols have a strong sense of security in their environment and feel that their property consists not only of the yurt, but also of the surrounding territory. They leave valuable possessions outside the yurt on their carts with no particular sense of concern that they may be stolen.

Privacy among Mongolian nomads has a much lower priority than in most other societies due to the limitations of the yurt and the fact that on the open steppe very little can be concealed. At the same time, depending on the wealth of the family, Mongols certainly are inclined to build larger yurts or a larger group of yurts when it is possible. The idea, common in Japanese society, of finding repose in a confined *cha-shitsu* or tearoom is quite foreign to Mongol thinking, with the possible exception of lamas, dedicated to *sam* or meditative discipline.

Mongols seldom have enclosures around their yurts, gardens, or other such private areas, although carts, which serve an important transportation function in nomadic life, are often placed a short distance from the dwelling and may set off an area considered somewhat more private than areas beyond the carts.

All this does not mean that there is absolutely no competition for territory among the Mongols, for, throughout history, there have been continuing struggles between tribes or clans for pastures and game areas. However, the Mongol relationship to the land is quite different from that in most other societies. In Asian agricultural societies particularly, there is great competition for position and control of land, and man's relationship is directly to land. In Mongolia, between man and land, there are animals. It is the *use* of land in a migrating society that is of greatest concern, not the *possession* of it. Many of Mongolia's territorial problems are not those of most Asian nations with a rapidly expanding population. Rather, the concern is a comparatively sparse population.

Although in premodern times, there was competition for grazing and gaming areas, the use of areas usually became set, and in normal circumstances trouble was avoided because seasonal migration is not haphazard or chaotic, but rather quite carefully defined. Except for close relatives, families tended *not* to group together on the steppe, but were strongly inclined to maintain some distance between their own yurts and those of neighboring herders. Except in abnormal situations of natural disaster or disruption, there were no conflicts or extreme competition for resources; there is no general theme in Mongolian society of competition between cattlemen and sheepmen as in the American West, for ordinarily families have mixed holdings of animals. However, there is a general view among many scholars that groups that specialize in horseraising are the "aristocrats" of nomadic society and tend to dominate people whose economic base is other animals.

On seasonal occasions, when Mongols come together for a festival, a tournament, or a visit to a temple, they usually leave their yurt and travel on horseback to the site and live temporarily in a tent. Even on these occasions, however, they are inclined to pitch their tents some distance from the festival area and ride in on horseback. In smaller gatherings, which involve only a few hundred or a few thousand people, there is no great problem with space, and, as people arrive, they choose a spot. During the empire period, when tens of thousands of people came together, it was necessary to have a more orderly system. Then priorities were established, and space was allocated according to the *kirü'es* system.

3
LIFE-STYLE OF THE NOMADS

BIRTH AND CHILDHOOD

Because conception and birth were mysteries not fully comprehended by premodern people, many taboos, sacred formulas, or mystic aspects are associated with them. A yurt in which a woman has given birth to a child is customarily taboo for a period of twenty-one days to a month, during which time visitors or strangers may not enter the yurt and in some cases even the family will not inhabit the yurt. Traditionally, upon birth of a boy, it is customary to hang arrows or a bow with arrows outside the yurt to frighten away evil spirits and to signify bravery for the boy just born. For a period of seven days, the woman is not moved, does no work, and is on a strict diet. When a baby is born, it also has been customary to put some liquor or fermented drink in the child's mouth to wash it out. This is also a type of "anointing" spoken of as *milaakh* (see section on Taboos and Customs below). The Mongols say the alcoholic drink has the significance of a blessing, but it very probably serves the purpose of a disinfectant. In ancient times, upon the birth of a baby it was common to call a shaman to pronounce some prayer or blessing on the new child, but after Buddhism became influential the custom changed and a lama was called in to chant a sutra or pronounce a blessing.

After birth, a child is customarily washed with a butter oil, wiped off, wrapped up, and placed in a cradle. The mother usually breast-feeds the child, but her milk may be supplemented with cow or sheep milk. In more wealthy families, a wet nurse may be hired. A Mongol who was cared for by a wet nurse during infancy will generally show great consideration and esteem for her.

As in much of Asia, it is customary to consider a child to be one year old when born and two years at the first new year. Since very early times, it has been common to calculate the birth of a child according to a calendar based on the signs of the Zodiac, a system that originated in China and was adopted early by the Mongols, Tibetans, and other Inner Asian peoples. Often, in noting the date of their birth, Mongols say that they were born in the year of the tiger, the horse, or one of the other twelve Zodiac animals.[1] A very common custom, which continued until recently, maintained that visitors born in a certain sign of the Zodiac, even including the father, could not view a particular new child. This divination is made by a lama. Mongols are still concerned with "good" or "bad" dates of birth.

The concept of spirits is closely connected with birth and death, and frequently myths and legends are associated with the birth of a great man or with remote ancestors. The following example is recorded in the *Secret History of the Mongols:*

> Following the death of Dobun Mergen, his wife, Alan Gho'a, gave birth to three sons . . . two older sons who had previously been born . . . were discussing the matter critically . . . and this was discovered by their mother. She [in order to explain] said, "Each night a man with a yellowish-white face entered the yurt on a beam of light, penetrating through a gap on top of the door. He massaged my stomach and the light penetrated my womb. When he left the yurt he also disappeared on the beam of sun and moonlight, wobbling like a yellow dog upward through the air. You must not speak confusingly of these things. From this it must be seen that these three are the sons of Heaven. You cannot compare them with the *kharachu* ['commoners']. Later they will be the khans of the *tümen* ['masses']. Then you ordinary *kharachu* will understand."[2]

This myth, associated with the origin of the Mongol khans in order to establish a tradition of heavenly ordination, is an example of the prevalent Mongol belief that pregnancy came not from intercourse, but from entrance of a spirit into the womb of a woman.

The institution or role of midwife has been common in Mongolia since ancient times. The Mongols speak of a midwife as a *kuisütü eej,* meaning "the mother who cuts the umbilical cord." In eastern Mongolian dialects, the word for midwife is *udghan,* which is derived from a classical Mongolian word, *idughan,* meaning "female shaman." In ancient times, the delivery of children apparently involved a female shaman.

There is very little recorded in early Mongol sources regarding the delivery of children, but the medieval traveler Rubruck and the Chinese General Hsü T'ing both noted that it was commonly felt that Mongol mothers needed no rest after childbirth (either their observations are not reliable or the custom changed later). In the *Hei-ta shih-lüeh,* Hsü T'ing noted that immediately upon delivery a Mongol child was wiped with sheep's wool, wrapped in lambskin, put in a cradle about one foot wide and four feet long, and immediately carried under arm on horseback in nomadic migrations.[3] This narrative is probably exaggerated or inaccurate, for it is quite unlikely a Chinese general or a foreign traveler would actually witness a Mongol birth. The *Secret History* records the birth of Chinggis Khan:

> Yesügei Ba'atur [father of Chinggis Khan] after capturing Temüjin-üge and Khori-bukha of the Tatar tribe was returning home when his wife, Kö'elün Üjen, being pregnant at the time, gave birth to Chinggis Khan at Deli'ün Boltagh in the vicinity of the Onon river. As he was born he held in his right hand a clot of blood the size of an ankle bone of a sheep. Because he was born on the occasion of the capture of Temüjin-üge he was named Temüjin . . . .[4] When Temüjin was nine years old his brother Jochi-khasar was seven, Khachi'un-elchi was five, Temüge-odchigin was just a three-year old tiger and his sister, Tümerün, was in her cradle.[5]

During the period of Chinggis Khan, a woman would ordinarily be at a settled camp to give birth, not traveling. At the time of birth, the nomads watch for some omen regarding the fate of the new child. An ancient belief held that it was a symbol of great power or strength for a child to be born with a clot of blood in its hand.

A young baby is customarily handled in a cradle, the term for which, both now and in the past as recorded in the *Secret History,* is *ölgei.* This cradle is probably the cradlelike object mentioned by Hsü T'ing; it is now about one foot wide and two feet long with rounded ends. The cradle has crossboards like rockers, so that it may be rocked, and many holes on both sides for tying the baby in. In the *Hei-ta shih-lüeh,* P'eng Ta-ya said, "Young babies are wrapped on a board (*ölgei*) and carried on horseback with their mothers as they come and go."[6] In both ancient and modern times, carts are commonly used for moving and since the women ride on these carts, it was not usually necessary to carry a child on a board on horseback.

The names given to children provide some insight regarding Mongolian culture as well as influences from other peoples. Names recorded in the *Secret History*, the *Altan tobchi*, and the *Yüan shih*, as well as modern names, are derived from many sources. Names may represent a very special occasion; for example, the commemoration of a victory: Temüjin, the childhood name of Chinggis Khan, was given to him to mark the capture of an enemy chieftain, Temüjin, by his father.

Animal names are given to many children due to the close association with hunting and herding: Khasar, "terrible dog"; Ghunan, "three-year-old tiger" or "three-year-old bull"; Khulan, "wild horse"; Nachin, "falcon or eagle"; Jali-bukha, "crafty bull"; Khara-gülüg, "black puppy"; Arslang, "lion."

A third category of names derives from foreign peoples with whom the Mongols had contact in their wide migrations and conquests. Examples of these are Tangghudai, meaning the Tangut or Tibetan people; Mantzedai, meaning southern barbarian—the Chinese; Uriyangkhadai, referring to the people of the clan of Uriyangkha; Nanggiyadai referring to the southern Chinese; and Sarkis, meaning Caucasian, (people of the Caucasus).

A fourth category of names indicates such characteristics as good luck, good behavior, virtue, and so forth: Batu, meaning "confident" or "immovable"; Möngke, "everlasting" or "eternal"; Bayan, "rich"; Khutugh, "blessed"; Ba'atur (Bator), meaning "brave," "courageous," or "hero"; Bilig, "intelligent." A fifth category refers to characteristics of preciousness, great strength, or durability: Khada'an, "rock"; Temür, "iron"; Altan, "gold"; Chila'un, "stone"; and Erdeni, "jewels."

In a sixth category are names associated with weapons or metal tools, such as Jebe, "arrowpoint"; Süke, "ax"; Toghon, "pot"; Toghon-temür, literally "pot iron," but in this case meaning "endless" or "continuous development." The famous Süke-bator thus is "a hero as sharp and powerful as an ax."

A seventh category of names is derived from color or some beautiful object and includes such names as Kökö, which means both "blue" and "everlasting"; Chaghan, "white," "pure," or "richness"; Gho'a, "beautiful lady"; Alan-gho'a, "red beautiful lady"; and Checheg, "flower."

An eighth category of Mongol names involves numbers or numerals: Jirghadai and Tabudai, the "sixth" and "fifth," referring to the number of the child in the family; also, Nayan and Jirandai, which mean "eighty" and "sixty" respectively—"eighty" refers to the fact that the child was conceived when the father was old. Yesüntai is a name associated with the number nine—a lucky number to the Mongols— meaning "abundant," and the largest number before ten, which is a reversion to 1 plus 0.

A ninth category is an interesting group of names having the connotation of something that is bad or despised. Examples of these are names like Eljigetei, "donkey"; Muu-nokhoi, "bad dog," or Büjir, "filthy." After the Mongols penetrated and occupied Chinese territory, new names of objects, again associated with despicable things, came into the language, including Tai-tu-lui, meaning a "donkey from Khanbalic"; Keüken, "girl," a name actually given to male babies since a boy in a nomadic society, as in most folk societies, is considered to have much greater value than a girl. Behind these bad names is the superstitious notion that spirits would more likely be attracted to that which is well named or beautiful, whereas a bad name may discourage and repel evil spirits.

A tenth category of Mongol names involves religious meanings or persons, such as the personal names Ananda, famous disciple of the Buddha; Ayushi, god of longevity; Lhamujab, "the goddess Lhamu will protect"- this goddess is the protecting deity of the Dalai Lama of Tibet. The suffix *jab,* common in Mongolian names derived from the Tibetan language, means "to be protected" or "to be blessed." Another example of this type of name is Lamajab, which means "protected by the Lama(s)."

The foregoing names generally are associated with Buddhism, but other groups of names are associated with or derived from Islam, Nestorianism, or some other form of western Christianity before the impact of Russian influence. Names in these categories would include Gorgis, Anton, Hasana, Nichola, and Uzbek (a Moslem saint). This last group of names dates from the period of the Mongol Empire and were borne by top leaders of the empire.

A later category of names is also derived from foreign names but is not necessarily associated with religion. The earliest seem to be Turkic names, such as Ülug-temür; Ülug, a Turkic word, meaning "large" is combined with Temür, a word common to both Turkic and Mongol, meaning "iron," thus deriving the name "large iron." Chelig is a Turkic word used as a name and means "hard" or "unbreakable." Another example is Kazan, a Turkic word for "pot."

The second group of foreign names appearing in Mongolia seems to have come in during the Kitan period (906-1125); an example is Sanbaonu from San-pao, a Chinese term referring to the three sacred objects of Buddhism (the Buddha, the scriptures, and the monk). *Nu* is a suffix commonly associated with Kitan names, the meaning of which is no longer known. Another example of a Kitan-derived name is Guanyinnu from Kuan-yin, the Chinese term for the Bodhisattva Avalokitesvara plus the Kitan suffix *nu*. Another group of names in this category was derived from the Chinese during the Yüan period including Khuashang, from Chinese *ho-shang* meaning "Chinese monk," and Choului, from Chinese *ch'o-lü* meaning "ugly donkey." Mongols who settled in the Persian area took western Asian names, for example, the Mongol Khan Abu-Said.

Another quite large group of names is derived from the Manchu language; Hujuri, "blessed," or Ürgüngge, "with happiness." Two other sets of Mongol names, pure Chinese or modified Chinese and pure Russian or modified Russian, became current in the late nineteenth or twentieth century. Two famous Inner Mongolian leaders, for example, are Wu Ho-ling and Pai Yun-t'i. Among the Buriyad and Kalmuck Mongols, Russianized names are common as in the cases of the scholar Galsang Gombuyev, the linguist Sanjiev, and the scholar Arash Bormanshinov. The most common names derived from a foreign influence, needless to say, are Tibetan. In this group, Dorji, "diamond" (a sacred object in Buddhism), Ochir or Wachir, "thunderbolt," and Sengge, "lion," are common personal names. All have religious significance in Buddhism.

According to Mongolian custom, the naming of children is usually done by the parents, but may also be done by a respected elder of the family or clan or by an official of the banner or tribe. Beginning with the general conversion of the Mongol nation to Tibetan Buddhism, it became customary for lamas, revered by the Mongolian people, to give the new child a name; thus Tibetan names become the most common.[7]

Universally, a birthday is a special, personal occasion and observances are associated with it. This has been true since ancient times in Mongolia. The old record *Altan tobchi* notes a comment by Chinggis Khan when he was discussing this matter with his sons. He asked them which day they regarded as particularly meaningful and important. One son replied that the most important occasion was New Year's, which brought many festivities and a new beginning for one's future life. Chinggis disagreed and stressed that even more important was a man's birthday. He reasoned that if a person's parents had not given them birth nothing whatever could be done; their very existence, name, and fame all stemmed from birth made possible only by one's parents. The Great Khan felt that it was important to commemorate this day with some special observance.[8] From ancient times, Mongolian celebration of birthdays, reflecting the injunction of Chinggis Khan, has involved a certain element of filial piety, a sentiment common among Mongols who have strong feelings of regard for parents and ancestors.

Particular birthdays are given special attention. These are calculated according to the zodiac cycle of twelve years symbolized by twelve animals. Thus, the birthdays that are considered to be unlucky and present a problem come at twelve-year intervals: thirteen, twenty-five, thirty-seven, forty-nine, sixty-one, and particularly seventy-three, since it is considered difficult for Mongols to live beyond this advanced age. Ironically, in a sort of reverse psychology, rather than avoiding these particular birthdays, Mongols tend to celebrate them in a sort of symbolic challenge, the conquest of evil represented by the unlucky year. While some Westerners choose to avoid the number thirteen in numbering the floors in an elevator, the Mongols would emphasize it even more prominently as a challenge.

A child ordinarily rides on the same horse with a parent until the age of three or four. By the age of five, a child is often taught to ride a horse alone with the parent galloping alongside, holding the reins. This practice is recorded in the *Hei-ta shih-lüeh*.[9] However, modern Mongols have seldom seen children shooting arrows while riding on sheep,[10] as recorded by Ssu-ma Ch'ien in the *Shih chi*.

Because of the great geographical expanse of Mongolia and the scattered and changing settlement patterns of the population, it is common for a child to have no close friend with whom to play.[11] Accordingly, children play mainly with their own brothers and sisters. It is obvious why Mongol children become very fond of pets, usually a dog. It is quite uncommon for Mongols to have other domesticated animals, such as birds, as pets because it is considered sinful to keep animals in a cage and because Mongol dogs are very ferocious, making it difficult to keep other types of pets.

A Mongolian family

Elderly Mongol people, especially grandmothers or aunts, often tell the children stories for amusement. Storytelling is a favorite form of amusement for the older people as well. The most common stories are those associated with nomadic life and adventure on the steppe. With the introduction of Buddhism, didactic Buddhist stories became very common.

From the age of seven or eight, Mongol children habitually follow their parents in caring for the sheep or animals. However, children are not allowed to participate in more dangerous or vigorous activities, such as herding camels and horses or hunting, until they are nearly fifteen. From the age of eight or nine, boys begin to learn the techniques of horse racing and to develop a keen interest in such sports as wrestling. Archery has continued only as a rather formalized, ceremonial sport, depending on the geographical area of Mongolia. Girls, in addition to assisting their mothers with sewing, cooking, sheepherding, and milking, commonly play games around the yurt, using a puck or game piece devised from the anklebone of an animal. A favorite winter activity of Mongolian children is the sport of kicking the anklebone of an ox or camel about on the ice; points are determined by the position in which the puck comes to rest. A variation of this game is played as far west as Norway. The game was a favorite of Chinggis Khan who played it with Jamukha, a childhood friend who became his mortal enemy in later life.[12]

Mongolian people, from ancient times to modern times, have paid close attention to their children's faces and particularly their eyes. The *Secret History* records a famous story that occurred during the youth of Chinggis Khan. His father took him to the tribe of his mother to seek a wife. On the way, they met Tei Sechen of the Onggirad tribe, and when Tei Sechen saw the boy Temüjin, he remarked that the child had fire in his eyes and a light upon his face. He then proposed that his daughter be given in marriage to young Chinggis and requested that the father, Yesügei, come to his yurt to examine the girl, Börte. When the father of Chinggis saw the girl, he is recorded as also having said, "The girl has a light on her face and fire in her eyes." Both parents were happy with the match and a marriage agreement was decided upon. History records that the father of Chinggis commented that the boy was nine years old and afraid of dogs.[13] Though the agreement was made according to custom, the marriage was postponed to a much later date. Observations such as these expressed by the fathers in the *Secret History* are still very common among the Mongols, and one may frequently hear a person referred to as having sparkling eyes, a shining face, or a bright countenance. To the Mongols, these attributes indicate a warm personality. Mongols feel an aversion to a child with a cold facial expression.

ADULTHOOD AND MARRIAGE

Many societies mark the transition from childhood to adulthood by rites of passage or some special ceremony. In Mongolia, however, there are no rites of passage, no clear-cut break between childhood and adulthood, no particular age marking arrival at maturity. In nomadic life, boys are introduced to the dominant activities of pastoralism, herding and hunting, at a fairly early age, which tends to push adult roles or functions to an earlier age than in many other societies. During the empire and Yüan periods, males were recruited for military service between the ages of fifteen and seventy,[1] indicating that a boy was considered mature at sixteen and that a man's full, active function in society was curtailed at the age of seventy. However later, during Manchu rule from the seventeenth century to 1911, conscription by law was set from eighteen to sixty years of age.[2] The change may have been due to need for fewer troops, but it may also indicate a change of attitude regarding the period of prime adulthood. The legal age at which a young prince received his seal of authority, assumed the role of *jasagh* ("ruler"), and took leadership in his banner is another sign of adulthood. This age, set through law and tradition extending back several centuries, has traditionally been eighteen.[3] If a *jasagh* died, a son or successor who was underage served under a regency until he became of age. Thus, while the transition from childhood to adulthood is not clear cut, there are indications of a general feeling.

Two functions generally reserved for adult males are drinking and smoking. A young boy is allowed to do neither, and even after he begins to drink and smoke as a young adult, he still does not do these things in the presence of older men except when given explicit permission. This form of etiquette also extends to older men in that while they may drink, they do not smoke before a person of some prestige, such as a venerable lama, their prince, or some other banner leader. Smoking seems to be regarded as informal and therefore restricted in more formal situations, while drinking is considered ritualistic and no restrictions are placed on it according to status. The vast majority of temples or Buddhist monasteries in Mongolia forbid their lamas to smoke or drink either domestic fermented drinks or liquor brought in from China or Russia, in the case of prerevolutionary northern Mongolia. An exception is made for *kumis,* however; no monastery will forbid its lamas to drink *kumis* on festive occasions. As the common people come to the temple, they put away their tobacco and pipes, but may on occasion secretly steal a smoke.

In Mongol society, marriage traditionally has been the event that identifies the passage from youth to adulthood. Some unique customs related to marriage developed in Mongolia, arising, like many other institutions, out of nomadic conditions, a widely dispersed and sparse population, and a very special historical experience. According to the common lore, nomads took wives in raids because of the demands of Mongolian exogamous mores,[4] and while this may have been the case sometimes, there were other, more usual, but less well-known marriage institutions.

The Mongol term most commonly used for marriage, *gerlekü,* refers only to males and more literally means, rather than marriage, establishing a separate *ger* or household. There is no definite age for marriage, but traditionally young men marry at an odd-numbered age—seventeen and nineteen being quite common. (It should be kept in mind that a child at birth is considered to be already one year old.) For females, the term *mordokhu* is commonly used to indicate marriage; restricted in usage, it means, literally, "to go off on a horse" (which is exactly what a bride does). The young woman has become mature and is now ready to become independent from her father's household.

Following marriage and the establishment of his *ger,* a son continues to migrate with the household and still depends greatly on his father in making major decisions. Unity and cooperation are important in the survival of the group; consequently, following the death of his father a son still defers to his mother in important decisions having to do with the family or lineage.

In Mongol society, there is no tradition of dating and courtship as a mode for young people to seek a mate and contract a marriage. The customary approach is for parents to arrange the marriages of their children. Naturally, in recent decades the bride and groom have had a greater voice. In beginning the betrothal process, the groom's side pays what anthropologists might call a bride price, but, later, after the engagement is contracted and the marriage consummated, the bride brings with her a dowry. These arrangements depend upon the individual case and are ordinarily set according to the social status of the family. In the pre-empire period, it was apparently customary for the groom to spend a short period with the family of the bride before the marriage took place,[5] but this custom has disappeared. The stereotyped ideal of the girl a family seeks as a wife for their son is changing, but one aspect may be seen in the common saying, "a sounding (thunderous) sky brings no rain and a girl with a reputation has no wedding banquet." The ideal is a more reserved girl, not a "belle of the ball" with a reputation for gaiety and romance.

Traditionally, engagements are made when children are fourteen or fifteen years of age, and the divination of a lama is obtained to decide whether an engagement will be successful. After an engagement is set, it is celebrated with a feast called *arki-uulghakh,* meaning "to cause [bride's parents] to drink wine." This feast takes the place of an ancient ceremonial feast, *bu'uljar.*[6] When the children have matured to an average age of eighteen or nineteen for boys and sixteen or seventeen years for girls, the marriage will be consummated.

A wedding in the steppe is a momentous occasion, and traditionally a lama is consulted to determine a propitious day and hour for the event. In ancient times, a shaman divined the day by considering the girl's appearance, her birthdate, a dream, or some such factor. The preparations at this time include sending an announcement to friends and relatives. When the groom goes to the bride's family to get her, many friends usually accompany him as an entourage in a procession of carts and horses, even though the distance may be more than a hundred miles. Before the groom's party arrives or while they are camped off some distance away, a good day is divined for the bride's "tea party" (*chai-uulghakh*). Friends and relatives of the bride present gifts to her at this time—usually clothing, ornaments, and money. The bridegroom's group do not attend on this occasion. When the groom's entourage arrives, the bride's family entertains them lavishly but does not formally receive them at this point. The groom particularly does not put in an appearance until later when he is formally presented.

When the groom comes to take the bride, he is, by custom, well dressed and carries bows and arrows. As his party approaches, someone from the bride's home ceremoniously goes out to meet the party and stops them so they do not come close to the yurt. Then a type of negotiating charade or protocol play takes place in which both parties have a speaker or representative who carry on a dialogue; the bride's speaker insists that the party must not advance to the camp, and the groom's speaker insists that they must—stating the purpose for the visit, reciting the clan genealogy and the exploits of the family, and sometimes including a recitation by the speaker (*khelmürchi*) of the important events of Mongolian history from the time of Chinggis Khan. This dialogue is not carried on in common conversation, but in a highly developed art of spontaneous poetry. The bride's speaker tries to make it difficult for the groom's spokesman by changing rhyme and meter. This, in turn, is matched and followed at every poetic turn by the spokesman of the groom. The poems are particularly important if the concerned families are elite, in which case the poems may even become part of the permanent oral tradition of the family—to be admired, recited, and analyzed carefully long afterward by the local people. Finally, regardless of what is said in this customary poetic tournament, the groom's party is allowed to come into the camp.

As the groom's party enters the yurt of the bride's family, the groom bows to the parents of the bride and remains silent while an older relative accompanying him presents gifts, pronounces a benediction on the family, states in a very humble and dignified manner the purpose of the visit, and asks for the goodwill of the bride's parents. The spokesman declares somewhat as follows:

In the season of ten thousand good blessings,
on this fortuitous day of tranquility and beneficence
as a symbol of the destiny of eternities past and eternities to come
We travel from a distant camp.

On behalf of the groom's father, mother, and relatives
in accordance with the tradition of our people
we cause your young son-in-law to grasp the good, sharp weapons,
to wear the sturdy, strong armor
to come forward to bow to the parents and relatives of the bride.

We now first present to the Buddha that you worship:
a beautiful lotus lamp and fragrantly ascending incense;
the long *khadagh*,[7] eight jewels without and seven jewels within;
a fine white sheep selected from our beloved herds;
dry fruit selected from the choicest food.
In order to complete the ceremony of the marriage
to establish the immortal blessings of their future
we now present to all relatives and friends gathered here
the holy, white *khadagh,* which has descended from heaven,
kumis and wine, which are the most delicious foods.

We rejoice in symbolizing the everlasting joy of the couple,
we come to receive the lovely young bride for him and to receive
mercy and love from you.
Here we pray that the youthful couple will always enjoy the
"ten best blessings,"
also happiness and well being.
May all their hopes come true.
May this blessed relationship continue for eternity.

While the groom remains kneeling, the bride's father states his acceptance of the party and their gifts, pronounces a benediction on the groom, and presents him with a complete set of new clothing from hat to boots. These the bride's father places on the groom himself, except for the boots which are merely presented. The bride's family also places on the groom a new set of bows and arrows. The wishes, blessings, and sentiments of gratitude spoken by the bride's father or his spokesman at this point may be translated as follows:

On this blessed occasion and on this auspicious day,
We desire to pronounce a benediction on our honored guests and

our son-in-law.
May our son-in-law's family and property prosper,
May their storehouse overflow.
We now robe you from head to foot with exquisite clothing,
    fine armor, and a helmet.
Mounted on a swift, strong horse,
We have you carry the golden bow and silver arrows.
We wish you a bounteous future,
May your blessings increase day by day.
You, our friends, have come with deep significance
To complete the marriage ceremony where the bride and groom
    are joined.
We desire all your best blessings and wishes
To be bestowed upon the new couple
That they may receive the greatest benediction from heaven
And enjoy inexhaustible happiness.
We now present to you, our honorable guests, the *khadagh* of heaven
And *kumis*—the best tasting of food and drink.

After much festivity, the bride and groom leave with their party on horseback and pass into the distant horizon; the bride's family stands at the door of their yurt, reciting good wishes and blessings, and trying to control their spontaneous tears since it would be a bad omen to openly express sad emotion. In ancient times, the mother would accompany the party to the home of the groom, but this custom has long been discontinued; however, one or two representatives of the bride's family and other friends or relatives may still accompany the bride to the new home of her husband.

The maternal uncle (*naghachu*) and his wife (*naghachu egechi*) often play a special role in both the engagement negotiations of a girl for a husband and again in the wedding ceremony. The uncle often goes with the bride and groom to the home of the groom in the process of completing the wedding ceremony. If he is not available, usually a senior relative accompanies the bride. This representative's role is referred to as *terigün khuda* ("the most important person in the marriage ceremony"). The maternal uncle plays no continuing role, but if trouble should arise between the young couple, he may be brought into the situation again. Paternal uncles are often quite active in the process of arranging a marriage; however, this is less so in the case of the groom than the bride. The groom's family may be represented by a paternal uncle or an older friend. Since cross-cousin marriages have been comparatively common in Mongolia, the role of maternal uncles has been increased.

The following sentiments are expressed by the parents of the bride as she departs:

Our daughter, your father is as heaven
And your mother is as earth to you.
We, your parents and relatives, bestow upon you bounteous presents.
In so doing, we proclaim that this auspicious day is set to bring
    you great future happiness.
In accordance with the ordinances of the nation, and the
    tradition of the people,
We have decided that you, our beloved child, shall go afar
To be the offspring of both families by mutual consent.
You, my child, my heart, my spirit, hear me!
The *Khan-kardi*[8] makes its nest on a high mountain.
When the wings and feathers of the young bird are mature,
It flys to *Khan-Tenggeri* ["God-heaven"].

Men's daughters, raised in love
By the custom of the people
Must also marry into a distant clan and be their offspring.
As the rocks of the steep and solid peaks
Are crumbled by the hoofs of campaigning horses,
Thus our daughter, as a round jewel,
Raised in the palm of us, her parents,
Must be given in marriage to a distant clan.
Oh, our beloved daughter,
Though iron and steel are strong,
They will bend in the fire.
Though the flow of the Ganges River is powerful,
It must follow the shape of the earth.
Take care always and be openhearted.
Thus, you may be friends with outsiders and honored by those within.
Persist in virtue, do not quarrel or struggle with others,
Then you will be loved by your husband
And praised by all, forever.

After the group has departed, the bride's family and friends continue the festivities with wine, fine food, and much happy singing. The songs praise the chastity of the girl and express the happiness of the family and other romantic sentiments. The virginity of the bride is symbolized in the ceremonies by a large jar of wine sealed by a skin that is ceremoniously cut by the thrust of a knife or an ivory chopstick, after which the new wine is given to the family and guests. This ceremony is accompanied by special blessings or recitations.

As the bride leaves her family, she is entirely covered with a cape, the color of which varies and is determined by the divination of a lama. The bride and groom journey—perhaps for several days—to their new home; at some spot enroute, at an auspicious time of day as determined earlier by a lama, the party stops and the marriage ceremony is completed with offerings of a sheep or some other animal to *Tenggeri* ("heaven"). A common Mongolian term for the process of marriage is *Tengri du mörgökü* ("bowing to heaven").[9] Mongol weddings traditionally do not take place in the yurt of either the bride or groom, but out on the open steppe. Only after the offering does the bride remove the cape. The new couple still do not enter the marriage bed, but continue the journey to their new home.

Without fail, the bridegroom's family prepares a new yurt for the couple. The yurt is not built in a hurry, but is rather ritualistically put together; each item is placed with care, and a spontaneous blessing, as the yurt is assembled. When the new husband and wife arrive at the home of the bridegroom, their first act is to bow to the family altar of worship. They then bow to each member of the older generation of the husband's family—a ceremonial obeisance which is customarily nine bows to the parents of a noble or elite family, but which may vary from six to as few as three among the common people. (None of these bows are formal prostrations of the Tibetan type, which are reserved only for the worship of deity.) At this time, the bride presents gifts to each of the older generation of her husband's family. The custom of excessive gift giving at weddings may result in near bankruptcy for some families. The bride of a rich family brings large amounts of clothing to last for many years—even a gown in which she will be buried. This practice, characteristic of traditional, aristocratic marriages has been dying out. Members of the older generation, upon receiving gifts from the new bride, give her presents in return. After these exchanges, the wedding festivities really begin, and the official representatives of the bride's family are seated in the place of honor. There is a formal exchange of good wishes and blessings between the representatives of the two families. If the head of a household is not a good speaker, he may invite someone else to represent him. The following is an example of the thoughts expressed on this occasion:

> It is your destiny to establish a new household.
> For you, our children who have tied the wedding knot,
> We, your parents and friends, rejoice and bestow upon you:
> The heavenly *khadagh,* most honored of all things;
> Gold and silver, treasured above all; *kumis,* the most delicious of
>   foods.
> Oh, our beloved children,
> We wish you the riches of Namsarai[10]
> And long life, as that of Ayushi.[11]
> May you always deserve the admiration and blessings of the people
> And have all the elements of peace and prosperity.
> May our age, spirit, destiny, and blessings
> Abound as the new moon which is enlarged day by day.
> May your hopes and good works be successful
> And complete according to your desires.[12]

The feasting usually continues for three days; on the third day, after breakfast or lunch, a representative of the bridegroom presents wine to the guests, ceremoniously reassures the friends of the bride that the girl is safe, reminds all that it is the destiny of girls to leave their family, and so forth. He then announces that the festivities are ended. Customarily, in play, some of the bride's party may insist that they would like to stay longer, and the bridegroom's family then ceremoniously drives them from the yurt with much laughter, even playfully throwing *argal* ("dried animal dung") at the guests. Thus, the wedding party ends with great merriment and joking.

Although the groom's family, the bride's family, or both seek a divination for a propitious date for the wedding, ordinarily a lama will not attend a wedding ceremony, unless it is a close blood relative, since marriage is contrary to the Lamaist doctrine of celibacy. For a lama, "leaving home" (*gerees gharkhu*) is the ideal rather than "establishing home" (*gerlekü*). Traditional marriage among the Mongols is associated not with Buddhism, but with Shamanism. The blessings of *Burkhan,* the Buddha, are not valued as highly on this occasion as those of the Shamanistic deity, *Tenggeri.*

Over the centuries, there has been significant cultural continuity in

marriage customs, even though changes have occured. The arrangement of the marriage of Chinggis Khan, as recorded in the *Secret History,*
is instructive in a number of respects:

> When Temüjin was nine years of age [his father] Yesügei Ba'atur took
> him to his uncle, Hö'elün's [his mother's] home in the clan of Ölkünüd, in
> order to marry one of the girls there. [On the way] . . . they met Tei
> Sechen of the Onggirad tribe . . . Tei Sechen said, "This, your boy, is a
> good boy with fire in his eyes and a light on his face. *Khuda* Yesügei,[13] I
> dreamed a dream last night in which I saw a white jer-falcon holding the
> sun and moon in its two claws and coming down to light upon my arm. . . .
> It must be the *sülder* [guardian spirit] of your Kiyad clan and it is a good
> omen. We, the Onggirad, from ancient times have paid close attention to
> the faces of our maternal grandsons and the beauty of our daughters. . . .
> *Khuda* Yesügei, I invite you to my home where I have a daughter who is
> still small; I wish you to see her." Thus saying, Tei Sechen took them to
> his home and they stayed with him. Seeing the daughter, he [Yesügei]
> noted that she was truly a girl with a light on her face and fire in her eyes.
> This was what he really desired. She was one year older than Temüjin,
> ten years at the time, and named, Börte. That night [the father and son]
> stayed there and the next morning [Tei Sechen] said, "It would be an
> honor to have [you] beg for her hand repeatedly—it would be despised by
> the people for [you] to have your request granted immediately. But, it is
> the destiny of a girl that she should never grow old at home so now I will
> give my daughter to you. Allow your son to become my son-in-law and
> remain here while you return home alone." So both sides agreed . . . and
> Yesügei Ba'atur . . . took his string of horses and presented them as a
> token of agreement to [Tei Sechen] and left Temüjin there as a son-in-
> law [to be] while he himself returned.[14]

The father of Temüjin was poisoned by Tatars on the way home, but
before dying he called for his son Temüjin to come to him. After his
father's death, the son experienced great difficulty, but finally regained
status and power and, in time, sent some of his followers to bring Börte
to be his wife. The *Secret History* continues, "Tei Sechen came part way
to see her off and then returned . . . . Jotan, the mother of Börte Üjen,[15]
came together with her daughter to . . . Temüjin's home. . . . When the
mother, Jotan, came she brought with her a black sable coat as a present
from her daughter to her parents-in-law."[16] Thus, it seems that when
Chinggis desired to claim his bride, Börte, he did not go himself, but sent
representatives, an exception to custom. According to the account, the

person who accompanied the bride to the home of the groom was not the father or some male representative, as customary, but the mother.

The *Secret History* reveals some of the ancient marriage customs of the Mongols, many of which are still practiced. As in more recent times, marriage was exogamous into another clan; recitations of genealogy indicate the importance of the exogamous tradition. The engagement or marriage contract was often decided by the parents while the children were very young, and this practice continued until the Communist period. The Wu-huan tribe of nomads of the later Han period (25-220 A.D.), however, based marriage arrangements on romantic love and courtship.[17] In some of the ceremonies surrounding Mongol weddings, there still can be seen the influence of the ancient nomadic custom of gaining wives by kidnapping.

The status of the family of the bridegroom and the physical appearance of the bride—both natural and fairly universal factors—were important. Also, as indicated by the remarks of **Tei Sechen, there** were apparently extended negotiations before a final agreement was made in obtaining a wife. Even such an influential leader as Chinggis Khan was refused in marriage negotiations with another tribe. The accounts would seem to indicate that at the engagement feast, *bu'uljar* (literally "sheep's neck"), a very tough piece of meat was eaten, symbolizing that the marriage must be strong and inseparable. This custom is still continued in some parts of Mongolia, but at the wedding feast rather than at an engagement banquet.

When the bride's family finally agrees to a marriage arrangement, a token gift confirming the contract must be given by the groom's family to the family of the bride; this custom also has continued from early to modern times. Apparently, in ancient times, the prospective bridegroom resided for a time with the family of the bride, but this custom has been abandoned. The token gift required by the bride's family has risen to a comparatively high value. In the Oirad law code of 1640 and also in the law codes of the early Ch'ing period, a ceiling was placed on the price. More recently, in the 1930s, under the Mongol government of Prince Demchügdüngrüb (De Wang), a law was promulgated that the bride price should not exceed five large animals.[18]

Upon first meeting her parents-in-law in her new home, the bride presents a gift to them. If her husband's parents are still living, she will stand on the left of the entrance just inside the yurt, facing the north. This symbolic, humble gesture shows obedience and demonstrates the bride's intention to respect the parents and elders of her husband's family. She does not sit facing the south in the honored position reserved for the head of the family.

Strict prohibitions against marrying within the same clan have persisted until recent times. Since a very high percentage of Mongol nobility (*taiji*) were of the Borjigid clan, marriage within this group was at times difficult or impossible; there were a limited number of eligible women, and it was customary, before the end of the Yüan period, for the Borjigid to intermarry with the Onggirad clan until the group was annihilated by the Chinese. The Borjigid then began to intermarry with the Uriyangkha clan or with the common people. Because of the great proliferation of the Borjigid and the increasing difficulty in making marriage contracts according to the old custom, the Borjigid clan was split into four subclans. The division was made along the lines of descendants of Chinggis Khan and his three younger brothers, Khasar, Khachiun, and Belgütei. It is not known just when this occurred, but it was after the Yüan period and in the early Ch'ing period.[19] From this time on, it was possible to marry within the extended Borjigid clan; however, there was a prohibition against marriage within the same lineages or more limited subclans. This prohibition applied to the paternal line but not to the maternal line.

There were differences between the more ancient exogamous marriage customs and those of later periods. During the early pre-empire, clan period, marriage between clans took place freely. However, after several centuries, the scope seems to have become much more limited, and marriages were contracted from family to family in particular lineages rather than from clan to clan. Thus, marriage between two particular lineages became increasingly more frequent, including cross-cousin marriages, which were, however, restricted to the maternal lineage. During the early clan period, it was possible for a man to marry the wife of his deceased brother or of some other deceased member of the clan. During later periods, while the paternal line was protected against intermarriage, there continued to be few restrictions upon marriage within the maternal line. Apparently, this change began to take place after the rise of the empire, but the transition was very slow and required several centuries.

Judging from the *Secret History,* no attention was paid to the closeness of relationship on the maternal side in contracting marriages. In this and in other particulars, the Mongols had more flexible marriage rules than the Chinese, which often caused difficulties. An account from the *Secret History* makes it clear that generational differences in mating were not particularly important to the Mongols; in this area, the Chinese were very strict. On the other hand, the accounts indicate that in Mongolia, as in China, the wedding and engagement feasts were very important. Chinggis Khan proposed a mutual marriage alliance between his own clan lineage and that of Ong Khan, powerful chief of the Kereyid Mongols. The proposal was rejected because of reservations on the part of the family or followers of the chief. However, Chinggis, still wishing to consolidate their friendship and expand his influence, insisted that Cha'ur Begi, the younger sister of Sengküm (son of Ong Khan) be given to his eldest son Jochi, and in return that his own daughter, Khochin-Begi, would be given to Tusakha, the son of Sengküm, in a marriage exchange or alliance. Sengküm proudly said, "Our daughter will go to his home and stand in the back of the door with her face to the north. Their daughter will come to our home and sit upon the main seat facing to the south." Thus Sengküm, with a proud and disdainful attitude, refused to give Cha'ur Begi in marriage, and because of his insult Chinggis Khan felt very cool toward Ong Khan and his son Sengküm. Later the Kereyid leaders plotted to kill Chinggis, and Sengküm said, "Because they have asked for our daughter Cha'ur Begi, we shall decide a date and have them come to partake of the *bu'uljar* feast [originally a marriage engagement feast] and when they come we shall ambush them." On the way to the engagement feast, Chinggis met an old vassal who felt there must certainly be a plot afoot and persuaded his lord to send someone else while he returned home.[20]

Another example occurred after the subjugation of the Kereyid by Chinggis Khan. Chinggis took as a wife, Ibakha Begi, daughter of Jakha-gembü, and took her younger sister Sorkhaghtani as a wife for his son Tolui.[21] Here again, although there were certainly customary restrictions on marriage, they did not pertain to the maternal line.

Sororal marriage, common among the biblical Hebrews, was also customary among the nomadic tribes of north Asia but has now disappeared. The Chinese, extremely strict in their own marriage customs, frequently wrote in their records from the time of the Hsiung-nu down to the time of the Mongols, "When a father dies the sons may take the father's wives (except for their own mother) and if an elder brother dies, a younger brother will take the widowed sister-in-law as a wife. This is the behavior of beasts." This strong view, still common among the Chinese, is arrived at without understanding the exogamous marriage customs and the kinship system among the Mongols. In contrast to the Chinese custom, upon the death of her husband, a Mongolian woman may return to her family or may remarry; the decision is largely left to her. There is no stigma on the remarriage of widows as in other Asian societies.

Polygamy was common among the Mongols, and among the wives of a household the first wife was senior and spoken of as *abali gergen* ("first legitimate wife") or *yeke ekener* ("major wife"). In contrast with the Chinese, who have very definite customs regarding concubines or secondary wives, the Mongols, comparatively speaking, did not develop quite such precise distinctions. *Ekener abakhu*[22] (literally, "to take a wife") was used for the second wife of a widowed man; *bagha ekener* ("minor wife") was the term for a secondary wife or concubine. Secondary wives were considered to have almost equal status with the first wife. However, among the Mongol rulers or nobility, only the son of the *abali gergen* could succeed the father and receive the greater part of the inheritance. Thus, while there was little discrimination between wives, the rules of succession and inheritance were close to those of the Chinese *ti-shu* system (*ti* refers to sons of legitimate wives, *shu* refers to sons of concubines). Chinese historians never attacked the Mongol rules of inheritance as they have done those of marriage. The custom of concubinage, as distinct from polygamy, common among the Chinese and greatly criticized in the West, was not introduced to the Mongols until after their occupation of Chinese territories during the Mongol expansion and did not become strong until during the Ch'ing period.

In the Mongol family, whether the marriage is monogamous or polygamous, the status of women is higher than in the traditional Chinese agricultural society. Very early in the Mongol Empire, many foreign envoys and travelers in Asia made special note of the fact that the wives of the khans were seated beside their husbands in audience, a practice unheard of in a Chinese court. Also, Chinggis Khan frequently mentioned occasions or ways in which his mother performed meritorious service in laying the foundations of the Mongol Empire. Thus, it was customary in traditional Mongol society for the voice of the women to be heard on matters of importance, and it was not uncommon for these views to find acceptance and be honored. It may be noted that two very important decisions of Chinggis Khan were urged upon him by his wife, Börte: the breaking of an alliance with Jamukha and the suppression of the powerful shaman, Kököchü.[23] Even such important matters as the decision of a successor to the khan were influenced by women. Chinggis made a decision regarding his successor, at the insistence of his wife, Yesüi, just before the great Middle Eastern campaign.[24]

In Mongol society, and even earlier in Kitan society, it was common for the wife of a prince or nobleman to succeed her deceased husband as the head of the household. At times she even controlled a fairly large and complex administrative structure. The higher status of women in nomadic society compared to that in most Asian agricultural societies may be, in part, due to great spatial mobility, which in turn influenced social mobility and status. It is impossible to develop strict controls within the family in a nomadic society to the degree that exists within the densely populated, sedentary, Chinese agricultural society. A greater degree of mutual consent on major decisions within the family, clan, or society is necessary to maintain stability and viability. The status of women declined in the eighteenth and nineteenth centuries due to the influence of Confucian philosophy and the quasi-feudalistic social system developed under the Manchu.

Mongolian poetry, literature, and songs reveal a greater degree of romantic love than Chinese counterparts, although romantic love never reached the point common in the modern period. Romantic love may result in marriage, but traditionally the occurrence is quite rare. Illicit relations naturally occur, but it is difficult to generalize on the matter on the basis of the available material. However, certain impressions, stereotypes, and trends may be set forth with some confidence. There is, for example, a divergence between the Mongolian ideal of chastity and actual practice. Strictness regarding sexual purity varies from region to region and differences are found from banner to banner in a particular league. People in the Üjümüchin Banner in the Shilin-ghol League, for example, are rigid regarding the matter of chastity and stereotype their Abagha Banner neighbors as being much more lax. (There are no statistics on such factors as illegitimate births to affirm or deny such impressions). Patterns also differ with class. The nobility or aristocratic families are generally more strict than the common people, but even here there are variations. As a rule, elite families are very stern concerning women marrying into their lineage, and great care is taken not to allow pollution of the family blood lines. Ironically, less strictness is exercised with their own daughters who will marry and leave the family in due course. The Mongolian attitude regarding illicit sexual relations is by no means as rigid as the Chinese, which is possibly the most strict of any major society.

One long-term trend that deserves more study is the obvious decline in sexual morality in Mongolia over the centuries. This is readily apparent in the area of law. During the early empire period and the Yüan dynasty, adultery was condemned as a most serious crime, and severe punishments were applied.[25] Following the collapse of the empire, records also show strictness in such matters. However, later, particularly during the Manchu-Ch'ing period, there was a significant relaxation regarding sexual relations, although the laws continued to be strict regarding the protection of the paternal line of the higher classes. The explanation for this trend revolves about several points. The sparsely populated and widely dispersed society found it necessary, over a period of time, to relax the traditional custom of exogamous clan marriage. This probably had some influence on relaxing the restrictions on the association between men and women. A second factor was the development of a few urbanlike centers, such as Urga, which resulted in a concentrated population, a change in attitudes, patterns of behavior, and personal relationships. A third factor, and possibly the most important, was the great growth of Lamaist or Tibetan Buddhism; a large percentage of the men were taken from society as celibate monks, thus disrupting the normal patterns of mating. Marriageable men became rare, and illicit liaisons became common as evidenced by the high incidence of veneral disease.

A number of foreign travelers or observers in Mongolia have referred to a custom of promiscuous hospitality. However, the incidences must have been greatly exaggerated for there is no cultural pattern or institutionalized form of this activity. A foreign traveler, impressed by a cultural aberration, probably generalized from a particular case in a rather sensational manner. No doubt, romantic affairs did occur as women had illicit relations with strangers; such affairs were an open secret in some places, but were generally condemned.

OLD AGE, ILLNESS, DEATH, AND BURIAL

Since ancient times, the Chinese chronicles, in commenting on the life of the northern nomads, note with a condescending and prejudicial tone that the barbarians "honor the strong and despise the old" (*kuei-chuang chien-lao*).[1] In fact this is a misperception. In contrast to the Chinese culture, which venerates old age, the Mongolian culture appears more youth-oriented; wrestling, hunting, fighting, and so forth are praised in song and poetry. However, this does not indicate lack of respect on the part of the Mongols for older, more experienced persons. Many passages in the venerable *Secret History* note that it is proper to respect age and heed the advice of the older generation. There is much evidence that older people in traditional nomadic society are honored. Ögödei Khan expressed these sentiments in his ambition to establish a condition in which "joy shall come to the old folk and the young folk shall grow up in peace."[2] There is no cultural pattern that could be construed to support the notion of disrespect for elders among the Mongols. As a rule, grandparents or the older generation are not lonely because they are customarily heads of the household and their advice must be gained on every important decision or problem unless they desire not to be involved.

A common task for grandparents among the nomads is the care of the young children around the yurt. They receive much attention and satisfaction from the children and are revered and respected by the whole household. Elderly men, incapacitated by age, do not engage in heavy work, but they remain involved in light work until death. Older women or widows may, on occasion, shave their heads and take the vows of a nun, but they remain in the household (monasteries for nuns did not develop in Mongolia). The everyday life of the elderly nuns is no different from the life of the average older person: they help with the chores around the home and tell stories to the younger children. Before the Communist period, the old folks would while away the time by fingering prayer beads and reciting Buddhist liturgical formulas.

Traditionally, in Mongolia, there has been virtually no institutionalized form of preventive medicine. Hygienic measures were unknown. Disease and sickness were regarded as the result of evil influences and wrongdoing. Accordingly, virtually the only measures taken against disease were those of the shaman: prayers and the exorcism of evil spirits. The *Secret History* notes that Ögödei Khan, in his campaign against the Chin (1231), suffered a stroke and that his mouth and tongue were paralyzed. The shamans, commanded to divine the reasons for the illness, declared: "the gods of the mountains and the rivers of the Chin territory have come to plague the khan. They are displeased because their people are plundered and their cities destroyed."[3]

In ancient times, the doctor and shaman were one and the same, and they were honored in society because of their mystic powers. The term *otochi* ("doctor") was a special name given persons with powers to cure sickness. Later, when Buddhism was introduced, the term *otochi* came to be translated as "god of medicine." Because white (*chaghan*) is a special color among the Mongols, a famous or prominent doctor is often given the title *chaghan-otochi*.[4] Following the establishment of the Mongol Empire, many physicians came from Persia, China, and other places and were generally highly honored.[5] A commendable attitude toward public health and charity is seen in the policies of the Yüan dynasty when the imperial hospital (*T'ai-i-yüan*) dispatched officials to such large centers as Taitu (Khanbalic) and Shangtu to dispense medicine to the common people.[6] While the role of the shaman in Mongolian society in this period was still very strong, medical practice was going through a transition, herbology and pragmatic traditional medicine, particularly from China, were being introduced.

At the end of the sixteenth century, Tibetan Buddhism became almost universally adopted in Mongolia, and the lama *emchi* or doctor came to hold a prominent position. Earlier, Buddhism had developed a very respectable, pragmatic medicine, and as the lamas came into Mongolia their role as doctors was an important factor in making converts and spreading Buddhism. Once, when Altan Khan was sick, the lamas came and, although there was considerable hostility against them in this early period, they were still invited to pray for the khan and to provide medicine. The khan was cured, and the incident was fortunate for the spread of Lamaist Buddhism.[7]

The studies of W. Heissig and others demonstrate how the role of the shaman as a doctor and exorcist in Mongolian society came to be assumed by the lamas and why Shamanism became weak.[8] The reading of sutras and the prayers of the lamas came to be relied upon to prevent illness, and, in the case of disease, traditional Buddhist medicine, imported mainly from Tibet, was used. Many of the most prominent Buddhist monasteries in Mongolia have, as one of their academic divisions, a *mampa-tatsang* ("medical college"). Due recognition and merit must be given to these institutions, which in the premodern period, with certain limitations, performed an important public-health function in Mongolia.

Lama doctors, known as *mampa* or *emchi,* who graduated from the medical colleges had spent many years training and studying the traditional Buddhist medical texts and pragmatic medicine. While lamas had some techniques for corrective medicine, they did practically nothing in the area of preventive medicine, except in the case of smallpox. To the Mongols, the most dreaded disease is smallpox (*jerlig,* literally "wild" or "untamed"). Long before the modern period, the lamas developed a unique form of vaccination that was a little dangerous for those who received it, but nevertheless was a very effective immunization. Acupuncture (*jigü-talbikhu*) has been practiced effectively by lama doctors for centuries and seems to have been introduced directly from Tibet rather than from China. The flora of Mongolia furnishes a wide range of herbs used by lama doctors, who very readily borrowed directly from the abundance of Chinese medicine.[9]

In addition to the sacred formulas of the lamas, since ancient times the Mongols have been attracted to special places in Mongolia called *arshan* (*arshiyan*), which means literally "holy water," or "water from a sacred source," but which also has the connotation of "springs." For centuries, the Mongols have come to these hot springs to take advantage of the healing qualities of the mineral waters.[10]

Nomads developed certain techniques to quarantine epidemics among both humans and cattle. Typhoid, a serious disease in premodern Europe which was known in Mongolia as sweating sickness (*kölüsütei ebedchin*), was effectively handled by the Mongols. They had some useful internal medicine, and few people died from typhoid. Naturally, the occurrence of such tropical diseases as cholera (*changkha*) and malaria were quite unknown.

Another serious disease was bubonic plague (*tarbaghan-u ebedchin*— literally "the disease of the marmot"). The Mongols knew of no way to cure bubonic plague, but realized that it was associated with or carried by marmots. For this reason none but the very poorest people eat this animal, which is quite tasty.[11]

From early modern times, syphilis, known to the Mongols as *Kitad yara* ("Chinese boils"), has been a serious problem in Mongolia. Lama doctors concocted various types of medicine and took measures against syphilis, but they seem to have been generally ineffective. The disease, unknown in earlier periods of Mongol history, came in with the Manchu rule as Mongol princes were constrained to take up residence in Peking and as Chinese merchants began their circuits through Mongolia or established business houses in Urga. Another common name for the disease is *yam,* from a Tibetan term meaning "bad blood." Social diseases are less common in eastern Inner Mongolia than in the west or the north. As strictness in morality began to break down throughout Mongolia during the Manchu period, eastern Inner Mongolia maintained a strict moral code, and persons who happened to contract a social disease often lost prestige and were stigmatized.

Tuberculosis (*menger*) is very rare in the nomadic areas of Mongolia, and the Mongols felt that drinking *kumis* was good protection against it. A common illness (in the past at least), although not a very serious one, was a fever that tended to recur periodically at intervals from five to seven days. Another affliction, restricted primarily to the Buddhist monasteries, is *bam,* the symptom of which is a swelling of the legs. This illness is virtually unknown among nomadic Mongols, and, therefore, it is commonly felt that it comes only upon people who live on "dead land" (*körös ügei*)—land that has been farmed or upon which buildings have been built and which, therefore, has "lost its skin." A common treatment for *bam* is to move the afflicted person from the monastery in the spring, have them live in a yurt on new, green, pasture land, and have them drink *kumis* and fresh milk. Internal surgery, including the amputation of infected limbs, was unknown in Mongolia until modern times. However, *khangginur,* a type of lancing of boils or other surface infections with a knife or a small ax, is practiced, and the Mongols are very capable of setting broken bones.

When a person was wounded in battle campaigns, it was common to suck a bloodclot from the wound as treatment.[12] Another common treatment was to cut open the stomach of a cow or a horse and place the wounded man or ailing member of the body in it. The *Yüan shih* notes that Kuo Pao-yü, a Chinese general in the service of Chinggis Khan, was treated in this manner, and cured, when wounded in a campaign against Khorezm.[13] These techniques, practiced in the pre-Buddhist period, were forbidden by the Third Dalai Lama in the 1570s and were discontinued.

The conversion of the Mongol nation to Tibetan Buddhism in the late sixteenth century brought about great changes in beliefs regarding birth, sickness, old age, and death. The Mongol was previously concerned with his relationship to *Tenggeri* ("heaven") and the suffering of the body and the spirit in death. Through the power of a shaman, a dead person passed to the next world. Apparently, until the introduction of Buddhism, there was no fear of retribution or of condemnation to hell or a fate from which one could escape only through the intercession of a diety. The Buddhist concepts of karma ("retribution"), hell, and reincarnation were eagerly accepted as an explanation of existence and as a means of liberation from successive incarnations. Buddhism superimposed upon the idea of *Tenggeri* the belief that the highest goal a person could strive for was the ascent of the spirit to *Burkhan-u oron* ("the dwelling place of the Buddha").

There has been a considerable proliferation of vocabulary for the phenomenon or concept of death in the Mongol language, but only a few will be mentioned here. The most common word, a neutral term used for both animals and men except for someone honored by the speaker, is *ükükü* ("death"). Another word, *öngerekü*, is used similarly to the English term, "pass away." A third term, *nasu bolkhu*, "life is completed," is used often in respect to the older generation. *Nasun buyan tegüskü* conveys the meaning "the blessing of long life is completed." A common expression for death is *taghal tegüskü*, meaning "one's love for the world is completed." An honorific term used for the khans and Mongol nobility is *Tenggeri bolkhu*, "ascent to heaven." Another term used only for a khan is *khalikhu*, "to soar on wing in the heavens." Still another term reserved for emperors is *jöb ese bolkhu* which conveys the idea that an event is irregular: the emperor should live a long life, but has prematurely died. There are also phrases like *Burkhan bolkhu*, "to become a Buddha," used by a person in reference to all those he honors. Another Buddhist expression is *nirvana gerel üjegülkhü*, "to show the light of nirvana," a phrase ordinarily restricted to the death of high lamas.

Mongolian Buddhists feel that the main concern in death should be with the fate or disposition of the spirit, and they have little or no concern with the body, which is considered but a vile receptacle. Taboos related to death make the disposition of the body troublesome to the family. Usually, when a person is on his deathbed, people around him do not move or disturb him. The dying person is to be left alone in meditation to direct or concentrate his thoughts on the Buddha. It is improper to cry, mourn, and otherwise disturb the dying person with concerns about earthly life and problems of the family. It is regarded as beneficial to call in a lama admired by the person to chant sutras while the spirit of the dying person departs. After death, a small butter lamp is placed near the body, symbolizing the wish that the person's journey to the world beyond may be in the light. In modern times, offerings of food may or may not be placed before the body, which customarily is not to be disturbed for twenty-four hours after death in order not to agitate the spirit. Grieving and sobbing in a restrained manner are acceptable, but it is inappropriate to mourn with great clamor and outcries as is common in many other cultures.

After a death, a member of the family, a friend, or a relative is customarily dispatched to a neighboring temple to request the lamas to divine the proper direction in which the spirit of the deceased may depart to the world of the Buddha or be reincarnated in a better situation. Then gifts and money in sizable amounts are customarily distributed to the lamas, and they pray for the well-being of the spirit of the deceased, for a release from hell, or for deliverance to the Buddhist "heaven." People also send gifts of animals and money to the family to be used for soliciting the prayers and assistance of the lamas.[14] The personal effects of the deceased person are given as gifts to favorite friends and relatives.

Although cremation is common among Buddhists over the world and is accepted among the Mongols, it is a means of disposition of the body that could be afforded only to honored lamas. Ordinary lamas and the common folk are regarded as unclean and their "dirty smoke" is not deserving of ascending to heaven. After the body of an honored lama has been cremated, the bone fragments (*sharil*) are gathered in an urn to be placed in a stupa within the temple compound as an object of worship.[15] But in south and southeastern Inner Mongolia, the bodies of nobility and commoners alike are usually buried in the ground.

In northern and western Mongolia, strongly influenced by Buddhism, it has been common to perform one last act of grace or compassion by giving one's body to famished animals as a demonstration of the high ideal of selflessness or non-ego. This disposition of the body, considered very barbaric among Chinese and Westerners, is held in high esteem by Buddhist Mongols. The dead person is dressed in new clothing and placed on a cart, which is then carried to the public burial grounds, a forbidden place not ordinarily visited by people, and here both the body and the cart are left for the wild animals. Since the turn of the century and the decline of Buddhism, this form of disposition is less common and may have even ended with Communist influence in Inner Mongolia. With the establishment of the Mongolian People's Republic, it was forbidden by law in former Outer Mongolia.

In recent centuries, each noble family had their own *ongghon* or burial ground.[16] The word is a Shamanistic term used in reference to a variety of divine objects. The institution of *ongghon* persists in pastoral areas but has been given up by Mongols in farming areas. In cases of death by a contagious disease, however, bodies are interred in the ground throughout Mongolia. Following a death, a memorial prayer or commemoration is held on set days in multiples of seven: the twenty-first day, the thirty-fifth day, and the forty-ninth day.

The ancient Mongol tradition of purification by fire has continued to modern times, and persons present at the unhappy and polluting occasion of death are compelled to cleanse themselves ritually by passing through, between, or near fire[17]—not over the fire, which is taboo. It is customary for the Mongols, upon a death in the family, to consult with the lamas regarding the handling or disposition of the body in order to avoid any further disaster upon the household or relatives. At this time, the lamas turn to a sort of Book of the Dead, the *Altan-saba* ("golden vessel").[18] From this book, a judgment is made regarding the disposition of the body based upon considerations of the dates of birth and death, the cause of death, and how its influence may be limited. This custom seems to stem from ancient Shamanistic influences and also reminds one of certain aspects of Tibetan Bon and Chinese Taoism.

Chinese sources furnish the most abundant data for a study of customs related to death. Hsiao Ta-heng, writing in 1594, made some very interesting observations. He reported that in ancient times, the Mongol khans and nobles were buried in a simple manner in a wooden coffin in a remote wilderness and that their armor and selected items of clothing were buried with them. Concubines and secondary wives, servants, and a favorite horse would be buried with them. The location of the burial was kept very secret. He added that during his time, as the Mongols were being converted to Buddhism, this custom changed and live offerings or the burying of persons to accompany the khan had been discontinued. Instead, the lamas had spread the custom of cremation. The ashes were gathered together and prepared in the form of a small image, which was gilded or covered with other precious metals and enshrined in a Lamaist temple, where it was honored in prayer ceremonies for forty-nine days following the death. Ordinary people, Hsiao noted, would at least have a lama pray for a departed family member for seven days. He added that the clothing, armor, horse, or personal belongings of the deceased person were given to the temple as an offering. All offerings brought as presents to the deceased were also given to the temple.[19] Early Mongol chronicles report that the Third Dalai Lama came from Tibet some time after Altan Khan's death, and, upon learning that the body had been buried, he instructed the Mongols to exhume the body, cremate it, and mold the ashes into a gilded image to be placed in the temple.[20]

Medieval European travelers[21] noted that in former times if a Mongol were ill, his spear would be stuck in the earth before the yurt and no one would enter except a person attending the sick. If the person died, relatives and friends mourned his passing and buried him immediately because of their belief that death is caused by evil spirits. The burial or mourning ceremonies included milk and meat offerings presented before the body by all the friends and relatives of the deceased. Two graves were used: one for the body of the dead person and one for his favorite horse—including the reins and saddle—bows and arrows, and other implements that may be necessary for the person's use in life beyond the grave. Following the burial, all those who attended would pass between two large fires in a ceremony of ritual purification. Next, the yurt in which the deceased person dwelled and all his possessions would be ceremoniously purified, and the family would continue to prepare food in the dead person's memory.

The body of a Mongol prince would be placed in a tent in a seated position, and before it would be placed a table set with a bowl of meat and a bowl of *kumis*. Not only the body of the prince, but also his yurt, a mare and colt, a stallion with full saddle and reins, and many other luxurious things belonging to him would be placed in the grave. The place of burial was kept secret, and someone was placed to guard the grave and prevent strangers from approaching it. The yurt in which the prince lived was disassembled, and it was customary that his name was not to be spoken by his descendants to the third generation.

P'eng Ta-ya, in the *Hei-ta shih-lüeh* (early 1200s), wrote, "No mound is made in burying the body and horses are caused to pass over the grave, to trample and obscure it in such a way that it appears like the rest of the surrounding area."[22] In a similar vein, Yeh Tzu-ch'i, an early Chinese authority on Mongol customs, noted in the *Ts'ao-mu-tzu* (late 1300s):

> The burial custom of the Yüan is to dig a very deep grave, bury the body and cause ten thousand horses to pass over the grave to make it level. After new green grass arises in this area, the prohibition will be raised [which forbids anyone from entering the area], the area will be level and all traces of the grave will be gone making it impossible to discover the site of the burial.[23]

In the section on traditional Mongol rituals in the Monograph on

Worship and Offerings (*Chi-ssu chih*) in the *Yüan shih*, interesting and valuable data is recorded regarding the elite burial of the Mongol khans who ruled China.

> When an emperor or empress is ill and death seems inevitable, they are removed from the palace to a yurt and should they die, the body is placed in a coffin within the yurt. Following this, a burnt offering or sacrifice (*shao-fan*) will be made of sheep for forty-nine days after the death. Then the yurt [in which the body had been placed] may be bestowed upon a favorite vassal. . . . When the deceased emperor is prepared for burial a coffin is made of the fragrant *nan* wood. A log is split in half and hollowed out in the form of the body. The length and the circumference will be only large enough to accommodate the body. The body is dressed in a sable gown and hat; the boots, stockings, and amulets hanging from the belt are specially prepared of finely tanned, white bleached hide. At the same time, two golden water vessels, a bowl, a dish, a pair of chopsticks and a spoon are also placed in the coffin. After this, the coffin is sealed and bound with four golden bands. The chariots on which the coffin is transported are covered with white felt and draped with bluish-green *na-shih-shih* [Persian, golden-embroidered silk]. In the funeral procession, a Mongol female shaman seated on a horse wearing a new coat leads a horse, covered with *na-shih-shih* and equipped with a gold saddle and reins, called "golden spirit horse." A sacrifice of a sheep is made three times each day during the journey to the burial. Each shovelful of dirt taken from the grave will be placed in a border at the side of the grave. After interring the coffin, the dirt is replaced in the grave in the sequence in which it was removed. Remaining earth will be transported to a distant place. Three special officials who accompany the coffin to the grave will reside five *li* away from the grave and a burnt offering will be made once each day for three years after which they return.[24]

Ssu-ma Ch'ien in his famous history, *Shih chi*, discussed the burial customs of the Hsiung-nu in the earliest account of the nomads and noted, "When they bury a dead person they use a coffin and gold and silver. . . . Vassals and wives whom they loved are buried together and may number up to a hundred."[25]

The burial customs of the nomadic Turks, discussed in the *Sui shu* (600s), indicate a somewhat different but related pattern.

> When a person dies he is placed in a yurt and his family and relatives slaughter cows and horses to make an offering. They ceremoniously circumambulate [walk around] the yurt seven times, moaning, crying, and cutting their face, mingling tears and blood to drop in the dirt. They then select a day for the burial and place the body on a horse to be burned.

The remaining ashes are then buried, the area of the grave is enclosed in a wooden fence, and in the center is erected a house. Within the house is placed a picture of the deceased and pictures depicting the battle scenes and events of his life."[26]

A comparison of these accounts of ancient non-Mongol nomadic peoples with what is known of the customs of the Mongols shows a certain continuity and many similarities during the peak of Mongol rule. Among the Mongols, a person nearing death was moved from the yurt in which he ordinarily lived to another place; even as great a person as a khan or emperor would not be allowed to die within the imperial palace if it could be avoided. Mongol scholars feel that this custom indicates a desire to die in a traditional dwelling rather than within a foreign structure. However, it was considered very meritorious to meet death in Tibet, the holy land. After a prince's death, favorite vassals, friends, and relatives came to make offerings of food to the deceased. A sacrifice or *tüleshi* ("burned offering") was made. This custom was transmitted from the old Kitan tribes through the Jurchen to the Mongols. In addition, the family burned objects that they wished to give to the deceased. This practice is strongly reminiscent of the sacrifices and offerings of the Hebrews of the *Old Testament*. The *Secret History* records an incident of an offering being made to the decapitated head of Ong Khan of the Kereyid Mongols by the mother of Tayang Khan of the Naiman tribe.[27]

Horses play an important role in the nomad's concept of and customs related to death. The Mongols firmly believe that the spirit of the deceased rides a horse to *Tenggeri* ("heaven") and, after the burial of a khan, horses are run over the grave. The Turks transported their dead on horseback.

The custom of burying prominent persons with many treasures is common in Asia. In addition to the Hsiung-nu, many other people practiced live or sacrificial burial of wives, concubines, or vassals with a deceased ruler. The incidence of this custom among the Hsiung-nu is confirmed by the discoveries of Kozlov at Noyan-ula where many bodies were uncovered beside that of the prince or noble. Black sables were also discovered in this digging, indicating a long and consistent tradition, from the ancient nomads to more recent Mongols, of using sable to bury royal leaders.[28] However, there is no indication from either the *Secret History* or the Mongol dynastic records in Chinese that the Mongols buried other people with the deceased rulers. A legend in the *Altan tobchi,* however, says that on his deathbed, Chinggis Khan said that he did not want to be alone and indicated certain companions and loved ones to accompany him in death. However, his ministers and counselors insisted that there was still much business to be completed in establishing the empire and helping his sons and they persuaded Chinggis to desist.[29] Persian materials record that Ögödei Khan "sent" forty beautiful girls to serve his father.[30] According to a passage in the *Erdeni-yin tobchi,* from the time of Altan Khan's conversion by the Dalai Lama, the custom of burying horses with a deceased person was forbidden.[31] According to the Yüan dynastic histories, in spite of the conversion of the Mongol court to Tibetan Buddhism, the practice of having a female shaman lead a "golden spirit horse" in the funeral procession still continued.[32]

From the Hsiung-nu of the pre-Christian era to the Mongols, the custom of holding a lavish funeral for rulers while interring the body in the ground and obscuring the area by having horses pass over the grave continued. Thus, the exact burial places of the great Chinggis Khan and Khubilai Khan are still a matter of debate. According to the *Yüan shih,* from the establishment of the dynasty to its end, Mongol khans were buried in the valley of Ch'i-nien-ku, but the location of this place is not known.[33] The traditional Mongol burial, without a raised mound or tomb, is in distinct contrast with that of the Turkic people who cremated the dead and built an enclosure for the grave. Only the Kitan, among the Altaic nomads, left impressive royal tombs. These great monuments still remain in the Ba'arin Banner of the Juu-uda League in Inner Mongolia.[34]

During his reign, Khubilai Khan established a *tai-miao* ("ancestral temple") in the Chinese tradition, centered at Khanbalic (Peking). At the same time, he established, according to Mongol tradition, the *naiman chaghan ger* ("eight white yurts"; Chs. *pa-pai-shih*).[35] These shrines were not limited to the veneration of Chinggis Khan, but were intended to commemorate in perpetuity all of the emperors in the imperial line. After the collapse of the Yüan dynasty, the ancestral temple was abolished by the succeeding Ming dynasty. As the Mongols withdrew into Mongolia, they continued to maintain the institution of the eight white yurts (*naiman chaghan ger*), but in time it came to be restricted to the veneration of Chinggis Khan and his wife Eshi Khatun (Börte).[36] This shrine was maintained in one of the Three Right Flank *Tümen* (a major division of the overall administration of the Mongol Empire after the end of the Yüan dynasty). One of the three *tümen* was called the Ordos, and, therefore, the area in which the cult or shrine came to be permanently located is known now as the Ordos. Ordos refers to a larger region, while the specific place in which the cult came to rest is known as Ejen-khoroo ("encampment of the Lord"). It was customary for a new khan to go to the shrine of Chinggis, wherever it was located, to pay his respects and worship before ascending the throne.

At present, the cult of Chinggis Khan remains at Ejen-khoroo in the Ordos area within the bend of the Yellow River. Whether this is actually the burial site of the Great Khan was and continues to be a matter of debate among Chinese scholars.[37] According to the *Altan tobchi,* the body of Chinggis was not buried here, but merely some articles of the khan's clothing and weapons:[38]

> When my Lord went [on an expedition] against the Tangut, he said, "I like this place." Therefore, the wheels of the cart [transporting the body] sank into the earth and would not move. A pretense of burial was made to the whole country and here they buried my Lord's long gown, a yurt, and one sock. As for his real body, some people claim it was buried at the Burkhan Ghaldan mountain, others say it was buried at Yeke Öteg, which was to the front [south] of the Kentei-khan mountains and to the rear [north] of the Altai-khan mountains.[39]

However, whether or not Ejen-khoroo is the burial site of the khan, it is regarded by all Mongols as a sacred place. During the war between Japan and China (1937–45), the sacred casket and other items belonging to Chinggis Khan were transported by Chinese troops to Hsinglung-shan in Kansu province in the interior of China, so they would not be captured and exploited for propaganda by the Japanese. After the establishment of the Communist government in China, this casket and other items were transported back to the Ordos, and a large mausoleum was erected on the spot to commemorate Chinggis Khan. The mausoleum is a symbol of the nationalistic sentiments of the Mongol people and the significance to them of the great emperor.

After the war, while the remains of Chinggis Khan were still at Hsinglung-shan, S. Jagchid visited the place with the head of the Ulanchab League, Prince Rinchinsengge, a descendant of Khasar, brother of Chinggis Khan, to pay formal respects to the remains.[40] They noted that the casket is about eight feet long by four feet high, rectangular in shape, and constructed of a dark metal (which metal is difficult to determine) with silver designs. The chief of the *darkhad* or guardians of the casket explained that it contains the remains of both Chinggis Khan and his wife Börte. Another similar but smaller casket was said to contain the remains of Khulan Khatun, another wife of the khan. Distilled spirits and a whole boiled sheep were offered on this occasion. The drink libation was in a large vase-shaped bronze vessel about one and a half feet tall. While presenting an offering, the priestlike *darkhad* guards chanted ceremonial praise in ritualistic, classical Mongol language. At the beginning of the ceremony, a representative of the group made an offering of a ceremonial scarf (*khadagh*). The group then offered incense and wine, performed three kneelings and nine kowtows. As the group kneeled, the *darkhad,* as their representative, recited a hymn or chant. He then took the wine that had been presented and told the group that it was a bestowal from the khan to those present; he took a drink, performed nine kowtows, and then offered it to those present according to rank. The ceremony seemed reminiscent of the ancient *ho-chan*[41] or royal wine party of the Yüan dynasty. Mongols of the twentieth century who have had such firsthand contact with Chinggis Khan, the emperor of emperors and most famous figure of Mongolian history, have considered it to be a very impressive and moving occasion.

After World War II, anthropologist Frank Bessac visited Ejen-khoroo where the shrine is traditionally kept, although at this time, the items of the shrine were in Kansu. In the ceremony, the leader, a "shaman" or non-Buddhist ceremonial and religious figure, after chanting and offering flour and distilled mare's milk to the four corners of heaven, had those present bow to some of the effects of Chinggis Khan that had not been moved. He then had them touch his bow ("for the first in line, which was I, the second touched the edge of my jacket and the third that of the second") while kneeling on one knee. He then tied a *khadagh* around the neck of those present, symbolizing that all had pledged themselves to the cause of Chinggis Khan—that all were part of the Mongolian confederacy, a sort of *ulus* (or nation) by adoption. (Bessac observes: "Perhaps this [wearing of the *khadagh*] is where the necktie really comes from!") The receipt of a *khadagh* meant the acceptance of vassalage of an individual to the Mongols, and with it went a certain degree of national identity.[42]

The punishment for commoners who committed serious crimes was decapitation. But royal princes or persons of nobility were not decapitated, even for serious offenses, because it was considered ominous for a royal Mongol to bleed to death; offenders were strangled instead. Jamukha, a friend of Chinggis Khan in his youth, became an enemy when they grew older. After his capture, since he was not willing to become a vassal of Chinggis Khan, it was determined that he must be executed. In spite of his great treachery, Chinggis sent him to an honorable death by strangulation rather than by the usual decapitation.[43]

DAILY LIFE AND RECREATION

The everyday life of nomadic Mongols revolves about the preservation, care, and increase of the herds. Most families arise before dawn to check the animals and pasture them or to attend to chores that must be done early. The sheep, especially, it is thought, should be pastured early to graze while the grass still has dew upon it—not only for the water content, but also because it is better for the nourishment of the animals. The women must prepare breakfast very early in the morning to meet the schedule of the day's work. After breakfast, the men take their *urgha*, a long pole with a noose at the end (counterpart of the Western lasso), and tend the herds of horses, cattle, or sheep. While the men are away, the women clean the yurt, do the daily chores, and spend their time on whatever project has priority. When the men are not busy looking after the flocks and herds, they repair carts, yurts, or other equipment. The early part of the day is the most quiet around the yurt because most family members are away at work. Three meals a day are customary. The men return home; eat lunch, which, like breakfast, is simple; rest; and then return to their work.

Evening is a very busy time for nomadic families. The sheep and cattle return to the vicinity of the yurt, and a chorus of bleats, moos, and other animals noises ensues. At this time, just once a day, animals are taken to water, milked, and settled for the night. Except for the sheep, the animals do not have to be driven to the well, for they know where it is and naturally go to the watering spot and wait for the herdsmen to draw the water.[1] The cows are freely milked anywhere, but sheep are milked while tethered to a long rope stretched out and staked on both ends to the ground. After the sheep are milked, the lambs are returned to their mothers. Mares are also hitched to a stationary post while they are milked, but this may or may not be at a set time of the day. Milking mares is a difficult job, requiring some skill and experience, and is usually done by the men.

When the evening chores are completed, it is dark, and the family gathers for the evening meal and some relaxation. This meal is the largest and best of the day. Music and singing often make the atmosphere of the yurt lively and cheerful. There is a close feeling among the family members, particularly between the children and the grandparents who delight in handling, caressing, or playing with them. In the winter, the warmth within the yurt contrasts greatly with the cold outside. Occasionally, the silence outdoors is broken by the baying of the wolves on the steppe.

There is a natural division of labor between males and females in the traditional life-style of nomadic peoples. The men look after military and administrative activities; engage in hunting, herding the larger animals, and caravan trading; and making and repairing carts, saddles, stirrups, and weapons. They generally build enclosures near the yurt for the animals, tan hides, and make felt and boots. The slaughter of animals is also customarily restricted to the males; in more recent centuries, some do this with ambivalent feelings because of Buddhist influences.

The work and activity of the women includes caring for the children and old folks, boiling tea, preparing meals, milking animals, sewing, doing general housework, making milk products such as cheese and butter, husking millet, working felt, making such domestic objects as cushions, rugs, and drapes, fetching water from a distant well by ox cart, gathering *arghal* ("dry dung") for fuel, herding sheep and goats in the vicinity of the yurt, and taking care of the very small animals. The women's work is comparatively heavier than that of the men, and they are generally more diligent in getting it done.

Certain types of activity are cooperative, involving both men and women, such as making and breaking camp during a migration, supervising and coordinating the carts and herds during the move, making felt, tanning hides.

Men have comparatively more leisure than women in premodern nomadic society and, hence, foreign travelers among the Mongols often comment on the laziness of the men—not really understanding their traditional life-style and the division of labor. Since the men are involved in taking care of the herds and hunting, they have few chores around the home. After the men have taken the herds out to pasture, they have considerable free time, except, of course, during bad weather when men must be with the horse herds both night and day to guard against stampedes, wolves, blizzards, or other problems. Contrary to the impressions of some foreigners, Mongol men are concerned about not appearing to be lazy. There is a certain social pressure within Mongol society in this connection, and even though a man may not have some important task to accomplish, he feels compelled to find some "busy work" and often occupies himself with "make work" projects (*aju-törökü*). Sometimes, these projects are actually more recreation than work.

When older persons have nothing to do, they often just sit and turn *kürel-mani* (literally, "bronze prayers"—drum implied); they rotate a prayer drum or wheel that has Buddhist prayers inscribed on it.[2] Older persons also while away the time by manipulating a Lamaist rosary (*erike*). Friar Rubruck observed this practice as early as the 1350s during his visit to Mongolia. "They also have in their hands wherever they go a string of one or two hundred beads, just as we carry our rosaries, and they always say these words, "On man baccam," that is "O God, Thou knowest" so one of them translated it for me and they expect to be rewarded by God as many times as they make mention of Him by saying this."[3] This would seem ostensibly to be pious religious activity, but much of it is just a habitual way of passing the time. The nomadic life on the steppe is very lonely; there are no neighbors and almost no noises, except for an occasional dog bark or the stir of some wild animal.[4] While the average nomad is quite well adjusted to a solitary life, Mongols who have spent some time in an urban environment and then returned to the steppe feel, at times, that the silence is almost overwhelming. Consequently, in their solitary abode, it is common for people to sing to themselves or to whistle some tune. Some old people consider this a vulgar way to pass the time, and a strict grandfather or father may allow some singing, but no whistling.

Carving is another important pastime, particularly for men, some of whom become quite adept at it and produce very attractive items such as sets of chess pieces. These handicrafts, however, are quite unknown outside of Mongolia because they have not been widely distributed commercially. Chess (*shitara*) is played frequently. Mongolian chess bears more similarity to European and Western chess than to the Chinese version.

In more well-to-do families, it is common to find the mother and daughters embroidering. *Dailur,*[5] a decorative pouch worn by men under the belt on the left hip is a popular object. Another very artistic and unique item is the decorative stocking top worn by both men and women. The men's stocking tops are more elaborate and colorful than the women's. Well-to-do families and those with better educations spend considerable free time reading various Mongolian stories and classics or Buddhist sutras.

In the evening, the older people drink a little liquor as they relax and sing and listen to the *morin-khuur,* a two-stringed "horse fiddle" played on the knee with a bow. In the winter season, particularly, older members of the family play games with the young people; one of the favorite games consists of finger flipping game pieces made from an antelope anklebone, in a manner similar to Western marble games.[6] Older people who live close to the *yamen* ("banner office") or in the vicinity of a Buddhist temple often gather at one of these places to chat about old times or current events.

Because of the widely dispersed settlements in Mongolia, visitors are few, and visits are occasions to learn the latest news or to chat about some interesting topic; nevertheless, a person who spends much time in leisure and rides from yurt to yurt constantly visiting people ordinarily would not have a good reputation.

The high points of the year and times most cherished for recreation are the great seasonal festivals or prayer meetings held at the temples or at the regional *oboo,* the Shamanistic shrine, at which many people gather wearing their best clothes and bringing their children for visiting and merrymaking. Another favorite occasion is the annual *dalalgha,* the "beckoning of wealth" festival: a family invites their friends or others in the region over to drink *kumis,* sing, and have fun.[7]

Forms of entertainment and personal practices that might be thought to have great appeal to persons living an isolated and lonely existence have not been popular in Mongolia. There has long been a resistance to drugs, and opium has never been introduced into the nomadic areas of Mongolia, although its use is not uncommon in the areas of mixed Mongol and Chinese population. The tobacco habit, alone, is universal in Mongolia except for children, who are prohibited from smoking.[8] While gambling is quite common among many peoples of Asia, there seems to be a singular lack of gambling among the Mongols, and they frown on it when it has been introduced by outsiders in modern times. Card games, introduced from Outer Mongolia, were one of the first forms of gambling brought in. *P'ai, da-liu* ("dominos"), a Chinese form of gambling using bamboo pieces, was introduced by merchants who came to do business in Mongol areas. Young people were the first to become involved in this activity, but they played in secret and tried to avoid being observed by the older people. The gambling game *mahjong* has become quite popular in this century in areas of mixed Mongol and Chinese population. Those who play, however, are subject to disapproval, social pressure, and feelings of guilt.

One of the most popular traditional forms of entertainment in Mongolia (particularly for children) is a type of storytelling (*üliger*), which may be performed without music by a person referred to as an *üligerchin* or by an instrumentalist called a *khuurchi* ("one who recites to his own accompaniment"). These individuals, always men, itinerate to Mongol encampments or temples where they recite, from Mongolia's rich oral tradition, stories based on the ancient exploits of warriors and religious figures, jokes, and adapted versions of Chinese tales. These fascinating old storytellers wander freely over the steppe and may remain for only a short time. The Ba'arin Banner in Inner Mongolia is most famous for its talented *khuurchi*.

Although the Mongols have a term for playing ball, the sport is quite uncommon except at gatherings at festival times. The Kitan, an earlier people ethnically related to the Mongols, took great delight in playing polo on horseback, which was also popular in T'ang China, quite certainly as an importation from Turkic peoples. The Mongols also played polo, but it seems to have been much less popular during the Mongol Empire and the Yüan dynasty than among earlier nomadic peoples.[9] Tracking and hunting game are common outdoor activities for men, especially in the winter. Young neophyte lamas commonly pass their leisure time in wrestling.

In recent decades, urbanization has obviously influenced traditional patterns of recreation and leisure; commercial enterprises, such as movies and government-sponsored talent groups, have become more prominent. The greatest single change is the widespread use of radios.

In the popular mind, a nomadic life-style is liberated from time and schedules and the tyranny of clock-watching. There is a good deal of truth in this view, however, Mongols are more time conscious than foreigners might expect and, while they are not clock-watchers in the Western manner, their concept of temporality should be given at least passing comment. Everyday life is timed according to the passage of the sun: on the steppe, people constantly watch their shadow, and within the yurt, the position of the sunbeam is observed as it comes through the ceiling and moves across the floor. Thus, activities of the day—meals, the handling of animals, and chores—are regulated. In temples and monasteries, a type of sundial adapted from a Tibetan model—usually cast bronze—is commonly used to calculate time and to schedule various temple functions and activities. Important events such as *nair,* a tournamentlike festival, ordinarily begin at a time considered to be auspicious. The concern to schedule special occasions at auspicious times is seen frequently in the *Secret History.*[10] The best time for an event used to be determined by influential shamans and, in more recent times, by the lamas. Troop movements in the great campaigns of the old Mongol Empire were very punctual. A fairly precise observance of time was necessary in order to rendezvous at particular times and places, often involving great distances.[11]

Like most Asian peoples, Mongols traditionally observed a lunar calendar and changed to the solar calendar only recently. The official calendar system of the Mongol Empire was quite complex. During the early part of the empire period, Western influence from Arabic or Moslem sources was great, and the Moslem calendar, noted in the records by the Chinese term *Hui-hui-li,* was also used by the Mongols in China.[12] However, after the Mongols conquered China, the Chinese calendar, introduced by Chinese advisers to the khans, was dominant in calculating chronology according to the reigns of the Mongol (Yüan) emperors.[13] With the rise of Lamaist Buddhism, a Tibetan calendar imported from Lhasa was most common in ecclesiastical affairs, but concurrently the banner princes throughout Mongolia ordered their schedule according to a calendar obtained yearly from the Manchu court.

With the Mongolian declaration of independence from the Manchu, a calendar was instituted with 1911 as the first year of the independent rule of the Boghda Khan, the Jebtsundamba Khutughtu, "living Buddha." Thus, 1911 became the first year of the new era *Bügüde-ergügsen,* literally "supported by all." The idea was that a new era had been ushered in for the Mongolian people. It has been speculated that the term was proposed by Deputy Minister of the Interior Khaisan,[14] a native from Inner Mongolia, and taken from the Chinese term *Kung-tai,* which has the same meaning.

In the 1930s, with the rise of the autonomous movement in Inner Mongolia, a calendar calculated from the reign of Chinggis Khan was used for a time. According to this system, years and notable events were set using 1206 as year 1; thus, the Mongolian government established in

Hohehot (later moved to Kalgan) was set at Chinggis Khan 731 (1937). This seems to have been the only unique and indigenous calendar system developed in Mongolia during recorded history and actually is more of a nationalistic or political phenomenon. The Western calendar system, imported with the rise of modernization, was used concurrently with other calendars for a time and is now common.

FESTIVALS AND SEASONAL ACTIVITIES

Festivals follow a seasonal cycle of the lunar calendar in Mongolia. The most important festival is the New Year; the first day of the first month is the most auspicious day and is referred to as the "rich white month" (*bayan chaghan sara*). Even the low temperature does not dampen the happiness of the festivities. Families arise earlier than usual and dress in their very best clothes. As the day breaks in the east, while there is only a white line on the horizon, everyone goes out of the yurt and bows in obeisance to each of the cardinal points, beginning with the east where the sun is rising.[1] They then make a sprinkled offering to *Tenggeri* ("heaven"), using the milk of a mare or a cow or some wine. This custom seems to have existed among the most ancient nomads, the Hsiung-nu, through the T'u-chüeh (Turks), and on down to modern Mongols.[2]

The family then returns to the yurt of the head of the family, gathers around a large fire, and makes obeisance to their Buddhist images. Then, while the head of the house and his wife are seated in the place of honor, other members of the family bow to pay their holiday respects. Customarily, the eldest son presents a bowl of *kumis* or milk on a *khadagh*[3] ("silk scarf") to his parents while kneeling on one knee. Before receiving the bowl, the father dips his middle finger into the *kumis* and sprinkles it towards the heaven three times as an offering to the gods.[4] Each of the children in turn present a *khadagh* to their parents, after which members of the family make a quick exchange, sampling each other's snuff bottles (also a well-established custom on other occasions). The exchange of *khadagh* is not really an exchange as such, but more often a mere touching of the ceremonial scarf of one person by another. The word for the "New Year's touch" is *jolghalgha*. A young person who makes this contact, much the same as a congratulatory handshake, places his hands under those of an older person. In a case of equals in age or rank, a left or right hand is placed one above and one below the other person's outstretched hands.

After this congratulatory salutation, members of the family bow to each other. Then the parents pronounce a sort of benediction upon the members of the family by addressing to them some ritual or ceremonial expressions of praise and well-wishing. The exchanges are directed first to the parents and then to each member of the family mutually in turn. By this time, the sun has risen, and members of the family gather around the hearth to partake of New Year's tea. They are careful throughout the day not to speak any bad words whatsoever. Whenever possible during the day, the men of the family go to the nearest Buddhist temple, worship the images, and pay their respects to the lamas.

After this, the men pay New Year's visits to friends and relatives according to the closeness of their relationship, going to their nearest relative first. In his writings, Marco Polo spoke of Khubilai Khan having dressed in a white robe, the honored color of the Mongols, to receive those who came to pay their New Year's respects.[5] The women usually stay at home unless the temple is quite close. On the steppe, it may take a number of weeks to make the visits. Although everyone travels on horseback and great amounts of meat and drink are consumed during this time, one never hears of anyone falling off a horse because of drunkenness.

From the fifteenth day to the end of the first month of the year, a great memorial service is held at the Lamaist temples. The adherents of the temple come to hear the lamas chant the sutras and to give gifts of money and goods. Many people bring their yurt and camp around the temple or even within its compounds, so the temple suddenly becomes a center of activity. For over a hundred years, Chinese merchants have used this occasion to come to the temples to barter and do business with the nomads; thus, over a long period of time, the significance of this occasion has changed from primarily religious to economic. Between the time of this festival and the beginning of spring, it is very bleak in Mongolia: cold, snow, dusty storms, dry grass, and emaciated animals are typical of this period.

The twenty-first day of the third month is an important spring festival: the memorial service in honor of Chinggis Khan. The occasion seems to commemorate a great victory by Chinggis after he had once been defeated by an enemy. There is no record as to its origin or reason for selecting this particular occasion for a festival, but the *Secret History* indicates it seems to have some connection with a situation in the period before Chinggis Khan became the undisputed ruler of all Mongols, when there were still three powerful competing tribes—the Kereyid, the Naiman, and a group that was later to become known as the Mongols. As Chinggis Khan became more powerful, Sengküm, son of Ong Khan and head of the Kereyid tribe, became very jealous and plotted to kill Chinggis Khan. He invited Chinggis to his camp to partake of a feast and receive Sengküm's daughter as a wife for his son. Chinggis, however, learned of the plot from an old vassal and did not continue the journey. He sent word that his animals were weak and unable to travel so far.[6] The Kereyid, finding that their plot had failed, attacked immediately, struck Chinggis before he could return to his camp, and defeated him.[7]

The scholar d'Ohsson, drawing upon the writings of Rashid ad-Din, a high minister of the Il-Khanate during the Mongol period of Persian history (1258-1335), says that Temüjin (Chinggis) was greatly outnumbered when attacked by the Kereyid and had no alternative but to retreat to Baljuna, near present-day Hulun-buir. Here, instead of fresh water, he found muddy water. Seeing his men in great distress, Temüjin looked toward heaven and made an oath: "From now on I will see both sorrow and joy together with you and if I fail in my word my fate will be as the waters of Baljuna." Then taking the muddy waters, Temüjin drank and passed his cup to the leaders accompanying him who drank in turn. These generals also made an oath that they would never forsake him. From this time on, those who were at the meeting became known as "drinkers of Baljuna," and they received special favors, gifts, and attention from Chinggis Khan.[8] Thereafter, the Mongols met no more decisive defeats in establishing the empire, and some Mongol scholars believe that the third-month festival commemorating Chinggis Khan stems from the incident at Baljuna.[9]

Until the middle of this century, on the occasion of this spring festival, many of the Mongol banners dispatched a special messenger or rider to Ejen-khoroo ("camp of the Lord"), the cult of Chinggis Khan in the Ordos region of Inner Mongolia, to pay respects and honor in behalf of the banner or league. Thus, on this festival, at the tomb or cult honoring Chinggis Khan, just inside the loop of the Yellow River, there appeared overnight a tent city reminiscent of the ancient glory of Mongol camps during the empire. Since the rise of Mongol nationalism, this holiday to honor the great hero of the Mongol people is celebrated wherever Mongols have settled, even outside of Mongolia.[10]

During the fourth month, the death of winter gives way to the beauty, green, and life of spring. As the season wears on, the animals give birth and become much more healthy and abundant in meat and milk. During this month, the nomads avoid killing their animals and live largely on a diet of *chaghan ide'e* ("white food"). Because of this practice, some Mongolists believe that before the establishment of the Yüan dynasty, the Mongol New Year was celebrated in the fourth month. According to their interpretation, which is open to dispute, the term designating the first lunar month, *bayan chaghan sara,* originated in or was borrowed from *chaghan ide'e,* the special month in the spring season.

Although the *Secret History* is a basic source of Mongolian history, it mentions specific dates only twice in the entire record and thus is of limited use in reconstructing the annual cycle of festivals. One incident for which a precise date is given is the capture and escape of young Chinggis Khan from the Taichi'ud tribe. According to the record, he escaped on the sixteenth day of the fourth month, while the people of the tribe were celebrating a special occasion.[11] The other specific mention of a date was in connection with a campaign against the Naiman tribe. It was a special day, called *khula'an tergel ödör* ("red round day")[12] because there was a full moon. Judging from the festivities, it must have been a special occasion, but we have no way of knowing what it commemorated. Some Mongol scholars have deduced that it must have been a New Year's Day. Whatever the origin, since early times, the birthday of Chinggis Khan has been celebrated on this day—the sixteenth day of the fourth month.

After the introduction of Buddhism, the Mongol people did not slaughter their animals during the fourth month; while there was an economic factor involved, the reason for abstention, according to the Mongols, was to honor the memory of the birth of Buddha. The Mongols felt that to kill animals during this special period would be very sinful considering the high regard for life in the teachings of the Buddha. Because the weather is pleasant, a greater number of people come on this occasion compared to the temple service in the first month, and the area around the temple is very lively.

Spring is also important in Mongol life because the manes of the horses are clipped then. There are two factors involved in this procedure: the hair is sold to the Chinese for making ropes and other things, and a distinction is made between stallions and other horses (the manes of the former are not clipped). In large herds, the horses are untamed and to catch and clip them is not child's play. The Mongols also carefully examine the herds and determine which horses will remain

A Mongolian religious festival

stallions and which will be castrated. Because many of the horses have never been ridden or trained, spring is also the time when young Mongol men show their prowess and courage in saddling, breaking, and training horses.

All agree the fifth month is beautiful: luxurious vegetation and flowers parade against the blue sky and white clouds; one may frequently see a mother and father crane walking across the steppe with their young; young Mongol couples, married and unmarried, gallop across the steppe, singing and enjoying themselves. Mongols feel that this is the most poetic or romantic time of the year and is the occasion to begin milking the mares to make *kumis,* the favorite drink of the Mongols.

While some seasonal observances have continued over the centuries in Mongolia, others are unique to a particular time and people. Customary festive assemblies of the ancient Hsiung-nu are noted in the *Han-shu* (ca. A.D. 100):

> In the first month all the chieftains gather in a small meeting at the court of the shan-yü [khan] and have some type of religious service. In the fifth month a large assembly is held at Lung-ch'eng ["dragon city"—probably

meaning the court of the ruler], for the worshipping of ancestors, heaven, earth, spirits and gods. In the fall when the horses are strong, another large gathering is held in a pine forest for the purpose of taking a census of all the men and animals.[13]

The *Hou Han shu* (ca. 400) also records: "According to the custom of the Hsiung-nu, they have three religious festivals which take place on the *wu* day [of the Zodiac calendar] in the first month and the ninth month to worship heaven . . . and to convene an assembly to discuss national affairs."[14] The small gathering and religious service in the first month must have been when the chieftains came to pay their New Year's respects to the *shan-yü* of the Hsiung-nu nation.

Some events or customs in the period from the fifth month to autumn have continued to modern times.[15] The tribelike banner, the center of the traditional administrative system among the Mongols for almost three hundred years beginning with the Manchu period, has commonly convened an important meeting during these months for the purpose of discussing taxes, promotions and demotions, the economical and political affairs of the banner, and so forth. At the end of the deliberations, a religious service is held to make offerings to the protective deities of the banner and to enjoy the songs, athletics, and other amusements. This occasion has become widely known as the *oboo* festival. The *oboo*, a common sight in Mongolia, is a large pile of rocks on top of a hill or some elevated place that may be laid out either with a large *oboo* in the center and six smaller *oboo* around it or with a large *oboo* in the center and small *oboo* extending to the four cardinal directions. A spear or a forked weapon is erected in the center of the stupalike pile of rocks and surrounding it, at the base of the rocks, are many tree branches, on which are hung fragments of silk and other cloths of varied colors. Sometimes the cloth scraps may be strung along a string or rope extending from the top of the main *oboo* out to the smaller *oboo* as flags. From a distance a decorated *oboo* is very striking.

An *oboo* is primarily a rustic shrine to the local deities *nibdagh, shibdagh,* or *luus. Luus* is most particularly known as the "dragon king." The deities come from the Shamanistic tradition, but gradually Lamaist Buddhism took over the functions and care of the *oboo.* Many of the *oboo* belong to local temples or to a group of people in a particular neighborhood; however, there is always one central, major *oboo* belonging to and identified with the entire banner. From the fifth month

Women gathered at a temple

to the middle of the eighth month, there are many *oboo* festivals
throughout the regions of Mongolia. When the festival is held at the
banner *oboo,* the *jasagh*—administrative head of the banner—the ranking
lama of the banner, and other important people gather to offer *kumis* and
make sacrificial burnt offerings. All worship and religious ceremonies
associated with the *oboo* festival are in the hands of men; it is taboo for
women to participate, although they attend the festivities that follow.[16]

The festivities following the religious ceremonies take place at the
foot of the hill on which the *oboo* is erected. A large tent (*chachir*) is
erected as a center, and other tents extend on two sides of the main tent.
The prince or a noble is seated, facing the south, on a high seat of honor
in the main tent. If the *oboo* belongs to a particular temple, the honored
seat will be occupied by the "living Buddha" or high lama of that
temple. Above the honored seat and attached to the ceiling of the high
tent is a canopy of beautiful fine cloth—a symbol of honor. Dignitaries
attending the festivities are seated on either side of the honored seat;
high lamas are seated to the right, which is the most honored position,
and visiting secular dignitaries to the left. To the south, in front of the
raised dais on which the prince or high lama is seated, is a passageway

about eight or ten feet wide and thirty to forty feet long; felt and rugs line the area on each side. On these are placed tables for the use of officials and honored guests. The seats closest to the dais have higher rank. There are no chairs apart from the special ones mentioned; common seating is on rugs spread on the ground. On each table are placed many cookies, milk products, and delicacies, and at the opposite end of the passageway from the honored seat is a large container of *kumis* and an official in formal dress to attend it. Many attendants fetch *kumis* from the bowl and carry it to the honored dignitaries and visitors. To the Mongols, this splendor and brilliance is reminiscent of the parties held in the imperial court during the empire period.[17] Only men are gathered in this area; the women are relegated to lesser positions in surrounding tents and areas. The common people may wander around as spectators in the areas occupied by the dignitaries. This is a very formal occasion, and all persons remain seated and in attendance until the gathering is dismissed. A wrestling space or tournament area is located in front of the tents. Still farther out are the tents and carts of the people attending the festival.

The activities of the *oboo* festival are much like a tournament, and the martial arts performed from early times, such as horse racing, wrestling, archery, and skilled or "trick" horse riding, have always been important. Since early times the Mongols have greatly admired the *böke* ("wrestler"—the term is also used to refer to a powerful man). They particularly respect a skilled archer (*mergen*). Khabtu-Khaser, the younger brother of Chinggis Khan was famous as a skilled archer. There is no precise English equivalent for *khabtu,* which was his nickname, but it connotes the quality of being skillfully precise. Another younger brother was commonly known as "Belgütei the Wrestler."[18] On these occasions, the wrestling participants are divided into two teams or groups, right and left, and a round-robin tournament of elimination is held. Winners are progressively matched together and losers eliminated from the competition. There is no set ring in which the matches take place, but when one of the participants touches the ground with anything but his feet he loses the contest. On the top part of the body, the wrestlers customarily wear a vestlike, tightly fitting garment made of oxhide; the small metal buttons that are attached make it difficult for all but a very powerful hand to grasp. Leather boots are part of the costume. In some regions, such as the Üjümüchin Banner of Inner Mongolia, which is famous for its wrestlers, the wrestlers wear a pair of

A typical Inner Mongolian wrestler

quite loose-fitting pants, while in the Khalkha region of northern Mongolia, tight-fitting shorts or trunks are worn instead of pants. The wrestling participants enter the arena with arms extended in a birdlike strut. Their names are announced by officials representing each team, and each side is cheered on by traditional songs sung by its supporters. A large tournament may have as many as 128 or 256 participants (matches always being in equal numbers). In the larger competitions, the last two participants receive prizes.

Horse racing is ancient and is still a national sport. Jockeys are ordinarily boys fifteen years of age or younger. Girls do not compete. The boys wear short, colorfully designed riding coats and no boots. This is to avoid falls caused by having a boot caught in the stirrups or saddle. Actually, no saddle is used; there is merely a triangular piece of felt tied to the back of the horse. The course is from twenty-five to thirty-five kilometers in length. The race is usually initiated in the early morning, before the offerings to the *oboo* take place, so that it can be completed by the proper time. The *sang* ceremony takes place at the beginning of the horse race. A brass or bronze vessel is set up on stones as a pedestal, and on this cedar or another fragrant wood is burned in a fairly large fire. The young riders on horseback circle the fire three times, singing a special song as they depart for the race. A few older men accompany the boy jockeys, carrying long poles with a lasso-noose on the end to retrieve lost animals if any of the boys fall off during the race. As the participants approach the finish line, they stretch themselves over the side of the horse toward its head and twirl their whip, as a sign of their riding prowess and as a signal for the trained horse to exert its greatest effort in completing the race. At the finish line are stationed a number of older people, each with a board two or three feet long with a number attached, and as the riders come in, the number one board is given to the leader, the number two to the following person, and so forth.

A third general activity typical of *oboo* festivals, archery, is participated in only by adult males. Sometimes archers stand and shoot at a stationary target in the distance, or they may participate in mounted archery planned to show the prowess of the men in shooting at a target while riding on horseback as in hunting.

Tournament prizes are given in multiples of nine, a magic or lucky number to the Mongols, and often the first winner in a large tournament will receive eighty-one prizes while those below him will receive a lesser number of prizes in multiples of nine. The prizes, which may be horses, sheep, pieces of cloth, brick tea, or other presents, are not merely a reward for the tournament, but also traditionally a strong incentive for the people to develop better animals and skills through long-range planning. As the prizes are conferred, a skilled poet will recite a spontaneous, running poem regarding a particular contest which praises the skilled winners and their fine animals, but which makes fun of those who lose. This announcement also serves to recognize and make known the winners, since there is no newspaper to serve such a function. The horse racing is ordinarily completed before noon; the archery usually follows, and wrestling is the last event of the day, after which the *oboo* festival is completed and everyone disperses, leaving the *oboo* and the area as desolate as it was before the nomadic festival convened. These festivals are common, favorite occasions of the Mongols over the steppe in all regions of Mongolia in the summer months.

In the sixth month, or in some regions in the seventh month, a summer worship service is held by the temple. Because the weather is ordinarily good, attendance is larger than at other times of the year, especially at some of the largest monastic centers. The event involves very impressive and inspiring dances having to do with the Buddhist tradition. The festival commemorates an ancient victory over the Tibetan king, Lang-dharma, who attempted to suppress Buddhism and support the Bon religion, Tibetan Shamanism. An important part of the activities is the famous *cham* dance, well known to Westerners, though mistakenly so, as a "devil dance." This mistaken concept is derived from the Chinese who speak of the dance as the *t'iao kuei* ("jumping devil"). In the symbolism of the dance, Buddhist representatives of good marshal the forces of heaven in the form of good spirits to suppress the forces of evil. In ancient times, in a critical struggle, the "evil" king, Lang-dharma, was killed. In the dance, his death is portrayed symbolically, but he is killed by heavenly messengers rather than by man.

Immediately following this dance, or the following day, there is a ceremonial trek or circumambulation around the temple. The image of Maidari (Maitreya) Buddha is carried in a sedan chair by the participants or pulled in a large cart by the people. Many lamas always participate, chanting sutras, sprinkling sacred rice, and pronouncing prayers while swinging vessels of burning incense. The people kneel down in order that the image might pass over them—a symbol of a prayer or wish that they be participants in the final great battle of Buddhism, the ushering in of Shambala, the "Kingdom of Heaven."

This great event is to be led by Maidari, Buddha of the Future, who is to deliver Buddhism from its enemies and usher in a new era of great peace. The belief is that the world is moving toward a crisis in which the present Law Wheel, being turned by the Buddha Gautama, will end with great destruction to Buddhists but that Maidari will usher in a new age with the next turn of the Law Wheel.

 The ceremonial walk or circumambulation dates back to early Mongolian and Buddhist history and is, among other things, symbolic of a desire for peace. The ceremony has varied in Mongolia over the centuries. During the Yüan period, at the Mongol capital, Khanbalic, they paraded the image of Dughur, a deity of the Saskya-pa sect, which was instrumental in the first introduction of Buddhism into Mongolia. Subsequently, Dughur became the protective deity of the Mongols during the Yüan dynasty. The symbol of Dughur is a white umbrella, and it was often actually this object that was ceremoniously paraded. In this connection, the "Book of Worship" of the *Yüan History* notes:

On the fifteenth day of the second month . . . every kind of military and civilian procession shall proceed the White Umbrella and shall make the circumambulation within the Royal City and without as a ceremony to drive out bad luck and evil spirits and to invoke the blessings of well-being upon the country and the people. . . . [Government] shall send one hundred and twenty drummers and umbrella bearers to follow the white umbrella in the procession and five hundred soldiers shall carry the sedan upon which is mounted the white umbrella. . . . Five hundred other men shall assist them. The Ministry of Religious and Tibetan Affairs (*Hsüancheng yüan*) shall direct the three hundred and sixty temples under their jurisdiction to supply all the necessary images, sedan chairs, flags, banners, umbrellas, and carts with drums, which shall total three hundred and sixty groups. In each group there shall be six sedan bearers and twelve monks to beat the gongs and drums. The capital district government (*Taitu lu*) shall furnish one hundred and twenty groups of every type to participate in the parade. The Bureau of Music and Drama (*Chiao-fang-ssu yün-ho shu*) shall supply four hundred men with seven types of musical instruments . . . and the Office for Administration of Professional Prostitution (*Hsing-ho shu*) shall send one hundred and fifty singing girls to participate in the drama with their costumes. The Administrative Office for Drama (*Hsiang-ho shu*) shall send a group of men and women with various costumes to participate in the procession. Also the Administrative Office for Music (*I-feng-ssu*) shall send three music troops of each type of division. In all they should number three hundred and twenty-four persons. The government shall distribute to the participants of this entire program all necessary armor, gowns, umbrellas, instruments; everything must be carried out in a very proper and formal manner. All dresses will be very stylish with gold, jewels, and fine embroidery—all shall be very luxurious. The entire procession from beginning to end will be thirty *li* [ten miles] and all the inhabitants of the surrounding countryside will come out to behold the magnificent procession.[19]

This ceremony disappeared after the fall of the Yüan dynasty.

The eighth month of the year in Mongolia is commonly termed "month of the rich autumn" because the animals are in good condition and there is much milk and many milk products. At this time, there is a ceremony called the *dalalgha* or "beckoning richness." In ancient times, this function derived from Shamanism, but it also came to be dominated by the lamas. In the ceremony, an arrow, the older the better, is taken and from the feathered end many different-colored ribbon streamers and *khadagh* are hung. The father of the family or his son takes the arrow outside of the yurt, and, against a background of chanted sutras, he will wave the arrow in a wide clockwise circle, repeating the words *khurai-khurai* ("gather together! gather together!"). While this phrase is repeated and the smoke from the sacred fire (*sang*) rises, someone drives the cattle around the yurt in the same clockwise direction. This ceremony of thanksgiving expresses gratitude to the deities for the bounteous blessing of flocks and herds and beseeches the gods to continue these blessings both for the family and for all men. Relatives and friends are invited to come and participate in a party, particularly the drinking of *kumis*. The party continues with eating, drinking, singing, and merriment until all are filled and drunk. This is the focal point of festive activity for the autumn season.[20]

Between the fifth month and the ninth month, or a little later, is the prime time for the Mongols to drive their animals to market. This is also the time when long trips or caravan journeys are undertaken, while the weather is not too harsh or cold. The caravans are large undertakings and must be sponsored ordinarily by a temple, a banner, or a group of more wealthy families. Today a caravan journey is spoken of as *ayan;* however, in ancient times, this term referred not to caravan trade but to a campaign for plunder.[21] Whatever the type of caravan, one of the older, more experienced men will be chosen to act as the *ghal-iin-akha* ("caravan head"). He has absolute authority while he is acting as head of the expedition, and his commands are law. This seems to be a continuation of the ancient tradition of a commander's authority during a campaign—authority even of life and death of the participants.

From the ninth month to about the end of the tenth month, there are no special activities or festivals except for observance of the day on which Tsongkha-pa, a Tibetan reformer of Buddhism, gained enlightenment or release to enter nirvana as a Buddha. The main activity on this day is saying prayers in the Lamaist monasteries. Until the Communist takeover and the establishment of the Mongolian People's Republic in Outer Mongolia, this day in old Urga (now Ulan Bator) was almost as active and festive as New Year's Day.

The tenth and eleventh months are especially good for hunting in the steppe because the animals' fur is at its best and they can be easily tracked in the snow. Professional fur hunters do not continue to hunt for pelts after the winter equinox because the fine hair of the animal begins to change and drop out.

The twelfth month, especially the latter half, is a busy time at home because it is the end of the old year. During this period and until the middle of the first month, the *tamagha* or official seals of the princes were traditionally sealed up to signify a period of rest from official duties. Before the *tamagha* is sealed, a special worship of fire is held.[22] The following is typical of this ceremony among the Kharachin Mongols of eastern Mongolia. First, a large iron brazier is set up and spread with white paper. Upon this is placed a large fire rack containing small pieces of new wood stacked together and interwoven to create a hollow center. A picture of a sheep is drawn on the white paper and various types of cheese, other milk products, cookies, fruits, and various offerings are then placed in the center of the hollow area. As this is set on fire and burned, the head of the family or an older son kneels down in silent worship while someone beside him reads or chants the *ghal-un sudur* ("fire sutra"). The fire frame and the iron platform on which it is placed are symbolic of the continuity of the family, and the fire offerings symbolize the hope for warmth and prosperity. This ceremony also serves to purify the home since fire is sacred. The picture of the sheep is a remnant of the ancient sacrifice of sheep as burnt offerings. Some feel that this may be a carry-over from an earlier influence of the Zoroastrian religion. This ceremony is reminiscent of the Chinese *tsao* ("hearth"); however, it is entirely different. In some regions of

Mongolia, the ceremony may take place in the eighth month or some other time, rather than the twelfth month.

On New Year's Eve, it is customary in Mongolian families to hold a ceremony in which the ancestors of the family are worshiped. This also is a very joyful and active time; lots of good food is prepared, and often an entire sheep is boiled. Before partaking of the food and singing out the old year, the family dresses in their best clothes, worships the image of the Buddha, and pays respect to the old members of the family by thanking them for their goodness and benevolence during the past year. The parents and grandparents in turn bless the younger generation. In preparing to partake of the sheep that has been cooked, the head of the house draws the symbol of an "X" or cross on the head of the animal with his knife, after which the head, part of the tail, and a hoof of the animal are placed as a special offering before the image of Buddha. This is symbolic of offering a whole sheep from head to tail and hoof. Although world Buddhism generally forbids offerings of meat, this persistent, ancient Shamanistic tradition continues in Mongolia. After the meat has been divided and eaten, the family retires early in order to be in good spirits the following day. There is no tradition of seeing out the old year and seeing in the new year as among Chinese and Westerners, except in those Mongol settlements close to the Great Wall.

BEHAVIOR PATTERNS, ETIQUETTE, AND ATTITUDES

It is difficult to generalize about some aspects of life in Mongolia because they vary greatly over the vast area and from group to group. However, through the ages, certain general patterns of conduct have developed, in part as a result of the nomad's migratory life-style.

The average nomad, riding over the steppe, keeps a sharp lookout on the horizon; if another person is sighted, they will come together to exchange information. The most common greeting is *sayin bainu* ("Are you well?"), *amur sayin bainu* or *mendü bainu* ("Are you at peace?"). Among the Buriyad minority group in eastern Inner Mongolia, a greeting gesture is made by extending one's hands palms up and outward to the sides in a sweeping motion with a slight bow. Traditionally, this may have indicated that one was not armed.

After a greeting, travelers usually dismount, squat on one boot, and chat while smoking a *ghans*—a traditional Chinese pipe with a small bowl still used in some northern Chinese villages and often carried by Mongol men in their boot. Usually, one man lights his pipe with a flint after which the other person cups his pipe over it in a friendly manner to get a light. (Mongol tobacco, called *duns*—from the Chinese word *tung-sheng*, which is difficult to identify etymologically—was imported from Manchuria and northern China in the seventeenth century. However, the custom of smoking appears to have been adopted from the Manchu, who had taken it up first after their invasion of Korea in 1637.) Ordinarily, persons who meet on the steppe are quite relaxed and informal. However, in old Mongolia, a unique "protocol posture" called *sükürkü* was used among the elite. Unlike the Chinese formal or ritualistic kowtow or the Japanese deep kneeling bow, the old Mongol form consisted of a sort of half-kneeling curtsey on the right knee while clasping one's two hands together over the left knee. This bow is somewhat different from a common posture associated with a formal meeting of the old Manchu elite in which the right knee was touched to the ground and the right hand was placed nearby just above the ground.

Mongols are not inclined to shout at a distance in greeting an acquaintance, except to draw the attention of a person, nor are they inclined to make any particular sign or motion to indicate whether they are friend or foe until they are quite close to each other. Traditionally, Mongols are well known for their keen eyesight and are amazingly able to judge at a distance whether a group is armed and hostile. In pure Mongol areas, where a person is familiar with the environment, there is a notable lack of concern about whether approaching persons are friend or foe; there is also a lack of conscious effort to take precautions against robbers or thieves, since common thievery is extremely rare in the nomadic areas of the steppe.

When visiting a yurt, one usually stops short of the dwelling and calls out for the owner to tend his dogs, for these animals are always present, rather vicious, and often a threat. It is extremely bad conduct for a person to whip another family's dog or otherwise abuse the animal, even in trying to defend oneself. Mongols also take great care to avoid urinating or otherwise relieving themselves in the vicinity of the yurt. Ordinarily, one takes care of this function at some distance.

Good treatment of travelers seem to be a Mongol custom from ancient times, at least from the period of Chinggis Khan.[1] Still, a stranger who approaches a yurt on the steppe often gets the impression that a Mongol host is quite cool or reserved compared with people in other parts of the world. For example, as a stranger approaches, the head of the yurt does not make an effort to stand or to smile, but maintains his position, hears what the stranger's business may be, and then with hardly a motion or gesture of cordiality, but a mere motion of the head with chin extended outward or upward, says *"suu"* ("sit"). Cordiality or hospitality develops very soon as the conversation begins, and the host spontaneously offers tea, other refreshments, or food and would never ask a guest to pay for the hospitality.

The situation is much different, of course, in a meeting between friends. The host arises, comes out of the yurt, and spontaneous conversation begins immediately, often after an embrace even between male friends who are happy to see each other. In the case of a somewhat formal visit after a long period of separation, the visitor would commonly bring a present for the friend. If a traveler comes upon a monastery or a home where he is known but not on intimate terms, and if he is not prepared with some special present, he must at least offer a *khadagh,* a greeting scarf, which Mongols customarily have in ready supply. Coming empty-handed creates the bad impression that the visitor is poverty-stricken, making those being visited feel uneasy.

Conversely, when a good friend is leaving, it is impolite to send him away empty-handed, and a parting gift from the host to the visitor is common; on special occasions, the gift may even be a horse. It is traditional, when a person leaves on a journey, especially to a big city, for friends to come from some distance with a *khadagh* upon which they place several pieces of silver and remark that they are assisting with travel expenses. Implicit in the situation is the traveler's obligation to bring them something from the city or place he is going to visit. This rather formal, customary exchange of presents was especially important among aristocrats or people of higher status and explains the problem encountered by many foreign travelers in Mongolia during the early empire period: when they requested an audience, they would be asked by attendants of the khan whether they had brought presents. Westerners were frequently distressed because they had not made arrangements for such occasions.[2]

Among Mongols of high social status, a visitor does not remove his hat as he approaches the host; the host will quickly put his hat on and both wear their hats during the initial exchange of greetings and remove them only after the conversation has relaxed and become more cordial. In traditional greetings, a ceremonial exchange of snuffboxes, with each person sampling the other's snuff, was another important part of the formalities.

Except for messengers who leave immediately, all visitors to a yurt or a Mongol home are invariably treated with tea or other refreshments. Not to offer tea is very impolite, and a common expression is *chai chi-ügei, charai chi ügei* ("no tea, no face/pride"). A guest, upon completing his refreshment, or food in the case of a meal, must very politely and properly place his eating utensils together and remark to the host, "*kürtelee*" ("I have received graciously"), meaning a thanksgiving to the host and to heaven for the hospitality. In partaking of refreshments or food, care is taken not to discard anything. The food in one's bowl or plate should be consumed entirely; to leave some uneaten would be an offense both to the host and to heaven.

At the beginning of formal banquets, those attending customarily wear hats, sit on one booted leg on cushions, and sing in a formal manner after a toast by the host. The singing, ordinarily in chorus, is followed by another toast. Then, as the singing, toasting, and conversation continue, the gathering becomes much less formal. On such occasions, it is usual to become drunk, but there is no stigma upon such behavior. When the festivities reach a point where they should end, it has been customary to remark, "*nair öndörlöö*" ("our friendship has been raised"), implying that there has been enough drinking and it is time to cease and to depart.

In many situations, Mongols prize formality, contrary to an expectation of a higher degree of informality among nomadic peoples; Mongols despise impoliteness or rudeness, but are lenient toward the behavior of one who is drunk. They are less inclined to frequently or spontaneously extend formal invitations to friends or acquaintances to come for a festival, or a visit; however, on such occasions as a funeral, or a marriage celebration, formal invitations are extended with a *khadagh*. A response to an invitation is obligatory, and someone from the family concerned must fulfill the invitation, pay respects, and extend condolences or whatever the situation demands. In more formal situations, hand positions are also very important among the Mongols. It would be impolite or insulting, for example, for one to stand before a group and make a report while holding one's hands behind the body or folding the arms. The conventional position is to clasp the hands together and hold them about waist high while talking.

Mongols are not as relaxed, informal, or free in their manner of wearing clothing as some peoples; they are quite precise in drawing their clothes about them in a proper fashion. Ordinarily, even the top button of the gown will be buttoned, although common herders may at times open the top of their gown for greater comfort. A coat is seldom draped on one's shoulders informally except, perhaps, very early in the morning or when a person is ill or old. Usually a person puts his arms in the sleeves and wears the coat in a proper manner. In the morning, a nomad may stroll about the yurt without boots on, but will quickly put them on if a visitor approaches, except, of course, for small children.

Etiquette is also carefully observed in seating arrangements and conversation; care is taken not to turn one's back on another while talking. Except among close friends, a Mongol will not usually sit in an informal manner, crossing legs or taking some other casual posture.

After meeting and greeting a friend, one commonly inquires regarding the friend's spouse and family. The stereotyped phrase is *tanai ger böl sayin bainu* ("Is your family well?"). Among officials, one extends greetings, asks about the other's banner, and then inquires regarding the animals and the situation of the grazing fields in the region. Mongols are very concerned about news and rumors (a fact commonly observed by strangers in Mongol society) and, after greeting, the first priority is to learn of the latest happenings and rumors. In conversation, particularly with older people, or in joking, Mongols take great care to avoid remarks or words that carry a bad omen or connotation. In meeting friends on the first day of a new year, everyone takes great care to avoid mentioning sickness, death, poverty, disturbances, or other matters of disaster or distress. Although lay people resist mentioning things of bad omen, the lamas feel that it is good to mention death at least three times a day in order to keep before one's mind the impermanency of life. This Buddhist sentiment does not have deep traditional roots in the Shamanistic past. At times, young Mongols feel impatient or distressed on special occasions when older people go to such great pains and make lengthy remarks, wishing them well, extending blessings, and so forth.

Personal interactions in Mongol society are rather formal, though in quite a different sense than in Chinese or Japanese society. Persons are generally very sensitive in relationships, while at the same time they are spontaneous—in a somewhat restrained way. For example, Mongols consider common Chinese conversation quite strange because the Chinese often talk loudly—almost shouting at each other in a manner that seems like arguing. (More traditional Chinese elite, of course, do not do this.) Foreigners also have noted this contrast. Mongols are not inclined to reveal strong feelings or allow spontaneous laughter or anger; men are much more inclined to be reserved than women, less given to an overt show of anger or strong emotion. Thus, common conversation is rather subdued, quiet, and orderly.

In manners and decorum, the Mongols are not as punctilious and ritualistic as the Japanese and Chinese; their manners and propriety seem to Western observers to be more natural and spontaneous. Nevertheless, Mongols do have particular mannerisms in walking, eating, talking, and so forth. In being seated, for example, a proper Mongol will not show the bottom of his foot toward an older person or one of higher status. They also have a particular way of clasping their hands during more formal conversation and of avoiding a loud voice even in common conversation.

In reciprocal relationships between socially superior and inferior persons and between older and younger persons, the former are expected to show consideration, benevolence, and care while the latter are to show respect and obedience. In Mongol homes, there is no stiff, rather formal relationship between different ages or people of different degrees of status, as there is in Chinese society; behavior is relaxed and informal. The home atmosphere encourages children to be more free in relation to their parents and grandparents than most other Asian societies.

Men of status take special care not to reveal their emotions. Outsiders dealing with Mongol leaders feel somewhat distressed that the response to important questions comes quite slowly. Restraint, it is believed, avoids rash deeds.[3] Khubilai Khan's injunction to his attendants was that if he ordered a man killed, the sentence should not be carried out immediately, but should be postponed for a day to allow for reconsideration. Khubilai explained that rash decisions made in the anger of a moment should be guarded against.[4] A standard Mongolian response to many questions (other than to close friends) is "I don't know" because an affirmative answer may lead to undesirable, detailed explanations and complications. Mongols tend to conceal an understanding or knowledge of particular matters to avoid embarrassment. To divulge secrets is a serious breach of propriety and shows a lack of morality. "Consultation is necessary for decisions, but from consultation comes the leaking of secrets" is a common expression. There is a keen awareness of the importance of keeping confidential information from anyone other than those in the inner circle.

The pattern of restraint is seen in tournaments where contestants are pitted against each other in exciting situations. Mongols are not inclined to cheer loudly and to fight with one another as fans for a particular contestant, like Latins, for example, among whom rioting is not uncommon. They are much more inclined to enjoy the match in a more orderly manner. The enjoyment then is somewhat subdued, and leaders are particularly restrained in their reaction to the contest.

Mongols are generally very sympathetic to persons in distress, and a person with a problem who might be ignored in the urban areas of Asia is likely to be assisted by Mongols. In purely pastoral areas, there are no beggars; but some existed in the old prerevolutionary city of Urga and in the mixed Mongol-Chinese areas of the border where, incidentally, beggars find a much more charitable reception in Mongol than in Chinese households. The *badarchin* (itinerant pilgrims making their way to a particular destination—Tibet, a temple, or a shrine) depend on people along the way for their sustenance. However, their begging activity is only temporary.

Friendships among Mongols are somewhat similar to those among other East Asians in that they tend to have few friends, but strong bonds, and they are restrained in establishing ties. Once a friendship has been established, it is very strong and enduring. There are several terms used for friendship. *Tanil* is used for an acquaintance—people who mutually recognize each other. *Naiji* implies a stronger relationship involving intimate friends. The two words most commonly used for a close relationship are *nökör* and *akha düü*. They were first used in the Mongol Empire period and meant companions-in-arms or men who had developed a strong relationship through close association in warfare or some other dangerous activity. In more modern times, *nökör* has come to mean partners in wedding (thus, a husband and wife may refer to each other as *nökör*) and also, in Communist areas, a party "comrade." *Akha düü*("brothers"—as Chinese *ti-hsiung* or Japanese *kyodai*) means, literally, elder and younger brother, signifying a very close relationship, an extension of a quasi-kinship relationship. All of these terms confirm the value placed on friendship and the comparative closeness of the relationship. In addition, a very special relationship *anda*—found as early as the *Secret History*[5]—is close to the common "blood-brotherhood" relationship known in some societies. It was revived by many young Inner Mongols in the late 1940s to characterize the fraternal relationship they felt in their struggle for self-determination.

Social mobility, or the lack of the same, is important in all societies, and while it is not possible to discuss this in any great detail here, it may be noted that the records tend to confirm a rather high degree of social mobility in Mongolia during the empire period. But mobility became greatly restricted during the several centuries of Manchu domination, after about 1650, when society became much more stable and restricted geographically to certain banner areas, according to a quasi-feudal system that consolidated the position of the traditional hereditary nobility. Since the turn of this century, there has been a much higher degree of social mobility, particularly with the rise of nationalism and the development of movements for self-determination. There are many cases of capable young nationalists or even former "bandits" who reached high positions on the basis of their personal merit and capability.[6] Throughout Mongol history, doers have had greater prestige and status than thinkers or those who could only speak eloquently. This is natural in a society where there must be great concern for survival in a harsh environment.

The nomadic Mongol's relaxed attitude toward work or life in general is somewhat unique in contrast to the Chinese or Japanese. The Mongol view is that other peoples are slaves to work; they lack free agency and are continually anxious about some particular undertaking or enterprise. To the Chinese, for example, the term *kuo-jih-tze,* "passing the day," means laboring industriously every day to maintain one's security. Mongols tend to reject the approach to life in which the work governs the person rather than the reverse. A nomad prefers to see himself as controlling his own life and destiny and commonly refers to his approach to labor as *aju-törökü,* meaning "being involved in productive labor." In short, the Mongols see themselves as freely and deliberately involved in work and the Chinese as rather unthinkingly, automatically working from dawn till dark with no real consciousness of the process.

In Mongolian society, there is a precedence of age over youth and of male over females. Ordinarily, men dominate in making decisions for the family, but they are greatly influenced by their wives. Relationships and decisions are not as democratic as in Western society, but, on the other hand, males are not as dominant in social arrangements as in Chinese or Japanese society. Mongols are quite free in relating to each other in such actions as entering or leaving yurts or in riding over the plains. On occasion there is no clear-cut status based on sex; age is more often a ruling factor in determining who has priority. In gatherings, younger persons reserve their remarks until those of greater age or status have opened the discussion. Deference is given particularly to grandfathers. Traditionally, the youngest son was favored in the inheritance of property on the death of the parents,[7] but in recent centuries, partly because of Manchu influence, the eldest son began to gain precedence in the inheritance of property.[8] However, unlike Chinese society—which stresses the *san ts'ung,* "three levels of obedience": obedience of a female to her father, to her husband, and to her son upon the death of his father—the Mongol society makes sons obedient to their mothers who make decisions for the family on the death of the fathers. In Mongolia, during the empire, the widows of khans became very powerful in the state structure on the death of their husbands, as in the cases of the mothers of the most famous Mongol rulers, Chinggis Khan, Güyüg Khan, Möngke Khan, and Khubilai Khan.[9]

In Mongol society, respect is given priority over popularity and learning is given more status than wealth in ideal typology, but there is a closer relationship between prestige and popularity than in Western society where many people gain great popularity, but lack real prestige or influence.

A social-linguistic view of Mongolian society sheds light on certain attitudes and customs. Children never address older persons or strangers by their name, but use a kinship term or a title. Thus, a common, formal term of address, even to older strangers, is *abughai,* originally a kinship term meaning "uncle." A more common and less formal form of this word is *ghu'ai.* In eastern Inner Mongolia, a common form of address corresponding to the Western term *Mister* is *baghshi* (literally, "teacher"). However, this term is not common in northern and western Inner Mongolia. In some western areas, Üjümüchin for example, a common term of address, particularly to a stranger is *akhuu (akha),* meaning "elder brother." Throughout Mongolia, a common formal term of address indicating some degree of status or honor is *erkim* ("honorable one").

Special terms are used for the Lamaist clergy. The most usual term of address to common lamas is *mam,* a shortened derivative of *lama.* For lamas of senior rank, the most common term is *lamkhai* (from *lama* and the suffix *-khai,* to show veneration).

In normal conversation, Mongols ordinarily call close associates by their given name—traditionally, there has not been a surname system in Mongolia, and most people have only a given name, which does not change from childhood to adulthood. Some people have several names—a given name and a religious name received from the lamas— but they ordinarily use one or the other, plus, possibly, a nickname.

Mongol names seem long to foreigners. A unique feature of the Mongolian system of address or referral by name is the custom of taking only the first syllable of the name as an abbreviated form and adding to it a title. Prince Demchügdüngrüb, a famous popular leader in Inner Mongolia, was generally referred to as De Noyan (Wang). Those close to him referred to him only as *noyan,* meaning "prince," because of a traditional avoidance custom that disallows the common usage of the given name of a respected person. In situations involving more than one prince and requiring some clarification, the first syllable of the name (De, for example) will be used, to which will be added *noyan* to denote which prince is referred to. A man whose name is Temürbator would not ordinarily be referred to by his full name, but rather by the abbreviated form Te plus *abughai* ("*Mister*") or Te plus *baghshi* ("teacher"). This illustrates the tendency to call people of distinction by a title instead of by their given name when it is clear to which person reference is made. In a banner region, people usually refer to the *tusalaghchi* (deputy administrator of the banner unit), or may refer to the right/west, the left/east, or the retired *tusalaghchi* if differentiation is necessary.

In smaller groups, with a more intimate relationship, it is common to refer to a person by a name that has no particular meaning, but which has been acquired and used over the years. Examples are *agha, ama, baba,* or *abughai.* These are the sort of nicknames used in American society; for example, everyone may refer to a particularly venerable old man as "gramps." Another form of address may be derived from a certain unique physical feature: *dogholang* ("the lame one"), *sokhor* ("the blind one"), or *khaljin* ("the bold one").

During the empire period, even prominent people were addressed by both name and title. But after the period of Khubilai Khan, the name was dropped and it became more common to address a person only by title.[10] Khubilai himself, for example, came to be most commonly known after his death as Sechen Khan ("the wise khan"). This pattern has been perpetuated to modern times. More recently, since the revolution in 1921, it has become common, beginning in Khalkha areas and spreading to Inner Mongolia, to refer to a person by his given name plus *nökör,* meaning "comrade."

Since Mongolian society is generally more formal, there is a marked paternalistic or patronizing attitude toward social inferiors. There are many different terms, both nouns and verbs, marking the person being referred to as being more honorable or more humble than the speaker. These are used to indicate differences of both social status or rank between persons and between the cultured and the common people. The more traditional nomads in northern Mongolia frequently spoke in rhyme, but this practice has declined as a result of modernization and external influence.

All groups have images of neighboring alien peoples and regional, stereotyped images of their own people. Since tribalism and regionalism have been such deep and continuing influences on Mongolian life, it is no surprise that various banners of subregions have been characterized in this way. Some stereotypes have their origins in the empire period, with the rise of the Mongols under Chinggis Khan, or even before. Others developed out of historical circumstances in more recent times. On occasion, Chinggis Khan ordered mixed groups of people to separate themselves according to lineage, clan, or region, in order to expose interlopers or infiltrators.[11] Throughout history, Mongols have been notably cosmopolitan in their views, but at the same time there was a concern about outsiders who might become a threat.

While Mongols have certain national characteristics as a people, which tend to be found more or less uniformly throughout the broad expanse of Mongolia, there are, at the same time, regional peculiarities. Nevertheless, Mongols, in their compulsion to show unity to the world, tend to minimize regional stereotypes or avoid drawing attention to them, considering them to be shameful: "showing one's bottom to outsiders." Mongol nationalists generally concede that negative regional stereotypes were one of the most important factors in perpetuating a fragmentation of Mongolia, thus retarding the unification of the Mongols and greatly complicating the task of defending themselves against incursions in modern times. The fragmentation began with the early Manchu policy of *divide et empira,* according to which an original three or four tribelike units were broken into eighty-six.

In the past, northern Mongols tended to simplistically view all southerners as Chakhar Mongols, and all western Inner Mongols collectively referred to all eastern Inner Mongols as Kharachin. Furthermore, many northern Khalkha Mongols generally stereotype people to the south in Inner Mongolia as *yamaan Chakhar*, "goatlike Chakhar"—unsettled, turbulent, and unstable. Conversely, the Inner Mongolian image of the brothers to the north has been that of *üker Khalkha*, "cattlelike Khalkha"—stubborn, slow to respond.

The Kharachin have been one of the most influential and thus quite controversial Mongol subgroups, so it is not surprising that they are the object of much criticism and the subject of many stereotypes. A negative Kharachin stereotype arises from their close contact with the Chinese. They had the longest association with and have been the most influenced culturally by the Chinese; therefore, they are often considered too "Chinesey." An extension of this stereotype is that they are shrewd, wily, and untrustworthy. This aspect of their image arises in part from an event during the period of Lighdan Khan (1604-34) in which the Kharachin surrendered to the Manchu and allied with them against their own Chakhar Mongol people. The Kharachin came in contact with the outside world very early, and their men were among the first educated in Peking and Japan. They also were among the first to become sedentary and to learn modern ways; consequently, they frequently have been found in places of leadership, have tended to dominate certain movements in modern Mongolia, and, in a sense, seem to be everywhere present. A common joke tells of a man who, despairing of life dominated always by Kharachin, decided to commit suicide and threw himself into a well. In the depths of the well, he found another Mongol, inquired as to the man's native place, and was once more distressed to find that he also was a Kharachin: in life or death, all is dominated by Kharachin bannermen.

The Kharachin Mongols, proud of their accomplishments and perhaps a little on the defensive, are jokingly boastful of their image or reputation. They speak of the "three *ba's*": *Shagja*-tuba ("the Buddha"), Tsongkha-*ba* ("great reformer of Buddhism"), and finally themselves, the "illustrious Kharachin-*ba*." The Tibetan grammatical element *pa*, read in Mongolian as *ba*, means a person. Thus, "Kharachin-*ba*" means a person from that place, and since this coincidentally matches the endings of the first two terms above, there is a play on words intended to mean that the Kharachin are so great as to rank with the Buddha and Tsongkha-pa.

The Dakhur Mongols of northeast Inner Mongolia are distressed by a persistent image of them as "unpure" Mongols,[12] which arises from the fact that they have been influenced by Manchu-Tungusic culture. This feeling was strengthened by the fact that few Dakhur Mongols converted to Buddhism. It has been traditional to regard "Mongolness" and Buddhism as inseparable, which creates a sort of self-imposed stereotype.

More narrow stereotypes are found within regional subgroupings. In the Shilin-ghol League, for example, Mongols of the Sünid Banner area are referred to as the "*köke* Sünid," or the "blue" Sünid, which really means that they are rather "dozy" and unperceptive. Chakhar Mongols tend to look condescendingly on the Tümed, who, like the Kharachin, are quite Sinicized and, therefore, are considered to be tainted. Mongols, as a whole, prize "purity" of nationality and have misgivings toward persons or groups who are too influenced by alien ways. Thus, Mongols all over the world now tend to look to the Mongolian People's Republic and to idealize it as a symbol, a focal point that comes closest to the Mongolian ideal. This tendency is now particularly marked in Inner Mongolia, which has been inundated by forced Chinese migration and settlement, and where there is serious threat to the purity of the Mongol people.

The Mongol antipathy toward the Chinese and toward Mongols who they feel are unduly influenced by Chinese ways is seen in the common epithet, tantamount to a swear word, *khara Kitad,*[13] "black Chinese." The use of this word caused a riot in a Mongolian prison camp in 1946, resulting in the death of several people. Khubilai Khan patronized Chinese Confucian teachers in an attempt to influence the thought of his family and the court, but his efforts had little effect. Togh-temür Khan (Wen-tsung), the most Sinicized of the Mongol rulers in China, was more influenced by Chinese values than other Mongol emperors, and earlier Jurchen emperors, but the Mongols, as a whole, never assimilated Chinese values. Crown prince Ayurshiridara, an important figure in the vast Mongol Empire of China, invited a number of Tibetans, Uighurs, and other Buddhist monks to discuss the various tenets of Buddhism for an entire night. He remarked that he had been taught the philosophies of China for many years and still did not understand them, but that in only one night he felt he had gained an understanding of Lamaist Buddhism.[14] This anecdote gives some indication of the cultural distance between the Mongols, even those in China, and their attitude toward Chinese thought.

A traditional, ideal image that the Mongols admire and try to project is one of reserved wisdom rather than open, flashy brilliance. A corollary follows: one should not attempt to persuade others to one's views because wisdom makes itself known and does not have to be openly propagandized. From this arises another prejudice against the southeastern Mongols who, it is felt, try too openly to persuade others to their point of view. The stereotype is that northern Mongols are doers while the southeastern Mongols are talkers.

Ordos Mongols of the Yeke-juu League are considered quarrelsome, always stirring up trouble. This view is possibly related to the fact that the famous "secret-society" type, *dughuilang*—rebellious or revolutionary groups—arose among the Ordos Mongols. Neighboring Mongols were distressed with the factional activities and felt that problems should be hidden from outsiders and resolved within the group. The common saying is that one should "cover one's arm in one's own sleeve if it is broken."

Regional stereotypes have become increasingly subordinate to a Mongolian national consciousness. In 1939, in the battle of Nomunkhan (Khalkha-yin ghol), the Japanese used the Mongols under their domination to attack an area of the Mongolian People's Republic that was allied with the Soviet Union. The attack failed when the Inner Mongols under the Japanese refused to fight their brothers. An overriding feeling of fraternity or national consciousness was also very evident at the end of World War II when the Inner Mongols felt a spontaneous compulsion to join with the people of the MPR in a new attempt at national unity.

SOCIAL THOUGHT AND VALUES

Closely related to attitudes and behavior patterns and to certain aspects of religion is the area of social thought. An attempt will be made here to touch on Mongolian thought as distinct from formal philosophy. Traditional Mongolian society is more sacred than secular on the "sacred-secular continuum" of social typology, since religion has permeated virtually every phase of society until quite recently. This orientation naturally appears in any broad analysis of social thought.

In common with many East Asian peoples, the nomads view heaven with a special regard or veneration, which is regarded by some as merely a persistence of early primitive religion or superstition while others interpret it, in a more philosophical vein, as having some characteristics of more profound philosophical thought, as seen in Chinese society. The thought persisted in Mongol society through many centuries that the khan received inspiration or revelation from heaven in directing his people, and that the destiny of the Mongols was in the hands of heaven. In everyday life, birth and marriage were blessed of heaven and in death the spirit of the deceased mounted to heaven on horseback. Thus, in all phases of Mongolian life and at all levels of society, there was a feeling that heaven should be honored and held in awe or fear and that everyone should take special care not to offend heaven in their social behavior. The concern for the "will of heaven" has functioned in the individual as a sort of conscience and seems rather inseparable from a moral concern or social consciousness. The individual character or conduct of a person in Mongolian society traditionally has been judged on this basis, and thus one must take great care in judging the traditional social thought of the Mongols on the basis of contemporary Western thought. One important implication of the extreme concern for the "will of heaven" is that it served as a useful check on what could have otherwise been a very despotic rule on the part of the khans. This, as well as other general circumstances, restrained abusive actions of the khans and secured the general welfare of the people. Chinggis Khan repeatedly showed careful regard for the "will of heaven" in his decisions and actions.[1] When Buddhism became widespread in Mongolian society, important changes took place in social thought, but the regard for heaven was not displaced: the Buddha became a focal point for veneration placed above or within heaven.

Primary group or interpersonal relationships have been very important in Mongolian society from early times and have had a concomitant influence on social thought, particularly since quasi-feudalistic, vassal-like relationships developed with the rise of the empire and particularly during the period of Manchu dominance after the 1640s. Great emphasis was placed on loyalty and faithfulness to one's lord. Vassal-like relationships that greatly conditioned actions and attitudes were promoted by Chinggis Khan and, in contrast to feudalistic thought or practice in the West, were much less egalitarian. Relationships were rather unilateral, demanding certain duties and performances from the subordinate vassal but making few demands upon the lord.

The Mongol ethic of loyalty must certainly have been reflected in the *jasagh* (*yasa*)—which cannot be studied—and can clearly be seen in the *Secret History*.[2] Loyalty became an iron rule in Mongolian society as Chinggis Khan set an important precedent of paternalistic concern for his subordinates and followers. The success of his concern can be seen in the fact that there was no notable rebellion or case of disobedience among his close followers and consequently no instances of execution, purge, or extreme punishment. This ethic of loyalty helps to explain why the descendants of Chinggis and their rule were maintained for over seven centuries. The stress on the principle of loyalty is further illustrated by the element *batu*, meaning "faithfulness," commonly found in many Mongol names.

After the Mongol alliance with the Manchu in the seventeenth century, which became in effect a subordination and exploitation of the Mongols in the conquest of China, the traditional Mongol loyalty was transferred to the Manchu emperor. One of the most outstanding examples of their loyalty, which continued to the end of the Ch'ing period, is that of Prince Senggerinchin (d. 1865),[3] the Mongol general who gained great honor for his valor in the Tai-p'ing Rebellion (1850-64) and also against the British and French forces in the Second Opium War (1856-60), and who lost his life later in action against the Nien-fei Rebellion (1855-68). For his loyalty, Senggerinchin was one of only two Mongols,[4] and one of the very few non-Manchu persons, enshrined in the Ancestral Temple of the Manchu emperors in Peking. Until recently, there were also many local temples, known as Seng-wang-miao (Prince Seng Temples), in Shantung province where he campaigned.

When nationalism developed and the nation rather than the lord became the focal point of loyalty, men such as Senggerinchin and Tsereng[5]—a prince of Khalkha who supported the Manchu in their war with the Jungar Mongols—were no longer revered as national heros, but were looked upon as traitors to the Mongols. Even with the growth of nationalism, loyalty still has remained a prime virtue and unloyal people are despised.

Filial piety (*achilaltu*) is another virtue or element of Mongolian thought that stretches back to earliest times and no doubt stems from early ancestral veneration. The behavior of Chinggis Khan, whose respect and obedience to his mother has been idealized, is an example of filial piety. Devotion to parents should not be attributed to Chinese influence, for the concept existed in the period before the Mongols had close contact with the Chinese. However, after the conquest of China, such thoughts or values were greatly strengthened and classics such as the *Hsiao ching* (classic of filial piety; Mong. *Achilaltu nom*) were immediately translated. Although many other Chinese classics that were translated into the Mongolian language during this early period have virtually all been lost, the *Hsiao ching* has been preserved, which is evidence of its place in Mongolian thought.[6]

An examination of the Mongolian language from the view of social linguistics reveals many terms commonly used among the Mongols that depict particular attitudes and values. One common term is *köörkii* (or *köörkön*), which has the connotations of "pity," "sympathy," "compassion," and also "loveliness." It expresses a spontaneous feeling of empathy toward others in social interaction, which seems to have predated the introduction of Buddhism and been strengthened when the Mongols became widely converted to Buddhism.

When Buddhism was introduced to Mongolia, such common Buddhist concepts and feelings as compassion, reincarnation, and causality (Mong. *irügel;* Chs. *yin-kuo*) greatly reinforced the traditional Mongol sentiment of *köörkii* ("sympathy"). It has long been customary for Mongols to show an extreme concern for lower forms of animal life that is rare in the Western world. Some have noted a certain Theravada Buddhist element in Mongol thought in viewing such "tragic situations" as a starving wolf eating a sheep. There is a feeling of *köörkii* or pity for the sheep being eaten, but also a feeling of *köörkii* for the wolf, which will perish if it does not eat. The sympathy for the wolf is prompted by the belief that its fate will be worse and its condemnation greater because of its actions. Thus, in theory (though not in practice), one should not harm the wolf, but rather one should pray for both wolf and sheep. On one occasion in the 1930s, the Panchan Lama urged the Mongols to refrain from killing wolves, so that their behavior would better conform to the tenet of Buddhism against taking life.[7]

Such sentiments, which became particularly strong as Buddhism gained great influence, was the greatest single factor in diminishing the martial spirit and aggressiveness ethic of the Mongols. But the martial spirit of the Mongols has not entirely disappeared. Many people continue to name their children Ba'atur (Bator), meaning "hero," "heroic," or "brave."[8] Although Mongols may be devout Buddhists, in crisis situations they fight as vigorously as their ancestors. Mongolian martial sentiments or tendencies reemerged in the late Ch'ing and early

Chinese Republican period on the China-Mongol border in the person of *Meng-fei* or "Mongol bandits," who were actually Robin Hood–type groups attempting to protect the Mongol people from roving Chinese bands and from groups backed by Chinese warlords who forced the Mongols from their lands.

Mongols definitely discourage private fighting or individual attacks by one person against another. Hostile feelings or aggressive behavior are to be directed against outsiders, not against one's in-group. During the thirteenth century, Western travelers in Mongolia made particular note of this trait. In recent decades, reports of murder and theft have been extremely rare.[9]

Foreigners commonly criticize Mongols for lying and stupidity. However, these generalizations often have been based on actions observed during campaigns, in extraordinary situations when it was important to mislead the enemy and when nomadic warriors could not be expected to behave as sedentary farmers or townsmen. Actually, there is considerable testimony that Mongols do place great value upon faithfulness to one's word.[10] There are many examples of this ethic in early Mongol records. When Chinggis Khan was suddenly attacked and defeated by the Kereyid, with whom he had a verbal pact, he dispatched a messenger to the khan of the Kereyid to rebuke him for not being true to his word.[11]

Most formal agreements of importance in Mongolia are stamped by a *tamagha* or seal. The practice began at the time of Chinggis Khan's capture of Tatatunggha,[12] a vassal of Chinggis's enemy the khan of the Naiman in 1204, and continued to modern times. However, because of the high rate of illiteracy among the nomadic peoples, there are many agreements, negotiations, and binding contracts made without any written form, but sealed by a handshake of the individuals involved. These agreements are strictly kept. Mongols are generally known for their faithfulness in keeping their word, much like the virtue of honor among men of the early American West. Customarily, a nomad's word is his bond, and verbal or written contracts are moral agreements. The presence of a witness is not a factor.

A common Mongol saying, *jaa gebel yoo geküei,* means "if you said yes, you cannot now say it hurts."[13] The idea is that if one has given one's word to a certain course of action, then one cannot retract it and should not bemoan the problem regardless of the consequence. Torture was common in the nomadic world as elsewhere, but the common view among the Mongols was that torture seldom brought forth confessions. Mongols admire a man who can take all manner of abuse and punishment and not disclose a secret.

In the stress and pressures of nomadic society, the honor of individuals often made the difference between life and death; thus, being dependable had great merit and high priority in the ranking of nomadic, that is, traditional, Mongol values. To call a person a liar or to otherwise indicate that they were unreliable placed a much greater stigma on them and was a much more serious charge among the Mongols than among most other Asian peoples.

A common aphorism, "do not lead a Mongol along a particular path for he will always follow the same route," refers to the straightforwardness and single-mindedness of the Mongols. For example, although it is quite difficult for Mongols to trust an outsider, once they do, the relationship will not be ambivalent. These traits are illustrated by Mongol behavior patterns after their conversion to Buddhism—they became extremely devout and followed the new faith without wavering. While single-mindedness is a virtue in some respects, it also allowed the Mongols to be exploited by shrewd foreign merchants who, in the course of time, brought them under a heavy bondage of debt.

It has often been observed that Mongols tend to take a definite position and to move toward a definite decision rather than maintaining neutrality or carefully attempting to balance two sides of a problem. It also has been said that once the traditional conditionings of a particular type of behavior, such as Buddhism, were broken, the average Mongol would behave as a horse that has lost its tether or hobbles and gallops freely and unrestrained, making it impossible to rein in or check it to return to old habits. A leader who changed a predetermined course of action in midstream is rare in Mongolian history. The tendency has been to pursue a chosen policy to the end.

Although the martial spirit has dominated the literary spirit, Mongols honor teachers. Particularly after Buddhism came into Mongolia, the respectful relationship, common in many Asian countries, of the student to the guru or teacher (the respect of the disciple for the master) has been very strong, and it is very uncommon in Mongolian society to find a person speaking badly of his teacher. Even if a student feels that his teacher has made a mistake, he will not criticize him openly.

In general, the traditional Mongol ethic is closer to that of other

Asians than to the West. There has been some influence from the Chinese, and the Chinese ethic often has tended to confirm and strengthen similar, native Mongolian tendencies. However, the greatest influence on Mongolian thought has not been Chinese Confucianism, but Mahayana Buddhism.

TABOOS AND CUSTOMS

Taboos and avoidance customs, found in all societies, evolve with the culture. Many old Mongolian taboos persist and still influence the attitudes and behavior of the people in modern society. Some are closely related to primitive religious patterns or superstitious notions of the common people; some are related to particular aspects of the traditional nomadic social system or institutions; others are related to the natural environment of the steppe and the unique life-style associated with it.

In the Mongolian language, the term that comes closest to the anthropological idea of taboo is *chigerlel*. However, the word actually has a broader usage and meaning than the strictly anthropological term taboo and applies much more generally to things that are to be avoided or restricted and to matters of propriety and protocol. In many instances, *chigerlel,* used in the sense of taboo, conveys a mystic impression of certain actions or things that should be avoided, but for which no rational explanation is given. Taboos of that nature have become established simply through long usage or custom. However, in other instances, there is a rational, practical reason for something that is *chigerleltei*. For example, a food that upsets someone who eats it is referred to as *chigerleltei*. If an official decides that he is not going to keep appointments with people who come to see him and therefore is "unavailable," his staff may say that he has *chigerlel.* In addition to mystic or practical taboos, behavior patterns and attitudes that Mongols consider impolite or improper are *chigerleltei*.

Some taboos are mentioned in the earliest Mongolian records. Another important source of information is the travelogues of men who journeyed through Mongol territory in the medieval period and whose observations are still useful. Were it not for such foreigners as John of Plano Carpini, William of Rubruck, and Marco Polo, much important data would have been lost. Some feel that foreign observers of Mongolian society were more perceptive than those within the society. There is some truth in this, but because they were generally unfamiliar with Mongolian society and culture, their observations were at times biased or distorted and must be considered with caution.

Important, albeit little known, observations of Mongolian society were made by Chao (Meng) Hung,[1] P'eng Ta-ya, and Hsü T'ing,[2] Chinese of the Southern Sung period (1127-1276). Another important observer, Hsiao Ta-heng of the Ming period (1368-1644), was a high-ranking Chinese general on the Mongol frontier for many years. Without his and other records, it would be impossible in many instances to find material on premodern Mongol taboos. A comparison of the observations of Hsiao Ta-heng with those of travelers in preceding centuries shows remarkable continuity in taboo patterns. One general trend is the weakening of some Shamanistic taboos and the strengthening of new Buddhist taboos. Important insights come from a deductive analysis of the *Yeke jasagh* ("Great Yasa"), the law code formulated by Chinggis Khan. Reference to certain taboos in this historical document is evidence of their importance in early Mongol society.

The famous study of d'Ohsson, drawn mainly from Persian, Arabic, and other western Asian records of the Mongol Empire, is another important source of information on taboos. He wrote of the Mongol taboo against urinating (or placing any unclean thing) in fire or water. It was even forbidden to step over a fire or to thrust a knife into a fire. A related taboo forbade urinating into rivers, lakes, or even the ashes of a fire. Strong taboos were related to fire in Mongol society, in part because fire was regarded as sacred and basic to the well-being and prosperity of the family.[3] Even today, Mongols believe that fire has qualities of purification, is sacred, and should not be played with or misused. There are a number of common expressions reflecting the belief that the disappearance or extinguishing of the family fire signifies a curse upon or an end to a family. These taboos were traditionally related to the family *gholomta* or hearth, a symbol of the continuity and integrity of the family. A threat to, or misuse of, the *gholomta* was considered an unforgivable sin because it would offend the fire god and threaten the good fortunes of the family.

In many cultures, there is a close correlation between that which is clean and that which is holy, but among the Mongols there is often a clear differentiation on this point, although some things may be considered both holy and clean. Shoes are an example of an item regarded as unholy, no matter how clean they may be. In contrast, a hat, no matter how battered and dirty, is regarded as special or holy. Naturally, that which is sacred or holy is much more important to the Mongols than that which is merely clean. The lower part of a person's body and the waste therefrom was regarded as both unclean and unholy. Therefore, any object pertaining to the lower part of the body was customarily not to be placed over the fire or over one's head.

Water is also considered sacred among the Mongols, and the word *eke*, "mother," is often found in names for rivers and lakes in Mongolia.[4] In all societies, water is valuable because it is so important to life; but to Mongols it is particularly critical because they were forced to establish certain migratory circuits according to sources of water. The scarcity of water has been a serious handicap in Mongolia. This, then, helps explain the reason for the existence of many strong taboos related to water. Ancient records mention the strictures placed upon the washing of dirty clothes, and this taboo is connected to the scarcity and necessity of maintaining pure sources of water, undefiled by such activities. Chao Hung, in his record the *Meng-ta pei-lu* (reference on the Mongol Tatars, dated 1221), and Hsiao Ta-heng, in his *Pei-lu feng-su* (customs of the northern barbarians, dated 1594), both mention the extremely filthy clothes of the Mongol people and the fact that they did not wash them.[5] William of Rubruck noted two and a half centuries earlier than Hsiao that Mongol women commonly did not wash and that when they did so, they customarily did not do it openly in the sun for fear of offending the gods of heaven and bringing down thunder and lightning.[6]

Through custom, the Mongols developed an avoidance of openly displaying soiled or dirty things that were felt to be offensive to heaven and the sun.[7] This taboo has largely disappeared, but some Mongols even now are still reluctant to openly display clothing worn on the lower part of the body to the sun and the heavens. A common injunction of some older people is that "certain clothing should be worn out from use on the body and not worn out from washing."[8] This notion seems to be due in part to the persistence of ancient taboos but is also a matter of necessity—a sense of thrift and the difficulty of obtaining cloth.

Some Mongol taboos stem from the fear of offending heaven. The common feeling among the Mongols and Chinese, traditionally, was that death by a thunderbolt was not an accident, but the result of sinful or shameful actions. It was punishment from heaven. Frequently, in the past, when a Mongol heard thunder, he would immediately lie down or wrap himself up in a piece of felt or skin. Chao Hung noted centuries ago, "their [Mongol] custom was to greatly honor Heaven . . . when they [troops] hear the sound of thunder they dared not march forward."[9] This action was not entirely due to superstition; it arose from actual frightening experiences in which nomads learned that a man with weapons standing on the barren steppe attracts lightning. Having no scientific explanation for this phenomenon, the Mongols colored it with religious or superstitious meaning. If a man's animals were struck by lightning, it was regarded as bad luck, and steps had to be taken for spiritual purification. In this connection, the Dakhur believed that the spirits of men killed in an unnatural manner are especially important and useful. Among these, the spirit of a man killed by lightning is most valuable when controlled by the shaman. The spirit obeys his commands and accomplishes his work.[10]

Mongols live very close to nature, and consequently a number of their taboos have to do with animals and natural life. In Mongolia, the wolf is the greatest enemy of herders and domesticated animals. Consequently, killing wolves on the steppe is ordinarily regarded as constructive activity to protect the flocks—but undertaken by some people with reservations. In addition, the pelt of the wolf may be sold or traded as a mat or wall hanging for both warmth and decoration. However, should a Mongol setting out on a long journey encounter a wolf, he will by no means attempt to kill the animal. He feels that the wolf is a very "strong-hearted," decisive animal, whose determination is to be admired, and he is reluctant to destroy or put down that which should be emulated during a journey.[11] Judging from evidence in ancient Mongol writings, this may be related to an ancient totemism which was part of the life of nomads in Mongolia. Ancient nomadic T'u-chüeh (Turkic) khans had a *tugh* ("standard"), which they prized as a symbol of authority and power and which was capped by the symbolic head of a wolf.[12] (Incidentally, Börte-chino'a ["spotted wolf"] is given as the name of a prominent ancestor of Chinggis Khan and thus of the Mongol nation.[13] The significance of this myth is a moot question.)

Snakes, rare in Mongolia, are symbolic of the *luus* deity, the "dragon god," and are regarded in many places as *nibdagh* or regional deities. Consequently, there is a taboo or customary avoidance to killing snakes in order not to provoke the *luus* deity who, according to circumstances, reacts to humans either positively or negatively.

For the Mongols, the *eliye,* a species of eagle, is a representation of evil spirits. They have a strong aversion to this particular bird and even more to the *shira shiba'un,* an owl-like yellow bird. The appearance and cry of the *shira shiba'un* in the night is regarded as a particularly bad omen. However, there does not seem to be any definite inclination as to whether or not the bird should be killed.

In a nomadic society, some taboos are invariably associated with animals—their care and activity. In selling or trading a horse, for example, although its reins or halter may be freely exchanged, it is taboo to give up or exchange the leather rope used to lead the animal. The animal itself may be sold or given away, but the rope used to lead it must be retained. All parts of domesticated animals that are slaughtered may be freely used, such as the hide, the wool, the meat, and so forth; however, the bones of an animal are considered special and are not to be sold, although they may be kept for personal use. The bones seem to be regarded as having some association with the origin of the animal. In recent decades, Mongols sometimes refused to sell the bones of animals scattered over the land to Chinese or Japanese merchants coming in to obtain them for use in manufacturing. There is also traditionally a reluctance to sell milk or milk products, which are regarded as special blessings not to be sold for financial gain. This custom or attitude has changed slowly with the inception of modern cooperatives. Some sedentary Chakhar Mongols by the 1930s readily sold milk to be used in the manufacture of a special glue. But Mongols in the more nomadic areas of Shilin-ghol continued to refuse to sell milk products; they felt to do so would decrease the blessings of the household. There is also a custom among the Mongols of setting apart or dedicating animals to temples as *seter* ("live offerings"), which are then not to be used, sold, or killed for food.[14] There are, however, no particular restrictions regarding their offspring. Generally the male animals are castrated.

Many taboos, needless to say, are related to matters of sex, and in this regard the great law code (the *jasagh* of Chinggis Khan), evidence from thirteenth-century travelers,[15] and the observations of Hsiao Ta-heng in the late sixteenth century confirm that the Mongols placed great value on chastity and that there were very strict taboos on illicit sexual relations. Hsiao Ta-heng made special note of the fact: "the barbarians regard illicit sexual relations as a most serious offense, and punishments associated with it are particularly severe."[16] In ancient times in Mongolia, the common result of serious sexual transgression was capital punishment. The severity of the punishment probably was related to a strong desire to maintain the integrity and purity of the patriarchal

lineage. However, it is common knowledge that the ancient concern for
sexual purity has greatly declined over the centuries as moral laxity has
increased. A decline occurred concurrently with the weakening of the
patriarchal system in Mongolia and more particularly with the spread
and almost universal domination of Lamaist Buddhism, because of
which large numbers of the male population joined celibate monastic
centers.

Most cultures have taboos or special customs related to the entrance
of a home or the greeting of guests. In this connection, Mongols also
have had strict observances. For instance, a guest, upon approaching a
yurt, is careful to approach from the left side and to raise the flap of the
door of the dwelling with his left hand. Conversely, in leaving the yurt,
one must take care to depart from the right side. A breach of this custom
is regarded not only as bad manners but also as an unlucky omen.
Actually, this particular custom may have arisen originally merely from
a point of utility in standardizing the mode of entrance and departure
from a dwelling. However, most traditional Mongols would regard it as
a matter of taboo and do not relate it merely to practical function.

Travel accounts record a strict taboo against stepping on the
threshold of a yurt when visiting, particularly the dwelling of a noble. In
ancient times, it was a capital crime for a common person to touch the
threshold of a noble,[17] and, while this custom has greatly moderated, it is
still impolite behavior. There is no rational explanation for the
existence of this taboo among the Mongols, but there seems to have been
a similar custom among the Koreans, other Altaic groups, and in North
China. In eastern Inner Mongolia, there is a popular, though not a
strong, feeling that stepping on the threshold of a yurt or house when
visiting is tantamount to stepping on the neck of the host.

Behavior in company always requires a certain amount of care, and,
traditionally, a Mongol seated in the presence of a superior person must
not expose the bottom of his feet toward him, toward a guest, or toward
the image of the Buddha. However, this taboo does not apply to persons
of lower rank, to one's children, or to servants. When talking with a
superior person, Mongols customarily take care as to how they position
their hands; a particular type of handclasp is regarded as acceptable or
proper. Interlocking the fingers of one's hands while talking with
another is regarded as an omen that the person doing so will be
imprisoned and placed in stocks. Moreover, a Mongol customarily uses
two hands in presenting an object to someone of rank.

The single most important weapon of the Mongols through history has been the bow and arrow; next came the sword and spear. But even before the turn of this century, these gradually fell into disuse as firearms were adopted. Now these old arms have come to be revered relics, and many homes permanently display, in an honored place, an old bow or sword.[18] These are handled with care and may not be commonly handled by children or strangers coming into the yurt. Traditionally, a menstruating woman was not allowed to touch weapons, even her husband's. Common custom held that an arrow, or in more recent times a gun, must never be pointed at a person in a careless, joking fashion, and even now parents do not allow their children to point a toy arrow or a toy gun at a person as is commonly done by American children.

The use of whips, a special item in a horse-riding nomadic society, involved certain taboos. Some old records note that there was a strict taboo against leaning on a horsewhip or touching it to the point of an arrow.[19] It was considered very bad and improper to point at objects with a whip. In the absence of careful fieldwork, it is not possible to judge whether any strict taboo persists regarding the touching of the point of an arrow with a whip since arrows are now obsolete except in tournaments; but there continues to be a taboo against touching another person's objects with a whip as a pointer. There was also traditionally a taboo against punishing a person with a horsewhip—only slaves or criminals would be so punished. A person never brought a horsewhip into the dwelling of someone else. If this were done deliberately, it meant that the officials had come to make an arrest. Of course, there was no objection to a person bringing a whip into his own dwelling. Dogs often come out in a savage manner when people arrive at a yurt on the steppe; but still it is taboo to use a whip to strike the dogs of the man being visited. A person may use a whip to punish his own dogs, but not another's animals.

An old taboo recorded by travelers forbade the throwing of food or the pouring of milk upon the ground.[20] This taboo, which has continued until the present, arises from the fact that Mongols consider food a blessing from heaven. There is a common feeling that heaven places a limitation upon the amount of food provided to man during life and that great care must be taken to properly use one's blessings and prolong one's good fortune. While it is not so strong as before, there is still a feeling that children should not take more than they can eat and must not waste what is given them. Adults are still very careful about what they take and try to consume it without waste. Among the variety of foods available in Mongolia, the most valued is white food, such as milk or milk products. Particular care is taken to avoid misuse or waste of these. This taboo, like others, naturally arises from the scarcity of food and the high regard accorded animal products. In some areas of Mongolia, there lingers a feeling that an article of food that accidentally drops to the ground should not be picked up; it is feared that the food has been deliberately taken by a wandering spirit.

While eating, a Mongol is customarily careful in slicing food to carve toward himself and not to display the sharp edge of a knife toward another person. This may not be regarded as a taboo, but rather as a matter of proper etiquette. Common etiquette also requires that a knife be passed handle first to another person. Common etiquette in the West requires the movement of one's spoon outward in eating soup; but according to Mongol custom, spooning outward is regarded as shoveling away one's blessings. Mongols have a strong aversion to the continued use of a bowl that has been cracked or broken because it may bring bad luck.

The traditional Mongol attitude toward food and its use has been closely related to other objects or behavior that are considered sacred or evil, and, accordingly, people's actions are often carefully prescribed in the handling of food. For example, one must avoid stepping over a small table on which food is to be served, placing one's feet close to food, or other such actions.

Taboos also forbid stepping over a person's head, his hat, or sitting on the collar of a garment, although it is permitted to sit on other parts of a garment. Women, regarded as less holy than men, are particularly forbidden to do so. For most taboos, the observances for females are stricter than for males.

The taboo forbidding the touching of certain items of another person's clothing is recorded in the historical visit of Ch'ang-ch'un chen-jen to the camp of Chinggis Khan while the khan was campaigning in Afghanistan. The Chinese Taoist sage noted in his *Hsi-yu chi*: "Ladies wear a special headdress called *ku-ku* (Mong. *boghta*) and it is strictly forbidden for other people to touch this."[21] It is quite clear that there were customary taboos against touching the headdresses of women, but there is no indication in the materials available of a taboo against touching the helmet or the armor of a warrior, although an ancient taboo, continuing until recently, forbade the touching of a wrestler's *jodogh* or special clothing, except during a match.

All cultures have taboos related to physical contact between persons, and one common among the Mongols forbids a stranger to touch the head of children he may meet because the hand is considered unclean while the head is regarded as sacred. Among the neighboring Chinese, there is no such custom. Ancient Mongols felt that a stranger from afar was unholy or unclean, and, accordingly, embassies visiting the camp of a khan were required to pass between two fires in a ritual purification.[22]

As in many parts of the world, there are taboos in Mongolia related to childbirth, menstruation, death, and illness. Contact with persons in any of these conditions is restricted, particularly in the case of strangers. There is no restriction on friends visiting a sick person during the morning, but visits in the afternoon are avoided because of a fear that a visitor might bring some evil influence. In his sixteenth-century record, Hsiao Ta-heng, noted:

> One of the most serious taboos among the Mongols is their avoidance of people with smallpox. Should a person contract this dreaded disease, even their parents, brothers, wife, and children hide and it is necessary for the ill person to be cared for by a Chinese. Should there be no Chinese to care for the person, their family places necessities at a certain location and the ill person takes the food after they have left. In the case of a husband or wife who contracts smallpox, they avoid contact with each other even after recovery until they hear the sound of thunder. . . . However, because Mongolia is cold, there are very few people who contract smallpox. . . . They regard the inner territories [China] as the land of the house of fire and avoid remaining there very long because they fear contracting smallpox.[23]

The Chinese general observed many instances in which the Mongols hired Chinese to substitute for them when taboos restricted action or contact.

With the conversion of the Mongol nation to Buddhism in the late sixteenth century, old taboos were changed and new ones introduced. For example, the lamas assumed the traditional role of the shaman in making divinations. They introduced new taboos such as the custom that a person born on a particular year and day should avoid contact with another person born at a particular time. This was so strict that even a parent was restricted in contact with his own child until it reached a particular age. A boy with this particular problem was carefully removed to the home of a relative or friend or placed in a monastery, though less care was taken with girls.

Certain Mongol taboos are related to the signs of the zodiac, or more correctly, to the broader East Asian time system of "heavenly stems and earthly branches" (Chs. *t'ien-kan ti-chih*). Accordingly, a person born at a particular time was restricted in his activity on a particular date. Demchügdüngrüb, prince and nationalist leader, born in the tiger hour on the tiger day in the tiger year, avoided doing business on the day of *Müchid*, one of the twenty-eight constellations. He even avoided conversations on a particular day lest he be involved in some unpropitious event.[24] Such taboo restrictions were more commonly observed among the Mongol elite than among the common people whose actions were less governed by such factors because of the necessity of making a livelihood. Hsiao Ta-heng noted almost four centuries ago: "the first, tenth, and fifteenth days of every month are the most auspicious."[25] For many centuries, the nomadic peoples of northeast Asia have persisted in observing particular, auspicious days.

Taboos regarding the different periods of the lunar month were also common traditionally, and the first part of the month from the new moon until the full moon was regarded as a more auspicious time than the latter part of the lunar month. The following is found in the *Shih chi*, in notes regarding the Hsiung-nu (Huns), dated first century B.C.: "When they mobilize their troops they give attention to the stars and the moon. When the moon is strong and full they will attack, but when the moon is waning they will retreat."[26] P'eng Ta-ya, in his *Hei-ta shih-lüeh* (1200s), confirmed this observation: "They choose an auspicious day for a particular activity and they will watch according to the fullness and the waning of the moon and on this basis they will advance or hold their position. . . . Just before the new moon, that is while the full moon is waning, is a period when they are inactive."[27]

Every society has taboos or avoidance customs associated with age, but Mongols, whether young or old, are not sensitive to direct questions about their age. However, they do avoid directly questioning a person regarding his birthday. If asked, a person ordinarily will avoid answering the question because it is common knowledge that in placing a curse on a person it is necessary to know the person's date of birth.

Customarily, the Mongols regard black as a color of ill omen and white as a color of good omen. Consequently, they carefully avoid wearing black apparel, particularly sashes or belts, which are regarded as particularly important items of clothing having symbolic significance of authority and power.

From early times to the present, Mongols have carefully differentiated between lucky and unlucky things. In Inner Mongolia, there is a saying: "Chinese do everything according to their money, but Mongols order their affairs according to their luck."[28] Proverbs such as this one demonstrate the importance of the idea of good luck and good fortune to the Mongols. Avoidance practices naturally have grown up around the beliefs in luck. Death is regarded as the most unlucky occurrence, and, therefore, after attending a funeral or burial rite, one customarily passes between two fires to cleanse oneself and avoids speaking to other members of the family until first bowing before the image of the Buddha. They then consider themselves cleansed and may converse with the family. Carts used to transport bodies to the graveyard or to a place for the disposal of dead bodies are not used again. Except to dispose of a body, it is customarily taboo to visit such places. However, unexpectedly happening upon a dead person during a journey is not regarded as bad luck; on the contrary, people compliment themselves or others on their good luck. This irrational reaction may be a matter of reverse psychology.

Mongols also avoid the use of what are regarded as unlucky words. They will, for example, take great care in the use of words referring to death, illness, or other misfortune. The words that are avoided may differ from place to place. For example, a prominent prince of the Üjümüchin Banner, who lived perhaps a century ago, was named Altan-khuyaghtu (*altan* means "gold"). Because of his prominence and the respect of the people for him, his name was avoided in conversation, and the word *altan*, commonly used throughout other parts of Mongolia, fell into disuse in this banner. Instead, the people use the word *shijir*, which means "raw gold." In the Kharachin Banner, according to custom in one prominent family, the word *makha* (from the Sanskrit *maha*, meaning "great") is avoided because it is an element of the name of an important ancestor of the family. Furthermore, *makha*, the Mongolian pronunciation of a common element in Sanskrit Buddhist terms, sounds very much like the Mongolian spoken word for meat (*makh*) as spoken in the Kharachin dialect. Consequently, this family did not commonly use the word to refer to meat; they adopted the Chinese word *jou (rou)*.[29]

The Mongols, like many people, have certain taboos regarding the exchange of gifts. It is especially bad to return or present an empty container to a person who has brought a gift; some small token is placed in it. In eastern Inner Mongolia, it is also regarded as particularly unlucky to happen on someone with an empty container while departing from one's home. It is regarded as inauspicious for all involved.

To have an antelope or some other animal cross one's path when traveling across the steppe is regarded as good fortune; but it is unlucky if the animal runs away without crossing paths. Taboos also regulate the movement of persons in relation to monasteries, religious shrines, common dwellings, and so forth. A circular movement around such a place must be clockwise to be considered lucky—a counterclockwise movement is unlucky, but in certain instances this is at variance with Shamanistic tradition.

Mountains are often held in awe by the Mongols, and many of them are sacred. If a stranger asks the name of a particular mountain in the vicinity, people may avoid giving the name even if they know it. Instead, they reply that the mountain is called *yeke ghajar,* "the great place." Similarly there is a strong avoidance of the use of the name of one's father, mother, or teacher.

Each Mongol region has unique local deities called by the generic terms *nibdagh* or *shibdagh.* Places set apart for the worship of a local deity are referred to as *oboo* and consist merely of a pile of rocks to form a Shamanistic shrine. The area is thus regarded as sacred, and a particular *oboo* associated with an important temple or a banner is held in high regard. Women are strictly forbidden to approach such a place. Sex-related taboos are also connected to lakes, particularly important ones such as Dabusun-nor in Üjümüchin Banner, Inner Mongolia, from which salt is produced. Women must avoid relieving themselves in this vicinity.[30]

The Mongols observe a custom, stemming from ancient times, called *milaakh (miliyakhu),* which best may be described as a sort of "anointing" or "blessing." The simple ceremony is carried out by placing a small amount of butter or animal fat on one's finger and then rubbing this on the object to be blessed. For example, a family or, particularly, a young newly married couple establishing a new yurt will rub a little butter or animal fat on the inside of the new roof near the opening in the ceiling used for ventilation. The anointer will pronounce some stereotyped words of blessing, such as a wish for many children, protection, or good fortune. It is also common to anoint the lintel of the door in a similar manner.

When the family has an extraordinarily good meal and prepares an entire sheep to be served, they will perform the *milaakh* ritual by taking a small piece of fat from the animal and putting it in the fire. This action shows a reverence for or places a blessing on the fire, a symbol of prosperity. It is also common on occasion for grandparents to *milaakh* the young children. This is simply a symbolic blessing or anointment, accompanied by the wish that the child will always have good food to eat, property, security, and so on.

In further ramifications of this ritual, it is customary to perform *milaakh* on specific occasions such as obtaining a new bow. A little fat is rubbed on the bow and the string, the intent being that the bow may be useful in obtaining game and otherwise beneficial to the family. When a young boy begins to follow his father in the hunt, it is customary for the father to rub a little animal fat on the son's thumb and index finger of the hand that draws the bow. The *milaakh* ceremony may also be performed by particularly devout or conscientious Mongols when they obtain some new furniture or some other object for which they feel they want to express gratitude. According to an incident recorded by d'Ohsson, Chinggis Khan was returning from a campaign in the West (1224) when he was met by his two grandsons, Khubilai and Hüle'ü, eleven and nine years of age, respectively. He saw that the boys had killed a rabbit and a deer, and, with praise and admiration, he anointed and blessed (*milaakh*) their bowstring fingers.[31]

The *milaakh* custom has been widespread among the steppe nomads from ancient times and is still found, for example, among the Kalmuck Mongols now living on the Don and Volga rivers of southern Russia. It has been common at the time of their fall *dalalgha* ("beckoning of wealth") festival for each of those attending to take a small piece of fat and anoint his mouth, while chanting, and then to swallow the piece of fat.[32]

A variation of the anointing ritual appears in the care of newborn babies. In this case, a little liquor or fermented drink is used as a type of anointment, although the actual purpose may be to wash the mouth of the baby. This also may possibly involve some traditional pragmatic medicinal function of disinfection. However, the Mongols feel that the anointing blesses the baby, and fermented drink, rather than tea, milk, or some other liquid, is used because it is considered to be *de'ed* ("superior") of *amt* ("tasty"). Three days after the birth of a male child, a special festival is held by the family at which time the *milaakh* ceremony is performed.

Old ladies particularly are inclined to feel impelled to bless (*irügel*) young people on special occasions; wishing them richness (*bayan*), preeminence (*noyan*) to "stand taller than others," to "be filial to parents at home and a credit to the banner in public," wishing their "progeny to be numerous," their "property to be bounteous," their "animals to become a numerous herd" (*sürüg*), and wishing "that any undertaking may prosper increasingly" (*ööd ösrög*).

4
RELIGION

SHAMANISM

Religion is often viewed as man's speculation regarding the unknown and his search for meaning in life. Linked to the development of a religious philosophy is a tendency to institutionalize beliefs in order to perpetuate a particular view of the world and man's relationship to it. Religion is an important aspect of human experience, and each religion reflects the unique cultural development of a particular society or people.

The influence of the natural environment on religion is inevitable, especially for people who live close to nature. The Mongols and other nomadic people of northern Asia, with the exception of a few forest peoples, live in a world dominated by two factors: the endless expanse of the sky and the boundless steppe. In this environment, the most overpowering and awesome factor is heaven with its fearful winds, threatening snows, rain, thunder, lightning, the bright sun, and the mysteries of the night sky. All natural phenomena confirm the dignity and glory of heaven in the minds of the nomads. Thus, *Tenggeri* ("heaven") became the prime object of worship among the nomads, and *etügen* ("earth"), which they and their animals depended on for a livelihood, came to be a second important object of veneration. It also follows that the natural phenomena between heaven and earth—the sun, moon and stars, high mountains, large rivers, forests, waterfalls, and fire—should all become objects of worship and have sacred meaning attributed to them by the nomads. The mysteries of birth, life and death, and the destiny of man's spirit are also key factors in the development of religious belief.

A concept of heaven is a common denominator among virtually all religions. Some peoples consider heaven to be the ultimate object of worship or an ultimate ideal. Others feel that in or above heaven there is a supreme intelligence that controls heaven itself. The northern Asian nomads seem to fit in the first of these categories. The first mention in recorded history of the worship of heaven by the ancient inhabitants of Mongolia is found in the *Han shu* and draws upon pre-Christian sources in discussing the Hsiung-nu: "In their country, they refer to their [ruler] by the title *Tenggeri ke'üd shan-yü*. The Hsiung-nu call heaven *Tenggeri* and a son they call *ke'üd*. The word *shan-yü* has a connotation that the object referred to has 'breadth' and 'greatness' and by extension means that a *shan-yü* is 'heavenlike.'"[1] This reference seems to indicate that the Hsiung-nu considered their ruler to be the Son of Heaven. They worshiped heaven and regarded it as the ultimate source of power. According to early Chinese observations, the Hsiung-nu were the first northern Asian nomads of record to worship *Tenggeri;* however, the evidence is too fragmentary to be conclusive. A discussion regarding the southern Hsiung-nu in the *Hou Han shu* gives another early indication of the worship of *Tenggeri* by the nomads: "According to Hsiung-nu custom, they have three annual religious festivals. These fall on the *wu* days of the first, the fifth and the ninth months and are occasions to worship the God of Heaven."[2]

Students of Mongolian history agree that the earliest religion among the Mongols was Shamanism, but whether it is, in fact, a religion is a question of definition. Shamanism, characterized by the worship of natural phenomena and by pantheism, is a primitive religion not restricted to the Mongols. Etymologically, the term *shaman* is derived from a Tungusic-Manchu word for witch. It does not exist in the Mongolian language, and, in ancient times, the Mongols were not aware that Shamanism might be regarded as a distinct religion. The Mongol word for witch, *bö'e*, is frequently found in the earliest Mongol record, the *Secret History*.[3] Among the Mongols, the word was not associated with any particular religion; however, the Mongols believed that the highest class of *bö'e* had supernatural powers and the ability to communicate with heaven or to understand and explain the "will of heaven" (*ji'arin*).[4] The Mongols revere a high shaman as a mediator between heaven and earth who possesses power from heaven to bless or to curse. Common shamans, Mongols believe, are limited to communicating with spirits, not with heaven. They can cast out evil spirits, invoke good spirits, curse, divine one's destiny, and heal various illnesses. Their role in society generally corresponds to that of the Westerners' witch doctor or medicine man. Now, common shamans have largely disappeared or have been greatly restricted in Mongolia. In the premodern era, Mongols believed that some shamans could control nature and cause rain, storms, or severe winds with a sacred stone called *jada.*[5]

In the pantheistic world of the Mongols, the shamans and the common people believed *Tenggeri* to be the supreme God of the universe, ruling over many other gods and such natural phenomena as mountains, rivers, stars, and the sun. Mongols also believed that shamans could utilize the spirit of a deceased person or of an animal, particularly the fox, to communicate with the unseen and to gain assistance in their work. A common activity of a shaman is the recitation of sacred prayers and formulas called *daghudalagha.*[6] Some of these chants have impressive poetic qualities, but others are meaningless and entirely devoid of any profound religious philosophy. Generalizations regarding chants are difficult because shamans or schools of shamans have different styles and forms. From ancient times to the present, Shamanism has shown little or no development, but has remained very primitive and generally is not highly regarded by students of comparative religion.

Traditionally, there were innumerable Shamanistic deities, but the most famous ones were Nemdü'ül and Khutugh,[7] both good deities from whom blessings are sought. Until recent times, in some places, the Mongol nobility worshiped a "god of blessing" known as Jula;[8] however, the ritualistic activity associated with this deity was secret and is not well known. There seems to be some evidence that the cult was a remnant of an earlier veneration or worship of ancestors.

A similar manifestation peculiar to the Chakhar Mongols is the belief in *Khara* or Tyrannical *Khara,* also a remnant of ancient ancestral veneration and associated secret rituals. One customary ritual associated with this deity was the placing of a new piece of cotton on the mouth of a dying person in order to catch the last breath. The cotton was then placed in a small sack as a fetish and hung in a secret place to protect the family against enemies and to bring a blessing to the household.[9] In more recent times, the Nemdü'ül deity has been changed into a deity of hunting because of the belief that a bounteous hunt is a great blessing to be gained from Nemdü'ül.[10] This deity was and by some probably still is known as *Manakhan-Tenggeri.*[11]

Divination of the cracks of heated clavicle bones was a ritual common to all shamans.[12] Until recently in a unique community in East Sünid of the Shilin-ghol region of Inner Mongolia, a whole settlement of *bö'e,* known as *bö'echül,* used a variation of this practice. Men of the community performed divinations, at least until the recent Communist takeover, without first exposing the bones to a fire, and it was common for people to seek their assistance in locating lost animals.[13]

Mongolian shamans, whether *bö'e* (male) or *idughan* (female),[14] have often shared a common characteristic that some would call eccentricity or deranged instability. Others use stronger terms, such as psychotic, to describe shamans. In some parts of Mongolia, until recently, *idughan* have been more influential than the *bö'e.* Shamans also often seem to have a special talent for poetic chants, ritualistic prayers, and an ability to entertain people with mystic stories or fairy tales. Mongolian shamans commonly live in inaccessible places and wear unique costumes, including picturesque hats and coats with rings on their belts or around their ankles; rings with small mirrors are sewed to their clothing. Part of their ritualistic equipment is a small one-headed drum.

A shaman begins the ceremony by beating the drum, chanting at a slow measured pace, and dancing to an increasingly rapid rhythm until the dance reaches a frenzied tempo. At the climax, the shaman collapses in a trance and is then able, it is believed, to communicate with the gods and spirits. After regaining consciousness, the shaman relates his or her spiritual travel, answers special questions, or makes a pronouncement on the problems of those who seek an oracle. It is also believed that shamans have the power to exorcise evil spirits and to remove sickness from a person by casting the spirit or the illness into an object such as a tree or an animal. These rituals and performances are commonly avoided by most Buddhist Mongols who believe they are evil and devilish.

The relationship of Chinggis Khan to heaven and to a shaman, is seen in the most ancient Mongolian chronicle, the *Secret History,* which begins with the words *De'ere Tenggeri*[15] ("heaven above"). The record proclaims that the birth of Chinggis Khan was destined and ordained of heaven. It is recorded that, later, on the occasion of Chinggis's confirmation as a ruler of a united group of Mongol clans, a proclamation was made by the powerful shaman Khorchi (who, it was believed, could speak for heaven) that Chinggis Khan took his position by virtue of *ji'arin,* the "will of heaven."[16] It was the custom of Chinggis before any great undertaking or decision to first worship heaven in prayer. Judging from Mongol records, he constantly had a feeling of awe or profound respect for heaven. He felt that he was ordained of heaven to a mission, protected by heaven, and destined to be lord over the whole earth. Many references indicate the importance of the worship of heaven among the Mongol people of that period.

Before the introduction of Buddhism, *Tenggeri* was the supreme deity or power in the universe to all northern Asian nomadic peoples. There are various forms of *Tenggeri,* but the supreme "godlike" *Tenggeri* was referred to as *Möngke Tenggeri* ("everlasting or eternal heaven").[17] An alternative to this term, but one that had the same meaning was *Odghan Tenggeri.* The Mongol concept of heaven seems to have been abstract— not personified or represented in any anthropomorphic form or image. However, their heaven did have personal qualities, such as the ability to see and hear, to be angry, to save, to kill, and so forth. Mongol *bö'e* or shamans speak of many heavens, and it is the common feeling that the heaven to the east is benevolent or lucky while the heaven to the west is malevolent and to be feared.

Traditionally, the Mongols felt that the sun, moon, and stars are manifestations of the glory of the supreme heaven, *Möngke Tenggeri,* and therefore objects of worship. Chinggis Khan, in his worship of heaven, bowed to the sun,[18] and, at the important New Year festival, the Mongols customarily begin by bowing first to the east, the origin of the sun.[19] The *Secret History* makes special mention of the fact that the sixteenth day of the fourth month of the lunar calendar was *khula'an tergel,* meaning "red round," in reference to the moon. It was customary to have a large evening feast on this day.[20]

Another important god of Shamanism is referred to by the Mongols as *Dolo'on-ebügen* or the "seven old men" (the Big Dipper).[21] The nomads, often migrating in the boundless steppe without set landmarks for navigation, give special regard to *Altan-khadaas* ("golden stake"), the North Star, for their bearing.[22]

The Mongols had certain ceremonies for the worship of *etügen,* the earth. In ancient times, decrees of the khans, certificates of envoys, and official papers began with the set phrase, "By the power of heaven and earth. . . ."[23] These words placed the highest stamp of authority and dignity on whatever they prefaced. The Chinese also place great importance on the reverence of heaven; however, according to Chinese custom, heaven is masculine (*ch'ien*) and the earth is feminine (*k'un*). It is

An *oboo,* Shamanistic shrine in Shilin-ghol, Inner Mongolia

unclear whether the Mongols originally made such a distinction, but by the time of the empire, they did use the term *idughan,* for "female shaman,"which is a cognate of the word *etügen* ("earth"). Thus, it would appear that they felt the earth had feminine or maternal qualities.

Natural phenomena play an important role in Shamanism. Mongols, roving over the steppe, feel that a mountain suddenly rising from the earth has certain mystic qualities. Moreover, they believe the raised earth to be the seat of local deities; this belief is reflected in the fact that all Mongol *oboo,* or Shamanistic shrines, are found on the tops of mountains or hills.[24] The Shamanistic worship of mountains extends back far into history and is demonstrated by Chinggis Khan's worship of Burkhan mountain and his instruction that his family and descendants should continue the practice. Rivers and streams are also important to the Mongols as a source of water for themselves and their animals and as a source of food. Thus, it is no surprise that they are often venerated. For example, the famous Onon River is referred to as *eke* or "mother,"[25] and Dabusun-nor, a salt lake located in the Üjümüchin Banner of the Shilin-ghol League, is referred to as *eej,* a colloquial word for "mother." Such terms of respect are indicative of the great importance to the livelihood of the Mongols of the salt—significant for both diet and trade—produced by the "Mother Lake" (*eej-nor*).[26] There are innumerable instances of the deification of lakes, rivers, and other natural features.

Fire, because of its light and warmth, also became an object of worship to Shamanistic Mongols. Some scholars conjecture that this is an influence from Zoroastrianism. While modern, educated persons feel no inhibitions, it is taboo for traditionally minded persons to cast anything considered dirty or polluted into a fire or even into the ashes of a fire. There is a strong feeling that fire has a cleansing quality, and there are many instances of its being used for this purpose. Foreign ambassadors to the khan, for example, were required to pass between two large fires to be purified before an audience at court.[27] Up until the time of Communist rule in Mongol areas, rituals connected with the worship of fire were common in Mongol families.

An important aspect of Mongolian Shamanism is a quite well-developed form of ancestral veneration, according to which it is customary to worship the spirit of the *de'edüs* ("those ascended above") or the *yekes* ("great ones").[28] This belief is a factor in the appearance of the cult of Chinggis Khan found in the Ordos in modern times. In earlier centuries, a remote ancestor or common progenitor of a Mongol kinship group was regarded as its protector. Thus, Chinggis Khan has also come to be regarded as the Great Protector of the Mongol nation.[29] A common belief that an ancestral spirit may either bless or curse a family, depending upon the family's attitudes and actions, extends back to early times. Examples are found in the *Secret History*. When Jamukha, a rival chief, was captured by Chinggis Khan and urged to serve him, he refused for personal reasons and urged Chinggis Khan to kill him, promising that his spirit would protect the descendants of Chinggis Khan in the future.[30]

Mongols also believe in local deities, referred to variously as *nibdagh* and *shibdagh*, who protect the region with which they are associated from trouble and outside invaders. These regional deities are typically Shamanistic gods with power to either curse or bless. When Ögödei Khan became sick during the great invasion of North China, his shaman counselor told him his illness was caused by the local deities of the Chin (Jurchen) land who had been offended by the attack on people and cities that the deities were protecting.[31]

Mongol tribes also have protective deities referred to as *sülder* or *sülde*, which are usually depicted as martial gods. They may or may not be identical with the clan god.[32] A tribal or military standard (*tugh*) displayed on special occasions is a symbol of the protective deity. Before important battles, it was customary to hold a ceremony and make offerings to the standard. In the Ordos region, one of the most important ancient relics is said to be the sacred *sülde* or standard of Chinggis Khan. The standard is regarded as the symbol of his protective deity and is also termed *sülde* because the deity may dwell in it. When Chinggis took power as khan in 1206, in order to honor his protective deity, he created a new standard or flag, which was white and mounted on a decorated staff with nine tassels or tails.[33] This flag became the standard of the Mongol Empire, but its exact nature or appearance is not known. Veneration of the relics of Chinggis Khan has continued over the centuries in Shamanistic tradition, and until recently each banner supposedly had a relic of Chinggis Khan which was worshiped at a secret and sacred place in the banner. The major focal point of this cult of Chinggis Khan has for centuries been located at Ejen-khoroo in the Ordos region.

A common feature of many Mongolian traditional ceremonies or rituals of worship is the sprinkling of mare's milk and the performing of three bows with nine kowtows. The sprinkling of *airagh,* fermented mare's milk, is called *sachuli.*[34] Since the horse is the supreme animal of the nomads and certain products of the horse are thought to be blessed, and since the color white symbolizes blessedness, goodness, purity, richness, and peace, therefore, the sprinkling of mare's milk is felt to be a ritual offering useful at all times and in all places whatever the object of worship may be. In a ritual associated with ancestral veneration, strips of meat are hung from a pole in a Shamanistic offering called *jügeli.*[35] Even to this day, in the Forbidden City of Peking, in the K'un-ning kung Palace there is an ancestral pole handed down from the Mongol-Yüan period and used, in ancient times, for the meat offering.[36] After the offering ceremonies are completed, the meat is distributed to be eaten by those participating and, in this case, is called a *keshig* or "blessing." A form of burnt offering or animal sacrifice (*tüleshi*)[37] has, from ancient times, been associated with the worship of ancestors. The most common object offered is a sheep, although a horse or some other animal may be used. This ritual follows the tradition of the earlier Jurchen and Kitan peoples.

Mongols customarily made offerings as a propitiation of the regional deities in order to avert any harm from them. From the time of the ancient Hsiung-nu to the period of the Mongol Empire, on rare occasions, a human was offered as a special sacrifice, though not necessarily in the form of a burnt offering. By the thirteenth century, this custom was changing, and in place of a sacrificial man, someone could be appointed as a *joligha*, not necessarily to be killed but to take upon himself a curse that would otherwise fall on others. The term has the connotation of an exchange, a ransom, or a scapegoat. Probably the most famous example is that of Tolui who offered to be the *joligha* for Ögödei Khan when he became ill during the North China campaign. Tolui took the curse upon himself at the request of the shamans and died, it was commonly believed, instead of his brother, the khan. The *Secret History* account of this incident seems to be exaggerated when compared to the one in the Yüan dynastic history, but nevertheless it is evidence of the Mongolian custom in such cases.[38]

In the early clan period of Mongolian history, before the empire, Shamanistic religious ceremonies within the clan were usually performed by the chief, since there was no strict division between religious and political functions. In other cases, they were performed by a shaman. Among the Mongol clans that anciently dwelled in the northwest forest areas bordering on Siberia, in a group referred to as the "people of the forest," Shamanism was particularly strong, and there it was very common for the roles of the clan shaman and the clan chief to be one and the same. A person in whom both the role of clan head and shaman converged was usually referred to as *begi* or *beki*. Two famous clan chieftains, who were also shamans, were Usun Ebügen and Khorchi, both of the Ba'arin clan and both of whom gave important support to Chinggis Khan in becoming the Great Khan of all the Mongol tribes.[39] Later, both of these shamans were accorded special honor and status. Khorchi was appointed as the head of a one-thousand household unit, and later, after the conquest of the "people of the forest," he became the head of a *tümen*, a ten-thousand household unit.[40] Usun Ebügen was given the special privileges by Chinggis of being clothed in white robes, of being seated on a white horse, and, on state occasions and assemblies, of being seated in the seat of honor and consulted to determine propitious days for important decisions. In his role as an exalted shaman, he received special treatment and many gifts from the khan and from other leaders and people.[41]

Throughout Mongolian history, it has been common for influential shamans (*bö'e*) to use their position to exploit the people and to seek personal gain or political influence. An early example was Kököchü

(Kökechü), the son of Menglig, an important vassal of Chinggis who had great power as a shaman in the court and among the leaders of the Mongol tribes and who was thought to have the power to communicate with heaven in the role of a Teb-Tenggeri.[42] He created a great deal of trouble because of his insults to the brothers of Chinggis, which was possibly an attempt to cause dissension between Chinggis and his inner circle. Eventually, it became necessary to remove this shaman, who posed a challenge, and it was only after his removal that Chinggis's undisputed power was established.[43] The influence of shamans in virtually every aspect of early Mongol life is indisputable, and it reached the highest levels of society. Some feel that there was a significant political implication in the case of Tolui, who was made a Shamanistic scapegoat for Ögödei Khan.[44] There is evidence that a plot by a shaman eventually caused a breach between the descendants of Tolui and his brother Ögödei—a split that later was a threat to unity within the Mongol Empire. Apparently, the manipulations and influence of a shaman were also behind the decree by Möngke, son of Tolui, that anyone who placed a curse on another person would be killed. This precedent was continued during the reign of Khubilai Khan, who also decreed a severe penalty for anyone placing curses on other persons.[45]

Religious images and symbols are referred to in the accounts of medieval Western travelers among the Mongols. These were not Buddhist images but rather *ongghon*, namely, images, symbols, and sacred paraphernalia used by shamans in their ceremonial activity and the worship of *Tenggeri*. A Chinese account records the capture, in a battle with the Hsiung-nu,[46] of a golden image that mistakenly has been identified by some scholars as a Buddhist image. Actually, it was a Shamanistic image, an *ongghon*. Western travelers also mention the divinations performed by the shamans at the Mongol court.

Unlike many religions, Shamanism is not exclusive but is comparatively accommodating in relating to other religions. Judging from the activity of various shamans and the behavior of the people, there was very little fanaticism associated with it. The deities of Buddhism or other religions were not condemned but, according to the pantheistic beliefs of Shamanism, were interpreted as special manifestations of Shamanistic deities. Thus, the shamans never saw any necessity to forbid the worship of other foreign gods. This helps to explain the tendency of the Mongol khans to have a tolerant policy toward other religions. All religions were seen to be good as long as they did not cause political problems or trouble for the empire; but religious leaders or priests under the Mongols were required to pray for the khan. All those who met this condition were exempted from taxes, military service, or other obligations. Thus, religious tolerance was one of the more successful policies of the Mongols during the empire period.

Shamanism is closer to Taoism than to other Chinese religions, and some interaction occurred between the two religions. Chinggis Khan invited the noted Taoist, Ch'ang-ch'un chen-jen (personal name, Ch'ü Ch'u-chi), to visit him from the distant Chinese province of Shantung. On a snowy mountain summit, during the Mongol campaign in Afghanistan, they discussed religion and Chinggis conferred upon him the title *shen-hsien* "the Immortal," the highest degree of Taoism.[47] As a result of the contact, all the Taoist temples and institutions of North China were exempted from taxes during Mongol rule. This is further evidence of the importance of the Mongol policy of religious tolerance. Chinggis apparently received no particular inspiration from his meeting with the Taoist priest, and Taoism as a religion has, at no time, had a significant influence among the Mongols. Nevertheless, the meeting was important for the career of Ch'ang-ch'un chen-jen, in that he was able to establish his preeminence as a religious leader in the Taoist sect known as Chüan-chen chiao.[48] This sect was especially promoted, tax exemption was received for all its institutions, and many religious officials and important Chinese scholars found refuge in its temples during the period of chaos that ensued during the conquest. Consequently, the Mongol patronage of the sect was an important factor in maintaining the cultural continuity of North China in a critical period. At the same time, because of this fortuitous development, Chinggis Khan received important support from the followers of the Chüan-chen chiao sect, who subsequently served as supporters during the Mongol takeover of North China. These events and developments can be indirectly attributed to the influence of Shamanism, which conditioned the attitudes of Mongol leaders.

Shamanism, from beginning to end, failed to develop any profound philosophy, organizational unity, or coherent priesthood, which could raise the status of the shaman above other classes in society as in many other Eastern and Western civilizations. The shamans never were consolidated, but did have considerable importance at times in their isolated roles.

The Shamanistic background was one reason for the rapid

assimilation by the Mongols of other forms of religion—Nestorian Christianity, Buddhism, Islam, and Catholicism. Because of the nature of the native religion and its response to new situations, its functions were gradually taken over by lamas or other persons in a progressive diminution of the role of the shaman in Mongolian society. The rulers of the khanates of Kipchak, Chaghadai, and Il-Khan were often converted to the religions of the areas over which they ruled.

After 1368 and the retreat of the Mongols from China, there was a rapid decline of foreign religions among them; Buddhism eventually disappeared, not to be reintroduced until the latter part of the sixteenth century. After the decline of the first introduction of Buddhism, Shamanism was once more revived and remained strong until the 1570s when Buddhism again spread into Mongolia and became virtually the state religion. Shamanism was once more suppressed and has become virtually extinct in some areas; the disappearance of Shamanism has been hastened by the secularization of society and Communist assimilation was easier because the role or many functions of the shamans of Mongolian society were usurped by the lamas. Although residual Shamanism continues, there is, nevertheless, generally no sentiment in Mongolia that Shamanism, as a native religion, should have special status. Although the worship of heaven, earth, mountains, rivers, and local deities continues to be strong, the ceremonial or ritualistic functions in such worship were taken over and performed by the lamas, and, in time, Shamanistic deities were absorbed into the lower strata of the Buddhist pantheon.

As Lamaism or Buddhism became dominant in Mongolia, shamans were persecuted in some areas and continued to practice only in secret. One of the more outstanding examples of the persecution of shamans occurred in the seventeenth century among the Oirad Mongols in far northwestern Mongolia. A famous and powerful Zaya Pandita Lama decreed that anyone having any association with Shamanistic ritual would have his property confiscated and dog dung spread on his face.[49] However, Buddhism never became dominant among the Dakhur Mongols of Hulun-buir or among some Buriyad Mongols in Siberia near Irkutsk on the west of Lake Baikal. In these areas, Shamanism continued to be strong.

After the introduction of Lamaist Buddhism, *oboo* shrines came under Buddhist influence, and Buddhist flags with Tibetan prayers on them are commonly found on Shamanistic shrines; Tibetan scriptures and prayers are also written on the stones of the shrines.[50] Spreading Tibetan Buddhism or Lamaism was not a simple process because a primitive Tibetan religion, known as Bon, which may be viewed as a sort of Tibetan form of Shamanism having many similarities to the primitive Mongolian religion, also influenced Mongolian culture and facilitated an amalgamation of Buddhism and Shamanism.

Probably the last time for public or official patronage of the shamans was on the occasion of the building and dedication in 1944 of a great temple to Chinggis Khan by the Japanese at Wang-yin süme (Wang-yeh miao, now Ulanhot) in an attempt by Japanese militarists to influence the Mongol people through their sacred, nationalistic symbols. Great crowds of people attended the ceremonies, and a group of shamans had a prominent part on the program.[51]

LAMAIST BUDDHISM

Many people consider Lamaism, the dominant religion in Mongolia and Tibet, to be a unique and distinct religion; however, the Mongols, unaware of this opinion, think of their religion simply as Buddhism. Some Western specialists also look with disfavor on the term *Lamaism,* but it is a descriptive term of long standing and wide use, and, although it is not precise, it is likely to continue to be used. The term *lama* comes into English from Chinese and was originally derived from the Tibetan word *bla-ma,* meaning "the superior one" or "the revered one."

Lamaism is actually a sect of Mahayana Buddhism and does have unique characteristics that differentiate it from other sects of Buddhism. For example, the general impression of Buddhism throughout most of the world is one of a very quiescent or subdued religion both in its spirit and outward manifestations. Buddhist ceremonies are not ordinarily considered to be dynamic or lively, and Buddhist temples or monks are not thought to be particularly flashy or brilliant in their dress or manner. In contrast, Lamaism has many very bright festivals and ceremonies and a much more highly developed pantheon than other Buddhist sects. The dress of the lamas and the images of the sect are quite colorful, and its religious art and music are certainly not conservative or subdued. Another distinguishing feature of Lamaist Buddhism is the tantric or mystic elements that it has assimilated and perpetuated, which particularly attract Mongols with Shamanistic background and conditioning. In contrast to many Chinese temples, which are built in inaccessible places as hermitages or retreats from society, temples in Mongolia are centers of social life, festivals, and economic activity. Mongols say that the religion with its bright decorations, music, robed monks, and settled monastic centers allays the loneliness and the emptiness which permeate the boundless steppe.

Lamaism originated in Tibet and arose in part from the marriage of Songsten Gampo (Srong-btsan sgam-po, 617-85), king of Tibet, to two Buddhist princesses: Wen-ch'eng of China[1] and a princess of Nepal.[2] Both wives were sources of Buddhist influence, and later the learned monk, Padmasambhava,[3] directly introduced Buddhism from India to Tibet (747). As Buddhism grew and flourished in Tibet, a syncretism developed between the new religion and the indigenous Tibetan Bon religion. In time, a conflict arose between the advocates of the more scholarly, intellectual form of Chinese Buddhism and the esoteric form of Indian Buddhism. An historic debate was held during the reign of King Trhisong Detsen (Khri-srong Ide-btsan, 743-97 or 730-85),[4] in which the respective merits of the two were discussed in detail, and, as a result, it was decided that Chinese Buddhism was not as acceptable to pastoral Tibetans as the tantric Indian type. The Mongols had the same preference, and Tibetan Buddhism eventually spread to Mongolia.

The succession of foreign religions introduced into Mongolia began with Nestorian Christianity, continued with Islam and then Taoism, Buddhism, and Catholicism. Buddhism was introduced into Mongolia comparatively late, probably in the T'ang period (618-907), although it had been introduced into China much earlier, during the later Han period (A.D. 25-220). The nomadic T'o-pa or Tabgach (386-557) invaded China from Mongolia and then became Buddhist; however, they were subsequently cut off from Mongolia by the Juan-juan (Jou-jan/Avars?), and thus Buddhism apparently did not spread into Mongolia even at this time. It appears that Buddhism was first introduced into Mongolia during the early T'ang dynasty in the reign of Bilgä Khan (ca. 710-30s),[5] through the T'u-chüeh, a Turkic rather than a Mongolian people, who occupied Mongolia at the time. Chinese forms of Buddhism had only a limited influence but did lay some foundation for Lamaism, which succeeded it. Manichaeanism was introduced among the Uighur Turks, by Teng-li-mu-yü Khan (759-80), while they occupied part of Mongolia for a brief period. Later, in the thirteenth century, Catholicism and the

Eastern Orthodox form of Christianity were introduced, but neither gained many adherents. The learned Taoist monk Ch'ang-ch'un chen-jen was honored by Chinggis Khan, but there was no noteworthy influence of Taoism in Mongolia. Yeh-lü Ch'u-ts'ai,[6] high minister of Ögödei Khan, was a profound scholar and sincere convert of Buddhism, but neither those men nor others were successful in converting the Mongol court to their religion. Even the Nestorian priests—who had long contact with Mongolian leaders, held high positions, and converted Sorkhaghtani, the mother of two khans—were unable to convert the Mongol khans themselves. In contrast, the Mongol khans readily accepted Lamaist Buddhism, with which they first came into contact in Tibet during their campaigns and occupation there. An examination of this process demonstrates that there was a tendency among the Mongols to accept this form of religion and that it was more readily adaptable to Mongol culture.[7]

The final and definite acculturation of the Mongols to Lamaism meant marked changes in the old tendency to struggle for a better station in life; the focus was shifted to less wordly concerns, such as improving one's incarnation after death and rebirth. A fixation on the next life militated against progressive adaptations necessary for successfully adjusting to a modern world. Due to the fact that, in some areas of Mongolia, from one-third to one-half of the male population led unproductive lives in monasteries, the natural expansion of the population was greatly curtailed and thus the main basis for labor and production declined. Many men, the most valuable human resource, were nonproductive. Moreover, much surplus wealth in Mongolia was attracted to the monasteries or temples, and, with money withdrawn from circulation, reinvestment for economic development was adversely affected. Social progress and reform were also hindered because the top level of ecclesiastical officials or lamas worked with the princes and nobility in the lay sector of society in a conservative system, which hindered social mobility and change and caused economic stagnation and political ossification. This hopeless decline was only broken by radical movements in recent decades. The resultant lack of development in Mongolia became the prime focus of reformers and revolutionaries among the Mongol intelligentsia.

However, while Lamaism was at its peak, the monasteries were the center of social life and contributed to a flourishing culture. There are strong parallels between the situations in Mongolia and in medieval Europe. In such fields as medicine (especially, the control of epidemics), literature, and art, the lamas made a noteworthy contribution to Mongolian achievements.

The first indication of the existence of Buddhism among the Mongols is found in the *Secret History;* the occasion was the campaign of Chinggis Khan against the Tanguts to the west of China (1227). The record notes that the conquered ruler of the Tanguts presented many *süme* to Chinggis Khan as a tribute. (The term *süme* is translated in the Chinese version of the *Secret History* as "Buddhist images."[8]) And although these objects were prized by the Tanguts, they seem to have made no discernible religious impression upon the Mongols at the time. When Buddhism was finally established among the Mongols much later, *süme* came to mean "temple" and lost its old meaning of "image." In its place, a new word, *burkhan,* a variant of the Sanskrit term Buddha, came to be used.

When they were conquered by the Mongols, the Uighur Turks were about equally divided between Buddhism and Islam, and the Buddhists among the Uighur may have played some role in the introduction of Buddhism into Mongolia.

Western travelers in the Mongol Empire reported seeing many images of worship among the people; these almost certainly were not Buddhist images, but the *ongghon* of Shamanism. The Annals of Hsien-tsung (Möngke Khan), found in the *Yüan shih,* mention that Möngke appointed the Chinese monk Hai-yün[9] as superintendent of Buddhist affairs and appointed Li Chih-ch'ang to supervise Taoist affairs,[10] and while such references have little broad significance for Mongolia, since they were limited to the Mongol royal household, Hai-yün's influence may have been a factor in the acceptance of Buddhism by the khans. However, the main influence seems to be more due to the Kashmiri monk Namo. According to the Biography of Tieh-ko [Tege] in the *Yüan shih:*

Tege . . . was a man from Kashmir. His father and uncle Otochi and Namo, devotees of Buddhism . . . accompanied him to visit the [Mongol] court and were received by T'ai-tsung [Ögödei Khan]. Ting-tsung [Güyüg Khan] made Namo his teacher . . . when Hsien-tsung [Möngke Khan] ascended the throne, he honored Namo as *kuo-shih* ["teacher of the realm"], gave him a jade seal, and the authority to supervise all Buddhist affairs under heaven.[11]

The form of Buddhism in Kashmir at the time was closely related to the form of the religion introduced into Tibet earlier, and it appears that Namo played a key role in the eventual acceptance of Lamaism by the Mongol court.

Another event related to the introduction of Lamaism into Mongolia occurred during the reign of Ögödei Khan (1229-41) when he dispatched his son, Kötön, to campaign against Tibet. After a successful campaign, Kötön ordered the Sa-skya Pandita, head of the powerful Saskya-pa branch of Tibetan Buddhism, to come to his court. He went, though not without reservations. His brilliant nephew Phags-pa,[12] who was later to become so famous, went with him quite happily as though on an adventure. By the time Phags-pa reached Mongolia from the camp of Prince Kötön, Möngke had become khan. Phags-pa lived in the khan's court for many years and became a close friend of young Prince Khubilai.[13] This situation was an entering wedge for Buddhism because a number of persons in the imperial court were converted.

During the rule of Möngke (1251-59), a great clash occurred at court in China between the Taoists and the Buddhists. The Buddhists were able to gain the support of Namo and Phags-pa, and the Taoists were eventually suppressed. Later, however, in the Yüan period, the Taoists were able to regain influence and on occasion were invited to perform religious ceremonies at court.

During Khubilai's reign (1260-94), Lamaism became even more influential. He honored Phags-pa with the title of *Kuo-shih*, "Teacher of the Realm" and later promoted him to *Ti-shih* or "Imperial Tutor." Khubilai also established a new office, the *Hsüan-cheng yüan*,[14] which had jurisdiction over the territory of Tibet as well as over all religious affairs of the realm. The head of the organization was under the direction of imperial tutors.

As Buddhism began to be accepted in the Mongol court and by the khans, the Saskya-pa sect and the Karma-pa sect were introduced at about the same time, resulting in keen competition between the two to gain influence in the court and among the nobility.

Generally, the Tibetan lamas who came to China and Inner Asia at this time to spread Buddhism had a high sense of morality and strict discipline; however, a few were very ambitious priests who sought power and wealth, became involved in plots and corruption, and caused trouble and considerable opposition from the Chinese. An example is the notorious Yang-lian-chen-chia who was appointed director of Religious Affairs over the area south of the Yangtze River. He made the serious mistake of becoming involved in local religious conflicts between the Taoists and the Buddhists and sided with the latter in a movement to destroy many Taoist shrines and temples, including even the tombs of the Southern Sung emperors who had been patrons of Taoism in an earlier period.[15] As a result of this type of activity, the Mongol rulers lost influence among the southern Chinese.

Another problem arose during the reign of Toghon-temür Khan, who succumbed to the influence of a crowd of lamas that dominated his court and involved him in esoteric rituals to such an extent that affairs of state were neglected, causing a still greater decline of Yüan power. With the fall of the Yüan dynasty, as Toghon-temür Khan retreated to Mongolia (1368), Buddhism continued to maintain its influence among the Mongols for a time, but finally gave way to the more traditional Shamanistic religion.[16]

During this period, as the Mongols lost power in China and as Buddhism lost influence among the Mongols, great changes, prompted by the famous reformer Tsongkha-pa, occurred in Tibetan Buddhism. The great leader was responsible for many important innovations, the most significant of which was to enforce stricter discipline among lamas to remain celibate—previously, they had married and had families. He also made a great effort to return Buddhism to its old orthodoxy and to eliminate many decadent esoteric practices. To emphasize his reform and set his followers apart from the old schools, Tsongkha-pa had his new sect of lamas dress in yellow robes, a symbol of wholeness or completeness. His disciples came to be known as the Gelug-pa and are commonly referred to in both Mongolian and English as the Yellow Sect. It is commonly thought that prior to these reforms all lamas were of the Red Sect, but this is a misconception for actually only the followers of the Nyingma-pa sect, founded by Padmasambhava, were of the Red Sect. Later, the Yellow Sect became the dominant and most influential sect of Lamaism in Tibet. Two of the most important disciples of Tsongkha-pa in their later incarnations came to be known as the Dalai Lama and the Panchen Tashi Lama.

After Dayan Khan reunified Mongolia in the latter part of the fifteenth century, his grandson Altan Khan, together with Sechen Khong Taiji, invited Tibetan lamas to return with them to Mongolia. The Mongolian classics, the *Erdeni-yin tobchi* and the *Altan tobchi,* both confirm that, in 1578, Sonam Gyatso (Mong. Sodnam-jamso, 1543-1588), head of the Tibetan Yellow Sect, was invited by Altan and other

Mongol leaders to come to Lake Kökönor to receive the veneration of the Mongol people.[17] On this occasion Altan Khan offered Sonam Gyatso the title of Dalai Lama—*dalai* having the connotation of "expansive as the ocean." Later, this lama came to be identified as the Third Dalai Lama, and his predecessors were posthumously designated as the First and Second Dalai Lamas.

Tibetan monks who introduced Buddhism to the Mongols found it very useful to manipulate the doctrine of reincarnation so as to trace their lineage and find roots in earlier Mongolian history. Through reincarnation, they laid claim to such important earlier leaders as Khubilai Khan and Phags-pa Lama. Later, many legendary stories were concocted to support Lamaism and to relate the Mongol khans to the ancient rulers of Tibet, even with the family of Gautama Buddha himself.[18] Thus, the spread of Buddhism in Mongolia was promoted by the notion that the Third Dalai Lama was a reincarnation of the famous Phags-pa Lama, who was so influential two centuries earlier in his association with Khubilai Khan, and by the claim that Altan Khan was the reincarnation of Khubilai Khan.[19]

Mongolian records note a miraculous event that supposedly occurred during Sonam Gyatso's journey from Tibet to Kökönor. According to the story, he assumed the form of the four-armed Bodhisattva Avalokiteśvara (Kuan-yin) when he was confronted by many strange deities, devils, and Shamanistic spirits, including camel-headed, horse-headed, and cat-headed spirits. All of these he converted to Buddhism, and they became protectors of the religion in Mongolia. Sonam Gyatso also obtained a promise from the Mongols to burn all Shamanistic *ongghon* images and honor Lamaist images in their stead, to supply the needs of the lamas, to recite scriptures on certain holy days, and to cease killing horses as an offering upon the death of a man. Mongol chroniclers consider this event a turning point, ending the "dark age" after the reign of Toghon-temür Khan and the collapse of the empire.

Stories such as Sonam Gyatso's assumption of the form of the four-armed figure of Avalokiteśvara were quite readily accepted and devoutly believed by the nomadic Mongols who had imaginative mentalities. The Tibetan lamas were able, in a comparatively short time, to assimilate the old Shamanistic gods of Mongolia, to subordinate them to Lamaist Buddhism, and to usurp the functions of the old traditional religion. Thus, the lamas found it very easy to supplant Shamanism with Buddhism in Mongolia. In a comparatively short period of time, such Shamanistic rituals as animal sacrifices were discontinued and replaced by Buddhist rituals. Soon Buddhist beliefs, such as causality, reincarnation, and compassion, grew firm roots in the minds of the Mongols.

Lamaism, fundamentally the same as other sects of Mahayana Buddhism, is distinguished mainly by outward ritual, religious art, priestly ceremonies, and many tantric or mystic elements, such as the exorcising of evil spirits. Due to these factors, Lamaist Buddhism naturally appealed to the Mongols and brought certain elements into Mongolian culture that enriched it and satisfied the natural feelings of the people. Although Lamaism emphasized respect for life and forbade killing, there was no dominant emphasis on vegetarianism. And although a celibate clergy was characteristic of Mongolian religious life, the monastic life of the lamas did not separate them entirely from their families; there was a continuity of association.

All these factors made the nomads of the Mongolian steppe more readily converted to Tibetan Buddhism than to Chinese Buddhism. After the eviction of the Mongols from rule in China and the decline of their empire, perpetual warfare and tribal feuds continued in the steppe lands of Mongolia, adding an incentive for many people to seek the security and consolation of Buddhism. Shamanism gave neither security for the struggle of life nor consolation in the hour of death, but Buddhism offered both with an emphasis on compassion, hope for a future life, benevolence, peace, and institutions for a more sophisticated culture. Consequently, Lamaism was accepted by both the elite of society and the masses. When Altan Khan accepted Buddhism, it spread rapidly not only in his area of western Mongolia, but became influential also in eastern Mongolia, which was under the rule of Jasaghtu Tümen Khan, and in northern Mongolia among the Khalkha.

When the Mongol nation accepted Tibetan Buddhism for the first time in the Yüan period (1260-1368), a close relationship developed between the rulers of Mongolia and Tibet. This relationship continued to be one of the dominant factors in Mongolian foreign relations for many centuries. Several times in the history of Tibet, the Mongols were a deciding factor in the establishment or support of a Lamaist theocratic type of government. On the first occasion, the Saskya-pa monastic center was established as the preeminent political power in Tibet during the reign of Khubilai Khan (1260-94). Later, at the end of the sixteenth century, Altan Khan sustained the Third Dalai Lama in power. Again, in the seventeenth century, Güüshi Khan of the Khoshod Mongols used his influence to put the Fifth Dalai Lama in power as the definitive ruler in Lhasa. From that time until the Communist takeover (1951), the Dalai Lamas continued to be "God-kings" in Tibet.

Conversely, Tibetan religious rulers had great influence on the social, political, and economic life of Mongolia as well as on religious matters. Under the influence of Lamaism, the idea developed that the *shajin* ("religion") and the *törö* ("state") should not only coexist, but also should be closely identified and support each other. Generally, Mongolian politics and religion were inseparable; the Mongol lay nobility and the high lamas are often referred to as "the twin pillars of feudalism" in traditional Mongolian society. An example of this philosophy may be seen in the case of the Fourth Dalai Lama, Yonten Gyatso (Mong. Yondonjamso), who was regarded as an incarnation or *khubil ghan* born in the house of the grandson of Altan Khan, after the death of the Third Tibetan Dalai Lama, Sonam Gyatso. There are many examples: the Chinggisid lineage or descendants of Chinggis Khan and the line of the Great Lamas were intertwined for centuries.

The reign of the last great khan, Lighdan (1604-34), was a long period of political chaos and civil war among the Mongols because of conflicts with the Chinese and feuds with Mongol tribes that had surrendered to the Manchu. Nevertheless, it was, paradoxically, a period when Lamaism greatly flourished among the Mongols. Under the patronage of Lighdan, the voluminous Kanjur canon of Tibetan scriptures was translated into Mongolian, a monumental accomplishment.

When the Yellow Sect began proselytizing in Mongolia, Tibetan monks of the Red Sect, as they were commonly but imprecisely called, also moved in to expand their influence. Keen competition and conflict between the two sects in the new mission field was a natural result, and the Mongols inevitably became involved on both sides. After Ligdan Khan was defeated by the Manchu, he allied with Choghtu Taiji of the Khalkha or northern Mongols as a defense against the Manchu. Eventually, Lighdan's forces retreated to Kökönor with the objective of entering Tibet as the patrons of the Red Sect, which they hoped to use in their struggle within Mongolia. Lighdan died during the retreat, and the troops of his ally, Choghtu Taiji, were exterminated by Güüshi Khan of the Khoshod Mongols who was struggling to sustain the Yellow Sect against the new threat. Güüshi Khan then entered Tibet, killed the lay rulers of Tibet, who supported the Red Sect, and established the Dalai

A Tibetan-style Mongolian monastery

Lama's line, the Yellow Sect, as the dominant political force. Thus, Güüshi became, as it were, patron khan of the succession of Dalai Lamas.

The first Lamaist temple in Mongolia was the Ta-chao-ssu (Yeke-juu)[20] built in Hohehot, Inner Mongolia, by Altan Khan in the 1570s. The first monastic institution built in northern Mongolia among the Khalkha was Erdeni-yin-juu (1586) at the old site of Karakorum, the capital of the Mongol Empire. From that time until this century, the number of temples continually increased, and the old class of mounted warriors, which earlier dominated Mongolia, gave way to yellow-frocked lamas living in settled institutions. For culture and society, this development was one of the greatest in the history of Mongolia, but it is also often cited as a cause for the decline of the Mongols.

As the Dalai Lama and Panchan Lama became supreme in Tibet, the Jebtsundamba Khutughtu,[21] the so-called Living Buddha, became supreme in Mongolia. Under these preeminent living Buddhas or reincarnations many other high lamas or *khutughtu* (a "blessed one" or "living Buddha," according to the Chinese) proliferated. Thus, in Inner Mongolia, the Jangjiya Khutughtu became the most influential figure in

Lamaism because of the patronage accorded him by the Manchu for political reasons.[22] Among the Oirad Mongols, the Zaya Pandita was the most noted patron and promoter of Lamaism.[23]

Manchu involvement in Mongolian society meant not only patronage for Lamaism, but also control; according to the law of the Ch'ing dynasty, each lama had to be registered. Also, the procedure for becoming a lama was strict, especially for the nobility, because the Ch'ing court desired to maintain Mongol society as a source of troops and to avoid the tendency for ecclesiastical power to flow into the hands of the lay nobility in Mongolia. Because the first and second Jebtsundamba Khutughtus in Urga were especially powerful men and gained great influence, the Ch'ing Emperor Ch'ien-lung controlled the selection of successive incarnations so that they were found among the Tibetans and not among the Mongols. However, this policy was not entirely successful: the independence movement in Mongolia was led by the Eighth Jebtsundamba, a Tibetan incarnation.

The Manchu emperors desired to maintain their source of military recruitment in Mongolia, but at the same time they encouraged Lamaism as a form of socio-political control even though the church drew men out of society.[24] Many common people allowed their sons to become lamas because they believed that it brought great merit and that it was extremely sinful to deter a man from taking priestly vows. Until modern times, Mongolian officials made no attempt to restrict the number of males entering the monasteries. Accordingly, in almost every period, there was an increase in the number of lamas, although it is not possible to give precise statistics.

The fate of most boys who became lamas was set by their parents while they were still infants; on the average, they were placed in monasteries at eight or nine years of age. In Mongolian monasteries, there are traditionally two stages of tonsure in the Buddhist priesthood: the first is *gesel* or acolyte; the second is *gelüng,* which is conferred when a lama takes higher vows to observe a very strict discipline including, at times, a period of mendicancy. Many Lamaist vows are similar to those of medieval Catholic monks. They enjoin, among other things, a code of obedience, celibacy, and renunciation of the temporal world.

Regardless of how much wisdom and learning is gained, unless a lama is an incarnation, or *khubilghan,* he is limited in upward mobility in the Lamaist hierarchy. However, there are generally no class considerations in the selections of incarnations. The common term among the Mongols

A young reincarnated lama (*khubilghan*)

for an incarnate lama is *gege'en,* meaning "enlightened,"which has come into English as "living Buddha." There are a number of rankings and titles for incarnate lamas, *khutughtu* being the highest. Lesser designations include *nom-un khan,* meaning "king of the law;" *chorji,* a Tibetan word with the same meaning; *pandita,* also Tibetan for "the learned one"; and *khambu,* a Tibetan term meaning "teacher." The last term is also used to designate a lama official who serves as a subordinate to a *khubilghan.*

There is no set size for Lamaist monastic institutions; they may house only ten lamas. But, at the peak of Lamaism in the late Ch'ing period, some (such as the Chaghan Dayanchi Temple [Chs. Jui-yin ssu], located among the East Tümed Mongols in Inner Mongolia) housed over ten thousand monks. Judging from observations and comparisons with other temples, the great monastic center of Urga, capital of old Outer Mongolia, must have housed an even greater number.

The monastic institutions of Lamaist Buddhism may be divided into five categories: (1) *küriyen,* a common monastic community of lamas; (2) *süme* (coll. *süm*), or common temple; (3) *khural,* smaller monastery; (4) *keid,* or retreat; and (5) *jisa,* an office or branch office, the function of which, in general, is to look after the economic interests of the temple and which may be located a long distance from the parent *süme* or temple. *Juu* is a general, inclusive term used to refer to *küriyen, süme,* and *keid.* The three most common Mongolian terms for a temple or monastery are *süme, keid,* and *juu.* Institutions that function as *küriyen, süme,* or *keid* are virtually indistinguishable in function or appearance. The famous temple center in Urga has generally been referred to as a *küriyen.* A small temple is ordinarily composed of only a *dughang* or main hall and modest quarters for the lamas. In a large temple center, the main hall, *tsogchin dughang,* has many minor halls and buildings clustered around it.

Monastic centers that are colleges (*tatsang*) or centers of study and learning are divided into four subcolleges: *choir tatsang, judpa tatsang, mampa tatsang,* and *doyingkhor tatsang.* A *choir tatsang* is a college of Buddhist studies, in which the pedagogy is mainly the reading of sutras and open debate. Within this college, there are thirteen degrees, and it may take a lama from sixteen to twenty years to complete the entire course of study. A top graduate from the course of study is awarded the title *ranjam-pa* or *kabchu-pa* in Outer Mongolia (Tibetan: *lharam-pa*), which is very roughly the equivalent to a doctoral degree in the West.

The *judpa tatsang* college specializes in the esoteric forms of Buddhism or Tantrayana, an especially difficult course of study. A graduate is awarded the title of *garim-pa,* "doctor of *tantra.*" The *mam-pa* college is a center of Lamaist medical studies. A candidate learns the various formulas or pharmacopoeia developed over many centuries of pragmatic Buddhist therapeutic techniques, medicine, or use of herbs; many medical texts are included in the Buddhist canon. The degree awarded is the *manran-pa.* In the fourth college, the *doyingkhor,* concentration is upon the study of astrology, mathematics, divination, and Tibetan grammar and rhetoric; the degree awarded is the *chirim-pa.* [25]

Because Lamaism originated in Tibet, the Mongols considered Lhasa to be the fountainhead of their religion, a Mecca-like holy land. The great ideal of the average Mongol was to make, sometime in his life, a pilgrimage to Lhasa. There are instances of people having traveled the entire journey by measuring the distance with their own body in an endless succession of prostrations. One who dies en route, it is believed, is assured of reaching the Buddhist paradise. Elaborate pilgrimages by the Mongol nobility to Tibet cause a great burden on the common people, who ultimately financed the undertakings. It is the desire of virtually every lama to study in one of the three great monastic centers in Lhasa, Tibet, or, falling short of that, to study in Labrang or Kumbum, great monasteries located in Kansu and Kökönor, respectively.

Nationalism, Communism, urbanization, and modernization greatly changed the role of Lamaist Buddhism in Mongolia.

CHRISTIANITY AND ISLAM

The first foreign religion introduced among the Mongols was the Nestorian version of Christianity, which gained influence in the steppe even before Buddhism came into Mongolia from either Tibet or China. Little is known of the Christian life-style of Mongol Nestorians apart from the fact that the religion was criticized as unorthodox by Catholics who had contact with it. [1] Therefore, the discussion of the sect is historical rather than cultural.

Nestorianism, which takes its name from its priest-leader Nestorius, was regarded by the dominant Western churches as a heretical sect of Christianity. Its believers were excommunicated and driven from the Byzantine Empire, and they and their beliefs rapidly spread from Syria to Persia, from where a branch spread to Ch'angan, the famous capital of China during the T'ang dynasty. Another branch spread into Inner Asia among the Uighur Turks and also found acceptance among the Naiman Mongols in the Altai mountain region and among the Kereyid Mongols located in the center of what is now the Mongolian People's Republic.

A legend of a powerful Christian prince, Prestor John,[2] became widespread in Europe during the Middle Ages. Some scholars believe the legend may have been prompted by the fact that Ong Khan, a powerful leader of the Kereyid Mongols, was converted to Nestorian Christianity. Some feel that most of the Naiman and Kereyid tribes were converted, but, judging from references in the *Secret History*, Shamanism continued to be influential,[3] although Nestorianism was widely accepted among these peoples. After Chinggis Khan conquered the two tribes, a number of prominent Mongols became Nestorian Christians; one was Sorkhaghtani,[4] the wife of Tolui, fourth son of Chinggis Khan, and mother of the two famous khans, Möngke and Khubilai. The *Yüan shih* notes that these Mongol emperors built a temple, the *shih-tsu ssu* ("temple of the cross"), for her, which indicates her influence and that of Nestorianism.[5]

In their western campaigns during the reign of Ögödei Khan, the Mongols came in contact with Greek Orthodox and Roman Catholic versions of Christianity. The Mongol appearance on the European scene in this period was interpreted by some as the "scourge of God," a curse upon Western peoples because of their unfaithfulness. On the other hand, because Christendom was deeply involved in the crusades against Islam in the Holy Land, the Mongols were viewed by the papacy as a possible ally, a powerful force in the rear of the Moslems which could help save Christendom.

Missionaries and envoys were sent to make contacts with the Mongol leaders for political reasons and to attempt to convert them. At the Conference of Lyons (1245), Pope Innocent IV instructed the Dominican and Franciscan orders to undertake missions to Asia to teach Christianity and to extend the influence of the church. Subsequently, the Franciscans dispatched John of Plano Carpini and the Dominicans dispatched Anselm as envoys to the Mongol khan. The objective of Anselm's group was to approach Mongolia via Persia, but in the camp of Mongol General Baiju, they made known their intention of converting the khan. The general apparently had some misgivings about the enterprise and refused to receive them. He treated them condescendingly and instructed them to return to Europe and urge the pope to surrender to the Mongols.

Carpini's group took a different route, via Russia, which brought them in contact with the Golden Horde. Here, through the assistance of Prince Batu, grandson of Chinggis Khan, they were able to witness the coronation of Güyüg Khan and then proceed to the Mongol capital, Karakorum. They also were unsuccessful in both their political and religious aims, but they did make some important contacts and observations.[6]

In a new attempt to establish relations, William of Rubruck, a Franciscan, was dispatched as an envoy to Mongolia (1253-56) by Louis IX of France and the pope. He proceeded along the same route as Carpini and received an introduction to Möngke Khan through Prince Batu. Rubruck mentioned, in his travel account, that there were many Nestorian monks active among the Mongols and that, around the imperial palace in Karakorum, many ceremonies were carried out by various and sundry sects, including Nestorians, Buddhists, Moslems, and Christians. He further reported that some of the Mongol nobility were Christian in the broad sense of the word. Some Chinese Catholic scholars claim that Möngke Khan was converted to Christianity,[7] but there is insufficient evidence to confirm this assertion. Later, the two merchant uncles of Marco Polo, Nicolo and Maffeo, were instructed by Khubilai Khan to urge the pope to dispatch capable and scholarly monks to the Mongol Empire. The Polo brothers on a subsequent trip to China were able to bring a letter from Pope Gregory X (1271) but failed to accomplish more, and the Roman Catholics missed an excellent opportunity to gain greater influence in the Mongol Empire.[8]

One year before the death of Khubilai Khan (d. 1294), Pope Nicolas IV dispatched John of Montecorvino, an Italian Franciscan, to Khanbalic (Peking). He was the first Catholic archbishop there, and during his thirty-seven-year mission in the Chinese realm of the Mongol Empire, some six thousand converts were baptized. In 1307, Pope Clement V appointed him, as archbishop of Khanbalic, to supervise all mission activities of Roman Catholicism in the East. Under him were seven bishops, and from that time many missionary priests were dispatched to the Yüan Empire.[9]

The sect of Nestorian Christianity was very active in both the

Mongol Empire period and later during the Yüan dynasty. Its archbishop was in Khanbalic. Khadagh, the high minister of Güyüg Khan,[10] and Burkhan, the high minister of Möngke Khan, were both Nestorian Christians.[11] An-t'ung (Anthony), the prime minister of Khubilai Khan, and Georgius, son-in-law of Khubilai and ruler of the Öngghüd tribe, were also Nestorian Christians.[12] Several empresses, mothers of khans, and other important women were converted to Christianity; however, among the male members of the royal house, apart from Sartagh,[13] son of Prince Batu, it is impossible to determine any who were Christian. Bar-saura, Mongol envoy of Khubilai to Syria, was later appointed patriarch of the Nestorian Church there.[14] The headquarters of Georgius, Nestorian Mongol ruler of the Öngghüd tribe, was located about thirty miles southwest of present-day Batu-kha'alagha (Pailingmiao) in the Ulanchab League, western Inner Mongolia. The site is presently called Olan-süme ("many temples") by the Mongols. Here still stands the cornerstone of an ancient building, marked with an interesting symbolic syncretism—a Christian cross superimposed upon a Buddhist lotus blossom.[15] Even in recent times, the peculiar cross of Nestorianism, worked in bronze, has been found in the desert of the Ordos.

During the Yüan period, some Christians were known by the term *Yeh-li-k'o-wen,* the precise meaning of which is debated, and Christian churches were referred to as *Yeh-li-ko-wen shih-tsu ssu,* "Christian temples of the cross."[16] At the end of Mongol rule in China, Christians in eastern and central Asia were isolated and cut off from the West because of Moslem expansion and the isolationism of the Ming dynasty. However, Christian groups or influence in Mongolia continued much later, according to the study of some Mongolists.[17]

In the late Ming period (1368-1644), when Christians once more established contact with China, they were unable to proceed to Mongolia because of the antagonism between Mongols and Chinese. Also, in the 1570s, the Mongols were rapidly accepting Buddhism, which also forestalled further Christian inroads among the Mongols.

Because of the liberal religious policy of the Mongols, the Russian Orthodox Church in the area occupied by the Golden Horde was given the same favorable consideration and exemptions as were Buddhist and Taoist sects and temples in China. Consequently, during this period, the church was protected and prospered,[18] and some of the Mongol nobility associated with the Golden Horde came in close contact with and were converted to Russian Orthodox Christianity. Even some of the saints canonized in the Russian church were Mongols—for example, Mongol Prince Peter.[19] Although some of the khans of the Golden Horde in Russia were converted to Islam, they did not oppress Christianity. Later, when Hüle'ü, younger brother of Möngke Khan, was campaigning in Persia (1250s), he also pursued a liberal policy and was particularly favorable to Christianity, including Nestorianism. Christians in Persia were severely persecuted prior to the Mongol invasion, but after their arrival, new freedoms were gained for the religion. One reason for the favorable policy was that the wife of Hüle'ü, Tögüs Khatun, was a Nestorian Christian. The policy was continued under Abagha, the succeeding khan, and resulted in a brighter era for Christians in the Il-Khan area of western Asia. As a result, the papacy decided to send envoys and missionaries further east. The liberal policy in the Persian area of the Il-Khanate continued until 1295, when Kazan Khan was converted to Islam and proclaimed it as the state religion with the result that persecution of other religions gradually set in.

From the time of the Mongol retreat from China after the Yüan period until the nineteenth century, while Catholicism disappeared among the Mongols, Nestorian Christianity lingered on for perhaps a century. By the middle of the nineteenth century, Christianity again was being introduced in China and Mongolia; however, this time it was in association with the imperialistic expansion of Europe and therefore was stigmatized. During the empire period, the Mongols had been very tolerant of other religions, but under Lamaist Buddhism in the modern period, they were quite intolerant, and it was very difficult for Christian missionaries to carry on proselyting activities in the social, political, and physical conditions of the steppe areas of Mongolia.

The first modern Catholic establishment in Mongolia was at Hsiwantse, some thirty miles northeast of Kalgan, just north of the Great Wall. Eventually, this community came to be populated entirely by Chinese settlers.[20] At the time of the Boxer Rebellion (1900), Mongols killed a few Christian missionaries[21] as well as some remnants of the Boxers, particularly in the Josotu League,[22] as they fled into Mongolia. There was great pressure by the Manchu court on the Mongol princes for revenue to assist the Ch'ing court in meeting indemnity payments demanded by the West. The levies were no great burden to the Mongols, but difficulty did arise from the fact that in the important Mongol pasture areas of Ulanchab, Yeke-juu, and Alashan,

land was confiscated and given to the Catholic mission as part of the
Boxer settlement in payment for damages incurred by the mission. At
Teng-ko in the Alashan area,[23] the Catholic occupation of a piece of land
created considerable hostility among the Mongols, who resisted
conversion to the church. Chinese Christian converts gradually came in
to cultivate the land. The problem was compounded by economic
troubles that arose between the church, the Chinese, and the Mongols.
Mongol grievances against the mission increased because the church was
so actively involved in settling Chinese farmers in the area. In part as a
result of the dispute, although the Catholics proselyted for more than
one hundred years in western Mongolia, there were not more than a
handful of converts made in the Ordos area of Mongolia. (A natural and
important obstacle to proselyting in Mongolia was the nomadic life-
style of the people).

The most successful area of Catholic mission work was in the
southern Ordos, south of the great Yellow River loop, at Borobalgha-
sun. Father Antoine Mostaert, a famous and brilliant Mongolist, worked
in the area. The history of the mission's activity has been well recorded
by the Scheut, Friar Van Hecken.[24]

Very little has been written of the activities of Protestant Christians
in Mongolia, who also began proselyting before the turn of this century
with very limited success.[25] At the time of the Boxer Rebellion, a
number of missionaries escaped from North China into Inner Mongolia;
they were not mistreated and eventually escaped through Outer
Mongolia to Europe. Protestant efforts, as those of the Catholics, were
retarded by the dominance of Lamaist Buddhism and its resistance to
any heterodox religious influence as well as by the difficulties of
proselyting among a migratory people. The political record of the
Protestants in Mongolia is comparatively good in that they did not gain
great concessions from the Boxer Rebellion and did not become
involved in any activity that was economically detrimental to the
Mongols.[26]

Protestant missionaries gained some influence in Inner Mongolia;
however, there were still very few conversions on any level of society.
The missionaries were comparatively more successful in Chakhar
because the area was not under the domination of princes and nobility,
and the people there were less migratory and more influenced by outside
factors associated with modernization. The missions most active in
Mongolia during the first half of this century were the Swedish

Mongolian Mission; the Scandinavian Alliance Mission (Chicago), later known as The Evangelical Alliance Mission (TEAM); the Canadian Pentecostal Mission; the British Foreign Bible Society; and the mission of the Church of the Brethren (Chs. *Ti-hsiung hui*).

After the 1920s and the People's Revolution in Outer Mongolia, no Christian missionaries were allowed to proselyte north of the Gobi. In Inner Mongolia, Christian proselyting activity ceased with the Japanese occupation in the 1930s. The subsequent collapse of the Japanese, the Chinese civil war, and a new Communist government precluded any further mission activity after the war.

The Bible, translated by both Catholics and Protestants, was published both in the traditional (Uighur) script and in the Toda Mongol (Kalmuck) script. In the late nineteenth century, the British Bible Society undertook a Mongol translation of the scriptures in the Siberian area of Buriyad Mongolia; however, as opposition arose from the Russian Orthodox authorities, they were evicted and the work was completed in London.[27] In the early 1950s, the New Testament was again published in a revised edition in Hong Kong by Protestant missionaries working with native Mongolian specialists.[28]

Islam was introduced into Mongolia after Nestorian Christianity. The contact began even before the Mongol Empire for the *Secret History* relates that when Chinggis Khan was defeated by the Kereyid tribe, he retreated to the Hulun-buir area and met a *sarta'ul* (the term for western Asians), named Asan.[29] Asan, no doubt a Moslem, traveled eastward across Mongolia in his circuit from the western Inner Mongolian Öngghüd area in the west to the area around the Ergüne River to trade in furs with the eastern Mongols. It seems safe to assume that he was not the only Moslem merchant active in Mongolia.

There was Moslem movement from western and Central Asia into Mongolia at an early date, but the evidence of influence is fragmentary, and aside from a few scattered notes of contact, there is no indication of any significant number of Mongol converts to Islam before the spread of the empire.

The campaigns of Chinggis Khan to the west liberated Moslems from the persecution of Buddhists in some areas, while in others Buddhists were liberated from Moslem oppression. In the conquest of Khorezm, although some mosques were damaged or destroyed in battle, Islamic priests were well treated. During Hüle'ü's campaign to western Asia, the Abbas dynasty of Bagdad was destroyed and the last caliph, al-Musta'sim, was imprisoned in a tower, in which he had attempted to hide his treasure, and left to starve. This incident had important political implications later because Berke, younger brother of Batu Khan and convert to Islam, was greatly angered by it. According to the data, Berke was the first of the imperial Chinggisid family to be converted to Islam. Later, in part because of the al-Musta'sim incident, bad feelings developed between the Mongol leaders and their armies and eventually civil war broke out. This was possibly the first clash among the Mongols over a religious problem. Although Berke became a Moslem, he did not declare Islam the state religion of the Kipchak (Golden Horde) Khanate. Later, when Uzbeg ascended the throne (1313), Islam became the state religion.

In Persia, the Mongols followed a liberal policy toward Christianity until Islam became the state religion; then the policy tended toward the persecution of Christians. Chaghadai, noted for his conservative tendencies, resisted Islam; his descendant Chenggechi, baptized a Roman Catholic, maintained a liberal policy toward Christians. In the Chaghadai Khanate of Central Asia, not until Tüglüg-temür ascended the throne (1347) did Islam become the state religion.

The conversion of the Mongol khans and leaders was due in part to the attraction of more sophisticated religions than their traditional Shamanism and in part to political motivations: most of their subjects were Moslems. The old Shamanistic Mongols had changed a great deal in their religious culture and intellectual outlook by the time of Temür (Tamerlane) who reunited the two western khanates of Il-Khan and Chaghadai, proclaimed himself "defender of the faith," and undertook a "holy war." The attitude of the Mongols toward religion in general, and Islam in particular, hastened their conversion and their assimilation to the Turkic stock of western Asia.

The tendency of the Mongol khans of Yüan China, particularly Khubilai, to favor Buddhism forestalled any rapid inroads of Islam in the royal court or among the Mongolian nobility in East Asia. A notable exception was Ananda, grandson of Khubilai, who was stationed in the Tangut area of Kansu and Ninghsia and was converted to Islam along with many of his troops. His conversion helps to explain the early influence and rapid expansion of Islam in this particular part of the China border area. The growth and influence of Islam in China during Mongol rule was largely due to the travel and residence of many Moslem merchants, envoys, military officers, and others. Many Moslem mosques were built in various places in the empire during Mongol rule, including China. Western observers of the religious situation under

Khubilai Khan noted that the khan felt that there were four great prophets—Jesus Christ, Mohammed, Moses, and Shakamuni (Buddha) —and that he honored and revered all of them hoping for the blessings of heaven.[30] Conflicts occurred with a strict and exclusive Islam in the west, but nevertheless, the Mongols generally tended to maintain a liberal policy toward all religions.

After the Mongol retreat from China at the end of the Yüan period (1368), Islamic influence was more marked in the west among the Oirad Mongols than among those farther east. For this reason the powerful Oirad leader, referred to in Mongol records as Batula, is referred to in Chinese materials as Mahmud. During the same period, some Mongol leaders were known by the Moslem name Ishmael. In the middle of the fifteenth century, tributary envoys came to China with Moslem names, indicating a continuing influence of Islam.[31] Other data confirms Islamic influence in Mongolia.

Over a long period of time, the influence of all foreign religions gradually declined in Mongolia, and the special privileges and exemptions they enjoyed under the khans were eventually lost. By the late sixteenth century, with the conversion of the Mongols to Buddhism, Moslems became the number one focus of opposition among the Mongols, which partly explains the small Islamic minority in Mongolia.[32] During the last century, there has been a particularly strong antagonism between the Moslem and Mongol peoples in western Inner Mongolia. The Mongols there were comparatively weak, and there were very few raids on Moslem centers; however, in the late 1800s, on a number of occasions, Moslems attacked some Buddhist Mongol centers (Kumbum and Tingyüanying in Alashan).[33]

At the present time, the only significant groups of Mongol Moslems are located in Alashan, west of the great loop of the Yellow River, and in western Inner Mongolia. Remnant communities of Mongolian Moslems still live in Afghanistan; they are descendants of former Mongol troops that were left there when the empire collapsed, and they still maintain a form of Mongolian language and culture. These groups have been studied by S. Iwamura and H. F. Schurmann.[34]

5
LETTERS AND ARTS

LANGUAGE

The Mongolian language is spoken by almost four million people—a comparatively small population spread over a very large and strategic geopolitical area that includes many groups and regions outside the political boundaries of the Mongolian People's Republic: the Inner Mongols, the Buriyad Mongols, the Mongols of Kökönor and Chinese Turkistan, the Kalmuck Mongols settled on the Volga River, and remnant Mongol communities in Afghanistan.

Mongolian stems from the Altaic language group, and its sentence structure is similar to other Altaic languages, including Turkic, Uighur, Kitan, Jurchen, and Manchu. A fairly large common vocabulary has developed because of the wide migrations and intermingling of these various peoples, all of whom have for centuries lived in Inner Asian pastoral areas. The sentence pattern of all of these languages is subject, object, predicate (like that of Japanese and Korean). A basic meaning is expressed in a root word, and variations of the meaning are expressed by adding suffixes or agglutinative grammatical elements in succession. The relationships of words within a sentence are determined by case particles.

Because speakers of the language occupy a great geographical area, many dialects have developed; however, the divergence of the dialects is not as great as those of other languages, and communication is not severely inhibited. As a standard written form of Mongolian finally developed, it tended to remain static and did not develop progressively to match changes in the spoken language. The divergence between spoken and written Mongolian is, therefore, greater than that found in

many other languages. Still, it is possible, though not easy, to read the
written language in a spoken language manner. Because of the
numerous nationalities included in the area inhabited by the Mongols,
many foreign loanwords have been taken into the language.

Data for studying the ancient, pre-empire, Mongolian language is
almost nonexistent, so knowlege of the languoge of that period is mostly
conjecture. A periodization for the study of the development of the
Mongolian language is generally set as follows: (1) the ancient
language, prior to the writing of the Secret History (1240s); (2) the middle
period, from the writing of the Secret History to the introduction of
Buddhism (1570s) and the translation of Buddhist sutras and the changes
that occurred with their diffusion over Mongolia; (3) the early modern
period from the time of the Manchu-Ch'ing conquest (1644) and the
effects of broad contacts with China, Russia, and Japan and many
modern influences.

Because of the difficulties of studying the ancient language, various
theories have developed. All Mongolian dialects contain elements of the
ancient language, but, according to some scholars, the language
perpetuated among the Mongols of Afghanistan preserves elements lost
by major dialects. Other scholars note that the Barghu (Bargha) and
Dakhur Mongols of the Hulun-buir region of eastern Mongolia have
preserved many linguistic elements of the earliest period. A
characteristic now lost or changed is a labial-dental f or ph before a
vowel. This element disappeared in the period previous to the writing of
the Secret History (1240s). For example, the early word for "ox" or
"cattle" was füker, but by the time of the Secret History, it was
pronounced küker (now üker).[1]

At the beginning of the middle period, when the Secret History was
written, spoken Mongolian possessed a glottal-fricative—an h, kh (q), or
k sound before an initial vowel—but it gradually disappeared after the
writing of the Secret History. "Ten," written as kharban,[2] for example, in
this record, has now become arban. The name of the Mongol prince who
directed the conquest of Persia is written as Hüle'ü in early records, but
the word from which it was taken has now become üle'ü or ülegü ("rich"
or "abundant").[3] This characteristic initial consonant is still preserved
in the Dakhur dialect.

The modern or early modern period of the Mongolian written
language can be considered to stem from the time of Manchu
domination over Mongolia during the late 1600s; the written style was

greatly influenced by the Manchu, and the form that evolved during that period has continued till recent decades. With the widespread acceptance of Buddhism, about the only materials preserved are sutras or classics, hence, there is very little data for a study of the spoken language of the early modern period. The People's Revolution of 1921 brought great changes in writing style and vocabulary. The formal adoption of the Cyrillic system (1946) is no doubt the most revolutionary phenomenon in the entire history of the Mongolian written language.

Mongolian independence and nationalism gave rise to the question, Which among various dialects was to be the standard language? The question was, in fact, moot because of the difficulties of political unification and great distances. The dialect spoken in Ulan Bator is recognized as standard, while linguists count as many as one hundred dialects and subdialects in other areas of Mongolia. Theoretically, there may be very many, but there is no great degree of divergence among them. Unintelligibility in conversation between dialects, from those in Hulun-buir in the far east to Kalmuck in the far west, is not a serious problem. The single exception may be the Dakhur dialect in eastern Inner Mongolia. A Mongol may travel widely through many areas speaking his own dialect and be understood.

The largest and most important dialect is the Khalkha dialect,[4] spoken in the Mongolian People's Republic and in some parts of Inner Mongolia. The dialects of Inner Mongolia are somewhat different from Khalkha, and some scholars count as many as seventy to one hundred of them. In the Mongolian People's Republic, generally speaking, there are two main dialect divisions: east and west. The one spoken in Ulan Bator predominates. In recent decades, the use of the Cyrillic alphabet and a great increase in the availability of published materials have contributed to great advances in the standardization of the language spoken in the MPR.

In the Inner Mongolian area, dialects may be divided into those of the northwest, the east, the southeast, and the southwest. The Chakhar–Shilin-ghol dialect, spoken in the geographic center of Inner Mongolia predominates; it is closely related to the standard Khalkha spoken in Ulan Bator and has tended to become the standard. Under the People's Republic of China, there has been some effort to establish a new standard dialect through a convergence of the language spoken in the Barin (Ba'arin) and Chakhar areas.[5]

Another large language grouping, the Buriyad dialect in the Lake

Baikal region, is divided into two parts, the southeast and the northwest. The southeastern dialect seems to be quite closely related to Khalkha.

Three subgroups of dialects are found among the Oirad or Kalmuck Mongols: the Dörbed dialects, spoken in the northwest region of the Mongolian People's Republic; the Torghud dialects in the area of Sinkiang (Chinese Turkistan); and the Torghud or Kalmuck dialects spoken by Mongols who have settled on the Volga River. The Mongols of Kökönor originally belonged to the Oirad group, but because of historical and geographical influences, they now speak a dialect that seems to be midway between Khalkha and Kalmuck.

An important group of dialects exists among the Dakhur Mongols in the northeast corner of Mongolia. Here, also, there are three distinct divisions: the language spoken in the Hulun-buir region and two subdialects, spoken east and west of the Nonni River. Characteristics of these dialects are the comparative abundance of $kh(q)$ and k used before the initial vowel and the assimilation of many Tungusic words. This dialect is virtually unintelligible to Mongols of other areas. Some scholars have even suggested that the Dakhur are ethnically Tungusic rather than Mongolian.

Finally, there is the section of the Mongolian language family spoken by the Mongols of Afghanistan. In this area, many Mongols have lost their original language and speak some other language; therefore, the number of people who speak Mongolian is considerably fewer than the number of ethnic Mongols actually living in the region. The dialect spoken by Afghan Mongols has a comparatively high incidence of ancient forms and a large number of Turkic and Iranian words, attributable to long isolation from the main body of the Mongols and mixing with other peoples.

It is not possible to discuss in detail the phonetic aspects of the Mongolian language, but it may be noted that it contains seven vowels, *a, e, i, o, u, ö,* and *ü;* and seventeen consonants *n, kh(k), gh(g), b, p, s, sh, t, d, l, m, r, y, j, ch, w,* and *ng*. Over the centuries, three more consonants have been added for expressing foreign words, namely, *f, ts,* and *k,* making a total of seven vowels and twenty consonants. Some studies count ten vowels in the Kalmuck dialects.

An important feature of the Mongolian language is vowel harmony. According to this principle, vowels are divided into three groups: (1) *a, o, u,* known to the Mongols as masculine vowels but now spoken of in the West by some Mongolists and linguists as back vowels; (2) *e, ö,* and *ü,* termed feminine vowels by the Mongols and spoken of in the West as front vowels; and (3) *i,* called a neuter by the Mongols and a middle vowel in the West. The Mongol terminology stems from the fact that the masculine and feminine vowels cannot be mixed in usage, although the *i,* or neuter, may be used with either. According to the principle of vowel harmony, the initial vowel of a word determines which vowels will follow—for example, *akha* ("elder brother") and *eke* ("mother"). A word with two middle vowels is *chichig* ("flower"); a back vowel–neuter combination is *mori* ("horse"), and a front vowel–neuter combination is *eki* ("source" or "origin"). Formerly, there was a notion that the principle of vowel harmony did not necessarily have to be preserved in the case of names. As a matter of fact, the rule does hold, and words that appear to be exceptions are invariably a combination of two words or a hyphenated name, such as Temür-batu. The question of whether vowel harmony is becoming stronger or weaker is disputed by students of the language.

There are variations in the principle of vowel harmony among different dialects. Generally, in the Khalkha (MPR) area, vowel combinations follow four basic patterns: (1) if the initial vowel is *e, i,* or *ü,* it must be followed by an *e;* (2) if the initial vowel is an *a* or *u,* it must be followed by *a;* (3) if the initial vowel is *o,* it must be followed by *o;* and (4) if the intial vowel is an *ö,* it must be followed by *o.* A subcategory of words with a different pattern of vowel harmony exists: if the initial vowel is an *i, e, ö,* or *ü, ü* follows. In a second subcategory, if the initial vowel is an *a, o,* or *u,* it must be followed by *u.*

Like other languages, Mongolian words may contain a single vowel, a double vowel, or a diphthong combination. Diphthongs follow the rules of vowel harmony. In order to insure a double vowel in the written language, at times a *gh* or *g,* which is absent in the spoken language, is inserted between two vowels. For example, the Mongol word for "paper," written as *chaghasu,* is spoken as *chaas.*[6] Omission of the *g* is characteristic of the language in the *Secret History.*

A few simple rules regarding Mongolian consonants may be noted. An *ng* combination will always occur after a vowel, never before. The *b* after a vowel sometimes becomes a *v. P* is rarely found in the Mongolian language; exceptions are invariably foreign loanwords, and in such cases, the labial-dental *f* is always changed into a bilabial *p.* For example, the word "France" in Mongolian is pronounced as "Prans." There are no words native to Mongolian that begin with a retroflexed *r.* Such words as occur are foreign loanwords, and the Mongols insert a suitable vowel preceding the *r*. For example, *Rus* ("Russia") in Mongolian is pronounced Oros.[7] Chinese knowledge of and contact with Russia came first through the Mongols; therefore, the Chinese word for Russia, *E-lo-ssu (E-kuo)*, is derived from Mongolian. Among Mongolian dialects, the elements *ch* and *j* of the southeast are changed and pronounced as a *ts* and *z* in northwestern Mongolia.

Mongolian accent patterns, contrary to common belief, tend to omit an accent on initial vowels. However, the initial vowel must be distinct while the following vowels in a word may be elided or weakened (unless they are a diphthong or double vowel). A single vowel at the end of a word is dropped unless it is to be emphasized.

Basic Mongolian sentence structure is different from English. In contrast to the English phrase, "I study history," the Mongolian phrase is "I history study" or, in earlier times, "history study I." Since Mongolian is an agglutinative language, verbs become complex as word suffixes, case particles, or other grammatical elements are attached to vary the meaning. There are generally three categories of words—nouns, verbs, and particles. Words in English ordinarily considered to be adjectives, adverbs, and pronouns may be considered in Mongolian to be nouns because they take the same case endings as nouns. There are generally considered to be seven cases in Mongolian: nominative, genitive, dative/locative, accusative, ablative, instrumental, and comitative. More complex grammatical constructs use double cases and reflexive; thus, case particles are important to avoid confusion. The noun *ger* is an example (see Table 1).

The following example may explain why adjectives and adverbs are put in a noun category. In the sentence *mori-iin khurdun* ("the speed of a horse"), *mori* means horse, *iin* (or *yin*) is a genitive case ending attached to *mori,* and *khurdun* means "fast" or "swift." The phrase *khurdun mori* is translated as "a fast horse," while the sentence *mori khurdun dabkina* may be translated as "the horse runs fast" (*dabki* meaning "to run"). Still another example would be *khurdun khurdun dabki,* meaning "quickly, quickly run." *Dabki* here is an imperative form, the base for all verbs.

A fairly complex verb conjugation is also characteristic of Mongolian grammar. A verb may be conjugated at considerable length by adding suffixes or grammatical elements one upon the other to the root. The conjugation of the verb *kel* ("to speak"/"to say") is shown in Table 2.

In addition to the flexibility seen in Table 2, the addition of suffixes can change verbs to nouns and nouns to verbs. For example, onto the word *kelelchi*, meaning to "talk together" or "to discuss," may be added the suffix *gen* to form *kelelchigen*, meaning "opinion." Another example, of many that could be given, is *yabu*, "to go," which, by the addition of the suffix *dal*, to form *yabudal*, comes to mean "behavior" or "deed." The root element of the word *nöö* (*negü*), meaning "to move," with the suffix *döl* (*del*), forming *nöödöl* (written form, *negüdel*), comes to mean "migration," as in a nomadic society. *Nöödöl*, which is a noun, may be made into a verb again by adding *öb* to form *nöödölöb* (*negüdellebe*), the past tense of "migrated."

Particles that are not verbs and that cannot take case particles form a third category of grammatical elements which includes exclamations, affirmatives, negatives, some adverbs, and the case particles themselves. Suffixes may be added to some of these elements to form verbs, as for example, the exclamation *aa!* (the English "ah!"), to which the addition of the suffix *ghal* forms the word *aaghal* meaning "to make an *aa!* sound." Needless to say, this is a complex, technical subject that cannot be fully treated here.

Every language has unique characteristics of vocabulary, and a metalinguistic or sociolinguistic study of vocabulary content in particular areas gives important insights into the form of the culture, the level of institutional development, modernization, and so forth. Because of the economic base and the nature of Mongolian nomadic life, there is a striking proliferation of words for such things as grass, so it is possible for Mongols to distinguish between many different types of grass. Also for animals, the most important element of Mongolian life, many different words have been developed to distinguish such factors as the age, sex, color, and the physical parts of an animal. For example, the generic term for horses or a horse herd is *aduu* (or *adughu*); a stallion is *ajiragha;* a mare is *güü* (*gegüü*); a castrated horse is *mori;* a military horse is *aghta;* an unbroken or untrained horse is *elmeg;* a one-year-old horse is *unagha;* a two-year-old horse is *dagha;* a three-year-old mare is *shüdleng* (*shidüleng*); a four-year-old horse is *kijalang*. There are also many different words for the various items of equipment used in raising or maintaining horses.

Another characteristic of the Mongolian language is the occurrence of honorific terms of respect. For example, there are special words to denote the head, arm, and leg of an honored man, such as *terigün, motor, ölmi,* whereas the head, arm, and leg of a common man would simply be

TABLE 1

Written	Spoken	English Translation
ger	ger	yurt (house/home/family)
ger-üd	gerüd	yurts
ger-yin	geriin	of the yurt
ger-tü	gert	at/in the yurt
ger-ig	gerig (geri)	yurt as an object in the sentence
ger-eyer	gereer	by the yurt
ger-eche	gerees	from the yurt
ger-tei	gertai	with the yurt
ger-tei-dür	gerteid	because of having a yurt
ger-tei-yi	gerteig	a person with a yurt, as accusative case
ger-tei-eche	gerteigees	because of having a yurt
ger-eyen	geree(n)*	action having to do with one's own yurt
	geriinkee(n)*	action having to do with something of one's own yurt
ger-tegen	gertee(n)	at/in one's own yurt
ger-tei-ben	gerteigee(n)	with one's own yurt
ger-tei-degen	gerteidee(n)	because of having one's own yurt
ger-eyer-ben	gereeree(n)	with/by one's own yurt
ger-tei-eche-ben	gerteigeesee(n)	while having one's own yurt

*In the reflexive suffix een, the n disappears in the standard dialect of the MPR.

TABLE 2

Written	Spoken	English Translation
kele	kel (kele)	speak or say (imperative)
kelegerei	kelerei	speak (imperative, more polite)
kelegtün	kelegtün	speak (imperative-classical)
kelechi	kelechi	(you) speak
kelene	kelne	will say
kelenü	kelnü	will say?
keleye	kelye	I will say (first person voluntative)
kelesügei	kelsügei	I will say (classical or written)
keletügei	keltügei	he will say (third person voluntative)
kelebe	keleb	said
kelejüküi	keljei	said (more definite)
kelekü	kelek	say (verb noun, present tense)
kelegsen	kelsen	say (verb noun, past tense)
kelejü	kelj	to say—actions occurring—consecutively, i.e., to speak and then perform another action
kelen	kelen	two actions occurring as one or simultaneously, i.e., talking while doing something else
keleged	keleed	one action preceding another
kelebesü	kelbel	if one says (conditional)
kelebechü	kelbech	although one says
kelechi	kelelch	talk together (imperative)
kelegül	kelüül	to cause to say
kelegde	kelegde	to be scolded (passive)
keledeg	keldeg	to say habitually
kelegseger	keleseer	to say while doing something (concessive action)
kelegmegche	kelmegch	immediately upon saying
	kelmen	because or after something was said another action resulted

referred to as *tologhai, ghar,* and *köl,* respectively. The general term for eating is *idekü,* but an honorific verb used for special persons is *jogholakhu.* Conversely, there are many terms showing a humble mood, used as polite forms in speaking to others, such as *khürtekü,* "to eat."

Mongolian has adopted many words from other languages and also has given words to other languages. The Mongolian steppe has been the cradle of many nomadic peoples, and there has been a certain linguistic continuity from ancient to modern times, despite the ethnic changes and migrations that have taken place. For this reason, there are a great many words held in common among the various peoples. The Hsiung-nu were the earliest people, and while there is virtually no material remaining from which to study their language, anthropological studies demonstrate that these people were proto-Mongol or proto-Turkic. Over a period of many hundreds of years, the ancient Hsiung-nu became differentiated into Turks on the one hand and Mongols on the other. No doubt the Turkic and Mongolian languages were even more closely related in ancient times than they are today. Some scholars have explained simplistically that similar words in Turkic and Mongolian are loanwords from Turkic into Mongolian[8] and that cases of similar Mongolian and Manchu words are assumed to be loanwords from Mongolian into Manchu. Actually, much work remains to be done in this area before any reliable generalizations can be made. The words *khaghan* ("emperor"), *temür* ("iron"), *bilig* ("wisdom"), *tenggeri* ("heaven"), and *khutugh* ("blessing") are used commonly by both Mongols and Turks. Similarly, the words *khan* ("emperor"), *ba'atur* ("hero"), *morin* ("horse"), and *erdeni* ("jewel") are used commonly by the Mongols and the Manchu. Examples could be multiplied endlessly, but it appears that Mongolian is more closely related to Turkic than to Manchu.

The writing system of the Kitan, a people who followed the Hsiung-nu but who have entirely disappeared, has not yet been deciphered, but there is no doubt that it belonged to the Altaic language group. An example is the case of a Chinese poem translated into Kitan and found in the *I-chien-chih,*[9] a book compiled by Hung Mai during the Sung period (960-1276). Two lines of this poem may be translated from the Chinese:

The birds dwell in the trees of the lake
a monk knocks on a door in the moonlight.

Hung explains that the Chinese lines are expressed in Kitan as:

moonlight in monk door knocks;
water of tree on crow sits

A direct, literal translation of the Kitan lines into Mongolian fits precisely and makes good sense:

Saran gegegen dur khuwaragh egüden-i toghshiju;
usun-u modun degere keriye saghumui.

At the beginning of the Mongol Empire, most clerical work was done by Uighurs, which helps to explain the abundance of Turkic words that came into Mongolian during this period. Apart from Turkic and other Altaic languages, the languages that influenced Mongols the most are Chinese and Tibetan; Russian terms have come in more recently. Mongolian borrowed most extensively from Chinese during the periods of the empire and the Yüan dynasty. Notable Chinese loanwords are *paitse,* a "tablet" or "credential" given to an official for identification on the imperial highway, and terms for noble ranks such as *gung,* meaning "duke," and *ong,* meaning "prince." During the Ch'ing period, *ong* gave way to *wang,* presently written *van* in the Mongolian People's Republic. In historic materials, there are many loanwords: Chinese *t'ai-tzu* ("crown prince") came into Mongolian as *taishi* in the empire period and later became *taiji;* Chinese *huang-t'ai-tzu* ("royal crown prince") became *khong-taiji* in Mongolian. Some common, everyday words are *chai,* from the Chinese word for "tea"(*ch'a*), and *toor,* the Mongolian word for "peach" from the Chinese *t'ao-erh.*

After Khubilai Khan became a patron of Tibetan Buddhism, many Tibetan words were assimilated into Mongolian, such as *baghshi* ("teacher"), which came originally from the Chinese term *po-shih* ("doctor"). This word went from Chinese into Sanskrit, into Tibetan, and from Tibetan into Mongolian. The term *Karma baghshi* was used in reference to the head of the Karma sect in Tibet. The Mongolian term *Burkhan* comes from the Sanskrit-Tibetan term "Buddha," and the term *tarani,* a "religious formula," also comes from Sanskrit via Tibetan. The most famous Tibetan loanword is *lama,* "a monk."

Many Mongolian personal names and other terms are adopted from

Tibetan and Sanskrit, especially after the latter part of the sixteenth century when, with Altan Khan as its patron, Lamaism rapidly gained popularity in Mongolia. Many monasteries were built, and many Tibetan terms, used in connection with monastic colleges (*tatsang* or *rasang*), were adopted. Other terms that were brought in were *gharagh,* to denote a "period of one week," *gharchigh,* a "catalog," and *labrang,* a "dormitory" or "hostel" for lamas. The extent of Tibetan influence on the Mongols may be judged by the fact that although a Communist system has been established for over a half century in the Mongolian People's Republic, Tibetan names are still very popular among the people.

Two and one-half centuries of Manchu domination over Mongolia greatly influenced the language, and many Manchu terms were taken into Mongolian. The Manchu term *güren* ("state") was adopted by the Mongols as well as *janggi* ("officer" or "official"), *amban* ("official(s) of various ranks"), and *yamen* ("office"), a Chinese term that came into Mongolian through Manchu. The relationship between the Mongolian and Manchu language is close. Common, everyday loanwords with an almost universal usage which have been adopted into Mongolian are *tamki* ("tobacco") and *chiker* ("sugar") used in the MPR (the variant *sheker* is found in eastern Inner Mongolia).

The Mongolian language has had some influence upon Chinese, but little work has been done in this area. A common term used in Peking and North China for a city lane is *hu-t'ung-tzu,* which seems to have been adopted from the Mongolian *ghutumji* ("lane"). The Peking opera term *chieh-mo,* "stage scenery," was adopted from the Mongolian term *chimeg* ("decorations"). In some rural areas of North China, a common slang term for a "specialist" or "expert" of various types is *pa-shih,* from the Mongolian *baghshi* ("teacher"/"master"). A common slang expression in Peking for a "cripple" or "one who limps" is *tao-go-lang,* adopted from the Mongolian word *doghlang* (*dogholang*) having the same meaning.

The most famous example of Mongolian influence on the Tibetan language is the title Dalai Lama; the term *dalai* means "ocean." Another example is that of the famous *erdeni,* which was an official title for the Panchan during the Ch'ing period and is the Mongolian equivalent of the Tibetan term *rinpochi,* meaning "jewel." During the reign of Emperor K'ang-hsi in the seventeenth century, *tiseri* or *tisri* was used in Tibet to designate the "prime minister" under the Dalai Lama. This term came into Tibetan much earlier, during Mongol rule in China, and was originally adopted from the Chinese term *ti-shih* ("teacher of the emperor").

The language of the Mongols of Sinkiang (Chinese Turkistan) has been influenced by borrowed Turkic terms. The Kalmuck Mongols in this area were especially influenced by Turkic and later by the Russian language. Still, because of Lamaism, there continues to be considerable Tibetan influence in the Kalmuck dialect.

Because Mongolia is landbound in the interior of the Eurasian continent and has been isolated from the ocean and from close contact with many developments in modern times, some people assume that the Mongolian language must be very limited in vocabulary and handicapped by a lack of more modern technical terms. Actually, there has been no serious problem in translating technical materials into Mongolian. Even in the 1600s, the voluminous Buddhist canon, the *Kanjur* and the *Tanjur* with their profound philosophy, was readily translated into Mongolian.

In the twentieth century, many new loanwords have come into Mongolian from both Chinese and Russian. Many of the terms entering through Russian originated in other European languages, particularly French. Linguistic geography is seen in the following example: in Inner Mongolia, an automobile is called *ch'i-ch'e,* adopted from the Chinese, whereas in Outer Mongolia the term is *mashin,* taken from the French *machine.* In Inner Mongolia, the common term for gasoline is the Chinese word *ch'i-yü,* although a native term *tosu* is also used. In the MPR, the Russian term *biyentsin,* originally a West European word, was common for a time, but the people of the Mongolian People's Republic are very nationalistic and have often resisted or rejected Russian terms; now, the native word *shitakhun* is used for gasoline. In Inner Mongolia, the Chinese term *yin-hang* is used for bank, while in the MPR *bangki* is common. Although the Mongols have adopted many terms from the Russians and the Chinese, many new native words have been developed for modern concepts, such as *aradchilakhu* ("democracy"), *aju-akhui* ("economics"), *khorishiya* ("a cooperative"). Currently, many changes, which merit continued intensive study, are taking place in the Mongolian language.

Even English has not escaped the influence of the Mongolian language. The common word "horde" is derived from Mongolian *ordo* ("court," "palace," or "great yurt"). The meanings seem unrelated unless one recalls the Golden Horde (*Altan Ordo*) of the Mongolian occupation of Russia. This *ordo,* with many men and animals, was seen by Westerners as a great mass of humanity, a "horde" of the khan. The Mongol term "khan" for an emperor is itself now common in English. A less well-known term is "argali" from the Mongolian *arghali,* a big-horned, wild mountain sheep.

WRITING SYSTEMS

In the transition from ancient to modern times, the Mongolian written language became divorced from the spoken language, and the spoken language itself, because of geography and other factors, evolved into many dialects. It is not far off the mark to consider the early written language as a "Mandarin" or official language of Mongolia.

When Chinggis Khan subdued the Naiman Mongols in 1204, he captured a Uighur scholar named Tatatunggha, a sort of chancellor of Tayang Khan of the Naiman tribe. When he was taken, he was wandering about clinging tightly to the official "golden seal," trying to find his lord in the chaos of battle. Chinggis was very impressed with the man's loyalty and appointed him as one of his personal clerks with the responsibility of looking after the imperial seals. The biography of Tatatunggha in the *Yüan shih* notes: "He was commissioned to teach the crown prince (*t'ai-tzu*) to write the Mongolian language in the Uighur script."[1] This is the first mention of the use of a written language by the Mongols.

In the same record, the biography of another Uighur official, Ha-la-i-ha-ch'ih-pei-lu, notes that at one point the Uighur rebelled against the Kara Kitai (1210s) and in the process killed the latter's envoy. Fearing retaliation, the Uighur envoy resident in Kara Kitai, Ha-la-i-ha-ch'ih-pei-lu (only the Chinese version of his name is known), escaped and fled to the camp of Chinggis Khan. According to the record: "T'ai-tsu (Chinggis) was very happy to see him and immediately appointed him to tutor the imperial princes."[2] This evidence reveals that there were at least two teachers of the Uighur writing system in the Mongolian court. One reason for the involvement of the Uighurs in such a role was an important affinity between the Mongol and Uighur cultures, particularly language. Assimilation by the Mongols in this case was facilitated because the Uighur script was phonetic and quite easily adapted to the Mongolian language.

The general consensus of Western scholars is that the Uighur script was derived from a Sogdian script through the agency of the Nestorian Christians. According to one theory, the Sogdian script was derived from or influenced by the Greek alphabet, other scholars feel that it was an adaptation of the Semitic or Aramaic alphabet. Not only the Mongolian script, but also certain items of vocabulary were influenced indirectly by Greek. According to some scholars, the word *nom,* meaning "book" or "scripture," was derived from the Greek through Sogdian and Uighur to Mongolian. The word *shijir* ("gold") is said to have the same etymology.

The famous medieval traveler, William of Rubruck, sojourning among the Mongols during the thirteenth century, observed that they had adopted the Uighur script and wrote lines vertically down the page but moved from left to right in contrast to Chinese, the dominant language of Asia.[3] This is the earliest observation of a Mongolian writing system by a Westerner. An alternative theory for the origin of the Mongolian script is found in many Mongol records, such as the *Jirüken-ü tolta*[4] and the *Kelen-ü chimeg.*[5] These accounts claim that the Mongolian script was devised by Gungga-jalsan,[6] the Sa-skya (Sakya) Pandita of Tibet, by the command of Kötön "Khan."[7] According to the account, in a dream, the monk saw a man approaching with a pole that had projections from the sides. Influenced by the dream, he invented the Mongolian script, which resembles this shape. Obviously, this story was concocted by the lamas to promote the expansion of Buddhism and to give prestige to the church. While the story is certainly apocryphal, it has been established that the monk, Gungga-jalsan, did reform and improve the Mongol script while he was in the camp of Prince Kötön engaged in the translation of Buddhist sutras from Tibetan into Mongolian (1240s). The same basic Uighur script is still used by many Mongols today, although the form has been somewhat changed over time.

From the reign of Khubilai Khan (1260-94) through the Yüan period (1260-1368), the official Uighur script was differentiated from the later Mongolian alphabet or script developed by Phags-pa.[8] The oldest remaining example of the Uighur-derived script is a stone inscription cut at the command of Chinggis Khan for Yesüngge, son of his brother Khasar, in the year 1225.[9] The second oldest example is another stone inscription, cut for Möngke Khan (1251-59).[10] From the thirteenth century to the seventeenth century, the Mongol script remained essentially the same, but after the seventeenth century, it changed.

The Uighur script of the Mongols has been in use for over seven centuries. In the early 1600s, the Manchu adapted the Uighur to their language with a few changes. Officially, the Manchu maintained this script until the present century, although the number of people who could read or write it was limited. The Uighur people, from whom this script was adopted, abandoned it in the fifteenth century as a result of their conversion to Islam and the growing influence of the Arabic script, which was adapted to the Turkic language.

During the reign of Khubilai Khan, the Mongol Empire was both splitting and expanding. Khubilai felt that such a large empire should have a flexible script capable of expressing all of the various languages within the empire. Accordingly, the work of developing such a script was assigned to his trusted teacher and head of the Saskya-pa sect of Tibetan Buddhism, Phags-pa. When Phags-pa completed the work, he had developed an entirely new script based on Tibetan and Sanskrit. In Yüan times, it was known as the New Mongolian Script (Chs. *Meng-ku hsin-tze*) and was referred to by the Mongols as *dörbeljin üsüg* or "square writing." Details regarding the development are given in the biography of Phags-pa.

When the script was presented to the emperor . . . the alphabet consisted of forty-one symbols and words were formed by linking these symbols together, thus making it possible to write words phonetically. . . . In general, words were formed by transcribing their sound. In the sixth year of Chih-yüan (1269) an imperial decree directed that this script be used throughout the realm.

The imperial decree declared: "written words are used to express language and language is used to record business. This is a common rule from ancient times to the present. Our state arose and expanded forth from the north. Our customs were simple and ancient and we had no time to develop new institutions. When we record matters, we use the Chinese and Uighur script to express the language of our dynasty. The Liao, the Chin, and other northern states before us developed their own writing system. Although our state and culture are developing, we lack a satisfactory system to express our written language. Therefore, Phags-pa, the Teacher of the Realm, was instructed to devise a new Mongol script with which to write and translate all languages in the realm, to facilitate communications and to convey our intentions. From this time on all imperial decrees shall be expressed in the New Mongolian Script and a bilingual copy shall be written in the language of the country concerned."[11]

This report gives some insight into the motivation and intent behind Phags-pa's commission to develop a new script.[12] It is also clear that much of the writing in the Mongolian language was being done with the cumbersome Chinese script,[13] the complex characters being used for their phonetic value rather than for their meaning as in the case of the *Secret History.*

After the new writing system was developed, there were many injunctions, as seen in the *Yüan shih,* to discontinue the use of the old Uighur script. Many people were not accustomed to the new script and continued to rely upon the old one. Finally, after 1368 and the collapse of Mongol rule in China, the Phags-pa script fell into disuse and eventually the old Uighur script became the only form of Mongolian writing in popular use. Some materials, particularly Buddhist texts and some imperial edicts in the Phags-pa script have been preserved. A number of bilingual temple texts with Chinese on one side and the Phags-pa script on the other exist. Most of the above are not actually Mongolian materials, but rather Chinese-language materials expressed in the phonetic Phags-pa script. Nevertheless, these materials are very useful for a study of Chinese phonetics of the Yüan period. There are also some Mongolian materials written in Uighur with headings in the Phags-pa script.[14]

The *Secret History* is the only existing history of a northern nomadic people written by themselves before the seventeenth century, and consequently great attention has been focused on it. Considerable debate has revolved around the question of the original script of this important record: Was it written in the Mongolian language in the Uighur script, the Mongolian language using Chinese characters phonetically, or the Phags-pa script?[15]

When the Communists assumed power in Mongolia, some lamas were still able to read the Phags-pa script; however, among them it was commonly referred to by the Tibetan term *hor-yig* (*hor* being Tibetan for northern nomads or Mongols and *yig* being the term for "words") rather than the colloquial Mongol term *dörbeljin üsüg* ("square writing"). Except for these lamas, no one used it, although it has the advantage of precision in phonetic structure. The complexity of the script worked against its widespread use.

With the introduction of Buddhism into Mongolia, many sutras or texts were translated, and in this process the writing system of the Mongols became more standardized or institutionalized. For this and other reasons, some scholars speak of a Mongolian Renaissance in the seventeenth century; great literary activity accompanied the spread of Buddhism. As a result, innovations were made in the Uighur script, and a secondary script was developed making it possible to be more precise in transcribing Tibetan or Sanskrit words. This script, called Galigh and derived from Tibetan, was used concurrently with the standard, unmodified Uighur script. However, because of its complexities, this script also is now disappearing with the decline of Lamaism in Mongolia.

Zaya Pandita, famous leader of the Oirad Mongols, noted deficiencies in the Uighur script and made certain innovations or reforms in 1648 to improve it. The results of his work—known as *Todo Mongol* or "clear Mongol" because of its greater preciseness—have been preserved, particularly among the Kalmuck Mongols.[16] Zaya Pandita hoped that his script would be accepted throughout the Mongol world. Unfortunately, because of the political breach between the Oirad and other Mongols and because of the geographical distances involved, the script was limited in use to the Oirad. A separate group of Oirad living in the Kökönor region never permanently adopted the *Todo Mongol* script because they were isolated from the main body of their people living on the Volga River. Another rare script that also never gained prominence is the *Soyombo* script, devised by the First Jebtsundamba Khutughktu (1633-1723), especially for use in religious texts.[17]

A notable attempt to reform the Mongol script was made by Agwangdorji, a Buriyad Mongol scholar, just before the Mongolian Revolution (1921); however, he gained little support and the attempt failed. Later in the 1920s, following the Communist revolution and the establishment of the Mongolian People's Republic and with the great rise of nationalism, there was another attempt by a number of Mongolian scholars to reform and standardize the written language. There was a great deal of discussion and activity among Buriyad, Khalkha, and Kalmuck Mongols, including a movement to romanize Mongolian by adopting the Latin alphabet.[18] The pan-Mongol overtones of this movement were not acceptable to the Soviet Union, and due to Soviet influence on Mongol leaders, the movement failed. Another attempt at linguistic unification through a Latin script was limited to Outer Mongolia; but this also failed. Consequently, the three Mongolian areas under Russian domination—the Buriyad, the Khalkha, and the Kalmuck—each gradually developed a new script adapted from the Russian Cyrillic alphabet. The subsequent divergence of the three dialects is reflected in both the written and the spoken language. In 1946, the Cyrillic alphabet was proclaimed the official script of the Mongolian People's Republic, and all formal documents are now printed in it. However, the traditional Uighur script continues to be popular among the people.

For a brief period following the conquest of Inner Mongolia by the Chinese Communists, the MPR, Russian, or Cyrillic script was used. But it was soon discontinued because the Chinese had reservations about Mongolian nationalism and an aversion to the persistence of a pan-Mongol vision. A second attempt was made, but it also failed because of a decision to keep the Inner Mongols culturally separated from the MPR Mongols. In the early 1950s, when the Chinese People's Republic planned, for a brief period, to romanize Chinese in a Latin script, an announcement was made that a new alphabet also would be developed in Inner Mongolia; however, until the present day the traditional Uighur script continues to be used. One of the crimes attributed to Ulanfu[19] when he was purged at the time of the Cultural Revolution (1967) was a pan-Mongol attempt to reform language. In the last two decades, there has been considerable displacement of the Mongolian language by Chinese in education and in other fields.

The adaptation of the Cyrillic script to written Mongolian lacks precision. Of the thirty alphabetical symbols adopted, some serve little useful function, such as the hard and soft signs of Russian and superfluous symbols for *y* and *i* connected with vowels. This script, like that of Phags-pa, was politically imposed upon the Mongols, and it seems questionable how long it would last if conditions changed. There seems to be a strong feeling that the Cyrillic script is an improvement over the old Uighur script; however, some feel that adopting the Latin alphabet would bring Mongolia in closer contact with the world.

LITERATURE

Nomadic literature, like that of other people, began with an oral tradition, an important part of which was poetry and epics that combined history and literature. However, it now seems impossible to find any form of Mongolian literature predating the *Secret History of the Mongols* written in the 1240s. Of the many known literary and historical works, only a few will be discussed here. A broad anthology of selections from the different genre of Mongolian literature has not yet been published in English.

The original name of the famous *Secret History* is *Mongghol-un ni'ucha tobchiyan* (Chs. *Yüan-ch'ao pi-shih*).[1] It is a narrative of the ancestors of Chinggis Khan, the career of the Great Khan, plus the exploits and accomplishments of his son Ögödei Khan. The term "secret" (*ni'ucha*) is misleading for it does not refer to something that is strictly secret, but rather to matters that are sacred, confidential, and not to be popularized. The word *tobchiyan*, found in the title, means "outline," and there is frequent reference in Chinese works of the Yüan period to the *To-pieh-chih-yan*,[2] a Chinese transliteration of the Mongolian term. It seems that each Mongol emperor had a "confidential" or "royal" record[3] patterned after the *Secret History;* however, in the battles and chaos of the fall of the empire and the retreat from China, these records were lost.

Next to the *Secret History,* the greatest Mongolian record is the *Altan tobchi,*[4] which may be freely translated as the "golden chronicle." It is generally believed by Mongolists that it was written in the early part of the seventeenth century.[5] There are many different versions of the text in existence. The version found in the Kharachin Banner of eastern Mongolia, published in Peking, is entitled *Chinggis khaghan-u chidagh;*[6] it has a unique appendix, which contains additional, valuable historical data not found in other texts. A different text with a similar name, known to Western scholars as the *Altan tobchi (nova),*[7] is a collection of Mongolian historical texts edited by a scholarly lama named Lobsangdanjin, who lived during the last part of the seventeenth and the first part of the eighteenth century in the religious centers of Inner Mongolia and Wu-tai-shan, Shansi province. His record contains about 80 percent of the *Secret History* and part of the *Altan tobchi,* plus additional material not found in either of these records. This work tends to confirm that a Mongolian text of the *Secret History* once existed.[8]

A third Monglian classic is commonly referred to, in the Western world, simply by the name of its author, Sagang Sechen, as though it were the title. The text, which has other titles, the best known being *Erdeni-yin tobchi* ("the precious outline or chronicle"),[9] is a mixture of history and legend regarding ancient Mongolia and its relationship with Tibet and India down to the early Ch'ing dynasty (1644-1911). Its author was greatly influenced by Lamaist ideas.

The *Secret History,* the *Altan tobchi,* and the *Erdeni-yin tobchi* all combine legend and history as literature. Virtually all Mongolian literature is characterized by a nomadic and hunting background and imagery. Typical poetic elements of Mongolian literature are illustrated in a selection taken from the seventy-eighth section of the *Secret History*. Kö'elün, mother of Temüjin (Chinggis Khan), rebukes him and his brother.

> You are like slut dogs that bite their own pups after birth
>   or like *khabulan*[10] that blindly crash
>   into the rocks.
> You are like lions that cannot control their anger or like
>   *mangghas*[11] that swallow their food alive and whole.
> You are like gyrfalcons that pounce upon their own shadow or
>   *chulakha*[12] that stealthily swallow their prey without
>   warning.
> You are like male camels that bite the heels of their
>   offspring or wild wolves that attack in a snow storm.
> You are like the *anggir*[13] that eats its own offspring if they
>   do not flee or treacherous wolves that attack those
>   wandering near their lair.
> You are like tigers seeking out their prey singlemindedly and
>   attacking in a flash or like the *barus*[14] rushing about
>   blindly.
> You are destroyers! You have no companions but your own
>   shadows, no whip but your own tails.

In the *Altan tobchi (nova)* poetic passages relate Chinggis Khan's instructions to the heads of army units. He warns of behavior to be avoided and stresses models of ideal behavior to be cultivated.

> Do not destroy the state merely because you are wounded by
>   the thrust of a male antelope's horn.
> Do not abandon your old lord and comrades merely because you
>   are gored by a ram.
> Do not mix with evil company merely because you are gored by
>   the horn of a bull. . . .
> While at home you must be more gentle than the spotted calf.
> On the battle field be more swift and agile than the gyrfalcon.
> When in contact with others you must be more gentle than a
>   small calf, but on a campaign more ferocious than a
>   terrible eagle.
> When in the company of friends be more gentle than a black

calf but when joined in battle be as merciless as the
black falcon.[15]

These passages are characteristic of the literary expressions in basically
historical texts.

Another genre of literature is inseparable from religious texts. Many
beautiful passages of prose and poetry are found in Mongolian
translations of Buddhist sutras. There are also novels, poems, plays, and
stories written on didactic Buddhist themes. Some are translations of
Tibetan literature; others were created by Mongol writers. Because of
the great influence of Lamaism in Mongolia, many of these works are
owned and read by the common people. Some examples are the
biography of Milare-pa, a famous Tibetan ascetic and poet,[16] and the
story of Shiditü Küür, a tale originating in India about a magic corpse.
The tale is not necessarily Buddhist, but exemplifies a body of literature
that flowed into Mongolia along with the sutras. The biography of the
goddess Dara Eke, popular among families throughout Mongolia, was
adopted from the original in a very free style of translation showing
great creativity and amounting virtually to a new piece of literature.

The *Üliger-ün dalai* ("the sea of parables")[17] is a collection of short
stories that is roughly analogous to the fables of Aesop; they are
commonly related by old folks to inculcate good manners among the
children.

> Once upon a time there lived two geese and a frog in a lake. As the water
> disappeared when the lake began to dry up, the two geese decided to
> move elsewhere. Beseeching the two geese the frog said, "My friends, be
> merciful, please take me to a place where there is water." The geese
> replied, "Tell us how we may transport you and we will do so." The frog
> then brought a small stick and explained, "I will grasp the middle of this
> stick with my mouth and each of you hold the two ends in your mouth and
> fly off with me." When the two geese flew through the air as instructed
> by the frog, people looking up exclaimed at the sight, "How wise and
> skillful are these two geese, see how they are able to carry the frog as they
> fly." They repeated this over and over again in great admiration for the
> geese. Finally, the frog could not contain himself and exclaimed, "This
> accomplishment is not due to the wisdom of these two geese, this is my
> idea." When he spoke, he lost hold of the stick and he fell to his death.
> The moral of the story is that men must overcome the compulsion to take
> vain pride in themselves without allowing credit to be given others.

Many heroic stories, such as those of Geser Khan and Jangghar Khan, are popular among the Mongols. Geser Khan is the legendary hero of a tale that originated in Tibet and eventually spread into Mongolia. Interestingly, it is an early tale devoid of Buddhist coloration. There are many different texts and versions of the tale and theories as to its origin. One questionable theory holds that the story stems from a tale about Caesar the Great, which spread to India and thence to Mongolia. During the Yüan period, the lamas promoted the notion that Geser Khan was the incarnation of a Chinese military god, Kuan Yü.[18]

Jangghar Khan, a legendary hero among the Oirad Mongols, plays a particularly important part in the oral tradition of the Kalmuck people living in the region of the Volga River. The stories about him are marked by great imagination and exaggeration. Such tales are not only conditioned by the nomadic environment of the Mongols, but are also strongly tinged with Shamanistic influences. Tales that come into vogue later naturally have a Buddhist coloring.

Many Chinese stories and novels have come into Mongolian by translation, notable examples are *San-kuo yen-i (Romance of the Three Kingdoms)*, *Chin-ku ch'i-kuan (Grotesque Tales Past and Present)*, and the *Hung-lo meng (Dream of the Red Chamber)*. Many Chinese works were translated directly from the Chinese, but most came into Mongolian via a Manchu version.

Another important genre of literature was the translation into Mongolian of many *bensen üliger,* a form of Chinese promptbooks or scripts (Chs. *ku-erh-t'se* or *Ch'ang-pen*) used by itinerant storytellers. Many of these are very free translations, even quite creative adaptations from the Chinese originals. They have long been popular, are generally sung in rhyme, and have served to disperse popular stories of Chinese origin and to influence Mongolian oral literature.[19]

Injannashi, a brilliant novelist and poet of the middle nineteenth century, was a Tümed Mongol who wrote many works, the most famous being *Köke-sudar (The Blue History),* a fictionalized form of Mongolian history. Injannashi's life and work has been ably treated by the Mongolian scholar John G. Hangin.[20]

With the rise of Lamaist Buddhism, Mongolian lamas became literate in the Tibetan language, and some of them wrote plays, Buddhist texts, and historical works, among other things, in Tibetan. The result, in spite of the foreign language, was a new and unique type of Mongolian literature. Indeed, because of the emphasis placed on the liturgical language of Tibetan, these essays or works are often easier for Mongolian lamas to read than items in their own language.[21]

Poetry seems to be more widespread and spontaneous among Mongol nomads than in Western cultures. Mongol poetry is characterized by alliteration and by rhyme, which occurs on the first words of a line rather than the last as is common in Western literature. In another type of poem, rhymes occur at both the beginning and the end of a line. The following is a popular poem in Mongolia.

> Saikhan chasutu chaghan aghulan dur
> Saran-u gerel dusabasu neng chaina
> Saraghul ukhaghantu merged-ün chikin dür
> Sain üge-yi sonosghabasu neng mergejine

> Beautiful/ snow-with/ white/ mountain/ on
> Moon's light/ strike-when/ more/ bright
> Brilliant/ wisdom-with/ wisemen's/ ears/ in
> Good/ word (obj.)/ cause-to-hear-if/ more/ wise

> Beautiful snow-clad mountains
> Are brighter yet when struck by moonbeams
> Wise persons with ears inclined to enlightenment
> Are made wiser yet on hearing good words.

Mongolian literature is particularly rich in epic poems, both long and short, that grew out of the nomadic heritage. Examples are *Dörben Oirad Mongghol-i darughsan tüüji (The Story of the Conquest of Mongolia by the Four Oirad)* and *Chinggis Boghda-yin durasghal-un tügübüri (Collection of the Memorials of Chinggis Khan).*[22] Even the originals of these pronouncements were in poetic form. Oral tradition was more important than written records in early Mongolian history, and there was a marked tendency to draw upon poetic forms as an aid to memorization, recall, and recitation. This characteristic carried over into the written tradition as it developed. One finds then, for example, that over one-third of the famous *Secret History* was set down in some form of poetry. *Törü-yin daghun (Song of the State),* a long recitation that is partly epic, has been frequently recited for generations at official feasts, particularly in such nomadic areas as Shilin-ghol and Ulanchab.

"Reminiscences of Khanbalic,"[23] a popular poem among the Mongols, is found in the *Altan tobchi* and commonly attributed to Toghon-temür Khan. Another poem known for its beauty is "Chinggis Khaghan-ü yeke üchig" ("Great Praises to Chinggis Khan").[24] Its recitation is a prominent part of the ceremonies of the annual festival held at the cult of Chinggis Khan in the Ordos region of Mongolia. Not surprisingly, there are many poems written to extol the greatness of Chinggis Khan, preeminent not only among Mongol heros, but also among world conquerors. Many noteworthy poetic chants and prayers have come from the shamans. They are beautifully expressed and greatly appeal to the people. Some work has been done by specialists to record and preserve these.[25]

A great deal of Mongolian poetry expresses romance as a characteristic of a nomadic heritage, more so than in most East Asian literature, which has been influenced by the Confucian tradition. The fire of martial songs and the expression of strong emotion, both sadness and joy, are additional elements of Mongolian literature.

A vast field of literature, a real product of the people which is only now drawing attention, is the important body of popular oral literature of the Mongols. It is not only rich, but also varies considerably from region to region.[26]

Another genre of Mongolian literature is short tales or anecdotes of an ironic nature intended to make fun of lamas, nobles, or other elites. They are a frequent source of amusement at gatherings of the common people. Their subtle criticism of the Buddhist clergy and princely class of former "feudal" Mongolia attracted the attention of socialist reformers, and Peking approved the publication and wide distribution in the 1950s of a collection of these anecdotes by Shaghdur, one of those rare, creative genius types from the Ba'arin Banner of Inner Mongolia who earned the sobriquet of "mad" (*suliyatu*).

A deeply set pessimism that long has been characteristic of the Mongolian nomad's view of life and of man's role in the world is evident in the literature. Juvaini, the medieval Persian historian who served the Mongol khans in Persia, recorded that during a visit to Karakorum in the reign of Möngke (1251-59), he heard the following lament:

> O thou, whose lifetime is certainly but a few days,
> What is even the empire of the whole world for a few
>   days?
> Enjoy the share of life as best thou canst
> For the few days will pass away.[27]

A pessimistic mood is found in a ritualistic folk song, "Tenggeri-yin salkin" of the Jerim and Josotu leagues of eastern Inner Mongolia. It is customarily sung at a banquet held on the occasion of the semiannual, shamanistic *oboo* festival. The Mongolian transliteration and an approximate translation follow.

Tenggeri-yin salkin tegshi ügei,
Törögsen beye chinü möngke ügei.
Möngke-yin arashiyan-ig kene chinü uughujubui?
Mönöken chilüge-degen jirghachighaya bidan-a.
Oghtorghui-yin salkin oghosor ügei,
Orchilang-un kümün chinü möngke ügei.
Möngke-yin arashiyan-ig kene chinü uughujubui?
Mönöken chilüge degen jirghachighaya bidan-a.[28]

The winds of the heaven are not balanced.
The body that comes of birth is not eternal.
Who has drunk the holy water of immortality?
In this limited moment let us enjoy ourselves.

The winds of heaven have no place on which one may
      grasp.
The men of this world are not eternal.
Who has drunk the holy water of immorality?
In this limited moment let us enjoy ourselves.

Shamanism and Buddhism seem only to have confirmed this spontaneous feeling born of what was often a bleak struggle for life in the steppe.

The last few decades have been a period of great change, but contemporary literature will not be discussed here except to note that after the revolution (1924), the main trend of literary development has been characterized as socialist-realism. Anyone pursuing a study of this era should give attention to the writing of the literary giant D. Natsaghdorj (1906-37), known mainly for his poetry, and to the brilliant work of B. Rinchin and Ts. Damdinsuren (Ch. Damdinsürüng), who not only made contributions in the literary field but also promoted a revival of traditional culture.[29]

EDUCATION

There is naturally great concern in Mongolia for the practical affairs of life and the continuing struggle for existence. Nevertheless, a learned person, a capable teacher in a temple school, or some other scholarly man of letters, such as Injannashi,[1] has long held great prestige. The prestige of learning extends far back into Mongolian history. The traditional attitude can be seen in the words of Chinggis Khan: "It is better to prove oneself with learning than to be concerned about outward appearances."[2] A close relationship between "virtue" and "learning" is seen in the Mongol term *erdem,* which, strictly speaking, has three meanings: (1) "learning" or "knowledge," (2) "virtue," and (3) "expertise" or "technique." In the latter connotation, a talented painter, a skillful wrestler, a capable horseman or bowman are all considered to have a type of virtue as well as aptitude (*erdem*).

Because the average father in a nomadic family is often traveling, hunting, and herding, he plays a less prominent role in the early informal education of his children than his equivalent in a sedentary society. Mongolian mothers often relate to their children on the children's own level, and baby talk is common. Fathers, however, are more inclined to relate to a child as an adult, though not so much as in more formal Asian societies. Fathers, and also older adults who come to visit, frequently relate to children by teasing, telling little stories, or discussing the child's activities, his pets, and playmates.

Because of the wide dispersal of Mongolian families, there has been little or no involvement of strangers or distant relatives in the education and training of children, except for the lama who occasionally visits the yurt and counsels the children. Traditionally, most families would have a particular lama come to their home periodically to read Buddhist scripture and also to informally advise and teach the children and encourage the parents themselves along certain lines in raising their family. All members of the family present give careful attention to the words of the lama who is considered to be a learned man and may often function as a personal counselor. (It is necessary to make a distinction here between a person who is highly regarded for his learning and experience and one who is politically influential, as many lamas have been. For example, an *emchi* or *otochi*—both medical men, the latter more traditional and the former more prominent in modern times—are given great honor, but this is due to their particular experience; they have seldom exerted influence in the area of politics and social affairs apart from their role of healing the ill. The average Mongol would not come to them with problems of a personal nature—apart from problems of illness, they have had little influence in society.)

There seems to be a relatively wide range among Mongol adults regarding a willingness to make a frank admission of ignorance or of having made a mistake. Some persons are very reluctant to admit they are wrong while others quite readily do so. There seems to be no particularly common cultural pattern in this area among the nomads; in this respect, they differ from Chinese who generally feel shame in admitting ignorance.

Although learning seems to be clearly more prestigious than wealth, paradoxically, in the average nomadic home, there are few books and those that exist are almost never openly displayed to gain prestige. At the same time, if a man is known to have books, it is assumed that he uses them and this fact gives him status. Actually, it is common for nomadic families who have books to put them in a Lamaist temple with a son or friend to protect them. One avoids carrying them around.

The high regard for learning has been slow to penetrate the attitudes and outlook of young children. When they are sent off to a banner school for education, their response is negative: education is to be avoided if possible. However, older folks take delight in sending the younger people off to handle the herds while they remain at home to read some book or scripture. Throughout the history of education in Mongolia, from the use of tutors around the turn of this century until the inception of what might be considered public schools sponsored by government officials, teachers have almost always been men.

All ancient Mongolian records indicate that, prior to the period of Chinggis Khan, education among the Mongols was limited to informal education based on oral transmission. A change came with the establishment of the empire and adoption of the Uighur script, which gave rise to written records and the development of a more formal system of tutoring. The first notable tutor in the Mongol court was Tatatunggha, the Uighur originator of the Mongolian script who taught the sons of Chinggis Khan.[3] A teacher roughly contemporary with Tatatunggha, also a Uighur, was Ha-la-i-ha-ch'ih-pei-lu (only the Chinese version of his name is known).[4] As was common throughout Asia, sons of the aristocracy were tutored along with the sons of the emperor.

Chinggis Khan and Shigi-khutughu, his supreme judge, ordered that certain records be kept and consequently an institution for scribes (*bichigchi*)[5] was developed within the *keshig* or royal guard. These highly skilled men were trained through an apprenticeship system.

Mongolian schoolchildren (1930s)

With the establishment of the Yüan dynasty under Khubilai Khan and the adoption of Chinese forms of administration, it became necessary for the Mongols to develop a more systematic way of learning Chinese language and culture in order to more effectively rule China. Khubilai set forth his own son Jinggim, the crown prince, as a model in a new training system. He appointed a number of scholars as his personal tutors, the most famous of which was probably the Tibetan, Phags-pa.[6] Khubilai gave each of them special titles; thus, the scholar Yao Shu, was appointed *T'ai-tzu t'ai-fu* ("exalted tutor of the crown prince")[7] and the scholar Hsü Heng was entitled *T'ai-tzu t'ai-pao* ("exalted guardian of the crown prince").[8] Unfortunately, this careful training came to naught because the crown prince died even before his father.

In imitation of the Chinese, Khubilai established a sort of imperial academy (*kuo-tzu-hsüeh*), within which there was a special department known as the Mongolian Academy (*Meng-ku kuo-tzu-hsüeh*).[9] The imperial instructions were that the great Chinese record *Tzu-chih t'ung-chien* (a voluminous survey of Chinese history) should be taught in outline at the academy in the Mongolian language.[10] Mongol leaders were concerned with training their young men to understand China as well as the successes and failures of previous dynasties with problems they had faced.

Khubilai appointed a famous Chinese scholar, Hsü Heng, as head of the imperial academy (*kuo-tzu chi-chiu*), with the responsibility of instructing the sons of the Mongolian elite.[11] Hsu taught not only the Chinese classics and Confucian philosophy, but also customary Chinese protocol, ritual, and decorum. The training included some ancient Chinese arts (archery was one and it had declined to a mere ceremonial form, which must have seemed quite ludicrous to the Mongols). The work and methods of Hsü Heng are an indication of the great efforts made to Sinicize Mongol leaders. There is also evidence of a conscious Mongolian effort to adopt Chinese methods in preparing Mongols to rule China. Hsü took special pains to bring young Chinese and young Mongol students together in the training and educational process in order that they could become better acquainted and be more integrated in their preparation.

Chinese advisers successfully urged the Mongol khans to adopt the Chinese civil-service examination system (*k'e-chü*). However, a revised examination system was developed, according to which different categories or *pang* were set up. Mongols and *se-mu* (mostly non-Mongol Central Asians) were given an examination separate from northern Chinese (*han-jen*) and southern Chinese (*nan-jen*).[12] The distinction was necessitated by the fact that although Mongols and *se-mu* could use Chinese, their standards were below that of native Chinese. Special, less exacting examinations were given to these persons. It is fair to assume that there were special schools or training centers for Mongols and *se-mu* preparing for the examinations.

The Mongolian rulers of China established a supreme scholarly institution, whose role is described in the *Yüan shih:* "The duties of the Mongolian *Han-lin* Academy (*Meng-ku han-lin yüan*) were to make official translations of foreign languages, to write the documents which would bear the Imperial seal according to the New Mongolian Script [Phags-pa script] with a secondary copy in the language of the foreign country concerned."[13] In addition to this institution, there was a Bureau of Arts and Literature, *I-wen chien,* which was responsible for translating into Mongolian all Confucian classics or commentaries and revisions pertaining thereto.[14] From such references, it may be seen that many men were trained both in the Mongolian language and in the foreign languages with which the Mongols were concerned. No doubt, there was some institutionalized means of training such individuals.

After Khubilai promoted the use of the Phags-pa Mongol script as the official script of the dynasty, official schools called *meng-ku hsüeh* were set up throughout China, and also in Korea, with the specific responsibility of training people to be able to handle the language problems of the realm.[15] There are numerous decrees in the Yüan records constraining the people to use the new Phags-pa Mongolian script. However, as previously noted, it was virtually impossible for the new script to compete with the more generally used Uighur script.

It is unclear from the records what type of educational system or institutions existed among the Mongols during the period from the collapse of the Yüan in 1368 to the reintroduction of Tibetan Buddhism in the late sixteenth century, but, as Buddhism grew in importance, the study of the Mongolian language and the translation of Tibetan texts flourished. From that time until Communist rule, temples were important centers of educational activity. A new, ecclesiastical class of lamas served as teachers in a system of formal education. Lamaist academies or schools modeled after those in Tibet were developed, and, eventually, the study of the Tibetan language gained greater prestige among the Mongols than the study of the Mongolian language. Tibetan lamas were active initially in Mongolia, but by early modern times they were rarely found. Mongolia had developed its own learned class and Lamaist luminaries. Mongols desired to travel to Tibet, the fountainhead of Lamaist Buddhism, and higher status was ascribed to those who had studied in Tibetan centers. In the temple centers of Mongolia, it was not uncommon for the lamas to teach the children of the families in the vicinity of the temple as well as the monks. These schools are analogous to the medieval *terakoya* or temple schools in Japan. Thus, the great temple center of Urga (Ulan Bator) in Khalkha became not only an ecclesiastical center but also a center of scholarly activity and education. When the thirteenth Dalai Lama visited there at the turn of the century, some of his followers were hard pressed to equal the standards of religious debate of Mongolian scholars.

During the Ch'ing period, the *yamen* or office of the *jasagh* head of each Mongolian banner also became a center of educational activity. *Yamen* centers and temple schools operated concurrently. The common people sent their children to the temple centers, and the nobility and officials sent their children to the *yamen* to be trained as future officials. Here they first learned to write, in time were advanced to clerks (*bichigchi*), and eventually were given greater responsibilities as banner officials. In some banners, special schools were developed in the vicinity of, but apart from, the *yamen* with virtually the same course of study and mode of operation.

Before the revolution and the beginning of real modernization, education in Mongolian schools, as in most places in the world where learning is a serious matter, emphasized reading and writing; almost no social activities or sports were sponsored by the school. Still, there was considerable "horseplay," generally in the form of wrestling. This was not criticized by the teachers and was found even in the temple schools among the young lamas when they were not involved in prayer masses or some other supervised activity.

Wealthier Mongolian families gradually adopted the practice of hiring private tutors to educate their children and perhaps those of their neighbors. The tutors taught reading and writing in the Mongolian script, simple Buddhist stories, and various texts distributed by the Manchu court. In the Chakhar, Hulun-buir, and Dakhur regions, the Manchu language was taught because those areas were often governed by Manchu *ambans*. Some Mongols of the present older generation are still proficient in the Manchu language from their early study.

As Chinese influence increased, the content of the studies became more influenced by Confucianism, and students studied such texts as the *Hsiao ching* (Chinese classic on filial piety), the Analects, and other Confucian classics.[16] The language of instruction emphasized in these schools differed; Mongolian and Manchu were more important in the *jasagh* schools, and Tibetan was more important in the temple schools. It was not uncommon in Mongolia for educated men to have some facility in at least two and sometimes three or four languages. The teachers were virtually all Mongols; Chinese tutors were introduced only in the late 1800s. While some Mongols scholars became very proficient in the Tibetan language, the common lamas and students seldom reached a very high level of literacy, but merely learned to memorize and chant Tibetan sutras.

During the nineteenth century, Mongols in Inner Mongolia, closer to the Great Wall, began to place increasingly greater value on learning the Chinese language; consequently, in many cases, Chinese teachers were hired as tutors in Mongol communities or in wealthy homes. This trend distressed the Manchu rulers at first, but not the Mongolian princes. A number of decrees by Manchu emperors forbade the study of

Chinese by the Mongols in accordance with Manchu policy, which was to maintain a separation of the two peoples.[17]

A similar development occurred among the Buriyad Mongols in Siberia and the Kalmuck Mongols on the Volga. As contact increased because of Russian expansion, these Mongols began to learn the Russian language and to travel to Russian centers for education. However, due to their great attachment to Buddhism, they learned the Russian language but did not rapidly assimilate Russian culture.

With the impact of Western imperialism on China, progressive Chinese leaders began to see the importance of developing modern learning, of adopting Western technology, and of making reforms in the traditional education system. A similar response came later in Mongolia which was more isolated. However, after the Boxer Rebellion in 1900, progressive leaders in Inner Mongolia became increasingly more interested in modern education. The most notable example was Prince Günsangnorbu[18] of the Kharachin Banner in eastern Mongolia, who was a man of scholarly inclination with a high level of proficiency in Chinese and Manchu as well as Mongolian. He traveled to Peking where he came in contact with Chinese scholars, learned to paint Chinese pictures, and compose Chinese poetry. He was an excellent calligrapher.

Güngsangnorbu perceived the decline of the Ch'ing Empire and was also aware of the rapid development of modern institutions in Japan following the Meiji restoration. Prince Gung, as he was called, visited Japan during her rise to power, just before the Russo-Japanese War (1904-5), to make a firsthand examination of the factors involved. He was very impressed with the stress on education and realized that it was imperative to prepare young Mongols to meet the modern world. He established three schools within his own banner and dispatched a dozen young Mongols, both male and female, to Japan to be educated in medicine, veterinary science, agriculture, military science, and education especially adapted to girls. The three schools established by Güngsangnorbu were the Ch'ung-cheng, an ordinary school that later became a teacher training institution; the Shou-cheng, a military academy; and the Yü-cheng, a girls' school. Establishing schools to educate even the children of commoners was in itself a great innovation in Mongolia; it was even more progressive to set up a girls' school. Schools for girls and coeducation were greatly opposed by the princes of other Mongol banners as well as conservative Manchu officials in

Peking. Prince Gung was supported in this work by his wife, a Manchu princess, and financed the schools from his own budget—even arranging to have special teachers come from Japan and from South China, both well known by that time for the excellent quality of their teachers. Some of the teachers who worked for Günsangnorbu later became well known; for example, Ch'ien Meng-t'sai, who in the 1930s became curator of the Palace Museum in Peking; Professor Torii Ryuzō, who became a famous Japanese archaeologist; and Kawahara Misako, who gained distinction as a pioneer educator and later married the president of the Bank of Japan.[19]

Güngsangnorbu maintained these schools, often with great difficulty, until the 1911 Republican Revolution. He was then called to Peking and became head of the Ministry of Mongolian-Tibetan affairs (*Meng-Tsang yüan*). After he moved to Peking, the girls' school and the military academy were discontinued, but he was able to persuade the Mongolian representatives in the new parliament of the Peking government to sponsor the establishment of a new educational institution in Peking, which became the well-known *Meng-Tsang hsüeh-hsiao* (Mongolian Tibetan Academy, founded in 1913).[20] At first, only preparatory classes were held, but with the addition of higher-level students, the school was raised to the rank of a college (1919). Specialized classes began to be developed in 1923 in politics, economics, agriculture, animal husbandry, and teacher training. About this time, nationalistic sentiment was becoming more apparent in both Outer Mongolia and Inner Mongolia as well as in China (the Kuomintang movement). Young Mongol students, including activists, began to participate in nationalist movements, and, once again, Güngsangnorbu became the object of attack and persecution, this time, ironically, as a symbol of the "feudalistic" princes. Nevertheless, it should be stressed that the work of Güngsangnorbu bore great fruit in preparing young Mongols as future leaders in Mongolia.

Because of the new situation in China under the republic and because of new ideas among the Mongols themselves, many young men began to go to Peking for education either in the Mongolian Tibetan Academy or in other private schools and universities in China. Soon it became a matter of prestige and status among Mongolian families to send a son to a good school. At the same time, primary schools sponsored by Mongol officials, began to appear, particularly in the Tümed and Kharachin banners—those Mongol areas near the Great Wall. After 1925 and the establishment of the Inner Mongolian People's Revolutionary Party, students from the Mongolian Tibetan Academy in Peking began to go to Ulan Bator and Moscow for special training. About the same time, an increased number of students began to go to Japan.

The rise of education sparked the printing of books in the Mongolian language. A pioneer in this work was Temgetü,[21] who set up a press in Peking. Earlier, there had been some Mongolian printing activity in Harbin promoted by the Russians and some printing in the Mongolian language was done in the Buriyad area of Siberia. Just after Temgetü began his work, modern printing began in Urga (Ulan Bator).[22]

Following the establishment of the Mongolian People's Republic in 1924, education was greatly promoted not merely as a privilege for the lamas or aristocracy, but also as a right and even duty of the common people. Public schools were established, and soon after this, in 1929, a Mongolian normal school (*Meng-ch'i shih-fan hsüeh-hsiao*) was established in Mukden (Sheng-yang), in eastern Mongolia, largely due to the efforts of Merse (Kuo Tao-fu),[23] an ardent Mongol nationalist who gained a concession from the Chinese warlord Chang Hsüeh-liang.[24] Many young Mongols who received their early education in this institution later became important leaders in Inner Mongolia.

After the Manchurian Incident (1931) and the Japanese occupation of Mongolia, the percentage of persons receiving an education rose from about 4 percent to 40 percent; a large part of the credit for this increase is due to those who received their education earlier in Merse's school. During the 1930s and 1940s, under the government of Prince Demchügdüngrüb (De Wang), great efforts were made to develop universal education.[25] However, the efforts did not extend to the Mongolian banners of Alashan and Ordos in far western Mongolia, which were beyond the scope of the governent.[26]

Presently, hundreds of schools and even a number of universities are operating in all parts of Mongolia. In Ulan Bator, the Academy of Sciences has been very energetic in pioneering and promoting studies in virtually every field of academic research at all levels of education.[27]

ART AND RELICS

Perhaps because of the vastness of Mongolia's steppes and the loneliness of the plains, the Mongols, yielding to an impulse to compensate for these conditions, tend to use bold motifs and bright colors. There is a lavish use of ornamentation, and usually motifs have a symbolic meaning associated with the nature of the article it adorns. Ornamentation and symbolism are much in evidence in the summer and autumn when Mongols customarily convene large festivals. A great blue tent (*chachir*) with a clear white design imposed on the blue background is set up. The pavilionlike tent is supported by red columns and has a golden spirelike decoration on the top. The clothing of the festival participants is bright and colorful. The Lamaist temples, which dot the landscape of Mongolia, are also very artistic. They are invariably white walled with red trimmings and often contain brilliant works of art. The yurt itself, in which the nomads dwell, has white felt walls and a beautiful red framework upon which the felt is placed. Because of the nomadic culture of life, there have been no great accomplishments in architecture in Mongolia, except for the temples.

Of prime importance in the historical development of Mongolian art was the introduction of Tibetan Buddhism as a vehicle in the adoption of many Lamaistic elements in the fine arts. Among the various artistic objects to be found in many temples are flags, mandalas, utensils, statues or images, and wall paintings.[1] Unfortunately, many of these works are products of anonymous artists, and the identities of outstanding men have been lost. An exception is the first incarnation of the Jebtsundamba who was, in his own right, a sculptor and architect who lived at the end of the seventeenth and the beginning of the eighteenth century.

Mongolian art is solidly painted, unlike much Zen-inspired, monochromatic painting of Japan or China, which makes creative use of unpainted, blank background and of line and space. Mongolian color contrasts are striking, their designs are bold, and there is none of the shading or indefiniteness found in many other forms of Asian painting.

One important theme common to traditional Mongolian artwork is the great compassion of the Buddha. Another common theme depicts the ferociousness of protecting deities or the guardians of hell of Lamaist Buddhism. Some Mongolian art images express a certain ambivalence, a duality combining both ferociousness and compassion. Doghor, a Buddha with a white umbrella, shows a complexity of feelings. Much creative art is found in the decorative work on Mongolian Buddhist wood-block prints, where great wealth was expended to decorate texts in gold, coral, and other colors.

Among the common people, art is everywhere present in the

Examples of customary Mongolian designs found on the felt trappings of yurt dwellings such as rugs, cushions, or doors; commonly done in brown thread on white felt background.

A traditional Mongolian painting portraying symbolic Buddhist elements of friendship, harmony, and cooperation.

decoration of knives, belt attachments, amulets, shoes, saddles, and many other personal items. Some of the most beautiful of these objects of art are done in steel and finely engraved with gold. Silver is the most common precious metal for decorations. The people of the Darighangha are noted for their talent in this field. One form of art unique to the Mongols is the creative designs found in the brands of their animals, each family has its own distinctive design. Unique designs are also found on horse saddles, harnesses, weapons, and in yurts, on the lintels of doors and upon the rugs and drapes used within tue yurt. Beautiful needlework on pillows, chaps, boots, stockings, and other clothing is common. Especially prized are sets of chessmen carved of wood or bone. Many techniques are employed in traditional folk art; the most common are carving, engraving, needlework, embroidery, knitting, wicker-work, appliqué, and filigree work. Old and new motifs are appliquéd on birchbark, paper, and other materials.[2] Craftsmen working in gold, silver, iron, wood, leather, and textiles, among other materials, tend to individual creativity rather than copying and standard production. The hereditary transmission of craftsmanship is still strong. In recent years, interest in the applied arts has increased in the MPR.

In ancient times, a great deal of notable artwork was associated with the images and paraphernalia of Shamanism; however, when Buddhism came in, this art was lost. Some persistent influence of Shamanistic art, still visible in the mirror or chest pieces of the shamans, indicates that the earlier art was very beautiful.

In the Mongolian People's Republic, many stone statues have been discovered that reportedly predate the Turkic T'u-chüeh period (500-750s). There is still hope that archaeologists may bring forth interesting finds from the numerous ruins of old city centers that have not yet been excavated. In eastern Mongolia, many pagodas, buildings, and other remnants of the Kitan-Liao period (907-1125) are still extant. The tombs of the Kitan royalty, found in Ba'arin Banner, are a most notable treasure.[3] Unfortunately, they have been plundered, but valuable remains or data are still to be retrieved. Occasionally, in the Ordos region, workers uncover brass belt buckles with artistic designs[4] from the Hsiung-nu, the earliest nomadic period. At Noyan-ula, another important dig for Hsiung-nu artifacts, a number of samples of ancient fabrics have been found with very early and interesting nomadic designs still visible.[5]

At Olan-süme, old capital of the Öngghüd tribe in the region of present-day Batu-kha'alagha-yin süme (Pailingmiao), numerous ruins dating from the thirteenth century await intensive study. A great deal of porcelain has been found here, but most of it has been crushed into small pieces and it may be impossible to analyze its artistic qualities.[6] Similarly, at the site of Khubilai Khan's old capital of Shangtu, also of the thirteenth century, in the region of present-day Juu-naiman süme, art items of porcelain, bronze, and stone are occasionally unearthed.[7]

During the Yüan period, under the patronage of the Mongols, there was a great deal of artistic production, particularly in temples and images. An outstanding artist of this period was A-ni-ko, a Nepalese specialist in Buddhist images who worked with the Mongols.[8] Many works executed by Liu Yüan,[9] a disciple of A-ni-ko, still remain, and a number of valuable items in the Taoist temple of Tung-yüeh miao in Peking are said to be his work. Unfortunately, the ancient capital of the Mongol Empire, Karakorum, was entirely destroyed in later civil wars, and the only remains are the foundations plus one or two relics, such as a stone tortoise from which the inscription has disappeared.[10] Fortunately, many of the stones from Karakorum were taken to build the famous old temple center of Erdeni-yin-juu, which still exists as a model of Mongolian art and architecture from the seventeenth century.

MUSIC, DANCE, AND DRAMA

Music, like virtually every other phase of Mongolian culture, is greatly influenced by the nomadic life of the people. Musical instruments and orchestras have existed since early times, but continual migrations have made it very difficult to bring together and maintain enough talent to have well-institutionalized orchestras or instrumental groups. It has been almost impossible for anyone other than a prince or a noble family to organize an orchestra.[1] There were elaborate entertainment groups and orchestras during the empire period and at the Mongol court, but their roots are lost in the dim beginnings of Inner Asian history. On the only specific date mentioned in the *Secret History* (the sixteenth day of the fourth lunar month),[2] the occasion of a great celebration, the people gathered together and danced—no doubt to music.

For the most part, therefore, solo instrumentation has dominated Mongolian music. Chinese records note that the *hu-ch'in* (Mongolian *khuur*), a stringed instrument common among the northern nomadic peoples, was imported into China from the steppes. The *p'i-pa*, a stringed instrument plucked by hand, also originated among the nomads and then spread to China. On the other hand, Chinese records also note the exportation of many musical instruments to the northern steppes, indicating a mutual cultural exchange with the nomads. As a consequence of this exchange, a number of instruments came to be used in common by both the Chinese and the steppe peoples. Mongolians have also adopted many musical compositions from China over the centuries, but in so doing have introduced changes or variations. Naturally, there are numerous native compositions.[3]

The most common instrument among the Mongols is the *mori-yin khuur,* which is about three feet long with a small box at the base and a long neck fitted with horsehair strings; it is played with a bow to produce a quite low, bass sound.

It is common on occasions of feasting and festivities to assemble an orchestra of stringed instruments to accompany vocalists. Formal pieces are often rendered by a vocal soloist who alternates with a chorus. If the program is not performed by a combined orchestra, soloist, and chorus, a vocal soloist is accompanied by the *mori-yin khuur* or by a person, who, without an instrument, emits a low bass sound that functions as an accompaniment and is called a *chor.* Mongols also enjoy an instrumental solo. In contrast to Chinese music, which is generally restricted to melody, Mongolian music uses harmony in a duet, which seems to be a natural result of a nomadic environment in which instruments are few and difficult to transport.

Spontaneous singing has long been characteristic of Mongolian society. The woman of the house, quite unlike Chinese women, will frequently sing to entertain guests. Also, young people commonly sing, hum, or whistle as they gallop over the steppe on horseback. There are many folk songs, which may be divided into four categories: (1) songs about nature and the countryside; (2) songs expressing joy, lamentation, or other strong feelings; (3) songs or chants of popular folk heros and their exploits; and (4) songs of romance and love.

The song-poem of D. Natsaghdorj is typical of the first category.[4] A very old popular song common both north and south of the Gobi was "Sheregün Khangghai" ("the cool Khangghai mountains"), a melancholy tune idealizing the beauty of this famous range. *"Köörkii"* *(kögörökei),* meaning "lovably tender," is a love song that originated in Chakhar and spread throughout Inner Mongolia. Such songs are frowned upon by the Chinese Communist Party as bourgeois decadence.

An old folk song popular in the late 1800s that still lingers in the minds of older Inner Mongolian adults is *"Seng-wang-yin daghan"* ("The Song of Prince Senggerinchin"),[5] which praises the exploits of the great Mongol general who supported the Manchu-Ch'ing when they were hard pressed by the great T'ai-p'ing Rebellion (1850-64) spreading from South China. This song was particularly popular in Chakhar and eastern Mongolia where Senggerinchin recruited his troops. While lauding the conscription, martial acts, and heroic exploits against the *ch'ang-mao* ("long hair ones"—meaning rebels), the song shows a singular lack of nationalism. The novelist Injannashi criticized the general for fighting Chinese battles rather than using his troops to promote Mongolian interests.[6]

One of the most popular old folk songs, arising in Inner Mongolia in the first decade of this century when Mongolia was troubled by Manchu and Chinese officials, was about the famous hero Toghtokhu Taiji.[7] One can see in it a rising Mongol national consciousness, but the content is mainly about the *ba'atur* ("hero"), the brave deeds of the nobleman Toghtokhu against treacherous and corrupt Chinese officials.

The revolution in Outer Mongolia (1921) and the establishment of the Mongolian People's Republic (1924) were important influences on the music of Inner Mongolia, which was forced to remain within the Chinese sphere in spite of its greater population and larger territory. A very popular song with a fast, catchy tune, but rather nonsensical content, was "Yanjuar" ("Cigarette"). Pipes had been traditional, but cigarettes became symbols of change and of life in a revolutionary era. This song was sung particularly in Ulanchab, Shilin-ghol, and Hulun-buir, regions adjacent to Khalkha where the song arose.

In the 1930s, a rapid rise of nationalistic songs in Inner Mongolia was concurrent with political activity and the movement for autonomy. One outstanding song was "Arban tümen" ("The Hundred Thousand"), popularly referred to as the "Chinggis Khan Marching Song." Its origin is unknown, but there is a common, though mistaken, notion that it comes from the old days of the empire. The song, rather heroic and militant in tone and reminiscent of ancient imperial glory, was informally adopted by the Köke-khota (Hohehot) regime and later the Kalgan Mongolian government as a sort of national anthem to be sung on special occasions.

A similar song, current in the 1930s and 1940s, was the "Köke tugh" ("Blue Banner"). It seems to have been an adaptation of "Red Flag," a revolutionary song from the neighboring Mongolian People's Republic, and it was frequently sung by Mongolian troops and the more radically inclined youth.

Many modern, Russian-influenced songs swept into the Mongolian People's Republic and then into Inner Mongolia after the collapse of Japan's expansion in northeastern Asia. Currently, the Chinese Communists have adopted old, popular Mongol music, but have rather skillfully adapted its content so that it praises Chairman Mao Tse-tung and the People's Liberation Army.

Another categorization of Mongolian musical compositions differentiates "old" and "new" forms; the old form is much longer and more formal. Newer compositions are faster in rhythm, lighter in spirit, and much less formal. Because of the great geographical expanse of Mongolia, there are many variations.[8] The general consensus among Mongols seems to be that Khalkha songs are the most appealing. More recent modern music is subject to foreign, mainly Russian, influence.

The music and ritual of the Mongolian emperors of China is treated in the Monograph on Ritual and Music in the *Yüan shih*. It is recorded that in the early years of his reign, Chinggis Khan (T'ai-tsu, 1206-27) accepted the advice of his Tangut adviser, Kao Chih-yüeh, and adopted into his court ritual the music of the Tangut (Hsi-Hsia).[9] Later, during the reign of Ögödei Khan (1238), a descendant of Confucius in the fiftieth generation, Hung Yüan-tso, reported to the khan that the court music of the former Jurchen-Chin dynasty was being scattered and lost and that it should be preserved. The khan agreed and appointed him to take charge of the enterprise and to establish a center for the dynasty's music and ritual at Tung-p'ing in present-day Shantung province.[10] On the advice of certain Chinese advisers and in order to preserve the court music (*ya-yüeh*) of the Southern Sung dynasty that he had earlier defeated, Khubilai gathered the musicians and performers of this school or tradition at Khanbalic (1282).[11]

The Yüan dynastic history also discusses various musical instruments used at court at the time. Included were several non-Chinese instruments. One, an "instrument of flourishing sounds" (*hsing-lung-sheng*), was a wind organ with ninety pipes and a bellows played by several men, which was given to the Mongol khan as a tribute by western Asian Moslems around 1260. A second instrument, identified as a "wooden peacock"(*mu-k'ung-ch'üeh*), was decorated with peacock feathers that were actuated when the instrument was played. A third instrument, a stringed guitar or *p'i-pa*-like item, was identified as an *huo-pu-ssu.* The *hu-chin,* a two-stringed instrument with a long neck decorated on the end with a carved wooden dragon head, was played with a horsehair bow. This can be identified as the modern *mori-yin khuur* of the Mongols.[12]

The orchestras described in the history include a liturgical group (*shuo-fa-tuei,* referring to its involvement in the preaching of the Law of the Buddha), whose function was to play the "music of the golden lettered sutra of Tibet (Hsi Fan)."[13]

Mongolian court music, thus, was a cosmopolitan mixture that included Mongolian, Chinese, western Asian, Tangut-Tibetan, and some Jurchen elements.

The Mongols have various forms of dance (all referred to as *büjig*), including folk dancing and social dancing involving males and females dancing together or separately, accompanied by instruments. In modern times, there was very little folk dancing among the Mongols until it was recently revived in the Mongolian People's Republic. An exception to the decline of traditional folk dances among most Mongol tribes is found among the Torghud, a branch of the Oirad or Kalmuck Mongols, who have many dances, the most famous being a popular chopstick dance. Many of these Torghud dances have been perpetuated for hundreds of years, while others seem to have been stimulated by contact with Turkic peoples.

The medieval observer Rubruck noted that "when it is a big feast they are holding, they all clap their hands and also dance to the sound of the instrument, the men before the master and the women before the mistress."[14]

The earliest Chinese reference to Mongolian dance is found in a discussion in the Monograph on Ritual and Music of the *Yüan shih* regarding activities carried out in the ancestral temple of the Mongol khans at Khanbalic (Peking). The record is detailed, but it is unclear whether the dance and music were Mongolian, Chinese, or a mixture of the two. Much of the ritual carried out in the temple involved both Mongolian shamans and Chinese participants, so one may speculate that the dance and music in question were also a combination of the two cultural traditions.[15]

The observances in the ancestral temple were commissioned by Khubilai Khan, and in 1275, a special military ritual dance was inaugurated that reviewed the glorious exploits of his forefathers from

Chinggis to Möngke Khan. The first stage depicted the defeat of the Kereyid Ong Khan. The second stage was the crushing of the Tangut (Hsi-Hsia), followed by a portrayal of the conquest of the Jurchen-Chin. The fourth stage was the occupation of the "western lands" (West Asia and Europe) and the pacification of Honan (the region south of the Yellow River). The fifth stage of the dance pageant was the conquest of western Ssuchuan and the pacification of the old Thai state of Nanchao. A sixth stage depicted the subduing of Korea and Vietnam.[16]

There is no evidence of any form of dramatic productions being presented in Mongolian society prior to or during the early empire period. It is difficult to develop institutionalized drama in a nomadic society. There must have been some form of drama in the great capital of Karakorum, but there is no record of any. However, with the consolidation of the empire, contact with foreign peoples, and the establishment of brilliant courts, notably Khanbalic (now Peking), the situation changed.

An important form of entertainment, particularly for Mongolian nobility during the Yüan dynasty, was the *ch'ü* or Yüan drama, which was developed by vulgarizing earlier Chinese forms and substituting many Mongolian words and phrases. It was designed for the pleasure of the Mongol elite who took great delight in viewing the theatrical productions. Later during the Manchu period, the forms evolved to become known as Peking opera. The term *shi* (Chs. *hsi*) came into the Mongolian language with the specific meaning of Peking opera. Mongolian influence continues in various forms, and, until recently, for example, a common item of terminology associated with Peking opera was the term *ch'ieh-mo,* which originally had no meaning in Chinese but which was taken from the Mongol word *chimeg* and refers to the scenery used in the drama. The Chinese use of the term is quite close to the original, but the Mongol word meant more specifically makeup, costumes, and stage hangings.

It is not possible to reconstruct the development of drama in Mongolia, but we know from old Mongol word lists or dictionaries that, even before contact with and influence from China, there was a form of drama referred to as *jüjüge.* While its origin is unknown, this theatrical form was apparently different from Chinese-influenced Peking opera. *Jüjüge* was a form of play in a broad sense in that it had a number of subcategories. One school or tradition was derived from Tibet, imported by the lamas, and consisted mainly of didactic or religious plays, commonly presented in the monasteries on special occasions by the lamas. Although these forms existed among the nomads, the limitations on them were severe and their full development was retarded until the modern period when various new forms of the theatrical arts began to come in or to be revived.

Separate and distinct from the religious plays classified in premodern times as *jüjüge* was a strictly religious theatrical form known as *cham*, originally a Tibetan word. The Mongols consider it a religious ceremony, but it takes the form of a play. *Cham* is actually a type of ritualistic dance-drama referred to in the West as "devil dance" (coming from the Chinese *t'iao kuei*).[17]

In Mongolia, *cham*, from the Tibetan word *'cham*, is a general term for Buddhist religious dance-dramas. There have been many kinds of *cham* performed in the great monasteries for centuries. In earlier days, in the Kharachin Right Banner and in the great monasteries at Dolonor, for instance, there were many different kinds of *cham* performed each year. The *cham* combines dance with music and the recital of Buddhist scriptures. The most popular *cham*, the one performed in the sixth month of the lunar calendar, commemorates the victory over the Tibetan king, Lang-dharma, who oppressed Buddhism in the tenth century and restored the Shamanistic Bon religion of Tibet. Eventually, the king, according to Tibetan history, was assassinated by a Buddhist monk.

The *cham* makes no attempt at historical accuracy. It relates, in a dramatic form of dance, that in the beginning there was peace and the people enjoyed life under the teachings of Buddhism; then the devils appeared and destroyed this peace. It was discovered by a great lama, Lobon-dayin, that the evil had been caused by an agent of Lang-dharma. Consequently, he invited the spiritual protectors of the Buddhist law to come down and defeat the evil spirits led by Chorjil, the king of hell. During the battle, in the drama, the evil spirits are encircled, and the protector of the law, masked as a deer, thrusts his horns into the encircled evil spirits and kills them, thus restoring peace again.[18]

The music and the recital of scripture during the *cham* presentation greatly appeal to the Mongols, but its symbolic presentation is not limited to the memory of a victory against an evil king. It is also a prayer that all evil spirits in the contemporary world will be defeated by the forces of heaven and that peace will be forever established in the human world.

After Urga became a settled community, Chinese plays were introduced there and later elsewhere. Subsequently, during the latter part of the Ch'ing period,[19] there were injunctions from the Ch'ing court in Peking forbidding the introduction of Chinese plays in Mongol areas. The ostensible reason was to protect the morality of the Mongols; however, the real reason seems to have been to restrict the introduction of Chinese influence into Mongolia, to keep the two peoples separate, and to perpetuate the ignorance of the Mongols. However, there was a strong countertendency in that the Mongol princes, who were required to present themselves annually or semiannually at court in Peking or Jehol, came into contact with Chinese opera and drama there. Their interest in these events naturally grew and soon, as the princes returned to their homes, they were introduced in various areas in Mongolia.

Mongols were not greatly attracted to Chinese *hsi* or operas. They attended out of curiosity, but they did not develop a strong interest. A notable development of Chinese-style drama in Inner Mongolia came only around the turn of this centry; examples are found in the Kharachin and Alashan areas. In both instances, the forms were introduced by the nobility and the common people were constrained to come to see the plays and to participate. Thus, one stream of drama developed with the introduction of Buddhism while a separate school developed concurrently with the growth of Chinese influence. Both forms of drama were popular until the Communist revolution.

The modern theater, opera, and other forms of dramatic production have had a remarkably flourishing development in the Mongolian People's Republic since its independence.[20] In Inner Mongolia, during the 1930s and 1940s during the Japanese occupation, modern forms of theater and drama were introduced in parts of eastern and western Mongolia through schools and troops of young people. These had some propagandistic content and were often characterized by nationalistic political sentiments. They have been continued by the Chinese Communists with the same objective of manipulating the sentiments of the people. Most notable are the theatrical and musical groups known as *ulaan-möchi* (Chs. *wu-lan mu-ch'i*), which tour the countryside entertaining the people.

6

THE SOCIO-POLITICAL STRUCTURE IN HISTORICAL PERSPECTIVE

THE CLAN-LINEAGE SYSTEM

The traditional Mongolian social system was based on kinship. The stem or nuclear family is the primary social unit, and the nomadic encampment is the secondary social unit. A third key unit is the common descent group or clan-lineage, usually referred to as *obogh*. As the number of clans increased, subdivisions called *yasun*, "sublineages," were developed. Naturally, clan, lineage, or sublineage shared the characteristics of a common blood relationship.

The ancient Mongolian tribal (*aimagh*) system was almost certainly patrilineal and has continued to be so. Even the few clans that seemed to have matrilineal tendencies attempted to trace their lineage to a legendary male ancestor. According to the genealogy of Chinggis Khan, found in the opening words of the *Secret History*, "By the mandate of heaven, Börte-chino'a, with his wife Gho'a-maral, crossed the Tenggis Sea [legendary] and came to the Burkhan mountain at the head waters of the Onon river, at which place Bata-chaghan was given birth."[1] Börte-chino'a and Gho'a-maral were the common legendary ancestors of Chinggis Khan and his people. The actual meaning of these names is uncertain because of problems arising from the phonetic reconstruction of the *Secret History* from Chinese characters. *Chino'a (chino)* means "wolf" and *Börte* may be an earlier form of *bordo*, which means "spotted"; the compound therefore may mean "spotted wolf." *Maral* means a "doe" or "female deer," but it is not certain whether the additive prefix should be *gho'a* ("beautiful") or *khu'a* or *khu'ai* ("yellowish white"). The *Secret History* was not translated into Chinese until the Ming period (1368-1644). Long after it was originally written,[2] the phrase was translated: "Originally, the ancestors of the Yüan people were a gray wolf and a yellowish-white deer. From the mating of these two a man was given birth named Bata-chaghan."[3] Many people interpreted this text to mean that the original ancestors of the Mongol people were animals. However, this seems to be a rather prejudiced interpretation of Chinese scholars, and it is very probable that these are not actually animals, but people bearing animal names. But, from the names, it may be deduced that the male was from a lineage with a wolf as family or clan emblem (totem) and the female from a lineage with a deer emblem. It was customary for kinship groups to feel a mystical relationship with such emblems or ritualistic mascots.

The *Secret History* contains a long and elaborate genealogy of Chinggis Khan traced through the paternal line, carefully identifying paternal ancestors, noting clearly which person was given birth by which couple, and also identifying the clan-lineage from which wives were taken in exogamous marriages. The manner in which maternal lines are treated indicates that women had important status in the system. In this genealogy, the *Secret History* notes that the great-grandson in the twelfth generation of Börte-chino'a was Dobun-mergen. After his death, his wife, Alan-gho'a, gave birth to three sons as the result of being impregnated "by a divine light penetrating from the yurt door."[4] Chinggis was a direct descendant of one of these three sons. Alan-gho'a may be a maternal ancestor of Chinggis Khan, and there is interjected into the genealogy an element of divine birth. At the same time, the genealogy is linked to a paternal line, which probably would not have been given unless it was felt to be of some importance.

There are strong centrifugal tendencies in nomadic society, including a common pattern of clan-lineages splitting into groups. The *Secret History* records that Du'a-sokhor, the older brother of Dobun-mergen, had four sons and that these sons split from the lineage, establishing a separate group known as the Dörben lineage.[5] The record also notes that the two sons born of Dobun-mergen and his wife Alan-gho'a became the progenitors of two separate lineages: Belgünütei was the founder of the Belgünüd lineage, and Büngünütei became the founder of the Bügünüd lineage. Also, the three sons born of Alan-gho'a after the death of her husband each founded separate lineages; thus Bukhu-khatagi gave rise to the Khatagin lineage; Bukhatu-salji gave rise to the Salji'ud lineage; and Botonchar was the founder of the famous Borjigin (singular form) or Borjigid (plural form) lineage.[6]

Traditionally, every Mongolian kinship group, as seen in these cases, had a male ancestor as a focal point of veneration. Ancestors were collectively spoken of as *de'edüs,* meaning "the ones above," or *ebüges,* meaning "forefathers." As a clan-lineage splits into groups, a new group may be called a *yasun* (sublineage), but over a period of time it evolves into an *obogh* (lineage).

The Borjigid clan-lineage, from which Chinggis Khan descended, split into a number of lineages including Nayagin, Barulas, Buda'ad, Adargin, Ulu'ud, Taichi'ud, Khongkhutan, Arulas, and Jürkin among others. In time, lineages that separated from the Borjigid ceased to be recognized as Borjigid. Some of these collateral lineages are extremely difficult or impossible to identify, and only the lineage of Chinggis Khan's father, Yesügei, the Kiyan or Kiyad sublineage,[7] retained its identification as a Borjigid group until the present time. All Mongol aristocratic families descended from Yesügei identify themselves as Borjigid, with the exception of those aristocratic kinship groups in the Ordos region of western Mongolia who identify themselves as Kiyad.

Because genealogy was a strong oral tradition among the people, the forming of confederations by lineage affiliations was greatly facilitated because groups were easily identified and knew their relationship. Needless to say, there were unrelated clan elements included in these confederations resulting in the formation of a tribe (*aimagh*), the members of which did not all trace their genealogy to a common ancestor. While raiding a neighboring lineage, Botonchar captured a pregnant woman, who gave birth to a boy; because he was the seed of an outside group, he was named Jajiradai and became the founder of the Jadaran lineage.[8] Later, this same woman gave birth to a son by Botonchar and, because she was a captive, the son was named Ba'aridei and he became founder of the Ba'arin (Bagharin) lineage.[9]

Clan confederations were complex and frequently included, besides those of the main trunk or genealogical line, lineages drawn into a close relationship through marriage. Exogamous marriage is an important characteristic of Mongol kinship groups. Marriage alliances or an exchange of marriage partners bilaterally between lineage *A* and lineage *B* could occur; however, this was not an exclusive matter, and kinship group *A* might also contract marriage alliances with other groups. In earlier periods, marriages with women of other clans who were captured during wars were not uncommon. But clearly endogamous marriages within a lineage were strictly forbidden. Many marriage alliances are recorded in the *Secret History,* among them those between the Borjigid and other lineages. Examples include Alan-gho'a, a member of the Khorilar lineage,[10] who married into the Borjigid lineage, and young Chinggis Khan, who was taken by his father, Yesügei, to the kinship group of his mother, the Olkhünüd, a sublineage of the Onggirad, for the purpose of finding a wife. The *Secret History* tells the story:

> While Yesügei was traveling, he met Tei Sechen of the Onggirad lineage, who said "*Khuda* Yesügei, where are you going?" and Yesügei replied, 'I am going to visit the maternal uncle of my son, the people of Oklhünüd, to find a girl for a wife." Tei Sechen then said, "Yesügei *khuda,* . . . we, the Onggirads, from ancient times have given close attention to the sons of our daughters and the beauty of our girls. We do not struggle with others for grazing fields, but we endeavor to have beautiful appearing daughters sit in the high-wheeled carts of your khan's family, to [let our daughters] ride in the carts pulled by the black camels and be seated with the *khatuns* [aristocratic wives].[11]

In this conversation, Tei Sechen used the term *khuda* in reference to the father of Chinggis Khan; this term is used only where there has been a previous marriage relationship between the clans. Tei Sechen also said implicitly in the conversation that their daughters were bred to ride the high-wheeled carts of the khans and to sit on special seats as their wives. This seems to confirm the existence of a marriage relationship over an extended period of time between the Borjigid and the Onggirad clans. This pattern continued for more than a century, at least until the end of the Yüan dynasty, for the Yüan history records that daughters of the Mongol imperial house were married out to the Onggirad.[12] Thus, there was apparently a long tradition of both matri- and patrilineal marriage exchange between these two clan-lineages.

The term *naghachu* ("maternal uncle") is found frequently in a number of the records, and it is obvious that this was an important role in the social system. Some have interpreted this importance as evidence of an earlier matrilineal system; however, there is little evidence to support such a conclusion. Moreover, it is now known, as a result of research on other societies, that the mother's brother played a role that was beneficial, in a number of ways, to his sister's son in a patrilineal society. He gave moral support and even practical assistance in times of need.

Before the rise of Chinggis Khan (1206), each kinship group had a chief, and his election or elevation to a leadership position depended upon his status within the clan or lineage. Because the system was patrilineal, succession of rule from father to son was most common, although the widow often served as regent until the son was confirmed. The genealogies in the *Secret History,* indicate that the writer was recording precedents to be followed as well as preserving genealogy. He also may have been creating or preserving a mythology regarding the ancestry of the khans.

In the twelfth century, titles given to lineage heads or clan chiefs usually followed a stereotyped form such as: *mergen,* meaning "an excellent archer," a term that later came to mean "a wise man"; *ba'atur,* meaning "brave" or "hero"; *sechen,* meaning "wise or virtuous"; *noyan,* meaning "noble" or "official"; and *beki,* a title of aristocrats or their daughters.[13] *Beki* or *begi* also meant an "honored shaman" and seems to have been derived from a time in which the head of a tribe was also the leading shaman within his tribe. A passage in the *Secret History* indicates the status and honor accorded a shaman in the role of a *beki.* Conferring rank upon his most meritorious followers, Chinggis Khan said: "Usun *Ebügen* (old man), you are a descendant of the oldest son of the Ba'arin and according to our custom *beki* are greatly honored. Usun, 'old man,' you will now be a *beki,* and as such you shall dress in a white gown, be mounted on a white horse and shall be seated on the honored seat among the people to determine which is the auspicious or ominous year or month and a time to be honored by the people."[14]

The head of a Mongolian clan-lineage held supreme authority before modern times, especially when his position also included religious functions. The main function of a lineage head were: (1) to maintain order in his group and preserve or protect their grazing fields and hunting grounds; (2) to coordinate large-scale hunting activity and long-distance migrations; (3) to take charge of battle campaigns; (4) to decide whether his group would join a confederation or break from such a union; (5) to take the lead in performing religious ceremonies and important rituals; and (6) to arbitrate disputes and confer punishments or rewards.

Most primitive or premodern societies were, in the sociologists' terms, "sacred" rather than "secular" societies—that is, religious practices permeated all the society's activities. Thus, the most important function in Mongolian society was the worship of *Tenggeri* ("heaven") and the *de'edüs* ("ancestors"). It was both an honor and a duty to worship the ancestors of one's lineage, and anyone excluded from this activity was, in effect, an outcast. Two instances in the *Secret History* are apropos. In the first case, the senior wife of Botonchar, founder of the famous Borjigid clan, gave birth to Khabichi-ba'atur and a secondary wife gave birth to a son named Je'üredei. While Botonchar was alive, he treated all his sons equally and allowed them all to participate in the ceremony of *jügeli* (a Shamanistic ceremony in which meat is attached on top of a pole as an offering to *Tenggeri*). However, after the death of the father, the son by the senior wife, Khabichi-ba'atur, did not recognize the junior son, Je'üredei, as a full brother; he forbade him to participate in the *jügeli* ceremony and drove him from the group. Later, the exiled son became the founder of the Je'üreyid lineage.[15] The exclusion from the primary kinship group was based upon bilateral reckoning—both sons had equal rights to inclusion within the lineage according to patrilineal reckoning.

Another example from the *Secret History* illustrates the importance of the worship of ancestors and the relationship between this function and formal kinship group membership.

> In the spring of that year, the *khatun* ["wives"] of Ambaghai Khan, Orbai and Sokhatai, prepared burnt offerings at the place for offerings to the ancestors. Kö'elün Üjen [the mother of Chinggis Khan] came late and, because they purposely did not wait for her, she declared, "Does this mean that because [my husband] Yesügei Ba'atur has died, my sons now will never reach maturity? Why did you purposely not wait until I arrived to distribute the meat of the offering to the ancestors [to be eaten by those present]?" There upon Orbai and Sokhatai replied, "You have no right to be invited . . . , but because Ambaghai Khan has died, [you] Kö'elün dare to speak out in such a manner. The settlement shall be thus: when the camp moves [you] both mother and children shall remain."[16]

The following day camp was broken, the whole tribe moved on; but Kö'elün Üjin and her sons were forced to remain behind. Even many people who previously followed her husband moved on with the rest.

Upon the death of the father, the mother, rather than an elder son, became head of the family. This tradition has continued into modern times. The implications of this custom can best be seen in the case of a ruling family. During the empire period, Ögödei Khan discussed state problems with Sorkhaghtani, the widow of Prince Tolui and the mother of Möngke and Khubilai Khan, because Sorkhaghtani was the head of the household or lineage.[17] Following the death of Ögödei Khan (1241), Törgene,[18] his wife, became the ruler of the entire Mongol Empire until her son, Güyüg, was established as khan in 1246. In a similar manner, after Güyüg died (1248), his widow, Oghulkhaimish,[19] became supreme ruler until Möngke was installed as khan (1251). When Khubilai was incapacitated by old age and did not receive court officials, his wife, Nambi, played an important role as a mediator in state affairs.[20] Thus, during early periods of Mongol history, at least beginning with the thirteenth century, women held considerable influence in politics. A family system, patrilineal in nature but with the mother becoming the head of the household upon the death of the father, has continued into modern times.

Although the status of women is not equal to that of men within the clan-lineage system, it is comparatively high and free considering the situation of women in most other parts of Asia. A nomadic life-style is not conducive to the subordination of women in a tight network of social relationships. Polygyny is common, at least among the elite.

"Property" in premodern Mongolia was defined only as movable property; there was no inheritance of landed estates as such. Landed institutions did not arise until the latter part of the sixteenth century, with the establishment of Buddhist temples. The common term for property in Mongolian is *khubi,* which also has the connotation of shares. The centrifugal tendency to subdivisions in Mongol society also extended into the political sphere and appears in the decentralization of rule and the awarding of fieflike grants of broad-ranging domains by the khan to his sons and generals or other vassals. Herds cannot be maintained or flourish after reaching a certain size, and from time to time it became necessary to divide the herds, resulting naturally in a division of families. Thus, no great family system (Chs. *ta chia-t'ing*) developed as in neighboring China. Wives in Mongolian society traditionally had rights to succeed to property. Some of the many royal tents, *ordo,* of Chinggis Khan were inherited by his wives upon his death.[21]

Some characteristics of the succession of property during the empire period (1206-1368) may be seen in the *Secret History.* In a number of cases, the record takes special pains to stress the unique position of the first son and the youngest son.[22] The eldest son of the first or senior wife held a privileged position in succession to leadership or domain, but the youngest son had a special role in inheriting herds and movable property not common in Asian societies. According to the system, which combines ultimogeniture and primogeniture, older sons receive their share of an inheritance while the father is still living, often at the time of marriage, but the youngest son inherits the father's property in a final settlement since he remains with his parents until their death. There are variations of this pattern. The father's heir, for example, may not be the youngest son but rather one considered to be more capable or a favorite son.

A passage in the *Secret History* records an example of the customary division of property made by Chinggis Khan to his wives, brothers, and sons in 1206 when Chinggis became the supreme head of the Mongol tribes. His decree was to "distribute the people to my mother, sons, and brothers." He continued, "It was my mother who ruled the people and exerted herself together with me to extablish the nation. The eldest among the sons is Jochi. And the youngest among my brothers is Odchigin."[23] On his mother and Odchigin (the youngest), he bestowed ten thousand people; to his sons, he distributed: nine thousand to Jochi (the eldest), eight thousand to Chaghadai, five thousand to Ögödei, and five thousand to Tolui. Four thousand were given to one brother, Khasar, and two thousand to Alchidai, another brother.[24] This record accords with the custom that the eldest and the youngest were especially favored.

Later, when the empire was larger and Chinggis drew close to the end of his career, he once more distributed the wealth of the empire to his sons. To his elder sons, Jochi, Chaghadai, and Ögödei, he bestowed the empire that he had conquered in Central Asia and Russia, excluding Mongolia. Mongolia proper or the Mongol homeland and the main armies were bequeathed to his youngest son, Tolui. After the death of Chinggis, Tolui became regent to handle state affairs until succession to the throne by Ögödei the following year (1229); thus, Chinese historians refer to Tolui as *chien-kuo,* "regent."[25] But the Mongols refer to him as *ejen,* "the lord," or "the owner," because of his role as the owner and protector of the family hearth (*gholomta*),[26] which entitled him to be the interim ruler of the entire empire and the overseer of the great Borjigid clan.

However, succession to khanship was not on the same basis as a son's succession to clan leadership. The throne was not part of the property that was passed on to a particular son. Ögödei achieved this position only by being sustained by all of the Mongol princes in a great *khuraltai* ("council of leaders"). The role or position of the eldest son (*odghan*) in relation to leadership is discussed in the *Secret History*: "In the beginning Khabul Khan had seven sons. Among these sons Ökin-barakhagh was the eldest. . . . and because he was the eldest of the sons of Khabul Khan, there was selected those men who had courageous hearts, a good bowstring thumb, and a feeling of pride and ambition, skillful, courageous and stout men, and they were made followers of [Ökin-barakhagh]."[27]

Later, during the Yüan dynasty (1260-1368), with the Mongolian political center being in China, while many positions did become hereditary, they did not customarily follow the rule of primogeniture in the Chinese pattern with khanship going to the eldest son. Instead, leadership fell to the son considered most capable. However, during the Yüan period, under Chinese influence, there was a tendency to reverse the roles of the first son and the last son. Later under Dayan Khan, with the fifteenth-century reunification of a nomadic empire, it was customary for the eldest son to succeed to khanship. However, property was still divided, and the eldest son did not receive the entire estate, as in Japan and Europe.

In the modern period, in cases of polygamy, the sons of the first wife usually have a more privileged position in receiving *khubi*, or shares of inheritance, than the sons of the other wives, but there are no strict customary restrictions or pressures upon the father of a household in dividing his property. Property may be divided evenly or particular sons may be given special consideration. A daughter is customarily given a dowry upon marriage, but ordinarily does not receive any *khubi* unless the father makes some special provision.

Within the modern Mongolian family, the father or grandfather makes all major decisions. Upon the death of these, the mother becomes head. Upon the death of both parents, the eldest son succeeds to chief responsibility for the family. The sons may remain together, but it is more common for them to divide and establish kinship units based on the conjugal family. In agricultural areas closer to the Great Wall, there is a tendency for the family to remain together, while in pastoral areas it is more common for them to divide. Even after the division of a family upon the death of the parents, the eldest son is still influential. In modern times, the maternal uncle continues to play a special role, giving advice, serving as sponsor, settling problems, and so forth. The *moghanda*[28] or "clan elder" may also be called in to arbitrate family problems.

In Mongolia, there is great concern to perpetuate the paternal bloodline, but not, however, to the degree found in Chinese society. If there are no male descendants in a family, it is customary to adopt a son from a relative to continue the lineage. (Adoption of orphaned children is also common.) It is extremely rare, however, for a family to contract a marriage for the purpose of having the son-in-law change his name to that of the family to continue their line (the Japanese custom of *mukoyoshi*). Though the son of a married daughter is a close relative, he has no right of inheritance in his mother's family since he is a member of an outside lineage.

Regarding the lineage or family, until the middle of this century there was the somewhat separate problem of celibacy; the matter of family continuity and inheritance as it related to unmarried lamas. With the rapid rise of Buddhism in the late sixteenth century, it became common for males to enter the Buddhist monasteries and become lamas. Although sons left the household to join the clergy and theoretically lost their rights of inheritance, in actual practice, they still received their *khubi* shares. However, perpetuating the family line took precedence over even highly stressed monastic vows, and, often, if the male progeny died out, a relative was brought back from the temple, giving up his vows as a lama, so that he might marry and perpetuate the family. Among common families, the lama ordinarily would be free to make a choice in the matter; however, in prominent families, the prince of the banner quite frequently constrained the lama to be secularized and honor responsibilities to the family.

Since the hearth (*gholomta*) is symbolic of the Mongol family, its continuity and unity, there is a traditional feeling and proverb to the effect that when the "fire goes out" the family continuity is broken, the family ceases. This is figurative and does not refer to accidental extinguishment in a storm or while traveling. Interestingly, in modern times, among families that have ceased to be nomadic and that no longer use the *gholomta* or hearth in daily life, it is still treasured and brought out on special occasions to be placed together with the Buddhist shrine and other special objects for obeisance and veneration by the family. In this connection, it should be noted that the guardian of the hearth and consequently the person responsible for the continuity of the family is termed *odchigin*. Historically, this role invariably fell to the youngest son, but in more recent times this rule was not strictly followed.[29]

The twentieth century has brought many changes to Mongolian society. These changes have accelerated greatly since the socialist revolution, and many of the traditions discussed here are no longer followed.

CLAN CONFEDERATIONS AND THE EMERGENCE OF STEPPE STATES

Given the unique relationship between man, land, and animals in nomadic society, mobility is more important than settlement. In the expansion of an agricultural state, the objective is to increase the amount of arable territory held; in a nomadic state, the objective is rather to gain control of pastures or to assimilate a greater number of clans or tribes plus pastures. Even in conquest situations, the concept of territory differs greatly between the two types of economy. Thus, the Chinese refer to important nomadic states as *hsing-kuo* or *ma-shang hsing-kuo*, "moving states" or "states on horseback."[1] Some Altaic scholars have been reluctant to use the term "state" to describe a Mongolian confederation or league and instead use the Mongolian term *ulus*. Because of its constant movement, its great striking power and its formation—a combination of many clan-lineages—a nomadic state in the steppe has been likened to a flash storm or a whirlwind. To the Chinese, it was like a dark cloud on the steppe. On the other hand, bad leadership and clashes between clans often brought the rapid disappearance of nomadic states.

The physical limitations of the steppe made it impossible for nomads to develop agriculture until very recently, and prejudices between the Chinese and nomadic peoples[2] made ordinary peaceful trade usually difficult, and often impossible. At times, a single clan or lineage was not able to manage by itself the difficulties of nomadic life, and large hunts, long-distance trade, war, or efforts to gain better pastures were only possible by combining the forces of a number of clans. The temptation of trade or plunder in China and the poor conditions in much of the Gobi or steppe lured the nomadic peoples southward to graze near the agricultural areas[3] along the Great Wall. Thus, the development of a powerful nomadic state was a perpetual threat to the Chinese, whose attempts to control and manipulate frontier trade to their advantage brought reprisals from the nomads. It must be kept in mind that obtaining grain, metal, and cloth from China was virtually an absolute necessity to the nomads.

The agricultural people lacked the nomads' great ability to attack and retreat, and their main means of defense was to establish walled cities or a defensive network of walls such as the Great Wall in North China. North of the wall, through history there appeared many nomadic states or empires such as the Hsiung-nu (Huns?), Hsien-pei, T'o-pa (Tobgachi), Juan-juan, T'u-chüeh (Turks), Uighur, and Kitan. The great Mongolian Empire was the classic example. The last nomadic state in the steppe was that of the Oirad and their descendants or successors, the Jungar. This state was crushed by the Manchu-Ch'ing dynasty in 1755.

As one wave of nomadic peoples moved into China, it was followed closely by another, and the pressure of one group upon another would at times force the earlier group to merge with or become absorbed by the Chinese. There were times when the Chinese would ally with a more distant wave of nomads to attack or subdue an earlier wave, which was already upon them or occupying Chinese territory.

Those who ruled China regarded peoples outside as barbarians, who were supposed to offer at least ceremonial tribute to China. But, at times, ceremonial tribute was accompanied by a considerable amount of real trade. Nomads who lived near China or along the trade routes to the West, the old Silk Route to Rome, were in a position to control the trade. As long as they did not challenge China directly, that is, in the ceremonial manner of status, then trade in China was allowed or rather winked at by Chinese officials. Thus, over the centuries, there were a number of nomadic or seminomadic states situated along the borders of China involved in trade. When China was weak, they struggled together to ascertain which would rule China. During periods of Chinese power, these states became vassals of the Dragon Throne or retreated into the steppe.

During the twelfth and thirteenth centuries, relationships between the Mongol lineages or clans were divided into three categories. The first category was a type of lineage in which all members shared a common ancestor and blood relationships. These were the most stable and most tightly knit kinship groups; but within this category, unity was a relative matter: a grouping of lineages was strong or weak depending on the degree of integration or the nature of relationships between the lineages. In the second category, lineages were related by marriage; individuals referred to each other as *khuda*.[4] A third category consisted of lineages grouped by coincidence or some special function such as hunting, but which had no blood or marriage relationships; in this case, lineage members spoke of others as *jad* ("outsiders").[5]

Another important grouping among the Mongols was the *aimagh,* or what is referred to as a tribe (here the word corresponds closely to the classical Roman), within which the members are ethnically closely related, possibly by distant blood ties. Within this tribal grouping, all the above relationships or units may be found. Tribes were subunits of the larger ethnic group (although we do not now have a clear picture of the borders of the ethnic groups of the time) and confederations of lineages. Yet tribes were not completely "secular" in that the myth of lineage relationships seems to have been maintained. Structurally, in early periods, tribes must have been very fluid, allowing rapid rise and fall of groups within kinship and quasi-kinship categories to justify incorporation. Virtually every nomad on the steppe must have been related to every other through one of several categories:

obogh—a patrilineal kinship group

yasun—a patrilineal sublineage

naghachu—a group related through one's mother's brother's lineage, one's mother's group

khuda—groups with an affinity through marriage including descendants of a daughter's as well as her husband's family as affinals

jad—people of the same ethnic group, but whose blood ties are unknown and who are therefore regarded as outsiders.

In the period before the empire, when the term Mongol was used in a narrow sense rather than in the broad, inclusive way that Mongol later came to be used, the Mongol tribe had within it all three types of the clan-lineage relationships (blood relatives, *khuda,* and *jad*). However, the kinship groups within this larger tribal structure were generally autonomous; they were quite loosely grouped except when there was a common objective, such as a war or an outside threat.

Blood ties between lineages *might not* be decisive in their relationship and working arrangements. For example, the Taichi'ud lineage and the

Kiyad sublineage, satellites of the Borjigid lineage, were closely related by blood; however, after the death of Yesügei Ba'atur, the Taichi'ud suppressed and mistreated the Kiyad and the relationship was greatly weakened. Later, however, after Chinggis Khan reestablished his confederacy with the Borjigid as the central group, the Taichi'ud were dissolved as a lineage; many people were killed, and many were distributed among other kinship groups as a result of feuds and a feeling that the Taichi'ud could no longer be trusted.

The famous Borjigid clan-lineage had a central position in the development of the Mongol Empire. However, there were other important tribes (*aimagh*); the Tatar, about which less is known, included the Ayiru'ud, Büirü'üd, Chagha'an, Alchi, and Duta'ud lineages. The well-known Merkid, a tribe that was an enemy of Chinggis Khan, included the following clan-lineages and possibly others: Üdüyid, Kha'ad, and U'as. The Kereyid, another tribal-like subunit of the Mongol ethnic group, included the Tübegen, Dungkhayid, and Ongghojid lineages.

An examination of the nature of the tribal groups of Mongolia confirms that, during the pre-empire period, there was a common pattern in interclan and tribal relationships. While materials are not available to definitely establish for what purpose lineages coalesced into tribes, one may arrive at some reasonable theories: it was probably necessary to gain or maintain control of larger or better grazing fields, and to provide mutual assistance and collective security in common campaigns or defense. One prerequisite to tribal linkage, of course, was a man with excellent leadership ability who was popular or acceptable to the clan or lineage heads.

The *Secret History* relates the coalescence of clan-lineages into a confederation, which led to the emergence of a larger tribal federation or a steppe state. Yesügei Ba'atur (father of Chinggis Khan) was the leader of a sublineage of the Borjigid clan-lineage. He was famous for his prowess in war and therefore was influential both in his own lineage and in neighboring groups. After his death, his son, Temüjin, was at first an outcast from his clan-lineage and was then attacked by the Taichi'ud. He was attacked again by another tribe, the Merkid, and very nearly lost his life. However, this talented young man, who in time was to emerge as the greatest leader in the history of the Mongol nation, utilized the former status of his father and shrewd clan or lineage politics to gain the allegiance of the Kereyid.

In time, Temüjin, or Chinggis, was finally able to reorganize and regain strength in his lineage and defeat his enemies. At this point, all clan-lineages that were closely related to his own were integrated, with the exception of the Taichi'ud. The regrouping or confederation resulted not from the single-handed work of Temüjin, but rather from a partnership between Temüjin and Jamukha of the Jadaran lineage. Later, however, the group was split into two large competing confederations led by these same two leaders.

Finally, because Chinggis Khan was the strongest chieftain among a number of possible leaders in his confederation of clan-lineages, he was appointed by the others as the prime leader of what may be referred to as a Mongol confederation. The exact date of this event is unknown, but it was at this point that Temüjin became recognized as Chinggis Khan. On this occasion, Ong Khan of the Kereyid is reported to have said, when he received Chinggis Khan's messenger reporting the newly established position of a khan over a new Mongol nation: "What can you Mongol people do without a *khaghan* (khan)? [His rhetorical question implies that this was a very important decision.] Now you must not break your word, you must not dissolve your union, you must not rend your own clothing."[6] It seems that the Mongols had not had a khan among them for a considerable period of time.

The newly organized union was looked upon by some neighboring tribal leaders as unstable and unpromising. In response to the new emergence of power among the Mongols, the lineage confederation led by Jamukha, including other breakaway fragments of the Mongols, strengthened its union and supported Jamukha as Gür Khan ("ruler of all"), with the objective of attacking the rival Mongol confederation under the leadership of Chinggis. The group under Jamukha was decisively defeated, and the remnants of his broken union eventually were reintegrated into the Mongol confederation under the leadership of Chinggis.

Mongol confederations had many difficulties until gradually, by shrewd decisions, Chinggis Khan was able to consolidate his organization and institutionalize his leadership into the great world empire of the Mongols. One such difficulty arose when two important leaders, Altan and Khuchar, became disaffected because Chinggis did not allow them to maintain booty they had plundered, but required that it be distributed equitably by the khan. Altan and Khuchar, with their groups, left the confederation and moved their allegiance to Ong Khan, leader of the Kereyid and a rival, though not an enemy, of Chinggis Khan and the Mongols.[7] Incidents such as this demonstrate the weakness and instability of the early Mongol nation.

Both Chinggis and Jamukha were supported as khans, but although they were elected and sustained as leaders of confederations of clanlike groups, they did not have definitive, despotic control of all kinship groups under them; they were not emperors as such. The main motivation in their elections was to guard against a threat from the outside rather than to gain strict control and ultimate power within the confederation. This explains, in part, why the clan-lineages under Jamukha left him when he was unable to fulfill the role of leader in protecting his union from its enemies. This same principle was involved within the confederation of Chinggis Khan when Altan and Khuchar resisted control, while Chinggis Khan desired to strengthen his own power within the confederation as well as against its outside enemies.

While the Mongols apparently had not had a supreme leader for a long period of time, it is recorded in the *Secret History* that the great-grandfather of Chinggis Khan, Khabul, had held the title of *khaghan* (khan).[8] After that, Ambaghai, a leader of the Taichi'ud, held the position. But after Ambaghai was captured by the Tatar tribe and sent to the Chin (Jurchen) where he was executed, his son was not appointed to succeed him as khan; Khutula, son of Khabul, succeeded to the position. According to the record, while there were earlier khans among the Mongols (Chinggis was not the first), there was no great confederation of strong, supreme khan, at least from the time of Khabul, if at all.

It may be useful to analyze the attitudes and actions of leaders of confederacies in the twelfth century, before the time of Chinggis Khan. According to the *Secret History,* when Ambaghai was traveling to the Tatar area, for the purpose of making a marriage for his daughter, and was captured, he is reported to have declared: "I, the *khagkan* of the people and lord of the nation, have been captured because I came to accompany my daughter. From now on learn from my experience and even though you work your five fingers off and even work your ten fingers to the bone, you must eventually come to gain revenge."[9] Apparently, the nomads had developed the concept of a role or institution considered supreme among the people, termed *khaghan,* and Ambaghai considered himself to be the head of state and the khan of the people. The word *ulus,* used here, is commonly interpreted as nation. Some scholars feel that *ulus* may have had the meaning of confederation, rather than state. However, the commonly used phrase *ulus-un-ejen,*[10] can hardly be interpreted as "Lord of the Confederation"; Lord of the Nation is more nearly the connotation. A stage had been reached in Mongolian history when the idea of allegiance to a body or organization larger than the lineage or clan confederation had developed. It is possible that the idea of a higher degree of integration, a larger governing unit, arose from contact with neighbors of the Mongols who already had more highly developed nation states. This seems to be the best explanation of the emergence of such ideas as Lord of the Nation and Emperor of the People. The words of Ambaghai also reflect a feeling of responsibility for the state in the sense of a father of the people. The idea of superloyalty to a nation-state had not yet become established, and the political entity or *ulus* over which Ambaghai ruled was little more than a confederation of diverse clan-lineages each based on blood relationship. The same may be said of the confederation of Chinggis Khan. The nuclear group of both of these confederations was the Borjigid lineage, and both of them descended from Börte-chino'a.

The kinship groups that supported Jamukha as *khaghan* to fight against Chinggis Khan in 1201 were a complex confederation of clan-lineages; for example, there was Jamukha's own lineage, the Jadaran, in addition to which there were four lineages related by blood, namely, the Taichi'ud and Salji'ud, the Khatagin and the Dörben, all having the common ancestor Börte-chino'a. Other unrelated Mongol tribes, such as the Ghorulas, and tribes that were related by marriage to the Borjigid, such as the Onggirad, were also in the confederation. All these clan-lineages, related to the "Mongol tribe," were in time integrated and identified as the Mongol nation. The Naiman, the Merkid, and the Oirad (a tribe of the "people of the forest") represented "non-Mongol" tribes—again using "Mongol" in the narrow sense of the word. Thus, under Jamukha, a group had come into being that was no mere lineage confederation, but a more complex tribal confederation.

The personal relationships between leaders of kinship groups were extremely important both in clan politics and in the making and breaking of alliances or confederations. The personal relationship between Chinggis and Ong Khan and Chinggis and Jamukha, which formed the basis of their alliance, was that of *anda* ("sworn brotherhood"). Ritualistic elements and formal oaths consummated the political relationship. The *Secret History* records a ceremony in 1201 during which a group of leaders supported Jamukha and swore allegiance to him: "[Eleven tribes and clan-lineages] assembled a conference (*khuraltai*) at Alakhui-bulagh and declared that they would . . . support Jamukha as *khaghan* (khan) and in unison [the chiefs] slashed a mare and a stallion with their weapons and thus established their oath and a confederation."[11] The *Secret History* notes, earlier, the oath of ceremony in which Chinggis was established as khan. "Altan, Khuchar, Sacha Begi, and others consulted together and declared to Chinggis Khan, 'In the time of thrusting through [war], if we disobey your order you may separate us from our wives, children and families, our property shall be confiscated and our heads shall be thrown into the wilderness. In time of peace, if we do not obey your instructions we shall be separated from our wives and families and shall be exiled into the wilderness.'"[12]

The procedure for deciding upon a khan or supratribal chief began with a formal *khuraltai,* or council, after consultation by powerful leaders. The agreement of vassalage was then formalized by a customary ceremony and a stylized oath. The details of the ceremony at which Jamukha was made khan are not given, and its nature cannot be determined. When Chinggis Khan became the supreme leader, a stronger commitment than customary was taken, which was not restricted to a high-level, overall jurisdiction, but also included internal clan-lineage obligations of a strict nature. When problems developed in the confederation and Altan and Khuchar attempted to throw off their obligations to Chinggis and escape, they were captured and Chinggis demanded fulfillment of the oath they had taken. They were constrained to stretch forth their necks for decapitation. Upon this important oath was founded the authority of Chinggis Khan and consequently the early Mongol Empire.

Ssu-ma Ch'ien (145?-90? B.C.), in discussing kinship groups among the Hsiung-nu—pre-Mongol nomads—noted: "They live in separate valleys and have their own rulers. On occasion when they gather together they have over one hundred barbarian groups, but it is impossible for them to unite."[13] At least during the first century B.C., nomadic clan-lineages were loosely organized, and although they, of necessity, maintained contact, they were still unable to perpetuate a strong unity for any length of time.

Following the decline of the Hsiung-nu, other groups came to dominate Mongolia, and in later Han records (*Hou Han shu*), the following comments are found regarding two Mongolian-type, nomadic peoples known to the Chinese as Hsien-pei and Wu-huan:

If there is anyone sufficiently strong, brave, and capable in arbitrating disputes [between clans], he will be put forth [by the clan chieftains] as a Great Leader (*ta-jen*), but without hereditary succession. The tribes (*i-lo*) have their own petty leaders (*hsiao-shuai*) and hundreds or thousands of groups are organized into a union . . . under a Great Leader while the individual tribes carry on their own life and pasture their own flocks. There is no interference from the outside in the internal affairs of the tribe. . . . When T'an-shih-huai [an outstanding Hsien-pei leader] was about fourteen or fifteen years old, he was very powerful, brave, wise and shrewd. Great leaders of other tribes plundered his herds in distant fields. When T'an-shih-huai went to pursue them alone, no one dared stand against him and he retrieved all he had lost. From that time, the clans and tribes feared and respected him. Then he proclaimed laws and prohibitions and made judgments regarding right and wrong. No one dared disobey and he was proclaimed [by the chiefs] as a Great Leader (*ta-jen*).[14]

The Chinese used the term *hsiao-shuai* to designate the leader of a smaller kinship group and *ta-jen* to designate a greater leader over a larger confederated group. Chinese records confirm that the main function of the *ta-jen* was to arbitrate disputes between clan-lineages and to maintain the unity and welfare of the overall confederation. The *ta-jen* it seems, had no control over the internal affairs of the individual groups, which still maintained a semi-independent role. The member units of a league were theoretically equal and autonomous.

A great assembly and a type of election procedure developed among tribal leaders very early (the first centuries A.D.). The assembly, found among the Kitan,[15] was the origin of the Mongolian *khuraltai*.[16] The chief of ancient nomadic confederations or leagues, like those of the Mongols, had to be an outstanding leader, a wise judge, a brave fighter, and a good organizer and administrator. The assembly over which he presided was a persistent element in nomadic society over centuries. A large confederation under a capable leader absorbed other groups either by negotiation or by force, and consequently, through confederation, a nomadic state was born.

FROM CLAN CONFEDERATIONS
TO A NOMADIC QUASI-FEUDALISM

The common understanding of the term *feudalism* is based upon the

classical European experience of the medieval period. Asia's development differed from Europe's, and scholars present various interpretations of the feudal-like phenomena that occurred in Asia. The nebulous,
distorted Marxist use of the term *feudalism* obscures more than it
clarifies, but there was certainly a quasi-feudalistic development in
social and political institutions in the steppe areas during the period of
Mongol expansion. For lack of a better term, the socio-political type or
model of feudalism will be used here.

Prior to the reign of Chinggis Khan, the *obogh* or clan-lineage, a unit
based on a blood relationship, was an economic, administrative, and
military unit within the *aimagh* ("tribe"). When clan-lineages drew
together, the *aimagh* often became very powerful. (Sometimes,
however, *aimagh*s became weak, disintegrated, or ceased to exist as
groups.) When a confederation was made of formerly independent
kinship groups, some authority was transferred to a supreme leader, but,
generally, certain prerogatives were retained by the group, which
maintained a measure of autonomy. Outside interference in the internal
affairs of the lineage was disallowed.

The rise of the Mongol Empire was accompanied by a decline or
change of the clan-lineage system and a strengthening and enlargement
of the authority of the khan. When Temüjin was established as Chinggis
Khan, the clan-lineages were effectively placed under his personal
control. His *jasagh (yasa)* or law code became the basis of all law in the
Mongol Empire. The tradition of clan independence and noninterfer-
ence by the khan in internal clan affairs passed away. Thus, in war or
peace, the command of the khan was supreme and obedience was
mandatory. Transgression of the oath establishing this relationship
usually meant exile or death.[1]

When Chinggis Khan unified the Mongol tribes in order to mobilize
the entire body, he immediately established various roles: the *bo'urchi*[2]
looked after the food supply; the *khonichi* looked after the sheep herds;
the *aghtachi* took care of the horse herds; and the *khorchi* were personal
guards to the khan. In addition, he commissioned other officials to
supervise carts and to handle intelligence activities. Thus, very early in
his career, Chinggis brought under his control every important aspect of
nomadic life: transportation, food supply, the herds, and men whose
role was to be his "eyes and ears."[3] In so doing, he took into his own
hands the power and authority that previously had been retained by
individual heads of lineages.

After the success of these initial policies, Chinggis developed a census system and a means by which he could recruit or conscript soldiers widely. The army was no longer just troops drawn from various clans of kinship groups; it became a general army, integrated and drawn from all important groups. Lineages, of course, were not abolished; Chinggis continued to recognize their existence and maintained them as units. However, after a census was taken, new groups were organized and superimposed upon the old clans or groups of common descent. A decimal system was inaugurated involving units of ten households, one hundred households, and one thousand households. Each unit had a commander with both military and administrative authority.[4]

Chinggis then established a new post, a superofficial called a *mingghan-u noyan* (head of one thousand households—including troops).[5] These commanders were a varied group: Chinggis's most meritorious generals, favorite vassals, royal sons-in-law, and former heads of lineages or tribelike units. This post was an important innovation in mobilizing the people and establishing the Mongol Empire.

The transition from the lineage system of the pre-empire period to a quasi-feudalistic social organization took centuries. During this time, some important kinship groups remained prominent and retained their identities, while many others were dissolved.

Some very important leaders did not have prominent backgrounds; as children, they were taken in battle, raised by the Mongols, and eventually given high positions. For example, Shigi-khutughu[6] and Boroghul[7] were former war orphans who eventually became generals and commanders. The thousand households under them consisted of remnants of lineages or nondescript groups, drawn from many places.

It was customary to take a defeated clan-lineage and distribute its members among a number of other lineages. For example, after their defeat, the Tübegen, Dungkhayid, and Jirgin lineages, formerly of the Kereyid tribe, were dissolved and their members distributed among other kinship groups.[8] At first, they had the low status of war prisoners or slaves. However, as time passed and as the population base of the Mongol Empire grew, people with humble backgrounds gained status on their own merit and some of them gained high positions. Some of the former importance of blood relationship and emphasis on genealogy or kinship was lost.

A sort of subinfeudation structure also developed during the reign of Chinggis Khan. He decided to divide the Mongol people as well as their subjects into units under his mother, brothers, and sons.[9] In the overall socio-political pyramid of the empire, the close relatives maintained a special status and under them were placed the old lineages of the Mongols and also those people who had been conquered and integrated. In the highest level of *noyan*, or nobility, in this feudal-like system, persons who had blood relationship to Chinggis were called the *altan-urugh*,[10] or "golden descendants." While it cannot be documented, there appears to have been a law in the old *jasagh* code according to which no person could assume the position of khan except those of the *altan-urugh*. The rank of *noyan* was established on the basis of hereditary perpetuity, and thus a hereditary nobility was established similar to that of the European feudal-elite or of China's early Han period under Han Kao-tsu, founder of the great Han dynasty. (In China, a person could not become a *wang* ["prince"] unless he were a member of the Liu family.)

There were a number of men of the first rank in this feudalistic system who were not descendants or blood relatives of Chinggis Khan. For example, among the *noyan* ("lords") of the first level was Mukhali,[11] commander of the left-flank armies of Chinggis who campaigned in North China, and also the brothers and/or the nephews of Börte, wife of Chinggis Khan, who were of the Onggirad tribe. Mukhali achieved a special rank of "king" (Mong. *gui-ong;* Chs. *kuo-wang,* "ruler of a realm"), which was rare, difficult to achieve, and passed down from generation to generation.

Another title, *ejen* ("lord"), was assumed by relatives or descendants of Chinggis Khan who expanded into western Asia and Europe and set up khanates or kingdoms of their own.[12] These *ejen* were established or supported by *mingghan-u noyan* (generals of over one thousand households) who had followed them in campaigns. Thus, all associated with Chinggis Khan, whether relatives or generals, received a sort of fief or stewardship in domain and people. The *Altan tobchi,* a Mongolian chronicle, records that when Jochi and Chaghadai were given personal realms over which to rule, Chinggis admonished them: "I do not wish to exile you and place you over your own realm, to have you control what I have conquered and administer what I have taken. You are to develop and enlarge the state and sustain the empire. You are to be a room of our mansion and an arm of my body."[13] In consolidating his empire, Chinggis Khan intended to distribute his holdings for effective rule to his vassals and relatives (as fieflike grants) and to attach the rulers to himself in an intimate personal relationship. His objective in establishing this new system was to confirm himself and his successors as the center and to supersede the old clan-lineage system with a new, more far-reaching and united social order.

The hierarchical system of administration in the Mongol Empire of ten, one-hundred, and one-thousand household units was enlarged later to include units of ten thousand households, which also had both administrative and military authority. Above these larger units were set the topmost nobility, the *altan-urugh*. Grazing domains were divided among the new units presided over by their lords. These fieflike areas conferred upon the *noyan* were spoken of classically as *nontug* (modern Mong. *notugh*).[14] During the Ch'ing period (1644-1911), *notugh* became commonly known by the Chinese term *yu-mu* ("grazing areas").[15] Originally the Mongol term meant "a camping area," but it eventually came to mean the area in which the new unit of approximately one to several thousand households resided and grazed their herds. The *Secret History* tells of an incident in which Sorkhan-shira, who had saved the life of young Chinggis Khan, requested the conferral of a *notugh* or pasture area: "If we receive your royal mercy and if we can have bestowed upon us a *notugh*, we desire to receive the land of the Merkid where we may pitch our tents freely."[16]

In 1206, when Chinggis Khan established the *mingghan-u noyan*, or the one-thousand household unit, the realm was already being divided into fieflike sections. This policy was enunciated later by Ögödei Khan: "I desire to establish peace among the people and to give them something that they may hold in their hand and a place whereon they may set their foot."[17] He meant that faithful followers should have their own grazing pastures. One purpose in setting determined grazing pastures was to end struggles over disputed migration circuits and to resolve intertribal wars over conflicting claims to pasturelands. This seems to have been the first occasion in Mongol history when a chief, his followers, and their herds were placed in direct relationship to a particular area of land. However, the important factor of the quasi-feudalistic situation at that time was not the relationship between man and land, but between man and man. The society remained nomadic, and between man and the land there were still the herds. Thus, while in an agrarian society, man and land were indivisible in the feudal relationship, the most important element in Mongolia was the relationship between lord and vassal; grazing fields of the vassals were a secondary consideration.

The feudal-like system in Mongolia during the Ch'ing period (1644-1911) was even a further departure from tradition and brought a much closer relationship between the people and the land.[18] The system was flexible, however in that even though a certain vassal and his followers would be given a particular realm or fief, if a situation arose in which his service was needed in some other area of the empire, the lord and his people would migrate to the new area.

During the empire period, the khan was the supreme ruler of the realm with all land and people belonging to him. He not only parceled out land in fiefs within Mongolia, but also gave lands south of the Great Wall in China, in the Moslem areas of West Asia, and in Russia to his sons and other relatives or vassals. The biography of Tei Sechen in the *Yüan shih* notes that his descendants received "fiefs" not only in Mongolia, but also in North China.[19] A Mongol lord who held "fiefs" both in the steppe and in the sown area would rule his steppe realm directly and the agricultural areas indirectly through administrative officials approved by the khan.

Besides distributing lands to sons, brothers, and vassals, the khan also retained certain areas under his direct control. As recorded in the *Secret History*, the people who were distributed to sons and vassals of the khan were referred to by the term *khubi*, literally "shares." The implication was that the empire belonged to the emperor and his family alone and that it was theirs to parcel out to subordinates as they saw fit. The precedent set by Chinggis Khan was perpetuated by his successors, and they, in turn, enfeoffed their own relatives and vassals as they gained power and lands. As in classical feudalism, the system was inseparable from the family institution.

The distribution of holdings was no problem as long as the empire was expanding. However, after the consolidation of the empire, when lands and population or other wealth became limited, great problems arose in the nomadic areas and the khanates. There was a proliferation of holdings, a fragmentation that mainly affected the domain of the khan. He was constrained to distribute his own lands to ensure the support of his vassals, and this, in turn, weakened the central government and eventually contributed to its fall. The Mongol process of distributing fiefs was less of a problem in China because the bureaucracy of the central government interceded between a domain and a lord who held it.[20]

Both during the era when clan-lineages were the key social units and during the quasi-feudalistic period that followed, the Mongolian nobility customarily had *omchu*,[21] or personal holdings, including both people and property. In origin, *omchu* holdings were usually hereditarily received from forefathers or gained by capture in warfare or received as gifts from a superior. *Omchu* moved with a lord wherever he went.

INSTITUTIONAL CHANGES
AFTER THE FALL OF THE EMPIRE

In 1260, Khubilai Khan established the great Yüan Empire with its capital at Khanbalic (modern Peking), thus shifting the political center of gravity of the Mongol Empire south into Chinese territory. Previously, the capital was at Karakorum in the steppe, an environment in great contrast to the rich and populated area south of the Great Wall. Most of the sons of Khubilai were enfeoffed or given domains south of the wall in China, and, from this time on, the former Mongol heartland became a mere province referred to as the *Ling-pei hsing chung-shu sheng* ("itinerant administrative office north of the mountains"). Other Chinggisid princes did not agree with Khubilai's policy of Sinicization or accommodation to China. The princes in the areas northeast and southwest of the old Mongol heartland resisted, making it impossible for the khan himself, seated in Khanbalic, to make changes within this area.

A crisis and second great turning point in Mongol history came in 1368 when Toghon-temür, hard pressed by rising Ming forces, retreated from China to the old Mongol pastures. According to the Mongolian historian, Sagang Sechen, of forty *tümen* (a unit of ten thousand troops with their families) quartered in China, only six *tümen* retreated north of the wall.[1] From that time on, the Mongols referred to themselves as the six Mongol *tümen*.[2] This retreat precipitated a radical change in the quasi-feudalistic system that had developed in Mongolia. Some who retreated to Mongolia were not originally Mongols. For example, the famous Arughtai, who resisted the invasion of Mongolia by the Ming Emperor Yung-lo (1403-24), identified himself as being of the Asud tribe or lineage, which was originally a Caucasoid group from the Caucasus mountain area known as the Aran. The Ming records also speak of the Uighurchin tribe, which evidently was a Turkic-Uighur remnant of the Mongol Empire.

After their retreat to the steppes in the early 1400s, the Mongols eventually split into two large warring factions: the Oirad (Chs. *Wa-la*) in the west and the Mongols (Chs. *Ta-tan*) in the east. For a short period, the Oirad were successful in usurping political power from the Borjigid royal clan. However, the Borjigid, clan-lineage of Chinggis, were later able to regain power and to unify most of Mongolia under the leadership of Dayan Khan (d. 1530?). During the period of civil war, many old social and political institutions were greatly changed.

Once peace was regained, Dayan Khan established a new structure according to which the six *tümen* were recognized as basic units: two flanks of three *tümen* on each side. The new Mongol nation that emerged was spoken of by the Mongols as the *Yeke-ulus* ("great nation").[3] The term *tümen,* a high-level military or administrative unit, was not used in the original sense, for actually there were many more families or people within each *tümen* than the original ten thousand. Dayan Khan set one of his sons over each of the six *tümen,* while he directly administered the affairs of the three *tümen* on the right flank with the rank of *jinong,* meaning "vice" or "deputy khan." Many of the old lineage names persisted, and all *tümen,* or units immediately under the *tümen,* were ruled by members of the Borjigid family. The clan names of kinship designations used at the time were only nominal because the population was very mixed.

The Oirad, who had been prominent in the civil war (1400-54), were defeated by Dayan Khan,[4] but did not come under his rule because they retreated west to the area of the Altai mountains. Thus, they escaped being redistributed among the six *tümen.* However, the war campaigns and accompanying problems caused internal turmoil and fragmentation within the various groups of the Oirad, so they also divided into four *tümen.* Eventually, they came to refer to themselves as the four Oirad (*ulus* or "nations"). Two Oirad tribes, the Dörbed[5] and the Jungar,[6] were ruled by two sons of Esen (d. 1454?), who previously had usurped power from the Borjigid and had assumed the role of khan for a short time. A third tribe, the Torghud,[7] was ruled by a descendant of the old Kereyid tribe, and the fourth Oirad group, the Khoshod,[8] was ruled by a descendant of Khasar, younger brother of Chinggis Khan.

In addition to the four Oirad nations to the west and the six Mongol *tümen* in the area of Inner and Outer Mongolia, to the east was the powerful Khorchin tribe,[9] also ruled by descendants of Khasar. There were also t o smaller groups, the Abagha[10] and Ongni'ud,[11] located in the area of present-day eastern Inner Mongolia. Their leaders were descendants of the younger brothers of Chinggis Khan. Of the six Mongol *tümen,* a prominent tribe of the left flank, the Uriyangkha,[12] were not descendants of Chinggis Khan, but of his important trusted general Jeleme.[13] Of all the tribes and groups, the most aristocratic in tradition were those whose rulers traced their lineage from the old Borjigid family.

When Dayan Khan began to reestablish a quasi-feudalistic structure centered on the *altan-urugh* ("golden descendants," the Borjigid nobles), he met great resistance from the elite of other lineages, particularly from the three right *tümen* that were actually under the khan's direct control. By the time of Lighdan Khan in the early seventeenth century, the power of the great khan was greatly weakened and the pattern of decentralized rule, characteristic of earlier quasi-feudalistic institutions, was confirmed. As a result, the smaller units or tribes within each *tümen* became petty realms ruled over by individual princes.

During this period, the topmost unit in the hierarchical structure was the *tümen,* also called *ulus* ("state" or "nation"). *Tümen,* in turn, were subdivided into *otogh* or *khushighun* (identified in later Mongol history as "banners"). The petty lords of most subunits within the *tümen* were sons or blood relatives of the lord of the *tümen* itself. By the early seventeenth century, the lord of the *tümen* had become a figurehead with no real power. By an inevitable process—the deaths of khans and problems of succession, the division of domains and giving of "shares" (*khubi*) to petty rulers—subdivisions took place that weakened the overall power structure or administrative unity in Mongolia (the Manchu later exploited this tendency to further weaken the Mongols). For example, the Ordos *tümen* in the loop of the Yellow River was divided into nine *otogh* or secondary units. The Khalkha, previously a mere subdivision of one *tümen,* was divided into seven *khushighun* (*otogh* or, later, "banners") ruled by three khans.

In the early Mongol Empire, the term khan (or *khaghan*) referred to the supreme ruler among the Mongols. Later, as the empire became subdivided into khanates, such as the Kipchak (Russia) and Il-Khan (Persia), less-powerful rulers of these areas also assumed the title of khan. However, as a matter of formality, the succession of rulers in the khanates had to be approved by the Great Khan even down to the later Yüan period. Thus, the Great Khan located in Khanbalic (Peking) was the symbol of supreme rule, and rulers of the khanates were vassals under his suzerainty. The Mongols referred to these rulers by the special term *keüd* or *kübegüd,*[14]meaning "the sons" (terminology is close to the Chinese *tsung-wang,* "prince of the royal blood"). After the establishment of the Yüan dynasty, Chinese terminology was actually adopted, and the general rank of lordship was referred to as *wang* or *ong* in Mongolian. Many *wang* or *ong* were not Chinggisid, but were generals, husbands of Chinggisid princesses, and so forth. In the early empire period, sons-in-law who became princes were referred to as *kürgen*.[15] Later the term *tabunang*[16] was used for this group.

Before Esen, the Oirad leader, no one is known to have transgressed the law of Chinggis Khan by attempting to assume, without justification, the title of khan. From the time of Dayan Khan, no one except him and his successors used the title of khan. During the rule of Daraisun-küden Khan (1551-71?), Altan, leader of the Tümed Mongols and grandson of Dayan Khan, demanded and received the title Sodo Khan ("minor khan"). Altan was the first man to hold this title, and with it, he was subordinate to the Great Khan. From the latter part of the sixteenth century, when the Mongols were converted to or greatly influenced by Tibetan Buddhism, the Dalai Lama began to confer the title of khan upon Mongol aristocrats who really had no claim to the title. Abadai, a Khalkha leader, was the first to receive the khan title in this way.[17] Such instances demonstrate that the title of khan had declined and was but a shadow of its former glory.

After the collapse of the Mongol Empire, particularly in Central Asia, those who developed political power on the base of the old empire, such as Timur (Tamerlane), did not assume the title of khan but took the title of *emir* (*amir*, meaning "commander" or "governor") and sought descendants of Chaghadai, second son of Chinggis, to be installed as khan. Later, the son of Timur, who succeeded him, adopted the title of *sultan* ("sovereign" or "king"). The pattern of kinship that persisted was a tradition stemming from Chinggis Khan.

Common terms for status and rank among the Mongols, aside from the exalted term *khan* and *jinong* ("deputy khan"), were *khong-taiji, taiji, tabunang,* and *khonjin*. The Mongol rank *khong-taiji* is actually a corruption of the Chinese term *huang-t'ai-tzu* ("crown prince"), which will be explained below. The term *taiji* also is a corruption of the Chinese term *t'ai-tzu* and became current among the Mongols before their takeover of China. For example, it is found in the early records used in reference to the uncle of Chinggis Khan, Nekün Taishi. Because the Mongol language has no sound corresponding to the Chinese *tze* or *tzu*, before the thirteenth century the term *t'ai-tzu* was adopted with the pronunciation *taishi;* but later, from the fifteenth century on, it evolved as the term *taiji*. The term *tabunang* is also a special term referring to those who gained rank by marrying into the Borjigid ruling family.[18] *Khonjin* was a title that could be conferred on virtually anyone, including the common people. Only the two roles or titles of *khong-taiji* and *taiji* were borne by men who really became lords in the quasi-feudal system. Generally, only men bearing these two titles had a domain or fief. Another common term of rank in the social structure was that of *noyan*—a broader generic term with the connotation of "nobility" or "official," which may include the ranks *khong-taiji* and *taiji*. Other terms used for nobility or superiors, terms with an honorific connotation, are *ba'atur* ("brave"), *sechen* ("virtuous"), *mergen* ("wise"), *sayin* ("good"), and *daiching* ("brave"). As noted previously, some of these rather exalted terms eventually became used as common personal names. During the period between the collapse of the Mongol Empire and the reunification of the Mongols under Dayan Khan, an important group of men with a distinctive role were referred to as *taishi;* but this term had a different origin from *taiji* and was taken from the Chinese *tai-shih* (title of a top court official in China).

The whole pattern of princely domains or so-called fiefs, which emerged during the period of Chinggis Khan and the Yüan emperors, was entirely changed or restructured during the civil wars and other disturbances following the collapse of the Mongol Empire. Two exceptions were the pasturelands bequeathed to Khasar, the younger brother of Chinggis, located in the valleys between the Nonni and Toor rivers in eastern Mongolia, and the area held by the Uriyangkha tribe northeast of Peking just across the Great Wall. Because of the fierce fighting, forced migrations, and other problems following the fall of the Yüan, it is virtually impossible to reconstruct the picture and locate all the old domains.

During the period of Dayan Khan's rule, the tribes became much more settled and consequently more precisely determined grazing areas or circuits were established. In the process, the forces of Dayan Khan drove the Oirad Mongols to the far northwest Altai mountain region and on west, but did not themselves settle there or in the territory vacated by the Oirad. Instead, the forces of Dayan returned to graze along the outer reaches of the Great Wall in the area of modern Inner Mongolia. Only the youngest son of Dayan Khan, Ghalsanjalair, was given holdings beyond the Gobi in the area of Khalkha Mongolia (MPR). The dividing line between the "great right flank" and the "great left flank" of Dayan's new empire ran along the western boundary of the modern Chakhar region. This is only an approximate picture because the situation was constantly changing and later the right flank to the west expanded into the Kökönor (Chinghai) area.

In the middle of the sixteenth century, Daraisun-küden Khan, leader of the left or eastern flank of the two great major divisions of the main body of the Mongols, moved his headquarters or base from the present-day Chakhar area to Ichou in modern Liaoning province. This action shows again that Mongol domain could be shifted from place to place within a large area. In the seventeenth century, the Torghud tribe of the Oirad Mongols made their famous move to the banks of the Volga River, and the Khoshod tribe of the Oirad Mongols eventually migrated into the Kökönor area and Tibet. These movements further demonstrate that vassalage relationships of the quasi-feudalistic conditions in Mongolia during the seventeenth century were between man and man, with only secondary consideration to land. Land was but pasturage for animals, which were the real units of value and which could be moved.

SOCIO-POLITICAL STRUCTURE
UNDER THE MANCHU

The period discussed here extends from the early seventeenth century, the era of the Mongol-Manchu alliance, to the twentieth century. The political and social systems of Mongolia prior to the Manchu dynasty were developed indigenously by the Mongols as they regulated their own affairs. However, when the Mongols surrendered to the Manchu in the 1600s and became their subordinated allies in the conquest of China, systems were often designed and implemented to facilitate control of the Mongols by their Manchu overlords.

The Manchu policy for the Mongols was "divide and rule"; by creating more ranks and titles, they reduced the actual power of petty princes and nobles. The Manchu fully realized the danger of allowing the Mongols to continue certain traditional patterns that might precipitate another rapid rise of nomadic power in the steppe. They realized that the customary migratory movement of nomadic tribes was a key factor in concentrating power and developing nomadic states and, furthermore, that the larger the sphere in which migrations took place, the greater the danger of a confederation of tribes. The threat of war from outside the steppe was traditionally not a danger to nomadic tribes; on the contrary, it was often a factor in pulling tribes together into a strong nation. Thus, the threat was actually to rulers south of the Great Wall.

To implement their policy, the Manchu divided the old *aimagh* or tribes into many smaller subdivisions. In the process, the old, titled nobility were left with vain glory and empty titles, but also rich stipends, which tied them to the imperial court in Peking. Overall, total power was watered down and spread over more leaders. Thus, men who were formerly mere nobles without realms now came into power as petty rulers within their own limited sphere. In addition to a vassalage-type relationship that had always been present, the Manchu added a new element by limiting the land area within which a petty ruler, or a *jasagh,* and his people could graze and hunt. Strict borders were established that could not be transgressed. The petty rulers jealously guarded their realms, and, with the loss of their former mobility, the Mongols also lost the possibility of developing great power.

In this new situation, every regional Mongol ruler was free and secure within his own area and had virtually no threat to his power and status unless he plotted rebellion against the Manchu. He had security plus protection from the emperor if he were threatened by a neighboring prince. While the vertical relationship between the petty rulers and the Dragon Throne in Peking became very intimate, the horizontal relationship between individual regional rulers within Mongolia was weakened. Thus, the motivation and tendencies of earlier days, when the Mongols, provoked by war or a threat, would unite, were gone forever. However, Mongols were allies of the Manchu and had higher status than Chinese subjects. The Manchu wanted to maintain the potential military strength of the Mongols, and therefore they maintained the old duality of a quasi-feudalistic administrative system of military groupings among the Mongols within the small realms that had been carved. These units were the key elements of the scheme designed by the Manchu to rule Mongolia to modern times.

During the Manchu-Ch'ing dynasty, the banner or *khushighun (khushuun)* was the basic and most important unit in the feudal-like system and had both administrative and military functions.[1] In the fifteenth century, the term *khushighun* was used in reference to a military unit and meant a "wedge" or "battalion." Before the Manchu invaded China, they adopted the *khushighun* unit as a basis for reorganizing their forces and thus created the "eight banner system."[2] At the same time, Mongol forces that were integrated into Manchu forces were organized as *khushighun* (the term now was used in the sense of "banner," came into

Chinese as *chi*, and continued until the present time to mean an administrative unit).

In creating banners, the Manchu made arbitrary divisions within existing Mongol units along lines of cleavage between noble families. They created new banners of any unit that could be separated and set up. For example, when the Khalkha came under the Manchu, they had four *aimagh* or tribes[3] within which were seven *khushighun,* in the original meaning of military units. The Manchu reorganization created eighty-six *khushighun* or banners, in the new meaning of administrative units.

The lord over each banner was a vassal of the Manchu emperor, and the banner included an inseparable unit of the lord, the people, and their grazing areas. There were many feudal-like characteristics of the system, which will not be discussed here, such as vassalage, tribute, a hereditary nobility and rigid class structure, decentralized rule in regional domains, a sort of tournament, and others. One important characteristic was the fact that a man was born into a banner unit and could not freely depart from it.[4]

During the Ch'ing period, most of the Mongol nobility were descendants from the old nobility of the Mongol Empire with few exceptions. In the early part of the seventeenth century,[5] before the Manchu invasion of China, Lighdan Khan attacked the old Kharachin *aimagh,* whose nobility was of Chinggisid lineage. The Kharachin nobility was exterminated and the common people became mixed with the Uriyangkha *aimagh* or tribe. The Uriyangkha name fell into disuse as Uriyangkha married into the Kharachin, assumed the more prestigious Kharachin name, and continued the title of *tabunang* ("imperial son-in-law"). In another instance, the Oirad in the far northwest of Mongolia, some of whom were not Chinggisid, used the imperial title of *taiji.*

After the Manchu took control of Mongolia and reorganized hereditary ranks in a hierarchical system, new terms came into use. Most were originally Chinese or Manchu terms such as *ch'in-wang, chün-wang, beyile, beyise, chen-kuo-kung,* and *fu-kuo-kung.*[6] The term *wang* is translated as "prince," and the term *kung* designated a "duke." *Beyile* and *beyise* had the connotation of "prince" among the Manchu before the invasion of China.[7] The new Mongol hierarchy was patterned after the Manchu model, but at the same time the rulers of northern Mongolia continued to use the title khan, as seen in the case of such Khalkha leaders as the Tüshiyetü Khan, Sechen Khan, and Jasaghtu Khan.

In addition to the above ranking of nobility, other terms of honorific address or reference came into use, such as *hosoi* (Chs. *ho-shuo,* a Manchu term) and *sechen* (Chs. *ch'e-ch'en,* a Mongol term), meaning "honor" and "wisdom," respectively. These terms were restricted to the upper echelon of the *taiji* and *tabunang* ranks of nobility. Lower echelons were subdivided into hierarchical ranks: first-, second-, third-, and fourth-class *taiji* or *tabunang.* A son born into a *taiji* or *tabunang* family of any rank would have, at least by birth, a fourth-class rank.

Rank was distinguished in many ways by insignia, dress, and sumptuary regulations. The Manchu bestowed titles and rank on most original Mongol nobility and upon others for meritorious service or outstanding loyalty. As a rule, noble rank was hereditary, but hierarchical position within the nobility varied from generation to generation, unless the emperor specified that a particular rank should remain unchanged. Promotions and demotions and the rewards attached thereto were decided entirely by the Manchu emperors, not by developments within Mongolia or by the Mongols themselves. This was an important factor in perpetuating the system of vassalage of the Mongol princes to the Manchu court.[8]

Noble rank and administrative power in premodern Mongolia did not go hand in hand. A person might have high rank, from *ch'in-wang* down to a first-class *taiji* or *tabunang,* but could not serve as the head of a banner government unless he were a *jasagh.* There were many men of noble rank within a banner, but only a noble with the title or role of *jasagh* held actual power. Other men of rank were referred to as "nobility of leisure" or *sula noyad.*[9] Within a banner, there would ordinarily be a limited number of nobles, but associated with them were ordinarily a number of *khariyatu,* "vassals" or "serfs." During the reign of Chinggis Khan, the term *jasagh* referred to military or constitutional law; however, as the term evolved it took on the present meaning, "one who administers the law" or "politics." There were actually two types of *jasagh,* those who gained their ranks strictly by hereditary transmission and those—a very small number of persons in northwestern Mongolia—without hereditary prerogatives,[10] who were appointed *jasagh* by the emperor in Peking.

The population of a banner traditionally was organized on the basis of a military system. Ordinarily, the basic unit was the *sumun* or "arrow," consisting, theoretically, of one hundred fifty fighting men and their families. Actually, they usually numbered around one hundred men, with the exception of the banners in the Jerim, Josotu, and Juu-uda leagues, which had larger populations and thus full strength. The *sumun* unit was led by a *sumun janggi,* "officer" of the *sumun.*[11] Under conditions of war, all the warriors in a *sumun* were combined under the leadership of a *jasagh* to form a battalion.

As with the case of the banner, it was virtually impossible for a person to transfer from one *sumun* to another. Thus, one could not transfer loyalty from one *jasagh* to another, nor could a person from one banner serve in any administrative capacity in another banner. The very strict regulations further illustrate the success of the Ch'ing dynasty in isolating banners from each other.[12]

Conflicts over private ownership of land did not develop among the early nomadic Mongols or during the Manchu period. Although the people were confined to a particular area, and the people and the land within a banner were under the administration of the hereditary post of *jasagh,* the land was still considered to be communal; it was not the private property of the *jasagh* himself. Strict boundaries were placed upon each banner, and the *jasagh* as well as the people could not transgress these boundaries in herding and hunting unless they were authorized to do so by the imperial court in Peking or by the *chighulghan-u darugha,* the "head of the league," within which the banner was included.[13] Thus, strict limitations on banner boundaries and loyalties, and the stricter relationship between the nomadic people and a given area of land, made feudal-like tendencies more pronounced in the Ch'ing period and greatly hampered the development of unity and strength among the Mongols in the modern period.

Above the banner unit was an administrative unit called the *chighulghan* or "league." Originally, the word had the connotation of "to gather together" or "to form an alliance." The English term league is taken from the Chinese *meng.* In the beginning of the Ch'ing period, the league was merely a temporary unit that gathered at a particular time and place and had no permanently designated head. A presiding officer was usually dispatched as a representative of the emperor to take charge of the league. From the 1750s on, it became customary to systematically appoint a banner head as the league head. Thus, the post of league head developed into an intermediary administrative office, with rather weak authority, between the emperor at the top and the banner on the local level. Significantly, the league post never became hereditary. Since the post was appointive, restrictive and arbitrary elitist tendencies, common in the banner, did not carry over into the league.

The perpetuation of a quasi-feudalistic system in Mongolia by the Manchu was promoted on the one hand by the need for control and on the other hand by a tendency to fragmentation in already existing institutions which could be sustained with little resistance from the society. Developing banners as petty kingdoms or fiefs served the purpose of the Manchu and, at the same time, satisfied the ambition for autonomy or some semblance of independent prestige for the ruling class among the Mongols. Ostensibly, such a policy could be construed as benevolent for the Mongols in that period.

In cases of treason or rebellion of a banner against the Manchu, their noble class and its feudalistic prerogatives were eliminated as an example to others. The Chakhar and Tümed, for example, two tribes that early recognized the overlordship of the Manchu but later rebelled, had their princely class eliminated and were then governed by *ambans* appointed by the court and put directly under the administration of Manchu *tu-t'ung* and *chiang-chün* ("governor generals").[14] Eliminating the princely privileges of Mongol lords who rebelled had a restraining effect on other banners that considered withdrawing support from the Manchu. The Chakhar and Tümed were subsequently reorganized administratively along the lines of the Manchu Eight Banners. Within the Manchu system, some Mongol officials were appointed to the post of *amban* (Chs. *tsung-kuan*), a type of local governor representing the court. The post of *amban* was not hereditary; officials were appointed from within the overall bureaucracy.[15] A man from one banner could be appointed as an official within another banner, but retained an identification with his original banner. The general view is that feudalistic tendencies in areas such as Chakhar and Tümed were much weaker than in banners in which the hereditary nobility continued. Despite the Manchu reorganization, some traditional features were maintained in the Chakhar and Tümed banners; for example, some *janggi* within a *sumun* continued to be hereditary. One hereditary *kung* ("duke"), in the Kübe'etü Shira Banner in the Chakhar area, referred to as Ö'elüd Kung,[16] was not originally a Chakhar, but from an Oirad Mongol group farther to the northwest. In the wars with the Manchu, he had surrendered and had been relocated among the Chakhar people. This, then, was a special case of a Mongol noble who had a limited number of hereditary *khariyatu* or "vassals," but very little influence.

The Manchu handled different groups in different ways. Some Mongol tribes recognized Manchu suzerainty, but the Manchu placed little importance on them and did not bestow important noble rank or feudalistic privileges upon them. The Manchu developed unique policies for other tribes. The Bargha (Barghu) tribes of the Hulun-buir area, under the commander in Heilungkiang and the Tannu-Uriyangkhai regions, were placed under the jurisdiction of the Manchu *amban* or governor general stationed at Kobdo.[17] Another policy was developed for the Budkha and Solon tribes in northeastern Mongolia, who were closely related to the Tungusic Manchu by culture, past contacts, and intermarriage. Top officials in these tribes were appointed by the Manchu, while lower functionaries were appointed by the Mongol officials. The Manchu felt that these people could be handled more nearly like the Manchu because of their cultural relationship. Although there were no hereditary princes or feudal-like privileges among them, a ruling clique or elite developed, and the appointment of officials was made along bloodlines in such a way as to be interpreted as feudalistic by some writers.

In the early seventeenth century and continuing through the Ch'ing period, a feudal-like ecclesiastical pattern that was associated with Lamaist Buddhism developed. Frequently, the literature on Mongolia notes that the Mongol princes and high lamas were the "twin pillars of feudalism" in Mongolia. At the end of the sixteenth century, with the second introduction of Buddhism, the nobility adopted the religion and constrained the common people also to accept Tibetan Buddhism. In time, it became the dominant religion. Some of the hereditary nobility became monks, while other monks or lamas gained such great prestige and so many privileges that they were regarded as nobles among the people. Though a noble took the vows of a lama, he still retained his rank of nobility[18] and still maintained his feudal-like privileges, such as holding *khariyatu* or "serfs." Also, over a period of time, many high lamas were given gifts by Mongolian nobles who wished to gain religious merit; at times these gifts consisted of people who became *shabinar,* or a sort of serf of the temple. *Shabinar* means literally "disciples"—in this case, lay disciples of a temple. From generation to generation, the *shabinar* belonged to the temple. Their sons could become lamas, but they themselves could not depart from the temple. From the time of the transfer of their status or service, they no longer served their old lord, but rather the temple.[19]

Feudalistic privileges in the temples were not transferred from generation to generation by heredity or by blood relationship, but rather through the institution of reincarnation. The *bodhisattva* ideal of Tibetan Buddhism holds that after death, a person does not enter nirvana but is reincarnated on earth in order to serve mankind. The Mongols speak of the incarnation of a high lama as a *khubilghan*. The determination of a new *khubilghan* was sometimes a complex process, involving, among other things, oracles and ecclesiastical politics. An indication may be given by the former incarnation before death as to where or in which direction the person may be reborn. Thus, on the death of an incarnation, the officials of the temple seek an oracle from a high lama who serves this function. Then, according to the instructions of the oracle, they seek several candidates of the approximate age which the new *khubilghan* should be. After two or three years, the candidates are tested in various ways to determine which will be recognized as the new incarnation. For example, a number of objects including relics of the former incarnation will be shown to them to determine if they can identify the proper objects. After a process of elimination, two or three remaining candidates will have their names submitted to the high lama of the temple for a final decision; in some cases an appeal may be made to the *choijung* or "protective spirit," to assist in the final decision. For a very prominent incarnation, an expedition may even be sent to Lhasa, Tibet, to seek the assistance of the Dalai Lama in making a final decision.

In the latter part of the eighteenth century, during the reign of the Emperor Ch'ien-lung (1726-95), in order to control or influence the decision of high *khubilghans*, a stipulation was made by the Ch'ing court that no high incarnation would be reborn in a noble family. This ruling was meant to establish a separation of the lay nobility and the ecclesiastical hierarchy. To carry out this policy, two *altan bomba* or "golden bottles" were established, one in Lhasa and one in the great imperial Lamaist temple, Yüng-ho kung, in Peking. The names of the candidates for the new incarnation of the great *khubilghan* were placed in the golden bottle, and, after special prayers and ceremonies, the names were drawn as lots under the supervision of the Manchu *amban* in Lhasa or by an official dispatched by the emperor to the temple in Peking.[20] As a result of this system, the greatest *khubilghan* of Mongolia, the Jebtsundamba of Urga, was reincarnated only two times in Mongolia, and every succeeding incarnation was found by direction of the Manchu emperors in Tibet.[21] The new incarnation was installed in the temple in the role of his predecessors.

All incarnations are referred to by the generic term *khubilghan;* but in addition they are commonly referred to by some title or designation of rank, the highest ranks being *khutughtu,* "blessed one," *nom-un khan,* "king of the (Buddhist) law," or *chorji,*[22] a Tibetan loanword having the same meaning as *nom-un khan.* All incarnations are commonly referred to by the people as *gegen, (gege'en,* "the enlightened one"). Another term of reference for incarnations is "living Buddha"; however, there is no corresponding term in Mongolian or Tibetan. It is an English translation of the Chinese term *huo-fo,* literally, "living Buddha."[23]

The role of the living Buddha in Mongolian life—secular as well as religious—was very important. He served as head of a temple and an object of worship among the people and the lamas. Apart from his role as ecclesiastical head of the temple, he was also overlord of the lay people (*shabinar*), who belonged to the temple as serfs. A high-ranking *khutughtu,* or living Buddha, might have possessed land and exercised administrative control over his *shabinar* grazing on that land. There was a great variation from region to region in Mongolia in regard to the power of the *khutughtu. Khutughtu* or incarnations holding sizable amounts of land and *shabinar* were the only ones who really could be compared to the Mongol princes and high-ranking nobility. The Jebtsundamba, Living Buddha of Urga, held such a large number of *shabinar* as to be equal in influence to the administrator of a league. Problems arose regarding the distribution of the herds belonging to the people and the pastures on which they grazed. If a minor living Buddha had only a limited number of *shabinar* or followers, they had no land of their own on which to graze their herds but were allowed to range freely as the other people of the banner. In such a case, a vassalage-type relationship was limited only to the living Buddha and his followers. A low-ranking incarnation had no influence in politics and very little administrative control, even in disputes among his own followers, and matters were settled by the banner officials.

Küriye Süm, a famous temple in eastern Inner Mongolia, which controlled pasturelands equal to those of surrounding banners and whose presiding lamas ruled their own domain, is an example of an ecclesiastical feudal-like phenomenon. Another is Chaghan Nom-un Khan, a Living Buddha in Kökönor, who also had large lands and herds and whose realm officially had the status of a banner.[24] The phenomenon of an ecclesiastical quasi-feudalism was not characteristic of the Mongol Empire of the Yüan period, but came into existence during the late sixteenth century and was really only institutionalized during the Manchu period. .

SOCIAL CLASSES:
THE NOBILITY AND THE PEOPLE

The *Secret History of the Mongols*, the most valuable early source describing the life of the Mongols, in recording the story of Alan-gho'a, an early female ancestor of the Mongols, makes note of two social classes, the *khaghan* and the *kharachu*.[1] One can infer, since the discussion centers on the legendary period of Mongol history, that class differentiation extended back into preclassical, that is, pre-empire, times. The *khaghan* (khan) was the highest rank of nobility. The original translation of *kharachu*, according to the Chinese from the *Secret History*, was "low people, subordinates", (Chs. *hsia-min*).[2] The Mongol term is roughly the equivalent of the Chinese term *ch'ien-shou* or "black-headed ones."

In modern times, Mongols speak of the nobility collectively as *noyad*, but the term *kharachu* is still used for commoners. The natural condescension of the nobility for the commoners is reflected in the root of the word *kharachu*: *khara* means "black." Customarily, the Mongols value white as the pure, superior, and lucky color; black has the opposite meanings. Thus, the noble class refer to themselves as the *chaghan yasutan* or "white lineages" and to the ordinary people as *khara yasutan* or "black lineages." Apart from the nobles or white lineages, all other people—slaves, captives, or free commoners—were considered black lineages. Used in this connection, and literally defined, the terms mean "white bone" and "black bone," which calls to mind a widely told story about a person of noble rank traveling with a common nomad. As the two came upon a number of animal skeletons, the commoner dismounted and bowed to the bones. The princely person inquired as to the reason for this strange behavior, and the commoner replied that he thought the white bones might be those of the nobleman's forebears and that it was only good propriety for him to pay due respect to the remains.[3] The manner and the situations in which the story is told indicate a certain class consciousness or reaction against the hereditary nobility of old Mongolia.

Captives taken in warring activity, a constant characteristic of nomadic society, became slaves, as in many other societies. As a result, below the common people was a class of slaves (*bo'ol* or *boghol*). It is not clear what the exact role of the so-called slaves in Mongolian society of the Middle Ages was, nor how slavery compared to institutions or classes in Europe or other parts of Asia. Even Communist scholars are debating this matter.[4] The *Secret History* records the case of To'oril, a vassal of Chinggis Khan, who separated from Chinggis and led a group to join Ong Khan of the Kereyid tribe. Chinggis sent a messenger to say:

> Go and tell younger brother To'oril—the reason I entitle you "younger brother" is because the slave captured by Tumbinai and Charkhai-lingkhu was Oghta. His son was Sübegei . . . [long genealogy given] and the son of Yegei-khongtakhar is you. Now whose people is it that you are going to take to Ong Khan to flatter him . . . the reason why I call you "younger brother" is because you were slaves in the threshold of my great-great-grandfather and slaves in the door of my great grandfather.[5]

By Mongol custom, this type of slave is referred to as *unaghan bo'ol,* which may be interpreted as "slave born into the household."[6] However, there was enough upward mobility that such a slave could in time gain status almost equal to that of a regular family member. This accounts for the fact that Chinggis Khan had this person's genealogy clearly in mind and referred to him as "younger brother." During the early empire period, slaves rose to become important vassals or comrades-in-arms.

Not all slaves were acquired as prisoners in war. The *Secret History* records how Chinggis Khan—after being recognized as the leader of a Mongol clan alliance and after defeating a rebellious Mongol group, the Jürkin—was approached by three brothers: Kü'ün-gho'a, Chila'un-khaichi, and Jcbüke (sons of Telegetü-bayan and members of the Jalayir lineage, a subgroup associated with the Jürkin lineage). The first brother, Kü'ün-gho'a, brought his two sons, Mukhali and Bukha, to Chinggis Khan and declared:"Let them be slaves [*bo'ol*] in your threshold and, if they pass out of your doorway, let the tendon of their ankles be cut. Let them be your personal slaves, and if they escape from your household, let their heart and liver be cut out." The second brother, Chila'un-khaichi, also brought his two sons, Tüngge and Khashi and said:

> I cause them to watch your golden threshold and I present them to you, O Khan. If they separate themselves from your golden threshold and attach themselves to another, let their lives be taken and they cast away. I cause them to open and close your broad door and present them to you, O Khan.

If they depart from your broad door and go to some other place, cut out their hearts and cast them afar.[7]

Thus, a slave class, so-called, arose because certain families presented their sons to a promising new leader with the hope that the way would be opened to them for future opportunities and success. Later, the two older brothers, Kü'ün-gho'a and Chila'un-khaichi, gave their younger brother Jebüke to Khasar, younger brother of Chinggis Khan.

According to early Mongolian records, even prominent families with wealth (often bearing the title *bayan*) were willing to present their sons or brothers to a Mongol ruler as "slaves." It is difficult to determine whether they can be accurately termed slaves or whether vassal is a better term. The "personal slaves" mentioned above are called, by the Mongols, *omchu bo'ol*,[8] which has the connotation of a very intimate follower of the lord himself. It is possible that in this situation very humble words were used in making a vassal-like relationship in a feudalistic context that actually did not amount to slavery. For example, it is common knowledge that, in addressing the emperor, Manchu officials of high rank used the term *nu-ts'ai*, literally "slaves," in reference to themselves. A similar manner of address was common during the Mongol Empire when vassals or lords addressed themselves to a khan or emperor. The boy in the story, Mukhali, later became a commander and chief of the left-flank army of Chinggis Khan. He was an important figure in the invasion of North China and later received the title of *kuo-wang* ("ruler of the realm").[9] His uncle, Jebüke, and his brother and cousin, Bukha and Tüngge, were all appointed *mingghan-u noyan* ("commander of one thousand troops") when Chinggis Khan ascended the throne as khan of the entire Mongol Empire (1206). Bukha also received the title *kürgen* or "royal son-in-law." Incidentally, cases involving men referred to in their early years as "slaves," but who gained high distinction in their later career, are used by Marxist analys.s to stress the existence of a slave class in early Mongolian society. The data is obviously questionable.[10]

Another role or group of status in Mongol society was that of *nökör*, which according to some scholars has the connotation of a vassal. Its function in society is not entirely clear. In the original Chinese translation of the *Secret History*, the term *nökör* is translated as *pan-tang* or "companion,"[11] indicating that it was a special role of both a companion-in-battle and a vassal. This position existed not only in the early "clan" or lineage period, but also through the empire era and the Yüan dynasty. Men in the *nökör* role were not restricted in service to the highest rank of khan, but were also found attached to the leaders of lower Mongol units (companies of one thousand and companies of one hundred). Apparently, *nökör* were even aides to higher officers who had such diverse origins as slaves, free men, or vassals.[12] The organization of the *keshig,* or personal guard, enlarged the *nökör* role and institutionalized a unique system and a new group (see Chapter 7, Political Structure: Unique Traditional Institutions). Bo'urchu,[13] son of a rich man of the Arulad lineage, voluntarily came to pledge loyalty to Chinggis Khan and serve him as a *nökör*-type vassal.

The following excerpt from the *Secret History* mentions the roles of the slave and the *nökör* or "vassal companion." When Chinggis Khan campaigned against the Kereyid tribe and overcame them, their leader, Ong Khan, escaped with the assistance of Khadagh Ba'atur, the courageous head of the Jirkin lineage. Later, Khadagh Ba'atur surrendered to Chinggis Khan and explained why he had assisted in his old lord's escape. Chinggis was very impressed and because Khuyildar, his own old *anda* ("sworn brother"),[14] had been killed in an earlier war with the Kereyid, he said:

> You did not forsake your *tus* ["original lord"], but fought very fiercely in order to assist his escape. Is it not a great man who would do such a thing? Such a man is indeed a *nökör.* The khan had mercy [on the man and] did not execute him. Because Khuyildar, the old *anda* of Chinggis had given his life [for him], in making judgment, Chinggis Khan said, "Let Khadagh Ba'atur, as the head of a hundred warriors of Jirkin (lineage), serve the wife and sons of Khuyildar. If sons are born to the company, let them also serve the descendants of Khuyildar. If daughters are born to them [the Jirkin group], they cannot marry out as they wish. They also must serve around the wife and daughter of Khuyildar."[15]

Obviously, such a loss of personal freedom places the person in question in a serflike position.

A man in the *nökör* role had to be very trustworthy. In cases such as the above, even though the person was a captive, he was given special service and maintained his title (*ba'atur*). Khadagh Ba'atur was given the position of a companion-in-arms and commander of troops; but at the same time, he was a vassal and bound by restrictions that made him less than a free man.

During the clan and the quasi-feudalistic periods, great emphasis was placed on the relationship between a *tus* ("lord") and his subordinates. *Tus* were originally heads of clans or lineages. Later, *tus* became *noyad* ("lords" or "nobility") and had subordinated to them, vassals, common people, and slaves in a feudal-like relationship. The clan-lineage and feudalistic systems were both based upon loyalty and obedience to an overlord or a type of *tus*.[16]

Men and their families who were sent to accompany daughters of nobles being married to other lineages belonged to another category of vassals called the *injes*.[17] The practice continued almost to the end of the Manchu period when Manchu royal princesses were married to Mongol princes and took with them their followers. Before the Ch'ing dynasty, these men were never eunuchs. (The eunuch system was not adopted among the Mongols until Chinese influence came in, and even then there is no known case of a Mongolian eunuch—all were Chinese.[18]

The majority of the population, needless to say, were classed neither as nobility nor as slaves. It is at times difficult to distinguish clearly, in the early social system of Mongolia, between vassals and free men with no obligation to a lord. "Free" men or commoners are referred to in the *Secret History* and the *Yuan shih* as *dure* (Chs. *pai-shen jen*). When Chinggis Khan was organizing his royal guard (*keshig* or *keseg*), he recruited men from among the sons and brothers of officers of the military units of one thousand, one hundred, and ten, and even from among the *düre* or common people who were not discriminated against.[19]

Other Mongol terms for commoners are *irgen*[20] and *aran*, which, according to the *Secret History*, were used in ancient times and were translated in the Yüan period by the Chinese as "lower people."[21] Today, the term *aran* has disappeared and only the plural form *arad* remains, with the meaning of "common people."

With the enlargement of the Mongolian Empire, many former *nökör*, vassals, and even slaves reached comparatively high positions. Many rose to become *noyad* ("officials" or "nobility"). There is some question whether there was a procedure or ritual for raising a man's social status from that of a slave to a free man; some scholars, who feel that a man was first made a *darkhan*,[22] support their theory by interpreting the term *darkhan* in the *Secret History*, according to the Chinese translation, *tze tsai* and hold this term to mean "to be free." *Darkhan* ("those without service") constitutes a separate and unique group, quite small and of little importance, which was neither of the nobility nor of the commoners (*albatu*). The most important group with this identity were people involved in the cult of Chinggis Khan in the Ordos,[23] who were exempt from other services in the pre-Communist situation. However, the term *darkhan* (*darkhad*), aside from the connotation of being free from obligation, has other meanings. It was also traditionally used to refer to those men who had a right to keep plunder that they took personally in war or to keep game that they killed personally. They were not compelled to share as was common. If they transgressed the law, *darkhan* were free from punishment for nine offenses.[24] Obviously, they had very special privileges not even allowed to some of the nobility, and it is very questionable that the term referred to a process of being freed from slavery.

It was customary for the Mongols to distribute captives taken in battle to various tribes or to place them in the direct service of the khan. However, it is difficult to determine whether these people were really slaves or free. Certainly their status was flexible because, as already noted, when the empire was enlarged, their status was raised and they often came to high positions. The system of distributing a captive population was, of course, not practicable when the Mongols invaded areas in which they were a minority. Even so, they still frequently took skilled craftsmen or artisans as captives and pressed them into special service. This particular group was spoken of, in the Yüan history, as *ch'üeh-lin-ko,* which seems to be a corruption of the Mongol term of *kiling,* meaning "guilt" or "anger," and the Chinese suffix *ko,* meaning "population" or "persons." The origin of the term cannot be found in Mongolian records, but it seems to be connected with the custom of taking captives in wartime for special service. There are other interpretations of the origin.[25]

Most commoners were referred to as *albatu* or "persons with duty," referring to their relationship with the princes or *jasagh.* Most of the social classes or roles discussed above continued from the Yüan dynasty until modern times and became more institutionalized as class lines became much more rigid. Consequently, there has been very little social mobility, except in situations created by the rise of nationalism, greater Chinese and Russian involvement, and the Japanese occupation.

The word *slave* is used in various contexts in modern Mongolia. It is a term of self-deprecation or humility as, for example, when one refers to oneself as a slave in addressing a person of nobility. A related term is *khariyatu* ("vassal" or "one under control"), which has been used until recently in reference to all people under a *jasagh* and has no connotation of real subjugated status.

Thus, there were three types of vassals (*khariyatu*) in Mongolian society until the Communist takeover: (1) people who gave special service to a lord; (2) persons attached to a temple (*shabinar*); and (3) special persons in the suite or service of a daughter of a noble family being married to another noble (*injes*). The only real slaves (*bo'ol*) were persons owned by the nobility or by wealthy commoners. At least until the Communist period, *bo'ol* were found in the Mongol areas near the Great Wall, but not in nomadic areas. A female slave is referred to as *shibegchin*. While the custom of slavery has continued to modern times, it is very rare. In more recent times, *bo'ol* or *shibegchin* originated from among the children of poor Mongols or Chinese refugees whose families could not support them and therefore sold them into slavery.[26]

A differentiation between (1) the common people, (2) *khariyatu* ("vassals"), and (3) slaves may be made: common people could serve in public office, but persons in the other two categories could not; *khariyatu* and slaves had no public duties or rights. However, in a limited number of Mongolian regions, *khariyatu* might fill some service. In a sense, all common people and even some petty nobility considered themselves *khariyatu* of the *jasagh* of their banner. However, to be precise, these people are generally *khariyatu* of the banner and not of the *jasagh* or chief official personally. This important distinction has not always been made, for, in some periods of history or in some places even in this century, some *khariyatu* were attached to the *jasagh* personally or to larger noble families. In some areas of Mongolia, these people have been listed in the census; in other places, they have not. In some places, they could serve in public office; in some, they could not, and, in still other places, they could serve with certain restrictions according to banner custom.[27] *Khariyatu* or vassals of temples and monasteries, as noted earlier, were followers of disciples of the institution (*shabinar*). Their duty or service was limited to the temple and not to the banner generally. Slaves were never listed in the census of the banner and had no status. They had neither public rights nor duties.[28]

From earliest clan times to the period of the Mongol Empire and quasi-feudalism, the duty of both vassals and the common people was to follow their lords in war, on expeditions, and in hunting, and to furnish service, tribute, or tax. Some of the terms of Mongol vassalage were recorded in the *Secret History*[29] in the account of the swearing of fealty by the lineage heads to Chinggis Khan and when Chinggis Khan rose to supreme power over the Mongol nation in 1206. Other examples of service and vassalage are found in the proclamation by Ögödei Khan on the occasion of his establishment of stages on the imperial road and the rate of tribute or tax to be given by the ordinary people. These various instances note the duties owed by a vassal to the state, to the khan, or to some other lord.[30]

Every vassal-type relationship involves service or duty, and persons under a lord were termed *albatu*. The types of duty owed by *albatu* were (1) military service whenever necessary, (2) civilian service or corvée, and (3) tax. Beginning with the Ch'ing dynasty (1644), all public offices in banner administration were filled by men who served without salary, but worked in fulfillment of their *alba*. The old basic terminology still persists under the socialist government in the Mongolian People's Republic, where common clerks and functionaries in the bureaucracy are termed *alba kha'aghchi* ("duty filler"). During the so-called feudalistic period, a man who retired from service in the higher echelons of banner administration was given the title *darkhan,* which meant he had filled his service. Corvée usually included such activity as service in the banner or some other public office; work at the residence of the *jasagh;* participation in long-distance caravan trade; service at posts or way stations on established routes; and common labor such as digging wells, repairing bridges, preparing carts, and supplying animals on requisiton for the service of the *jasagh* or banner.

Taxes were paid according to quota and in kind from the herds. Taxes on the Mongol people during the empire period, as seen in the *Secret History,* were very light. Ögödei Khan assembled a great *kuraltai,* or assembly, and announced:

> In order to supply . . . the sheep for the royal soup, a two-year-old sheep shall be given as tribute from every herd. . . . A one-year-old lamb shall be given to the tribe for every one hundred sheep of the herd to relieve the distress of the poor people. . . . In order not to disturb the people, a definite road shall be established for use of those officials who come and go in service, and men shall be dispatched to serve at the stations and to look after the horses.[31]

The custom of taking one sheep per one hundred in a herd as a tax or tribute is also mentioned in the *Ta-yüan ma-cheng chi* (record of the horse policy of the great Yüan dynasty),[32] and it may be seen from these records that the tax, service, or tribute was comparatively light at the beginning of the dynasty; however, as disturbances and trouble increased toward the end of the dynasty, exactions were greatly increased.

During the later part of the sixteenth century, with the conversion of the Mongol nobility to Tibetan Buddhism, a great burden was added to the people. A custom developed wherein *jasagh* or higher nobility made gifts to the Buddhist temples and high lamas of *alba* or service of the people under them. After the Mongols became subordinated to the Manchu during the Ch'ing period, a limit was placed upon the amount of tax or *alba* that could be required of the people. As noted in the *Ta-Ch'ing hui-tien* (collected institutes of the great Ch'ing dynasty) of the 1640s:

> The princes (*wang-kung*) and nobility (*taiji*) may requisition of their people every year, one sheep from a man who has five cows or more and twenty sheep; two sheep will be taken from a man who has forty sheep, and even if the herd is larger no additional animals may be taken. From a man who has two sheep, six pots of grain shall be assessed. From a man who has but one sheep, one pot of grain will be taken. On special occasions such as in sending tribute to the emperor, league council meetings, migration, and a marriage of the nobility, tax will be taken according to the number of vassals held by the lord. If he holds more than one hundred families there shall be assessed from he who is head of ten families, a cow, a horse, a cart, and in addition, from those families who have cows, shall be taken a stomach sack of butter. From a man who has five or more cows shall be taken a bottle of milk wine, and from a man who has more than one hundred sheep shall be taken a piece of felt. If more than this quota is taken there shall be a punishment.[33]

The mention of grain in the record seems to indicate that these regulations were set up in the early period when groups of Mongols first came under the subordination of the Manchu in eastern Inner Mongolia. In actual practice, the burden on the people of the Mongol nobility was greater than the official record indicates. It was customary for the *jasagh* or higher nobility to make arbitrary requisitions from the people, which were filled by distributing the burden among the people of the banner. On occasions, even the punishment of a *jasagh* by the Manchu court was not assumed by him personally, but was distributed among his people. Personal debts of the *jasagh* also were often handled by a requisition from the people. This is spoken of as *alba duusghakhu* or "distributing the tax."

The burden on the common people became particularly unbearable later in the Ch'ing period when the nobility were required to make regular trips to the capital in Peking or to follow the court during the imperial hunt. The animals and supplies for the caravans had to be furnished by the people.

Alba was also extracted from the *shabinar* or serflike disciples of the Lamaist temples. But it was light in comparison to the burden on the banner in general since their tax or service was only to the temple, and lamas were exempt from military service, participation in large hunts, and so forth. During the eighteenth and nineteenth centuries, people tried to escape the heavy burdens of *alba* by becoming *shabinar* of temples, in much the same way as men in feudal Europe escaped taxes by attaching themselves to monasteries (commendation).

A particularly important development occurred in the second decade of the present century during the emergence of an independent government in Outer Mongolia (1911). A large number of people had escaped taxation by becoming *shabinar* and had come under the jurisdiction of the high lamas. The expenditures and budget of the newly independent state increased, and there was an uneven tax burden upon the common people because the lamas had exempted their own *shabinar*, since they themselves held power in the government. There was great discontent among some lay nobility and others who experienced a growing desire to give up independence for a return to the less-exacting Chinese jurisdiction. To complicate matters, many of the lay nobility were greatly indebted to Chinese and Russian merchants, and these debts were being transferred to the shoulders of the lay people in addition to new taxes required by the newly independent government. The compounded discontent gave rise to a revolutionary sentiment leading to Communist rule in the 1920s.[34]

THE END OF NOMADIC EMPIRES

Expanding nomadic empires and peoples from the most ancient nomads to the Mongols had a great impact on the premodern world—for China and Russia, ancient Rome, and medieval Europe they were a traumatic experience. Although many nomadic peoples have disappeared from the world, the Mongols are still with us and give strong evidence of a resurgence, albeit not in the old sense of a "yellow peril." The question remains in the minds of many, Why have the Mongols been obscured from world view for so long? This question can only be touched on in passing, but it cannot be ignored because of its momentous implications for the nomads of Mongolia and for their society and culture.

But, in 1757, after seven decades of struggle with the powerful Manchu Empire, the Jungar Mongol state, the last nomadic empire,[1] was crushed; from that time on, the nomadic peoples of North and Central Asia failed to establish another empire.

A central theme of Asian history has been the continuous interaction between the northern steppe peoples and the Chinese to the south; their contact involved wars and trade, competition and cooperation. The focus of the historical geography of the Middle Kingdom was to the north in perpetual vigilance against invasion by nomads. But when a Chinese state was strong, it expanded its influence to the south and sought to include smaller states in its tributary system; when China was weak, she neglected this quarter. There were only mystic notions and general ignorance in ancient China regarding the realm beyond the seas to the east, which were viewed as natural protection. Chinese commonly thought of their land as the *hai-nei*—"the regions within the seas." There was a puzzling lack of curiosity and exploration beyond their boundaries.

Conversely, the nomadic peoples were always concerned with what they considered to be oppression from the south. If there was no threat from China, the nomads peacefully followed their herds, hunted game, and led a quiet life—except when pressing needs for certain goods or alien groups forced them to move south of the Great Wall.[2] To the nomads, the areas north and west of Mongolia were boundless areas for continual expansion. The hunting or forest peoples of these areas were always subjugated to them. Under pressure of the Chinese agricultural people from the south, these regions of Inner Asia became a refuge for defense of the nomads.

During the period of powerful Chinese dynasties, emperors—such as Wu-ti (140-87 B.C.) and Ho-ti (A.D. 89-105) of the Han and Yung-lo (1403-24) of the Ming—mounted great campaigns into the northern steppes and even defeated some nomadic forces; but they were never able to occupy or control the land for any length of time because of the nature of the Gobi. Even when Chinese forces entered the "dry sea" or Gobi, the nomads could move farther west and bide their time for another opportunity. Thus, an army from the south never posed a permanent military threat, but merely caused a temporary retreat into the refuge of the steppe. In contrast, the nomads always reappeared on the frontier in some new threat, which invariably involved nomadic movements to the south to pasture animals in the fertile areas along the Great Wall. The game of military hide-and-seek never definitely crushed the nomadic people. However, attempts to mount great campaigns into the steppes often caused dislocation, conflict, and trouble for the agricultural Chinese. Men were conscripted and taxes were levied.

The process often caused a chain reaction: the Chinese attacks pushed the nomads west, and the peoples in the west were affected.[3] Conversely, some pastoral nomads withdrew from Europe, to the western sector of the Eurasian continent, or from the Persian sector into Inner Asia, causing turbulence and conflict. Turks, Kazaks, and others also formed nomadic confederations and displaced neighboring nomadic groups.

From ancient times, the nomads and the Chinese shared a mutual aversion to living on each other's lands. The attitude was expressed in the second century B.C. by the wife of the great Hsiung-nu *shan-yü* (khan) Mao-tun on the occasion of the siege of the Chinese Emperor Han Kao-ti inside the Great Wall: "Now we have occupied Chinese territory, but over the long run it is not the place where you, the *shan-yü*, are able to live."[4] The Chinese repulsion to living in the steppe was stated in the late first century by the great Chinese historian Pan Ku:

> Mountains, valleys, and the great desert separate them from us. This barrier which lies between the interior [China] and the alien [Mongolian] was made by Heaven and Earth. Therefore the sage rulers . . . neither established agreements with them nor subjugated them. . . . It would involve our troops in vain and cause the enemy to fight back if an invasion were carried out. Their land is impossible to cultivate and it is impossible to rule them as subjects.[5]

The expressed mutual discomfort supports our theory that no dynasty of steppe peoples successfully occupied China without the collaboration of some of the Chinese elite. It was impossible to rule China without Chinese help. Similarly, with but a few exceptions along the Great Wall, Chinese migrated and settled in Mongolia only comparatively recently.

Beginning in the eighteenth century, with the eastward expansion of the Russians, the old Inner Asian refuge was lost. The nomadic peoples of Central Asia were pressed north by the irresistible force of the Manchu Empire in China, and at the same time they were thrust upon from the rear by the expansion of tsarist Russia. Thus, the nomads who had occupied China and Russia for centuries were now caught between these two great powers. There was no escape. China and Russia made direct contact (the first treaties between a European and an Asian power)[6] and set boundaries, which, for the first time, curtailed the movement of the nomadic peoples of the steppe. This event signaled the end of nomadic empires.

The last of the nomadic empires, the Jungar, established by Galdan, was defeated by the great Manchu Emperor K'ang-hsi in 1696. This was the first defeat of the nomadic cavalry in battle by cannons, developed with the assistance of the Jesuit missionaries in Peking. It was also the first time that Mongol tactics were ineffective against modern weapons. Thus, the Mongols felt the impact of the Western penetration of Asia, but were themselves isolated in the confines of Inner Asia by the natural boundaries of Siberian wastelands and by the isolation policy of China. They were unable to contact Western peoples and adopt their modern technology, without which they were at the mercy of the more advanced science of their neighbors (particularly with respect to guns and railroads). It was not until the turn of the twentieth century that the Mongols began to learn modern ways.[7]

Apart from external factors, which forced an end to nomadic migrations, confederations, and empires, there were important internal trends that weakened the nomads. Internecine wars decimated the people and the herds and fragmented the tribes and clans. The Manchu-Ch'ing policy successfully hastened the division of the Mongols. The conversion of the Mongols to Lamaist Buddhism had great influence upon the attitudes and values of the nomads, particularly a negative influence on population growth.

The complex ramifications of the forced end of wide-ranging, nomadic migrations for the Mongols has implications for almost every section of this study. While traditional attitudes and behavior show considerable continuity, there were, naturally, many changes in social and political structure, in basic economic life, and in many other areas of culture and society. Some changes came by radical revolution and the socio-economic engineering of Communism. In other instances, there was an evolutionary tendency toward a more sedentary way of life and a gradual assimilation or accommodation of the nomads to the dominant

Chinese or Russian society, which pressed into areas such as Inner Mongolia and Buriyat. The changes in question are all the more complex in that, with modernization and the change of traditional institutions, there has also been a new consciousness and a resurgence of Mongol nationalism.

7
ECONOMY AND POLITY

From ancient times, the economy of the Mongolian society has been based primarily upon herding and secondarily upon hunting, both of which were supplemented by trade and raiding. The development of a marginal agriculture came very late and industry only in recent decades.

Herding and hunting were discussed in Chapter 2, but it should be noted here that products gained from these activities were used not only for domestic consumption, but also for barter and exchange with other peoples. Although trading was very important to the Mongols and they depended very greatly upon it, little or no effort was made to consciously cultivate a merchant class; nor did a significant Mongolian merchant class arise naturally. Thus, trade was seldom smooth and never really well established or institutionalized. It was carried on mainly by tribal leaders, rather than by a special class. Even in modern times, mercantile activity was invariably in the hands of the Chinese until the situation changed in Outer Mongolia after the establishment of the Mongolian People's Republic.

Development of society in Mongolia comes very close to a case of economic determinism in that not only diet but also products for barter and trade depend upon the type of animals raised and hunted. Based on the situation in the Shilin-ghol League, a purely pastoral area of Inner Mongolia, if annual consumption and taxes were limited to around one-tenth of the herds, an increase could be sustained. If consumption and various requisitions were to rise above 10 percent of the animals, it would be difficult or impossible to maintain any continued increase. An important factor for the nomads is the incidence of natural catastrophes. Ordinarily, in a given year, one-third of the hides of the above 10 percent would meet the necessities of the people, and two-thirds of the hides and most of the wool could be considered as a surplus for exchange.[1] Until recent decades, milk products were never considered objects for trade or barter for several reasons. First, there was no real demand from the only potential market, China, in which the consumption of milk products has been customarily very low. Secondly, there were insurmountable problems of distribution. Important also was a general feeling among the Mongols, from early times, that milk is a blessing and is not to be sold for profit.

During normal times, the consumption of the people and the natural increase of the animals are well balanced. During the period of the 1930s and 1940s, for example, the average household of the nomadic area of Shilin-ghol was between four and five persons, and this manpower was sufficient to care for a herd of forty to fifty horses or the same number of cattle, plus three to four hundred sheep. Comparatively speaking, a pastoral family in Shilin-ghol had a higher income or standard of living than the average Mongol family of the same size in sedentary areas, who were using adequate but relatively primitive Chinese techniques of agriculture.[2] Though it is possible for a family of five to handle herds of this size, this ideal was seldom reached. The average mixed herd of horses, cattle, and sheep was about one hundred head during this period. However, these statistics are rather tentative because there was a very uneven distribution of wealth: some wealthy families held herds of thousands of animals, and very poor families had but a few head. Wealthy commoners with large herds employed poorer people to handle their sheep, and these people were paid with the milk and wool of the animals concerned. However, the hide was to be returned to the owner if the animal died. For larger animals—horses or camels—hired help would be brought in by more wealthy families and paid a monthly or seasonal rate.[3]

A number of events limited the natural increase of wealth in the herding economy of Mongolia. Historically, internecine warfare destroyed the economic base in Mongolia, which was well developed before and during the Mongol Empire. The destruction of tribal groups and their herds occurred for more than one century during the period extending from the end of the Yüan dynasty (1368) until the time of Dayan Khan (d. 1530?). A second factor was the burden upon the common people of service and taxes to their lords under the quasi-feudalistic, traditional division of labor in Mongolia. The burdens especially increased after the Mongol princes were subjugated as vassals to the Manchu and were required to make frequent and expensive trips to Peking, to follow the royal hunt in Jehol, to give expensive gifts, to buy expensive mansions in the capital, and so forth. Many demands were placed upon the people in a pastoral economy that was limited and unstable. This problem was compounded when the princes, whose resources came from a pastoral economy, became involved in a money economy and the demands of urban centers such as Peking or Mukden. The wealth of Mongol leaders in animals was changed into money by Chinese merchants, both out in the districts and in the capital; but as the princes and aristocracy became indebted, the burden on the people became heavier.

A third factor tending to depress the economy was the conversion of the Mongol population to Lamaist Buddhism and the rapid rise of monastic or temple centers. Great demands were made upon the people for gifts and sacrifices, and a large institutionalized, unproductive class appeared on the scene. Much of the wealth of Mongolia flowed to the temples and was lost for reinvestment in future development for the society at large. In addition to the unproductive drag of the lamas in Mongolia, there was a great outflow of wealth in pious donations to Tibet, the fountainhead of Lamaist Buddhism. The Mongolian biography of the Zaya Pandita, an incarnation of the seventeenth century, mentions that on two different occasions over twenty thousand head of horses were gathered in Mongolia and sold to Chinese merchants, and the proceeds were sent to Tibet as a donation.[4]

From the end of the sixteenth century to the twentieth century, many Mongol sons became lamas; in some areas this practice absorbed from one-third to one-half of the productive male population. Much of the manpower of Mongol society was lost to monastic institutions and became part of the consuming class. Even after the Communist revolution of the 1920s in Outer Mongolia, when the class structure was radically changed, a rapid increase in production still did not occur, essentially because of the limitation of manpower.

Barter and trade are a natural part of every society, but there are some unique aspects of the mercantile activity of the nomadic peoples of Mongolia, arising from the fact that the nomads were the turbulent, militant "have nots" of the premodern world. Some internal barter and trade existed among the nomads from ancient times; however, most of their trade was with the agricultural peoples to the south of the Great

Wall, the oasis city-states in Central Asia, and with Persians, Turks, and Arabs of western Asia. In contrast, the Chinese were much more self-sufficient and, as a nation, did not place high priority on external trade. However, during some periods, they struggled with the Hsiung-nu, Tibetans, Turks, and others for control of the Silk Route extending through the Kansu corridor into Chinese Turkistan, Central Asia, and to the West.

The rulers of China were well aware of the economic circumstances of the northern nomads and their need for agricultural products, but they failed to develop a policy or workable arrangement for mutually beneficial trade. They generally tended to espouse a policy of embargo or economic strangulation of their nomadic neighbors. The Chinese, historically, are very pragmatic, so it is all the more ironic that they never developed a good trade policy or modus vivendi with the nomads, who were a continual threat. The constant disorders and conflict on the Chinese-Mongolian frontier must be viewed from this perspective. When the nomads were victorious in border clashes, they invariably demanded regular, peaceful trade. When the nomads were able to establish a dynasty by conquest or infiltration in North China, they still demanded tribute from southern Chinese dynasties in the form of goods. The treaty of T'an-yüan in 1004 between the Kitan and the Sung is a well-known example. Thus, the general pattern of relations between the Chinese and the nomads was that the nomads gained by warfare those things they could not gain in peace and the Chinese often gained peace only by "buying off" the nomads.

Differences between the nomads and peasant farmers were so great that it is easy to see why peace could only be established on a long-range basis of mutual exchange and co-prosperity. As noted by Ssu-ma Ch'ien in his history:

> After ascending his throne, Emperor Wu-ti [140-87 B.C.] clearly made it his policy to continue the establishment of kinship through marriage [with nomadic leaders] in order to tighten his control over frontier affairs, to treat outsiders hospitably, to open broader market places, and to give more goods to foreigners. Therefore, the Hsiung-nu from the *Shan-yü* (khan) down to the ordinary people, all became pro-Chinese and the nomads came and went freely at the Great Wall.[5]

This indicates a very early precedent for peaceful trade between the nomads and the Chinese and a relationship with great potential for resolving the natural animosity between the two. In a sense, the border trade between the Chinese and the Hsiung-nu, during the Han period, had a good beginning but a sad ending. During the early period of Han Wu-ti's reign, border markets were established, and, as Chinese treatment was fair, the nomads making contact were favorably inclined toward the Chinese and the exchange of goods flourished.

This situation lasted only a short time. A subordinate Chinese commander in the vicinity of the wall used the new trade arrangement to lay a trap to capture the leader of the nomads and demonstrate his personal heroism. Ssu-ma Ch'ien commented on this incident.

> The [Chinese officials] made the old man Nieh I of the city of Ma-i[6] their spy, in the exchange of goods with the Hsiung-nu. Luring in the Shan-yü[7] he pretended to betray the city of Ma-i, and the Hsiung-nu invaded the border of Wusai[8] with a hundred thousand cavalry. The Chinese ambushed the Shan-yü with three hundred thousand troops . . . and tried to capture and kill him. After that, the Hsiung-nu discontinued the practice of intermarriage . . . and continued increasingly to invade the borders of China.[9]

This was but one of many such occurrences; but with the fall of the Han dynasty, the whole issue of border markets ceased to be a problem to the nomads because various nomadic peoples came to dominate North China as dynasties of conquest or infiltration. However, when the T'ang (618–907) once more consolidated Chinese rule on the frontier, they moved toward a tough policy, and border markets once more became a source of contention. Over time, the possibility for a continuing peace and profitable exchange was lost, resulting in many centuries of mistrust and bloodshed between the two peoples. While hostility and conflict dominated the relationship, there were times of sporadic trade.

Moslem traders appeared very early in Mongol areas. Even before the establishment of the Mongol Empire, a Moslem merchant, Asan, traveled widely from the area of the Öngghüd tribe near the Great Wall to the vicinity of the Ergüne River, at the headwaters of the Amur, to buy sable, ermine, and other rare furs.[10] From this it would appear that Moslem merchants from Central Asia were active in distant, eastern Mongol areas at a very early period. During the Mongol Empire, Uighur, Persian, and other western Asian Moslems gained high positions in the Mongol bureaucracy because of their excellent abilities.

But the main current of trade was still between Mongolia proper and China; Mongolian trade with Central and western Asia was less developed. The nomads of Mongolia looked to their neighbors for most commodities; complex manufacturing never developed in the steppe areas because of the natural limitations of climate and resources, the primitive level of productive techniques among the nomadic peoples, and other factors noted above. There was little alternative to dependence upon the agricultural peoples south of the Great Wall.

Chinggis Khan and other Mongol leaders had a liberal policy toward caravan trade. They utilized caravan merchants for the purpose of gathering intelligence and, therefore, generally protected and encouraged them. The pretext of Chinggis Khan's attack on Khorezm—the killing of his envoy and the execution of caravan men under his protection[11]—is evidence of the high priority placed upon caravan activity by Mongol leaders, who were naturally prompted by economic needs and not necessarily political or military factors. However, Mongols were not usually directly involved in caravan trade until later centuries, although they worked closely with others who were.

Moslem merchants of Inner Asia cooperated very well with Mongolian leaders during the empire period, and they were particularly active in money lending and tax collection. Lending activity was called *örtög*,[12] which has the connotation, in modern times, of usury. The Mongol khans decreed laws in an attempt to regulate or abolish lending by Moslem merchants, but they were unsuccessful. This is the earliest example of exploitation by merchants in Mongolia, a trend which became an especially great problem in modern Mongolian history and one of the causes of Mongolia's independence movement and separation from China.

With the end of the Yüan period, the large caravan activity of Central Asian Moslems was gradually reduced in Mongol areas. The Moslem merchants were later replaced by Chinese merchants who came into Mongolia after the establishment of the Manchu-Ch'ing dynasty (1644) and by Russian merchants who came into northern Mongolia with the expansion of tsarist Russia. During the Ming period (1368-1644), border markets were opened only under duress as the Chinese were forced to recognize the demands of Altan Khan (1507-83?) in the western region of the Great Wall. The use of trade and war as alternatives to gain the same end can be seen in the policies of Altan Khan, which stemmed from the intense economic demand for regular channels of exchange in order to export the surplus products of a growing cattle-raising industry in return for the importation of Chinese handicrafts and agricultural goods.[13] In spite of the fact that the Chinese were forced by Altan Khan to open markets, they ironically gave him the title of Shun-i wang or "prince of righteous obedience." Following the death of Altan, his successors so desired to continue border markets that, on occasion, they returned plunder taken in raids on Chinese cities when Chinese officials threatened that the border markets would be abolished if they did not. The Mongol nation was split during this period, and the western Mongols fared rather better in the Chinese trade than the eastern Mongols who continued as a great threat to the Chinese. There was no formal agreement between the eastern Mongols and the Ming rulers, so generally the old Mongol style of "trade"— raiding and plundering—continued.

Except for the dynasties established by the Mongols and the Manchu, the Chinese were generally inclined toward isolationism; they tended to restrict goods from leaving the empire and flowing across the Great Wall into the steppes. Even the dynasties established by non-Chinese, such as the T'o-pa Wei and the Jurchen-Chin, tended to follow the Chinese example to restrict free trade abroad. Consequently, these dynasties fell into the same trouble or trap as the Chinese and were continually threatened by new waves of northern nomadic peoples.

A departure from the traditional pattern of contact and trade came with the establishment of the Ch'ing dynasty by the Manchu (1644). Their innovative policy allowed trade to develop in nomadic areas, which, in part, explains the long period of comparative peace that resulted: the needs of the nomadic peoples were satisfied, and there was no necessity for warlike activity. Trade, however, was not an unmixed blessing for either the Mongols or China. For the latter, it was one of the main reasons for the declaration of independence of Outer Mongolia from China (1911). For the nomads, it presented a new problem— exploitation by Chinese itinerant traders.

As Chinese merchants penetrated Mongol areas, they easily and peacefully carried on trade from tents which they pitched as they traveled. This was a great improvement for the Mongols over earlier times when it was necessary to obtain important items by raiding and plundering. However, studies of this trade confirm that while it was convenient, it was also very usurious and exploitive. The Chinese established a close relationship with Mongol princes, lending them money at high interest rates which had to be repaid by levies on the common people. At the same time, the merchants established a close working relationship with various Manchu *amban* and other officials in Mongolia to protect their trade and financial activities, which were very inimical to Mongolia's welfare. The Russians used Chinese as contact men or agents, backed by great sums of Russian money. Because of the great inflow of foreign capital, many Mongols became indebted to Chinese and Russian traders, as a result of the exploitation, the Mongols generally developed a very negative attitude toward commercial activity.

There are three general terms in the Mongolian language for merchants: *maimai* or *naimai,* a loan word from the Chinese; *araljigha,* which comes from "exchange"; and *khudaldugha,* "one who sells or buys." The root of the last word, *khudal,* has the connotation of cheating or lying, indicating the Mongol attitude toward merchants. *Araljigha* indicates that all mercantile activity in Mongolia was by barter. (Gradually, during the Ch'ing period, a money economy, using various forms of silver or brick tea as units of exchange, developed.) Although Mongols greatly needed trade, they despised merchants as liars and cheaters and never developed a strong merchant class of their own. Chinese records of the Ming period mention a group of *mao-i-jen,*[14] who were Mongols and apparently traders; but they were an insignificant group in Mongolian society. In modern times, in the Mongolian People's Republic after the Communist revolution and in Inner Mongolia during the late 1930s and early 1940s, institutions were developed with the objective of ridding Mongolia of exploitive middlemen. In both cases, these institutions, *khorishiya,* took the form of cooperatives. Under their own leadership, the Mongols gathered and processed animal products for marketing.

The trade commodities between Mongolia and China remained fairly constant for many centuries. Goods flowing from the steppes were animals, furs, and hides, and the commodities flowing from China were grain, silk, cloth, and various manufactured items. Tea became an important trade commodity from China to Mongolia only in the late sixteenth century. From ancient times, there was a constant embargo against Chinese traders shipping metal or weapons into the frontier. However, from the beginning, the embargo on metal was a dead letter, and great profits were gained by Chinese merchants from the trade of metal goods. On the other hand, although the horse was the primary factor in Mongol warfare and the key to mobility and power, the great needs of the nomads forced them to export great numbers of them.[15]

In spite of the aversion of the nomads to the agricultural Chinese, it was impossible to prevent entirely Chinese political influence from flowing naturally into nomadic areas along with the trade. Because of the high level of sophistication and great penetrating power of the Chinese economically and culturally, there was a tendency over the centuries for nomadic people to be amalgamated with or assimilated by the Chinese. As early as the first century B.C., the Herodotus of China, Ssu-ma Ch'ien, saw this problem and recorded an interesting anecdote. After his surrender to the Shan-yü or khan of the Hsiung-nu, a Chinese official, Chung-hang Yüeh, became a trusted adviser to the nomadic leader. And, although the Hsiung-nu desired silk, cloth, and food from the Chinese, Chung-hang Yüeh said:

> The entire population of the Hsiung-nu is not as large as a single province of China. However, the reason you are still powerful is only because your clothing and food are different and nothing is needed from China. Now if you, the Shan-yü, change the culture or custom and if you long for the goods from China, then the Chinese by mobilizing only two-tenths of their wealth may bring all of the Hsiung-nu under China's rule." Then he [Chung-hang Yüeh, the Chinese official], wearing the silk and cloth of the Chinese, rushed on horseback among the bushes and thorns, letting his coat and trousers be entirely torn to pieces to prove that the material was inferior to garments made of wool and pelts. He also rejected all Chinese foods to demonstrate that they were not as good and desirable as milk and curds.[16]

A similar story is found in the *Chiu T'ang shu,* history of the T'ang period (618-907), according to which Tonyugug (Tün-yu-ku), a Turkic minister, pointed out to his lord, Bilgä Khan, the threat of assimilation by the Chinese if the Turkic people should become too dependent upon China.[17] From these and other records, it may be established that some far-sighted nomadic rulers realized that a critical balance must be maintained in their relations with China. They perceived that the nomads, of necessity, were dependent upon agricultural products, but also that the influence of this dependence must not be allowed to go beyond a certain point. While many foreign peoples were attracted to Chinese culture, the Mongols generally valued their own style of life over that of the agricultural people, and in their contacts and trade they resisted assimilation, which would mean their extinction.

Between the nomads and the Chinese, there were five categories of historical contact or exchange, which were related to trade. The first, the bestowal of goods and presents upon the nomads by the rulers of the Middle Kingdom, generally took place when China was united and strong and the nomads were disunited and weak. The objective of this policy was to appease the nomads and dissuade them from raiding attacks along the border. This shrewd strategem deterred the nomads from unifying and attacking the Chinese for economic gain.[18]

The second pattern was arranging a marriage between a royal Chinese princess and the khan of the nomads or another leading noble. The marriages were always accompanied by large dowries, which served the same purpose as trade, and usually took place when the nomads already had established a powerful state in the steppe area. The objective again was to develop good relations and avoid conflict. The dowries had the effect of temporarily alleviating the economic drive of the khan and his people to gain luxury goods or necessities by attacking China. Three main factors motivated these intermarriages. In some cases, the rulers of China hoped to develop an alliance with powerful nomads in order to gain their assistance against other internal or external enemies as well as to lessen the chance of destructive raids into China. In other cases, an ambitious nomadic ruler desired to become a son-in-law of a Chinese ruler in order to further his own political and economic aims. Other marriages resulted from the defeat of Chinese armies and the nomads' demand of a royal princess as one of the conditions for peace.[19]

Tribute from the nomads to the Chinese was a third type of exchange or contact. Tribute implied that the nomads were obedient to the demands of the Chinese, although in reality it was often merely a form of trade. The term tribute is very imprecise to characterize all the forms of exchange that took place under so-called tributary conditions, of which there were at least three. In many cases, leaders among the nomads, while yet disunited and weak, were willing to send tribute to a rich and powerful Chinese ruler in order to obtain needed grain and other commodities. In other cases, nomadic rulers defeated by a powerful Chinese dynasty often had no alternative but to send tribute in response to the demands of the Chinese and in recognition of the "mandate of heaven." In these instances, when the nomads presented tributes they would generally receive gifts in return, which were the same as goods desired in trade. The third group of cases were those of powerful nomadic rulers sending envoys to a powerful Chinese emperor in order to establish better relations. These powerful khans were by no means capitulating; but such nomadic delegations were invariably termed by the Chinese "tribute-bearing vassals."[20]

The fourth category of exchange occurred when a powerful nomadic ruler demanded an annual quota of goods from an acquiescent Chinese ruler who wished to avoid trouble and was willing to send tribute to the nomads. While, in fact, this was a tribute granted under duress from a Chinese state to a nomadic state, in Chinese records it is invariably termed a *sui-pi* ("yearly stipend"). This exchange was hardly trade because of its one-sided nature. Whatever its inception, in some periods it supplied the nomads with important commodities.[21]

A final category of exchange was actual trade that took place at certain points along the Great Wall in frontier markets called *pien-shih* ("border markets" or "custom markets") or *kung-shih* ("tributary markets"). This activity, usually beneficial for both the Chinese and the nomads, was sporadic, was seldom given high priority by the Chinese, and was institutionalized, only for a short period by the Ming[22] as a measure to stabilize frontier turbulence.

Of these forms of exchange and contact, the most important were tribute and border markets. There are voluminous Chinese records regarding tribute matters; the obedience of the barbarians and the rich bestowals of benevolent Chinese emperors upon the nomads is always emphasized. There is also frequent mention of incidents in which the nomads petitioned for permission to send a tributary mission to the capital, but were refused by the Chinese; border attacks usually followed. The major reason the Chinese rejected petitions of nomadic tributary missions was because they realized that the motive of the nomads was economic gain and not recognition of the benevolence or greatness of the Son of Heaven or the Dragon Throne. The records confirm that economic necessity, rather than recognition of a superior Chinese culture, was the main motivation of the nomads. The Chinese were motivated, in these contacts, by political, defensive objectives; the expansion of Chinese suzerainty; and the influence of Chinese culture on their so-called barbarian neighbors.[23] When profitable tributary arrangements were not forthcoming, the nomads attempted to gain what they wanted or needed by force.

From frequent mention in the *Ming shih-lu* of tributary contact

between the Chinese and the Mongols, we learn that tributary delegations generally included a chief delegate and a deputy head, plus
many men, women, and *mao-i-jen* ("traders"), often totaling two or
three thousand people.[24] Ming dynasty records indicate that during some
periods a fairly large number of persons came on tributary missions in a
single year. The Oirad, for example, at first sent around fifty people, but
later groups came in with over one thousand persons. A characteristic
function of these tributary groups was the presentation of official gifts
and large quantities of horses, wool, pelts, and so forth as an official
exchange. Upon receiving these gifts, it was customary for the emperor
to give a "bestowal" in return. A standard rate of exchange, listing the
set value of horses in terms of silk or grain, was developed. If the
emperor did not desire to receive all the items brought by the Mongols,
the mission was free to sell them in the public bazaar. The so-called
tribute was actually a form of trade carried on by official caravans,
approved by the ruler of the nomads and allowed by the Chinese
emperor, which came into designated cities or the capital to exchange
goods at a standard rate. After receiving official tribute caravans, a
Chinese ruler usually dispatched an envoy to the Mongol rulers to
present gifts and the cordial regards of the Chinese emperor.

A discussion of trade is not complete without reference to the
monetary system. Inasmuch as Mongolia's traditional economy
operated on a barter system, people's wealth was held in the form of
livestock, which was exchanged for necessities or luxuries. However,
there have been other forms of wealth used for exchange. Silver was
often even more important than livestock for certain types of exchange.
It was used in several forms, the most important being ingots of the same
size and shape as those found in China. Actually, these ingots originated
in China in ancient times, perhaps by the Han period (206 B.C.-A.D. 220)
and were no doubt used in Mongolia from early times; but as yet the
details of their use are unknown. The Chinese refer to them as *yüan-pao*
and the Mongols by the loan word *yimboo*. They bore stamps of
certification according to the Chinese merchant or banking house from
which they originated. These ingots or tael were graded in size from
five to fifty *liang,* a Chinese unit of measurement. (One *liang* equaled 1.2
English ounces of silver or U.S. $1.63 from 1600 to 1814. By 1900, its
value had dropped by 50 percent.) In addition, there was "black silver"
(*khara mönggü*) or "local silver" in circulation, which had no mark or
stamp of certification. When buying a prize horse, a person most often

paid in silver. On other occasions, beginning in the early Ch'ing period, it was common for the nomads to use parcels of tobacco, bricks of tea, or ceremonial scarfs (*khadagh*) as units of exchange. Silver coins, introduced in the Ch'ing period, were used later; but the Mexican or Chinese silver coins were not valued as highly as pure silver ingots. The Mongol term for the coins is *tögürig* (*tügrik*), meaning "round" and corresponding to the Chinese *yüan* or Japanese *yen*, which have the same meaning. Concurrently with the use of silver ingots—and even before the use of silver coins—copper coins were introduced and circulated, particularly in the Mongol regions adjacent to the Great Wall. The most common form was the well-known copper coin with a hole in the middle which could be tied in strings for easy handling. Various types of coins continued through the Ch'ing period and into the Chinese republican period, although the form was changed.

Paper money was also used widely in the Mongolian Empire, especially in the Yüan period. However, with the decline of the empire, this currency also fell into disuse and was reintroduced only in modern times. Various forms of paper money came into Mongolia as a result of modern influences, the most common was Chinese notes circulated by the Ta-Ch'ing yin-hang, a bank of the Ch'ing period, which gave way to currency distributed by the Bank of China after the revolution (1911). In addition, particularly in Outer Mongolia or eastern Inner Mongolia, paper money circulated by tsarist Russia was used; but it fell into disuse following the Russian revolution. The Mongols, like most people, tended to distrust paper money or *chaas* (*chaghasu*) and valued pure silver, which they often buried in some secret place for safety.

Among the Mongols the role of moneylenders has never been highly developed, and Mongols tend to have a negative attitude toward this activity. Early, during the empire period, most institutionalized money lending was in the hands of the Uighur and was referred to as *örtög* (this came into Chinese as *wo'to*).[25] This system of money lending was notoriously usurious, and the Mongols placed a stigma on it and tried to avoid *kölüsütei mönggü* ("sweat silver") or *keütei-joos* ("money with sons")—money that perpetuates itself in interest without end. Mongols feel strongly that the honorable way to help a person in need is to lend them money without interest. *Damjikhu* is the special Mongolian term used in reference to lending money or other objects without strings attached. Borrowing or lending money with interest is spoken of as *je'el* (*jegeli*), a word taken from the Chinese *chieh*. The fact that these important Mongolian words having to do with money lending have been derived either from the Uighur or, more recently, from the Chinese and that, earlier, there was no common word in the language covering this activity indicates that the Mongols traditionally had no customary activity of manipulating money to exploit people.

THE ECONOMY:
AGRICULTURE AND MANUFACTURING

A number of factors have hindered the development of agriculture in Mongolia. Climate and geography make the Mongolian steppe unsuitable for agriculture. Mongolian nomads have been psychologically conditioned for centuries to feel that toiling in the soil is not a proper way for humans to make a living. The nomads' customary view has been that it is better to work on horseback and look after one's animals than to dig in the dirt. However, through history, Mongols and earlier nomads sometimes constrained war prisoners to cultivate for them. These traditional prejudices were further confirmed by Tibetan-Buddhist influences, according to which land should be preserved in its natural form. To cultivate the soil, according to the Tibetans, harms the surface of the world, the "skin of the earth" or the *"körösü,"* as the Mongols express it. This angers the local deity, the *luus* or the "dragon king," who may harm those who break the soil as well as others living in the vicinity.

In ancient times, when Mongolia was under the rule of the Hsiung-nu and particularly during the Han dynasty (206 B.C.-A.D. 220), some land seems to have been cultivated by captives taken by the nomads in their frequent battles with the Chinese. Later, under duress, some Chinese seem to have gone over to the Hsiung-nu during periods of conflict within the Great Wall to farm for them. At times, the work was done under the supervision of the Hsiung-nu or of Chinese leaders who surrendered with their men and were resettled in areas that could be cultivated.[1] Following the decline of the Hsiung-nu, the Hsien-pei (ca. 100 B.C.- ca. A.D. 400) and the Wu-huan (100 B.C.-A.D. 200) peoples occupied the southeastern part of Mongolia, just outside the Great Wall, in a turbulent period from the latter part of the first century to about the fifth century. Chinese historians record that they carried out some simple agricultural production and also produced liquor from their grain.[2] The ethnic relation of these early people to modern Mongols has not been established.

A prominent nomadic people, the Juan-juan, occupied Mongolia during the fifth and sixth centuries. In the Account of the Juan-juan, discussed in the *Wei shu*, a passage states that, in A.D. 522, the Juan-juan needed "seeds," but this seems to be a reference to a need for grain. There was a famine among the Juan-juan, and grain had to be imported.[3] These people customarily wintered near the Great Wall, but moved north of the Gobi for the summer.[4] Such a pattern of movement would almost certainly preclude agricultural activity.

When the Turks or the T'u-chüeh were the overlords of Mongolia (ca. 550-740), they followed the precedent of the earlier Hsiung-nu people and had Chinese captives or migrants from China cultivate for them at various places in Mongolia. Bilgä Khan of the nomadic T'u-chüeh even considered establishing a capital in Inner Mongolia involving permanent buildings and some kind of agricultural development. However, his plan was abandoned on the advice of the famous minister Tonyugug (Chs. Tün-yu-ku), who reasoned that, if the Turks followed a sedentary Chinese style of life, they would be assimilated very easily and overcome by Chinese power.[5]

Later, the Turkic Uighur, who occupied Mongolia from the 740s to the 840s, made some attempts at agriculture. At first a purely nomadic people, they helped the T'ang dynasty pacify rebellions in China in the 760s and, following this involvement, a Uighur khan and a number of his followers were converted to Manichaeanism.[6] The vegetarian doctrine of the religion caused the Uighur to try to develop gardening in the vicinity of their capital in Mongolia; but from the records available it is unclear as to what happened with the experiment. However, later, in the 840s when the Uighurs were driven west by a related group of Kirgiz, they pursued agriculture in the oasis areas of Chinese Turkistan, which may suggest that they had actually developed some form of agriculture before they moved into Turkistan.

There is some textual and archaeological evidence that agriculture may have become somewhat more important in Mongolia by the Kitan period (Liao dynasty 907-1125). Aerial reconnaissance of some northern Mongolian Khalkha areas reveals what appears to have been regions of agricultural activity; however, it is not known whether these areas were worked by the Chinese, the nomadic Kitan, or someone else. In Inner Mongolia, some agriculture developed; however, it was probably not carried out by the Kitan, but by Chinese who for one reason or another fled into Mongolia or had been captured. These farmers were located near urban centers especially developed for them, particularly around the Shira-müren area of southeastern Mongolia, just north of the Great Wall. They farmed under the supervision of and for the Kitan. During the twelfth century, the Jurchen (Chin) people built a secondary wall north of the Great Wall of China in order to protect themselves against marauding Mongols, and, in the Chinese pattern, they rather strictly resisted trade with the nomads. The remains of these walls are still to be seen in certain areas of Shilin-ghol, Ulanchab, and in eastern Inner Mongolia near Lin-hsi, Juu-uda League.[7] The dynastic history of this period, the *Chin shih*, makes references to *t'un-t'ien*, which were unique settlements established by troops stationed on the frontier who simultaneously carried on agricultural activity.[8] The earliest mention of this system of combining farming and military defense on the frontier was in 241 B.C., during the Ch'in dynasty,[9] in the Ordos area of Mongolia against the Hsiung-nu.[10]

The transitory agriculture practiced in the China-Mongol border area during the empire of Chinggis Khan in the thirteenth century was also not by Mongols, but by Jurchen and possibly some Chinese. At the time of the rise of the empire, according to Chinese records, the Mongolian diet was predominantly meat and milk products with little or no grain.[11] It seems definite that agriculture was not practiced. Later, however, after the rise of the empire, the situation changed and the city of Chimkhai (Chs. Chen-hai) was established for the purpose of supplying agricultural products for people north of the Gobi. This city appears to have been located in the region of the Orkhon River of northern Mongolia, but this has not been definitely established. The term Chimkhai was originally taken from the name of the minister who supervised the city, and the farming was carried on by captives, not by the Mongols themselves.[12] There is evidence of later agricultural activity near the great Mongol capital, Karakorum, in the vicinity of the Erdeni-yin-juu temple, in what is now the Mongolian People's Republic. An inscription on stone found there mentions some problems of agriculture, grain production, and transportation, but it is difficult to believe that this involved Mongol farmers.[13]

All farming settlements or cities in Mongolia seem to have totally disappeared with the collapse of the Mongol Empire, and there was a lapse of two centuries before there was another mention of agricultural activity in the Chinese records: Altan Khan gathered Chinese farmers escaping from the Ming Empire because of heavy taxes and other problems. The agricultural developments under Mongol rule after the collapse of the empire were carried out in southwestern Inner Mongolia in the vicinity of Köke-khota (Hohehot), the present capital of the Inner Mongolian Autonomous Region. The Chinese settlements were called *baishang* (Chs. *pan-shieng*) by the Mongols and were the first instance of free Chinese settlement and cultivation in Mongolia under Mongol protection. Most of the Chinese involved in the farming were adherents of the White Lotus Sect (Pai-lien chiao) who had fled from China. This secret Buddhist sect, at times, took a rebellious or revolutionary attitude toward the existing regime. Society members who were persecuted by Chinese officials escaped to Mongolia and sought refuge under Altan Khan.[14]

When Mongolia came under the rule of the Manchu-Ch'ing dynasty, Manchu emperors adopted a negative policy toward Mongolian development of agriculture in order to preserve their cavalry potential and exploit Mongol nomadic military power. Nevertheless, there was some agricultural activity in southeastern Mongolia along the Great Wall, mainly by Chinese, which went on in spite of the restrictive policy. Still, the majority of the Mongolian people were limited by Manchu policy as well as by tradition and climatic factors, and they did not cultivate the land. The limitations of the Ch'ing policy were eventually loosened when the Russians moved eastward and posed a threat to China's frontier areas. The Manchu Empire was threatened not only from the north, but also by great rebellions and many natural disasters that took place inside the wall area during the nineteenth century. As a result, many Chinese peasants lost their lands and livelihood and migrated to Mongolia to escape the ravages in China proper. They sought refuge in the territories of the Mongolian banners and cultivated the land, usually under the patronage of some Mongolian overlords.

As Chinese immigrants later became more and more concentrated in particular spots, they began to rent lands more freely or independently and to pay land rent or taxes under various arrangements to the Mongols. Since Mongolian lands were held in common by all people of a banner, Chinese peasants usually became tenants of the Mongolian banners. With time and exposure to Chinese influence, some Mongols began to follow a Chinese life-style and cultivate their own land, though this transition only occurred in Inner Mongolian areas in the vicinity of the Great Wall. This not only changed the life-style of many people, but also eventually gave birth to a new idea—private possession of land among the Mongols. Still, farming was not widespread.

As the Ch'ing dynasty felt more threatened by Russian expansion and there was more pressure to solve the problem of population increases, the government encouraged more Chinese to immigrate into Inner Mongolia, even as far as Urga, the capital of Outer Mongolia, to cultivate the land and secure the border. Following the great influx of Chinese frontier colonists, the Manchu-Ch'ing government established an administrative system to handle Chinese affairs in Mongolian territory.

The first stage in Chinese frontier political development was the establishment of *t'ing, chou,* or *hsien* district administrative units. Eventually, the power of the Chinese administrative organizations increased and posed a great threat to the self-rule of the Mongols; this led to Outer Mongolia's declaration of independence in 1911. Many so-called Mongol bandits (Chs. *Meng-fei*) burned Chinese settlements in Inner Mongolian territory along the Great Wall, killing Manchu and Chinese officials and settlers.

The basic cause for the uprisings was the fact that the Chinese farmers occupied the better grazing fields and Mongolian herdsmen were forced to move their animals to inferior pastures. In the face of many economic and political problems, sporadic uprisings gave way to movements for reform and revolution and eventually to the Mongolian Autonomous Movement of 1933, led by Demchügdüngrüb (Chs. Te Wang).[15] Thus, agriculture and economic problems concerning land were linked to political problems concerning self-determination.

It is very difficult to determine from historical records exactly when Mongols began to farm their land themselves, but it appears quite definite that during the Ming period Mongols living several hundred miles just northeast of Peking came to trade with the Chinese for plows and seeds. These people are now known as Kharachin Mongols. From the Ming period to the present, some of the Mongols in this region have carried on agriculture. Continuous records over a long period from Ming times note that Mongols came to trade horses and pelts with the Chinese for plows, grain, and other products. It is possible that the Mongols made weapons out of the plows and did not actually use them for farming.

The earliest references in the Ch'ing records to Mongolian agriculture is a decree by Emperor T'ai-tsung (1626–43), which documents the existence of Mongolian settlements in eastern Mongolia near the old Manchu home regions in which agriculture was carried on.[16] A later reference (1650) in the *Ta-Ch'ing hui-tien*, notes: "every fifteen men among the subordinate Mongols shall be given a piece of land twenty *li* in length and one *li* in width."[17] The reference is to land given to Mongol men enlisted in the ranks of the imperial banner troops and is further evidence of Mongolian agricultural activity in very early Ch'ing times. This was an exception to Manchu policy, for soon after this a general policy decision of the emperor forbade Mongols from engaging in agriculture. However, by the end of the 1800s, there was a continual flow of Chinese migrants into Mongol territories. This influx marked the real beginning of Mongolian agriculture, copied or learned from Chinese settlements in Mongol territory. Originally, the Mongols were not concerned with protecting their pastures, and thus an inherent contradiction between herders and peasants developed soon after the inception of agriculture in traditionally nomadic areas. Eventually, the great pressure and tension between the Mongols and the Chinese farmers provoked movements for Outer Mongolian independence and Inner Mongolian autonomy.

In spite of the political problems, many Mongols living along the Great Wall gradually adopted Chinese methods of cultivation, tilled their own land, and made the transition from herdsman to peasant. Some even became landlords, hiring both Mongolians and Chinese to plant for them. Over several decades, serious problems arose as Mongols rented their lands to Chinese settlers. Land problems became worse toward the end of the Manchu-Ch'ing period and particularly during the warlord period of the Republic of China (1916-28). Some problems were temporarily settled by the Japanese after they occupied Inner Mongolia; much land was returned to the Mongolian banner governments as public property. But it was not possible to return many land parcels from Chinese tillers to the Mongols because the claims and titles were too complicated. A definite rent and tax settlement that was more or less acceptable to the Mongols was made; or in other cases, a set price was negotiated for a sale to the Chinese settlers, usually in terms to be paid over a period of twenty-five years. The revenue received from these former banner lands was then used to develop Mongolian education with the result that many schools were built and many students sent to study in Japan.[18]

A unique type of grain planting and harvesting was developed by the Mongols who lived away from the Great Wall, though still south of the

A farm family in eastern Inner Mongolia

Gobi Desert. This form of farming, known in Mongolian as *Mongghol tariya,* was practiced mostly in the northern part of the Juu-uda and Jerim leagues. A special sickle with a long handle, which made it possible to stand upright to cut and remove grass, was used, after which seeds were broadcast freehand and the herds were moved away from the site until the fall harvest of the crop. While the production was very poor using this approach, it was better than nothing. The development of *Mongghol tariya* further confirms the attitude of the nomadic or pastoral Mongols who needed some agricultural products, but did not want to dig in the dirt or stoop in the back-breaking manner necessary when using the short-handled sickles of the Chinese farmer.

Manufacturing and industry developed very late in Mongolia, although premodern forms of handicraft industry did exist very early. The Mongols were very adept at such work as blacksmithing and the production of armor and weapons. From very early times, an artisan class, referred to as *uran* which now means "art," had high status in Mongol society. Chinggis Khan greatly favored this group and called his favorite weaponsmaker *yeke uran,* the "great artist."[19] After Chinggis ascended the throne in 1206 and reorganized Mongol society according to units of one thousand households per unit, Güchügür, a woodworker, was appointed as the head of one of these large units.[20] It was a common policy during the Mongol conquest to immediately select the artisans from among the common people of a newly occupied area. Certain individuals were reserved for the khan, and the remaining artisans were then divided among the Mongol generals and nobility. Artisans received considerably better treatment under the Mongol conquerors than did the common people. A Frenchman, William Bucher, a Paris goldsmith captured in Hungary, worked in the palace of Möngke Khan.[21]

The early development of modern industry and more advanced manufacturing among the Mongols was retarded by several factors, chiefly the nondevelopment of urban life, the far-flung migrations of the Mongolian people, and the recruitment of all ablebodied males for military service. The high incidence of warlike activity in Mongol history was also, in the long run, a contributing factor. There was a general tendency in the society for men to be involved in handicraft or manufacturing activity only as secondary work; no class that specialized strictly in the production of goods developed.

In more recent history, even during the long period of peace in the Ch'ing dynasty (1644-1911), industry and manufacturing failed to develop in Mongolia because Chinese goods flowed even more freely into the steppe areas and Chinese artisans settled in monastic centers, hindering the development of an indigenous class of Mongol artisans. It was not until the third or fourth decade of the present century that manufacturing activity and artisans began to develop in Mongolia under the patronage of far-sighted nationalist leaders.

In early handicraft forms of manufacturing, the Mongols developed techniques for weaving textiles with very appealing designs. They also developed a very effective means of fashioning belt hooks with artistic animal designs. Important discoveries of these have been made by the Russian archaeologist, Kozlov, in Noyan-ula.[22] Belt hooks or fasteners have also been frequently discovered in recent decades in the Ordos Desert.[23] All demonstrate the highly artistic talents of the nomadic people. The Chinese official histories mention Turkic or T'u-chüeh blacksmiths in the khan's service of the Juan-juan period, who were apparently quite talented in making weapons and armor for their nomadic rulers.[24] This capability in the manufacture of arms was quite likely a factor in the nomads becoming a dominant power and subduing the Juan-juan north of the Gobi.

Museum collections of traditional Mongol ethnographic artifacts show that the Mongols were adept at making durable and artistic boots with very intricate designs in various color combinations. Even after fine Chinese-made footwear became common in Mongolia, the people still preferred domestically produced boots, which were more expensive but which were regarded as more beautiful than the Chinese products. Most Mongol banners have traditionally had a few well-known gold or silversmiths or blacksmiths talented in the manufacture of knives, bowls, ornaments, and other items. Some Mongols are also adept at working steel with inlaid gold in a very beautiful manner, which has produced priceless masterpieces. For centuries, Mongolian artisans have independently produced Buddhist images and temple ornaments of rare quality. However, the work has always been done by individual artisans; large-scale production was never developed. The Mongolian word for a "smith," *darkhan*, had the same pronunciation during the Mongolian Empire period as the title for a high-ranking officer who was exempt from certain duties, indicating the honor awarded to the smith and perhaps accounting for the name, Darkhan, given to the new industrial center established a few years ago in the northern part of the Mongolian People's Republic.

It is not the intent here to exaggerate the capacity of the various nomadic peoples of Mongolia in manufacturing products for their nomadic way of life; moving from place to place is not suitable for the development of industry, and it is quite difficult to pass beyond the stage of handicraft into the standardized processes of mass production in industry. Nevertheless, the Mongols and other Inner Asian nomads did for many centuries produce their own implements for daily life. They produced, for example, their own cattle carts, the wooden frames of the yurt dwellings, the felt to cover it, as well as the furnishings for the inside of the yurt. Only recently did Chinese merchants transport these items to Mongolia and come to dominate their production and distribution. Traditionally, the items were mainly prepared by the Mongols themselves.

POLITICAL STRUCTURE: LEAGUES AND BANNERS

The political structure of Mongolian society has always been marked by a comparatively high degree of instability, characterized by a cycle of disunity, unity, and return to disunity (with disunity predominating).

The dominant feature over the centuries has been fragmented, political units, extending from smaller clan-lineage groups to larger clan confederations, with the appearance at historical peaks of larger pastoral nomadic empires like that of Chinggis Khan.

An analysis of political structure and function must deal with several levels of institutional size and complexity. For the lowest level, that of the clan-lineage (*obogh*), the approach of the social anthropologist seems to be most useful. The second administrative level, the tribe (*aimagh*) or the subtribe (*otogh*), is closely related to the clan-lineage. The third level, the *tümen*, a larger political and military administrative unit which usually combined several confederated tribes or *aimagh*, ceased to exist three centuries ago with the final conquest of the Mongols by the Manchu. (These units as social institutions were treated in Chapter 6.)

This leaves two areas to be discussed: (1) the political institutions of the league and the banner, which will be analyzed in this section, and (2) certain special political institutions (most of which ceased to exist over six hundred years ago) that were very important at the zenith of Mongolian history during the empire period. These will be discussed in the following section.

The purpose of the Manchu policy that instituted a fragmented or compartmentalized system of banners loosely held together in leagues was to weaken the *horizontal* ties between important Mongol groups and to strengthen the *vertical* ties between these units and the central government in Peking. This system of control continued for over three centuries, even after Chinese rule came in, and left a deep imprint on Mongolia.

The roots of the banner and league system (*khushighun* and *chighulghan*, respectively) extend back to the old tribal-clan socio-political system of pre-empire Mongolia; but both of these institutions, as known in modern times, stem from the Manchu-Ch'ing period. An understanding of their structure, function, and purpose is important in any consideration of Mongolia, both past and present.

Under Manchu domination, the Mongols and their lands were subdivided into *khushighun*, a term that originally meant a wedge or contingent of troops, but has come into English as "banner," taken from the Chinese word *chi*. It is basically an administrative unit. On a level above the *khushighun*, *chighulghan* were established by combining a number of banners in a broader regional unit. The Mongolian term *chighulghan* has come into English as "league," again because of its

Chinese translation *meng,* meaning an "alliance" or "league" of smaller units. The old tribe (*aimagh*) or subtribe (*otogh*) was the basis for the establishment of the *khushighun,* but the term *aimagh* itself continued only as a historical term and was not applied to any administrative institutions of the Ch'ing period.

A banner consisted of both people and territory structured in a broad quasi-feudalistic system of political and economic control that had some vassalage-like characteristics. The banner was also a traditional military unit organizing those within it into fighting units. Although basically a political unit of local administration, the banner traditionally had related judicial functions.

Within each banner, the people—actually households—were organized into *sumun,* which means "arrow" in Mongolian (Chs. *tso-ling*). Traditionally, *sumun* were basic military units consisting of one hundrd and fifty ablebodied men headed by a *sumun-janggi* (Chs. *tso-ling chang-ching*). Theoretically, one *sumun* administered one hundred and fifty households, but actually there was no strict rule and the number of men involved varied from time to time and from banner to banner.

Because of the Mongolian nomadic life-style, households and *sumun* did not live continually in a definite area but migrated over the territory of the banner. Thus, while *sumun* served as units of local administration and military organization, they were not restricted to territorial boundaries in quite the same manner as banners. Under Manchu rule, a *jalan* (Chs. *tsan-ling*) or magistrate was appointed over every six *sumun,* although in some cases the number was less. The *jalan* were key administrators and liaisons between the banner and their subordinate *sumun.* The number of *sumun* within a banner was not fixed; thus, the Tümed Right Banner of the Josotu League, as an example, contained ninety-seven *sumun,* while the Left Banner, Right Flank of the Chichirlig League, Sechen Khan *aimagh,* only contained a half (*khondogh*) *sumun.* The Manchu carried out a greater degree of fragmentation of Mongolian administrative units in Outer Mongolia than in Inner Mongolia in order to further weaken and control them.

Above the banners (*khushighun*), leagues (*chighulghan*) were organized; there were some banners that were not under the jurisdiction of any league, however. Leagues or *chighulghan* as larger, regional administrative units also had certain military characteristics, but were not as feudalistic, so-called, because a league governor was appointed by the central government, meaning the Manchu court; his position was not

A banner administrative office and officials in Shilin-ghol

held hereditarily among the Mongolian nobility. All leagues were directly under the administration of the *Li-fan yüan,* the Ministry of Dependencies—a special office over non-Chinese border areas.

The lords or princes over banners were usually entitled *taiji* or *tabunang,* "royal descendants" and "royal sons-in-law," respectively, and were divided into four ranks. Aside from their general status, they were also given specific noble titles: *ch'in-wang, chün-wang, beyile, beyise, chen-kuo-kung,* and *fu-kuo-kung.*[1] These ranks were set according to the merits of a prince or the service of his ancestry as judged by the Manchu rulers.[2] These lords were mainly descendants of earlier tribal leaders. Rank and title were hereditary privileges among the nobility, but even if a man held high rank and title, he might not be appointed as a *jasagh* and authorized to administer a banner. Nobility who were not hereditary *jasagh*s were known as "leisure lords" (*sula noyad*) and were not involved in the administration and military leadership of the banner. Thus, there was a separation between title and real power.

*Jasagh*s, that is, banner administrators, usually had hereditary princely titles, but there are several cases of *jasagh*s in this century and before who were not hereditary princes. As top administrators of the banners, *jasagh*s were key figures in the governmental system. They had authority to make decisions concerning banner administration, taxation, litigation, recruitment of troops, and so forth as long as their actions did not conflict with the laws, ordinances, and policy of the Manchu central government or with the league governors. While *jasagh*s had important judicial powers, they did not always make all final decisions for in disputes there was a process of appeal to the league governor or even to the Ministry of Dependencies in the capital, Peking.

The administrative center of a banner was a group of yurts situated near the *jasagh* and officially known as the *jasagh-un tamagha-yin ghajar* (literally, "the place of the *jasagh*'s seal"; the term *tamagha*, meaning "seal," has also by extension come to mean "office," i.e., the place of the seal). Also known as the *jasagh yamun* (Chs. *ya-men*, meaning "office"), particularly by the Manchus and the Chinese, it functioned as the military headquarters of the banner. A *jasagh* himself commanded the troops of the banner, at least nominally. Under the *jasagh*, according to law, the *jakiraghchi* was head of the troops as a sort of chief of staff. In larger banners, for example, the Kharachin Right Banner and the Üjümüchin Right Banner of Inner Mongolia, a special official in charge of military affairs, a *cherig-ün meiren*, was ordinarily appointed to look after the military affairs of the banner.

A *jasagh* exercised broad and rather arbitrary power and freely appointed or discharged officials within his banner, with the exception of several higher administrators, regarding whom action had to be confirmed by the league governor or by the central government. The role of a *jasagh* was similar to that of a feudal lord because of the broad powers that he traditionally held on a hereditary basis. Unless he resigned or offended the central authority, he held his post for life. Upon his death, on the basis of both custom and law, his son was traditionally confirmed as his successor by recommendation of the league governor to the central government. If the son was not eighteen years of age, the administration was temporarily carried out by a regency under a *tusalaghchi*.

The staff or bureaucracy of a banner under a *jasagh* was fairly uniform and ordinarily included two *tusalaghchi*—a senior and a junior—a *jakiraghchi*, a *meiren*, and several *jalan*. The post of *tusalaghchi* (Chs. *hsieh-li t'ai-chi*) was limited to the nobility (*taiji* or *tabunang*). It was a very important position in banner government after the *jasagh*. All official documents in a banner were customarily cosigned by both the *jasagh* and a *tusalaghchi* as a matter of custom. The appointment or dismissal of a *tusalaghchi* had to be authorized by Peking. He was the prime authority to administer the affairs of a banner in the absence of the *jasagh* or if the latter happened to be a minor.

A *jakiraghchi*, as the title implies, was actually the official most directly concerned with the administrative affairs of a banner. His full official title was *khushighun jakiraghchi janggi*—literally, "banner controlling official," the last term being a Manchu word. This post was open to both the nobility and the common people. As a key official, he did not merely assist the *jasagh*, but rather freely handled administrative decisions, apart from basic policy.

The comparative roles of the *tusalaghchi* and *jakiraghchi* differed from place to place and over time according to custom and the relative capabilities or merits of the men holding the posts. In southeastern Inner Mongolia, the power of the common people was greater than, for example, in western Inner Mongolia, and, accordingly, the *jakiraghchi* post, being open to commoners, tended to be more powerful in some places than the *tusalaghchi*.[3] In areas of Inner Mongolia where the common people were less powerful, the hereditary nobility were less inhibited or had greater initiative, and the *tusalaghchi* tended to be more influential than the *jakiraghchi*.[4] In many cases the relative predominance of one or another of these officials was naturally determined by merit as to which man was the most influential leader in a banner next to the *jasagh*.

A third official in a banner administration was the *meiren* (also known as *meiren janggi*). This Manchu word was the title given to one who served as an assistant or deputy *jakiraghchi*. It was an important post that was also open to either the nobility or commoners.

Apart from the key offices noted, banner bureaucracies included other minor functionaries and clerks, including at least one *jalan*, who assisted in the affairs of the *jasagh*'s office. The key *jalan* was entitled the *tamagha jalan*, meaning the *jalan* assigned to the *jasagh*'s office (*tamagha*). Concurrently, he served as the chief of several *sumun*. In addition, there were other *jalan* (the number depended on the size of the banner), known generally as *sumun jalan* or officials who looked after the affairs of a number of *sumun*.

The lowest, and perhaps the busiest, functionaries in a *jasagh*'s office traditionally were the *bichigchi* or "clerks." The number of men serving in this role depended on the size of the banner and the volume of the administrative work involved. Directed by their superiors, *bichigchi* dealt mainly with paperwork and the records of a banner. There were customarily no restrictions on who might serve as clerk and candidacy was open to capable sons of commoners, but this role tended to be filled mainly by the fifteen- or sixteen-year-old sons of higher officials. The post of *bichigchi* served as an apprenticeship for future appointment to a higher official post. Training as *bichigchi* may have lasted for as long as fifteen years or even more before one was regarded as a fully qualified clerk. During this period, a young man learned of the complexities of the politics and finances of the banner. Several *boyida* or "managers," served in a banner office. While a *jalan* supervised the clerical functions, *bichigchi* and so forth, the *boyida* was concerned with the housekeeping chores of the office, servants, guards, food, horses, herds, and yurts.

Under Manchu and Chinese rule, the egalitarianism, flexibility, and upward mobility of earlier Mongolian political structure—the characteristics of purely Mongol rule—were largely lost. No definite tenure was set on the positions, and a person frequently continued in the same post for an extended period of time assuming that he committed no unpardonable transgression that would bring his dismissal. Naturally, deaths, retirements, or dismissals in the higher levels of the hierarchy opened the way for those below to be promoted.

Planning and policy for handling banner administration were discussed in council among the higher officials of the banner: the *tusalaghchi*, the *jakiraghchi*, the *meiren*, and sometimes even the *jalan janggi*. After a consensus was arrived at, proposals were presented to the *jasagh* for a final decision. The decisions thus arrived at were then carried out through the various subdivisions of the banner by the *sumun* officials (*jalan*), who represented or acted as a liaison with the various *sumun*.

Within these *sumun* units of around one hundred and fifty households, there was a hierarchy of petty officials to whom orders and policies were transmitted. The head was the *sumun-janggi* ("official") and below him the various *bushugh* (Manchu, *kundu*), who were the heads of units of fifty households. On the next level were the *arban-u darugha* or heads of units of ten households.[5] These minor functionaries received and carried out orders and made reports.

Thus, there were two levels of officials within the top administration of a banner. Men in the higher posts, those of *tusalaghchi* and *jakiraghchi* or *meiren*, usually rose from among the more capable and experienced *bichigchi* of the banner office (*tamagha* or *yamun*) after having served as *jalan* or *meiren*. According to Manchu law, all offices were open to qualified *sumun-janggi* or *bushugh;* however, as a matter of custom, seldom did these men rise into top banner leadership. Ordinarily, they filled only the post of a head over several *sumun (sumun jalan).*

Taxes were collected throughout a banner by the *arban-u darugha* on the lower levels and transmitted to the *jasagh's* office through the chain of command of the *sumun-janggi* and *sumun jalan,* who were over a number of *sumun.* Although the Manchu promulgated certain laws and regulations for Mongolia during their period of domination, tax laws were usually very loose.[6] Therefore, the *jasagh* or banner officials determined tax policy and had the authority to set a levy on the people at whatever level they desired. At the beginning of Manchu domination there seems to have been few tax problems, but in the modern period, taxation seems to have grown much heavier and to have become more arbitrary.

In judicial matters, minor cases within a banner were handled on the *sumun* level by the officials concerned (the *janggi* or *jalan*), and more difficult problems were passed up to the officials in the banner office and arbitrated in the name of the *jasagh.* If a judgment was not satisfactory to either the plaintiff or defendant, they might appeal to the league governor and finally to the Ministry of Dependencies (the *Li-fan yüan* in Peking).

It was traditional, until recent decades, for a banner to hold a council (*khural*) annually in the early summer at the central shrine (*oboo*) of the banner, at which time official offerings were made and matters such as the promotion and discharge of officials, the budget, taxation for the coming year, and so forth were handled.[7] Because the banner was handled much in the manner of a feudal domain, decisions might be either authorized or vetoed by the *jasagh.*

Matters of a broader range, which concerned the league, were traditionally handled at an important council held every three years; decisions regarding political affairs were made and military forces were reviewed. Leagues, which were a Manchu innovation, often took their names from the place of the meeting. Thus, the famous Josotu League met at a place known as the *Josotu-yin chighulghan* or "the gathering of Josotu," now translated as the Josotu League (Chs. *meng*). The Shilinghol League assembled at a place on the Shilin River, and the Ulanchab League met at a hillock by the same name.

Originally, the Manchu emperor dispatched a special envoy to a league conference to represent him, to conduct the proceedings, and to review the military forces. However, after 1751, the Emperor Ch'ien-lung decided to appoint an outstanding man from among the banner leaders to be head of each league. He came to be called in Mongolian, *chighulghan-u darugha* or "league governor."

The relationshp between league and banner leaders was ambivalent for two centuries. A *jasagh* was all-powerful within his domain, and because a banner is fairly autonomous, traditionally, the power of a league governor was quite limited. At the same time, the Manchu rulers decided to further limit the power of the league governor and his connection to the various Mongolian banners by not establishing a definite, separate, and continuing office with an administrative apparatus for league governors. Thus, from the 1750s until the middle of this century, the head of a league found himself in a strained situation in that he had to depend on his own banner office to administer his affairs or fulfill his role as head of a league. If he were not *jasagh* of a banner, he lacked the bureaucratic apparatus to really exert influence in league affairs. Nevertheless, in his role as a league governor, he did have certain important functions that strengthened his hand. For example, by his authority, the succession of a *jasagh* was confirmed and the appointment and dismissal of *tusalaghchi* was made within the various banners. Also, league governors administered or arbitrated matters concerning two or more banners. Furthermore, in some leagues, he served concurrently as the military commander (*cherig-ün jasagh*) of the league and had authority to report on or make recommendations to the central government regarding the various banners under his juris-diction.

In each league, there was a vice-governor who had no real power, unless for some reason the governor himself could not administer the affairs of the league. He had some potential influence in that it was common for the vice-governor to succeed to the leadership of a league upon the retirement or death of the league head. The league bureaucracy was traditionally quite small. In addition to the posts of governor and vice-governor, some leagues in Inner Mongolia had an official known as the *shidgegchi* ("administrator" or "one who handles matters"—Chs. *pang-pan meng-wu*), who assisted the governor and vice-governor in administering the affairs of the league. The *shidgegchi* was found in larger leagues such as Jerim, Juu-uda, Josotu, and Yeke-juu. Traditionally, there was no other staff such as clerks in the league, and therefore, league officials drew on their banner staff to fulfill their responsibilities.

The league was a comparatively late development, and the triannual conference (*chighulghan*) of banner leaders was one of the most important functions of the league government for over two centuries and up into the modern period. All decisions of the conference were carried out by the various *jasagh*, as heads of banners, under the coordination of the league governors. Another important earlier function of the leagues was to serve as an intermediate institution between the Manchu-Ch'ing court in Peking and the many individual Mongolian banners out beyond the Great Wall. As such, leagues served at times as important liaisons between the two levels in military, judicial, and administrative functions. However, because of the compartmentalized structure of the banners developed by the Manchu emperors, the power of leagues was rather restricted by the power of the central government in Peking on the one hand, and by the banners' great resistance to interference in internal affairs on the other. This situation continued for over two hundred and sixty years of Manchu rule.[8]

In areas where the unique Manchu and quasi-feudalistic banner system was not developed—for example, in Chakhar and in the Dahkur and Bargha banners associated with the Hulun-buir region—administrative units are still traditionally called banners, though some were called *sürüg*, meaning "pasture" or "herding" areas (Chs. *ch'ün*). Here, the administration was not in the hands of a hereditary *jasagh*, but a Mongol or Manchu, who was dispatched or appointed by the court in Peking with the title of *amban* (Chs. *tsung-kuan*). These areas were also organized along military lines in *sumun* subdivisions, and a number of *sumun* were combined by the Manchu under the supervision of a *jalan* as in the regular banners. The "herding" or "pasture" areas were for the care of the imperial herds of the Manchu central government.[9] An example of such areas in the Chakhar region is *T'ai-pu-ssu* ("the royal servants bureau") or, in other words, pastures, horses, chariots, and so forth attached to the particular imperial office. Another such area was the *Darighangghai* pasture area, which belonged to the Royal Horse Bureau (*shang-ts'ung yüan*) and has now come under the jurisdiction of the Mongolian People's Republic and been reorganized as the *Sukebator aimagh*. A third example is the Mingghan pasture of Chakhar, which in the early Ch'ing period was a "herd" under the jurisdiction of the Military Ministry (*ping-pu*). Officials who administered these pasture areas below the *amban* were termed *ghali-yin da* (Chs. *i-chang*). These pastures or banner areas were not organized into leagues, but were under the command of a Manchu official dispatched from Peking with the title of governor general (*tu-t'ung* or *chiang-chün*).[10]

In this century, under the Chinese republic and extending through the period of Japanese domination (1937–45), there was a growing feeling that the league level of administration should be strengthened as a regional structure of government in order to bring greater coordination above the banner level. Accordingly, during both the Chinese period of domination and the Japanese period of occupation, there were attempts to reform and strengthen administration on the league level.

Another debate of importance in this century arose from the growing feeling among Mongolian intellectuals that the "feudalistic" league and banner institutions must be either abolished or greatly reformed to facilitate greater progress into the modern world. Banners, it was felt, should be more democratic in order to strengthen Mongolia and the Mongols and to preserve the nation and culture. While there was considerable criticism of league and banner institutions on this basis, there were, on the other hand, strong feelings among both conservative Mongolian officials and progressive Mongolian intellectuals that, in view of outside pressures, the league and banner governmental system must be protected and perpetuated, even though reforms were made, in order to prevent further interference in local Mongolian affairs by Chinese or Japanese as the latter gained dominance during certain periods.

One of the most prolonged and bitter conflicts in this century between Mongols and Chinese has been the confrontation between Chinese provincial and district (*hsien*) governments and the administration of the Mongolian leagues and banners. The Manchus originally forbade Chinese to migrate into Mongolia, but this policy was changed in the middle of the eighteenth century because of population growth, famines, and other natural disasters in China proper as well as the threat of Russian expansion into the Mongol border areas. The Manchu reversed their policy of restricting Chinese land development in Mongolia even before 1900 and then actually encouraged Chinese to migrate into Mongolian frontier areas in order to solve internal problems while strengthening border defenses. As a result of this policy change, a large number of Chinese peasants colonized areas of Mongolia beyond the Great Wall in a century-long period of migration, penetrating particularly deeply into the lands of eastern Inner Mongolia.[11]

Following long-established tradition, Chinese administrative institutions followed the migration or expansion of Chinese society and culture. In the process, many Chinese *hsien* ("districts" or "counties") were established in Mongolian territory, and many officials were dispatched into the area to administer border affairs, including both military and civilian personnel. Officials and functionaries, variously termed *tu-t'ung, chiang-chün,* and *amban,*[12] strengthened Manchu-Chinese influence and interference in local Mongolian administration.

Administrative, political, and even military conflicts naturally arose out of this situation, and the general tendency was for Manchu or Chinese administrators to be supported by the central government in Peking against local Mongol leadership. Problems of land, administration, the economic exploitation of merchants, and so forth were the main reasons behind the Mongolian Independence Movement (1911) and the Inner Mongolian Autonomous Movement (1933).

From its independence in 1911 until the revolution of 1921, Outer Mongolia was under a conservative leadership in Urga, and change in the traditional local or regional governmental system was effectively blocked. Officials of the newly independent state were drawn largely from the old nobility of traditional society, and, hence, political institutions were also perpetuated with very little change. However, in 1921, the Mongolian People's Revolutionary Party seized power in Urga, changed the name of the capital to Ulan Bator (Red Hero), and began to carry out socialistic reforms including many changes in the administrative institutions of the country. The new leadership also, for a transitional period, continued the general political structure and organization of leagues, banners, and *sumun*.

The Mongolian People's Republic was formally established in 1924, and from then on many socialist reforms and reorganization of governmental administration were carried out. In the process, leagues (*chighulghan*) were abolished, and the old Mongolian term for tribal unit, the *aimagh*, was reinstituted as a designation for a broad regional administrative unit. The old six leagues of the Manchu period of domination over Outer Mongolia were reorganized into eighteen *aimagh*, and all banners (*khushighun*) were abolished along with their "feudal" characteristics. The *sumun*, the old basic local governmental units, were maintained in name, although their internal organization and function were greatly changed by the new socialist leadership. In the new situation, the various *aimagh* could be roughly equated with provinces and the old nomadic military and administrative unit of the *sumun* became much more like a county or district administration.[13]

The situation in Inner Mongolia, which remained a subregion of the Republic of China, diverged greatly from that in Outer Mongolia. Nevertheless, the Outer Mongolian Independence Movement greatly influenced Inner Mongolia, creating considerable political instability. The new Peking government (1912), being rather shaky and weak, decided to temporarily perpetuate the status quo in Inner Mongolia, and thus the feudal-like league and banner system was continued as a measure to gain support for the new Republic of China, particularly among the conservative nobility and the powerful princes and *jasaghs* throughout Inner Mongolia.[14] Nevertheless, much of Inner Mongolia had superimposed on it a Chinese system of Special Administrative Districts. A fragmented, weak, and anachronistic Inner Mongolia— caught between the changing political institutions of socialism in the People's Republic of Mongolia to the north and the modernizing Republic of China to the south—was exploited by rising Chinese warlordism and ambitious officials in the Chinese *hsien* within Inner Mongolia. There was continual political, economic, and military interference by Chinese warlords or officials within the administrative areas of the Mongolian leagues and banners.

A new situation began to emerge with the Northern Expedition (1926-28), the Kuomintang unification of China, and the establishment of a new national government at Nanking (1927). A fervent reformist and revolutionary spirit sparked a strong inclination to abolish the traditional local and regional governmental institutions of Mongolia. The Mongols were faced with a crisis. The Special Administrative Districts were arbitrarily reorganized as provinces to be ruled by Chinese governors because there was no inclination for the new central government of China to allow autonomy or self-government for the Mongolian people. There was pressure to cancel out Mongol institutions and to integrate Mongolian areas into the expanding administrative network of the new governmental system being established under the Republic of China.[15]

In response to the threat, Mongol leaders and intellectuals, particularly those in Peking and in touch with the Chinese, drew together and presented the Mongolian view of Mongolian problems to the national government in Nanking; in particular, they presented counterdemands to proposals to abolish the league and banner system.[16] The Mongols were successful in gaining recognition of their demands, and the traditional system was continued; however, at the same time the central government tended to reinforce the Chinese administrative institutions in Inner Mongolia, such as the provincial governors and other officials. This really reinforced the Chinese warlord rule in the border areas. By this time, Chinese frontier administrators had been greatly strengthened by railroad communications, guns, and other modern technology, and the conflict between Chinese and Mongolian administrative systems was more critical than ever.

In response to Mongolian pressures on the Chinese government, a Mongolian Conference was finally held in 1930 in Nanking, and, after much debate and ominous warnings by Mongol leaders, a new basic policy was drawn up. Known as the "Law Regarding the League, Aimagh, and Banner Organization," it was later authorized by the Nanking government (1931). The new law confirmed the traditional Mongolian administrative structure of leagues, banners, and *sumun*. It also set forth in theory the right of local Mongolian self-government and projected certain reforms. At the same time, the hereditary *jasagh* system was abolished in favor of a more democratic approach to leadership. Unfortunately for the Mongols, the new law remained a dead letter and was never really implemented. Conservative Mongolian princes blocked its implementation in the banners, and the situation was further complicated by Japan's invasion and occupation of Inner Mongolia, which brought its own repercussions in the administrative system of Inner Mongolia. Only one banner, the Kharachin Right Flank, was reorganized according to the new law.

Chinese and Russian influence on Mongolian institutions are of long standing, but Japanese influence is much more recent and really began with the Manchurian Incident of September 1931. Japan rapidly occupied all of eastern Inner Mongolia, and, with the establishment of Manchukuo (1932), the traditional system of leagues was abolished, although banners were maintained and treated on an equal basis with the Chinese *hsien*. To unify and coordinate administration for the Mongolian banners, the Japanese established Hsingan province and allowed considerable Mongolian self-government on the banner level. The Japanese also gave sympathetic consideration to traditional cultural differences in eastern Mongolia, and radical changes were not made in social or political institutions. The Japanese acted in accordance with the consensus of even progressive leaders who were suspicious of any Japanese interference. However, the hereditary *jasagh* system within the banners was abolished, and a new system of appointing qualified leaders as banner heads was instituted. From one point of view, this change was an important, progressive phase in Mongolian administrative development; but on the other hand, the abolition of the traditional system, however feudalistic it may have been, made it possible for the Japanese to more easily interfere in Mongolian affairs.

During the 1930s and 1940s, although all of Inner Mongolia was occupied by the Japanese, eastern Mongolia and western Mongolia were maintained as separate administrative regions in spite of Mongolian wishes for unification.

In western Inner Mongolia, in 1933, an autonomous movement directed against Chinese rule began.[17] The Chinese were reluctantly forced to recognize a new Mongolian Regional Autonomous Political Council as a unifying administration over most of the banners in western Inner Mongolia. However, the new council was weak and experienced continued confrontation with Chinese governmental institutions and officials in the area.

Japanese expansion into western Inner Mongolia and North China followed almost immediately, and there was not time for Mongolian leaders to carry out reforms of their own in local government structure and operation. Inner Mongolia fell under the domination of the Japanese militarists, and the Mongolian Autonomous Government of Allied Leagues was established at Köke-khota (Hohehot) in 1937. Later, it was reorganized as the Mongolian Federated Autonomous Government and moved from Hohehot to Kalgan. Under Japanese domination, it was very difficult for Mongolian leaders to govern their territory as they wished, and the old league and banner system with its hereditary nobility and traditional structure remained one of the few instruments that the Mongols could utilize to resist the interference of Japanese "advisers" in local affairs. This situation allowed the league governments to be reformed and reinforced, but opposed any basic changes of the structure and function of the banners.

After World War II, Inner Mongolia gradually fell under the Chinese Communists, and Mongolian political and governmental institutions were radically changed after the establishment of the Chinese People's Republic. At first, the Communists acquiesced to the pressure of the Mongolian nationalist movement and allowed the Mongols to establish an Autonomous Region of Inner Mongolia covering all Mongolian territory under Chinese domination except areas in Sinkiang and Ch'inghai. But after two decades, the Autonomous Region of Inner Mongolia has been cut back and restricted to part of western Inner Mongolia. Although nominally labeled the Mongolian Autonomous Region, this region has, in reality, followed the changing pattern of Chinese Communist policy, and a great number of Chinese colonists continue to be settled in the territory. Furthermore, a majority of the political leaders of this region are Chinese, not Mongols.

The Chinese Communists have changed the traditional Mongolian system of local government and have abolished its so-called feudalistic character. Nevertheless, the term *khushighun* or banner was still used for a time as the basic unit of local administration. Under the banners, the various *sumun* were also continued, but after the Cultural Revolution, they were converted into "people's communes." Above the banner, the higher unit of the league or *chighulghan* remains as an intermediary political organization between the banners and the regional government of the overall Inner Mongolian Autonomous Region. Recently, the Mongolian term *chighulghan* has been giving way to a reintroduction of the old term *aimagh,* although the Chinese term *meng* continues to be used for this level of administration.

Civil administration was only part of the government of the Mongolian society because the steppe nomads traditionally maintained a "sacred" rather than a secular society. Lamaist Buddhism permeated all aspects of society, and a large percentage of the population was not under the direct administration of the banners, but under an ecclesiastical administration of temples and monasteries (see Chapter 4). Buddhist centers in Mongolia were not included in banner governments and had intricate internal bureaucracies with their own hierarchies of officials administered by a *jasagh* lama or a *shangtsad-pa* lama. Temple institutions as a whole were under the jurisdiction of a Bureau of Lamaist Affairs (*lama tamagha*) located at Dolonor and Peking. The bureau mainly controlled the number of men becoming priests, the succession to power in the monasteries, and so forth. It, in turn, was governed by the Ministry of Dependencies (*Li-fan yüan*), an important office of the Manchu central government.

For centuries, at different times, most notably during the Mongol-Yüan period (1260-1368) and the Manchu-Ch'ing period (1644-1911), ultimate political power over Mongolia rested in China. At other times, for example, during the Ming period (1368-1644), important, though often turbulent, relations between Mongolia and China had vital implications for all the political, social, and economic institutions of Mongolia. Accordingly, a note on the Chinese institutions involved in Mongolia's contact with China has relevance for the discussion.

From before the Middle Ages, the foreign affairs of the Chinese empire were under the administration of the *Hung-lu-ssu;* after the conquest of China by the Mongols and the integration of the Tibetan area into the empire, a new agency, known as the *Hsüan-cheng yüan,* was developed. The office was concerned with Tibetan affairs—since under Lamaist Buddhism, Tibet was virtually a theocracy—and with other religious affairs of the entire empire including Mongolia. Naturally, during Mongol rule, secular matters were handled by a dual administration of Mongolia and China. When a new Chinese government was formed under the Ming (1368-1644), the Board or Ministry of Ritual (*Li pu*) handled relations with Mongolia because foreign peoples came within the tributary system and a ritualistic orientation was the key element of Chinese foreign relations.

After the Manchu conquest (1644), jurisdiction over so-called foreign dependencies—namely, Mongolia, Tibet, and Chinese Turkistan— came under the Ministry or Board of Dependencies (*Li-fan yüan*), which dominated governmental affairs in Mongolia. It generated overall policy, adjudicated league and banner problems, set forth guidelines for league and banner leadership, served as a high court of appeals, and so forth. In the late Ch'ing period, this institution was renamed the *Li-fan pu.* After the Chinese revolution (1911) and establishment of the republic, the term *li-fan* was abolished because of a derogatory connotation that its function was "to rule the subordinate." General foreign diplomacy was placed under the Ministry of Foreign Affairs (*Wai-chiao pu*), which stemmed from an earlier office, the *Tsung-li yamen,* while Mongolian areas and Tibet were placed under the jurisdiction of a new office, the Ministry of Mongolian and Tibetan affairs (*Meng-Tsang yüan*). This ministry continued until the establishment of the Nationalist government in Nanking (1927), at which time the office was downgraded as the Mongolian Tibetan Affairs Commission (*Meng-Tsang wei-yüan-hui*) in the new governmental reorganization. The commission was influential in Mongolian affairs until the Japanese occupation and the Chinese Communist takeover, both of which presented unique problems of governmental administration.

After the Chinese Communists came to power and through the 1950s and 1960s, the main agency concerned directly with Mongols and other minorities was the Nationalities Affairs Commission (*Ming-tsu shih-wu wei-yüan-hui*). However, since the Fourth People's Congress (1975), the commission has dropped out of sight and may have been absorbed by other governmental agencies.

POLITICAL STRUCTURE:
UNIQUE TRADITIONAL INSTITUTIONS

A few rather unique institutions existed in the clan and empire periods of the historical experience of the steppe. Actually the political institutions of the Mongols are patterned after those of earlier nomadic peoples. Under the Mongols, these institutions became more systematized and in many instances were strengthened. Attention will be focused on several key areas: the process by which khans, the supreme leaders, were selected, the problems of succession, and the *khuraltai*, a council-like institution.

Clan heads, who originally had limited power, evolved over time as heads of state with unlimited power. But this did not take place until after Temüjin became Chinggis Khan (1206). Originally, the khan (or *khaghan*) as head of state achieved his position through an elective process, in that he was sustained by the heads of powerful, autonomous clans or tribes. The process was essentially the same from the most ancient nomadic group, the Hsiung-nu down through history to the Hsien-pei, the Wu-huan, the Kitan, and others. The process of selecting a key leader, the khan, was important, and the assemblies that served this purpose and decided other important matters of state became institutionalized as *khuraltai*.[1] With the rise of the Mongols, these assemblies became much more important than in earlier centuries, and Chinggis Khan himself was confirmed as the khan over all Mongol tribes through the support of clan heads in a *khuraltai* or council. The *khuraltai*, then, was an assembly of elite leaders acting somewhat on democratic or parliamentary principles to decide succession to khanship, establish fundamental law or policy, and handle other important matters of state. This custom continued over centuries. Because of the nature of the assembly, writers in both the East and the West speak of it as a parliament or a diet. We just cannot tell how a consensus was determined, but quite certainly it was not by balloting. In the transitory Mongolian government, in modern times in Kalgan, voting was by a voiced response to a proposal or by clapping.[2]

Previous to the time of Chinggis Khan, the election of a khan, that is, head of a large confederation of clans, drew candidates from only two collateral lines of the famous Borjigid clan. The first leader known in Mongolian history to hold the title was the Khabul, the grandfather of Chinggis Khan. He was head of the Kiyad subclan of the Borjigid and was succeeded by Ambaghai, leader of the Taichi'ud, a clan that had earlier separated from the Borjigid. Ambaghai's successor was Khutula, son of Khabul of the Kiyad.[3] Thus, there seems to have been some alternation of leadership between the lineages and succession was flexible, allowing support for a capable leader who had proven himself rather than a strict following of hereditary lines from father to son. Naturally, a man would not be elected unless he had some real power to support his bid. Customarily, a khan could recommend a candidate to be considered as his successor; however, this was not binding upon the tribal heads and could or could not be accepted. Also, on occasion, two candidates were nominated by a former khan, with the final choice of a successor being left to the heads of clans and tribes assembled in *khuraltai*.[4] Chinggis Khan seems to have been elected without any supporting nomination by a former khan. In the *Secret History,* Chinggis Khan rebukes some powerful clan heads who had sworn allegiance to him, but then behaved contrary to their oath.

> You, Khuchar are the son of Nekün Taishi [the elder brother of Chinggis Khan's father], and in the beginning we supported you as the khan, but you refused the position. Altan, your father was Khutula Khan, who previously ruled [the state] and therefore we requested you to be the khan and you also refused. In our senior generation we have the sons of Bartam-ba'atur, Seche and Taichu, and we asked them to lead us but they also refused. Then, because all of you asked me to be the khan, I had no alternative but to serve.[5]

From this account, it would seem that when there was no definite candidate sent forth by an earlier khan, it was customary for clan leaders to make nominations. At times, men declined the position, but those who were sustained had to have superior standing among the tribes to secure the leadership role. In this case, a number of men were qualified to become the khan: Khuchar, as the son of Nekün Taishi, held leadership among the Kiyad subclan; Altan, son of a previous khan, also had status; Seche and Taichu could bid for power as leaders of the powerful Jürkin clan.⁶ But the election of Temüjin as Chinggis Khan seems to have been due mainly to his native ability and popularity.

While the nomination of candidates by a retiring khan was not binding, it was, as noted, influential. According to the *Secret History*, Khabul Khan of the Borjigid, forerunner of Chinggis, held control of the entire Mongol nation (*ulus*), but he turned rule over to Ambaghai of the Taichi'ud, even though he had seven sons.⁷ When Ambaghai was captured by enemy Tatar, handed over to the Jurchen-Chin, and executed, his will named his son Khada'an and also Khutula, the son of Khabul, as candidates to be khan.⁸ The Mongols and the Taichi'ud then assembled in the vicinity of the Onon River and sustained Khutula. This is but one example of candidates for khan being set forth by a previous ruler and of a succession that was not within narrow limits of lineage. However, from the time of Chinggis Khan, without exception, the khans elected were Chinggisid, that is, descendants of Temüjin.

As a general rule, there was a smooth succession of power on those occasions when a khan nominated his successor; but problems arose when there was no clear-cut nomination. The *Secret History* confirms this pattern in the smooth succession of Ögödei as khan (1229).⁹ Following his death, there were several occasions during the empire period when no clear-cut candidate was set forth and when, consequently, bitter struggles for power broke out. This was especially true after the death of Möngke Khan (1259). Two brothers of Möngke, Khubilai and Arigh-bukha, each convened a *khuraltai* to gain support as the next khan.¹⁰ Khubilai was victorious and, with the one hand, ruled as supreme khan of the Mongol Empire while, with the other, he filled the role as Son of Heaven, seated on the Dragon Throne of the great Chinese empire. From this time on, the Mongols maintained a dual system of administration over their vast empire: a Mongolian structure superimposed on Chinese institutions. However, in China, the traditional system predominated. But problems arose from the time of Khubilai because he did not adopt the Chinese method of succession and he weakened the traditional Mongol custom of the *khuraltai*.

Later, powerful ministers pressured or threatened the *khuraltai*. The biography of Bayan relates that when Shih-tsu (Khubilai) died (1294) and Ch'eng Tsung (Temür, grandson of Khubilai) ascended the throne at the palace of Ta-an-ke in Shangtu, some royal princes were inclined to go their individual ways and Bayan (the prime minister) stood on the steps of the palace with sword in hand, proclaiming the precious ancestral law and declaring that the principles of legitimacy established Ch'eng Tsung (Temür) as the emperor. According to the biography, "The countenance and words of Bayan were terrifying and all of the imperial princes trembled and rushed forward to bow before the palace."[11] Although not clearly stated, it seems apparent that the customary norms of succession required the sustaining vote of a *khuraltai* to establish Temür as the legitimate successor to Khubilai. But in this case, the decisive words of a powerful minister were of great importance, and from this time on the *khuraltai* became a hollow form. When there was no clear-cut succession to the throne, the matter was decided by an inner group of powerful ministers and royal princes. The long-term result was the weakening and eventual collapse of the Yüan dynasty.

After the establishment of the Mongol Empire and the codification by Chinggis Khan of the *Yeke jasagh* or the Great Law, all men who ascended the throne as ruler of the empire from that time forth had to be *altan-urugh,* or "golden descendants," that is, Chinggisid in lineage. The *Secret History* and important Persian records regarding the Mongol Empire confirm that a particular oath of fealty or loyalty to the khan was mandatory of all princes and other Mongol leaders. A typical oath was as follows: "Although your descendants have only a scrap of meat which is thrown in the grass and which the cows will not eat or a scrap of fatty meat which even the dogs will not eat, still we will be faithful to you and will not support a ruler from another lineage to sit on the throne."[12] Implicit in this oath was support only for descendants of Chinggis Khan.

Although the Mongol princes were not entirely consistent in supporting such an oath, over the centuries, no one but a Chinggisid ever became a khan with but a single exception. For a very brief period in the fifteenth century, Esen, the Oirad leader, assumed the title. Moreover, from the time of the empire until the modern period and the Communist takeover, power in Mongolia or the leadership of the banners was almost always in the hands of Chinggisid princes. The only important exception came in this century when the famous Eighth Jebtsundamba Living Buddha of Urga, a Tibetan, was supported by the princes of Outer Mongolia as emperor of a new state that declared its independence from the Manchu-Ch'ing Empire (1911). When an autonomous Mongol government was set up in Inner Mongolia in the 1930s, the head, Prince Demchügdüngrüb (De Wang), was a descendant of Chinggis Khan in the thirty-first generation.[13] There are many examples that demonstrate the great continuing influence of the law of Chinggis Khan over seven centuries in the important matter of succession to high office. Moreover, in the dynamics of rule, Chinggis Khan established the precedent that the khan was not only overall ruler of the realm, but also absolute ruler within the tribal units, that is, supreme lord in a quasi-feudalistic system.

From the collapse of the Yüan dynasty (1368) until the reconsolidation of a Mongolian state under Dayan Khan (d. 1530?), a period of about one century, although the khans were supported by the powerful princes of Mongolia, there is no record of a *khuraltai* being held to determine the succession to khanship. Be that as it may, there are records to confirm that *khuraltai*-type assemblies were held to determine important matters of state. And it is well known that from the reign of Dayan Khan on, succession to the position of khan and that of other important lords or regional rulers became hereditary. Succession fell to the eldest son. While the *khuraltai* continued as an institution, it seems that it was no longer used for the purpose of electing khans.

Interestingly, the succession and the comparative power of the khan of the Kitan-Liao (907-1125), long before the rise of the Mongols, reveals a similar pattern. Originally, the khanship was rotated among the leaders of powerful clans every few years by assembly. However, when Yeh-lü A-pao-chi was sustained as khan (A.D. 907), he had sufficient power to abolish the custom of rotation. He served for life and made the succession to khanship hereditary through his own posterity.

In this century, new political currents and the rise of national consciousness revived the *khuraltai* institution. In 1911, with the declaration of independence by Outer Mongolia and the establishment of a new state, the old tradition of voting for or sustaining the khan in a great *khural* or assembly was restored. The Eighth Jebtsundamba was installed as head of state by the princes of Khalkha assembled in a *khuraltai*—referred to more generally by the generic term *khural.* Also, in accordance with East Asian tradition, a new "reign period" was established—*Bügüde-ergügsen,* literally, "supported by all."[14]

The old *khuraltai* tradition also carried over in the 1930s in Inner Mongolia. During the important autonomous movement and even during the Japanese domination, top leadership and important policies were established by a council or conference (*khural*). Examples are those held in Üjümüchin (1933 and 1935), Batu-kha'alagha (Pailingmiao,

1933), and Köke-khota (Hohehot, 1937). Even after the socialist revolution in the Mongolian People's Republic (1924), the outward form and ancient title was still used, and the national assembly of the Mongolian People's Republic is the *yeke khuraltan* or "great assembly."[15]

Historically, the main function of the *khuraltai* was to enthrone a new khan or to consider the will left by a deceased khan. No person dared assume the title and power without the approval of a *khuraltai*. The assembly also decided important matters of state. The famous assembly held in 1229 established Ögödei as khan and voted to carry out three great military expeditions. According to the policy set in council, the khan himself undertook an expedition against the Jurchen (Chin), while Chormakhan undertook the conquest of Persia and Sübe'etei undertook the conquest of Kipchak (Cuman) and Bulgar in southern Russia.[16] This same *khuraltai* also decided such matters as how to mobilize horses and men and the grand strategy for a projected conquest. On certain occasions, the traditional *khuraltai* was supplemented by feasting, tournaments, and entertainment. Juvaini, in the *History of the World Conqueror*, records that after Ögödei established the capital at Karakorum (1235), feasting and entertainment for one month accompanied a great *khuraltai* at which Ögödei distributed riches gathered from the time he ascended the throne until the assembling of the *khuraltai*.[17]

The Yüan dynastic history also notes in the Annals of Tai-tsung (Ögödei): "In the fifth month of the sixth year [1234] the Emperor assembled all the princes at Dalan Daba'a and here proclaimed the laws and ordinances. Also, it was announced that all those who should have come to the *khuraltai*, but who absented themselves for a personal feast, would be executed."[18] Attendance at the *khuraltai*, which in ancient times was a duty but flexible, had now become mandatory. In the biography of the famous statesman Yeh-lü Ch'u-ts'ai (1190-1244), as recorded in the *Yüan shih*, the *khuraltai* of his day was referred to as the *tsung ch'in* conference, which implies that it was a great conference of royal relatives.[19] For the period concerned, this gives some idea of the nature of the assembly. However, with the expansion of the base of the empire and with a great increase in the number of representatives attending the assembly, it was no longer restricted to Chinggisid leaders and their relatives. For example, the great *khuraltai* held by Ögödei, after the death of Chinggis (1227), was attended by the princes of the right and left flank, the center column, the princesses and royal sons-in-law, all of whom can be included as royal relatives. But in addition, there were many generals, ministers, and others who belonged to other clans and who were related neither by blood nor marriage. In the great *khuraltai* that elected Möngke (1251), the main spokesmen for his support were Prince Batu and Mangghasar, and the main spokesmen for the opposition were Elji'etei and Baragh, a Uighur vassal—obviously influential men who were neither Chinggisid nor royal relatives.[20] Thus, in only several decades, the composition of the *khuraltai* had greatly changed.

A note establishing the antiquity of the *khuraltai* is found in the *Han shu* regarding the Hsiung-nu: "In the fall when the horses are fat they meet in the pine woods to count the men and horses [to assess their forces]."[21] A later Account of the Southern Hsiung-nu in the *Hou-Han shu* notes: "In the ninth month they assembled the tribes to discuss important affairs."[22] Such references indicate that the institution of the *khuraltai* goes back to the prehistory of the nomadic peoples. The census or assessment of men and animals, which was vital in planning campaigns and strategy, continued down to the Ch'ing period (1644–1911), the last imperial dynasty of China, and was one function of the system of leagues (*chighulghan*) set up as a *khuraltai* council. The term *chighulghan*, widely translated as league, has the connotation of an assembly. However, by this later period, the league council, so-called, was limited in its function.[23] Its scope or authority—a shadow of what it was in the old days—was restricted to a count of the fighting men plus limited discussion of the affairs of the league. Earlier, other important *khuraltai* were held, long after the fall of the Mongol Empire but before the Manchu domination. Ba'atur Khong-taiji of the Jungar, for example, assembled a great *khuraltai* and proclaimed the famous Law Code of the Oirad (1640).[24] Throughout Mongolia, during the Ch'ing dynasty, it was customary to hold a *khuraltai* periodically even on the banner level to discuss important matters. After the end of the dynasty and the establishment of the Chinese republic (1912), the custom continued.[25]

During the rise of the Mongol Empire, military affairs were naturally the matter of greatest concern. Thus, the leaders of ten, one hundred, one thousand, and ten thousand households commanded their respective military units and, at the same time, had a dominant role in handling matters considered in most societies to be civil affairs. The more important leaders—heads of one thousand and ten thousand households—served directly on the staff of the khan, planning and executing policy. In addition, a select group of these officials served in the royal guard or *keshig (kesegten)*.

The *keshig*, an important traditional institution that fell into disuse over the centuries and disappeared, has been the object of much attention and controversy among specialists in Altaic studies. We will only present an introduction to the institution, not attempt to survey the various conflicting interpretations. Although some of the best sources on many areas of Mongolian studies are in the Chinese language, the *keshig* was little understood by the Chinese during or after the Yüan period, and they tended to view it merely as a royal guard or part of the imperial entourage without perceiving its political aspects and general importance. The late Professor Yanai Wataru has made an excellent study of the institution.[26]

Several possible origins, from the pre-empire period, have been suggested for the name of the institution. One theory is that it stems from two similar sounding words: *keshig*, a "blessing" or a "favor," and *keseg*, a "part" or a "division." Thus, according to the first alternative, a particular elite group in the entourage of the khan (the *ordo*) was "blessed" or "favored" (*keshig*) and served certain special functions. According to the second possibility, the same elite group was a special "division" or was "set apart" (*keseg*) with a unique role or assignment. In modern times, a military division on the regimental level is referred to as a *keseg*. Also, there is the famous Keshiktan Banner of Juu-uda League, eastern Inner Mongolia, which still exists—a tribal group or administrative unit that was "favored" or "blessed," probably during the old empire period, for some reason now unknown. A third possible origin, which seems quite reasonable, is that the term *keseg* comes from the Turkic verb *kese*, meaning "to watch," with a suffix *g* added to make it a noun. In modern Mongolian, there is the verb *kesekü*, "to patrol" or "to investigate," which adds credence to this theory.

The original *keshig* of the early khans was no doubt very simple in structure, but when it became more complex with the rise of the empire and included thousands of men, it was divided into four parts, each having subunits. During, if not before, the time of Chinggis Khan, the various assignments, roles, or functions of the *keshig* (cooking, handling weapons or animals, for example) became hereditary. This gave the units a certain stability and continuity.

Another feature of the *keshig* was the periodical rotation of the groups or the personnel in each of the four divisions. As one staff went to the field for action or home for a rest, another set of staff members assumed their duties.[27] There were a number of reasons for this arrangement, but a strong one seems to have been that the custom of rotation made it possible for the khan to become acquainted with a broader group of leaders, to train them better at close hand, and to watch for men of particular brilliance or aptitude who could be given special assignments and responsibility. It is not a distortion to say that the *keshig* was the center of the *ulus*—the "state on horseback" or nomadic empire—since it served to guard the person of the khan, to serve his royal yurts (*ordo*), to aid in the formulation of policy, and to carry out any assigned course of action decided upon by the *khuraltai* or the khan.

Originally, the *keshig* was a rather rudimentary organization in which the labor was divided according to the needs of a limited group of warriors; but it had no real administrative functions over broad lands and people. It helped coordinate a federation of tribal warriors in nomadic military functions. However, as the empire evolved, so also did the role of the men in the *keshig*. Thus, as but an example, Bo'orchu,[28] who was originally a modest supply officer in charge of providing food for Chinggis Khan's staff and entourage, soon took on much more important positions in the imperial administration and was appointed to high office because he was known and trusted from service in the *keshig*.

The position of the *keshig* during the career of Chinggis Khan deserves special attention. The administration of Chinggis Khan combined both military and political functions. Its main role was to organize a home base or general staff. In this context, the *keshig* was the single most important institution above clans and tribes, and, therefore, its significance cannot be minimized. It is not an overstatement to call it "the government."

Immediately upon assuming the role of khan over a somewhat limited grouping of Mongol tribes, Chinggis's first undertaking was to mobilize troops. He appointed a responsible man to superintend logistics or the army's food supply and charged him to "see that breakfast is sufficient and that supper is not delayed." This man held the title of *bo'urchi*. Chinggis also appointed officials to superintend the sheep herds (*khonichi*) and men to be in charge of the carts (*ula'achi*). The general superintendent of the horse herds was called *aghtachi*. Archers (*khorchi*) were organized. These positions later were included within the general system of the *keshig* and were expanded with the rise of the empire and the power of the khan. The number of men within the *keshig* was enlarged from eighty to one thousand and later from one thousand to ten thousand.[29]

A large number of the men of the *keshig* were directly or indirectly associated with administrative affairs and had close personal contact with the khan; therefore, Chinggis used the institution for the important purpose of training young men for specialized service. After proper training, they were appointed to responsible positions in the empire. Chinggis once said, "when Shigi-khutughu is making a judgment, let the men of the *keshig* be sent to observe [and learn]."[30] This and other such examples demonstrate the use of this institution to apprentice young men in leadership and administration. A key group of men among them were specially trained to serve as clerks (*bichigchi*) and keep important documents.

Of special interest are the four top officers of the *keshig* who served Chinggis Khan: (1) Boroghul[31] who was captured as a young boy and raised by the mother of Chinggis Khan as his adopted brother; (2) Bo'orchu, the overseer of Chinggis's entire staff, who was concurrently leader of a ten-thousand household unit and chief commander of all right-flank Mongol forces; (3) Mukhali,[32] who bore the title of *gui-ong* (Chs. *kuo-wang*) "prince of the realm" was chief commander of the left-flank forces (when Chinggis Khan invaded western Asia, Mukhali dealt with the problem of the Jurchen, a powerful Inner Asian enemy who were occupying North China); and (4) Chila'un,[33] who had saved the life of Chinggis Khan when the latter was a captive of an enemy tribe. These powerful men were naturally involved in administration and politics, and the two most important, Boroghul and Bo'orchu, were responsible for superintending the cooking for the royal household. Later, during the reign of Khubilai Khan, the grandson of Bo'orchu held such a high post that he was not referred to by his personal name, but only by an honored title Ülüg Noyan, or "The Grand Official." As a result of Chinese influence on the Mongolian government, a unique "censorate" institution was adopted, and Ülüg Noyan was assigned the role of "censor-in-chief." In this powerful position, he had several functions, including the traditional censor that was to become the control staff in the modern Chinese government. In conjunction with this post, Bo'orchu and his descendants continued to directly supervise the kitchen of the khan. On occasion, he personally filled the wine cups of the royal family, but he was no common servant and members of the imperial family rose to their feet as he served them.[34]

As young men were trained in the *keshig*, gained trust, and demonstrated ability, they were appointed to important positions in the field and were often given missions in some distant operation, upon the completion of which they returned to the khan's camp or the capital to again assume some responsibility in the *keshig*. During the reign of Ögödei Khan, Chormakhan, who held the role of *khorchi*, or "quiver bearer," in the *keshig*, led an expedition to western Asia. The chief of staff during the famous European campaign that reached far into Poland and Hungary was Sübe'etei, who held the title of *ba'atur*. Chinese records confirm that when these men were at court, they were high ministers and in the field, they were top generals. All without exception were from the *keshig* and were given appointments on the general staff. The Chinese writers of the Mongol dynastic history (*Yüan shih*) were puzzled by and critical of the khans' custom of assigning men to high positions in the field and calling them back to the court to return to what the Chinese considered rather humble posts.[35] The Chinese reaction is surprising since the system or administrative style changed but very little through the entire period of the Yüan dynasty, and even many important Chinese officials[36] recruited by Khubilai Khan had served him earlier in his personal residence in, what appears to have been, the Mongolian institution of the *keshig*. Thus, it seems all the more strange that the *keshig* and its role in the dual administrative system of the Mongol Empire was little understood by Chinese scholars and historians, who made but passing mention of it.

The Monograph on Military Affairs in the *Yüan shih* records the following regarding the *keshig* (or imperial entourage).

The four *keshig* [heads] were meritorious ministers of T'ai-tsu [Chinggis]. They were Boroghul, Bo'urchu, Mukhali, and Chila'un and were spoken of as the "*dörben külüg,* meaning the four heroes. T'ai-tsu appointed them hereditary heads of the *keshig*. Their duty was to serve as the imperial guard on a rotating basis. The descendants of those heads of the *keshig* were the trustworthy associates of the Sons of Heaven [the successors of emperors]. They were recommended by the prime-minister and succeeded to their office by seniority. They maintained their post hereditarily and served as an encircling guard [of the khan]. Even though their rank was low [from the Chinese point of view], this was not important. As for the commander of the four *keshig*, the Son of Heaven himself served in this role or appointed a high minister to the post. However, it was ordinarily vacant. Those appointed to serve in the *keshig*

who dwelled within the forbidden area were divided into the following
various categories according to their duties and whatever it was to which
their assignments pertained: the headgear and clothing, bows and
arrows, food and drink, records and clerical work, horses and chariots,
camps and tents, barns and storage areas, medicines and herbs, divination
and prayer. Men with these duties maintained their post from generation
to generation. Although on occasion they were appointed to high office
because of their ability and became very powerful and honored, still if
they were released from their position and returned to the imperial
household they resumed their former responsibilities [in the *keshig*]. The
younger generation of their descendents continued in the same manner.
Unless they were trustworthy men they did not receive such a post [as
keshig].

The titles of the functions of the *keshig* are: those who looked after the
bows and arrows, the hawks and falcons—men called *khorchi* and *shiba'-
uchi* [respectively], also *göröchi* [a hunter]; those who recorded the
Imperial ordinances were called *jarlighchi* and men who kept the records
and handled clerical work were called *bichigchi;* those who personally
prepared the imperial meals were entitled *bo'urchi;* men who carried
swords, bows and arrows and served the emperor are called *ildüchi* and
kötöchi [*ildüchi* were swordsmen, *kötöchi* were keepers of the reserve
horses]; the keeper of the gates and doors were *balkhachi* [the original
Chinese text is mistaken—*balkhachi* looked after the barns—gateguards
were *e'üdenchi*]; men in charge of the wine were called *darachi;* men who
cared for the horses and carriages were *morinchi,* men who looked after
the imperial wardrobe and the storehouses were entitled *sükürchi;* men
who cared for the camels were called *teme'echi;* shepherds were called
khonichi; men who served as police were entitled *khulaghanchi;* musicians
were called *khu'urchi;* the loyal and courageous ones were known as
ba'atur and men of surpassing bravery were called *batu.* There were many
names for various functions and roles but men who bore them all served
the Son of Heaven in his personal entourage [*keshig*]."[37]

The dual aspect of the Mongolian administration during the Yüan
period (the ruling of native areas by native institutions and the ruling of
China by a combination of Chinese and Mongolian institutions) was
only vaguely recognized by the writers of the Yüan dynastic history.
They were concerned only with administrative institutions established
by Khubilai Khan and interpreted them along the lines of a Chinese
system with which they were familiar. They largely ignored the

Mongolian elements of the dual system including the *keshig*. The Monograph on Officials of the *Yüan shih* notes:

> At the beginning of the establishment [of the Mongolian state, the khans] naturally had no time to set up a stable and durable regime. But after Shih-tsu [Khubilai] ascended the throne, he appointed many experienced scholars [Chinese] and began to organize the government on a grand scale. . . . Then the administrative system of the dynasty began to function. For a hundred years, his descendants had institutions to rely upon.[38]

The same negative view is also seen in the Monograph on Law of the *Yüan shih*, which is really concerned with institutions: "In the beginning of the Yüan period, there was no law code"[39] (meaning no systematic institutions). The institutions or governmental systems that the Mongols perpetuated, many of them dating from the early Hsiung-nu and T'u-chüeh peoples and having deep roots in their nomadic traditions, states, and empires, were not recognized or given legitimacy by the Chinese, unless they had some precedent in the Ch'in, Han, or T'ang dynasties. Therefore, in the Annals of T'ai-tsu (Chinggis Khan), there is very little mention of the important administrative systems and institutions that he developed. The foremost Chinese record of the period, the *Yüan shih*, merely states:

> T'ai-tsu arose in the northern territories and began to control the people. The tribes lived in the wilderness with no system of cities and their customs were simple and unrefined. They had no complicated organization, but merely a head of ten thousand households to control military affairs. They only appointed *tuan-shih kuan* [*jarghuchi*] to control politics and administer the law. Such men as were appointed were, but one or two from among the high nobility or important ministers.[40]

Most discussions of traditional Mongolian government focus mainly on military affairs because of the dominant role of this activity in the brilliant rise of the Mongols. A detailed discussion of military structure and function and its relationship to government and politics is found in the subsection Military Institutions: Structure and Function (this chapter). It will only be noted here that in the empire, the chief responsibility for military affairs was divided between a commander of the right flank and a commander of the left flank in a great threefold division of Mongolian forces. These posts were held by commanders of ten thousand households, while the pivotal, center column was usually controlled by the khan himself. Clan politics persisted, and close relatives of the khan always had key roles in military affairs.

The judicial function of the Mongolian government was naturally important. The administration of law in the Mongol Empire was conducted by various *jarghuchi* (Chs. *tuan-shih kuan*); the top law official was the *yeke jarghuchi* or "supreme judge." Important records were maintained by *bichigchi* ("scribes") under the supervision of the secretary general (*yeke bichigchi*). In addition, these two chief men were roughly equivalent to prime ministers.[41]

The primary source on government, the *Yüan shih*, comments on the role of the *jarghuchi* in the *chung-shu sheng* (the agency in the imperial administration over matters other than military affairs and the censorate): "At the beginning of the dynasty, the post [*tuan-shih kuan/jarghuchi*] was filled by prime ministers. The responsibility and honor of this post was very heavy and it was filled by men in the personal service of the Emperor, the Empress, the Crown Princes, the Royal Princes, or men of the *keshig*[*ten*]."[42] The Chinese record reverses the order and importance of the two offices in question; actually, as the Mongols viewed it, the supreme judge (the *yeke jarghuchi*), served as prime minister, not the reverse.

After the establishment of the Yüan dynasty (1260) and the consolidation of governmental institutions, the Chinese system of bureaucracy was increasingly adopted. In the transition, the administrative functions of the *yeke jarghuchi* were placed into the hands of the prime minister (*ch'eng-hsiang*) and the censorate functions of the *yeke jarghuchi* were placed in the hands of the chief censorate (*yü-shih tai-fu*). After this, only very important cases, such as those involving arbitration between two members of the royal family, were handled by the *yeke jarghuchi*.[43] There is documentation in the *Yüan shih* that the *jarghuchi* post was filled by a royal prince or a man from the *keshig*, which is added proof of the great importance of that institution.

The first mention of the *jarghuchi* is in the *Secret History*; the post was filled by the brother of Chinggis Khan, Belgütei.[44] Later, the first supreme judge and prime minister (*yeke jarghuchi*) was Shigi-khutughu,[45] an adopted brother of Chinggis Khan. Hsü T'ing's commentary on P'eng Ta-ya's *Hei-ta shih-lüeh*, refers to him as Hu Ch'eng-hsiang, meaning "prime minister Hu (Khutughu)."[46] Other Chinese records of the period also speak of the *jarghuchi* role as a *tuan-shih kuan* or minister (*shang-shu*). For example, in the key periods of Ögödei Khan and Möngke Khan, there is mention of Mahmud Yalavaj having been appointed as minister of North China, and the title of his office is given as *shang-shu sheng*, the Chinese term for the prime minister's office.

When Möngke ascended the throne (1251) he established three *jarghuchi* or prime-ministerial offices. One of the offices had jurisdiction over western Asia and was referred to in Chinese as the *shang-shu sheng* of Amu Daria. Another was centered at Besh-balig with jurisdiction over Central Asia, and the third was at Yenching (Peking) with jurisdiction over North China.[47] To each of these offices was appointed a prime minister or *yeke jarghuchi*. Interestingly, the new institution, the *shang-shu sheng*, later evolved into the Office of the Itinerate Prime Minister, in China, known as the *hsing chung-shu sheng*. Later, during the Ming and Ch'ing periods, *hsing-sheng*, a shorter form of the title, became commonly used, and it led to the establishment of the provincial (*sheng*) system of China.

After the collapse of the Yüan (1368) and the retreat of the Mongols into Mongolia, the office of *jarghuchi* continued, arbitrating cases of a more serious nature. Then the function of the institution more nearly corresponded to the actual meaning of the title of the office or the official holding it as one who makes judgment. The institution and role continued through the Ming period and into the Ch'ing period until the establishment of the league and banner system, at which time it was abolished.[48] (The judicial function in Mongolian society under the new arrangement was discussed in connection with the institutions of leagues and banners.)

Bichigchi has been translated as "secretariat"—a depository of documents—but it was more than that. In addition to merely keeping records, it superintended government administration in the same manner as many national or international institutions in the contemporary world. The term seems to refer to both the role and the official who holds it. The institution existed prior to the Mongol Empire, but the concern here is its later development.

Men who were close associates of Chinggis Khan before his rise to power were later given high office and functioned in the empire as *bichigchi* or "secretary generals." Some information on the beginning of the role is found in the Biography of Esen-bukha in the *Yüan shih:*

The grandfather of Esen-bukha, Shira-oghul, had contact with T'ai-tsu (Chinggis Khan) while he still had little power. Later, Chinggis treated him very kindly as an old friend, showed him greater favoritism than other clan leaders and appointed him as chief *bichigchi*. At court and banquets he sat in the honored place. When Shira-oghul died early, his son, Borokhon, served Jui-tsung (Tolui) as *keshig(su-wei)*. When Hsien-tsung (Möngke Khan) ascended the throne [1251], he, together with Mangghasar, planned all important and secret matters. Therefore, Borokhon was promoted as a prime minister (*chung-shu yu ch'eng-hsiang*) and held state affairs in his hand. From the time of Khubilai, Esen-bukha's post of *bichigchi* became hereditary.[49]

When Möngke Khan ascended the throne, according to Juvaini, Mangghasar and Borokha (Borokhon) led all other officials in the court ceremonies.[50] The foregoing may be compared to a similar account in the *Yüan shih*, and it may be concluded that both of these men, Borokhon and Mangghasar, served as prime ministers. The *yeke jarghuchi* was more powerful than the *yeke bichigchi*. The role of chief *bichigchi* became hereditary and was also important in the *keshig*.

When the Mongols took rule of China, finding Chinese equivalents for Mongol terms presented problems, and a rather free translation of the title of *yeke bichigchi* ("prime minister") in Chinese was devised as *chung-shu yu ch'eng-hsiang*. Naturally, it took time for Mongolian administration to adapt to Chinese institutions and to make a transition in terminology. The title *chung-shu ling*, held by the famous Yeh-lü Ch'u-ts'ai,[51] was also a free translation of the Mongolian title *yeke bichigchi*. Thus it seems that Yeh-lü Ch'u-ts'ai, Borokhon, and others were all of approximately equal status and performed the functions of prime minister. It may be further concluded that the chief *bichigchi* and chief *jarghuchi*, as prime ministers of the Mongolian governmental apparatus, were drawn from the *keshig* and continued to maintain their status there even after they assumed the new posts.

In the Chinese part of the dual administration of the Mongol-Yüan dynasty, a functional division of institutions and responsibility evolved along three lines: the administrative, the military, and the censorate. There was a "prime minister (*ch'eng-hsiang*) of the right" and a "prime minister of the left," whose offices came to be known in Chinese as the *chung-shu sheng* (roughly, "office of document concentration"). By a similar process, an office of military affairs (*Shu-mi yüan*) was derived from the Mongol office of the head of ten-thousand household units, namely, the *tümen-ü noyan*, dating from the time of Chinggis Khan.

Under the Mongolian administration of China, an institution or agency very close to the traditional censorate (*yü-shih tai*) was perpetuated with the usual function of investigating governmental operations, impeaching, and so forth. It was constituted by assuming part of the former functions of the Mongolian office of the *yeke jarghuchi*. The officials who filled these various offices were drawn largely from the *keshig* and still maintained their association with this unique institution. Thus, officials who filled high posts in the Chinese part of the dual system of the bureaucracy were still associated with the *keshig*, the Mongol part of the dual system.

In the khanates of the empire, much less change took place in Mongol governmental institutions, and they remained much closer to the earlier empire system. Still, as may be expected, various Mongol administrative structures were influenced in each case by the unique environment and native institutions of the area.

With the end of the Yüan dynasty and a return to the steppe, the Mongols and their institutions were under continual threat both from within and from without. For a time, they attempted to maintain the governmental institutions developed in China during their rule there. However, in time, they reverted to institutions closer to those of the old nomadic states of Inner Asia. Unfortunately, sources are lacking for a full and detailed institutional analysis of this period. Some sources indicate that the highest office under the khan was that of the *ürlüg* (literally, "hero"), an official concerned with military affairs.[52] According to Mongolian sources, the post of *jarghuchi* continued to exist, and within the court bureaucracy, the "prime minister," known by the term *chingsang*, a corruption of the old Chinese term *ch'eng-hsiang*, continued to function. The powerful Oirad leader Batula (Mahmud in Chinese records) is known to have held the title of *chingsang*. *Tsai-hsiang*, a less-formal Chinese term for prime minister, was also perpetuated in Mongolian governmental terminology in the corrupted form *tsaisang*. This office or term continued for several centuries until the early Ch'ing period and even later in some regions. However, the function of the office changed, and it came to have jurisdiction over petty affairs of the common people.

To rule the immensely expansive territories under the jurisdiction of the Mongol Empire, the khan dispatched a prime minister (*jarghuchi*) to administer particularly large territories. To smaller areas, a *darughachi* ("head" man or "chief" governor) was dispatched.[53] It was common for the *darughachi* to be superimposed upon the existing government and to give direction or command to the indigenous administrative head. His primary function was to deal with financial and civil affairs. *Darughachi* have been looked upon as the trunk or main body of the great Mongolian bureaucracy. As a general rule, Mongols were dispatched to fill the posts of *darughachi;* however, often the position was filled by other Inner Asians (*se-mu*) and even by Chinese.

The Mongol Empire and the Yüan dynasty naturally included many different peoples. These nationalities were treated with differing degrees of status and priority. Only the case of the Chinese realm will be considered here. Uppermost were the Mongols, referred to as the *kuo-tsu*, "state nationality." The peoples of Inner Asia who were neither Mongols nor Chinese were commonly referred to as *se-mu*. Northern Chinese were called *han-jen* and were given precedence over the people of South China known as *nan-jen*. The Mongols even today, like the Russians, refer to the Chinese as Kitad (a term derived from the plural form of the name of an earlier proto-Mongol people—the Kitan). Interestingly, the current Mongol term for Southern Chinese is Nanggiyad, which has an element of condescension. Some have referred to the hierarchical arrangement developed during the Mongol period in China as a four-class society.[54] However, the classification was not clear cut; there was overlapping and blurred lines of distinction. It is well known that there was sufficient mobility within the Mongolian governmental structure for many Chinese to fill high posts as ministers.

The quasi-feudalistic socio-political structure of the Mongols, which developed following the Yüan dynasty and continued to the present century, will not be discussed further here. However, a few unique institutions of the Jungar Mongols will be noted. Below the nobility with the title of khan or of *khong-taiji,* there were four categories of officials: (1) *tüshimel,* high officials who functioned as administrative assistants to the khan and other top-level nobility; (2) *jarghuchi,* officials who dealt with law suits, arbitration, and judgment; (3) *demchi,* officials who dealt with the matters of tax, finance, and domestic affairs of the court (*ordo*); and (4) *tsaisang,* minor officials in civilian affairs.

Among the Chakhar, at the time of their surrender to Manchu suzerainty (1636), there were a number of official posts that are mentioned in the Ch'ing records. Among them were the *jarghuchi; khushighuchi,* the head of a group of soldiers or a vanguard; and a military official, *jasaghul,* who acted as an honor guard. Earlier, in Yüan times, there were *jasaghulsun* who served as superintendents or inspectors of post roads. At the time, the Chakhar were the most important Mongol group tracing their lineage from the great ruler Dayan Khan (d. 1530?), and the various official roles at that time may have been modeled on the earlier structure of the Dayan Khan period. Also, they may be models of most Mongol *aimaghs* or tribes of that time for which we lack records to make a detailed study.[55] Needless to say, much study is yet to be done on the function of the many roles and institutions noted above.

LAW

Different environments, traditions, and social systems give rise to different forms of law, and the legal institutions of nomadic peoples naturally differ from those of sedentary agricultural people. Mongol law is generally an extension or continuation of the legal traditions and common law that were customary from very early times among nomadic peoples. Due to the inadequacy of materials, nomadic law previous to the Mongols cannot be studied in depth. While much more is known about Mongol law than the legal institutions of other nomadic peoples, even here, full materials do not exist. Some law codes or commentaries of peoples who conquered China previous to the Mongols are extant, but these records were written after the occupation of Chinese areas and are really adaptations, not original law codes. They do not clearly set forth the legal institutions of these people before they migrated from the steppe and came into close contact with the Chinese.

Of the many peoples from beyond the Great Wall, the Kitan were closest culturally to the Mongols, and their customary law sheds some light on that of other nomadic peoples; however, it is very difficult to reconstruct early, preconquest Kitan law from the records of the Liao period (907-1125).[1] Similarly, it is possible, but very difficult, to reconstruct the broad outlines of Mongolian law prior to the empire. Some of the best data is found in the famous collection of imperial decrees and adaptions of Mongol law in the *Yüan tien-chang*[2] and the important records of the *Hsing-fa chih*, the law section of the Yüan dynastic history. However, these records preserve laws, regulations, and directives developed for the rule of Chinese territories and not for the administration of purely nomadic Mongol territories.

The most important point of departure for a study of Mongol law is the period of Chinggis Khan because he unified many tribes and at the same time brought together their customary laws, recodified them, and added some innovations of his own. It was necessary in the process to unify and standardize many diverse laws of different peoples. Many laws were abolished and new ones added. The famous code of Chinggis Khan is now known generally by the Turkic term *yasa* (*jasagh* in the Mongolian language). The term *jasagh* was in general use prior to the ascendancy of Chinggis Khan as the ruler of the Mongol tribes and will be used here. In the Chinese translations of the *Secret History, jasagh* is translated as "law" or "military law."[3] At the present time, among the Mongols, *jasagh* means "politics," "administration," or the title of the leader of a Mongol banner. This usage became current during the Ch'ing dynasty.

During both the empire and the Yüan period in China, judges were called *jarghuchi* (Chs. *tuan-shih kuan*).[4] The office existed prior to the reign of Chinggis Khan, but he raised it to the status of supreme judge and adopted the term *jasagh* with the unique meaning of "constitutional law" or "law of laws."

When Chinggis Khan commissioned Shigi-khutughu as the supreme *jarghuchi* or judge of his empire, he enjoined him saying:

> You will punish all thieves in the entire realm. You will investigate all rumor makers, killing those who should be killed and punishing those who should be punished. All this you will do according to reason. You will record the distribution of all the people of the entire realm [meaning the establishment of feudal-like vassalage and the assignment of a type of fief] and record all law suits and judgments; all things which are assigned and judged shall be written in the Blue Book (*Köke-debter*). This shall be a permanent record forever for the generations of our sons, our grandsons, and great-grandsons. All things [law and policy] which Shigi-khutughu and I discuss and settle shall be written down in black words on white paper and this shall be compiled as a *debter*. From now on, this shall never be changed, and the man who tries to make changes shall be punished.[5]

This order to the supreme judge initiated work by many scribes to establish a new law code that came to be known as the *jasagh* (*yasa*). They began just after 1206, when Chinggis assumed supreme power. From an examination of the records, it seems that the *Köke-debter* or Blue Book was an attempt to bring together and rationalize previously existing customary law and also to institutionalize it by creating a written code from the oral tradition. This was done through a series of discussions between Chinggis Khan and Shigi-khutughu, and the results seem to be a combination of criminal law and the establishment of legal precedent through the recording of various law suits. The work also included a record of certain regulations or decisions regarding administration or government, such as the division and jurisdiction of the people.

Unfortunately, this law code, which was greatly influential and considered to be the fundamental law of the empire to be observed by the successors and descendants of Chinggis Khan and by the common people, was lost after the collapse of the empire. A great effort has been made by scholars to reconstruct the *jasagh* code from existing historical materials, but it is impossible to retrieve the exact record. According to studies made of the laws of the *jasagh,* it may be divided into four sections: (1) the laws and regulations of the royal household; (2) the laws and ordinances of war and political administration; (3) criminal and common law; and (4) commercial law and regulations regarding the welfare and assistance of people during times of crisis or disaster. It seems to have been a very comprehensive law code.[6]

It is very difficult to determine whether customary law among the nomadic peoples prior to the Mongol Empire was oral or written. Some of the people had a written language, but among those who did, no examples have been discovered of a written law. The famous *jasagh* code itself was not recorded at one time, but was the result of an evolutionary process. A beginning was made in about 1206, but later, when important *khuraltai* or assemblies were held, the record was revised. Most laws of the Mongol Empire were codified during the reign of Ögödei Khan. For example, in the *Yüan shih,* the "Annals of Tai-tsung" note: "In the summer during the fifth month of the sixth year of the reign of T'ai-tsung [1234], the emperor held a large conference of all princes and officials at a place called Dalan-dabaa for the purpose of promulgating the law."[7] These important laws pertained to the basic law of the empire and no doubt were recorded in the *jasagh.*

In addition to the *jasagh,* there were other regulations, ordinances, or decrees of the khans that seem to have been regarded as law, although distinct from this code. These may be divided into three categories. First, the *jarligh* (*yarlig* in Turkic), which seems to have been pronouncements, decrees, or instructions of the khans and included appointments or proclamations, which were, in effect, ordinances. A second category was the *debter,* a record of cases that set precedence for administrative policy and jurisdiction. Third was the *bilig,* a collection of proverbs or words of wisdom of Chinggis Khan, at times referred to as *Khutughtu bilig* ("blessed wisdom"). Among these, the first two had the actual force of law, and the third was more like moral injunctions or admonitions for a good life and success. Complete copies of these collections also no longer exist, but of the three, the last, the words of Chinggis Khan, has been most completely preserved. This is evidence of the prestige and regard for the great khan among the Mongols up to the present and also confirmation of the fact that he is regarded not only as a great warrior, but also as a man of inspired wisdom and administrative ability.

The most reliable Mongol source for the career of Chinggis Khan, the *Secret History,* makes it clear that he placed great value upon obedience to law.[8] His second son, Chaghadai, another outstanding leader, was also well known for his strict observance of law. One of the main reasons these Mongol leaders emphasized law was their keen interest in stabilizing the chaotic nature of the steppes and bringing about order and organization.

Mongol law resulted from the experience and conditioning of nomadic life, and therefore, its comparative strictness or flexibility in arbitration differed from the patterns of law found among settled agricultural societies. The law of nomads cannot be fairly judged solely on the basis of statutes found among agricultural people. For example, according to Mongol law, one who killed a person, by accident or murder, might quite easily ransom his life by paying a certain sum in animals. In contrast, one found guilty of stealing horses from the *kirü'es,* or horse-hitching station outside the royal tents, was executed or beaten with one hundred and seven strokes and then banished to the eastern Siberian frontier.[9] Often, the punishments would be reversed in agricultural societies. Stealing a horse would be a minor offense while killing a person would be very serious.

Some of the problems arising from conflicting interpretations of law by the Chinese and the Mongols can be found in the *Yüan tien-chang.* These differences can also be seen in the preface of the law section (*Hsing-fa chih*) of the Yüan dynastic history, which was compiled after the collapse of Mongol rule. Phrases such as, "The Yüan dynasty was established but at first there was no law,"[10] demonstrate that the Chinese compilers or critics of Mongol law tended to ignore the existence of any form of law prior to the establishment of the dynasty. Their cultural prejudice led to the notion that anything other than law in the Chinese tradition was not really worthy of consideration. As noted in the *Hsing-fa chih:*

When [Yüan] officials judged cases they continued to use Chin Dynasty law which was too strict. Later, Shih-tsu [Khubilai Khan] overcame the Sung, unified the realm, and from then on the complicated and strict law codes began to be simplified. New law codes were developed and promulgated to officials as the New Laws of the Chih-yüan period (*Chih-yüan hsin-ke*). Then in the era of Jen-tsung [Buyantu Khan] there was once more a collecting of various law codes and a re-codification compiled, which was called the Comprehensive Law Survey (*Feng-hsien hung-kang*). Still later, during the reign of Yin-tsung [Gegen Khan], the prime minister and scholarly ministers were commanded to revise former law codes, to delete those items considered unnecessary, and to add new ones deemed important. This work was entitled General System of the Great Yüan (*Ta-Yüan t'ung-chih*).[11]

The revisions and recodifications of law made during the Mongol-Yüan period were necessary for the task of ruling China, not for the Mongols themselves. They show a realization on the part of Mongol rulers that Mongol law was not applicable to the Chinese situation and also indicate the dual administrative system maintained by the Mongols during their occupation of China. Apparently, Mongol administrators wished to reduce conflict in Chinese areas under their rule and thus depended to a great extent upon earlier Chin dynasty law. As for the Chinese criticism of an excessive strictness of Chin law, the Mongols can hardly be held responsible for codes developed by an earlier dynasty.

New law codes developed during Mongol rule were devised mainly by Chinese scholars, but were greatly influenced by the Mongols. Regarding Yüan-dynasty law, the writers of the law section of the dynastic history stated:

> Their emperors and ministers emphasized the reduction of punishments and consequently in one hundred years all under heaven was settled and peaceful; this was not by chance. However, the defectiveness of their law was that they had a different system in the south than in the north. Also all the provisions and articles [of the law] were too complex. . . . however, a positive aspect of Yüan law was that criminal punishments were merciful and liberal, while their defect was that the codes were too loose and lacked effectiveness.[12]

According to these comments, the administration of law under the Mongols was liberal and punishments were comparatively light. This is due, in part, to the influence of a Mongol legal philosophy that tended to oppose punitive law. As for the criticism that the Mongols maintained two different sets of law for Chinese and non-Chinese areas and that the law systems were too complex, it should be kept in mind that a different legal approach was required for the two different types of society. Also, it was inevitable that law would be complex in such a far-flung, cosmopolitan empire as that of the Mongols, which included many diverse peoples. This was a natural result of what might be termed a policy of plurality maintained by Mongol rulers. The impact of Mongol law or legal institutions differed greatly according to the various regions of the empire.

In Persia, Central Asia, and Russia, legal development was much more influenced by Mongol rule than in China, which may be explained by the comparatively higher level of sophistication, stability, and integration of China before the Mongol conquest.

After the collapse of Mongol rule in China, their realm was divided into two great parts—the "Ta-tan" Mongols in the East and the Oirad Mongols in the West. These two warred incessantly, resulting in a breakdown of their legal systems, with a great loss of records, which makes it virtually impossible to study legal institutions of this period in depth. The office of *jarghuchi* ("supreme judge") continued, and it seems that the legal system developed during the Yüan period continued for a long time. This, however, is impossible to confirm.

The term *Oirad* means "alliance," and from the tribes brought together in the union, there developed a common or customary law known as the Old Oirad Law Code (*Khaghuchin chaghaja-yin bichig*). Unfortunately, only eight articles now exist. When the Oirad regained power in 1640, a Jungar chief, Ba'atur Khong-taiji, assembled a great *khural* of the Oirad and the Khalkha nobility at the court of Jasaghtu Khan of the Khalkha Mongols. On this occasion, the customary laws of the various tribes were codified, and a new system of law was developed for the Mongol tribes north of the Gobi Desert. This was called the *Yeke chaghaja-yin bichig* ("The Great Law Record"), more generally known as the Oirad Mongol Law Code, and included one hundred and twenty-one articles divided as follows: laws having to do with political affairs between the *aimagh* ("tribes") and the *ulus* ("nation"); laws having to do with religion; laws pertaining to social conditions, family, and marriage; laws regarding herding, hunting, and war; and laws concerning property in general. A later code was developed, again among the Mongols north of the Gobi, known as the Law Code of the Seven

Khushighun of the Khalkha Tribe; however, all the articles of this law code have been lost.[13]

In 1709, another stage in the legal development of the Khalkha tribes was reached when the three *aimagh* heads of Sechen, Tüshiyetü, and Jasaghtu set down a common law code, the *Khalkha-jirüm*, for their areas. This code is known to have been revised in 1718, 1722, 1724, 1728, 1736, 1746, 1759, and 1770. During its evolution, it came to be divided into twenty-four parts, all of which cannot be commented upon, but which include statutes in the following categories: religion, politics, military affairs, post-road stations, temples, criminal law, and private law. This system of laws continued up to the time of the socialist revolution in 1921, when its application was gradually reduced until it was used only among the *shabinar* ("disciples") of the Jebtsundamba, Living Buddha of Urga.[14]

All the law codes show a common feature: a continued tendency to de-emphasize punitive law and to punish by fines. However, beginning from the eighteenth century, punitive law rapidly rose because of the influence of Chinese law, which expanded into Mongol areas during Manchu rule. All the law codes had special provisions for Buddhism and the high regard accorded lamas.

After the Mongols both north and south of the Gobi came under the rule of the Ch'ing dynasty, there was a continual growth in the influence of Chinese law. In 1667, Emperor K'ang-hsi recodified all available earlier law and promulgated a new code, the *Meng-ku lü-shu* ("Law Book of Mongolia"). His grandson, Emperor Ch'ien-lung, also promulgated a new code, the *Meng-ku lü-li* ("The Laws of Mongolia") in 1741. Still later, in 1789, Ch'ien-lung instituted the *Li-fan yüan tse-li*,[15] a collection of cases of precedents, laws, and ordinances of the *Li-fan yüan*, or Board of Dependencies. This law code continued some of the earlier precedents in such areas as politics, military affairs, civil law, and criminal law. During the reign of Chia-ch'ing (1796-1820), the latter code was revised, and at the end of the Ch'ing period, when the *Li-fan yüan* was reorganized (1906) as the *Li-fan pu*, the code was again changed and called the *Li-fan pu tse-li;* a comparison shows the contents to be almost entirely the same. This last work is a collection of the main laws promulgated in Mongolia during the Manchu period. In addition to it, the *Ta-Ch'ing hui-tien* was developed, a voluminous compilation of precedents, commentaries, and interpretations, which were important because the laws of the *Li-fan pu tse-li* were rather obscure and difficult to interpret. Still, problems arose, and it was necessary to refer to the *Ta-*

Ch'ing lü, the most important general law of the Ch'ing dynasty.

While legal institutions and law changed in Khalkha areas (Outer Mongolia) after independence (1911) and the rise of Communist influence (from 1921), essentially the same old legal system continued in Inner Mongolia during the entire period of its rule under the Republic of China. There were no new law codes for Mongol areas developed under the Chinese central government until after the Chinese Communists came to power. The government was weak in the border areas, and the warlords dominated. In addition, there were very few problems with common criminals and no necessity to give careful attention to criminal law and punishments. Changes in the legal codes under Japan's occupation, during the period of the Kalgan government, pertained only to the Chinese population of Mongolia. There was virtually no attention given to problems of criminal law in the Mongol areas of Inner Mongolia, partly because Mongol leaders were concentrating on politics, economics, and education. Also, it was wartime: many men were conscripted into the army, much reform activity was under way, and there was no significant urbanization (which ordinarily precedes important changes in legal systems in modern times) taking place. Traditional controls and punishments still served the needs of the Mongol banners.

We look now at the judicial system and procedures among the Mongols during almost three centuries of Manchu rule. Within the Mongol banners, there was no sharp separation between law and administration; rather the two were merged. In cases of dispute within a banner, first, the head of the ten household unit (*arba*) attempted to solve the problem and bring a reconciliation. If necessary, he brought the problem to the attention of the *sumu-nu janggi,* the next level of jurisdiction, and if it was still not solved, the case was appealed to the *jalan* (head of several *sumun*). If the case then remained unsettled, it was brought to the *yamun* (*yamen*), or office of the *jasagh,* where a jury of the higher banner officials was constituted to review the case and make a judgment in behalf of the *jasagh.*[16] This procedure, as outlined in the *Ta-Ch'ing hui-tien,* stipulated:

> Law suits among the Mongols shall be heard by the *jasagh.* If the *jasagh* cannot satisfactorily solve the case, it may be appealed by the defendant or the accuser to the head of the league for a review. If the case still cannot be solved, it shall be referred to the *li-fan yüan.* Also, if a *jasagh* or the head of a league finds a case which cannot be solved they may refer it

to the *li-fan yüan*. In cases where the accuser or the accused feel a *jasagh* or a league head are not just in their judgment, they may appeal the case to the [Li-fan] yüan.[17]

Thus, the last legal court of appeal, the authority of final decision, passed from the hands of the Mongols to the Manchu.

Under Manchu rule, if a man from banner *A* transgressed the law within banner *B*, he was extradited to his home banner for trial. In cases of crime involving both banners, the case was settled jointly by cooperation between the officials of the two banners. When a crime was committed by a non-Mongol, even in Mongol territory, the case fell under the jurisdiction of the Chinese *hsien* ("district") courts. If a dispute involved both a Mongol banner and a Chinese *hsien*, then the case was settled jointly by officials of both jurisdictions. The following reference in the *Ta-Ch'ing hui-tien* outlines important points of jurisdiction:

At the beginning of the dynasty [Ch'ing], it was determined that if people within the border [Great Wall] transgressed the law outside the border, the case shall be tried according to the laws of China's Board of Punishments (*Hsing pu*). A man from outside the boundary [Great Wall] who transgressed the law within the boundary, shall be tried according to Mongol law. The people of the Eight Banners [Mongols organized in the Manchu Eight Banner system and treated as Manchu] and people of the pastures [Khalkha, etc.] who transgress the law shall be judged according to Mongol law.[18]

Over a period of time, the integrity and authority of Mongol law broke down under Manchu rule, and a Mongol transgressing the law of Chinese areas was tried by Chinese courts with a Mongol adviser in attendance. However, a Chinese committing a crime in Mongol areas was turned over to be tried in Chinese courts, and Mongolian authority was weakened. This was due, in part, to Chinese politics and in part because Mongol officials themselves abdicated their jurisdiction. By the turn of the century, rebellions among the Mongols and other political complications led eventually to Mongolian movements for autonomy and independence.

Generally speaking, and contrary to popular belief, traditional Mongol law was not as punitive as the law in many other premodern societies. Capital punishment and cruel or inhumane punishments were infrequent. In general, Mongol punishment for the transgression of law seemed to allow greater provision for satisfying justice through the payment of a fine rather than through a strict execution of punitive law. In making retribution, there seems to have been particularly wide latitude. For minor crimes, the tendency was to exact a fine from the transgressor, payable to the person offended, usually in the form of animals or goods. In the *Secret History*, the most common punishment seems to have been beating, which was gauged, according to the seriousness of the crime, from three strokes to thirty-seven strokes.[19] However, transgression against public order or the welfare of the state (*ulus*) was met with more severity and a greater incidence of punitive law. In the case of murder, a great deal depended upon the status or roles of the defendant and the victim; thus, law was relative to the situation and the persons involved. Because of this, people in countries occupied by the Mongols complained that they practiced a double standard; all were not equal before the law. For example, killing a Chinese was not as serious an offense as killing a fellow Mongol soldier or a Moslem from western Asia.[20] A person who stole a horse from the *kirü'es*, or hitching area, while the khan was holding a conference, was punished more severely than a person who killed another commoner because the first offense was considered a crime against the state. The record notes that certain persons, upon breaking an oath with Chinggis Khan, were "to be thrown into the wilderness"[21](this probably meaning killed in the wilderness). Cases of execution, which do occur in the record, are obscured by circumlocution; there is no clear mention of capital punishment as such. Moreover, it is not possible to determine how this was carried out.

From ancient times almost to the present, there has been a clear tendency, arising from a Shamanistic, superstitious aversion to the shedding of blood, to find some form of capital punishment other than spilling the victim's blood. (Probably the most extreme curse throughout Mongol history is "may you have your blood spilt!" [*chasaar üküsen;* classical, *chisu-bar-ükügsen*].) Various early records indicate the most common forms of capital punishment were strangulation, smothering or crushing the victim in a sack, or breaking the spine of the victim. In the *Hsing-fa chih* (section on law) of the Yüan dynastic history, an important form of execution customary in Chinese history, known as *chiao* or strangling, is not mentioned because it was reserved to the Mongolian imperial house and was thus left out of the record that dealt with punishments for common criminal law.[22] It is interesting that this punishment, common in earlier periods, should be reserved to the imperial house during Mongol rule of China.

It is not clear from the scanty records available what forms of corporal punishment were used from the end of the Mongol Empire to the Manchu period. However, there are ample records to document the situation during the Manchu-Ch'ing period (1644-1911). Authority for legal punishment was taken out of the hands of the Mongol princes and reserved to the Manchu court in Peking. No Mongol prince or *jasagh*, for example, could carry out capital punishment of any form within his domain in Mongolia. The death sentence was often carried out secretly, but according to law, a *jasagh* did not have this authority.[23]

The most common official form of punishment in Mongolia during the Ch'ing period was the *khara tashuur* (*tashighur*), the "black lash." Another form of punishment commonly used was imprisonment in the *khara ger*, meaning the black or "bad" yurt. In more sedentary areas in Inner Mongolia, this "jail" is more often referred to as the *giyandan*. In other instances, the prisoner was placed in a sort of chamber (*shorun*) or hole dug into the ground. A form of punishment used independently or in association with imprisonment was the use of chains and stocks on both head and hands. Travelers in Urga frequently reported that common criminals were placed in small cages, which were then exposed in public regardless of the weather. Because the nomads moved continually, it was not possible to put a person in a cage and abandon him; therefore, it was common, up to modern times, to put a criminal in stocks, chains, or a cage and place him on an ox cart that was sent on a circuit.

A unique punishment was practiced until recently in western Mongolia in the area of Alashan, one of the harshest desert areas of Mongolia. A prisoner was taken far into the desert by camel to a small oasislike place where he was set up with a yurt and left. Periodic deliveries of food maintained him. He was not bound in any way, since it was impossible to escape on foot over such a broad desert; an attempt to do so would mean certain death.[24]

Most reports by Western observers regarding punishment and torture in Mongolia were based on events in Urga before the revolution. The reports give the impression that Mongolian punishments were very cruel.[25] However, that one urban situation was unique, and in most areas of Mongolia, extreme and torturous punishments were comparatively rare. Buddhist influence tended to ameliorate judgments and punishments. For example, in Üjümüchin, the "black lash" (khara tashuur) fell into disuse naturally because it was considered too cruel, and it became customary in recent times to beat a criminal with willows, which did less damage to the body than the black lash. However, until the 1930s and the establishment of the Mongolian Autonomous Government, the black lash was conspicuously displayed at the entrance of some banner yamen or administrative offices. When the Kalgan government was established (1939), modern young leaders felt that the khara tashuur, symbolic of primitive and cruel punishment, gave a bad image, and it was abolished.[26]

Following Mongolia's independence movement, the revolution, and the establishment of the Mongolian People's Republic, as a matter of course, the handling of criminal matters was entirely according to socialist law. Purges, executions, and punishments were carried out according to the Communist system by the cadre.

In spite of the fact that horses and cattle are valuable property among the Mongols, rustling was virtually unheard of in both ancient and modern times. Investigations have failed to turn up significant instances of theft of this sort. Some animals were stolen by the Meng-fei, "Mongol bandits," few of whom were Mongols but most of whom were renegade Chinese.[27] During the warlord period of disruption, cattle rustling did occur across the border northward into old Outer Mongolia into what had now become the revolutionary area of the Mongolian People's Republic; this area was a new independent state under the jurisdiction of Ulan Bator, but in a confrontation it was considered a no-man's-land.

In pure pastoral areas, such as Ulanchab or Shilin-ghol, common criminals were so infrequent as to be negligible, and it is not possible to generalize regarding their crimes or punishment.[28] Along the Great Wall, where there are Inner Mongolian areas of mixed Mongol-Chinese population, there has been, from the turn of the century, a rising incidence of crime. Here also, in such areas as Jehol or Chakhar, those imprisoned or punished seem to be almost entirely Chinese.[29] Common criminals are rare among Mongols.

MILITARY INSTITUTIONS:
STRUCTURE AND FUNCTION

In the thirteenth century, through their great military power, the Mongols established an empire unprecedented and unequaled since that time. The great military strength of the nomads, whose numbers were few, naturally stemmed from the mobility inherent in their broad, perpetual migrations and from their matchless ability in handling horses, the swiftest animal of the time that could be adapted to warfare. This powerful element corresponds to important technological advantages of our own day, such as aircraft or artillery. In addition, the Mongols possessed valuable skills, naturally inculcated by their hunting activities. The Mongol nomad of the medieval world was a well-trained, mounted warrior who learned to ride as a small child and who was continually in the saddle, hunting and herding. Not the least factor in the Mongol military triumph was the superior leadership of the historic figure Chinggis Khan and his staff.

The general structure of Mongol military organization was a simple pyramidlike arrangement of units of ten thousand households, one thousand households, one hundred households, and ten households. All of these units were, in turn, organized into an overall structure of three broad sections, a center and two flanks.[1] When Chinggis became khan (1206), he established ninety-five units of one thousand households each.[2] This was the basic unit, the single most important group in the pyramid. At the same time, Chinggis Khan organized a royal guard (*keshig* or *keseg*) by recruiting the sons and brothers of his top generals as leaders of units of ten thousand, one thousand, and one hundred households. The *keshig* was the core and general staff of his army, and it served as a training institution.[3]

The Mongol system of graduating military units in size by multiples of ten up to ten thousand households is discussed in important Chinese sources. According to the *Hei-ta shih-lüeh:* "The system of their households is such that ten persons are organized under one *p'ai-tzu-t'ou* ('head of a unit of ten family groups'), from ten to one hundred, from one hundred to one thousand, and from one thousand to ten thousand, each having a head."[4] The military section of the *Yüan shih* notes:

> The Yüan state originated from the northern steppe with a very simple military system. T'ai-tsu and T'ai-tsung [Chinggis and Ögödei] crushed the Hsia and obliterated the Chin, as a thunderbolt and hurricane and then occupied the Middle Kingdom. Their military power, it may be said, was strong and powerful. . . . At the beginning of the dynasty the rank of their military officers was determined according to the number of soldiers under a man's command. The *wan-hu* was commander of ten thousand men, the *ch'ien-hu* was commander of one thousand, and the *pai-hu* was commander of one hundred men.[5]

Actually, this model of organized military units—in multiples of ten up to ten thousand, and the entire force divided into center and right and left flanks—did not originate with the Mongols; it was an ancient tradition extending back to the time of the Hsiung-nu.[6]

When the Mongol Empire was first established, there were only three units of ten thousand households.[7] (The basic unit of ten thousand households was not actually limited to ten thousand. The unit of one thousand under the noted *noyan* Jürchedei, for example, was actually four thousand households, mainly from the Ulu'ud clan.[8]) Later, when the empire expanded, Chinese and other alien people were integrated into the Mongol structure. Therefore, the number of leaders commanding units of ten thousand greatly increased over the original three as the empire expanded.

The Mongolian approach to mobilization was simple: all functions, either military or civil, were combined into a single administration. The Chinese records emphasize the combination of a military function in conjunction with the pyramiding of households in units of multiples of ten. Again, according to the *Hei-ta shih-lüeh*, "The ranks of the troops were expanded to include the entire [male] population from fifteen years of age and older. They had only cavalry—no infantry."[9] The military section of the *Yüan shih* states, "All [Mongolian] sons from fifteen to seventy, even an only son, must serve in the army."[10] By custom, the Mongol khans, before undertaking a great campaign, made a very careful census or calculation of their manpower to determine the limits of their strength.[11] After completing a major stage of conquest, they again made a careful examination to reassess the strength of their forces for the next campaign. Chinese historians speak of this practice as *kua-hu,*[12] which has the concept of counting as people are scooped up and refers to the strategy of integrating new forces from among conquered peoples.

Military service without pay was mandatory for all males. In a sense, it was service to the khan as his vassals and did not therefore increase the burden on the khan's personal resources. As the Persian historian Juvaini commented, in contrast to other peoples of the world, Mongol warriors not only did not receive pay but also had an additional duty to present as tribute each year a certain number of horses, other animals, felt, and so forth to their leaders. No one was exempt from taxes because of service in the army; a man's wife or others living in his tent had to fulfill the quota in his stead duting the Mongol expansion.[13]

Naturally, the fruits of battle were an important element in motivating and rewarding troops. A battle or a campaign was often an opportunity for a man to establish the basis for his future career, and plunder and booty was his right. The *Secret History* points out that in the first campaign of Chinggis Khan against the Jurchen (Chin), the enemy was defeated and, along with much other tribute, a princess was presented to the khan as a wife. "They sent a princess with the rank of *gung-chu* ("imperial daughter") from the capital, Jungdu [Chungtu = Peking], with much tribute in gold, silver, silk, and other materials, which the khan allowed his soldiers to take . . . each man took as much silk and other valuables as could be loaded upon his horse, they even used valuable bolts of silk to wrap up and carry the booty."[14]

The equipment of an army is second only to its men, and Juvaini noted that besides bows, arrows, and axes, Mongol troops had honing instruments with which to sharpen their arrows. Each man was also required to equip himself with a large needle, a small needle, and some thread to be able to make minor repairs and keep his body covered during a campaign. If a man were found short in any of these things, he was punished. The better-equipped men had a curved sword. A Mongol soldier ordinarily wore a leather helmet and leather jerkin, on which was sewn metal strips as armored protection.[15] The Chinese envoy to the Mongols, P'eng Ta-ya, noted in his *Hei-ta shih-lüeh* that each man had two or three horses and that some even had six or seven.[16] Another envoy, Hsü T'ing, in his annotation of the same record, said "the officers are mounted on horses and in addition take with them, some five or six, some three or four horses to assist them in time of emergency. Even the poorest warrior will have two or three horses."[17] These early Chinese records give some information regarding the nature of the equipment of the average Mongolian soldier. D'Ohsson also noted, in his *History of the Mongols,* that each warrior carried a small tent, a leather bag in which to carry milk, a pot, and all he needed for his personal maintenance.[18] When an army advanced, a herd of animals followed to supply its needs. Chinggis Khan and his successors organized logistics by forming various units termed *a'urugh* (a "supply base" or "group"), which were mainly concerned with the necessary replacement of troops and supplies.[19]

The Mongols were masters in the utilization of weapons. Their long-distance weapons were bows and arrows. The weapons for close combat were swords, axes, spears, and forks. The Mongolian bow was shorter, but heavier, than the usual instrument of the period. The Mongols

A Mongolian bowman

reportedly had a quicker draw because of the shorter bow and placed western Asians and Europeans at a disadvantage in the western campaigns. Mongols were very skilled at shooting from horseback, and a common tactic was to attack in waves, shooting rapidly, while peeling off to one flank, and even shooting effectively in retreat. The effectiveness in the use of weapons was coupled with a rare capacity for endurance. All Mongols, men or women, were accustomed to long-distance, forced rides during hunting activity. This was naturally excellent training for war campaigns, and the nomads always had a high level of military preparation.

The *keshig* or royal guard was a key institution that made it possible for Mongol leaders to closely observe potential leaders for replacement, promotion, or special assignments. Because the royal guard was in the personal service of the khan, it was particularly exacting and rigid. Since candidates for the *keshig* were recruited from prominent families, Mongol leaders had close contact with them and an opportunity to seek the best talent. After an initial apprenticeship in the *keshig,* men were assigned in the field for a time, after which they returned again for a period of further training.[20] The continual rotation of officers from the field made it possible for the khan to keep in close contact with important developments.

Because of the advantages of mobility and surprise, Mongol strategy was to fight a moving war rather than one of fixed lines. Upon attacking a point, if they found too large a concentration of enemy troops, they circled to evade a dangerous confrontation and struck in some other area. They generally had excellent sources of intelligence and were aware of the weak points of the enemy. They also made effective feinting attacks. As a general practice, they avoided a decisive confrontation that would lock their troops with an enemy in a battle, the outcome of which was uncertain.

The Mongols gave careful attention to timing in troop movements and attacks, which made it possible to coordinate troops from different areas so they could converge simultaneously on a particular target.[21] This had the added psychological advantage of making it appear that they were much more numerous than they actually were. In some cases, if the Mongols found a target to be invulnerable, they feinted a retreat and drew the enemy out of its stronghold into a trap laid in the shape of a large U. The enemy forces were drawn into the center, and the Mongol cavalry then converged to annihilate them.

Another tactic that added to Mongol effectiveness and victory was bypassing important strongholds and destroying the surrounding countryside, isolating the strategic point so that it lost its effectiveness and would fall because its communications and transportation were cut off from the outside world. The old center of Peking fell in this way. Khorezm and other important areas in the west fell in part as a result of large encircling movements.[22] Ordinarily, Chinggis Khan dispatched a small scouting group to observe a particular city or stronghold, while his main forces sought out enemy groups that did not have the advantage of walled defenses.

The most common approach of Mongol commanders was to send in light-cavalry units to make the first engagement with an enemy in a rapid strike and retreat tactic. After the enemy had tired, heavy cavalry and troops engaged in close combat with spears and axes. Whereas many commanders of the period would strike and then consolidate their hold, the Mongols would drive in, and, as the enemy forces were defeated and fled in disarray, they would rapidly pursue and destroy them as completely as possible. Mongols were often more adept than others at exploiting the topography of a particular region because of their superior experience in hunting. Their commanders could judge at a glance the advantages and disadvantages of a particular geographical area. Moreover, they made the best possible use of seasonal changes. In the famous Naiman campaign, Chinggis attacked in late spring when the horses and herds on the steppe were still weak from the winter.[23] In so doing, he exploited a Naiman supposition that no attack would occur in that season. The famous Russian campaign of Sübe'etei was also initiated during what was considered off-season. In that case, Mongol cavalry moved in the winter of 1238 and rapidly crossed frozen rivers to strike the enemy and advance still further into southern Russia before the spring thaws. Although the Mongols were adept at judging and using continental climate, they were unfamiliar with the situation of sea regions. This accounts in part for the miscalculation and failure of Khubilai Khan's attack on Japan (1281).

In the early stages of the North China campaign, the Mongols did not use siege equipment with which to attack walled cities; they did not have any nor were they experienced in using it. However, after they acquired siege equipment, they used it effectively in China and particularly in their Persian campaigns.[24] They were very flexible in adapting new techniques, and, thus, when they acquired even better siege equipment in Persia, it was turned to advantage in the Southern Sung campaign in South China.[25] Another example of Mongolian progressiveness in adopting new techniques of warfare was the adaptation of Chinese rocketry. The Chinese had used rocketry largely for defense, but the Mongols learned to use it for offensive warfare.

Contrary to the popular view, Mongol hordes did not rampage about destructively with no rational method in movements. Before a great series of battles was undertaken, Mongol leaders held a great council (*khuraltai*) for the purpose of carefully assessing their forces and determining necessary preparations and strategy, the strength and weaknesses of the enemy, and the main objectives for future campaigns.

After making decisions for a campaign, Mongol khans carefully explained to all commanders the precise goals of the campaign and its justification as they viewed it. After a successful attack, as the main body of troops would pursue the enemy or move on to the next phase of a major campaign, smaller groups were left behind to consolidate the ground gained and to take a census or make an assessment as soon as possible of artisans and resources that could be used to advantage in the campaign. In a few isolated cases, the Mongols utilized the people of one conquered area as the vanguard in striking the next objective. This technique was more common in western Asian campaigns than in eastern Asia. Mongol commanders were more careful in the use of their forces than was often the case in their day, so that men and resources were not wasted. By careful tactics, coordination, and rapid convergence of forces, they overwhelmed a comparatively powerful strongpoint with a small number of troops. Commanders were adept at accomplishing complex tasks in the simplest possible way.[26]

The khans and commanders were very aware of the importance of psychological warfare, and they carefully exploited every opportunity to shatter the morale of enemy leaders, troops, or the general population. A careful differentiation was made in the treatment of an enemy that rapidly capitulated as compared to one that reisted. Because of the rapid and continuing successes of the Mongols, their enemies were generally in a state of terror and, in effect, were already defeated psychologically before they were even engaged in battle.

The Mongols had a very tolerant view of alien religions and were at times able to appear as the liberator of peoples in situations of religious discrimination and injustice. Thus, they were able, in some instances, to make their campaigns a positive movement. In the Kashgar region, where Moslems were oppressed by Buddhist rulers, the Mongols, under General Jebe, appeared as their champion and were able to take a strategic point without a battle. The Mongols exploited conflict between religious groups, while at the same time, because their forces were composed of many different religious types, they were able to neutralize the Moslem idea or strategy of a "holy war." Mongol leaders carefully adopted a very tolerant policy in areas they occupied, and usually the ecclesiastical classes were exempt from tax, military service, corvée, and so forth. Thus, religious reasons for resisting the Mongols were usually avoided. This was probably more of a factor in the east than in the west. Religion, a key factor in traditional societies before the trend to secularization, was shrewdly manipulated or neutralized by Mongolian leaders in many important situations.

Long before Chinggis Khan and the rise of the Mongols, nomads felt that warfare constituted a positive, productive activity. The traditional embargo maintained by the Chinese agricultural state, which retarded the flow of foodstuffs into the steppe area, deprived the nomads of necessities, which they could gain only by military activity. The economic motivation of the nomads was carefully channeled and manipulated by Mongol leaders for great effectiveness in fulfilling their needs, in strengthening their people, and in expanding their influence or control. The standard of living of the people was frequently raised by an equitable distribution of plunder taken in campaigns. The morale, motivation, and loyalty of troops and leaders were prompted by distributing not only booty, but also the lands and people taken in battle. Thus, Chinggis Khan and his generals viewed war—generally a wasteful activity depleting the resources of a people—as a productive enterprise, a source of greater wealth. On balance, the Mongols had everything to gain, their enemies had everything to lose, and the outcome of battle tended to favor the Mongols in economic terms. Chinggis Khan made the enemy the main source of supply, so battle did not mean unacceptable hardship and an outlay for the Mongols. Battle usually meant victory with greater wealth, resources, and security.[27] In addition, Chinggis Khan considered overt fighting an extreme action, but an effective means of settling perpetual disturbances. Chinggis himself was raised in an unsettled, chaotic, clan life of constant struggle and insecurity. This seems to have developed within him and those close to him a compulsion to bring order out of chaos by warfare. His hope was to use warfare to prevent prolonged, destructive wars. If the enemy was not overcome, the smaller Mongol clans would perish.

Mongol leaders clearly understood the supreme importance of good political or military intelligence, and, from the beginning, the Mongols gave careful attention to certain merchant groups, particularly caravan men, the main link between many distant and divergent centers. By special privileges and careful cultivation of this group, the Mongols developed a very excellent network from which they derived important information, and this made the difference between their success or failure in a campaign. Because the Mongol general staff was often familiar with factional politics and personality conflicts among the enemy, they were able to take advantage of schisms within their camps or governments.

In expanding the empire, Mongol generals constantly added new resources and important talent to their forces through a deliberate policy of seeking out and recruiting leadership and talent wherever they could find it, including among their enemies. The Mongol staff, both military and civil, was a cosmopolitan group with divergent religious backgrounds, and it integrated new leadership from many quarters and assigned responsibility and status on the basis of merit even to former enemies. Thus, as the Mongol armies moved forward, they were constantly enlarged by a snowballing action that drew upon new sources. This was particularly true when they moved west in Turkic areas. Turkic forces were assimilated by the Mongols to a greater degree than any other people.

If Mongol forces were separated from their horses or pasture reserves, their strength was greatly diminished. The khans of the Yüan empire in China could not control the western khanates because they lacked horsepower. This factor was a constant concern and point of strategy with Mongol leaders. Ssu-ma Ch'ien, in his discussion of the Hsiung-nu, before the Christian period, concluded that the nomadic peoples would pursue warfare if there was economic gain to be had; otherwise they would withdraw. He said they felt that it was no shame or cowardice to retreat.[28] This pattern continued into modern times as a general philosophy of warfare among the northern nomadic peoples who built empires on horseback, and helps to explain the survival and strength of the Mongols even after the collapse of their empire. They retreated as quickly as possible from China, conserving their strength without attempting a "do or die" struggle. Later, when the situation changed and the Ming state weakened, the Mongols once more gravitated south to the Great Wall and attacked when there was some gain to be had.

At the latter part of the seventeenth century, the Jungar Mongols used their traditional tactic of coordinating light and heavy cavalry in attacking the Manchu, but they were defeated because of the famous "red coated cannons" (*hung-i ta-p'ao*) cast for the Manchu by the Jesuits. This is the earliest example of nomadic tactics being forced to bow before technological developments. At the same time, the Jungar Mongols lost their former advantage of an endless refuge in the northwest because of Russian occupation of the area. Because they could not retreat and regroup as in earlier times, they were forced to meet the Manchu in a decisive war, which meant the end of Mongol power in this era.

From the ancient clan period of the Mongols to their subjugation by the Manchu in the seventeenth century, although many important political and social changes occurred in their institutions, the duty of all Mongol men to give military service in a time of crisis remained constant. Upon their alliance with and eventual subordination to the Manchu, this old custom became more formalized under Manchu overlords and through the organization of *sumun,* military units of one hundred to one hundred fifty households. The *sumun-janggi* became not only a civil administrator, but also a military leader. According to the new arrangement, the entire male population from eighteen to sixty years of age was enrolled on conscription lists. Then, within each *sumun,* fifty men were given a special assignment as *khuyagh* or standing troops; the remainder were called up only in a general mobilization. Customarily, the head of a banner would periodically make a careful examination of all men in the *sumun* within his domain, and every third year the head of a league would make a general inspection of the men on the military rolls and make a report to the Manchu emperor regarding the level of military preparedness in the area of his jurisdiction.[29] These forces, spread throughout Mongolia, were an important reserve for the Manchu emperors in case of an emergency. The best example is the forces of the Mongol general Prince Senggerinchin who recruited a Mongol army and fought valiantly for the Manchu against the Tai-p'ing (Chinese rebels) and also against French and British invading forces in the 1850s and 1860s.[30]

POSTSCRIPT ON
MODERN CULTURE

No contemporary society or culture has escaped the impact of the complex process of modernization, the inroads of science, technology, and modern ideologies. While the impact of these factors came later in Mongolia than in most parts of Asia, certainly after the turn of the present century their penetration and influence increased. Many changes have been imposed on the Mongols as a result of contact with Chinese, Russians, and Japanese. In addition, many changes have been implemented internally, as progressive young Mongols educated abroad deemed it imperative for their people to develop new approaches to national life in order to preserve their culture and identity as a nation. Most of the societal and cultural patterns discussed in this book are changing, but many have been continued.[1] Modernization has been accompanied by the inevitable processes of Sinicization in southern Mongolia and Russification in northern Mongolia. These processes are inseparable from the broad trends in politics, imperialism, and forced acculturation.

One of the most important transitions in Mongolian culture in many areas has been from a wide-ranging, full nomadism to a more restricted, semisedentary pastoralism. The gradual transition has been the result of outside influences and the realization of Mongol leaders that innovations and changes in their traditional life must be made. Progressive persons saw that nomadic migration was one of the greatest hindrances to modernization, and they moved to make an accommodation with the modern world. While herding is still a basic activity, agriculture, traditionally rejected by the Mongols as a means of production, is increasingly accepted and is now an important supplement to herding in the economy.[2]

The Mongols have learned the benefit of drilling wells, establishing schools, and setting up agricultural cooperatives—all of which could not be accomplished unless the people were more settled. With a more sedentary pastoralism have come many changes in herding techniques:[3] technological advances in the shearing of the sheep, scientific breeding of animals, drilling of wells for new water sources, modern packing plants for processing meat and dairy products, and establishment of shelters to protect animals from the harsh winters on the Mongolian steppe.

Hunting continues in modern Mongolia not only for amusement, but also for the old economic reasons: to supplement the diet and to have pelts to sell. However, the methods and the instruments of the hunt have greatly changed with the adoption of firearms. The old mass hunt, the battue or *aba,* has disappeared, and hunting no longer has the important political implications of inculcating discipline and training troops. The romantic characteristics of the great hunts are largely gone.

As the nomadic life is given up and new forms of economic activity and institutions are adopted in the society, there is naturally a concomitant change in aspects of daily life. In diet, for example, while one may still hear the old folks claim, "meat is for man, but grass [vegetables] is for animals," and while Mongols still probably consume more meat than any other people in the world, the diet is now being diversified with grains, fruits, and vegetables. Mongols are also once more beginning to fish, a common activity in ancient times that was discontinued when the Mongols converted to Lamaist Buddhism. As nomads give up yurts and live in modern dwellings, the means of preparing food also changes, and some people in the Mongolian People's Republic are giving up traditional chopsticks for forks and knives.

Western or modern dress for both men and women is being rapidly adopted. In general, dress has become more drab, and the very old, very colorful costumes, female hairstyles with jeweled ornaments, and beautiful gowns are becoming rare. Now one seldom sees the characteristic boot of the nomad, which was not only very colorful, but also designated the particular region or tribe from which a person came. The standardization and mass production of clothing has given rise to a more uniform type of dress, probably more functional but certainly less attractive and colorful. While people in the MPR are being acculturated to Western dress, in Inner Mongolia, the Chinese sphere, people are

A monastery looks out upon factories near Ulan Bator

rapidly adopting various forms of Chinese dress: peasant clothing for the common people, Mao Tse-tung jackets, or other forms of contemporary dress. This situation prevails particularly in areas of mixed population.

As the population of Mongolia is becoming more settled, dwellings are changing, and, although the *ger* or yurt may be seen even on the outskirts of such cities as Ulan Bator, most buildings are modern in style, and there is increasing pressure to reduce the use of the traditional yurt. In the present transitional period, the use of both traditional and modern forms of dwelling is mixed uniquely. Mongols may dwell in modern houses or apartments during part of the year, but many have a strong nostalgic urge during the summer season to move out and live in the dwelling of the past. The design and construction of the yurt has changed very little, but there may be some new features, like a more permanent floor. Furnishings particularly have greatly changed; radios, television, electricity, modern style stoves, sewing machines, and many other modern conveniences have become popular. Some changes are due to convenience and changing style, but others are due to economics. For example, it is becoming more and more expensive to change the wool and felt coverings of the yurt each year.

The complex process of urbanization has greatly influenced Mongolia. The ratio of urban to rural population in Mongolia is one of the greatest in the world. It is estimated that over 20 percent of the population lives in the capital city of Ulan Bator. In northern Mongolia (MPR), where modern cities are being built and where there is considerable Russian influence, a Mongolian flavor, personality, or style is still retained. Urban development progresses with excellent city planning.

However, in southern Mongolia, where Chinese settlement has been pushed with great pressure, former Mongol centers have been overwhelmed and have lost their traditional Mongol character. Only recently has attention been given to rational planning of the urbanization process in this area. Here, many formerly nomadic people are moving from the countryside into communes or coming to work in factories, where they are naturally greatly influenced by both Chinese and modern ways. But in the Inner Mongolian hinterland, many traditional ways strongly persist among the people, who still pursue some form of modified pastoralism. But, even these people are taking on new ways or using some modern materials, such as tools, radios, and methods of communication and transportation.

Most traditional festivals closely associated with Shamanism and Lamaist Buddhism have been largely given up, although more conservative families still maintain some minor observances on special occasions. The forces of nationalism and Communism have worked to abolish traditional religious festivals in favor of state festivals. The most prominent contemporary holidays are those commemorating the revolution, independence, the birthdays of the leading revolutionary figures, and the October Revolution of the Communist world. No longer observed are the old brilliant and festive holidays, such as the birthday of the Buddha, the anniversary of Tsongkha-pa, the *cham* festivals of the monasteries, the festival commemorating Maidari

(Maitreya), with its circumambulation of the temples, the *oboo* shrine festivals, and others. The traditional tournament festival of *na'adam* continues in much the same manner, emphasizing prowess; however, it has been converted to a mass athletic meeting held in stadiums, with comparatively more spectator observation than participation. The national sports are the old three *erdem* or "talents of men": wrestling, horse racing, and archery. Mongols still take great delight in these activities, are still very adept in them, and take pride in honors.

Transportation is changing, but the horse is still very important in many parts of Mongolia and caravans are still seen, although they are much fewer in number than in the old days. In cities like Ulan Bator, it is cheaper to maintain a motorbike than a horse, and for cross-country travel, caravans rapidly become more expensive than truck transportation. Mongolia is now traversed from north to south by a railroad, and a number of branch lines have been built. Also, the airplane has become very important in reaching outlying areas and in linking Mongolia to the outside world. Buses, trucks, jeeps, and passenger cars are more numerous and are increasing in number.

Superstitious or mystic notions of birth and death are rapidly giving way to more scientific views. Hospital care and midwives are almost universal, and daycare nurseries and kindergartens have become very popular for young children. Even the stories told by the old people to the children are changing as the old didactic religious tales and heroic legends of ages past give way to modern stories, often with political implications or elements of nationalism and socialism. Still, Mongolian youth are not ignorant of their tradition; they take increasing pride in their history and learn a great deal from their elders through informal education.

Personal names of children is one area in which there has been a thrust for continuity and a resistance to outside influence and change. Mongol children are still given names originating from Buddhism or from Tibetan and Sanskrit sources, but there is an increasing tendency to use indigenous Mongol names. In Inner Mongolia, there has been a tendency to adopt Chinese names, and in government listings, it is often difficult to tell which persons are Chinese and which are Mongolian. Some persons take new names with revolutionary connotations, such as Ulanfu[4] ("red son"), but these names seem somewhat unnatural to Mongols and there are very few of them even among more radical leaders.

Marriage has not escaped change. There is now much greater

freedom in contracting marriages, and the considerations of the young people involved receive more attention. The use of fortune-tellers to divine a suitable mate is no longer common, and parents have much less influence in making a match or determining arrangements; also divorces have increased in frequency. In many areas of life, family considerations have been replaced by other factors, such as the interests of the party or the country as dictated by ideas of planned nationhood. The old forms of courtship are gone, and the marriage rituals have now given way to much more simple civil ceremonies. Now people marry at somewhat later ages than previously, but it is difficult to generalize on this matter. The population problem of Mongolia is just the reverse of that found in many developing nations. Due to a sparse population, rewards and great encouragement or incentive is given by the government to couples who have many children.

As a result of hygienic and medical development, longevity has been greatly increased; many diseases and illnesses have been brought under control. Syphilis, once a great curse to the Mongols, has now been largely eradicated. More people are living to a much older age, and life expectancy has almost doubled to an estimated sixty-four years. The composition of the population is also changing; almost half of the people are under twenty-five years of age.[5]

The old practice of exposing bodies in remote places as a form of final sacrifice of one's last and only possession, the body, to wildlife has been abolished. Also, most of the old taboos having to do with death— removal of the body from the yurt and so forth—have changed. Many other taboos are naturally forgotten as the society becomes more secularized and modernized.

The clan and lineage system of Mongolia had greatly changed even before modern times, but changes continue to take place. Old Mongol *obogh* names, originally clan or lineage names, have now become "surnames" for some people. However, many people have forgotten their lineage identification. In more recent decades, there has been a move in the MPR to deemphasize surnames with the hope of abolishing the old clan names of the nobility and elite families. Instead, generation by generation, sons adopt their father's name as their own surname in a manner that would remind some Westerners of the Scandinavian surname system. This practice makes it easier for the government to maintain a record of a person's family and class background and genealogical records.

No radical change has occurred within the nuclear family of Mongolia in the transition to modern times. There was never a well-developed extended-family system, and the stem or nuclear family structure has continued to be the husband, wife, and their children, and perhaps a grandparent. There must be some differences in this situation between the Mongolian People's Republic and contemporary Inner Mongolia within the Chinese sphere; however, fieldwork cannot be freely carried out at present to determine precisely just what these differences are and to ascertain what particular changes may have resulted from the impact of such events as the People's Commune Movement and the Cultural Revolution (1966-68).

Distinct social classes continued to exist in Mongolia until the Communist revolution and the radical restructuring of society. But from the evidence available, it is not possible to document any strong class consciousness among the Mongols until very recent times. Traditionally, in the minds of the Mongols, social classes meant broadly (1) the "black" (*khara*) or lay society and (2) the "yellow" (*shira*) or ecclesiastical segment of society, plus various sublevels or subclasses within these. Two main groups in the lay society were the nobility (*noyad*) and the common people (*arad*). Among the common people, social levels or distinctions existed in that some non-nobility were very wealthy. As for the "yellow" (*shira*), the large and important religious segment of society, the two main classes were (1) the "incarnations" (*khubilghan*) or high lamas and (2) the common lamas together with the lay disciples (*shabinar*) who were subject to the religious authorities.

The development of class consciousness was retarded by such Buddhist concepts as *üile-üri* or karma—the belief that status was determined at birth by one's deeds in preexistent lives. The common belief was that class distinctions and different stations in life were natural according to birth. However, as young Mongols went to foreign areas and as modernizing influences penetrated Mongolia, these attitudes changed and, even before the inception of socialist ideas, there were many manifestations of discontent; subservience was rejected, and young men who felt that their fate should be in their own hands rebelled against the ruling class. Class consciousness really only developed to a notable degree upon the stimulation of Communism. It then became common to use such phrases as *khara-shira peudal*[6] ("feudalistic lay and ecclesiastical upper classes"). In present-day Mongolia, the old classes have disappeared and have been replaced by a new elite arising from the party.

Changes in the political structure and administrative system of Mongolia are far too complex to discuss here, but many of the old, traditional names continue to be used in the Mongolian People's Republic. For example, the local district units are still called *sumun,* and these are brought together in a larger regional or provincial unit, the *aimagh.* In Inner Mongolia, the units are virtually the same, although different terms are used; the local banner unit is called a *khushighun,* and these basic administrative units are brought together in larger regional units, commonly spoken of in the West as leagues (*chighulghan*). Needless to say, these are no longer controlled by a hereditary nobility, but rather by functionaries of the Communist party.

In Inner Mongolia, although political administration changed hands—from the Manchu to the Republic of China to the Japanese followed by the Communists—the units of the banner and league have continued and have been heroically defended by both conservative and radical Mongols and by traditionalists and nationalists alike as a defense against the incursions of Chinese colonists. Very recently (1970s), the old term for a league administrative unit, *chighulghan,* has been dropped in favor of the MPR term *aimagh;* the Chinese version of the term continues to be *meng.* Former Mongolian local units known as *sumun* have been converted to people's communes.

In the political structure of the modern Mongolian People's Republic, the national assembly is now a very important institution (*khuraltan*). This is not the old convocation of princes and leaders of the empire period, but "representatives of the people" in a People's Congress.

The famous basic law of the Mongol Empire, the *jasagh* (*yasa*) of Chinggis Khan, broke down following the end of the empire. The Ch'ing dynasty or Manchu law, which succeeded it, continued until the Communist takeover with very little change. At the turn of the century, when Ch'ing power declined, Outer Mongolia gained its independence, and in the 1920s the revolutionary administration that came to power developed new law codes called the national constitution (*ündüsün kha'uli*).

In Inner Mongolia, Manchu law continued with little change among the Mongols through the period of the Chinese republic and the Japanese occupations until the Communist takeover. In areas of concentrated Chinese settlement, there were some changes in the law codes, but they related only indirectly to the Mongolian population.

The legal codes that have been developed in the Mongolian People's Republic tend to emphasize the socialist nature of property and to stress duty to the state over private citizen's rights. In addition, the law regulates many aspects of life that never were controlled before and that are not controlled in most other modern societies. An entirely new criminal code has been developed, and there is an emphasis on equal rights for women. One element that has carried through from traditional Mongolia to the modern Communist period is the tendency to consider crimes committed against the state as more serious than crimes committed against private persons. One of the key words of the old legal codes was *chaghaja*, which has the connotation of prohibition or that which is forbidden. The great emphasis was on negative restrictions. In contrast, a key word in the codes that have developed under socialism in the MPR is *erke*, meaning "rights." While the tone has definitely changed, many civil rights are still missing, and many prescriptive regulations are set forth to guide the relationships of the people in various phases of life, to define the limitations of their activity, and to interpret their duties in what the party feels is the best interest of society.

The military aspect of society has continued to be important in Mongolia in the modern period. Today, as in the past, military men have high status in society, and men continue to have a certain natural aptitude to adapt to military life and be effective in battle situations. However, the old reliance on cavalry is rapidly giving way to mechanization, and now the ratio of troops to civilians, that is, the comparative size of the military segment of society, is much smaller than in former times. Mongol troops have demonstrated valor in modern warfare as amply documented in the studies of the Khalkhin-ghol (Nomunkhan) Battle (1939) against the Japanese.

Two of the most significant changes in the domestic economy of Mongolia are the development of agriculture and manufacturing. The role of agriculture in economic planning in this century has been very controversial, and the trend in Inner Mongolia has differed from that in Northern Mongolia, the MPR. In Inner Mongolia, a Chinese sphere, there has been a strong inclination to associate agriculture totally with Chinese immigration, and consequently, during recent decades, leaders have tended to resist the development of agriculture, which would almost certainly lead to Chinese domination of Mongol lands.

During the 1930s and 1940s, Inner Mongolian leaders were strongly inclined to move the pastoral society toward manufacturing, but not toward agriculture.[7] They hoped to gradually settle the population in modified pastoral activities, avoiding agriculture and developing industries for the processing of meat, hides, and textiles, which would be compatible with the traditional economic base of Mongolia and which would also encourage self-sufficiency. For a brief period, during the rule of the Kalgan government (1939-45), cooperatives were developed, planned, and administered in such a way as to bring the economy of Inner Mongolia into the hands of the Mongols and eliminate exploitation by outside peoples, such as the Chinese or the Japanese. However, the collapse of Japan's occupation of Mongolia ended these efforts, and Inner Mongolia fell so completely under the domination of Communist China that the economic planning of Inner Mongolia after 1950 must be considered as a function of China proper. As such, it was subject to such economic programs as the Great Leap Forward, the Commune Movement, the Cultural Revolution, and the subsequent Production and Construction Corps Movement.

As a result of the various essentially Chinese programs, a concerted effort has been made to develop some manufacturing in Inner Mongolia, such as the mining operating at Paotou and, at the same time, to turn pastureland into farmland. Apart from any evaluation of attempts at land development, this change in the economic base of Inner Mongolia has greatly influenced all other areas of society and culture, if for no other reason than that the ratio of Chinese to Mongols has radically changed and has greatly subordinated the Mongol minority to the Chinese.[8]

The economic development of northern Mongolia in this century must be considered separately from that of Inner Mongolia. After centuries of exploitation by Chinese merchants, a radical break was made with the independence movement, which brought a shift to Russian domination or assistance—depending on one's interpretation— in exchange for the former Chinese economic involvement. This situation has now continued for over half a century and has resulted in a socialist economy.

The traditional pastoral economic base continues, but industry and agriculture are gaining new importance. Only recently, the MPR has become self-sufficient in grain production, and advances are being made in various types of manufacturing; nevertheless, pastoralism remains the dominant segment of the economy. Here also, however, changes are being made, and the tendency is to restructure and redirect pastoral activity and to link it with agricultural and industrial development. While pastoralism and agriculture have been divorced in Mongolian history, the tendency is now to bring these together by settling the herds, building shelters for them, developing new techniques of feeding, and thus bringing about a more sedentary form of pastoralism, much like ranching in other parts of the world.

For a short period during the high point of the Sino-Soviet alliance, China sent considerable aid into the MPR, mainly in the form of construction groups. But this rapprochement did not last long, and after the Sino-Soviet confrontation, Mongolia once more came totally under Russian influence and has now been integrated into COMECON, the East European counterpart of the European Common Market. The significance of this development is that Mongol trade patterns, traditionally oriented toward China, have been changed and the economy and trade of Mongolia have now been integrated within the patterns of Soviet and East European exchange. Until recently, over 90 percent of the MPR trade was with Russia, but now trade is being developed with other areas, mainly eastern Europe but also Japan.

In the transition to the modern period, the Mongolian language has demonstrated a great vitality and a remarkable persistence of linguistic purity. However, changes are inevitably induced from the outside; thus, while Inner Mongolian language is increasingly influenced by words, phrases, and ideas from the Chinese sphere, the Mongolian People's Republic is greatly influenced by Russian language and thought. Still, there is a strong impulse among the Mongols to look to their own language to find elements for modern terms rather than to adopt loanwords from foreign languages.

There has been a great evolutionary linguistic change over the eight centuries from the time of the empire. The result is a wide divergence between the spoken and the classical written forms of the language. Nevertheless, the old traditional script has served a useful purpose in the thrust for unity among many widely separated and diverse Mongol groups over the centuries. Much linguistic divergence and diversification came with the political changes in this century. The Buriyad Mongols, the Oirad (Kalmuck) Mongols, and the main group of the Khalkha (MPR) have all adopted a Cyrillic or Russian script, but with certain differences.

The development of the written language in Inner Mongolia has also been very complex. The traditional script continued until the 1940s, but was changed to the Russian script after the Chinese Communist takeover, in an attempt by Inner Mongolian leaders to facilitate greater communication between the two spheres of Mongolia. The move to the Cyrillic script was short-lived. After the Sino-Soviet split, the Chinese pressured the Mongols to give up publishing materials in the Russian script and to revert to the old form. Later, there were several similar, but unsuccessful, attempts to change the written script. Ulanfu, the long-time head of the Inner Mongolian Autonomous Region, whose "crimes" consisted of promoting language reform and "separatism," was purged during the Cultural Revolution but is rehabilitated.

Before the revolution, there was considerable literature written in Mongolia, but most of it was Buddhist and thus infused with religious ideas. Since the revolution and the establishment of an independent Mongolian People's Republic, there has been a great promotion of art and literary activity, secular in nature and extending over a broad spectrum both in form and content. While much of the literature has been very commendable, most of it has not been art for art's sake. A political theme has been subtly infused in most literary and artistic production.

Contemporary Mongol art and literature contain new and modern themes. The original typically Asian tone with a strong Buddhist influence is now much more secularized and more closely related to the external modern world. Many modern international masterpieces have been translated into Mongolian, and the stage and screen show definite modern influences. Ballet, Western music, cinematography, and so forth are all to be found. Traditional themes and a low-key, but undeniable, spirit of nationalism has continued in spite of strong Russian disapproval.

In Inner Mongolia, where the Mongols have actually become a minority and where the Chinese Communists have been particularly active in promoting many cultural programs, it has not been possible for the Mongols to escape acculturation or to be free agents in developing a distinctly Mongol form of culture. There has been considerable publishing activity and energetic development of Mongolian music, dance, drama, modern cinema, and literature—but all are infused with a certain Chinese tone.

The growth of education in this century in all areas of Mongolia has been one of the most spectacular developments. Kindergartens, primary and secondary schools, and institutions of higher education are found everywhere. Particularly notable is the establishment of the Academy of Sciences in the MPR, where the greatest development in education has taken place. One may gather from reading the works of such people as academician Rinchen that, while there has been a remarkable development in education since the revolution, there has been a rather misleading tendency to play down educational development before the revolution and to give the impression that there was none.[9] In recent years, an increasing number of young Mongols have gone abroad to study. This is a renewal of an earlier trend in which young Mongols of Inner Mongolia went to Japan or to China for education and many youth from Buriyad and Kalmuck areas went to Kazan and other areas of Russia for education. There were even important groups who went to France and Germany in the 1920s.[10] Thus, education in Mongolia is much more related to the outside world in this century than in the past.

In the area of social thought, there have been major changes with many implications, but it will only be noted here that the old dominance of Buddhism over attitudes and values has given way to the influence of socialism. It is difficult to sort out the complexities of philosophy, religion, and social thought in Mongolia, but in practical terms the constitution grants both the right to believe and the right to oppose religious beliefs. Moreover, the state has been strongly biased in favor of subordinating religious influences to party or governmental authority. Some tolerance for Buddhism, which actually is no longer a strong force in the life and thought of the nation has only recently developed. The dominant themes that replaced the old ideas of Lamaist Buddhism are service to the state and the people, progress toward modernization, counteracting bourgeois class consciousness, and the promotion of science and technology. Also, great lip service is given to democracy. Still, the traditional Mongol virtues of loyalty, prudence, respect for age, and faithfulness to friends and family are still strong. Naturally, there has been a transfer of values from the princes and khans to the new state and from the old religion to the new dogma of socialism. All in all, Mongols are still very much Mongols and will continue to be in spite of foreign and modernizing influences.

IDENTIFICATION OF MAJOR REFERENCES

The most important documentary sources used in this study are primary Chinese and Mongolian works. Identified below and arranged alphabetically, the references may be grouped separately in several categories:

1. Important Mongolian chronicles and classics.
2. Official Chinese histories devoted to alien dynasties of conquest and rule over China, including the *Wei shu, Liao shih, Chin shih,* and the *Yüan shih.*
3. The histories of major Chinese dynasties which include important accounts of major contemporary nomadic peoples; such as the *Shih-chi, Han shu, Sui shu, T'ang shu* and *Ming shih.*
4. Uniquely important personal accounts by Chinese that are virtually unknown in the West and to which reference is frequently made. These include the *Meng-ta pei-lu,* the *Hei-ta shih-lüeh,* and the *Pei-lu feng-su.* Included in each of the various records, implicitly or explicitly, is information on the life-style or culture and society of the Mongols and other nomadic peoples that preceded them.

These notes do not include such standard Western works as those by Marco Polo and C. d'Ohsson. Regarding the Chinese sources, one must constantly keep in mind that while they are often virtually the only source available regarding a particular nomadic people, they have a strong inherent bias, having been written by Chinese about alien enemies who are viewed as uncivilized barbarians.

For all works listed here that are not also listed in the "Key to Short Title References," the Po-na edition (reprinted, Taipei,

Taiwan: Commercial Press, 1960s) was used.

1. *Altan tobchi* (Golden chronicle): Next to the *Secret History of the Mongols* this is the greatest early Mongolian record important as a source for information on Mongolian history, society, and culture. There are many versions of the *Altan tobchi,* but the one used in this book was edited by Lobsangdanjin in the 1600s from materials written by unknown Mongolian authors. It actually contains about 80 percent of the material included in the *Secret History.*

2. *Chin shih:* This is the history of the Chin dynasty (1115-1234), the third alien dynasty of conquest over China, established by the Jurchen, Tungusic ancestors of the Manchu people, who ruled as the last alien dynasty from 1644 to 1911. Compiled under the name of Toghtogh (Chs. To-to), it is drawn on for information on the Tungusic branch of the Altaic family whose life-style was a mixture of pastoralism and agriculture.

3. *Chiu T'ang shu:* This was the first of two standard histories for the T'ang dynasty (618-907). Edited by Liu Hsu (d. 937?), it contains accounts of the Turks, Uighur, and Kitans among other nomadic peoples of the China-Mongol border area. Later, a revised edition known as the *Hsin T'ang shu* (new history of the T'ang dynasty) was completed, which contains accounts of the same peoples and is essentially the same as the *Chiu T'ang shu.*

4. *Chou shu:* This history of the Chou dynasty (557-81) was the work of Ling-hu Te-fen (d. 666), a scholarly minister of the T'ang dynasty. Although it is a minor dynastic history, the Account of the T'u-chüeh Turks contained therein supplies important material for studies of this early Turkic people.

5. *Erdeni-yin tobchi* (Jeweled chronicle): Also commonly referred to as Sagang Sechen, the name of its author, this Mongolian classic is a mixture of history and legend written in the seventeenth century during the period when great changes were taking place in Mongolian society and culture under Manchu domination and with the conversion of the Mongol nation to Lamaist Buddhism.

6. *Han shu:* This history of the former Han dynasty (206 B.C.-A.D. 8) in one hundred chapters is largely the work of the second great Chinese historian Pan Ku (d. A.D. 92). The Account of the Hsiung-nu contained therein duplicates, but also supplements, the work on these nomads written by Ssu-ma Ch'ien almost two centuries earlier.

7. *Hei-ta shih-lüeh* (Brief record of the Black Tatars): Originally written by a Sung dynasty official P'eng Ta-ya, with a commentary by Hsü T'ing (both P'eng and Hsü were envoys to the Mongol court about 1234), this work, together with the *Meng-ta pei-lu*, provides an authoritative primary account by contemporary Chinese of the lifestyle and customs of the Mongols in their early empire period. The book was written in 1237.

8. *Hou Han shu:* This history of the later Han dynasty (A.D. 25-220) is mainly a work of Fan Yeh (d. 446?). The Account of the Southern Hsiung-nu and the Account of the Wu-huan and Hsienpei recorded therein include important materials for the study of these nomadic peoples who inhabited Mongolia for the first two centuries following the meridian of time.

9. *Liao shih:* This is the best primary source for studies of the culture and history of the alien Liao dynasty (907-1125), the second dynasty of conquest over China under the nomadic Kitan people whose origins were in Mongolia. It was compiled under the direction of To-to (Toghtogh, d. 1355), a Mongolian chancellor of the Yüan dynasty.

10. *Meng-ta pei-lu* (Reference on the Mongol-Tatars): This is a personal travel record written in 1221 by Chao Hung, a Chinese officer of the Sung dynasty dispatched to the headquarters of Mukhali, commander of the Mongolian forces invading North China. This is a record of his observations made during a sojourn among the Mongols, and it virtually stands alone as a firsthand Chinese account of Mongolian life and customs during this period.

11. *Ming shih:* This history of the Ming dynasty (1368-1644) contains an account of the Ta-tan (Eastern Mongols), the Wa-la (the Oirad Mongols in western Mongolia), and the three Mongolian garrisons of To-yen, Fu-yu, and T'ai-ning (in southeastern Inner Mongolia). Edited by Chang T'ing-yu (d. 1755), it is useful as a source on the Mongols following the decline of the empire and for making comparisons with earlier periods.

12. *Pei-lu feng-su* (Customs of the northern barbarians—the Mongols): This is another rare firsthand Chinese account of the Mongols written by Hsiao Ta-heng, commander of Ming China's force stationed along the central section of the Great Wall in the sixteenth century. Later becoming Minister of War (1594), Hsiao gave a detailed record of the Mongols of his day, particularly regarding the major new trend of their conversion to Tibetan Buddhism.

13. *San-kuo chih:* This history of the Three Kingdoms (Wei, Wu, and

Shu Han, 220-80) edited by Chen Shuo (d. 297) contains important information on the Wu-huan and Hsien-pei peoples. It records part of the history of these two Altaic peoples of the later Han period who were successors to the Hsiung-nu.

14. *Secret History of the Mongols (Mongghol-un ni'ucha tobchiyan;* Chs. *Yüan-ch'ao pi-shih):* This is the most important and the earliest literary monument of the Mongols. It is the source most often referred to in this study. The term "secret" is misleading, for actually it was a sacred or confidential chronicle handed down by the inner circle of the Mongolian ruling clan. Written in the thirteenth century, its most important contributions are a quasi-historical account of the origins of the Mongols or more particularly the lineage of Chinggis Khan—his early struggles and an account of the early rise of the Mongol Empire up through the early reign of Chinggis's successor in the 1240s, Ögödei Khan. It virtually stands alone as a source of information regarding earliest Mongolian society and culture. Written in Mongolian, the original was lost in the chaos following the fall of the Mongol Empire and now is preserved only in a complex and much studied version written phonetically in Chinese characters.

15. *Shih chi:* The *Shih chi,* or Historical Records, is a famous work in 130 chapters by China's first great historian, Ssu-ma Ch'ien (145?-90? B.C.). It is broader in scope and more sophisticated in scholarship than anything which precedes it. Its coverage extends from the earliest mythological emperors up through the period of the Emperor Wu-ti (140-85 B.C.) of the Han dynasty. The section, Account of the Hsiung-nu, contained therein is the most complete record of the earliest nomadic people of North Asia who formed a great confederation outside the Great Wall as a challenge to the Chinese.

16. *Sui-shu:* A history of the Sui dynasty (581-618), edited by Wei Cheng (d. 643), this work is a basic reference regarding several Inner Asian peoples, including the Turks, Western Turks, Tölös, Hsi, and Kitan.

17. *Ta-Ch'ing hui-tien* (Collection of the law code of the Ch'ing dynasty, 1644-1911): This was the major collection of laws and statutes compiled by the Ch'ing court. In 1934, the Mongolian-Tibetan Affairs Commission of the National Government in Nanking edited out those parts especially related to Mongolia and Tibet and published a new compilation under the title *Ch'ing-tai pien-cheng t'ung-k'ao* (General survey of border area administration in the Ch'ing dynasty). Among

other functions, it is a valuable source of information and analysis of the administrative and judicial institutions and the policies of the Manchu for their rule of Mongolia. The latter work was actually based on the *Li-fan tse-li* (Statutes of the imperial board of dependencies).

18. *Wei shu:* A history of the Wei dynasty (38-557), this work was written mainly by Wei Shuo (d. 572). This first dynasty of conquest over China was established by the T'o-pa tribe, a non-Chinese people related to the Hsien-pei arising out of Mongolia. This history also contains an Account of Juan-juan originally known as the Jou-jan, another purely nomadic power north of the Great Wall, referred to in the study.

19. *Yüan shih:* This history of the Mongolian Yüan dynasty (1206-1368) by Chinese scholars is frequently cited in this study. It covers the period from Chinggis Khan (1206-27) to the end of the dynasty in 1368. This was the fourth dynasty of conquest to rule over China, the last established by pure nomads. Compiled under the chief editor Sung Lien (d. 1381?) it is a most important source of information on Mongolian social institutions.

KEY TO SHORT
TITLE REFERENCES

Altan tobči (nova)   *Altan tobči (nova)*. Scripta Mongolica ed. Cambridge: Harvard University Press, 1953.

Bawden   Bawden, C. R. *Modern History of Mongolia*. New York: Praeger, 1968.

Chao Hung   Chao Hung. *Meng-ta pei-lu*. Meng-ku shih-liao ssu-chung ed. Taipei, 1962.

CTPCTK   *Ch'ing-tai pien-cheng t'ung-k'ao*. 4th ed. Taipei, 1959.

Damdinsürüng   Damdinsürüng, Ch., ed. *Mongghol uran jokiyal-un degeji jaghun bilig orušibai* [A Hundred Selections from Mongolian Literature]. Ulan Bator, 1959.

Damdinsuren and Sodnom   Damdinsuren, Ts. (Ch. Damdinsürüng) and B. Sodnom, eds. *D. Natsagdorji zohiolund* [The Works of Natsaghdorj]. Ulan Bator, 1961.

Dawson   Dawson, Christopher, ed. *The Mongol Mission: Narratives and Letters of the Franciscan Missionaries in Mongolia and China in the Thirteenth and Fourteenth Centuries*. Trans. by a Nun of Stanbrook Abbey. London and New York: Sheed and Ward, 1955.

d'Ohsson   d'Ohsson, C. *Histoire des Mongols*. The Hague and Amsterdam: Les Frères van Cleef, 1834–35.

Hsiao Ta-heng   Hsiao Ta-heng. *Pei-lu feng-su* [The Customs of the Northern Barbarians]. Reprint. Peking, 1930s.

Jagchid, *Pei ya yu-ma min-tsu*   Jagchid, S. *Pei-ya yu-mu min-tsu yu chung-yüan nung-yeh min-tsu chien ti ho-ping chan-cheng yü mao-i chih kuan-hsi* [Peace, War, and Trade Relationships between the North Asian Nomadic Peoples and the Agricultural Chinese]. Taipei, 1972.

Jagchid, *Pien-chiang*   Jagchid, S. *Pien-chiang chiao-yu* [Education in Chinese
    chiao-yü   Border Areas]. Taipei, 1961.

Juvaini   Juvaini, 'Ala-ad-Din 'Ata-Malik. *The History of the
                      World Conqueror*. J. A. Boyle, trans. Manchester,
                      1958.

Meng-ku yüan-liu   *Meng-ku yüan-liu*. Chien-lung Chinese ed. of *Erdeni-yin
                      tobchi*. Reprint. Taipei, 1965.

P'eng Ta-ya   P'eng Ta-ya. *Hei-ta shih-lüeh*. Commentary by Wang
                      Kuo-wei. Meng-ku shih-liao ssu-chung ed. Taipei,
                      1962.

Sagang Sechen   Sagang Sechen. *Erdeni-yin tobchi*. Ulan Bator, 1961.

Secret History   *Secret History. Mongghol-un ni'ucha tobchiyan*. Ssu-pu
                      ts'ung-k'an ed. Taipei, n.d.

Vernadsky   Vernadsky, George. *The Mongols and Russia*. New
                      Haven, 1953.

Wada Sei   Wada Sei. *Toa shi kenkyu-Moko hen* [Studies on the
                      History of East Asia, Mongolia]. Tokyo, 1959.

Yüan-tien-chang   *Yüan-tien-chang* [Collection of Yuan Dynasty Docu-
                      ments]. Taipei, 1964.

Yule   Yule, Henry. *Cathay and the Way Thither: Being a
                      Collection of Medieval Notices of China*. 3rd ed., rev. H.
                      Cordier. London, 1921.

NOTES

CHAPTER 1. LAND AND PEOPLE

1. S. Jagchid, "Trade, Peace, and War," *BICBAS* no. 1 (1970):35-80.

2. Ibid.

3. According to the traditional Chinese official view, the acceptance of the imperial calendar (*feng cheng-shuo*) by alien peoples was symbolic of their acceptance of the suzerainty of the Son of Heaven of the Middle Kingdom.

4. *Han shu,* Vol. 94b, Account of the Hsiung-nu, 32ab.

5. *Shih chi,* Vol. 110, Account of the Hsiung-nu, 1b-2a.

6. Ibid., 8ab. This passage discusses the struggle for land between the Hsiung-nu and the Tung-hu and also gives the statement of Mao-tun, khan of the Hsiung-nu: "land is the root of a country."

7. "State on horseback" is a translation from the Chinese *ma-shang hsing-kuo*. *Hsing-kuo* here means a state on the move, a nomadic state on horseback. The term was first used by Ssu-ma Ch'ien in his *Shih chi,* Vol. 123; see Account of Ta-wan, entries on Wu-sun and K'ang-chü, 4a.

8. See P'eng Ta-ya, *Hei-ta shih-lüeh,* commentary by Wang Kuo-wei, Meng-ku shih-liao ssu-chung ed. (Taipei, 1962), p. 1a.

9. Sagang Sechen, *Erdeni-yin tobchi* (Ulan Bator, 1961), p. 87. See also *Meng-ku yüan-liu,* Ch'ien-cheng ed. of the *Erdeni-yin tobchi* (reprint ed. Taipei, 1965), 3:11b. This translation of Sagang Sechen is rather odd, but is still the basic Chinese translation. This text was introduced to the Western world by Isaac Jacob Schmidt, *Geschichte der Ost-Mongolen und ihres Fürstenhauses, verfasst von Ssanang Ssetsen Chungtaidschi der Ordus; aus dem Mongolischen übersetzt, und mit dem Originaltexte, nebst Anmerkungen, Erläuterungen und Citaten aus anderen unedirten Originalwerken herausgegeben von Issac Jacob Schmidt* (St. Petersburg, 1829). Prince Khorjurjab (d. 1945) of the Sünid Banner, Inner Mongolia, a well-known scholar versed in both Mongolian and Tibetan literatures, was a widely known

exponent of this idea. Sayinbayar and Erinchin Kharadaban were others. This theory was an interesting element in encouraging the national consciousness of many young Mongols at the time of the Inner Mongolian Autonomous Movement in the 1930s and 1940s.

10. "Song of Ch'ih-le" was sung by Hu-lü-chin, a military leader at the court of the Northern Ch'i, from the Ch'ih-le, an early Turkic tribe. See Pei-Chi shu, Vol. 2, Annals of Emperor Shen-wu (b), 14a, and Vol. 17, Biography of Hu-lü-chin. For the text of this song, see Kuo Mu-ch'ien (Sung dynasty), *Yüeh-fu shih-chi* (reprint ed., Taipei: Shih-chieh shu-chü, 1967), 86ab. For an alternate translation of this piece, see Ogawa Tamaki, "The Song of Ch'ih-le, Chinese Translation of Turkic Folk Songs and Their Influence on Chinese Poetry," *Acta Asiatica*, no. 1 (1960):43-57.

11. Li Chih-ch'ang, *Ch'ang-ch'un chen-jen hsi-yu chi,* Meng-ku shih-liao ssu-chung ed. (Taipei, 1962), p. 16b.

12. During the T'ang dynasty (618-907), the Chinese court officially designated the area under the rule of the Sung-mo *tu-tu-fu,* namely, the Office of the Governor-General of the Land of Pine Trees and Desert; the title of *tu-tu* was conferred upon the leaders of the Kitan people for several centuries.

13. *Mongghol-un ni'ucha tobchiyan* (the Secret History of the Mongols), Sec. 239. The version of this most important reference used throughout this study is the readily available *yüan-ch'ao pi-shih* transcription, Ssu-pu ts'ung-k'an ed., reprinted Taipei, n.d. It will be cited hereafter simply as *Secret History.* For a discussion of this monumental record see the subsection Literature.

14. Dashdorjiin Natsaghdorj (1906-37) has been acclaimed as the founder of modern Mongolian literature. Active in both political and military fields at the time of the revolution (1921), he graduated from a school of journalism in Leipzig and became recognized at an early age as a major poet, prose writer, dramatist, and translator.

15. The poem was translated by Gombojab Hangin, the founder of the Mongolia Society (US) and best known for his work in Mongolian linguistics and literature. For the original text of this poem, see Ts. Damdinsuren (Ch. Damdinsürüng) and B. Sodnom, eds., *D. Natsagdorji zohioluud* [The Works of Natsaghdorj] (Ulan Bator, 1961).

16. Harrison E. Salisbury, *War Between Russia and China* (New York: W. W. Norton and Company, 1969), pp. 19, 26-27.

CHAPTER 2. NOMADIC CULTURE

Herding

1. *Shih chi,* Vol. 110, Account of the Hsiung-nu, 1ab.
2. *Wei shu,* Vol. 103, Account of the Juan-juan, 1b.
3. *Sui shu,* Vol. 84, Account of the T'u-chüeh, 1b-2a.

4. This is a common maxim of elderly people in the pastoral areas of both Shilin-ghol and Ulanchab leagues in Inner Mongolia and possibly elsewhere.

5. According to the account in both the *Secret History* and the Annals of Tai-tsu in the *Yüan shih.*

6. *Altan tobči (nova)*, Scripta Mongolica ed. (Cambridge: Harvard University Press, 1953), 2:55-57.

7. *Secret History*, Secs. 190, 193.

8. This is a common proverb in northern Inner Mongolia.

9. The practice of sacrificing a horse for a deceased person at the time of burial was discontinued after the Mongols were converted to Lamaist Buddhism in the latter part of the sixteenth century through the efforts of the Third Dalai Lama; see *Meng-ku yüan-liu* (Sagang Sechen, *Erdeni-yin tobchi*), 7:4a.

10. *Ta-Ch'ing hui-tien*, Vol. 68, 4a. The *Jou-yüan ch'ing-li ssu* section of the *Li-fan yüan* states: "Each year the Jebtsundamba Khutughtu sends envoys to present one white camel and eight white horses [to the emperor] and this is acknowledged as the [tribute of] nine whites. Both the Sechen Khan and Tüshiyetü Khan also send envoys to present the nine whites."

11. *Secret History*, Sec. 216.

12. Horses of mixed colors were particularly prized by one of the Mongol khans of the Yüan dynasty about 1330; see the *Ta-yüan ma-cheng chi*, Wen-tien-ko ed. (Peking, 193?), p. 3.

13. The *Ch'ing-tai pien-cheng t'ung-k'ao (CTPCTK)* states:

Formerly it was decided that any Mongols trespassing the border to pasture their animals would be fined [as follows]: a *wang* ten horses, a *jasagh, beyile, beyise* or *gung* seven horses, a *taiji* five horses, and a commoner one ox. Again the law has been revised so that for anyone trespassing the border limitations to pasture animals, the fine is as follows: a *wang* one hundred horses, a *jasagh, beyile, beyise* or *gung* seventy horses, a *taiji* fifty horses. In the case of a commoner, all their property will be confiscated and given to the person reporting the matter.

Edited from the *Ta Ch'ing hui-tien* by the Meng-Tsang wei-yuan-hui, 4th ed. (Taipei, 1959), p. 254.

14. *Liao shih*, Vol. 32, Monograph on the Royal Camp Garrison (*yin-wei chih*), 1a-3a.

Hunting

1. *Shih chi*, Vol. 110, Account of the Hsiung-nu, 1b.

2. P'eng Ta-ya, 7b.

3. *Secret History*, Sec. 9.

4. *Hou Han shu*, Vol. 90, Account of the Wu-huan and Hsien-pei, 8b. The *na* is described as a type of monkey, but it is impossible to determine just what animal it was.

5. Chao Hung, *Meng-ta pei-lu*, Meng-ku shih-liao ssu-chung ed. (Taipei, 1962), 8a.

6. *Liao shih*, Vol. 32, Monograph on the Royal Garrison Camp; see entry on the winter *nai-po*, 3a.

7. *Chin shih*, Vol. 6, Annals of Shih-tsung, I, 20b.

8. Juvaini, 'Ala-ad-Din 'Ata-Malik, *The History of the World Conqueror*, trans. J. A. Boyle (Manchester, 1958), 1:27.

9. Christopher Dawson, ed., *The Mongol Mission: Narratives and Letters of the Franciscan Missionaries in Mongolia and China in the Thirteenth and Fourteenth Centuries*, trans. by a Nun of Stanbrook Abbey (London and New York: Sheed and Ward, 1955), p. 35.

10. Translated by C. R. Bawden and S. Jagchid from the original Mongolian verse, see Lobsangdarjin, *Altan tobci (nova)*, 1:24-25.

11. *Secret History*, Sec. 123.

12. *Ch'ing shih*, (Taipei, 1966), Vol. 90, Monograph on Rituals, IX, entry on autumn imperial hunt, 1118-19. There is a very detailed record of the Manchu emperors' hunting activities in *Chin-ting Je-ho chih* (1781; reprint ed., Taipei, 1966), Vols. 45-49. See also CTPCTK, pp. 306-10.

13. *Altan tobci (nova)*, 2:57.

14. *Liao shih*, Vol. 32, Monograph on the Imperial Guards (*Ying-wei chih*), 1a-3b. See also *Chin shih*, Vols. 6-8, Annals of Shih-tsung. There are many records on hunting and the eagle aviary of the Yüan emperors and the Mongolian nobles in *Yüan shih*, Vol. 84, Monograph on Officials (*Pai-kuan chih*) I, entry on Ping-pu, 27b-38b; Vol. 88, entry on *Chung-cheng yüan*, 19b, 21ab, and 22b; Vol. 89, entry on *Chao-kung wang-hu tu-tsung-shih ssu*, 26b; Vol. 101, Monograph on Military Affairs, IV, entry on aviary and hunting, 17a-20a.

15. The primary reference used in this study for Marco Polo's account is Henry Yule, *Cathay and the Way Thither: Being a Collection of Medieval Notices of China*, 3rd ed., rev. H. Cordier (London, 1921), 1:400-406.

16. Yeh-lü Ch'u-ts'ai, *Chan-jan-chü-shih chi*, Ssu-pu-t'ang kan ed. (Taipei: Shang-wu Press, n.d.), 10:100. The version of the poem used here is paraphrased.

17. Ibid., 10:102-3.

18. Juvaini, 1:28.

19. P'eng Ta-ya, 8b.

20. *Ch'ing shih*, Vol. 90, Monograph on Rituals, IX, entry on autumn imperial hunt, 1118-19.

21. Hsiao Ta-heng, *Pei-lu feng-su* (reprint ed., Peking, 1930s), pp. 12-13.

22. P'eng Ta-ya, 17b.

23. *Sui shu*, Vol. 84, Account of the T'u-chüeh, 1ab.

24. The best reference in this area is J. Damdin, *Bural angchinnii temdeglel* [Record of a Gray-Haired Hunter] (Ulan Bator, 1963).

25. *Yuan shih,* Vol. 1, Annals of Tai-tsu, 4b; *Secret History,* Sec. 239. Several presentations of white gyrfalcons to Chinggis Khan by Central Asian tribal leaders are mentioned in the *Ch'in-cheng lu,* Meng-ku shih-liao ssu-chung ed., 72ab.

26. *Yüan shih,* Vol. 99, Monograph on Military Affairs, II, 2b, and Vol. 95, Monograph on Economics, III, 30b. See also Yule, 1:90, 158, 269, 402; 2:282, 397, 411, 431.

Food

1. See Namio Egami, "Kyodo no inshokubutsu ni tsuite" [On the diet of the Hsiung-nu], *Toyogakuho* 20, nos. 4, 5 (1932).

2. *Shih chi,* Vol. 110, Account of the Hsiung-nu, 2a, 12b, 13a, 16a.

3. Chao Hung, 9b.

4. P'eng Ta'ya, 6a-7b.

5. *Secret History,* Sec. 12.

6. Ibid., Secs. 19, 27.

7. Ibid., Sec. 28.

8. Ibid., Sec. 74.

9. Ibid., Sec. 75.

10. Ibid., Sec. 87.

11. Ibid., Sec. 89.

12. Ibid., Sec. 130.

13. Ibid.

14. Ibid., Sec. 200.

15. Ibid., Secs. 229, 280.

16. See observations of Carpini and Rubruck in Dawson, pp. 62, 108-9.

17. Ibid., pp. 98-99

18. Ssu-ma Hsiang-ju, a famous poet of the former Han dynasty. For his biography, see *Han shu,* Vol. 57.

19. Chia I, a famous reformer, official, and poet of the former Han dynasty. For his biography, see *Han shu,* Vol. 48.

20. Yeh-lü Ch'u-ts'ai, *Chan-jan Chu-shih Wen-chi,* Ssu-pu ts'ung-k'ang ed. (originally published in Shanghai; reprint ed., Taipei, n.d.), 4:38.

21. *Altan tobči (nova),* 2:3.

22. Sagang Sechen, p. 246; see also *Meng-ku yüan-liu,* 7:2a.

23. Hsiao Ta-heng, pp. 13-14.

24. *Yüan shih,* Vol. 118, Biography of A-la-wu-ssu ti-chi hu-li, 10b.

25. C. d'Ohsson, *Histoire des Mongols* (The Hague and Amsterdam: Les Frères van Cleef, 1834-35), Vol. 1, Chap. 10, pp. 411-12.

26. *Yüan shih,* Vol. 2, Annals of Tai-tsung, 7b-8a.

27. Ibid., Vol. 146, Biography of Yeh-lü ch'u-ts'ai, 9a.

28. *Altan tobči (nova),* 2:162.

29. *Ming shih,* Vol. 330, Account of the Western Regions, II, sec. on garrisons of the western barbarians (*Hsi-fan chu-wei*), 9b-10a.

30. See Tsevel, "Mongoliin tsagaan idee" [The Mongolian milk food], *Studia Ethnografhica* Tomus 1, Fasc. 6 (Ulan Bator, 1959).

31. *Yüan shih,* Vol. 74, Monograph on Worship and Offerings (*Chi-ssu chih*), III, 16a-17a.

Dress

1. *Shih chi,* Vol. 110, Account of the Hsiung-nu, 12b-13a.

2. Umehara Suiji, *Moko Noin-ura hakken no ibutsu* (Tokyo, 1966). This work is a study of the site of Noyan-ula.

3. *Secret History,* Sec. 252.

4. Ibid., Sec. 238.

5. *Shih chi,* Vol. 110, Account of the Hsiung-nu, 2a.

6. *Secret History,* Sec. 55.

7. Ibid., Sec. 56.

8. Ibid.

9. Ibid., Sec. 74.

10. Ibid., Sec. 96.

11. Ibid., Sec. 97.

12. Ibid., Sec. 99.

13. Ibid., Sec. 92.

14. Ibid., Sec. 103.

15. Ibid., Sec. 112.

16. Ibid., Sec. 114.

17. Ibid., Sec. 135.

18. Ibid., Sec. 146.

19. P'eng Ta-ya, 7b-8a.

20. See *Kuan-t'ang chi-lin* [A collection of Wang Kuo-wei's work], Vol. 22, *Hai-ning Wang-shih tsen-ting tsai-pan,* rev. ed. by Wang family of Naining, (reprint ed., Taipei, n.d.).

21. *Yüan shih,* Vol. 78, I, 2a-14b.

22. Dawson, pp. 7-8, 61.

23. *Yüan shih,* Vol. 78, Monograph on Chariots and Costumes (*Yü-fu chih*), I, 2a-14b.

24. Ibid., 7b.

25. Dawson, p. 154; also pp. 101-3.

26. *Jirüken-ü tolta-yin tayilburi* (reprint ed. with Russian translation, Ulan-Ude, 1962), p. 39.

27. Hsiao Ta-heng, pp. 14-15.

28. *Yüan shih,* Vol. 77, Monograph on Worship (*Chi-ssu chih*), VI, see entry regarding Mongolian traditional rituals, 17b. In 1930, when the famous prince of Kharachin, Güngsangnorbu, died in Peking, a sable pelt was hung on the front of his coffin at his funeral.

29. Yano Jinichi, *Kindai Mokoshi kenkyu* (Kyoto, 1923); see chapters on the Uriyanghkai problem.

30. *Secret History,* Sec. 96.

31. Ibid., Sec. 102.

32. The story, which was still remembered by many old Mongolian scholars during the 1940s, is also recorded by Chang Mu in his *Meng-ku yü-mu chi,* Kuo-hsüeh chi-pen ts'ung-shu ed. (Taipei, 1968), 7:139-40.

Transportation

1. See C. R. Bawden and S. Jagchid, "Some Notes on the Horse Policy of the Yüan Dynasty," *CAJ* 10, nos. 3, 4 (1956).

2. *Secret History,* Sec. 281.

3. *Yüan shih,* Vol. 101, Monograph on Military Affairs (*Ping chih*), IV, entry on *jamchi,* 1a-12a. See also, Haneda Toru, "Moko ekitenko," *Toyo kyokai chosabu gakujutsu hokoku,* 1 (Tokyo, 1909).

4. S. Jagchid, "Shuo *Yüan-shih chung ti ch'üeh-lieh-ssu*" [On the *kirü'es* of the Yüan dynasty], *Ta-lu tsa-chih* (Taipei) 26, no. 4 (1963).

5. *Secret History,* Sec. 131.

6. *Yüan shih,* Vol. 164, Monograph on Law and Punishment (*Hsing-fa chih*), II, 12ab.

7. *Secret History,* Sec. 245.

8. Ibid, Secs. 6, 56.

9. Ibid., Sec. 64.

10. Ibid., Sec. 85.

11. Ibid., Sec. 101.

12. Ibid., Sec. 121.

13. Ibid., Sec. 124.

14. See Liu Ping-chung's biography in *Yüan shih,* Vol. 157.

15. See Liu Ping-chung's *"Ts'ang-ch'un-chi,"* unpublished manuscript in the Central Library, Taipei, Taiwan.

Dwellings and Concept of Space

1. *Secret History,* Sec. 24.

2. Ibid., Sec. 44.

3. Ibid., Sec. 90.

4. Ibid., Sec. 80.

5. Ibid., Sec. 121.

6. Ibid., Secs. 229, 232, 234.

7. Ibid., Sec. 184.

8. Yang Yün-fu, *Luan-ching tsa-yung* [Poems on the capital of Luan River], rare publication in collection of Central Library, Taipei, Taiwan.

9. The Kharachin Right Banner of the Josotu League is the home banner of S. Jagchid.

10. The original Chinese term for *baishing* is *pan-sheng;* see *Ming shih,* Vol. 327, Account of the Ta-tan, 21b.

11. Dawson, p. 8.

12. Manuel Komroff, ed., *Contemporaries of Marco Polo* (New York, 1928), pp. 239-40.

13. P'eng Ta-ya, 5ab.

14. *Shih chi,* Vol. 110, Account of the Hsiung-nu mentions: "In the morning the Shan-yü [Khan] goes outside [his camp] to bow to the rising sun" (11a). *Chou shü,* Vol. 50, Account of the T'u-chüeh states: "The door of the yurts opens toward the east in order to honor the rise of the sun" (5b).

15. *Secret History,* Sec. 112, mentions that Bülgütei, a brother of Chinggis Khan, in searching for his mother, rushed in from the right side of the door while his mother rushed out from the left side and therefore he missed finding her.

16. Dawson, p. 127.

17. The hearth is also a symbol of the continuity of a household and therefore is honored.

18. Yanai Wataru, "Gencho orudo ko," *Toyo gakuho* 10, nos. 1, 2, 3 (1920).

19. *Secret History,* Sec. 229.

20. Ibid., Secs. 90, 129.

21. Rubruck mentioned the Mongolian great pavilion for the celebration of the new khan, Cuyue (Güyüg): "By the time we got there, a large pavilion had already been put up made of white velvet, and in my opinion it was so big that more than two thousand men could have got into it. Around it had been erected a wooden palisade, on which various designs were painted"; see Dawson, p. 61.

22. See H. Perlee, *Hyatan nar, tednii Mongolchuudtai holbogdson ni* [The Kitan and their relationship with the Mongols] (Ulan Bator, 1959), pp. 84-93, for a discussion of the cities that were built by the Kitans in northern Mongolia.

CHAPTER 3. LIFESTYLE OF THE NOMADS

Birth and Childhood

1. The zodiac animals, "twelve earthly branches," are the rat, cattle, tiger, rabbit, dragon, snake, horse, sheep, monkey, cock, dog, and pig. In Mongolia, the usual answer to "How old are you?" is: "I was born in the year of such and

such an animal," for example, *moritai* ("horse") or *nokhaitai* ("dog"). The zodiac year-cycle is so well known, even among the common people, that with such a reference or reply the age of the person in question is readily understood.

2. *Secret History,* Secs. 20, 21.

3. William of Rubruck mentioned: "They [Mongol women] never lie down on a bed to give birth to their children"; Dawson, p. 109; P'eng Ta-ya, p. 17b.

4. *Secret History,* Sec. 59.

5. Ibid., Sec. 60.

6. P'eng Ta-ya, 17b.

7. People commonly inquire regarding a Mongol's surname, but actually, as in many parts of the world, there has not been a traditional surname system. Traditionally, persons often identified themselves by their personal name plus a clan designation. Thus, a clan name served roughly as a surname. However, by the early modern period, as this social unit was weakened, the Mongols had forgotten clan identity. With the growth of a national consciousness plus an awareness of how some modern peoples identify themselves, some Mongols began to readopt clan names; thus Sechin Jagchid revived the old clan name Jagchid as a surname. In the Mongolian People's Republic, it is common for persons to place the name or initial of their father preceding their own name as a sort of prefixed or abbreviated patronymic. As certain groups of Mongols began to assimilate Chinese culture in the modern period, many persons in Inner Mongolia acquired Chinese-style surnames and also given names. Thus, persons of the Borjigid lineage became identified by the family name Pao; Uriyangkhai adopted Wu; Chimid became Chen; Khanud became Han; Öelüd became Liu, and so on.

8. *Altan tobči (nova),* 2:2.

9. P'eng Ta-ya, 17b.

10. *Shih chi,* Vol. 110, Account of the Hsiung-nu, 1b.

11. For a discussion of childhood life in eastern Inner Mongolia, see Pao Kuo-yi, "Childbirth and Child Training in a Khorchin Mongol Village," *Monumenta Serica* 25 (1966):406-39.

12. *Secret History,* Sec. 116.

13. Ibid., Secs. 62, 66.

Adulthood and Marriage

1. *Yüan shih,* Vol. 98, Account on Military Affairs, I, 2a. After 1270 (the seventh year of Chih-yüan), the recruiting age for the Chinese population was changed from fifteen to twenty.

2. *CTPCTK,* p. 26.

3. Ibid., p. 21.

4. *Secret History,* Secs. 54-56.

5. Ibid., Sec. 66.

6. Ibid., Sec. 168.

7. *Khadagh* is a white or light blue silk scarf about three to six feet long with Buddhist designs on it. The presentation of a *khadagh* is a symbol of wishing the receiver blessings and further flourishing.

8. Legendary sacred bird of Lamaist Buddhism.

9. For a liturgy of the marriage ceremony, see Henry Serruys, "Four Manuals for Marriage Ceremonies Among the Mongols," *Zentralasiatische Studien* (Wiesbaden) no. 8 (1974) and no. 9 (1975).

10. God of wealth of Lamaist Buddhism.

11. Ayushi is the god of long life.

12. All the poetic pronouncements, blessings, and dialogue mentioned here are translated from Ch. Damdinsürüng, ed., *Mongghol uran jokiyal-un degeiji jaghun bilig orusibai* [A hundred selections from Mongolian literature] (Ulan Bator, 1959), pp. 100-117.

13. *Khuda* is a special term indicating that two families are related by marriage. At the time of the *Secret History* in the early empire, the word *khuda* seems to refer to relationships established through intermarriage of two particular clans.

14. *Secret History,* Secs. 61-64, 66.

15. *Üjen,* an adopted word, is a corruption of the Chinese *fu-jen* meaning "lady."

16. *Secret History,* Secs. 94, 96.

17. *Hou Han shu,* Vol. 90, Account of the Wu-huan, 1b.

18. The gifts to the parents of the bride (the bride price) was limited by the law of the Manchu Ch'ing court: "The gifts for the marriage engagement between two households will be two horses, two head of cattle, and not more than twenty sheep. In any case where these limits are exceeded, the animals will be confiscated"; see *CTPCTK,* p. 27. Similar strict limitations were set by the Oirad law code of 1640. On marriage regulations of the Oirad, see V. A. Riasanovsky, *Fundamental Principles of Mongol Law* (Tientsin, 1937; reprint ed., Bloomington: Indiana University, 1965), p. 100; see also, Tayama Shigeru, *Moko hotten no kenkyu* (*A Study of Mongolian Law Codes*), (Tokyo, 1967), pp. 144-45. Inner Mongolian custom traditionally sets the gift limit at one big animal or one *boda,* which equals five small animals, i.e., sheep or goats. Therefore, the number of animals is lower than that set by Ch'ing laws.

19. According to the personal observation of S. Jagchid of the marriage relationships among the nobles of the ten banners of Shilin-ghol League, the thirteen banners of Juu-uda League, and the six banners of Ulanchab League.

20. *Secret History,* Secs. 165, 168.

21. Ibid., Sec. 186.

22. A higher level of diction is used for the nobility: *sula tatakhu* replaces *ekener abakhu* and the wife is referred to as *sula khatun* ("secondary lady").

23. *Secret History,* Secs. 118, 245.

24. Ibid., Sec. 254.

25. In the thirteenth century, Carpini observed: "They also have a law or custom of putting to death a man or woman they find openly committing adultery; similarly, if a virgin commits fornication with anyone, they kill both the man and the woman"; see Dawson, p. 17. By the end of the sixteenth century, according to Hsiao Ta-heng, there was a death penalty for committing adultery with the wife of a noble, and a heavy punishment for adultery among the ordinary people; see his *Pei-lu feng-su,* pp. 4-5. However, the *Khalkha-jirüm,* law code of Khalkha Mongols (the amendment of 1709), states that the penalty for adultery is a fine of an animal rather than the death penalty; see also Tayama, pp. 246-47.

Old Age, Illness, Death, and Burial

1. *Shih chi,* Vol. 110, Account of the Hsiung-nu, 2a, states: "The strong ones eat the best food and the elderly ones eat the remainder. They honor young and strong persons, but despise old and weak ones." Later, this became a traditional stereotyped description of all North Asian nomadic peoples to be found in all historical records, including those regarding the Mongols.

2. See *Altan tobči (nova),* 2:56-57.

3. *Secret History,* Sec. 272.

4. *Yüan shih,* Vol. 125, Biography of Tege, 13b-14a.

5. Ibid., Vol 88, Monograph on Officials, IV, 5a, entry on the imperial hospital (*T'ai-i-yüan*) in the section regarding the *Tai-tu Shang-tu hui-hui yao-wu yüan.*

6. Ibid., 5b, topical entries on *Tai-tu hui-min chü* and *Shang-tu hui-min ssu* of the *Tai-i yüan* office.

7. Sagang Sechen, pp. 261-66; see also *Meng-ku yüan-liu,* 7:8a-9b.

8. See Francis W. Cleaves, "A Medical Practice of the Mongols in the Thirteenth Century," *HJAS* 17 (December 1954):428-44.

9. In Inner Mongolia, which is under Chinese Communist rule and where Lamaist Buddhist medicine is still in vogue, traditional prescriptions are studied together with modern, scientific medical technology.

10. Khujirtu (or Hujirt), the well-known recreation area of the Mongolian People's Republic, is a hot, mineral-spring area. In Inner Mongolia, Khaluun-arshiyan ("hot springs") of the Hulun-buir region is the most famous mineral-spring area. It is also known as the "land of Otochi," the god of healing and medicine. Also famous is the seashore at the mouth of the Ta-ling River, in the

Po-hai Gulf in eastern Inner Mongolia, where people can go to be healed, to be cleansed of sin, and to meditate and gain spiritual comfort.

11. After a great epidemic of the plague at the beginning of this century, the city of Bayantala (T'ung-liao), in eastern Inner Mongolia (Manchuria), remained a center of the contagious disease which continued to be a problem almost to the end of the 1930s. Finally, it was brought under control through the efforts of medical and public-health workers during the so-called Manchukuo period.

12. *Secret History,* Secs. 145, 173.

13. *Yüan shih,* Vol. 149, Biography of Kuo Pao-yü, 12a.

14. C. R. Bawden, "The Supernatural Element in Sickness and Death according to Mongol Tradition," *Asia Major,* n.s. 8, no. 2 (1961):215-57 and 9, no. 2 (1962):153-78.

15. Sagang Sechen, pp. 268-69; also *Meng-ku yüan-liu,* 7:10b.

16. There were four methods of burial or *ongghon* of Mongolian nobles. (1) The body of the deceased person is put on a small hill or in a mountain valley: an example is the *ongghon* of the prince of the Abagha Left Flank Banner of the Shilin-ghol League. (2) Another custom is to bury the body and build a small platformlike tomb structure of stone as seen in some burials or tombs of the princes of Üjümüchin Right Wing Banner in the Shilin-ghol League. (3) The body may be buried in large tombs as in the case of the princes of Kharachin Right Wing Banner. (4) The bodies of high lamas are customarily cremated and the bone fragments (*sharil*) are picked up and placed into bronze or mud stupas located within or in the vicinity of a temple.

17. See Carpini's observations in Dawson, p. 14.

18. John R. Krueger, "*The Altan Saba* (golden vessel): A Mongolian Lamaist Burial Manual," *Monumenta Serica* 24 (1965).

19. Hsiao Ta-heng, pp. 7-8.

20. Sagang Sechen, pp. 268-69; *Meng-ku yüan-liu,* 7:10b.

21. Dawson, pp. 12-13.

22. P'eng Ta-ya, 29b-30a.

23. Yeh Tzu-chi, *Ts'o-mu-tzu,* Yeh Fu-te, ed. (Fuchou, 1516), Vol. 3, rare book preserved at the Central Library, Taipei, Taiwan.

24. *Yüan shih,* Vol. 77, Monograph on Worship and Offerings (*Chi-ssu chih*), VI; see entry on old rituals and national customs (*kuo-su chiu-li*), 17b-18a.

25. *Shih chi,* Vol. 110, Account of the Hsiung-nu, 11a.

26. *Sui shu,* Vol. 84, Account of the T'u-chüeh, 2a.

27. *Secret History,* Sec. 189.

28. P. K. Kozlov, *Comtes rendus expeditions pour l'exploration du.Nord de la Mongolie* (Leningrad, 1927).

29. *Altan tobči (nova),* 2:104-5.

30. Juvaini, 1:189.

31. Sagang Sechen, p. 252; see also *Meng-ku yüan-liu*, 7:4a.

32. *Yüan shih*, Vol. 77, Monograph on Worship and Offerings (*Chi-ssu chih*) VI; see entry on old rituals and national customs (*kuo-su chiu-li*), 17b-18a.

33. According to the annals of the emperors recorded in the *Yüan shih*, almost all deceased khans were buried at Ch'i-nien-ku in Mongolia. For instances, see *Yüan shih*, Vol. 17, Annals of Shih-tsu (Khubilai Khan), XIV, 24a, and Vol. 37, Annals of Ning-tsung (Rinchenbal Khan), 5b.

34. Tamura Jitsuzo, *Ch'ing ling* (Kyoto, 1953), Vols. 1, 2.

35. According to the *Yüan shih*, the "eight rooms" (Chs. *pa-shih*), system of the ancestral temple (*tsung-miao*) was established by Khubilai Khan (Shih-tsu) in 1266 (the third year of Chih-yüan); see *Yüan shih*, Vol. 6, Annals of Shih-tsu, III, 8b; also Vol. 74, Monograph on Worship and Offerings, III, entry on *tsung-miao*, 2b.

36. According to Sagang Sechen the "eight white yurts" were established when Chinggis Khan was buried in a valley somewhere between the Altai-khan and the Kentei-khan mountain ranges; see Sagang Sechen, p. 132; see also *Meng-ku yüan-liu*, 4:8b. Later, he indicated that the "eight white yurts" became a sacred place of worship, which a new khan must visit to pay his respects and which was located in the realm of the Three Right Flanks; see Sagang Sechen, pp. 213, 219; also *Meng-ku yüan-liu*, 6:8a, 12a. The same source indicates that the Ordos Mongols were the guards of the "eight white yurts"; see Sagang Sechen, p. 21, and *Meng-ku yüan-liu*, 6:6b.

37. This was an open debate (1915-17) between Chang Hsiang-wen, a historical geographer, who maintained the Ejen-khoroo site was the real tomb of Chinggis Khan, and Tu Chi, author of the well-known Mongolian history *Meng-wu-erh shih-chi*, who claimed the tomb of the khan was in northern Mongolia.

38. *Altan tobči (nova)*, 2:104-5.

39. Ibid.

40. Richinsengge, the son of Babudorji, was appointed governor of the Ulanchab League by Prince Demchügdüngrüb at the time of the Kalgan Mongolian Government. It was later reported that he was killed by Chinese Communists by 1950.

41. This ceremony is seen in the *Secret History*, Sec. 154, But no explanation is given. According to several Chinese records of the Yuan time, such as Yu Chi's *Tao-yüan hsüeh-ku lu* (Vol. 16) and T'ao Tsung-i's *Ch'o-ching lu*, Ssu-pu ts'ung-k'an ed. (1363; reprint ed., Taipei, 1963), it seems that after the Son of Heaven (the khan) drank from the cup, he passed it to his high generals and ministers. The late Professor Yao Ts'ung-wu collected most of the Chinese records concerned and refers to them in his new Chinese translation of the *Secret History*, Sec. 154; see *Wen-shih-che hsüeh-pao* (Taiwan University), no. 10 (1961):192.

42. Personal interview of Paul Hyer with Frank Bessac, December 1974.

Bessac notes that the ceremony at Kansu did not impress him as much as the simpler one at Ejen-khoroo "perhaps because I did not understand the former."

43. For an account of the execution of Jamukha, see the *Secret History*, Sec. 201.

Daily Life and Recreation

1. This routine was observed by Hsü T'ing as early as the thirteenth century; see P'eng Ta-ya (with Hsü T'ing's commentary), 18b.

2. There are also many large prayer wheels (*kürel-mani*), which pilgrims turn, in the courtyard of temples. The Lamaist Buddhist formula *om-ma-ni-pad-me-hun* ("hail to the Jewel of the lotus"—meaning the Buddha) is written inside these "bronze prayers."

3. Dawson, p. 139; the "On man baccan" seems to be a mistranslation of *Om-ma-ni-pad-me-hun*.

4. If a dog continually bays like a wolf, especially at night, many Mongols take it as a bad omen.

5. *Dailur* is a word borrowed from the Chinese *ta-lien* having the same meaning.

6. For Mongolian games, see N. Namjildorf, *Mongolian Togloom* (Ulan Bator, 196?). Also see, Skallsjo Steffan, "Hsia (a Mongol game)," *Ethnos* 17 (1952):15-23; and George Soderbom, "The Mongolian game Norbo," *Ethnos* 15 (1950):95-100.

7. On the *oboo* and *dalalgha*, see the section on Festivals and Seasonal Activities.

8. Most temples prohibit the use of tobacco, especially in the main hall where images of the Buddha are placed.

9. Mongolian polo was observed by early Chinese visitors to Mongolia; see Chao Hung, 13b.

10. *Secret History*, Sec. 216.

11. On this and related topics, see Denis Sinor, "On Mongol Strategy," *Proceedings of the Fourth East Asian Altaistic Conference* (Taipei, 1971), pp. 238-49.

12. *Yüan shih*, Vol. 52, Monograph on the Calendar, I, 2b-3a; also ibid., Vol. 90, Monograph on Officials, VI, the entries on *ssu-tien chien* and *hui-hui ssu-tien chien*, 22a-23a.

13. Ibid., Vol 146, Biography of Yeh-lü Ch'u-ts'ai, 2a.

14. Khaisan was a Kharachin Mongol official who fled to Outer Mongolia because of political persecution by the Manchu Ch'ing government. He was one of the Mongolian delegates who went to tsarist Russia for assistance for the Mongolian independence movement. Later he became the vice-minister of internal affairs of the new Urga government. He worked for the unification of both Inner and Outer Mongolia but failed, and, finally, because of political

disagreements, he returned to Kharachin, was received by the Peking government of the Republic of China, and was given the noble rank of *beise*. He was accomplished in both Mongolian and Chinese literature and published a Chinese-Mongolian dictionary, *Wu-fang yüan-yin* (Peking, 1917).

Festivals and Seasonal Activities

1. *Shih chi,* Vol. 110, Account of the Hsiung-nu, mentions: "In the morning the Shan-yü [khan] goes outside [his camp] to bow to the rising sun" (11a). *Chou shu,* Vol. 50, Account of the T'u-chüeh (Turks), states: "The door of their yurts opens toward the east in order to honor the rising of the sun" (5b).

2. *Hou Han shu,* Vol. 89, Account of the Southern Hsiung-nu, records: "According to the custom of the Hsiung-nu they have three religious festivals which take place . . . in the first month, the fifth month, and the ninth month to worship heaven" (7ab). *Chou shu,* Vol. 50 also notes: "In the middle of the fifth month, [they] gathered and worshipped the god of heaven" (6a). On the sprinkling of the *kumis,* see note 4 below.

3. *Khadagh* is a white or light blue silk scarf about three to six feet long with Buddhist designs on it. To present a *khadagh* is to wish the receiver blessings and further good fortune.

4. This practice is also known as *sachuli* in the *Secret History.* Originally a Shamanistic ritual, it was later adopted as a Lamaist Buddhist ceremony.

5. Yule, 1:390.

6. *Secret History,* Sec. 168.

7. Ibid., Secs. 170-75.

8. For the background and details of this incident, see d'Ohsson, 1:79 ff.

9. See Tsyben Zhamcarano, "Kul't Chingis v Ordose—iz puteshestviya v yuzhnuyu Mongoliya v 1910g" [The cult of Chinggis in the Ordos—from a journey to southern Mongolia in 1910], *Central Asian Journal* 6 (1961):194-234. See also Sechin Jagchid, "Cheng-chi-ssu-han ta-chi-jih ti li-shih i-i" [The historical significance of the great memorial day of Chinggis Khan], *Central Daily News* (Taipei), May 5, 1961.

10. The Mongols in Taiwan have celebrated this holiday every year since they escaped from Inner Mongolia and Chinese Communist rule in 1949.

11. *Secret History,* Sec. 81.

12. Ibid., Sec. 193.

13. *Han shu,* Vol. 94a, Account of the Hsiung-nu, I, 7b.

14. *Hou Han shu,* Vol. 89, Account of the Southern Hsiung-nu, 7ab.

15. *Chou shu,* Vol. 50, Account of the T'u-chüeh (Turks).

16. On the ceremony of the *oboo* cult, see Magdalene Tatar, "Zur Fragen des Obo-kultes bei den Mongolen," *Acta Orientalia* (Hungary), Tomus 24, Fasc. 3 (1971):301-30.

17. Yule, 1:386-92.

18. *Altan tobči (nova)*, 1:79.

19. *Yüan shih*, Vol. 77, Monograph on Worship and Offerings (*Chi-ssu chih*), VI, entry on the traditional rituals of the Mongols (*kuo-chao chiu-li*), 18a-19b.

20. Descriptions of the *dalalgha* ceremony and the fire cult in the Kharachin area are based upon the personal observations of S. Jagchid.

21. See *Secret History*, Sec. 199 for *ayalaghulurun*, and Sec. 275 for *ayalarun*: references where these terms are used to mean a campaign.

22. Harnod Hakanchulu, "Fire Worship in the Jarud West Banner of Inner Mongolia," *Proceedings of the Fourth East Asian Altaistic Conference* (Taipei, 1971), pp. 114-27.

Behavior Patterns, Etiquette, and Attitudes

1. This seems to be one of the injunctions of Chinggis Khan in his *jasagh* code. Reference to warm hospitality is frequently found in the travel literature on Mongolia.

2. An example is Carpini's difficulty at the court of Prince Batu; see Dawson, p. 56.

3. *Secret History*, Secs. 244-45, records that before Chinggis Khan made his decision to dispose of the ambitious shaman Teb-Tenggeri, he first kept silence and pondered for a time. On another occasion in a quarrel over succession to the throne, Chinggis kept his counsel in silence before making any decision; see ibid., Secs. 245-55.

4. *Yüan shih*, Vol. 102, Monograph on Laws, records: "If We are angry against one who is judged guilty and command you to execute him, do not kill him immediately but wait for one or two days and then report to Us again for the final decision" (I, 3a).

5. *Secret History*, Secs. 96, 117.

6. At the end of the Manchu-Ch'ing dynasty (1644-1911) and the beginning of the Chinese Republic (1912), many Mongol people fought against Chinese settlers who occupied their grazing lands and who were supported by the Chinese government. These Mongolian rebels were referred to by the Chinese as *Meng-fei*, "Mongol bandits."

7. The youngest son was usually known as *odchigin* and was privileged to look after the *gholomta*, the hearth or fire frame, a symbol of the continuity of the household.

8. According to Manchu-Ch'ing law, rank and title were mainly passed down to the eldest son of the first legitimate wife.

9. The mother of Chinggis Khan (Kö'elün) and the mother of Möngke Khan and Khubilai Khan (Sorkhaghtani) were all influential in national affairs. A special case was Naimanjin Khatun, the mother of Güyüg Khan, who served as regent before Güyüg was enthroned.

10. While Temüjin was commonly known by his title Chinggis Khan and while Ögödei was commonly known as either Ögödei Khan or Khaghan Khan, both Güyüg and Möngke were each known only by one name and title: Güyüg Khan and Möngke Khan. However, after Khubilai Khan, all khans were endowed with an honorary name, which was used for address or reference rather than their personal name. This, no doubt, is the influence of the Chinese system of *miao-hao* ("imperial title" or "ancestral temple name").

11. *Secret History*, Sec. 156.

12. Under Chinese Communist rule, the Dakhur area was organized into an autonomous district in the Inner Mongolian Autonomous Region established in 1947 because it was felt that the people were ethnically different from other Mongols. After the Cultural Revolution (1966-68), the Dakhur region was reorganized, separated from the Autonomous Region, and put under the administration of the Chinese Heilungkiang province, People's Republic of China.

13. The term *khara Kitad* as used here has no relationship to the historical Kara Kitai or Kitata state established in central Asia in the twelfth century.

14. *Yüan shih*, Vol. 46, Annals of Shun-ti (Toghon-temür), 8b.

Social Thought and Values

1. See *Secret History*, Secs. 1, 121; also P'eng Ta-ya, 12b-13a. The Mongolian concept "will of heaven" (*tenggeri-yin jiyagha*) is similar to the Chinese idea *t'ien-ming*, "mandate of heaven."

2. *Secret History*, Secs. 149, 185, 200.

3. See *Ch'ing shih*, (Taipei, 1966), Vol. 405, Biography of Senggerinchin.

4. The other was Tsereng; see *Ch'ing shih*, Vol. 297, Biography of Tsereng.

5. Ibid.

6. Ch. Damdinsürüng, *Achalalt nomín tuxai* [A study of the *Hsiao-ching*], (Ulan Bator, 1961).

7. Personal knowledge of S. Jagchid.

8. *Yüan shih*, Vol. 99, Monograph on Military Affairs, II, entry on the four Ch'üeh-hsüeh (*keshig*), 3a.

9. Note Carpini's observation: "Fights, brawls, wounding, murder are never met with among them. Nor are robbers and thieves who steal on a large scale found there. . ."; Dawson, pp. 14-15.

10. d'Ohsson, 1, Chap. 1; Carpini also noted: ". . . nor do they lightly lie to them [their masters]. They rarely or never contend with each other in word, and in action never"; Dawson, p. 14.

11. *Secret History*, Sec. 177.

12. *Yüan shih*, Vol. 124, Biography of Ta-ta-tung-a (Tatatunggha).

13. This is a common saying in Üjümüchin, Shilin-ghol League, Inner Mongolia.

Taboos and Customs

1. Chao Hung, 1a.
2. P'eng Ta-ya, pp. 525-28.
3. See Carpini's observations in Dawson, p. 11.
4. *Secret History,* Sec. 75. The well-known salt lake of Üjümüchin, Dabusun-nor, is also called *Eej-nor* (*eej* is the spoken form of *eke*)—"Mother Lake"—by the local people.
5. Hsiao Ta-heng, p. 16.
6. See the observations of William of Rubruck in Dawson, p. 103.
7. Personal observation of S. Jagchid.
8. This is a very common saying among the elderly people of eastern Inner Mongolia.
9. Chao Hung, 12b.
10. From a conversation with Mr. Jirghalang (Te-ku-lai), a leader of the Inner Mongolian Dakhur group, which has continued its belief in Shamanism.
11. This has been a particularly strong tradition of the people of the Shilin-ghol League.
12. *Chou shu,* Vol. 50, Account of the T'u-chüeh (Turks), 4b.
13. *Secret History,* Sec. 1.
14. Rashidungdok Shiliembu (C. T. Hsi), "On *Seter,*" *Proceedings of the Third East Asian Altaistic Conference* (Taipei, 1969), pp. 210-12.
15. Dawson, pp. 15, 17.
16. Hsiao Ta-heng, pp. 4-5.
17. Dawson, p. 127.
18. Kao Ch'ü-hsün, "The Chin-lu shen Shrines of Han Sword Worship in Hsiung-nu Religion," *CAJ* 5 (1959/60):221-32; see also Henry Serruys, "A Note on Arrows and Oaths Among the Mongols," *JAOS* 78 (Oct./Dec. 1958):279-94.
19. Dawson, p. 11.
20. Ibid.
21. Li Chih-ch'ang, *Ch'ang-ch'un chen-jen hsi-yu chi,* Meng-ku shih-liao ssu-chung ed. (Taipei, 1962), p. 22b.
22. Dawson, p. 56.
23. Hsiao Ta-heng, pp. 17-18.
24. Personal experience of S. Jagchid.
25. Hsiao Ta-heng, p. 18.
26. *Shih chi,* Vol. 110, Account of the Hsiung-nu, 11a.
27. P'eng Ta-ya, 9b.
28. Personal experience of S. Jagchid.
29. Ibid.
30. Ibid.

31. d'Ohsson, 1, Chap. 7, p. 323.

32. From a conversation with Dr. Sandja Stepanov, an elder of the Kalmuck Mongol community in Philadelphia.

CHAPTER 4. RELIGION

Shamanism

1. *Han shu,* Vol. 94a, Account of the Hsiung-nu, I, 7a.

2. *Hou Han shu,* Vol. 89, Account of the Southern Hsiung-nu, 7ab.

3. For examples, see *Secret History,* Sec. 181.

4. Ibid., Sec. 121.

5. Ibid., Sec. 143. Tao Tsung-i noted: "In times past I have seen Mongolian rain sorcerers . . . take only a basin of clean water and soak several stones in it. The larger ones were as big as chicken eggs. . . . [The man] then recited some secret formulas while washing the stones. In doing this the rain usually fell. The stones were called *cha-ta (jada).*"T'ao Tsung-i, *Ch'o-ching lu,* Ssu-pu ts'ung-k'an ed. (1363; reprint ed., Taipei, 1963), 4:13b.

6. See B. Rintchen, *Les Materiaux pour l'etude Du Chamanisme Mongol,* (Wiesbaden, 1959).

7. *Secret History,* Sec. 105.

8. From personal experience of S. Jachid in the Josotu and Shilin-ghol leagues of Inner Mongolia.

9. From personal experience of S. Jagchid in Chakhar, Inner Mongolia.

10. Information on this matter comes from Wangchindorji, a Chakhar scholar who assisted in translating the Mongolian New Testament in Hong Kong in the late 1940s.

11. "Manakhan Tenggeri-yi takikhu yosun" [The ritual of worshipping Manakhan Tenggeri—the king of game], in Damdinsürüng, *Mongghol uran jokiyal,* pp. 122-23.

12. See the section on worship *(chi-ssu)* of Chao Hung, 12a; see also the observation of William Rubruck in Dawson, p. 164.

13. From personal experience of S. Jagchid in the Shilin-ghol League.

14. Albert E. Dien, "A Possible Occurrence of Altaic *idughan,"CAJ*2, no. 1 (1956):12-20.

15. *Secret History,* Sec. 1.

16. Ibid., Sec. 121.

17. *Secret History,* Secs. 256, 275. The Chinese translation of the term is *ch'ang-sheng-tien.* See Güyüg Khan's letter to Pope Innocent I V (1246) in Dawson, p. 85.

18. *Secret History,* Sec. 103; see also *Shih chi,* Vol. 110, Account of the Hsiung-nu, 11a.

19. Personal experience of S. Jagchid in Mongolia.

20. *Secret History,* Sec. 81.

21. See "Dologhan ebügen kemekü odon-u sudur," in Damdinsürüng, *Mongghol uran jokiyal,* pp. 131-35.

22. Noted also by Carpini in Dawson, p. 10.

23. P'eng Ta-ya, 12b.

24. On the subject of *oboo,* see Magdalene Tatar, "Zur Fragen des Obo-kultes bei den Mongolen," *Acta Orientalia* (Hungary), Tomus 24, Fasc. 3 (1971); see also C. R. Bawden, "Two Mongol Texts concerning *Obo-*worship," *Oriens Extremus* 5 (1958):23-41.

25. *Secret History,* Sec. 75.

26. Personal observation of S. Jagchid in the Üjümüchin Banner.

27. Dawson, p. 56.

28. *Secret History,* Sec. 70.

29. "Chinggis Khaghan-u yeke üchig" [The great prayer of Chinggis Khan], in Damdinsürüng, *Mongghol uran jokiyal,* pp. 73-87.

30. *Secret History,* Sec. 201.

31. Ibid., Sec. 272.

32. Ibid., Sec. 63.

33. Ibid., Sec. 202; *Yüan shih,* Vol. 1, Annals of T'ai-tsu, 14b.

34. *Secret History,* Sec. 193; see also Rubruck's observation in Dawson, p.184: "When [Mongols] were about to drink, they sprinkled their felt idols [*ongghon*] with cosmos [*kumis*]."

35. *Secret History,* Sec. 44.

36. This "ancestral pole" is called *tsu-tsung kan-tzu* in Chinese. Imperial marriages of the emperors or the crown princes took place in the K'un-ning kung Palace.

37. *Secret History,* Sec. 161.

38. Ibid., Sec. 272.

39. Ibid., Sec. 120.

40. Ibid., Sec. 207.

41. Ibid., Sec. 216.

42. Francis W. Cleaves, "Teb-Tenggeri," *Ural-altaische Jahrbücher* no. 39 (1967):248-60.

43. *Secret History,* Secs. 244, 245.

44. Ibid., Sec. 272.

45. *Yüan shih,* Vol. 3. Annals of Hsien-tsung, 4a.

46. *Han shu,* Vol. 194a, Account of the Hsiung-nu, I, 20ab.

47. Li Chih-ch'ang, *Ch'ang-ch'un chen-jen hsi-yu chi,* Meng-ku shih-liao ssu-chung ed. (Taipei, 1962), pp. 6b,8b, and 9a.

48. Yao Ts'ung-wu, "Chin-Yüan Ch'üan-chen-chiao ti min-tsu-ssu-hsiang yu chü-shih-ssu-hsiang" ("World Salvation and Nationalistic Aspects in the Thought of the Ch'üan-chen-chiao of the Chin and Yüan Period"), in *Tung-pei-shih lun-ts'ung* [Essays on the Northeast-Manchurian History], (Taipei, 1959), 2:175-204.

49. Radnabadara, "Zaya Bandita-yin namtar" [The biography of Zaya Bandita], in Damdinsürüng, *Mongghol uran jokiyal*, p. 325.

50. Personal experience of S. Jagchid.

51. Paul Hyer, unpublished manuscript on the Chinggis Khan Temple at Wang-yin süme.

Lamaist Buddhism

1. *Chiu T'ang shu,* Vol. 194A, Account of Tu-fan (Tibet), I, 2a-4b.

2. *Hu-lan deb-ther,* Japanese trans. by Inaba Shoju and Sato Hisashi (Kyoto, 1964), pp. 92-94.

3. Ibid., p. 94.

4. Ibid.

5. See the *Chiu T'ang shu,* Vol. 194, Account of the T'u-chüeh, I, 14b, for mention of Bilgä Khan's plan to construct a city and Buddhist temples.

6. *Yüan shih,* Vol. 146, Biography of Yeh-lü Ch'u-ts'ai; see also entry for "Seng-ko-lin-ch'in," in A. W. Hummel, *Eminent Chinese of the Ch'ing Period* (Washington, D.C., 1944), p. 632-34.

7. S. Jagchid, "Why the Mongolian Khans Adopted Tibetan Buddhism as Their Faith," *Proceedings of the Third East Asian Altaistic Conference* (Taipei, 1969), pp. 108-28.

8. *Secret History,* Sec. 167.

9. Ch'eng Chü-fu, "Hai-yün Chien-ho-shang t'a pei," [Inscription on the Pagoda for the Abbot Hai-yün Chien], in *Hsueh-lou-chi,* Vol. 6, rare book in the Central Library, Taipei, Taiwan.

10. *Yüan shih,* Vol. 3, Annals of Hsien-tsung, 3a.

11. Ibid., Vol. 125, Biography of T'ieh-ko [Tege], 13b-14a.

12. Ibid., Vol. 202, Biography of Pa-ssu-pa [Phags-pa]; see also S. Jagchid, "Ta-Yüan-ti-shih Pa-ssu-pa la-ma shih tsen-yang-ti i-ko-jen" [What kind of person was Phags-pa Lama, the Imperial Teacher of the Great Yüan?], *Chung-hua wen-i fu-hsing yüeh-k'an (Chinese Cultural Renaissance Monthly)* 4, no. 4 (April 1971):12-19.

13. S. Jagchid, "Hu-pi-lieh ko-han yu Pa-ssu-pa la-ma" [Khubilai Khan and Phags-pa Lama], *Shih-hsüeh hui-k'an* no. 2 (Taipei, 1969):165-72.

14. S. Jagchid, "Shuo Yüan-tai-ti Hsüan-cheng yüan" [On the Hsuan-cheng-yüan of the Yüan dynasty], *Shih-hsüeh chi-k'an,* no. 3, ed. by the Chinese Historical Association (Taipei, 1971):39-62.

15. Tao Tsung-i, *Cho-ching lu,* 4:63-69.

16. S. Jagchid, "Buddhism in Mongolia after the Collapse of the Yüan Dynasty," in *Traditions religieuses et paza-religieuses des peuples altaiques,* ed. Irene Melikoff (Paris, 1972), pp. 49-58.

17. Sagang Sechen, pp. 241-61; see also *Meng-ku yüan-liu,* 6:30a; 7:7b; *Altan tobči (nova),* 2:181-84.

18. *Altan tobči,* 1:1-6; *Meng-ku yüan-liu,* 1:3.

19. Sagang Sechen, pp. 247-48; *Meng-ku yüan-liu,* 7:2ab; *Altan tobči,* 2:183.

20. The Chinese name of this temple is Wu-liang ssu; see "Shen-chiao-chih" [The records of religion], 3b-4a, in *Kuei-sui hsien-chih* [The gazeteer of Kuei-sui], (Peking, 1934).

21. *The Jebtsundamba Khutukhtus of Urga,* English trans. and notes by Charles R. Bawden (Wiesbaden, 1961).

22. Hjigs-med nam-mkhah, *Chen-po hor-gyi-yul-du dam-paihi-chos-ji-ltar-byun-bahi-tshul-bsad-pa rgyal-bahi-bstan-pa-rin-po-che gsal-bar-byed-pahi-rgron-me;* Japanese trans. by Hashimoto Koho, *Mokō ramakyōshi* [A history of Mongolian Lamaism], (Tokyo, 1940), pp. 279-310. There is also a German translation by J. Huth, but the authors were unable to consult this work.

23. See Radnabadara, pp. 320-34.

24. S. Jagchid, "The Manchu-Ch'ing Policy Towards Mongolian Lamaism," paper presented at the 184th Meeting of the American Oriental Society, Santa Barbara, Calif., 1974.

25. Hashimoto Koho, *Mokō no ramakyō (Lamaism of Mongolia),* (Tokyo, 1942), pp. 233-44.

Christianity and Islam

1. See the comments of Rubruck in Dawson, pp. 137-39.

2. See Robert Silverberg, *The Realm of Prester John* (Garden City, N.J.: Doubleday, 1972).

3. *Secret History,* Sec. 189.

4. Juvaini, 2:549-53, section on "Ulugh-Noyan and Sorqotani Beki." There is also a short biography on Sorkhaghtani in the *Yüan shih,* Vol. 116.

5. *Yüan shih,* Vol. 38, Annals of Shun-ti, I, 14a: "On the *ping-shen* day of the third month, the first year of Chih-Yüan (1335), the minister of the *Chung-shu sheng* reported: 'Now the mother of Emperor Shih-tsu [Khubilai], Pieh-chi [Beki] T'ai-hou, is worshiped in the Shih-tsu ssu of Kanchou lu, Kansu Province. The rituals to be followed have yet to be decided.' This memorial was accepted [by the Emperor]."

6. Dawson, pp. 3-72.

7. Ibid., p. 180. The Catholic Church in Taiwan, China, recognizes Yüan Hsien-tsung (Möngke Khan) as a church member.

8. Yule, Vol. 1, Chaps. 7, 12.

9. Henry Serruys, "Early Mongol and Catholic Church," *Neue Zeitschrift für Missionswissenschaft* 19 (1963):161-69.

10. d'Ohsson, 3:234.

11. Ibid., 5:260.

12. Chen Yüan, *Yüan Hsi-yu-jen hua-hua k'ao* [A study of the Sinicization of

Central Asians in the Yüan period],(reprint ed., Taipei, 1953), 22b-24a.

13. See Rubruck's observations in Dawson, pp. 117-19.

14. See E. A. W. Budge, *The Monks of Kublai Khan, Emperor of China* (London, 1928).

15. S. Jagchid visited this area several times in the late 1930s and the first half of the 1940s and saw the sculptured palace cornerstone. For an archaeological study of this city, see Namio Egami, "Olon-sume et la de'couverte de l'eglise catholique romaine de Jean de Montecorvino," *Journal Asiatique* (Paris) 240 (1952):155-67.

16. *Yüan shih,* Vol. 38, Annals of Shun-ti, I, 14a.

17. Okada Hidehira, "Virgin Mary in Fifteenth Century Mongolia," *BICBAS* no. 1 (1970).

18. Vernadsky, pp. 377 ff.

19. Ibid., p. 384.

20. On the development of Catholic work in this China-Mongol border area, see J. Van Hecken, *Les Missions chez les Mongols aux temps modernes* (Peking: Imprimerie des Lazaristes, 1949).

21. Tai Hsüeh-chi, "1900 nien Nei-meng-ku hsi-pu ti-ch'ü ko-tsu jen-min ti fan-ti tou-cheng" [The anti-imperialistic struggle of the people of the different nationalities of Inner-Mongolia], in *Yi-ho-tuan yün-tung liu-shih chou-nien chi-nien lun-wen-chi* [Collection of theses for the 60th anniversary of the Boxer movement], ed. by the Institute of History, Shantung Branch of the Chinese Academy of Sciences (Peking, 1961), pp. 211-36.

22. Hsing Chih-hsiang, *K'a-la-chin yu-ch'i cha-sa-k'e chin-wang Kung-sang-no-erh-pu chi lueh-shih* [A brief history of prince Gungsangnorbu, jasagh of the Kharachin Right Flank Banner], (Kharachin, Inner Mongolia, 1938).

23. Teng-ko was originally known as San-sheng-kung, actually the name of a Chinese shop. After the Catholic Church received a tract of land from the Alashan Banner, it attracted Chinese to settle and cultivate the land, eventually forcing the Mongolian herdsmen to retreat; in the late 1920s, the Ninghsia provincial government organized a prefecture (*hsien*), which posed a Chinese political threat to the integrity of the Mongolian banner administration.

24. See Van Hecken; see also Carlo Van Melckebeke, *Service social de L'Eglise en Mongolia* (Scheut, 1968).

25. John C. Brown, *First Fruits of a Mission to Siberia* (Capetown: Solomon Co., 1847); W. P. Nairne, *Gilmour of the Mongols* (London: Hodder and Stroughton, n.d.); Gerda Ollen and Joel Ericksson, *Vid Gobiöknens Gränser* (Stockholm: Svenska Mongol Missionens Forlag, 1943).

26. An exception was the Protestant Church at Patse-bolang, Dalad Banner, Yeke-juu League, which gained land in a post–Boxer Rebellion settlement through the pressure of the Chinese governor-general of Suiyuan.

27. Richard Lovett, *The History of the London Missionary Society 1795-1895*

(London: Oxford University Press, 1899), 2:597-98.

28. This work was coordinated mainly by Reverend Stuart Gunzel of the Evangelical Alliance Mission. He was assisted by a Mongolian preacher, Erinchen, and by the Mongolian scholars Wangchindorji and Mathew Magadburen Haltod.

29. *Secret History,* Sec. 182. The Mongol term *sarta'ul* referred, at times, to Persians, but more particularly to West Asian Moslems during the rise of the Mongol Empire.

30. Yule, 1:348.

31. The head of one Oirad "tributary mission," for example, was a man named Pir Mahmed; Ming-shih-lu, Vol. 160, sec. on Ying-tsung; see entry for the *chai-ch'en* day in the eleventh month of the twelfth year of the Cheng-tung reign period.

32. See Ts. Zhamtsarano, "Khotons: The Muslims of Mongolia" (English trans.), *Mongolia Society Bulletin* no. 6 (Spring 1967).

33. Large stones piled on the city walls of Tingyüanying as weapons in preparation for Moslem attacks were still there when S. Jagchid visited the city in the summer of 1949.

34. Herbert Franz Schurmann, *The Mongols of Afghanistan: An Ethnography of the Moghals and related peoples of Afghanistan* (The Hague: Mouton, 1962).

CHAPTER 5. LETTERS AND ARTS

Language

1. For an example see *Secret History,* Sec. 120.

2. Ibid., Sec. 81.

3. This is the reason his name was recorded in Chinese materials as Hsü-lieh-wu.

4. See John Charles Street, *Khalkha Structure* (Bloomington: Indiana University Press, 1963).

5. Sun Chu, "Language News from Inner Mongolia," trans. Jerry Norman from *Zhongguo yu-wen,* no. 6 (1964), in *Mongolia Society Bulletin* 4 (1965).

6. At the time of the Kalgan, Inner Mongolian Government, Prince Demchügdüngrüb wrote a pamphlet on the proper reading of Mongolian words: *Daghudalagha-yi töb bolghakhu minü sanal* [My opinion on proper pronunciation] (Kalgan, 1943).

7. This feature is of long standing and may be seen in the *Secret History,* Sec. 274.

8. Gerard Clauson, "The Early Turkish Loan Word in Mongolian," *CAJ* 4 (1958-59):174-87.

9. Hung Mai (Sung period), "Chi-tan sung shih" ("A Kitan Reading a Poem"), in *I-chien-chih* (*ping* part), Shang-wu chi-cheng ed. (reprint ed., Taipei,

n.d.). See also Shimada Masao, "Ts'ung jen-lei-hsüeh shang k'an Liao-tai ti wen-hua" [Observations on Liao culture from the viewpoint of anthropology], *Ta-lu tsa-chih* (Taipei) 19, no. 11 (1956).

Writing Systems

1. *Yüan shih,* Vol. 124, Biography of Ta-ta-tung-a [Tatatunggha].
2. Ibid., Vol. 124, Biography of Ha-la-i-ha-ch'ih-pei-lu.
3. See the observations of Rubruck in Dawson, p. 140.
4. It is reported that the original text was written by Choiji-odsar in the fourteenth century and that the *tayilburi* ("explanation") was compiled by a learned lama Danzan-daghwa in the 1700s with co-authors Nomundalai and Junduijumtso, two learned lamas, one Urad and one Kharachin. This work has many editions and was reprinted in Ulan-Ude in 1963 by P. B. Baldanjapov with a Russian translation and notes.
5. The author of the *Kelen-ü chimeg* was Agwangdandar, a famous and learned lama of the Alashan Banner. In the 1800s, this work was produced by wood-block process by a Makhasadwa lama. It has several editions and was also reprinted in Ulan-Ude in 1962 by P. B. Baldanjapov, with Russian translation and notes.
6. Gungga-jalsan was a great abbot of the Saskya-pa sect of Tibetan Buddhism and an uncle of the great Phags-pa lama. He visited the camp of Prince Kötön in the 1240s and converted the Mongolian prince to Buddhism, thus opening the way for the spread of Lamaist Buddhism in the Mongolian imperial household and among the nobility.
7. Kötön was not a khan but a prince, the son of Ögödei Khan and brother of Güyüg Khan.
8. *Yüan shih,* Vol. 202, Biography of Pa-ssu-pa (Phags-pa) in the *"shih lao chuan"* [Biographies of religious leaders].
9. Murayama Shichiro, "Chingisu Kan sekihimon no kaidoku" [An explanation of the Chinggis Khan inscription], *Toyogo Kenkyu* 19 (1948).
10. See N. Poppe and Kun Chang, "Notes on the Monument in Honor of Möngke Khan," *CAJ* 6 (1961):13-23.
11. *Yüan shih,* Vol. 202, Biography of Pa-ssu-pa (Phags-pa), 1b-2a.
12. Ibid.; see also N. Poppe and John R. Kruger, *The Mongolian Monuments in Phags-pa Script,* 2d ed. (Wiesbaden, 1967).
13. *Yüan shih,* Vol. 202, 1b-2a.
14. Francis W. Cleaves, "The Sino-Mongolian Inscription of 1335 in Memory of Chang Ying-jui," *HJAS* 13, nos. 1-2 (1950): plates 17-35.
15. Cf. Takashiro Kobayashi, *Gencho hishi no kenkyu* [A study of the Yüan-ch'ao p'i-shih], (Tokyo, 1955), pp. 306-80.
16. Radnabadara, "Zaya Bandita-yin namtar" [The biography of Zaya

Bandita], in Damdinsürüng, *Mongghol uran jokiyal,* p. 326.

17. B. Rintchen, "Sojombo-emblemat wolno'sci i niepodległo-sci narodu Mongol-skiego," *Przeglad Orieialistyczny* (Warsaw) 1, 15 (1955):319-24.

18. See Isidorzi, *Mongoliin sine ysegiin zaabar* [Introduction to the new Mongolian writing system], (Ulan Bator: Aradiig Gegeeryylke Jaamanii Keblel, 1931).

19. Paul Hyer and William Heaton, "The Cultural Revolution in Inner Mongolia: Local Nationalism and Party Disintegration in a Key Border Region of China," *China Quarterly* (London) 36 (Oct.-Dec. 1968):114-28.

Literature

1. William Hung, "The Transmission of the Book Known as *The Secret History of the Mongols,*" *HJAS* 14, nos. 3, 4 (1951).

2. For mention of *tobchiyan,* see *Yüan shih,* Vol. 181, Biography of Yü Chi, 10a.

3. The Chinese term for this record is *shih-lu.* For an important study, see Kobayashi, particularly the section on the "royal record" or "national history," the *to-pieh-chih-yan,* pp. 72-83.

4. Charles R. Bawden, trans. with comments, *The Mongolian Chronicle, Altan Tobči* (Wiesbaden, 1955); see also Takashiro Kobayashi, *Moko Kogon shi* (Tokyo, 1941).

5. See C. Z. Zamcarano, *The Mongol Chronicles of the Seventeenth Century,* trans. Rudolf Loewenthal (Wiesbaden, 1955).

6. This work was reprinted by Temgetü's Meng-wen shu-she (Peking: Mongolian Book Company, 2d ed., 1925).

7. Reprinted by Harvard Univ. Press, Cambridge, 1955, with an introduction by Antoine Mostaert and Francis W. Cleaves.

8. Ibid., Introduction, pp. xviii-xx. Also see S. Jagchid, "Meng-wen huang-chin-shih i-chu" ("A Chinese Translation of the *Altan-Tobči*—a Brief History of the Mongols, with Annotations"), *Chung-kuo tung-ya hsüeh-shu yen-chiu-chi-hua wei-yüan-hui nien-pao* (The China Council for East Asian Studies, Bulletin, Taipei), 2 (1963):92-95.

9. The *Khad-un ündüsün-ü Erdeni-yin tobchi,* as given in full title, was translated into both Manchu and Chinese in the 1700s. The Chinese edition, well known as *Meng-ku yüan-liu,* is Sagang Sechen's *Erdeni-yin tobchi.* It was first introduced to the West by I.J. Schmidt, Petersburgh, 1829. It was reprinted in the Series Scripta Mongolica 2 by the Harvard-Yenching Institute, 1956, with a critical introduction by A. Mostaert and an editor's foreword by Francis W. Cleaves.

10. *Khabulan* is the old name of a type of wild beast that cannot be identified.

11. *Mangghas* or *manggus* is a large, legendary, pythonlike snake, also known as a monster.

12. *Chulakha* is a large fish.

13. *Anggir* is a type of red swan; the Chinese term is *yüan-yang*.

14. The *barus* is a legendary tiger, the name of which seems to be derived from the word *bars* ("tiger").

15. *Altan tobči*, 2:67.

16. *Mila-yin namtar* [Biography of Milaraspa in its Mongolian version by Sieregtü Güüsi Corjiva, with an introduction by James E. Bosson], (Taipei, 1967).

17. There are several editions of *Üliger-ün dalai*, all from woodblock. It was widely read in Mongolia. According to Damdinsürüng, it was originally translated into Mongolian from Tibetan by Güüsi Chorji of Köke-khota (Hohehot); see Damdinsürüng, *Mongghol uran jokiyal*, p. 297.

18. The temple of Kuan Yü, within the Imperial Lamasery of Yüng-ho kung at Peking, is also known to the Mongols as Geser-ün süme, the temple of Geser.

19. For instance, *Yeke Jünken Khatan* [The great lady Jünken], intro. D. Tserensodnom (Ulan Bator, 1963).

20. See the annotated translation and analysis of John Gombojab Hangin, *Köke Sudar (The Blue Chronicle); A Study of the First Mongolian Historical Novel by Injannashi* (Wiesbaden: Harrassowitz, 1973).

21. See Sh. Bira, "Mongolian Historical Literature of the 17th-19th Centuries written in Tibetan," trans. from the Russian by Stanley N. Frye, Mongolia Society *Occasional Paper*, no. 7 (1970).

22. Reprinted by Temgetü's Mongolian Book Company, Peking, 1926.

23. Damdinsürüng, *Mongghol uran jokiyal*, p. 73.

24. Ibid., pp. 73-87.

25. See B. Rintchen, *Folklore Mongol*, vols. 1-6 (Wiesbaden, 1960-65).

26. See D. Dashdorj and I. Gur-Rentsen, eds. *Ardiin aman zohioloos* [Popular oral texts], (Ulan Bator, 1958); see also Antoine Mostaert, *Textes oraux Ordos, Monumenta Serica*, Fu-jen University, Monograph Series no. 11 (Peking, 1947).

27. Juvaini, 1:198.

28. From the recollection of S. Jagchid.

29. See L. K. Gerasimovich, *History of Modern Mongolian Literature (1921-1964)*, trans. from the Russian (Bloomington, Ind.: Mongolia Society, 1970); see also David B. T. Aikman, "Mongolian Poetry Since the Revolution," *Mongolia Society Bulletin* no. 5 (1966).

Education

1. See Hangin.

2. *Chinggis Boghda-yin dorosghal-un tegëbüri* [A collection of memories of the sacred Chinggis], (Peking: Meng-wen shu-she, 1926), p. 41.

3. *Yüan shih*, Vol. 124, Biography of T'a-t'a t'ung-a.

4. Ibid., Vol. 124, Biography of Ha-la-i-ha-ch'ih-pei-lu.

5. See also S. Jagchid, "Shuo Yüan-shih chung-ti *pi-che-ch'ih pin-chian-lun Yüan shih chu-ti chüng-shu-ling*" ("On the *Bichigchi* and the *Chung-shu-ling* of the Mongolian Empire and the Yüan dynasty"), *BICBAS* no. 2 (1971).

6. Wang P'an (Yüan period), *Ti-shih Pa-ssu-pa hsing-chuang* [The life of the Imperial Tutor, Phags-pa], in *Fuo-tsu t'ung-tien* of the Chinese *Ta-tsang ching* (reprint ed., Taipei, 1972).

7. *Yüan shih,* Vol. 158, Biography of Yao Shu.

8. Ibid., Vol. 158, Biography of Hsü Heng, 8a.

9. Ibid., Vol. 81, Monograph on Election (*Hsüan-chü chih*), see entry on schools (*Hsüeh-hsiao*), 14a-15a.

10. Ibid., 1a.

11. Ibid., Vol. 158, Biography of Hsü Heng, 19b.

12. Ibid., Vol. 81, Monograph on Election, see entry on subjects (*K'o-mu*), 5b-8a.

13. Ibid., Vol. 87, Monograph on Officials, II, entry on the *Meng-ku han-lin yüan,* 4b.

14. Ibid., Vol. 88, Monograph on Officials, IV, entry on the *I-wen chien,* 7ab.

15. Ibid., Vol. 91, Monograph on Officials, 7, 9a, 14a.

16. In the Mongolian Yüan period (1260-1386), most of the Confucian classics were translated into Mongolian; however, except for *Hsiao ching,* all were lost after the collapse of the dynasty. Later, during Manchu-Ch'ing period (1644-1911), most of the Confucian classics were again translated into the Mongolian language. In the 1920s, the "Four Books" were reprinted in Peking by Temgetü's Mongolian Book Co. (*Meng-wen shu-she*) and were recently reprinted by the Mongolian-Tibetan Affairs Commission (*Meng-Tsang wei-yüan-hui*), Taipei, 1971.

17. During the Ch'ing period, there were many prohibitions restricting the Mongols from cultural contact with the Chinese. In 1839 and again in 1853, the Manchu court promulgated special prohibitions against Mongols learning the Chinese language; see *CTPCTK,* p. 380.

18. See Hsin-chih-hsiang, *K'a-la-ch'in cha-sa-k'o ch'in-wang Kung-sang-no-erh-pu chih lueh-shih* [A brief history of the prince of the Kharachin Banner, Güngsangnorbu], (Kharachin, Inner Mongolia, 1938). Paul Hyer and S. Jagchid are presently collaborating on a comparatively complete biography of Prince Güngsangnorbu.

19. See Kawahara Misako, *Moko miyage (Mongolian Souvenir),* (Tokyo, 1909), pp. 141-84; also Torii Kimiko, *Dozokugakujo yori mitaru Moko* [Ethnographical observations on Mongolia], (Tokyo, 1927), pp. 26-29.

20. S. Jagchid, *Pien-chiang chiao-yü* [Education in the Chinese border areas], (Taipei, 1961), pp. 14-15.

21. Temgetü, a Kharachin man, was also known by his Chinese name Wang Jui-ch'ang. He was one of the students sent by Prince Güngsangnorbu to Japan

to study. After returning, he was appointed a teacher in the Mongolian Tibetan Academy in Peking. He began printing works in the middle of the 1920s and published many Mongolian classics, novels, textbooks, and Buddhist scriptures. In the 1930s, he was appointed an official of the Ministry of Education in Nanking. After the Manchurian Incident (1931), he returned to eastern Inner Mongolia and became a teacher at the Hsingan (Mongolian) Military Officers School and died there in the early 1940s.

22. See A. Dashnyam, *Mongol orond heblel üüsch högjsön tüühees* [A brief history of the development of the printing industry in Mongolia), (Ulan Bator, 1962).

23. From Paul Hyer's discussions with Hukjintai, a former student of this school. Merse was a militant young Dakhur Mongol who studied at the *O-wen fa-cheng chuan-k'o hsüeh-hsiao* (a Chinese law school specializing in Russian law and politics) in Peking and collaborated with Pai Yun-ti in 1925 to establish the Inner Mongolian People's Revolutionary Party, also known as the *Nei-Meng-ku Kuo-min-tang*. When this party became defunct in 1927, Merse studied and worked in Ulan Bator for a time, and then, in 1929, undertook an independence movement in the Hulun-buir region of eastern Inner Mongolia. This brought him to a confrontation with Chang Hsüeh-liang, and the Mongolian school came out of a compromise between the two. Also known as Kuo Tao-fu, see his views as expressed in "Modern Mongolia," *Pacific Affairs* 3, no. 8 (1930):754–62.

24. Chang Hsüeh-liang, son of the Manchurian warlord Chang Tso-ling, was the warlord of Manchuria when it was taken over by the Japanese in 1931. In 1936, he carried out a coup d'etat against Chiang Kai-shek and imprisoned him for about two weeks. As a result, Chang was placed under house arrest in Taiwan, where he has remained until the present.

25. S. Jagchid, *Pien-chiang chiao-yü*, pp. 46–47.

26. Ibid., pp. 26, 33–36.

27. Y. Rinchen, "Books and Traditions (from the History of Mongol Culture)," trans. Stanley Frye, in *Analecta Mongolica*, ed. by John G. Hangin and Urgunge Onon, Mongolia Society *Occasional Papers*, no. 8, pp. 63–76.

Art and Relics

1. Mongolian Buddhist paintings are similar to those of Tibetan monasteries. The best work on this subject is Guiseppe Tucci's *Tibetan Painted Scrolls*, 2 vols. (Roma: La Libreria della stato, 1949).

2. See *Orchin üeiin Mongoliin gar urlig* [Modern Mongolian art], (Ulan Bator: State Publishing House, 1971).

3. See Tamura Jitsuzo, *Ch'ing-ling* (*Tombs and Mural Paintings of Ch'ing-ling, Liao Imperial Mausoleums of Eleventh Century in Eastern Inner Mongolia*), English summary by Iwamura Shinobu and Wilma Fairbank, 2 vols. (Kyoto: Kyoto University, 1952-53).

4. See Max Loehr, "Ordos Daggers and Knives: New Material, Classification and Chronology, First Part: Dagger," *Artibus Asiae* 12, no. 1/2 (1949): 23-83;"Second Part: Knives," *Artibus Asiae* 14 (1951): 77-162.

5. See Petr Kuzmich Kozlov, *Comptes rendus expeditions pour l'exploration du Nord de la Mongolia* (Leningrad, 1927).

6. See Egami Namio, "Olon-sume et la de'couverte de l'eglise catholique romaine de Jean de Montecorvino," *Journal Asiatique* (Paris) 240, no. 2 (1952).

7. Ishida Mikinosuke, "Gendai no Joto ni tsuite"[On the city of Shangtu of the Yüan period], *Nihon Daigaku Soritsu 70 nen kinen ronbunshu,* 1960.

8. *Yüan shih,* Vol. 203, Biography of A-ni-ko; see also Ishida Mikinosuke, "Gendai no kogeika Neparu ozoku Aniko no ten ni tsuite"[On the master artist A-ni-ko, as member of the Nepalese royal household], *Moko gaguho* no. 2 (1941).

9. Biographical information on Liu Yüan is found in the Biography of A-ni-ko, *Yüan shih,* Vol. 203.

10. See E. D. Phillips, *The Mongols* (New York, 1969), pp. 94-103 and related notes on Karakorum. See also Francis W. Cleaves, "The Sino-Mongolian Inscription of 1346," *HJAS* 15, nos. 1-2 (1952):1-123.

Music, Dance, and Drama

1. The orchestras of the Üjümüchin and Sünid banners of Inner Mongolia were well known in the first half of this century.

2. *Secret History,* Secs. 57, 81, 193.

3. Taki Ryochi, "Moko no ongaku ni tsuite" [On Mongolian music], *Mokogaku* no. 3 (1938). Henning Haslung-Christensen, *The Music of the Mongols: Eastern Mongolia* (New York, 1971).

4. For the original text, see Damdinsuren and Sodnom, *D. Natsagdorji,* pp. 115-17. For a translation and note, see chapter 1, this volume.

5. *Ch'ing shih,* Vol. 405, Biography of Senggerinchin.

6. This information was learned by S. Jagchid from Prince Demchügdüngrüb in the early 1940s. During the Manchu-Ch'ing period, the statements of Injannashi were sensitive or potentially dangerous in that they could have been taken as a scheme for rebellion. The usual punishment in such cases was the extermination of the entire household. Moreover, it was Senggerinchin's duty to report this to the court. In order to avert a tragedy, Prince Senggerinchin rejected Injannashi's proposal; but fearing that he might be personally implicated if it became known, Senggerinchin asked, "Are you insane?" Thus, on the one hand, Senggerinchin avoided involvement in a serious crime against the Manchu emperor, and, on the other, he saved the lives of Injannashi and his family. From this time on, the great writer Injannashi behaved strangely, like a psychotic playing a role. Jagchid's aunt (Injannashi was a brother of her grandmother) also reports that Injannashi was eccentric. Sometimes he dressed

as the great strategist Chu-ke Liang of the famous Chinese novel *San-kuo yen-i* (*Romance of the Three Kingdoms*), and at other times as Chia Pao-yü, the romantic key character of the novel *Hung-lo meng* (*Dream of the Red Chamber*). His actions, it was said, were to give the impression that he was insane.

7. Toghtokhu (or Toghtogh) was a noble of the Khorchin Banner, eastern Inner Mongolia, with the rank of *taiji*. He was known as a great *Meng-fei* or so-called Mongolian bandit. After fighting a successful guerrilla campaign against the Chinese, he retreated into Outer Mongolia, and later, at the time of the Mongolian Independence Movement (1911), he was appointed vice-minister of Military Affairs in the new Urga government; see also Bawden, p. 193.

8. See Takeda Ichiro, "Moko no Uta" ("Mongolian Songs"), *Toyo ongaku kenkyu*, Oriental Musical Studies, 16/17 (1962).

9. *Yüan shih*, 1a.

10. Ibid., 1ab.

11. Ibid., 6b.

12. Ibid., Vol. 71, Monograph on Ritual and Music, V, 8a-9a.

13. Ibid., 14a.

14. Dawson, p. 97.

15. *Yüan shih*, Vol. 70, Monograph on Ritual and Music, IV, entries on music and dance in ancestral temples, 4b-17b.

16. Ibid., Vol. 68, Monograph on Ritual and Music, II, 6a.

17. Before the Communist revolution, the "devil dance" of Yüng-ho kung, the great lama temple of Peking was one of the most important sightseeing programs for Western tourists.

18. Emil S. Fischer, "The Sacred Lamaist Dance," *Journal of the North China Branch of the Royal Asiatic Society* no. 72 (1946).

19. According to the important record *Ta-Ch'ing hui-tien*, the Emperor Chia-ch'ing twice forbade Chinese plays in Mongolia: once in 1815 and again in 1818; see *Ch'ing-tai pien-cheng t'ung-kao* (*CTPCTK*).

20. For the development of music, dance, and drama in the contemporary Mongolian People's Republic, see F. S. Bischoff, "In the Gobi with the Songsters," *Mongolia Society Bulletin* 8 (1969); see also G. Dolgorsuren, *Mongol ardiin bujig* (Mongolian People's Dance), (Ulan Bator, 1962).

CHAPTER 6. SOCIO-POLITICAL STRUCTURE

The Clan-Lineage System

1. *Secret History*, Sec. 1.

2. The date of the translation is not definite, but the generally accepted date is 1369. An alternate theory gives 1382 as the date.

3. *Secret History*, Sec. 1.

4. Ibid., Sec. 21.

5. Ibid., Sec. 11.

6. Ibid., Sec. 42.

7. Ibid., Sec. 63. The word Kiyad or Kiyaten was mistranslated by the editors of the *Yüan shih* as "chi-wo-wen."

8. Ibid., Sec. 40.

9. Ibid., Sec. 41.

10. Ibid., Sec. 9.

11. Ibid., Sec. 64.

12. *Yüan shih,* Vol. 118. Biography of Te-hsüeh-chan [Tei Sechen].

13. *Secret History,* Sec. 165.

14. Ibid., Sec. 216.

15. Ibid., Secs. 43, 44.

16. Ibid., Secs. 70-72.

17. Juvaini, 2:549-53.

18. Ibid., 1:239-44.

19. Ibid., 1:262-66.

20. *Yüan shih,* Vol. 114, *Huo-fei chuang,* [Biographies of Empresses], a biography of Empress Nambi (Nan-pi), 4ab.

21. See Yanai Wataru, "Gencho orudo ko" ("On the *Ordo* of the Yüan Dynasty"), *Toyo gakuho* 10, nos. 1-3 (1920); also reprinted in his *Moko shi kenkyu* (Tokyo, 1930). See also Matsumura Jun, "Shin taishu no kohi" ("The Empresses and Royal Concubines of the Emperor Ch'ing T'ai-tsung"), *BICBAS* no. 3 (1972). In this article, Matsumura discusses problems regarding the transferral of property in the case of the *khatuns* of the last Mongol khan, Lighdan.

22. *Secret History,* Sec. 242.

23. Ibid., Sec. 242. Here the title or role known as *odchigin* became like a name.

24. Ibid., Sec. 242.

25. See *Yüan shih,* Vol. 1, Annals of T'ai-tsu (Chinggis Khan), 23b.

26. The *Altan tobči (nova)* refers to both Tolui, the youngest son of Chinggis Khan's first wife and to Arigh-bukha, youngest son of the first wife of Tolui, as *ejen.* These are examples of the role and the term concerned. It also refers to Jochi, the eldest son of Chinggis Khan as *ejen,* which presents a problem that requires further study to explain satisfactorily. It may be that the term was applied to him only as the lord of his own limited domain, the Jochi *ulus.*

27. *Secret History,* Sec. 139.

28. *Moghanda* is a Manchu word. Batsarghurda, nominal director of the Mengchiang Bank in Kalgan in the 1930s and early 1940s, was the *moghanda* of the *taiji* (Borjigid clan) of Abakhanar Left Banner of Shilin-ghol League. He was influential because of his role and actually was often referred to as Moghanda rather than by his personal name.

29. B. Vladimirtsov gives special attention to these matters in his *Le Régime social des Mongols: Le Féodalisme nomade* (London, 1963), pp. 60, 67, 126, 152.

Clan Confederations and the Emergence of Steppe States

1. *Shih chi,* Vol. 123, see entry on Wu-sun in the Biography of Ta-wan, 4a.

2. The writer of the *Han shu,* Pan Ku, in a colophon to his Account of the Hsiung-nu, noted:"The barbarians are covetous for gain . . . human faced but animal hearted" (Vol. 94b, 32a). Observations of this type are found throughout traditional Chinese historical materials on nomadic peoples.

3. S. Jagchid, "Objectives of Warfare in Inner Asia," *BICBAS* no. 4 (1973).

4. *Secret History,* Secs. 62-64.

5. Ibid., Sec. 40; see also B. Vladimirtsov's observations on *jat* (or *jad*) in pp. 64, 74, 76, 78, 81.

6. *Secret History,* Sec. 126.

7. Ibid., Secs. 153, 166.

8. Ibid., Sec. 48.

9. Ibid., Sec. 53.

10. Ibid; *ulus* may also mean "the people" or "the masses," an ethnic group, nation, or state.

11. Ibid., Sec. 141.

12. Ibid., Sec. 123.

13. *Shih chi,* Vol. 110, Account of the Hsiung-nu, 5a.

14. *Hou Han Shu,* Vol. 90, Account of the Wu-huan and Hsien-pei, 1b.

15. Yao Ts'ung-wu "Ch'i-tan chün-wei chi-ch'eng wen-t'i ti fen-hsi," ("Analysis of the Problems of Succession to the Kitan Throne"), in *Tung-pei-shih lun-ts'ung* [*Essays on the Northeast-Manchurian History*], (Taipei, 1959), 1:248-83.

16. Yanai Wataru, "Moko no kokkai sunawachi *kurirutai* ni tsuite" ("On *khuraltai,* the Mongolian National Assembly"), *Shigaku zashi* 8, nos. 4, 5, 7 (1917); reprinted in his *Moko shi kenkyu* (Tokyo, 1930).

From Clan Confederations to a Nomadic Quasi-Feudalism

1. *Secret History,* Secs. 123, 136.

2. S. Jagchid, "Shuo Yüan shih chung ti po-erh-chih" ("On the *bo'orchi* of the Yüan shih"), *Asiatic Studies in Honour of Dr. Jitsuzo Tamura On the Occasion of His Sixty-fourth Birthday* (Kyoto, 1968), pp. 667-82.

3. *Secret History,* Sec. 124.

4. P'eng Ta-ya, 16a; see also *Secret History,* Sec. 124.

5. *Secret History,* Sec. 202.

6. Shigi-khutughu, an orphan from an enemy camp of the Tatar tribe, was raised by the mother of Chinggis Khan. Later, he became the *Yeke-jarghuchi,* the grand judge or prime minister of the Mongolian Empire; see the *Secret History,* Secs. 136, 203, 234, 262, 252, 257. In his comments in the *Hei-ta shih-lüeh,* 15b, Hsü T'ing called him "Hu Cheng-hsiang," prime minister Khu.

7. Boroghul, an orphan from an enemy camp of the Jürkin tribe, was also raised by the mother of Chinggis Khan; he eventually became a great general in the empire. (see *Yüan shih,* Vol. 119, Biography of Po-erh-hu).

8. *Secret History,* Sec. 187.

9. Ibid., Sec. 242.

10. Henry Serruys, "Mongol *Altan* 'Gold'-Imperial," *Monumenta Serica* 21 (1962):357-78.

11. *Secret History,* Sec. 106; *Yüan shih,* Vol. 119, Biography of Mu-hua-li.

12. *Altan tobči (nova),* 2:105-6, records Jochi, the eldest son of Chinggis Khan, as Jochi *ejn.*

13. Ibid., 2:86-87.

14. *Secret History,* Sec. 219; *Yüan shih,* Vol. 118, Biography of Te-hsüeh-ch'an [Tei Sechen], 5b.

15. *CTPCTK,* p. 1.

16. *Secret History,* Sec. 219.

17. *Altan tobči (nova),* 2:56-57.

18. Manchu rulers forbade the Mongols to freely pasture or hunt beyond the border of their own *notugh (yu-mu).* Persons transgressing received heavy punishments as recorded in the *Ta-Ch'ing hui-tien;* see *CTPCTK,* pp. 14-15, 245.

19. *Yüan shih,* Vol. 118, Biography of Te-hsüeh-ch'an, 5b-7a.

20. Ibid., Vol. 146, Biography of Yeh-lü Ch'u-ts'ai, 7a.

21. *Secret History,* Secs. 139, 180, 186.

Institutional Changes after the Fall of the Empire

1. Sagang Sechen, p. 158; *Meng-ku yüan-liu,* 5:3a. The rest of the *tümen* were killed or assimilated; see Henry Serruys, *The Mongols in China during the Hung-wu Period (1368-1398)* (Burges, 1959), chap. 8, "Sinicization of the Mongols in China," pp. 158-71.

2. See "Dayan khaghan-u khariyatu jirghughan tümen Mongghol-un maghtaghal" [The praise of the six *tümen* of Mongols under Dayan Khan], in Damdinsürüng, *Mongghol uran jokiyal,* pp. 183-84: here it is recorded that the Chakhar, the Khalkha, and the Uriyangkha are the three *tümens* of the Left Flank.

3. Sagang Sechen, pp. 213, 215.

4. See Wada Sei, "On Dayan Khaghan," *Toa shi kenkyu—Moko hen (Studies on the History of East Asia-Mongolia),* (Tokyo, 1959), pp. 425-520, with English summary.

5. The Dörbed were progenitors of the majority of the population of the western part of the present Mongolian People's Republic.

6. The Jungar people were exterminated by the Manchu in the Manchu-Jungarian War (1688-1755).

7. The Torghud were the progenitors of most Kalmuck Mongols now living in southern Russia and the Mongols in Chinese Turkistan (Sinkiang).

8. The Khoshod are the ancestors of the Mongols of present-day Kökönor (Chinghai).

9. By the Ch'ing period, six of the ten banners of the Jerim League of Eastern Mongolia belonged to the Korchin *aimagh.* At the present time, some of these banners still exist under Chinese Communist administration.

10. From the Ch'ing period (1644-1911) to the Chinese Communist takeover (1949), the Abagha *aimagh* was divided into four banners: the Abagha Right and Left and the Abakhanar Right and Left banners. At the present time, they have been reorganized into two banners within the Shilin-ghol League.

11. The Ongni'ud eventually became two banners of the Juu-uda League. At present, these people are settled in an area northwest of the city of Chihfeng (in former Jehol).

12. The Uriyangkha (Uriyangkhan or Uriyangkhai) was a powerful tribe in southeastern Inner Mongolia, and its members were ancestors of the present-day Kharachin Mongols—not to be confused with the Uriyangkhai people of Tanuu Tuva (Wada Sei, English summary, pp. 3-7; Japanese text, pp. 107-423).

13. See *Secret History,* Secs. 97, 145, 211.

14. Ibid., Sec. 269. The original Chinese term was *ta-wang* ("great prince").

15. Ibid.; the word *kürgen* in this meaning equals the Chinese term *fu-ma* ("royal sons-in-law").

16. *CTPCTK,* pp. 16, 46. All nobility of the three Kharachin banners and Eastern Tümed Left Banner are known as *tabunang.* All were the old Uriyangkha.

17. See Charles R. Bawden's English translation of *The Jebtsundamba Khutukhtus of Urga* (Wiesbaden, 1961), pp. 35-41.

18. *Secret History,* Sec. 269; *CTPCTK,* pp. 16, 46.

Socio-Political Structure under the Manchu

1. S. Jagchid, "Chin-tai Meng-ku chih ti-fang cheng-chih chih-tu" [The Mongolian local political system in the modern period], in *She-hui k'o-hsüeh chi-k'an (Bulletin of Social Sciences,* Peking University) 6, no. 3 (1936): pp. 703-36.

2. The Manchu Eight Banners (Man. *jakun gusa)* was a combined military-civilian administrative system established by Nurhachi (1560-1619), founder of the Manchu-Ch'ing dynasty (1644-1911). The system divided the eight banners into two groups each identified by a symbolic flag (banner). Four flags were solid colors: yellow, white, red, and blue; and four flags had a solid field with a different colored border.

3. These were the Sechen Khan Aimagh, Tüshiyetü Khan Aimagh,

Jasaghtu Khan Aimagh, and the Sayin Noyan Aimagh. No leader bore the title of khan until the late Ch'ing period.

4. Jagchid, "Chin-tai Meng-ku."

5. Wada Sei, Sec. 15, "On the Battle of Joo Khota of Tümed," English summary, pp. 16-17; Japanese text, pp. 889-99.

6. These are recorded in detail in the *Ta-Ch'ing hui-tien;* see *CTPCTK,* pp. 15-20, 46-55.

7. *Beyile* was an old title among the Jurchen-Manchu nobles. In the *Chin shih,* history of the Jurchen Chin (1115-1234), the term is recorded as *po-chi-lieh;* see Vol. 3, 1(b).

8. *CTPCTK,* pp. 16, 20-21.

9. Jagchid, "Chin-tai Meng-ku."

10. Ibid.

11. *CTPCTK,* pp. 25, 61.

12. Ibid., pp. 14-15.

13. Ibid., pp. 28-30, 61-62.

14. Ibid., pp. 33, 62, 73-75, 143, 212-15.

15. Ibid., pp. 224-28.

16. Ibid., p. 180.

17. Ibid., pp. 61, 73-75. The Chinese title of the *amban* at Kobdo is K'o-pu-to *ts'an-tsan ta-chen.* The governor-general over the Hulun-buir Bargha was the Heilungkiang *chiang-chün.*

18. For instance, Danjin Lama who was the leader of the Sayin Noyan Aimagh of the Khalkha at the time of the rise of the Manchu-Ch'ing power.

19. S. Jagchid, "Mongolian Lamaist Quasi-Feudalism during the Period of Manchu Domination," *Mongolian Studies* 1 (1974):27-54.

20. *CTPCTK,* pp. 66-67.

21. It is still impossible to find any official document to support this historical fact.

22. Jagchid, "Mongolian Lamaist Quasi-Feudalism."

23. First seen in the *Ming shih,* Vol. 331, Account of the Hsi-yü [Western regions],III, 4a; see the entry for Wu-ssu-tsang *ta-pao fa-wang* [the Great Jeweled King of the Buddhist Law of dbUs-gTsang, Tibet]. This account entitled the great lama (1506) as *huo-fo,* the "living Buddha."

24. Jagchid, "Mongolian Lamaist Quasi-Feudalism."

Social Classes: The Nobility and the People

1. *Secret History,* Sec. 21.

2. Ibid.; the Chinese translation of the word *kharachu* is *hsia-min,* from the original text, and means the "lower people."

3. This joke is quite popular in eastern Inner Mongolia especially in the Kharachin banners.

4. Che. Natsagdorj, "Main Characters of Feudalism of the Nomads" (Paper presented at the XIV International Congress of Historical Sciences, San Francisco, 1975). Cf. Chu Jung-chia [*sic*] (Jurunggha), "Research Institute of Inner Mongolian History Discusses Historical Questions of Mongols," *Li-shih yen-chiu* (*Historical Studies*) no. 5 (1961). This reference may most easily be consulted in *The Survey China Mainland Magazine* (*SCMM*) no. 289 (November 27, 1961):12-16. These two Mongolian writers, both Communists, one in the MPR and the other under Chinese influence, obviously have very differing interpretations of the issue.

5. *Secret History*, Sec. 180.

6. B. Vladimirtsov's classic work on traditional Mongolian society discusses in detail this slave class (which he transliterates as *boghol*); see pp. 80-88, 91, 94-95, 107, 112-13, 123, 125-27, 132, 140, 154-56.

7. *Secret History*, Sec. 137.

8. Ibid., Sec. 137.

9. *Yüan shih*, Vol. 119, Biography of Mu-hua-li records: "In the eighth month of the year *ting-ch'ou* [1217], [T'ai-tsu] bestowed [upon him] the title of *T'ai-shih kuo-wang* [and assigned Mukhali] to supervise the provinces and promulgate decrees to carry out administration. Also, a tablet inscribed with his oath and a golden seal were given him. [On the seal] was written: 'The state [*kuo*] will be passed on to his descendants unceasingly from generation to generation'" (4a).

10. Che. Natsagdorj; Chu Jung-chia.

11. *Secret History*, Sec. 92.

12. Mori Masao, "Nöhör ko josetsu" ("An Introduction to the Study of Nöhör"), *Tohogaku* no. 5 (1952); also "Nöhör ko" ("A Study on *Nöhör*"), *Shigaku zashi* 61, no. 8 (1952).

13. *Secret History*, Sec. 90-93; *Yüan shih*, Vol. 119, Biography of Po-erh-chu.

14. *Secret History*, Secs. 171, 175; *Yüan shih*, Vol. 121, Biography of Wei-ta-erh.

15. *Secret History*, Sec. 185.

16. Ibid., Secs. 149, 185, 200.

17. Ibid., Sec. 208; see also Valdimirtsov, pp. 70, 82, 85, 127-28; see also Francis W. Cleaves, "The Sino-Mongolian Inscription of 1335 in Memory of Chang Ying-jui," *HJAS* 13, nos. 1-2 (1950): note 44, pp. 37-38.

18. There are only two biographies of eunuchs in the *Yüan shih*, Vol. 204: one Li Pan-ning, an old Chinese eunuch of the Sung court, and another Pu (or Piao) Pu-hua, a Korean. No Mongolian eunuch is mentioned. The text praises the fact that the Mongolian institution of the *keshig* ("royal guard") avoided involvement in the Chinese problem of the eunuch institution.

19. *Secret History*, Secs. 191, 224; see also *Yüan tien-chang* (Taipei, 1964 edition), *Hsing-chi* section, entry on Li-pu, 1a-2b.

20. *Secret History*, Sec. 29. The Chinese translation for the term *irgen* is *pai-*

hsing, "people," or "common people."

21. Ibid., Sec. 55. The original text is *kharan.* The initial *kh* disappeared in the late thirteenth century, resulting in the modern term *aran.*

22. On this important group, see Vladimirtsov, pp. 78, 119, 147, 153-54, 212, 215, 217-18, 229-30.

23. Henry Serruys, "A Field Trip to Ordos: The Cult of Chinggis -Qan, the Darqad, and Related Subjects: A Newspaper Report from 1936," *Mongolia Society Bulletin* 9, no. 1 (1970):39-54.

24. *Secret History,* Secs. 187, 219.

25. Cf. Francis W. Cleaves, "The Sino-Mongolian Inscription of 1335 in Memory of Chang Ying-jui," *HJAS* 13, nos. 1-2 (1950): note 170.

26. By the early Yüan period, some Mongols had already been sold as slaves. After reviewing the problem, the Mongolian khan freed all Mongol slaves; see *Yüan tien-chang,* 57:15b.

27. In the Kharachin region, the personal *khariyatu* of a *jasagh* or prince were not customarily listed in the files of the banner office; therefore they were not allowed to serve in public office. In the Üjümüchin Banner of Shilin-ghol, they were allowed to serve in public office with the exception of the top office of *jakiraghchi.* In other banners, even this limitation was later ignored. In some places until recent times, notably Khalkha areas and the Ordos, the term *khamjilagha* has been used instead of *khariyatu.* The term is seen in Ch'ing period records and is translated in Chinese as *tsung-ting.* In both cases, it means able-bodied men attached to or followers of a particular noble. Some consider these persons to be "slaves."

28. Jagchid, "Mongolian Lamaist Quasi-Feudalism."

29. *Secret History,* Sec. 123.

30. Ibid., Secs. 279, 280.

31. Ibid., Sec. 31.

32. The *Ta-yüan ma-cheng chi* [The horse policy of the great Yüan], originally compiled at the latter part of the Yüan dynasty, was reprinted in the 1930s in Peking by the Wen-tien-ko Book Company.

33. *CTPCTK,* p. 256.

34. S. Jagchid, "Wai-meng-ku ti tu-li tzu-chih ho cheh-chih" [The independence, autonomy, and abolition of autonomy of Outer Mongolia], *Chung-kuo hsien-tai-shih ts'ung-k'an* (Taipei, 1962), 4:39-142.

The End of Nomadic Empires

1. Walther Heissig, "The History of the Dzungaria," *Central Asian Review* no. 13 (1965):17-80.

2. Jagchid, "Objectives of Warfare in Inner Asia," pp. 11-23.

3. Fredrick J. Teggart, *Rome and China: A Study of Correlations in Historical*

Events (Berkeley, 1939), treats Asian influences in the West.

4. *Han shu,* Vol. 94a, Account of the Hsiung-nu, I, 9a.

5. Ibid., Vol. 94b, Account of the Hsiung-nu, II, 32a.

6. The Sino or Manchu-Russian Treaty of Nerchinsk, 1689, and the Treaty of Khiakta, 1727.

7. S. Jagchid, "Reasons for the Nondevelopment of Nomadic Power in North Asia Since the Eighteenth Century," *Proceedings of the Second East Asian Altaistic Conference* (Seoul, Korea, 1968), pp. 35-39.

CHAPTER 7. ECONOMY AND POLITY

The Economy: Trade and Tribute

1. Observations of S. Jagchid based on personal experience as an administrator in Shilin-ghol League (1943-45).

2. Observation and experience indicate that it is unwise to attempt to develop agriculture in marginal areas under natural conditions. Forced cultivation by the Chinese Communists in the Mongol frontier tends to confirm this belief, although it is still a moot question.

3. Observations of S. Jagchid.

4. See Radnabadara, "Zaya Bandita-yin namtar," in Damdinsürüng, *Mongghol uran jokiyal,* pp. 320-34.

5. *Shih chi,* Vol. 110, Account of the Hsiung-nu, 20b-21a.

6. Presently Shuohsien in Shansi Province.

7. This *shan-yü* (or khan), according to the *Shih chi,* was Chün-ch'en Shan-yü.

8. Presently the Yenmenkuan district in Shansi Province.

9. *Shih chi,* Vol. 110, 21ab.

10. *Secret History,* Sec. 182.

11. Juvaini, 1:77 81.

12. Otagi Matsuo, "The Ortag-qian [loan of Ortaq] and Its Background," *Toyoshi-kenkyu* (Tokyo) 32, no. 1 (June 1973):1-27; no. 2 (September 1973):23-61, English summary.

13. S. Jagchid, *Pei-ya yu-mu min-tsu yü chung-yüan nung-yeh min-tsu chien ti ho-ping chan-cheng yü mao-i chih kuan-hsi* [Peace, war, and trade relationships between the North Asian nomadic peoples and the agricultural Chinese], (Taipei, 1972), pp. 147-50, 527-84.

14. Entry on the *wu yin* day of the first month of spring, the seventh year of Cheng-te (1942), *Ming shih-lu,* Yin-tsung, Vol. 88.

15. Jagchid, *Pei-ya yu-mu min-tsu,* pp. 467-528.

16. *Shih chi,* Vol. 110, 15b-16a.

17. *Chiu T'ang shu,* Vol. 194, Account of the Tu-ch'üeh, I, 14b.

18. Jagchid, *Pei-ya yu-mu min-tsu,* pp. 338-60.

19. Ibid., pp. 183-254.

20. Ibid., pp. 255-309. Henry Serruys, *The Tribute System and Diplomatic Missions* (Brussels, 1967) is a good study on the Ming court's (1368-1644) economic relations with the Mongols.

21. Jagchid, *Pei-ya yu-mu min-tsu,* pp. 311-37.

22. Ibid., pp. 361-467.

23. Ibid., pp. 529-84.

24. *Ming shih-lu,* Ying-tsung, Vol. 96, see entry for the keng-ch'en day of the ninth month of Cheng-tung, seventh year (1442); see also Jagchid, *Pei-ya yu-mu min-tsu,* pp. 295-96.

25. Otagi "The Ortag-qian."

The Economy: Agriculture and Manufacturing

1. B. Shirendev, Sh. Natsagdorj et. al., *Bugd nairamdah Mongol ard ulsyn tuuh* (*The History of the Mongolian People's Republic),* (Ulan Bator, 1966), pp. 89, 91.

2. See *San-kuo chih,* Account of the Wu-huan and the Hsien-pei in the *Wei chih,* Vol. 30.

3. *Wei shu,* Vol. 103, Account of the Juan-juan, 20a.

4. Ibid., 1b.

5. *Chiu T'ang shu,* Vol. 194A, Account of the T'u-chüeh, I, 11a, 14b.

6. Teng-li-mu-yü Khan (759-80); see also E. E. Chavannes and P. Pelliot, "Un traite manichéen retrouvé en Chine," *Journal Asiatique* I, Vol. 190 (1913):146-94.

7. Yao Ts'ung-wu, *Tung-pei-shih lun-ts'ung* [Essays on the Northeast-Manchurian History], Vol. 1, "Shuo A-po-chi shih-tai ti Han-ch'eng" [A discussion on the Chinese cities in Mongolia at the time of Yeh-lü A-pao-chi], (Taipei, 1959), pp. 193-216.

8. Toyama Gunji, *Kincho shi kenkyu (Studies in the History of the Chin Dynasty),* (Kyoto, 1964), pp. 472-76, 487-95.

9. Ibid., p. 476 ff; see also *Chin shih,* Vol. 44, Monograph of Military Affairs, 18a.

10. *Han shu,* Vol. 194A, Account of the Hsiung-nu (I), 4b.

11. P'eng Ta-ya, 6a.

12. *Yüan shih,* Vol. 120, Biography of Chen-hai [Chimkhai], 10ab.

13. Chen Lu, *Chih-shih pi-chi* [The notes of Chih-shih], (first published in 1917 in China; reprint ed., Taipei: Wen-hai, 1960s), p. 48.

14. *Ming shih,* Vol. 327, Account of the Ta-tan, 20a-21b.

15. For the Batu-kha'alagha süme (Pailingmiao) "Declaration of Mongolian Autonomy," see Huang Fen-sheng, *Meng-ku tze-chih yun-tung chi-shih* (*True Record of the Mongolian Autonomous Movement),* (Shanghai: Chung-hua Book Co., 1935).

16. This decree is now preserved at Academia Sinica, Taipei, Taiwan.

17. *CTPCTK*, p. 248.

18. Many personal friends of the authors were involved in this problem in both land and education.

19. *Yüan shih*, Vol. 203, Biography of Artisans—Sun Wei, 8b-9a.

20. *Secret History*, Sec. 223.

21. Dawson, pp. 157-58, 175-77.

22. P. K. Kozlov, *Comptes rendus expeditions pour l'exploration du Nord de la Mongolia* (Leningrad, 1927).

23. Max Loehr, "Ordos Daggers and Knives: New Material, Classification and Chronology," *Artibus Asiae* 12 (1949):28-83, and 14 (1951):77-162.

24. *Chou shu*, Vol. 50, Account of the Tu-chüeh, 2a, 3ab.

Political Structure: Leagues and Banners

1. See Socio-Political Structure under the Manchu," Chap. 6, this volume.

2. During the Manchu-Ch'ing period, there were many promotions and demotions in the titles and ranks of the Mongolian nobility because the system of ranks and titles was used by Manchu rulers to check the Mongolian lords and to insure their loyalty to the court. There is considerable detailed data on this matter in the *Ta-Ch'ing hui-tien;* see *CTPCTK*, pp. 16-20, 48-55, 124-78.

3. For example, the three Kharachin Banners of the Josotu League.

4. This situation has long prevailed in some of the Ordos banners of the Yeke-juu League.

5. To organize ten households into one military and administrative unit was traditional in the Mongol Empire. To group fifty households together under a *bushugh* was also in keeping with Mongolian tradition. But the *sumun*, a unit of one hundred and fifty households, was a Manchu innovation. In the thirteenth century, P'eng Ta-ya reported that every fifty Mongolian cavalrymen were organized into one *chiu;* see his *Hei ta shih-lüeh*, 19a.

6. At the beginning of Manchu rule, the tax paid by the common people to their lord was set; see *CTPCTK*, p. 256. However, later, the regulation was entirely neglected by the banner authorities, and tax exactions became more burdensome and arbitrary.

7. Conferences of this type have a long history. In Asian nomadic society, they may be traced back to the time of the Hsiung-nu, roughly 200 B.C.- A.D. 200. The *Han shu*, Vol. 94, Account of the Hsiung-nu, notes: "In the fifth month, they have a great gathering at the Dragon City (Lung-ch'eng) to make offerings to their ancestors, to heaven and earth, and to their gods and spirits. In the autumn, when the horses are powerful, a great gathering takes place in the forest to count the people and their animals" (7b).

8. See S. Jagchid, "Chin-tai Meng-ku chih ti-fang cheng-chih chih-tu" [The Mongolian local political system in the modern period], in *She-hui k'o-hsüeh chi-*

k'an (*Bulletin of Social Sciences,* Peking University) 6, no. 3 (1936):703-36.

9. See Socio-Political Structure under the Manchu, Chap. 6, this volume. See also David F. Aberle, *Chahar and Dagor Mongol Bureaucratic Administration, 1912-1945* (New Haven, 1962), for information from native leaders Gombojab Hangin and Urgune Onon on the Chakhar and Hulun-buir regions (including the Dakhur areas in the Nonni River valley). These regions, in 1931, were nominally recognized as *pu* (Mong. *aimagh*)—that is, tribal administrative units directly under an official appointed by the capital—largely because of the persistent demands by Mongolian leaders on the new Nanking central government; however, no action was actually taken to implement this agreement before Japan's takeover in Manchuria and eastern Mongolia in 1931. Chakhar was again nominally recognized as a league by the Chinese government at the time of the Inner Mongolian Autonomous Movement (1933), but it was not until after the area was occupied by Japanese forces that the Mongols themselves actually implemented the organization of the league in 1935. After World War II, the Chinese authorities reneged on their commitment and refused to recognize either Chakhar or Hulun-buir as leagues.

10. For instance, the Chakhar *tu-t'ung* and the Suiyüan ch'eng *chiang-chün* (the governor general at Köke-khota) who governed the Tümed Mongols.

11. S. Jagchid, "Agricultural Development and Chinese Colonization in Mongolia," *Proceedings of the Montana Academy of Sciences* 28 (1968):134-43.

12. *Amban* here refers to the *amban* stationed at Urga (Chs. *Ku-lun pan-shih ta-chen*).

13. Regarding more recent changes affecting the *sumun,* see Trevor N. Dupuy, et al., *Area Handbook for Mongolia* (Washington, D.C.: U.S. Government Printing Office, 1970), p. 207.

14. Yüan Shih-k'ai's Peking government, the Republic of China, promulgated, on August 21, 1912, the "Meng-ku tai-yu t'iao-li," (Regulations for the treatment of Mongolia), in which the government guaranteed the "feudalistic" privileges of the Mongolian princes and the self-rule of the banners. This regulation was promulgated again as a concession in 1919 concurrent with the forced cancellation of Outer Mongolian autonomy.

15. In 1928, the central government in Nanking proclaimed the establishment of six new provinces: Jehol, Chahar, Suiyüan, Ninghsia, Chinghai, and Hsikang. Hsikang covers the Kham area of Tibet, but the remaining five provinces cover territory traditionally included in Inner Mongolia and Kökönor Mongolia.

16. In 1928, under the influence of the leading Inner Mongolian Prince Güngsangnorbu, a "Mongolian delegation" was organized to negotiate with the new Nanking government on Mongolia's status and other outstanding problems. Prince Güngsangnorbu was assisted by others, notably Wu Ho-ling, in this endeavor. The group traveled to Nanking under the leadership of Wu

Ho-ling as secretary general and there proposed a comprehensive Inner Mongolian policy to the new Kuomintang Party government.

17. This autonomous movement was led by Prince Demchügdüngrüb (De Wang) whose aim was the full independence of all Mongolia. The movement was soon overshadowed by the Japanese invasion and the Second Sino-Japanese War, 1937-45.

Political Structure: Unique Traditional Institutions

1. See Yanai Wataru, "Moko no kokkai sunawachi *kurirutai* ni tsuite," *Shigaku zashi* 28, nos. 4, 5, 7 (1917); republished in his *Mokoshi kenkyu* (Tokyo, 1966).

2. S. Jagchid attended various *khural* in Inner Mongolia during the late 1930s and early 1940s.

3. *Secret History,* Secs. 52, 57.

4. Ibid., Sec. 57.

5. Ibid., Sec. 179.

6. Ibid.

7. Ibid., Sec. 52.

8. Ibid., Sec. 53.

9. Ibid., Sec. 269.

10. *Yüan shih,* Vol. 4, Annals of Shih-tsu (Khubilai), I. See also Tamura Jitsuzo, "Arikubuka no ran ni tsuite—Mongoru teikoku kara gencho e" (On the rebellion of Arigh-bukha—from the Mongol Empire to the Yüan dynasty), *Toyoshi kenkyu* 14, no. 3 (1955).

11. *Yüan shih,* Vol. 127, Biography of Po-yen [Bayan], 19b.

12. *Secret History,* Sec. 255.

13. This relationship, which was common knowledge in Inner Mongolia, was supported by a genealogical record that had been preserved in the Sünid Right Banner, but destroyed by the invading Soviet forces in the fall of 1945. The lineage of Prince Demchügdüngrüb can also be confirmed by using the materials of Chang Mu's *Meng-ku yü-mu chi,* Kuo-hsüeh chi-pen ts'ung-shu ed. (Taipei, 1968), Vol. 4, Sec. on Sünid, and the *Ta-Ch'ing hui-tien,* see excerpt in *CTPCTK,* p. 24. See also *Meng-Tsang-hui wang-kung cha-sa-ke hsien-ming tsung-piao,* Meng-Tsang yüan, ed. (Peking, 1919).

14. The Chinese translation of *Bügüde-ergügsen* is *Kung-tai.*

15. See the Constitution of the Mongolian People's Republic, Chap. 3, Art. 18-36, quoted in R. Rupen, *Mongols of the Twentieth Century,* Uralic and Altaic Series, Vol. 37 (Bloomington: Indiana University, 1964), pp. 416-19.

16. *Secret History,* Secs. 269, 270.

17. Juvaini, "Of the Second Quriltai," 1:196-200.

18. *Yüan shih,* Vol. 3, The Annals of Tai-tsung, 4ab.

19. Ibid., Vol. 146, Biography of Yeh-lü Ch'u ts'ai, 3a.

20. Ibid., Vol. 124, Biography of Mang-ko-sa-erh [Mangghasar], 13a; see also Juvaini, 2:557-63.

21. *Han shu,* Vol. 94a, Account of the Hsiung-nu, I, 7b.

22. *Hou Han shu,* Vol. 79, Account of the Southern Hsiung-nu, 7ab.

23. See Jagchid, "Chin-tai Meng-ku."

24. This law code is also known in Mongolian as the *Shine chaghaja-yin bichig.*

25. The laws concerning Mongolia, such as the *Li-fan yüan shih-li* of the *Ta-Ch'ing hui-tien* and the *Li-fan yüan tse-li,* compiled and promulgated during the Ch'ing period, were recognized in 1929 by the Supreme Court of the new national government in Nanking as continuing in effect until the codification of new laws could be accomplished.

26. Yanai Wataru, "Gencho kyogetsu ko" [On the *keshig* of the Yüan dynasty], *Toyogakuho* 6, no. 3 (1916); also reprinted in his *Mokoshi kenkyu.*

27. *Secret History,* Secs. 227, 278; see also *Yüan shih,* Vol. 99, Monograph on Military Affairs, II, entry on the four *keshig (ch'üeh-hsueh),* 1b-2a.

28. See *Yüan shih,* Vol. 119, Biography of Po-erh-chu [Bo'orchu].

29. *Secret History,* Secs. 225, 226.

30. Ibid., Sec. 234.

31. See in the *Yüan shih,* Vol. 119, Biography of Po-lo-hu [Boroghul].

32. Ibid., Vol. 119, Biography of Mu-hua-li [Mukhali].

33. Chila'un was the son of Sorkhan-shira who saved the life of Chinggis Khan. He was also one of the "four heros" associated with the khan; see *Secret History,* Secs. 82-86, 177, 219.

34. *Yüan shih,* Vol. 119, Biography of Yü-hsi teh-mu-erh [Üshi-temür], 20ab.

35. See *Yüan shih,* Vol. 99, Monograph on Military Affairs, II, 1b-3a.

36. Examples are the Chinese scholars, Liu Ping-chung and Chang Wen-ch'ien. The latter was a scribe in the princely residence of Khubilai, which in reality meant that he was a *bichigchi* of the *keshig;* see their biographies in the *Yüan shih,* Vol. 157.

37. *Yüan shih,* Vol. 99, Monograph on Military Affairs, II, 1b-3a.

38. Ibid., Vol. 85, Monograph on Officials, I, 1b-2a.

39. Ibid., Vol. 102, Monograph on Law, I, 1ab.

40. Ibid., Vol. 85, Monograph on Officials, I, 1a.

41. See S. Jagchid, "Shuo Yüan-shih chung ti cha-lu-hua-chih pin chien lun Yüan-chu ti shang-shu sheng" ("On the *Jarghuchi* and the *Shang-shu sheng* of the Mongolian Empire and the Yüan Dynasty"), *BICBAS* no. 1 (1970):147-257. See also S. Jagchid, "Shuo Yüan-shih chung-ti *pi-che-ch'ih pin-chian-lun Yüan shih chu-ti chüng-shu-ling*" ("On the *Bichigchi* and the *Chüng-shu-ling* of the Mongolian Empire and the Yüan dynasty"), *BICBAS* no. 2 (1971):12-112.

42. *Yüan shih,* Vol. 85, Monograph on Officials, I, the entry on the *tuan-shih kuan* of the *chung-shu sheng,* 1ab.

43. See S. Jagchid's comments on the *jarghuchi* and the *shang-shu-sheng* of the Mongolian Empire and the Yüan dynasty, *BICBAS* no. 1 (1970):147-257; and no. 2 (1971):12-112.

44. *Yüan shih,* Vol. 117, Biography of Pieh-li-ku-t'ai [Belgütei], 1ab.

45. *Secret History,* Secs. 203, 234.

46. P'eng Ta-ya, 13b.

47. *Yüan shih,* Vol. 3, Annals of Hsien-tsung [Möngke Khan], 3a.

48. *Altan tobči (nova),* 2:191-92; according to this reference, a member of the Manchu delegation to negotiate an alliance with the Kharachin Mongols had the title of *jarghuchi.*

49. *Yüan shih,* Vol. 134, Biography of Yeh-hsien-pu-hua [Esen-bukha], 25a.

50. Juvaini, 2:139-40.

51. *Yüan shih,* Vol. 146, Biography of Yeh-lü Ch'ü-ts'ai, 4b.

52. *Altan tobči (nova),* 2:139-40.

53. S. Jagchid, "Shuo *Yüan-shih* chung ti ta-lu-hua-chih" ("On the *Darughachi* of the *Yüan shih*"), *Wen-shih-che hsüeh-pao (Bulletin of Literature, History, and Philosophy,* Taiwan University), no. 13 (1963):293-441.

54. Yanai Wataru, "Gendai shakai no san kaikyu" ("The Three Classes of the Yüan Society"), *Man-Sen chiri rekishi kenkyu hokoku* no. 3 (1916); also reprinted in his *Mokoshi kenkyu.*

55. These official titles appear in various law codes and documents. See Tayama Shigeru, *Moko hotten no kenkyu (A Study of Mongolian Law Codes),* (Tokyo, 1967), pp. 67-72, 199-200.

Law

1. See Shimada Masao, *Ryo sei no kenkyu* [A study of Liao law and institutions], (Tokyo, 1954).

2. This is a very valuable collection of recorded cases on Yüan-period administrative decisions and law. It is difficult to read due to the fact that much of it is a literal translation in colloquial Chinese of the Yüan period from original Mongolian documents now lost. One needs to know Mongolian grammar to determine the meaning of the Chinese. These historic texts are preserved in the Palace Museum in Taipei, Taiwan. A Ch'ing-period edition (1858) was reprinted in Taipei, 1964. The best recent research on these texts is by a group of Japanese specialists headed by the scholar Iwamura Shinobu at Kyoto University.

3. *Secret History,* Sec. 152.

4. Jagchid, "Shuo Yüan-shih chung ti cha-lu-hua-chih pin chien lun Yüan-chu ti shang-shu sheng."

5. *Secret History,* Sec. 203.

6. Vernadsky, *The Mongols and Russia,* pp. 99-110.

7. *Yüan shih,* Vol. 2, Annals of T'ai-tsung, 4a.

8. *Secret History,* Sec. 203.

9. S. Jagchid, "Shuo *Yüan-shih chung ti ch'üeh-lieh-ssu*" [On the *kirü'es* of the Yüan dynasty], *Ta-lu tsa-chih* (Taipei) 26, no. 4 (1963).

10. *Yüan shih,* Vol. 102, Monograph on Law, I, 1ab.

11. Ibid., 1b.

12. Ibid., 2b.

13. V. A. Riasanovsky, *Fundamental Principles of Mongol Law* (Tientsin, 1937; reprint ed., Bloomington: Indiana University, 1965), pp. 57-62.

14. Ibid., p. 69.

15. Shimada Masao, "Moko ritsurei to rihanin sokurei" ("Mongolian Law and the *Li-fan Yüan* Code"), *Hosei shi kenkyu* (Tokyo) no. 18 (1968).

16. Jagchid, "Chin-tai Meng-ku."

17. *CTPCTK,* p. 84.

18. Ibid., p. 390.

19. *Secret History,* Sec. 227.

20. Juvaini, 1:207.

21. *Secret History,* Secs. 123, 136.

22. *Yüan shih,* Vol. 102, Monograph on Law, I, 2a.

23. See Shimada Masao, "Moko ritsurei to rihanin sokurei"; see also Te-tsung shih-lu in the *Ch'ing shih-lu,* Vol. 526, entry for the *wu-shen* day of the first month of the thirtieth year of Kuang-hsü (1904).

24. Personal experience of S. Jagchid.

25. G. Nawangnamjil, *Öbgön bicheechin Ügüülel* [Tales of an old secretary], (Ulan Bator, 1956).

26. Personal experience of S. Jagchid.

27. There is a list of thirty-one so-called Mongolian bandits (active during the early Republic of China) in Huang Yüan-yung's *Yüan sheng yi-chu* (Peking, 1919), 2:141-44. But not one was a Mongol; all were Chinese.

28. Personal experience of S. Jagchid.

29. Mr. Sechinchoghtu (Chs. name, Yang-tsün-sheng), former head of the Ongni'ud Right Banner at Ulaankhada (Ch'ihfeng, in former Jehol) during the Manchukuo period, reported in an interview that the eight hundred persons in the prison at Ch'ihfeng were all Chinese; not a single Mongolian was in the group.

Military Institutions: Structure and Function

1. *Secret History,* Secs. 205, 206, 226.

2. Ibid., Sec. 202.

3. Ibid., Secs. 191, 226.

4. P'eng Ta-ya, 16ab.

5. *Yüan shih,* Vol. 98, Monograph on Military Affairs, I, 1ab.

6. *Shih chi,* Vol. 110, Account of the Hsiung-nu, 10ab.

7. *Secret History,* Secs. 205, 206, 226.

8. Ibid., Sec. 208.

9. P'eng Ta-ya, 19a.

10. *Yüan shih,* Vol. 98, Monograph on Military Affairs, 2a.

11. *Secret History,* Sec. 191.

12. *Yüan shih,* Vol. 2, Annals of T'ai-tsung, 3b, and Vol. 3, Annals of Hsien-tsung, 4b.

13. Juvaini, 1:30-31.

14. *Secret History,* Sec. 248.

15. Juvaini, 1:30; see also John of Plano Carpini's observations on the Mongolian army in Dawson, p. 33.

16. P'eng Ta-ya, 19a.

17. Ibid., 19b, commentary of Hsü T'ing.

18. d'Ohsson, Chap. 10.

19. Iwamura Shinobu, "Moko oruko" ("A Study of the Mongolian *a'urugh*"), *Kita Ajia gakuhō* no. 1 (1942).

20. *Yüan shih,* Vol. 99, "Monograph on Military Affairs," II, entry on the "four *chüeh-hsüeh,*" 2ab.

21. Hsiao Ta-heng, p. 26; see also Denis Sinor, "On Mongol Strategy," *Proceedings of the Fourth East Asian Altaistic Conference* (Taipei, 1971).

22. *Secret History,* Secs. 247, 248, 257.

23. Ibid., Sec. 193.

24. See Hsü T'ing's commentary in P'eng Ta-ya, 20a.

25. *Yüan shih,* Vol. 203, Biography of A-lao-wa-ting; also the Biography of I-ssu-ma-yin.

26. See Carpini's observations on the Mongolian army in Dawson, pp. 32-38, 43-50.

27. P'eng Ta-ya, 20b; see also S. Jagchid, "Objectives of Warfare in Inner Asia," *BICBAS* no. 4 (July 1973):11-23.

28. *Shih chi,* Vol. 110, Account of the Hsiung-nu, 2a.

29. *CTPCTK,* pp. 263-74.

30. For a brief biography of Senggerinchin (Seng-k'o-lin-ch'in), see Arthur Hummel, ed., *Eminent Chinese of the Ch'ing Period* (Washington, D.C., 1944), pp. 632-34. See also Charles Leavenworth, *The Arrow War with China* (London, 1901).

POSTSCRIPT ON MODERN CULTURE

1. S. Jagchid, "Traditional Mongolian Attitudes and Values as Seen in the *Secret History of the Mongols* and the *Altan-Tobči,*" paper presented at the Eighteenth Meeting of the Permanent International Altaistic Conference (PIAC), Bloomington, Ind., 1975.

2. Mongolia has reportedly now become self-sufficient in wheat. For occasional articles on the development of both agriculture and industry, see *Mongolia Today,* English-language monthly published by the Information and Broadcasting Department of the Mongolian People's Republic, Ulan Bator.

3. In the Mongolian People's Republic, sedentary pastoralism has been promoted along with the establishment of state farms. In Inner Mongolia, the Kalgan Mongolian government set up the *Mongghol-yin choghchilakhu anggi* (Mongolian reconstruction groups) in the early 1940s. These experiments were disrupted by the defeat of the Japanese and by the Chinese civil war, but cooperatives or communes and a more settled life have been pushed by the Chinese communists.

4. Ulanfu, a Tümed Mongol, was originally known by his Chinese name Yün Tse. But, in the 1920s, he was sent by the Inner Mongolian People's Revolutionary Party (also known as the Inner Mongolian Kuomintang) to study in Ulan Bator and the Soviet Union. There he adopted the revolutionary name Ulaan-keü ("red son"), transliterated into Chinese as Wu-lan-fu and into English as Ulanfu.

5. For date and some tentative analyses regarding the population of Mongolia, see Trevor N. Dupuy, et. al., pp. 26-30.

6. In colloquial Mongolian, there is no consonant *f,* so all *f* sounds are pronounced as *p.*

7. From the personal experience of S. Jagchid as an official in the Shilin-ghol League at the time of Kalgan Mongolian government.

8. Paul Hyer, "The Mongolian Nation within the People's Republic of China," in W. A. Veenhoven, ed., *Case Studies on Human Rights and Fundamental Freedoms—A World Survey,* Foundation for the Study of Plural Societies (The Hague: Nijhoff, 1975), 1:472-507.

9. Y. Rinchen, "Books and Traditions (from the History of Mongol Culture)," trans. Stanley Frye, in *Analecta Mongolica,* ed. by John G. Hangin and Urgunge Onon, The Mongolian Society *Occasional Papers,* no. 8, pp. 63-76.

10. Serge M. Wolff, "Mongolian Educational Venture in Western Europe (1926-1929)," *Mongolia Society Bulletin* 9, no. 2 (December 1970):40-107.

INDEX

Index